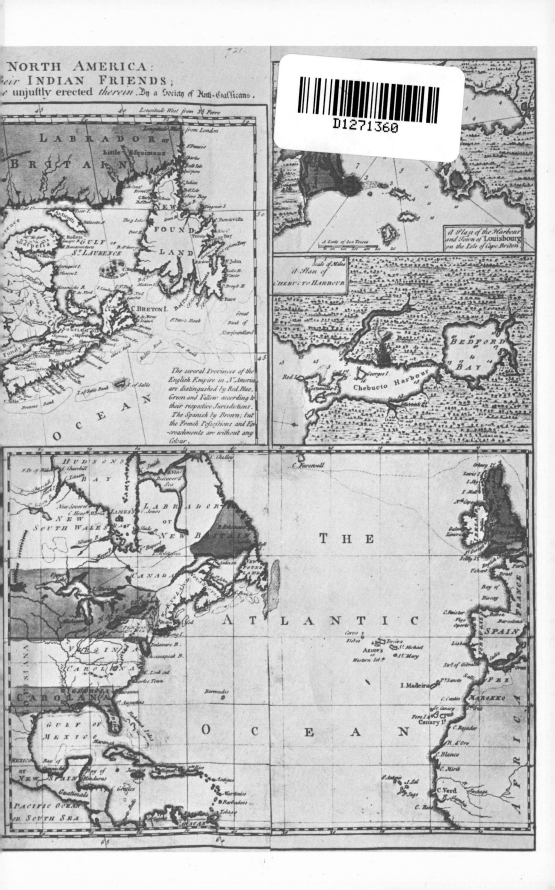

THE ORIGINS OF AMERICAN DIPLOMACY:

The International History of Angloamerica, 1492-1763

AMERICAN DIPLOMATIC HISTORY SERIES

GENERAL EDITOR: *Armin Rappaport*

Prelude to World Power: 1860–1900
FOSTER RHEA DULLES

The Uncertain Giant: 1921–1941
SELIG ADLER

Challenge and Rejection: 1900–1921
JULIUS W. PRATT

The Origins of American Diplomacy:
The International History of Angloamerica, 1492–1763
MAX SAVELLE

THE ORIGINS OF

American Diplomacy:

The International History of

Angloamerica, 1492-1763

BY

MAX SAVELLE

WITH THE ASSISTANCE OF

Margaret Anne Fisher

THE MACMILLAN COMPANY, NEW YORK

COLLIER-MACMILLAN LIMITED, LONDON

Library of Congress Catalog Card Number: 67-20734

FIRST PRINTING

The Macmillan Company, New York
Collier-Macmillan Canada Ltd., Toronto, Ontario

Printed in the United States of America

CONTENTS

List of Maps

Front End Paper: "A New and Accurate Map of the English Empire in North America . . ." (1755). Courtesy of the William L. Clements Library.

Back End Paper: Partie de la Mer du Nord, où se trouvent les grandes et petites Isles Antilles, et les Isles Lucayes. Par le Sr. Robert, Géographe ordinaire du Roy, Avec Privilège (1750). Courtesy of the Library of Congress.

Maps other than the historical prints were drawn by Joan Emerson.

List of Abbreviations

A.É., Corr. Pol., Ang. Archives du Ministère des Affaires Étrangères, Paris. Series "Correspondence Politique," sub-series "Angleterre."

A.É., Corr. Pol., Esp. Archives du Ministère des Affaires Étrangères, Paris. Series "Correspondence Politique," sub-series "Espagne."

A.É. Divers. Archives du Ministère des Affaires Étrangères, Paris. Series "Divers."

A.É., Méms. et Docs: Amer. Archives du Ministère des Affaires Étrangères, Paris. Series "Mémoires et Documents," sub-series "Amerique."

A.É., Méms. et Docs: Ang. Archives du Ministère des Affaires Étrangères, Paris. Series "Mémoires et Documents," sub-series "Angleterre."

A.G.S. Archivo General de Simancas.

A.H.N. Archivo Historico Nacional, Madrid.

Amer. Hist. Rev. American Historical Review.

A.N. Cols. Archives Nationales, Paris, series "Colonies."

B.M. British Museum, London.

B.N. Bibliothèque Nationale, Paris.

B.N., Ff., na. Bibliothèque Nationale, Fonds français, nouvelles acquisitions.

B.N.M. Biblioteca Nacional, Madrid.

C.A.O. Public Archives of Canada, Ottawa.

C.A.O., A.É., Cor. Pol., Ang. Public Archives of Canada, Ottawa: Transcripts from the Archives du Ministère des Affaires Étrangères, Paris, series "Correspondence Politique: Angleterre."

C.A.O., P.R.O., F.O.90 (B.T.Mss.). Public Archives of Canada, Ottawa, Transcripts from the British Public Record office: Foreign Office Papers, series 90 (Board of Trade Manuscripts).

C.A.O., P.R.O., F.O.90: France. Public Archives of Canada, Ottawa. Transcripts from the British Public Record Office, Foreign Office Papers, series 90 (France).

C.L. William L. Clements Library, Ann Arbor, Michigan.

C.S.P., Col., A.& W.I. Great Britain, Public Record Office: *Calendar of State Papers, Colonial, America and West Indies.*

C.S.P., Spain, 1580–86. Great Britain, Public Record Office, *Calendar of State Papers, Spain.*

Eng. Hist. Rev. English Historical Review.

G.B., P.C., Jud.Cee. Great Britain, Privy Council, Judicial Committee.

H.L., El. Huntington Library, Elsmere Manuscripts.

H.L., H.M. Huntington Library, Huntington Manuscripts.

H.L.R.B. Huntington Library, Rare Book Room.

H.M.C. *Reports of the Royal Commission on Historical Manuscripts.*

L.C. Library of Congress, Washington.

L.C., B.M., Add. Mss. Library of Congress: Transcripts of the "Additional Manuscripts" Series in the British Museum

L.C., H.L. Mss. Library of Congress, Transcripts of Manuscripts in the Library of the House of Lords.

L.C., A.É., Méms. et Docs., Amér. Library of Congress, Transcripts and Photostats of Documents in the Archives du Ministère des Affaires Étrangères, series "Mémoires et Documents," sub-series "Amérique."

M.N.M. Museo Naval, Madrid.

Méms. des Comms. du Roi. *Mémoires des Commissaires du Roi et ceux de sa Majesté Britannique* . . .

N.Y.C.D. *Documents Relative to the Colonial History of the State of New York,* edited by E. B. O'Callaghan and Berthold Fernow.

N.Y.P.L. New York Public Library.

Pac. Hist. Rev. *Pacific Historical Review.*

P.R.O., Chatham Corr. Public Record Office, Chatham Correspondence (mss.).

P.R.O., C.O. Public Record Office, series "Colonial Office Papers."

P.R.O., S.P. Public Record Office, series "State Papers" London.

Recueil des Insts. *Recueil des Instructions données aux ambassadeurs et Ministres de France depuis les Traités de Westphalie jusqu'à la Revolution Française.*

PREFACE

THE INVOLVEMENTS OF the English colonies in America, and of the territories in which they grew, in the international relations of the western world prior to the War for American Independence were of superlative importance, both as a factor in the history of the North Atlantic community of states and for the history of the colonies themselves and of the nations that they later became. And yet, prior to the present study, no narrative history of those involvements has ever been written. The only American historian of stature ever to interest herself in this almost completely neglected but profoundly important area of American history was Miss Frances Gardiner Davenport, whose magisterial collection of *European Treaties Bearing Upon the Territory of the United States and its Dependencies*[1] still remains the only significant work on the subject in existence.

Miss Davenport, of course, was not interested in writing a narrative history. Her interest lay in making a collection of treaties, in writing scholarly historical introductions to them, and in providing adequate bibliographies of material with regard to them for other scholars who might follow her in this field of study. Her contribution to the study of the international history of Angloamerica, therefore, is in the nature of a series of brilliant and scholarly, but unconnected, essays upon specific documents, together with an extremely valuable bibliography for each one.

For an advanced student of European and American diplomatic history, these short essays, in themselves, constitute a sort of diplomatic history of

[1] 3 vols.; Washington, D.C.: The Carnegie Institution of Washington, 1917–1934. Volumes II and III of the collection were brought to publication after Miss Davenport's death by J. Franklin Jameson, and a fourth volume, covering the period from 1716 to 1815, but without editorial introductions or bibliographical supports, was made by Charles O. Paullin (Charles O. Paullin, ed., *European Treaties Bearing upon the History of the United States and its Dependencies*, Vol. IV, Washington, D.C.: The Carnegie Institution of Washington, 1937).

America. Unfortunately for most students of this subject, however, Miss Davenport's work is not, and never was intended to be, a coherent narrative history. Her essays on individual treaties cover only the international agreements made down to and including the Peace of Utrecht (1713) and her collection omits many treaties that do not deal directly with American questions, even though such treaties might indirectly affect—as many do—American international relations. Her work also assumes an advanced knowledge of a number of European languages, especially French, which relatively few American students have.

The present book is an effort to fill the need for a narrative history of the international involvements of the English colonies in America during the period prior to the American Revolution. Since Miss Davenport's work is so thorough, the first eight chapters of the present narrative history rest heavily, although by no means entirely, upon the Davenport collection. The other chapters of the present work, especially those covering the period between 1715 and 1763, rest almost entirely upon original research in the archival collections of Europe, collected documents of a diplomatic and colonial nature, and contemporary imprints. This history is, of necessity, general in nature.

It is a pleasure to acknowledge my profound indebtedness to the directors and the staffs of the archives and libraries that have aided me so patiently and effectively in the finding and the use of material, particularly those of the Archivo de Indias, Seville; of the Biblioteca del Museo Naval, the Biblioteca Nacional and the Archivo Nacional, Madrid; of the Archivo General de Simancas; of the Bibliotèque Nationale, the Archives Nationales, and the Archives du Ministère des Affaires Étrangères, Paris; of the British Museum, the Public Records Office, and the Library of the House of Lords, London; of the Public Archives of Canada, Ottawa; of the New York Public Library, of the William L. Clements Library, Ann Arbor; of the Library of Congress, of the Huntington Library, and of the Library of the University of Washington.

My hearty thanks are due to the Public Record Office, London, the Library of Congress, and the W. L. Clements Library for assistance in finding appropriate contemporary maps, for reproductions, and for permission to use them, as, also, to the *Canadian Historical Review* for permission to print the map which appears on page 198 of volume XXXVIII, No. 3 (September, 1957) of their *Review*. I am especially grateful to the Carnegie Endowment for International Peace for permission to reprint, with a slight revision, as parts of the present book, certain paragraphs and pages of my book *The Diplomatic History of the Canadian Boundary, 1749–1763*, published by the Endowment (Yale University Press) in 1940.

I am also indebted and deeply grateful, for aid of a more material sort, to the Social Science Research Council, the American Philosophical Society, the United States Committee for the International Exchange of Persons ("The Fulbright Committee"), and the Graduate School of the University of Washington. For an infinite amount of note-checking, editorial reading and collation of the manuscript, and bibliographical assistance, I am heavily indebted to Mrs. James (Judith) Wilson.

I owe a very special debt of gratitude to Miss Margaret Fisher, who began her work with this project as a graduate-student research assistant. Her superlative work in reading and digesting microfilm copies of archival documents in a variety of foreign languages and in finding, reporting, and coordinating documents in printed collections led to the drafting of the preliminary texts of the manuscripts of several of the chapters of the book, and she drew the sketches of the maps in the text. She thus became a true collaborator in this work, wherefore her name appears on the title page, where it belongs. Without Miss Fisher's assistance this book could not have appeared in its present form at this time; I am deeply grateful to her.

Unless otherwise noted, all the dates given in the work are in the new style. Translations from foreign languages, with a few exceptions, are my own.

I am conscious that in a study of this sort there must be errors; the responsibility for these errors is mine alone.

MAX SAVELLE

University of Washington
April, 1967

THE ORIGINS OF AMERICAN DIPLOMACY:

The International History of Angloamerica, 1492-1763

CHAPTER I

The Pre-Columbian Precedents

THE DIPLOMATIC HISTORY of America begins, strictly speaking, with the discovery of this continent by Christopher Columbus. For that discovery precipitated a chain of international rivalries, actions, correspondence, wars, and treaties relative to the American continent that continued at least until the nineteenth century, and also opened an era of experience in the "new world," national and international, which significantly contributed to the formulation of many of the principles of modern international law and policy.

In a certain sense, however, the diplomatic history of America begins long before Columbus's discovery, because that discovery, although probably bound to happen, sooner or later, was only an accidental incident in a much larger phenomenon, the so-called expansion of European civilization around the world—or, to put it more accurately, the progressive enlargement of the Europeans' knowledge of the geography of those parts of the word that lay outside of Europe, to the point where they finally arrived at an accurate knowledge of practically all of the earth's surface. As they went along discovering, exploring, and exploiting the "new world," the Europeans laid claim to it, or parts of it, "by right of prior discovery." These national claims to territory in the "new world," which often overlapped, and to the right to exploit them commercially, provided much of the basis for the international exchanges that took place with regard to them.

This extension of geographic knowledge with regard to lands around the Atlantic may be said to have begun near the beginning of the fifteenth century, with the exploratory work sponsored by Prince Henry of Portugal (1394–1460), sometimes called Henry the Navigator.[1] It was Prince

---

[1] The commercial and colonial expansion of the European cities and states actually had begun much earlier. But this pre-Portuguese expansion was eastward, and it was confined to lands bordering upon the Mediterranean and the Black Sea. See Verlinden, *Precedents médiévaux de la colonie en Amérique.*

Henry who, from his modest palace at Sagres, on Cape St. Vincent, directed the voyages of his sea captains down the coast of Africa, beginning about 1419, until, step by step, they had explored the coast of that continent as far as Guinea. Henry's captains also rediscovered the Madeira Islands (1418–20), the Canaries (1425), and the Azores (1427?), all of which had been known to the ancients, and discovered the Cape Verde Islands in 1456. The Portuguese colonized them all.

Prince Henry's interest in the expansion of geographic knowledge was in large measure intellectual and scientific, and he gathered about him at Sagres a "college" of mathematicians, astronomers, and geographers to aid him in his work. At the same time, Henry, who was a devout Catholic with a crusading zeal, hoped to make contact with the semi-mythical people of the East "who were said to worship the name of Christ," and to form with them an alliance that might roll back the flanks of Islam. But his efforts in the more mundane interests of economic expansion, to say nothing of those of the merchants of Lisbon who profited from his work, were always focused upon the establishment of commercial relations with the coast of Africa and, eventually, the Far East. It was continued, after his death, by the kings of Portugal, and it reached a dramatic justification when Bartholomew Díaz rounded the Cape of Good Hope in 1486 and sailed some distance along the east coast of Africa before turning back toward home, where he arrived in December, 1487, certain that he was at last on the longed-for all-sea route to the Indies. It reached a fabulous climax ten years later, in the voyage of Vasco da Gama, who, in 1497 and 1498, sailed around Africa to India and returned to Lisbon with cargoes said to have been worth sixty times the value of those he had carried on the outward voyage.

Henry's work in the opening of western Africa aroused the rivalry of the kingdom of Castile. In the first place, Castile had a plausible claim to the Canary Islands, based upon a long series of historic grants; in the second place, the merchants of Cadiz and Seville, especially, recognized the wealth-producing potentialities of the new territories on the mainland of Africa, and early began, even before Henry's death, to send their ships for trade into the areas Henry's captains had explored for Portugal. It thus fell out that when, in 1454, a Portuguese vessel seized a Castilian ship that had been trading in Africa, King John II of Castile complained to the King of Portugal with regard to the Portuguese occupation of the Canaries, and, most vehemently, about the Portuguese seizure of Castilian ships trading to "Guinea," which, he claimed, really belonged to him. King Alfonso V, of Portugal, then appealed to the Pope, Nicholas V, as a neutral power, as the generally accepted arbiter of international disputes, and as the recognized authority in matters pertaining to relations between Christians and non-Christians, to decide the question of ownership. This the Pope did, in the famous bull "*Romanus Pontifex*," of January 8, 1455.[2]

In this bull the Pope recognized the work of Prince Henry as expanding the bounds of Christendom and as establishing the title of Portugal to the territories Henry's captains had explored. He recognized Portugal's title to the new lands "that have already been acquired and that shall hereafter come to be acquired," beyond Capes Bojador and Não to the southward, and gave Portugal an exclusive monopoly of trade with them, together with the right to conquer, enslave, and Christianize them; further, he prohibited all others from "meddling" therein without special license from Portugal. This bull thus recognized an exclusive Portuguese possession, together with a commercial and religious monopoly in the "new world." As the first significant international pronouncement relative to the overseas colonial possessions of European nations around the Atlantic, it may be said to mark the beginning of the history of international relations with regard to them.

The bull *Romanus Pontifex* of 1455 was revised slightly in 1456 by a new pope, Calixtus III, who, hoping to encourage Portugal to a greater crusading zeal against Islam in the "new world," extended the religious concessions granted to that country by Nicholas V. Thus the bull *Inter Caetera* of 1456[3] specifically granted to the Portuguese Order of Jesus Christ the ecclesiastical jurisdiction over the newly discovered lands, as well as that of any other lands that might be taken from the Saracens, in the islands or along the coasts of Africa, "all the way to the Indians."

It was hardly to be expected that Castile would forever accept this ruling by the Pope giving Portugal an exclusive possession of the "new world" of exploration. On the other hand, King Alfonso V of Portugal laid claim to the throne of Castile itself, and in 1475 invaded Castile in an effort to make good his claim. The war that resulted was extended to the Canary Islands, and the Castilians actively revived their trade with the coasts of Africa. In the Treaty of Alcaçovas, which ended the war in 1479, Portugal recognized Castile's title to the Canaries, while Castile, now under the rule of King Ferdinand of Aragon and Queen Isabela of Castile, recognized Portugal's exclusive monopoly of the land and the trade of "Guinea," the Azores, the Madeiras, and the Cape Verde Islands, as well as whatever new lands "shall be found." Under the terms of the

[2] Davenport, ed., *European Treaties bearing on the History of the United States and Its Dependencies*, I, 9-26.

[3] Davenport, ed., *European Treaties*, I, 27-32.

treaty the rulers of Castile agreed to forbid their subjects to go into the Portuguese sphere; the King of Portugal, on his part, instructed his captains to seize the ships of interlopers and throw their officers and crews into the sea. The ships might have value; the lives of interloping sailors had none.

But the authority of the Pope as the arbiter of international relations was still strong, especially in matters involving relations between Christians and the heathen. More particularly, King John II of Portugal, who succeeded to the throne in 1481, had reason to distrust Castile's disinterestedness in the carrying out of the treaty. Furthermore, he himself was actively interested in carrying forward the exploratory work of his uncle, Prince Henry. He, therefore, appealed once more to the Pope, now Sixtus IV, for confirmation, not only of the former papal bulls but even of the Treaty of Alcaçovas itself. The Pope, in response to King John's request, in 1481 issued another bull, *Aeterni Regris*,[4] to lend papal sanction to the international arrangements hitherto made. This bull, therefore, confirmed the arrangements made in the Treaty of Alcaçovas, especially the mutual provisos of the two signatories not to molest each other in their respective spheres, and reiterated the positions taken and the privileges granted in the bulls of 1455 and 1456.

Thus had it come about that certain practices and rules of international behavior with regard to the "new world" were laid down in the four decades before Columbus sailed westward from Palos in Castile in 1492. The overseas colonial world was divided by mutual agreement between Castile and Portugal, and this agreement was ratified by papal sanction. The principle of the "closed door" in the colonies was established; and the right of the proprietary state to punish interlopers in its colonies was recognized. The colonies of both Castile and Portugal had proved their profitableness. They had already become an important "stake" in European international diplomacy.

[4] Davenport, ed., *European Treaties*, I, 49-55.

CHAPTER II

Columbus and the Hispano-Portuguese Lines of Demarcation

UPON HIS RETURN to Europe after his first voyage of discovery to America, Christopher Columbus, driven by a westerly storm, took refuge in the mouth of the Tagus River, in Portugal, where he dropped anchor on March 4, 1493. He asked of King John II permission to go up the river as far as Lisbon; the king gave him the permission, but summoned him to the court.

Columbus related to the King the story of his voyage, whereupon the King expressed the opinion that Columbus had been in the part of the world assigned to Portugal by the Treaty of Alcaçovas. This was, of course, not true, since that treaty recognized as a Portuguese sphere only the lands discovered in Africa and the Madeira, Azores, and Cape Verde Islands and other lands and islands "down toward Guinea." Columbus replied that he had not seen that treaty; he knew only that his orders had strictly enjoined him from going to Guinea or to the southward, and that, in fact, he had actually sailed to the westward.

King John was not satisfied by Columbus's answer, and he seems to have gathered a fleet at Lisbon to go out and verify Columbus's data. Meanwhile, Columbus had written to King Ferdinand and Queen Isabela, who were at Barcelona, of his adventures together with a report of the suspicions of King John. He then went on to Palos, in Spain. Ferdinand, upon receiving Columbus's letter, immediately sent off messengers to the Pope, asking for papal confirmation of Spain's ownership of the lands Columbus had discovered, and summoned Columbus himself to Barcelona.

1. The Papal Bulls of 1493

In response to Ferdinand's appeal the Pope, Alexander VI, who was a Valencian and a personal friend of Alfonso, issued a series of bulls recognizing Spain's title to the new lands.

The first of these, the bull *Inter Caetera*,[1] was dated May 3, 1493. It formally granted to Spain the "countries and islands" discovered by Columbus, and others "to be discovered hereafter," provided only that they should not be in the possession of any Christian prince. It also gave Spain complete political dominion over the new lands, and enjoined upon Ferdinand and Isabela the duty of sending missionaries to them for the conversion of the inhabitants to Christianity. At the same time, the Pope prohibited anyone from going to the new countries for trade or any other purpose, without permission of the Spanish rulers, thus giving them an absolute monopoly of the external relations of the new territories. The Pope also specifically recognized the grants to Portugal already made by former popes, of Guinea, the islands and the southern coasts of Africa, and extended to Spain, in its own westward sphere, all the privileges and immunities formerly granted to Portugal in Africa.

The second bull, *Eximiae Devotionis*,[2] although it also bears the date of May 3, 1493, was probably not actually issued until the July following. It repeated the grant contained in *Inter Caetera*, of new lands "lying toward the western parts and the ocean sea." But it placed particular emphasis upon the fact that all the privileges, liberties, and immunities hitherto granted to Portugal in Africa and the islands were now fully granted to the Spanish rulers.

The third bull issued by the Pope to ratify Spain's title to the lands discovered by Columbus, also called *Inter Caetera*,[3] was dated May 4, 1493. This bull repeated the provisions of *Inter Caetera* of May 3rd and those of *Eximiae Devotionis*, but it added a factor of extreme importance in the provision that there should be drawn a line, north and south, from pole to pole, in the "Ocean Sea" one hundred leagues west of the Azores or the Cape Verde Islands, and that lands discovered and to be discovered to the westward of this line should belong to Spain, regardless of who discovered them, even if they were found in the direction of India, provided only that such lands did not actually belong to any Christian prince. Within this huge zone, Spain was to have a monop-

---

[1] Davenport, ed., *European Treaties*, I, 56-63. See also Harrisse, *The Diplomatic History of America*, and Van der Linden, "Alexander VI and the Demarcation of the Maritime and Colonial Domains of Spain and Portugal," *Amer. Hist. Rev.*, XXII, (1916), 1-20.

[2] Davenport, ed., *European Treaties*, I, 66-70.

[3] Davenport, ed., *European Treaties*, I, 71-78.

oly of trade and of the propagation of the Christian religion—no one was to enter this sphere without the king of Spain's permission.

No provision was made in this bull for any rights Portugal might have to the eastward of the papal line. It is also to be noted that since the existence of the Pacific Ocean between the lands discovered by Columbus and the continent of Asia was not yet suspected by Europeans, the provision that lands discovered by Spain while sailing westward, even if in the direction of India, should belong to Spain indicated that it was expected that the Spaniards would eventually arrive in India by this, their exclusive route.

In the summer of 1493 the Spanish sovereigns asked the King of Portugal not to send his armada to occupy the lands Columbus had discovered, at least until it could be clearly determined to whom they rightfully ought to belong. The King of Portugal, on his part, asked Ferdinand and Isabela to prevent their subjects from going into the Portuguese sphere in the direction of Africa, as provided by the Treaty of Alcaçovas. Furthermore, since Columbus had told King John that he believed there were lands to the southward of those he had discovered, the King of Portugal suggested that, in addition to the north-south line of demarcation drawn by the Pope, an east-west line be drawn at the latitude of the Canary Islands, with a restriction of Spaniards to the area north of this line.

Negotiations to these ends were begun in Barcelona by representatives of both countries in the summer of 1493, but in the midst of the negotiations Ferdinand again appealed to the Pope for a confirmation of his claims. The Pope complied, and on September 26, 1493, he issued a fourth bull, *Dudum Siquidem.*[4] This bull repeated the grant of lands discovered west of the line of demarcation to Spain, but it was especially explicit in its provision that those lands should belong to Spain, even though they might be "islands and mainlands that belonged or belong to India," and no one was to go to or occupy these lands without the Spanish king's permission, notwithstanding any grants made by the Pope's predecessors or some other ruling monarch, provided that the lands granted under these other concessions were not actually occupied. This provision apparently refers to the grants to Portugal by former popes, and seems to be a sort of safeguard against any later Portuguese claim that Spain, by sailing westward, might be trespassing upon Portuguese territories which might have been found by Portuguese sailing southward and eastward.

The appeal of the Spanish rulers for papal sanction for their title to the lands discovered by Columbus and the issuance of the four bulls of 1493 to allocate to Spain a large portion of the unknown territory of the world are indicative of the fact that the Pope was still looked upon as an

---

[4] Davenport, ed., *European Treaties,* I, 79-83.

arbiter of international disputes. While the four bulls clearly favored
Spain, they embodied the "rules of the game" with regard to the exploration and exploitation of the "new world" laid down in the earlier papal
bulls and the Treaty of Alcaçovas. Thus, under the terms of these bulls,
Spain was given exclusive, monopolistic ownership of all the lands it might
discover to the westward of the line of demarcation, together with the
monopolistic and exclusive rights to religious penetration and of commerce with them. These basic monopolistic principles were accepted by
both of the two great rivals for colonal empire.

2. *The Treaty of Tordesillas, 1494*

The chief problem in the Hispano-Portuguese negotiations at Barcelona
in the summer of 1493 was that of agreeing upon clear and recognizable
boundaries between the spheres of interest of the two countries in the
"new world." But the negotiations broke up because, in the words of the
Spanish negotiators, the Portuguese delegates "do not come [correctly]
informed as to what is ours." Another effort at negotiation was made in
the fall of 1493, and yet another in the spring of 1494. In the latter case,
the Portuguese agents, Ruy de Sousa, Toão de Sousa, and Ayres de
Almada, talked directly with the Spanish rulers at Medina del Campo,
near Valladolid, in Spain.

The Portuguese delegates complained that the line of demarcation
drawn by the Pope lay too close to the Azores and asked that the line be
moved farther west by agreement. Incidentally, of course, they hoped that
by moving the line to the westward their sphere of interest might be made
to include more lands—as it actually was.

The Portuguese proposal was accepted, and a treaty was signed at
Tordesillas, near Valladolid, on June 7, 1494.[5] Under its provisions, the
line of demarcation was moved to that of the north-south meridian 370
leagues west of the Cape Verde Islands. It was clearly stated that all lands
already discovered or to be discovered on "This [eastern] side" of the line
should belong to the King of Portugal, and that all lands already discovered or to be discovered "on the western side of the said bound,"
should belong to the King and Queen of Spain. The treaty provided, also,
that Spain would keep its ships and subjects from going into the Portuguese sphere; Portugal promised to keep its ships and subjects from
entering the Spanish sphere, for any purpose whatsoever, whether exploration, trade, or conquest. Should the ships of either party enter the
sphere of the other, they were to be seized and confiscated, and any lands
discovered by them were to be delivered up to the royal proprietor of that

---

[5] Davenport, ed., *European Treaties*, I, 84-100.

sphere. However, since Spanish ships going toward the Spanish sphere to the west of the line must sail over the "seas of the said King of Portugal" to the east of it, they are permitted to do so, but they must take the most direct route, so as not to spend too much time in the Portuguese sphere nor be tempted to take anything therein that was Portugal's. If, however, lands already occupied by Spain were found to be east of the line, those lands were to remain in Spain's possession.

Provision was made in the treaty for a survey of the location of the line by a joint commission of mariners and surveyors, but this provision was never actually carried out. The line appeared (for the first time) on the famous Cantino map of 1502.[6]

Thus did Spain and Portugal coolly divide the "new world" between them, with, they thought, the sanction of the Holy See. Thus, too, did they reiterate the "rules of the game" as between themselves; they just as coolly assumed that the other nations of the world would respect their agreements.

When, in 1500, Pedro Alvarez Cabral, on his way to India, landed on the coast of what later came to be known as Brazil and discovered that much of the large eastern bulge of South America lay to the eastward of the Tordesillas line, it was realized that Portugal had, indeed, added a great body of new land in America to its empire under the terms of the Treaty of 1494. Shortly thereafter, having heard of the lands discovered by English explorers, Portugal sent the Corte-Real brothers, in 1500 and 1501, to explore the northeastern coasts of North America, which were thought also to lie to the eastward of the line, and which, on the basis of these explorations, Portugal proceeded to claim.

In view of the fact, however, that M. A. Pinzón and Diego de Lepe had both taken possession of the coasts of South America for Spain, King Emanuel of Portugal appealed to the Pope, now Julius II, to confirm the Treaty of Tordesillas, and, thereby, extinguish the new Spanish claim. Julius complied, and on January 24, 1506, issued the bull *Ea Quae*,[7] which specifically confirmed the Treaty of Tordesillas, although it did not mention the treaty by name. The bull also contained a polite warning to Spain not to molest the Portuguese in their possession of lands discovered and occupied under the agreement, which would include, of course, those lands discovered and claimed by the Portuguese east of the line in America.

In the years following the voyages of Vasco da Gama (1497) and Pedro Cabral (1500) to India, the Portuguese colonial empire in the East Indies advanced steadily farther and farther eastward. Malacca was conquered by Albuquerque in 1511, and the Moluccas were reached in 1512. As the Portuguese moved eastward, serious questions began to arise as to

[6] Davenport, ed., *European Treaties*, I, 101.
[7] Davenport, ed., *European Treaties*, I, 107-111.

whether—since no one dreamed, as yet, that the broad Pacific lay between the continent discovered by Columbus and the east coast of Asia—these rich lands being occupied by the Portuguese might, indeed, lie on the Spanish side of the line drawn in the Atlantic by the Treaty of Tordesillas.

It was apparently to forestall claims by Spain that might arise out of these questions that King Emanuel of Portugal, now in great favor with the Pope, Leo X, turned to the Holy See for such a ruling as to his title to his Far Eastern possessions as might guarantee him against Spanish challenges in that area. The Pope complied again, and on November 3, 1514, issued the bull *Praecelsae Devotionis*.[8]

In this bull the Pope confirmed all the concessions made by his predecessors to Portugal. But he added "other and new privileges" to inspire King Emanuel to further efforts in spreading Christianity among the infidels. Thus, the King was assured of the rightness of his title to all the lands hitherto discovered "or in future to be recovered, acquired, discovered and found by the said King Emanuel and his successors," both from Capes Bojador and Não (on the west coast of Africa) to the Indies, "and in any place or region whatsoever, even though perchance unknown to us at present"; all faithful Christians were prohibited from hindering King Emanuel in any way.

The logical effect of this bull was to nullify the line of Tordesillas, since it guaranteed the Portuguese title to any land to be discovered "in any place or region whatsoever." Practically, Portugal still respected the Tordesillas line; all it wished to be assured of was that it might take and hold whatever it might find in this island paradise off Southeast Asia.

3. The Line in the Pacific, 1529

Apparently, Balboa's discovery of the Pacific off the Isthmus of Panama in 1513 had little direct effect upon European thinking or diplomacy with regard to the "new world." It remained for Ferdinand de Magellan to demonstrate the significance of the Pacific in the distribution of the earth's colonial riches. In 1519 Magellan, a disgruntled Portuguese captain who had previously sailed to the Moluccas, took service with King Carlos I of Spain, and having convinced him that the Moluccas could be reached by sailing westward, actually sailed around South America and arrived in the Philippines in 1521.

Since Magellan had reached the Philippines by sailing westward for Spain beyond the line of Tordesillas, did not these islands rightfully belong to Spain? Did not the Moluccas, visited by Sebastián Elcano in Magellan's ship, the *Victoria* (Magellan was killed in a skirmish with the natives in the Philippines), also belong to Spain, since the native chieftains made

[8] Davenport, ed., *European Treaties*, I, 112-117.

treaties with Elcano and declared themselves to be the vassals of Spain? Of course, the Portuguese were already there and sought to destroy Elcano and all his works.

Elcano and the *Victoria* escaped from the Portuguese and completed their epic voyage. They had not only demonstrated the huge size of the Pacific; they had also demonstrated that the Tordesillas line was useless, at least with regard to the East Indies, so long as Spanish ships might reach the very heart of the Portuguese colonial empire by sailing westward; and they had dramatically proved, to the Spanish and Portuguese rulers, the urgent necessity for a new line to define their respective spheres of interest in the Pacific and the Far East.

The two courts, therefore, almost immediately began a series of negotiations with regard to the new situation. These negotiations concerned themselves with three basic problems: (1) that of drawing a new line of demarcation in the Pacific, (2) the question of who actually possessed the Moluccas, and (3) who really owned those islands. Both sides claimed they had effectively occupied the Moluccas; the Portuguese, since they had found the islands, claimed them, even though they might lie within the Spanish sphere under the terms of the Treaty of Tordesillas; if they did lie in the Spanish sphere, at least Spain should petition for their return. The Spaniards demanded just the opposite.

An agreement was arrived at in Victoria, in Spain, on February 19, 1524.[9] According to this agreement, since there had arisen some doubt as to whether the Moluccas, under the provision of the Treaty of Tordesillas, belonged to Spain or to Portugal, there should be named a joint commission composed of "three astrologers [navigators] and three pilots and sailors" for each side to determine in which sphere the Moluccas lay according to the Treaty of Tordesillas. Another commission, composed of three lawyers for each side, was to decide which of the two countries actually possessed the islands. While the two commissions were deliberating, neither country would send trading expeditions to the islands.[10]

Accordingly, in execution of the terms of the treaty, the so-called *"junta* of Badajoz" was held at Badajoz, on the Spanish-Portuguese frontier, in the spring of 1524. The *junta* broke up without accomplishing anything, however. There was disagreement as to the location of the line of Tordesillas, to begin with, and while the Portuguese commissioners found the Moluccas to be 21° east of the line of Tordesillas, the Spaniards found them to be an even greater distance to the west of it—as well they might. Both of them could have been right, but the question of ownership remained: it simply could not be decided under the Treaty of Tordesillas.

Because the *"junta* of Badajoz" was a complete failure, the problem of the demarcation of spheres of influence in the Pacific and the Far East

[9] Davenport, ed., *European Treaties*, I, 118-130.
[10] Davenport, ed., *European Treaties*, I, 127-128.

remained unsolved. It was not until 1529 that, in the Treaty of Saragossa, a working arrangement for the resolution of the problem was devised.

An effort was, indeed, made in the year 1526, and representatives of the two countries drew up a draft of an agreement on the subject of the demarcation of colonial spheres. According to this proposed agreement, the question of the ownership of the Moluccas was to be settled by a joint "tribunal" of lawyers and "astrologers" or mariners on the basis of the Treaty of Tordesillas. But this agreement was never signed.[11]

It was not until 1529 that an agreement was finally arrived at, in the Treaty of Saragossa of that year.[12] In this instance, the renewed negotiations grew out of the need of King Carlos I of Spain, now the Holy Roman Emperor, for money. It occurred to him and his advisers that he might sell his claim to the Moluccas to Portugal. The proposal met with an interested response from Portugal, and the treaty was signed on April 23, 1529.

This treaty was in effect a contract by which the Emperor, King of Spain, pledged Spain's claim to the Moluccas against 350,000 ducats in gold to be advanced to him by Portugal. It was not an outright sale, for Spain had a right to renew its claim by the repayment of the money. Needless to say, the claim was never renewed.

The most significant provision of this treaty, however, was the agreement to draw a new line of demarcation in the Pacific Ocean, drawn north and south from pole to pole, through the Islands of Santo Tomé de las Velas, situated 17° east of the Moluccas. Spaniards crossing the line, going westward into the Portuguese sphere, were to be regarded as trespassers; Portuguese crossing it eastward into the Spanish sphere were to be condemned and punished as interlopers in the Spanish zone. As for the Moluccas, a joint commission was to attempt again to determine the ownership of the Moluccas in view of the conflicting claims of the two countries under the terms of the Treaty of Tordesillas. If the commission should favor the King of Spain, Spanish ownership was not to be recognized until the Emperor had repaid the 350,000 ducats advanced to him by Portugal. This was a futile gesture, of course, since it was impossible to determine the ownership of the Moluccas under the old treaty, as already noted.

By the drawing of the new line, since the Treaty of Tordesillas remained in force, the world was now effectively divided into two north-south zones. The zone between the two lines, going westward from that of Tordesillas in the Atlantic toward that of Saragossa in the Pacific, which included America, was recognized as Spanish, although the Spaniards could enter their zone only by sailing westward. The zone between the Tordesillas line on the west and the Saragossa line on the east was recog-

[11] Davenport, ed., *European Treaties*, I, 131-145.
[12] Davenport, ed., *European Treaties*, I, 169-198.

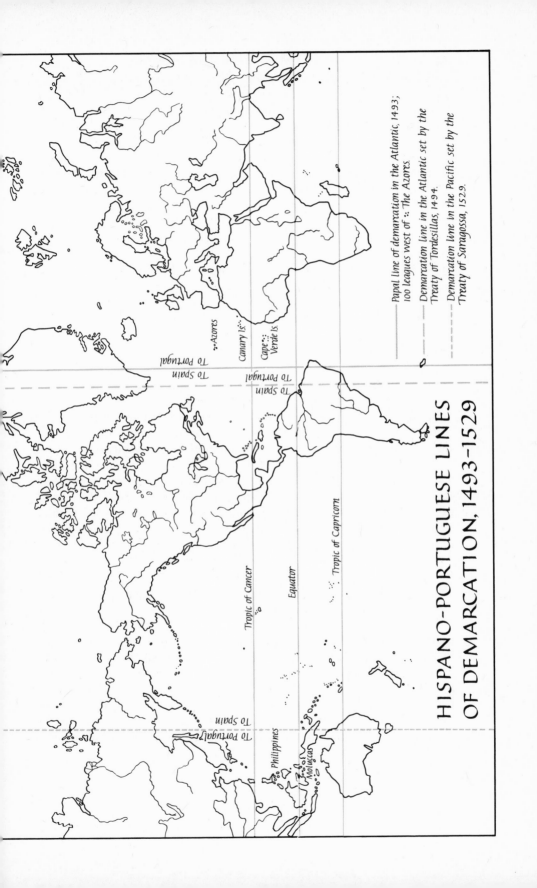

HISPANO-PORTUGUESE LINES
OF DEMARCATION, 1493–1529

Papal line of demarcation in the Atlantic, 1493;
100 leagues west of ∴ The Azores.

Demarcation line in the Atlantic set by the
Treaty of Tordesillas, 1494.

Demarcation line in the Pacific set by the
Treaty of Saragossa, 1529.

Azores

Canary Is.

Cape
Verde Is.

To Portugal

To Spain   To Portugal

To Spain   To Portugal

Tropic of Cancer

Equator

Tropic of Capricorn

Philippines

Moluccas

To Portugal?   To Spain

nized as Portuguese, but Portuguese ships could enter it only by sailing southward from Europe and eastward around Africa. The treaty was to be submitted to the Pope for confirmation.

It is to be noted that, although Spain never again claimed the Moluccas, the Philippine Islands, discovered by Magellan, lay to the westward of the line of Saragossa, and, therefore, within the Portuguese sphere as delimited by the Saragossa line of demarcation. The Portuguese, therefore, laid claim to these islands, and when, in 1542–43 Spain sent a colonizing expedition there from Mexico under Rez Lopez de Villalobos, the Portuguese entered a vigorous protest. Another expedition in 1568 elicited another protest; but the union of the Spanish and Portuguese crowns in 1580 ended for a time the debate over the ownership of these islands. Upon the separation of the crowns of Spain and Portugal again in 1640, however, the dispute was revived, and Portugal again laid claim to the Philippines under the Treaty of Saragossa. The Hispano-Portuguese quarrel over the Philippines was not ended until the "American" treaty between them, made in 1750. Under this treaty Spain retained title to the Philippines.[13]

By the Treaty of Saragossa of 1529 the first phase in the international history of America came to an end. During the years between 1492 and 1529 Spain and Portugal, among the states of Western Europe, had enjoyed an almost unchallenged monopoly of overseas discovery, exploration, conquest, colonization, and exploitation of the hitherto unknown, or little known, world outside of Europe. They had divided the "new world" between them, and they had laid down, as between themselves, the basic rules governing their respective colonial empires: the closed, exclusive sphere of colonial possession, a national monopoly of exploration, commerce, and religious activity within each sphere, a recognition of the sharp demarcation of spheres provided by the two lines set up in the Treaties of Tordesillas and Saragossa, and an acceptance of the principle that the seas "beyond the lines" were the property of the owners of the spheres as well as the land, and that, therefore, those seas were closed to "interlopers" of any other nation.

These two states had assumed, without much thought, that these principles, fully accepted between themselves, would also be accepted by the other states of the world. This, of course, was not to be; for already, by the time of the signing of the Treaty of Saragossa, the other commercially expanding states and societies of Western Europe were challenging the arrogant assumptions and procedures of the Hispano-Portuguese monopoly. That challenge—or those challenges—would introduce what was one of the most dramatic international dramas of modern times.

[13] See Chapter XII.

CHAPTER III

The French, English, and Dutch Challenges to the Hispano-Portuguese Monopoly

I T WAS HARDLY to be expected that the other expanding commercial peoples of Western Europe would either accept or respect the arrogation to themselves by Spain and Portugal of the entire undiscovered world, with or without the blessings and encouragement of the Pope. The sanction of the Pope, indeed, actually gave an additional and powerful motive for opposing it, to those peoples who, as the Dutch and the English, in the sixteenth century became Protestant. But the economic motive alone was sufficiently strong to make a series of challenges to Hispano-Portuguese monopoly almost inevitable, by Catholic France as well as by Protestant England and Holland.

1. The French Challenge

France was one of the first of the Western European countries to challenge the self-declared Hispano-Portuguese monopoly of the hitherto unexplored world.

France, indeed, after the ravages of the Hundred Years War and the final emergence of Louis XI (who died in 1483) as monarch of a stabilized and unified kingdom, had entered upon an era of prosperity, with full participation of the merchants of Marseilles, Lyon, Bordeaux, Nantes, Dieppe, Rouen, and other mercantile seaports in the benefits of the great overseas expansion of Western European commerce. Investment capital accumulated in these cities, and the merchants supported many an exploratory expedition into the prospective new markets of the non-European world, even into the gradually opening areas of western Africa. French interest and participation in overseas expansion was thus well established before Columbus's discovery. It has even been suggested that

French mariners may have discovered Brazil in 1488, and that Columbus may have been encouraged to make his voyage by a knowledge of their discovery.[1]

At about this time, certainly, the French fishermen of the coast towns of Brittany and Normandy began to exploit the fabulously rich fisheries of the Grand Bank of Newfoundland, and a number of exploratory voyages went from Honfleur and Rouen to study the land of the area in 1506, 1508, and 1509; the last of them brought back to France a number of American Indians. Other voyages in the same period took the French to the coast of Brazil.

Presently, French corsairs and privateers began to reap a rich harvest from preying upon Spanish and Portuguese ships returning to Europe with the wealth of the Indies, West and East. Complaints and reprisals multiplied; Spain and Portugal claimed that the mere presence of French ships in the areas of the world closed by papal bulls and Hispano-Portuguese treaties was *ipso facto* sufficient justification for their destruction, since they were interloping in the closed spheres of interest proclaimed by the Hispano-Portuguese monopoly. Francis I, who mounted the French throne in 1515, vacillated, but he generally supported his mariners on the ground that the seas were open to all.

After the Spanish conquest of Mexico in 1523, when the treasures of Mexico were shipped in quantity from the "new world" to Spain, French "entrepreneurs" from the French coastal ports found it profitable to pounce upon the Spanish treasure ships on their way home from America. The greatest and most powerful of these French promoters was Jean Ango, of Dieppe, whose raiders, under the cover of the war (1520–26) between Francis I of France and Carlos I of Spain, laid heavy toll upon the Spanish galleons. Later, Ango's ships visited Madagascar, Sumatra, and Brazil, all in the Portuguese sphere of the "new world" of discovery and exploitation.

Meanwhile, in 1523, a group of silk merchants of Lyon, headed by the Italian Tomascino Guadaqui, one of the King's bankers, interested in a direct route to China, engaged a Florentine navigator, Giovanni da Verrazano, to search for a route to the Orient around the northern shores of Europe. Driven back by storms, Verrazano crossed the Atlantic westward and examined the eastern shore of North America from about Cape Fear to Newfoundland. As he reported to King Francis on his return, he was surprised and chagrined to find such an obstacle in his path and hoped to try again. This he did in 1526 and again in 1528. His expeditions were unsuccessful, but they gave Francis I a basis for claiming the territory of North America, which Verrazano had called New France.

It was upon the basis of this claim that the government of France subsidized two voyages to New France—or "Francis-land"—under the

[1] Roncière, *Histoire de la marine française*, II, 401-405.

leadership of Jacques Cartier, of St. Malo, in 1534 and 1535. Cartier explored the Gulf and River of St. Lawrence, ascended the river as far as Montreal, and brought back a little gold and some sand crystals that were thought to be diamonds. Because of events in Europe, however, no further efforts were made by the French in that area at that time.

A new war began between Francis I and Carlos I in 1536 (the second in the series), and Francis I, in order to win the benevolent neutrality of Portugal, which stood very much in fear of Spain, made a treaty with Portugal [2] which assured the neutral Portuguese commerce of friendly treatment by the French corsairs and permitted the French privateers and warships to bring their prizes into Portuguese ports. In practice, this meant that the French corsairs could use the ports of the Portuguese colonies in the Azores as bases from which to attack the Spanish treasure fleets returning from America. Under the friendship established by this treaty, also, Francis I prohibited French ships from voyaging into the prohibited Portuguese sphere in Brazil, Guinea, or other lands claimed by Portugal.

Thus, while Francis I won Portugal's acquiescence in French violations of the Spanish sphere of influence as established under the Treaty of Tordesillas, he acknowledged, in effect, the Portuguese claim to a closed sphere in its own colonial empire, and promised to respect it. Francis I actually prohibited his mariners from going to the Portuguese colonies; but his prohibition lasted only until 1540.

This second war between Francis I and Carlos I was ended in 1538 by the so-called Truce of Nice. In the four years of peace that followed, France again became active in overseas enterprises, and Francis I, hoping to found a French colonial source of national wealth, authorized François de la Rocque, the Seigneur de Roberval, to found a colony in the lands Cartier had explored along the St. Lawrence. This colony failed; but the work of Verrazano, Cartier, and Roberval had given France a fairly solid basis for a claim to a large slice of North America—a slice that included both the future Canada and the future United States.

More important was the fact that the activities of the French in North America, and especially Roberval's colony, were extremely distressing to both Spain and Portugal, for these activities were clearly a violation of the Hispano-Portuguese monopoly of the "new world" proclaimed in the Treaty of Tordesillas in 1494. Carlos I even sent a ship to follow and report upon Cartier's new expedition to Canada. But to the Emperor's demand for French recognition of the exclusive Spanish possession of all the land west of the Line of Tordesillas, Francis I replied, "The sun shines for me as for others; I should like to see the clause in Adam's will that excludes me from a share in the world." [3]

[2] Davenport, ed., *European Treaties*, I, 199-204.
[3] Quoted by Roncière, *Histoire de la marine française*, III, 300.

Francis I, by this and other pronouncements, thus emerges as one of the earliest champions of the doctrine of the freedom of the seas. And it was the rivalry of the colonizing powers in America which first called that doctrine into being.

In July, 1542, Francis I again declared war upon Carlos I. This war was disastrous for France, for Carlos I and his English allies invaded France and very nearly took Paris. The war was concluded by a treaty of peace signed at Crépy-en-Laonnois, September 18, 1544,[4] to which was added a secret article with regard to the Indies, providing that France would not colonize the East Indies or the West Indies. Spain did permit the French to go to the Indies, but only for trading purposes. France was willing, it seems, to accept this limitation because of the failure of Cartier and Roberval to discover riches for France in Canada. Even this concession, however, was disliked by the Spanish Council of the Indies and the Spanish Council of State because it permitted the French to trade in the hitherto totally sealed Spanish colonial sphere and to sail over the exclusively Spanish ocean. It was feared that not only would the French not trade according to the rules, but that this loophole would provide the French with a perfect cover for the French corsairs who had hitherto preyed upon Spain's American commerce with such devastating effect. The Council of the Indies urged that this treaty, as others hitherto made by Spain, omit the Indies. The Portuguese also objected to this concession to the French, on much the same grounds.

Probably because of such opposition this article of the treaty was never officially ratified. Nevertheless, Francis I, abandoning, for the moment, his noble principle of the freedom of the seas, in 1545 prohibited his subjects from going to the Spanish colonies.[5]

In 1555, a French colony under the leadership of Nicholas Durand de Villegagnon was established on the coast of Brazil, only to be destroyed by the Portuguese. Meanwhile, in 1552 Spain and France had gone to war once more. This war had spread to America, and Spanish privateers had preyed upon the French fisheries at Newfoundland while French privateers raided Spanish fleets and colonies in the Caribbean area; Havana fell to the French admiral Jacques de Sores in 1555. A truce was arranged at Vaucelles, in France, in 1556,[6] according to which France agreed that its subjects would not trade in the Spanish Indies without special licenses from the Spanish king, now Philip II. France thus again abandoned its claim to a right of its mariners to sail anywhere in the Spanish sphere, even that recognized by Spain in the Treaty of Crépy-en-Laonnois.

But the truce of Vaucelles did not last; fighting began again less than a year after it was signed. The new hostilities were ended by the Treaty

[4] Davenport, ed., *European Treaties*, I, 205-214.
[5] Davenport, ed., *European Treaties*, I, 206-207.
[6] Davenport, ed., *European Treaties*, I, 215-218.

of Cateau-Cambrésis, signed April 3, 1559.[7] The situation in America, which now included French raids upon Spain's Caribbean colonies, played an important role in the discussions. The Spanish negotiators reasserted the old Spanish claim to an exclusive right to the seas and the lands to the westward of the line of demarcation stabilized by the papal bulls and demanded the abandonment of Villegagnon's colony. But the French negotiators now reaffirmed the principle that the sea everywhere was open and free to all nations and asserted the principle of "effective occupation," that is, that lands not effectively occupied, wherever they might be, might be occupied and claimed by any nation. This doctrine, if accepted, would have nullified the monopolistic claims of Spain and Portugal, whether under the papal bulls or the various treaties between Spain and Portugal. The French were willing, however, to omit all mention of the Indies from the treaty, with the understanding that the French would continue to operate in the Indies upon the basis of their own principles and that if Frenchmen went into areas actually occupied by the Spanish, they might be punished; it was understood that such punishment would not be considered a cause for war between the two countries. This was, in effect, an informal agreement between France and Spain that "might makes right beyond the Line," a significant antecedent or an elementary form of the later "doctrine of the two spheres," that is, that Europe constituted a sphere in which a certain body of international law and precedent prevailed, and the "new world" constituted another sphere, with a different set of laws and conventions. Violence "beyond the Line," under this doctrine, was not considered a *casus belli* in Europe.[8]

Thus stood the outcome of the French challenge to the Hispano-Portuguese monopoly in 1559. Under this *modus vivendi*, French expeditions of all sorts to America continued. A new French colony was founded in Florida in 1562 under Jean Ribaut and René de Laudonnière, only to be destroyed by the Spanish in 1565. Despite the fact that France was wracked by internal religious and dynastic strife for the next several decades, other efforts were made to plant French colonies in the northeastern parts of North America in the last two decades of the century, efforts that culminated in the successful founding of Acadia by Samuel de Champlain in 1604 and of Quebec in 1608.

Yet Spain was far from ready to relax its claim to an exclusive monopoly of the entire American hemisphere. The question of recognition of a French right to go there came up in the negotiations for the Treaty of Vervins (1598), which made peace between Henry IV of France and Philip II of Spain after Philip's intervention in the French religious wars, but Spain was unwilling to admit in writing that any other nation might go to the

[7] Davenport, ed., *European Treaties*, I, 219-222.
[8] Davenport, ed., *European Treaties*, I, 220-221, fn. 9.

Spanish Indies in America. It was finally decided to leave the matter as it had been left in 1559, that is, as one of the French negotiators recalled,

He [the king of Spain] spoke to me privately of certain complaints that had been made of prosecution of certain people who had taken some Spaniards in the Indies, and he said that we need not favor the said Spaniards; and since they did not wish to permit anyone to trade in the Indies, Brazil, or other places beyond the line, and at the last treaty [1559] nothing had been done in that direction, he did not intend that any prosecution be made of what our people had done in that area [America]; and since they took our vessels when they found them there it was only fair that we should be allowed to do the same.[9]

Philip simply did not wish to give the appearance of legality to the presence of French ships in American waters by putting into a public treaty provision for prosecuting them for deeds they committed while there!

In any case, Spain's policy of sticking its head in the sand in order to avoid seeing that other nations were actually going to America was of no avail. The founding of Acadia and Quebec, in territories theoretically claimed by Spain, marked the beginning of the successful conclusion of the French challenge to the Hispano-Portuguese monopoly and the opening of a new era in the relations between France and Spain in the colonial world of America.

2. The English Challenge

The second of the European commercial nations to challenge the self-proclaimed Hispano-Portuguese monopoly was England. If France's challenge was begun and developed by means of poaching, piracy, privateering, and war, English infiltration into the profitable exploitation of the "new world" was achieved, at first at least, through the channels of legitimate commerce and peaceful penetration.

So far as Portugal was concerned, ever since the marriage of a daughter of John of Gaunt to King John of Portugal, the father of Prince Henry the Navigator, late in the fourteenth century, the commercial relations between England and Portugal had been friendly. By the end of the fifteenth century, during the reign of Henry VII in England, there was an active commerce between the two countries.

It was Henry VII who, in 1497, sent John Cabot across the Atlantic to look for China and to establish relations with that country. On his first voyage he found a land that was probably eastern Labrador; he thought he was in Asia and might find China by sailing southward. On his second voyage, in 1498, he tried it, but he did not find China. No one, as yet, had any idea that there was a great continent and a vast ocean still standing

[9] Quoted in Davenport, ed., *European Treaties*, I, 213, fn. 8.

between Europe and eastern Asia. John Cabot's son, Sebastian, repeated his father's efforts a little later; it may be that Sebastian realized the true situation, for he seems consciously to have been seeking a passage around America toward the northwestward. When the Arctic ice field blocked his way he turned southward, and he apparently skirted a long stretch of the eastern shore of North America.

In any case, the explorations of the Cabots fell into the area claimed by Portugal under the Treaty of Tordesillas; and Portugal, in order to verify this fact, sent out two exploratory expeditions under the Corte-Real brothers in 1500 and 1501, as has been noted.

Meanwhile, the trade between England and Portugal was flourishing, and certain merchants of Bristol entered into a direct trade with the Azores and sent new expeditions to the northeastern parts of North America for fishing and fur trading, and to search for the northwest passage to China. During the reign of Henry VIII, English merchants of Plymouth, Southhampton, and London established direct trades with Portuguese Guinea and Brazil.

In 1527, King Henry VIII sent John Rut to explore the possibility of finding a northwest passage, but Rut followed the Cabot route: he found Labrador, was blocked by ice, and turned southward to explore the coast as far as the West Indies. He visited the Spanish colonies at Puerto Rico and Santo Domingo, thus apparently becoming the first English explorer to intrude upon the closed Spanish colonial sphere in the Caribbean area.

In 1530–32, despite the protests of the Portuguese government, William Hawkins of Plymouth made a series of voyages to Brazil by way of Guinea. One of his ships, in 1540, brought home to England a valuable cargo of ivory from Africa and "brazil-wood" (dyewood) from Brazil. Portugal took steps to stop the interlopers, however, and the English contact with Brazil came to an end, at least for the time being.

Thus, during the reign of Henry VIII in England, English ships, seamen, and trade had penetrated both the Spanish and the Portuguese spheres established by the Treaty of Tordesillas.

The direct trade with Brazil died out about 1540; but English voyages to Africa—the Gold Coast and the Bight of Benin, for example—in the Portuguese sphere continued; and in 1553 an English syndicate began a profitable trade in that area for grain, ivory, and gold. Portugal protested these intrusions, as was to be expected; the English government replied that the merchants traded only with African chieftains in areas not effectively occupied by the Portuguese—thus asserting what came to be known as "the doctrine of effective occupation" and disregarding both the papal bulls and the Spanish and Portuguese claims under the Treaty of Tordesillas. When Mary Tudor succeeded Edward VI in 1553, she, joining with her husband, Philip II of Spain, accepted the Portuguese and Spanish positions and prohibited her merchants from entering the Portuguese sphere. The trade went on, nevertheless, and when Elizabeth I succeeded Mary in 1558 it was more or less publicly reopened, with a general encouragement from the Queen. One of the most notable voyages of this period was that made in 1562–63 by John Hawkins, who went to the Guinea coast, took a cargo of slaves after plundering a number of Portuguese vessels, and then proceeded to the Spanish West Indies, where he sold the Negroes to Spanish colonists, as some have reported, at the points of his guns. He thus violated the Spanish exclusive policy in those parts, effectively defied the Portuguese claim to a monopoly of African colonization and trade, including the *asiento* (the monopoly of the carrying of African slaves to the Spanish colonies in America), and initiated the English trade in African slaves to that hemisphere.

Both Portugal and Spain bitterly objected to these violations of both their spheres. When Portugal sent ambassadors to protest, Queen Elizabeth replied, on one occasion, that she would, for the sake of peace, prohibit her people from visiting places in Africa actually occupied by the Portuguese, but that she could not accept exclusion, under the orders of the Portuguese court, from areas not effectively occupied by Portuguese subjects. Meanwhile, English voyages to Africa and the Spanish West Indies continued, to the great profit of the English merchants.[10]

In 1567 John Hawkins made his most spectacular voyage to America. He stopped at San Juan de Ulloa (Vera Cruz) for repairs to his ships, only to be attacked by a fleet of Spanish ships that arrived shortly after he did. All but two of his ships were destroyed; Hawkins escaped on one of these, the young Francis Drake got away on the other.

Disappointed in its efforts to get Queen Elizabeth I to prohibit her subjects from trading in Africa, Portugal sent warships to the African coast to stop the visits by interlopers. There ensued several years of undeclared war. Negotiations for peace began in 1571, but since Queen Elizabeth would not budge on the principle of effective occupation, nothing was achieved except, in 1576, an agreement to end hostilities. Eventually, the principle of effective occupation came to be accepted, at least tacitly, by Spain and Portugal; it was upon the basis of this principle that England could claim a sort of quasi-legal justification for the settlement of its first colonies in America later in the century.

As for Spain, the English began to benefit from the trade of the Spanish colonies almost from the beginning. King Henry VII had cultivated commerce with Spain, and by the commercial clauses of the Treaty of Medina del Campo, of 1489, which was primarily a military alliance against France, it had been agreed that the ships of each nation should be permitted to visit all the territories of the others. At that moment, of

[10] For a further discussion of the doctrine of effective occupation see Chapter XII.

course, Spain's only overseas colony was the Canary Islands; Columbus's discovery and its international impact did not come until three years later. Under this treaty, however, England assumed that the trade of the Spanish colony of the Canaries was to be open to English traders, as, indeed it was.

After the opening of America by Columbus and his successors, English merchants, either resident in Spain or through factors there, participated in the commerce of the Spanish colonies by way of the *Casa de Contratación*, the official Spanish agency for the conduct of trade with America, and the ports of Seville, Cadiz, and San Lucar de Barrameda. All this commerce with Spanish America was handled by the official Spanish monopoly, and the English merchants were at first subject only to the same restrictions as those under which Spanish citizens were permitted to participate in the trade. Some even had English factors resident in the Spanish colonies.

This happy situation was not to last, however. With the growth of an English inclination to go directly to the new trading areas of the world and the consequent invasions of English seamen in both the Portuguese and the Spanish spheres, the economic harmony between Spain and England began to be dispelled, and to economic tensions were added political tensions sprung from religious differences engendered by the Protestant Reformation in England under Henry VIII and Edward VI. The Spanish Inquisition began to bring its fires to bear upon the Protestant English merchants resident in Spain, and they suffered both personal persecution and the loss of their commercial privileges. To these, again, was added a bitter resentment against "Spanish treachery" when Spain withdrew in 1544 from the joint Anglo-Spanish war against France by the separate Treaty of Crépy-en-Laonnois, already noted.

It was in line with this new English enmity for Spain that, in 1545, John Reneger, an English merchant-privateer, in professed retaliation for the abuse of Englishmen in Spain, seized a Spanish ship, the *San Salvador*, off Cape St. Vincent, homeward bound from the Indies.[11]

The "Reneger incident" marked a sharp turning point in Anglo-Spanish relations, for it initiated the beginning of a period of increasingly bitter tension between the two countries, a tension that was at once political, economic, and religious, and which mounted steadily, with the exception of the reign of Queen Mary Tudor (1553–58), from that time until it reached its climax in the war of the Great Armada.

Spain immediately protested Reneger's action through diplomatic channels and demanded a return of the gold seized by him. At the same time, English ships in Spanish ports were seized as hostages, an action that only made the English more adamant in their refusal to restore the *San Salvador* and its gold. The English, on their side, explained that the

[11] See Connell-Smith, *Forerunners of Drake; A Study of Trade with Spain in the Early Tudor Period, passim.*

San Salvador had been seized in retaliation for the seizure of English ships in Spain; when those ships were released and Protestant English merchants assured they would be safe from the persecutions of the Inquisition something might be done toward a restoration of the *San Salvador's* treasure.

This quarrel was eventually patched up; but the tension between the two countries continued, both in Europe and in America. It was exacerbated by the aid given the Low Countries by England in the course of their rebellion against Spain. In the meantime, the seafaring and commercial classes of England continued, at an increasing pace, their penetration, through privateering, piracy, or brazen violations of the Spanish restrictions upon Spanish colonial commerce, of which the "Reneger incident" was only one early example. The French had already been challenging Spain's maritime and colonial monopoly in America; by its varied maritime aggressions, England now asserted and carried out a challenge of its own, one that was to culminate in the activities of the "Elizabethan seadogs" and the colonizing activities of Humphrey Gilbert, Walter Raleigh, and their successors.

From the destruction of Hawkins's fleet at San Juan de Ulloa onward, it was Francis Drake who personified the English challenge to Spanish colonial and commercial supremacy [12]; and it was Drake who, a decade later, made his spectacular raid on the Spanish colonies on the Pacific coast of South America and took possession of "New Albion" (California), the first actual territory in America claimed for England.

Spain vigorously protested Drake's voyage. The Spanish ambassador to England, Bernardino de Mendoza, pointed out to Queen Elizabeth the "scandalous nature of the case," and demanded the restitution of the plunder Drake had taken from the Spaniards in the South Sea.[13] But the Spanish protests were met with evasion, and the English piracy continued.

Meanwhile, the colonizing fever had seized England's mercantile classes,[14] and in 1578 Humphrey Gilbert received from Queen Elizabeth a patent for land on the east coast of America, some of which he subgranted and part of which (Newfoundland) he himself attempted to colonize.

The grants issued by Queen Elizabeth to Gilbert and others were based upon the doctrine of effective occupation, that is, Gilbert was enjoined

[12] See Corbett, *Drake and the Tudor Navy, with a History of the Rise of England as a Maritime Power, passim,* and Mattingly, *The Defeat of the Spanish Armada, passim.*

[13] The King (Philip II) to Bernardino de Mendoza, Nov. 14, 1580, P.R.O., *C.S.P., Spain,* 1580–1586, 65-66.

[14] See J. H. Rose, A. P. Newton, and E. A. Benians, eds., *The Cambridge History of the British Empire,* I, Chapters 3, 4.

from settling in territory already occupied by any other country; but it was taken for granted that lands not effectively occupied by Europeans might legitimately be taken and colonized by Englishmen.

Spain protested the Gilbert enterprise, also, which the Spanish ambassador at first thought was directed at Florida. Mendoza reported that the Queen, to encourage colonization, had offered to make a special dispensation for Catholics who would aid Gilbert, sparing their lives and their property in England and granting them freedom of worship in America, if they would go with him. Mendoza warned the English Catholics that to go with Gilbert would be dangerous, since his colony would surely be destroyed by Spain as the French colony of Jean Ribaut had been; besides which, the encouragement of this heretic enterprise, he assured them, would be very displeasing to His Holiness, the Pope.[15]

The Spanish protests against the English interlopers in America, against Drake and against Humphrey Gilbert's projects, were generally based upon Spain's claim to exclusive ownership of America in its entirety, both land and sea, by reason of prior discovery, the papal bulls, and the Hispano-Portuguese Treaty of Tordesillas. Furthermore, since Portugal and its colonial empire had been annexed to Spain in 1580, Spain could now claim, not only America, but also the whole of the Portuguese Empire in the East, along with Portugal's own claim to exclusive ownership of all the lands and all the seas in the Portuguese sphere, created by the same bulls and treaty. However, since the bases for the Hispano-Portuguese claims were now being challenged by the French, Dutch, and English governments, the tone of Spanish protests accentuated Spain's right by discovery rather than that by papal donation.

In her reply to Mendoza's protests, Queen Elizabeth denied the validity of the papal donations, and reiterated the English doctrine of effective occupation. "For that their [the Spaniards'] having touched only here and there upon a coast," she was reported to have said, "and given names to a few rivers or capes, were such insignificant things as could in no ways entitle them to a propriety further than in the parts where they actually settled and continued to inhabit." [16]

The mood of England, its government and its mercantile interests in particular, was in these years aggressively focused upon overseas expansion, and it involved motives that were at once economic, nationalistic, and religious. Moreover, there was a considerable body of pamphlet literature written to rationalize and justify England's aggressiveness. Probably the most famous of these rationalizations was written by Richard Hakluyt,

[15] Bernardino Mendoza to the King (Philip II), July 11, 1582, P.R.O., *C.S.P.*, *Spain, 1580–1586*, 384-385.
[16] Quoted in *The Cambridge History of the British Empire*, I, 185.

popularly known under the title *A Discourse Concerning Western Planting*.[17]

Hakluyt's essay gave many good reasons why England should plant colonies in America, among which were a number that bore directly upon England's relations with Spain. Starting with the religious problem inherent in the fact that Spain felt no scruples about destroying or persecuting Englishmen in any of the Spanish dominions anywhere, since they were Protestants, he went on to show that apart from the commodities they might furnish to the national economy, English colonies in America would be "a greate bridle" to the power of Spain. The planting of two or three colonies on the coast of North America between Florida and "Cape Briton" would provide bases for a constant threat at the Spanish treasure fleets bound for Spain. This would be of extreme importance to the British nation, said Hakluyt, for

if you touche him in the Indies, you touche the apple of his eye; for take away his treasure, which is *nervus belli*, and which he hath almoste [all] oute of his West Indies, his old bandes of souldiers will soone be dissolved, his purposes defeated, his power and strengthe diminished, his pride abated, and his tyranie utterly suppressed.[18]

Hakluyt described the actual settlements of Spaniards as occupying relatively sparse areas; and he urged the implementation of the doctrine of effective occupation by the speedy settlement of English colonies in the unoccupied areas; if England doesn't do it, he says, other nations assuredly will, and soon.

As a matter of fact, Hakluyt adduced ancient accounts, in Welsh and English, of early discoveries of America, long before Columbus, which gave England unquestionable title to these western lands by reason of prior discovery. He refuted the donations to Spain and Portugal contained in the papal bulls, since the Pope had no authority whatever to give away to the kings of Spain and Portugal great areas and peoples of the earth to which he had no claim; and he cited the Spanish historian, López de Gómera, to show that God "laughed them [Spain and Portugal] to scorne, and made them ridiculous and their partition in the eyes of the worlds and in their owne consciences." [19]

It seems clear that Hakluyt's thinking was typical of his time, and it probably represented the general mood of most of those English merchants and statesmen who were concerned with colonial affairs. In any case, the ideas and arguments expressed by Hakluyt found their way into

[17] Hakluyt's title was "A particular discourse concerning the great necessitie and manifolde comodyties that are like to growe to this Realme of Englande by the Westerne discoveries lately attempted . . ." The pamphlet, or letter, is printed in the *Collections of the Maine Historical Society*, 2nd Series, II, 1-167.

[18] *Hakluyt, Discourse, loc. cit.*, 2nd Series, II, 59.

[19] Quoted in Hakluyt, *Discourse, loc. cit.*, 2nd Series, II, 142.

English diplomacy with regard to the colonies throughout the next two centuries.

The English challenge, like the French, reached its climax shortly after the turn of the sixteenth century into the seventeenth. When Queen Elizabeth I died and James VI of Scotland ascended the English throne as James I, the Anglo-Spanish conflict came to a temporary end in the Treaty of London, of 1604. By the terms of this treaty Spain and England agreed to reciprocal trading privileges, and Philip III promised not to molest English merchants in Spain on account of their religion. But Spain insisted that the treaty's provisions relative to commerce, which were, in effect, a restatement of similar provisions of the old Anglo-Spanish Treaty of Medina del Campo of 1489, did not apply to the Spanish Indies. Spain was not disposed to admit, even in 1604, that any other nation might legally enter the sphere of the world claimed by both Portugal and Spain (Portugal had been annexed to Spain in 1580) under the papal bulls and the Treaty of Tordesillas. The English negotiators insisted, however, that the terms of the old treaties, such as that of Medina del Campo, extending reciprocal rights of trade to *all* the dominions of both countries, included the Indies. Furthermore, they also insisted upon the principle of effective occupation. This principle had long been sponsored by both the English and the French; it had been written into the instructions to British explorers and was incorporated into Queen Elizabeth's charter to Sir Humphrey Gilbert for a colony in America (1578), in Sir Walter Raleigh's charter for Virginia (1584), and in the charter of the East India Company (1600); and it was later included in the charter to the Virginia Company (1606).

Since clear agreement could not be reached, the negotiators agreed only to leave in the treaty a vague provision that "there shall be . . . free commerce between [the subjects of the two kings] . . . in all and singular their kingdoms, dominions [etc.] . . . agreeably and according to the use and observance of the ancient alliances and treaties before the war. . . ." [20] This, in effect, left each of the parties to interpret the treaty as he saw fit. Naturally, the Spanish continued to maintain that it did not apply to the Indies, since "the said Indies are a new world," and that the English might not go to the Indies, either East or West, under the treaty. The English government and people, on their side, continued to insist both that the old treaties applied to the Spanish dominions in America and that, under the doctrine of effective occupation, the English had a perfect right to settle in any area "not actually possessed of any Christian Prince, nor inhabited by Christian People. . . ," as Raleigh's charter had put it.

Indeed, the instructions to the English negotiators were explicit on this point:

[20] Davenport, ed., *European Treaties*, I, 256.

And likewise it is no reason by a large naming of the Indies, to barre our marchantes to trade in any places discovered or to be discovered by our own people, being places where neyther in the tyme of the Emperor Charles, nor of the King that now is, any Spanyard, Portingale, or any other Christian people have had any habitation, residence or resorte.[21]

It was under this interpretation of the situation and of the treaty that the Virginia Company sent out its ships in 1606 to found Virginia, the first permanently successful English colony in America.

The English challenge to the Hispano-Portuguese monopoly thus culminated, in 1607, in the founding of a permanent English colony in America, at almost exactly the same time that the French challenge was culminating in the founding of Canada.

3. The Dutch Challenge

The Netherlands, at the time when Columbus discovered America, were a part of the dominion of the dukes of Burgundy. When Carlos I, prince of the House of Burgundy (later the Holy Roman Emperor, Charles V) became king of Spain after the deaths of Ferdinand and Isabela, the Netherlands had been joined to Spain. The Low Countries were thus part of the Spanish Empire and shared richly in the wealth of the Spanish Indies, via Seville and Cadiz (they were prohibited from direct trade with Spain's American colonies).

In 1565, or thereabouts, after Philip II had become king of Spain, the Low Countries, the northern provinces of which had now become Protestant, rebelled against their Spanish masters, and there began the long and bloody conflict which eventuated in the splitting of the Netherlands into the northern (Holland) and the southern provinces (Belgium) by the diplomatic policies and the military skill of the Spanish governor, the Duke of Parma, in May, 1579, and the eventual independence of Holland. In Parma's settlement, the southern Catholic provinces (Belgium) made peace with Spain. The Protestant northern provinces (Holland) continued the struggle, under the leadership of the valiant Prince William of Orange and with the aid of Queen Elizabeth and England. This war continued until a truce was arranged in 1609; it was renewed and merged with the Thirty Years War in 1621.

In the course of their war for independence, the Dutch, whose very economic existence depended upon commerce, laid a heavy toll upon Spanish shipping, whether in the straits, upon the ocean, or among the treasure fleets from America. Formerly participants in the trade of both the eastern and western Indies via Lisbon and Seville, they now began to send their own ships directly into both spheres. And, since Portugal,

[21] Quoted in Davenport, ed., *European Treaties*, I, 247, fn. 4.

after 1580, was annexed to Spain, the Dutch preyed upon Portuguese shipping in the Indian Ocean as well as upon Spanish fleets in the Atlantic.

In 1593 certain Dutch merchants formed companies for the promotion of their commerce into the East Indies. The profits were fabulous, and the merchants were encouraged to go further. Three years later, in 1596, the Dutch States-General joined a league with France and England against Spain,[22] under the terms of which the Dutch assisted the English in their maritime war against the Spaniards. But Henry IV made a separate peace with Spain at Vervins in 1598, as already noted, and the alliance collapsed.

The war was too profitable for both the Dutch and the English to give up, besides the fact that their joint war against Spain was really a war to break the Hispano-Portuguese maritime and colonial dominance, so England and Holland formed a new treaty of mutual assistance at Westminster in 1598.[23] Under the terms of this treaty, apart from its arrangements having to do with Europe, the Dutch undertook to cooperate with the English in offensive naval warfare against the Portuguese Azores Islands, in the Indies, both East and West, and, in particular, in operations against the Spanish treasure fleets returning to Europe from America.

Encouraged by this agreement, a group of English merchants formed the English East India Company in 1600, and the Dutch merchants formed the Universal East India Company in 1602. The Dutch Company traded exclusively with the East Indies, where it enjoyed a monopoly of trade, so far as Dutchmen were concerned. Almost immediately after its organization, groups of Dutch merchants began to send explorers into the western hemisphere, where they searched for a westward passage to the Orient and exploited the economic possibilities of trade in North America, Guiana, and Brazil. It was on one of these expeditions that Henry Hudson sailed up the river that bears his name and opened a profitable trade with the Indians of the Hudson Valley.

In these circumstances, with Holland prospering from its war, King James I of England in effect deserted his Dutch allies by making peace with Spain in the Treaty of London, which has been noted. The Dutch-Spanish conflict dragged on, nevertheless, until 1609, when both sides agreed upon a twelve-year truce. This truce, the so-called Twelve-Years Truce of 1609,[24] was actually a great international triumph for all the challengers of the Hispano-Portuguese monopoly, as well as for the Dutch, since it marked the first legal break in the monopoly, the first explicit recognition of the right of any non-Iberian people to sail to the "new world." The Spanish negotiators tried rather desperately, in fact, to hide

[22] Davenport, ed., *European Treaties*, X, 229-231.
[23] Davenport, ed., *European Treaties*, I, 243-245.
[24] Davenport, ed., *European Treaties*, I, 258-269.

the Spanish admission under obscure language; but the admission was clear enough for all the world to see.

As finally drawn up, this agreement provided that both countries, Spain and the United Netherlands, would remain in possession of the places they held at the time of making the truce. The citizens of both were to be free to trade with each other and to reside in the territories of both. This privilege, however, extended by the King of Spain to the citizens of the United Netherlands was to be restricted to Spanish possessions in Europe

and the other places and seas [in Europe] where the subjects of the kings and princes that are his friends and allies enjoy the said traffic mutually [with the Dutch]. And as for the places, towns, ports and harbors which he [the King] has outside the said limits, the said Estates [of the Netherlands] and their subjects may not exercize any traffic there without the express permission of the said King [of Spain].

However, they may carry on the said traffic, if it seems good to them, in the countries of all other princes, potentates, and peoples, who are willing to permit them, even outside the said limits, so that the said King [of Spain], his officers, and his subjects, who depend upon him, will offer no impediment of any kind on that account to the said princes, potentates, and peoples, who shall have permitted them or who shall permit them, nor, equally, to them or to the private citizens with whom they have carried on or will carry on the said trade.[25]

What this meant was that, while the subjects of the two countries might trade with each other in Europe, Spain recognized the right of the Dutch to trade with any prince or country outside of Europe that was willing to trade with them. Spain preserved the fiction of permitting the Dutch to sail to and to trade in the "new world"; but the recognition of this right, obscure as it was, also involved the right of the Dutch to sail the seas of the world hitherto claimed as *mari clausa* by Spain and Portugal.

As a sort of addendum to the truce, the ambassadors of France and England who were present at the negotiations issued a certificate to the effect that by the provisions of the truce, although it was not specified, all the parties to the negotiations understood that it was intended to mean that whereas the Dutch promised not to visit the Spanish Indies without permission, the Spanish King also promised that he would not permit "his subjects to traffic in the ports, towns, and places which the said Estates possess in the said Indies without their permission." [26]

This was the tacit additional admission that the United Netherlands might—and did—own colonies in the "new world" as well as the right to trade there.

[25] Davenport, ed., *European Treaties*, I, 266-267.
[26] Davenport, ed., *European Treaties*, I, 268.

The Twelve-Years Truce was, thus, the first legal break in the Hispano-Portuguese monopoly, a breach of which the challengers were not slow in taking advantage. Furthermore, since Portugal was at the time annexed to Spain, it applied to both the original partners in the monopoly. Curiously enough, the Dutch challenge to the monopoly reached this *dénouement* at approximately the same time that the French and English challenges were achieving theirs in the form of permanent colonies established in the American hemisphere. This breaking of the monopoly was the beginning of the end of the first phase of the diplomatic history of the American hemisphere.

CHAPTER IV

Virginia, the Thirty Years War, and the
End of the Hispano-Portuguese Monopoly

THE FOUNDING OF permanent colonies in America by the French, the English, and the Dutch in the first two decades of the seventeenth century marked a *de facto* end of the Hispano-Portuguese monopoly of the "new world" that was initiated by the papal bulls of 1493 and the Treaty of Tordesillas of 1494. It was not a *de jure* end, however; for Spain, despite the "temporary" admissions contained in the Twelve-Years Truce (1609), was not yet ready to admit that these powers, or any other, had any legal right either to go to the new world "beyond the Line" or to establish colonies there. That break did not come until the Peace of Westphalia in 1648.

1. Virginia and the West Indies in Anglo-Spanish
Diplomacy, 1606-20

In the two decades between Humphrey Gilbert's ill-fated attempt to plant a colony in Newfoundland and the death of Queen Elizabeth, English colonizers, to say nothing of English privateers, pirates, and interlopers in Spanish-American colonial trade, flouted the Spanish and Portuguese claims to exclusive ownership of the American continent and the seas surrounding it by making a number of attempts to plant colonies there. Walter Raleigh's attempt to locate a colony in Virginia was followed, in 1593, by an English exploratory voyage to the St. Lawrence River, in an area claimed by Portugal, and this voyage was followed in 1597 by an attempt by Charles Leigh to plant a colony of English separatists in that area. Walter Raleigh sent a series of expeditions to Guiana between 1594 and 1597, and in 1604 Charles Leigh again tried colonizing, this time in Guiana. In 1605, the *Olive Branch*, which failed to land in

Guiana, left settlers on the island of St. Lucia. None of these efforts succeeded. Spanish efforts to stop them were sporadic and vicious,[1] but ineffectual, because neither Spain nor Portugal was powerful enough or vigorous enough to mount a really effective defense of its colonies. Besides which, they were preoccupied with the war in Europe (the War of the Great Armada lasted until the Treaty of London, 1604).

The first permanently successful English colony in America was Virginia, the charter for which was issued by King James I to the Virginia Company in 1606. The Company sent out two "plantations," one to the coast of New England and the other to present-day Virginia. Of the two, the New England colony failed, while the one sent to Virginia, after a very uncertain beginning, managed to take permanent root.

This colony, centering in Jamestown on the James River, lay in territory claimed by Spain, and Spain was not slow in protesting its creation. Through an extensive organization of spies in English official circles and in the Virginia Company itself, Spain was well informed of the project, almost from the moment of its conception. The Spanish ambassador in London, Don Pedro de Zuñiga, kept his king, Philip III, fully informed, and, when the colony had landed in Virginia, vigorously protested to James I that it was a violation of Spanish territory.[2]

The Spanish protest, apparently, did not appeal directly to the authority of the Pope, perhaps because the Spaniards knew very well that Englishmen, being Protestants and not recognizing the Pope's authority in anything, least of all in the disposition of the unoccupied lands of the world, would be likely to hold such a claim in derision, as, indeed, they did.[3] The protest was based, rather, upon Spain's claim to America by prior discovery and upon the Treaty of London of 1604, under the terms of which Spain understood that Englishmen were not to be permitted by their government to go to the Indies.[4] But back of these arguments lay a real Spanish fear—the fear that an English colony in Virginia, as a base of operations against the Spanish treasure fleets returning homeward through the Bahama Channel, would be a deadly threat to Spain's very lifeline to its vital American wealth.[5]

[1] In December of 1604 the Venetian ambassador in London wrote to his home government: "News arrived yesterday that the Spanish in the West Indies have captured two English [salt-harvesting] vessels [at Punta Araya, in Guiana]. They cut off the hands, feet, noses and ears of the crews and smeared them with honey, and tied them to trees to be tortured by flies and other beasts. The Spanish here [London] plead that they were pirates, not merchants, and did not know of the peace. But the barbarity makes people here cry out." Quoted in Burns, *History of the British West Indies*, 175.

[2] Brown, ed., *The Genesis of the United States*, I, 44-45; Zuñiga to the King, Apr. 30, 1607, *ibid.*, I, 38.

[3] "Certayne briefe answers to the Bul of Donation, with reasons why the English may trade into the West Indies," Brown, *Genesis*, II, 673.

[4] Zuñiga to the King, Oct. 8, 1607, Brown, ed., *Genesis*, I, 120-121.

[5] Juan de Cirica to Andres de Pedastra, Madrid, May 7, 1607, Brown, ed., *Genesis*, I, 100-101.

Worse than that, it was known that the settlers in Virginia hoped to find a quick route overland to the South Sea (the Pacific Ocean), and it was presently reported in good faith that

The English desire nothing else so much as to make themselves Masters of the South Sea in order to secure their share of the riches of the Indies and to cut off the trade of the King of Spain; and to seek new worlds for themselves. With a view to this end: to make themselves Masters of the South Sea they have determined to erect a fort at the end of every days march of these ten days march which lie between the head of their river and the South Sea, to secure themselves on this route . . .[6]

It was in view of these considerations and these fears that both Zuñiga and the Spanish Council of State urged King Philip III, in 1607, to lose no time in sending a sufficient force to destroy the settlement at Jamestown. Such an action, by taking possession of Virginia in the King's name, would be a *de facto* establishment that would obviate the English argument based upon the doctrine of effective occupation. But the King vacillated; he feared that the delay which would be necessary to prepare a fleet to destroy Virginia might postpone the ejection of the English for a long time. Apparently, he hoped that the same end might be achieved by a negotiation with a friendly King James I of England.[7]

When Zuñiga had protested to King James, as Zuñiga reported it, the King had pled ignorance of what was going on; as for Virginia, he said he never understood that Spain "had any right to it," that it was very distant from any Spanish territory, and that in England's treaties with Spain (as that of London, 1604), English subjects were not prohibited from going there. He recognized that Englishmen were prohibited from going to the "Indies"—meaning Spanish colonial territories actually occupied by Spaniards—and if they did go there they did so at their own risk and might be punished if caught; England would not protect them. On the other hand, if Spaniards could go into hitherto unexplored areas of the world and discover and possess new land, so, also, might the English.[8]

In this reply to Zuñiga James reiterated the favorite English doctrine of effective occupation and fully accepted that of the two spheres and that of the closed national colonial empire. His position was reinforced by the Earl of Salisbury, Lord Treasurer of England, who also talked to Zuñiga. But Salisbury, according to Zuñiga, went so far, apparently, as to admit that the settlers in Virginia had, indeed, no right to even be there, and that, if Spain should drive them out, England would not complain. However, should he order the return of the Jamestown settlers, as Zuñiga

---

[6] Report of Francis Maguel, an Irishman, on Virginia, to the Spanish Council of State, July 10, 1610, Brown, ed., *Genesis*, I, 397-399.

[7] Zuñiga to the King, London, October 5, 1607, Brown, ed., *Genesis*, I, 118-119; Report of the Spanish Council of State, November 10, 1607, regarding the communication from Zuñiga on Virginia, *ibid.*, I, 125-126.

[8] Zuñiga to the King, London, Oct. 8, 1607, Brown, ed., *Genesis*, I, 120-121.

had requested, it would be tantamount to acknowledging that Spain owned all of "the Indies," which England could not, of course, do. Even to ask for the pardon of prisoners taken in American waters would be a confession of guilt in going there, and thereby indirectly recognize the Spanish King's sovereignty there. Salisbury almost encouraged His Catholic Majesty to chase the English out of Virginia, but he could not possibly order them out himself![9]

The colony of Virginia did not prosper, and the Virginia Company was reorganized under a new charter in 1609. Zuñiga assiduously reported all the English activities relative to the colony, as well as the widespread popular and religious interest in it as a sort of Protestant outpost against Catholic Spain. In one of his reports, in April, 1609, he again expressed the urgent hope that His Catholic Majesty "will give orders to have these insolent people quickly annihilated." [10]

The English, both in England and in Virginia, constantly feared an expedition from Spain that would annihilate Virginia as Ribaut's colony in Florida had been annihilated half a century earler, and reports of plans for such expeditions were rife in Spain in 1611, 1612, and 1613; these plans were now said to include the eradication of the English colony on Bermuda as well as Virginia.[11] But as reports of the languishing condition of the colony continued to circulate, both in England and in Spain, the Spanish government became convinced that the Virginia colony would disappear of its own inanition, without any effort on Spain's part.[12] King Philip III therefore abandoned, for the time at least, all thought of forceful eradication of the colony.[13]

In the same years in which Virginia was slowly struggling to its feet, other English attempts at colonization were being made in the Caribbean area, near the heart of the Spanish colonial empire, all of which failed. Then, in 1617, Walter Raleigh, the "father of Virginia" once more entered the arena of colonial adventure. He was released from the Tower of London, where he had been imprisoned under sentence of death since 1603, upon the strength of his promise to find gold in Guiana, now thought of as an English colony, and to bring it home to England. He was warned,

[9] Zuñiga to the King, London, Oct. 16, 1607, Brown, ed., *Genesis*, I, 173-174; Abstract of Bacon's report to the House of Commons (June 17) of Salisbury's speech at the conference of the Lords on June 15, 1607, *ibid.*, I, 119.

[10] Zuñiga to Philip III, Apr. 12, 1609, Brown, ed., *Genesis*, I, 258-259.

[11] John Digby (English ambassador to Spain) to Salisbury, Dec. 15, 1611, Brown, ed., *Genesis*, II, 530-531; Digby to Sir Dudley Carlton, June 20, 1612, *ibid.*, II, 562; Digby to James I, September 13, 1612 *ibid.*, II, 588-589; Digby to Carlton, September 22, 1612, *ibid.*, II, 590. See also, Brown, *Genesis* II, 602-603.

[12] Zuñiga to Philip III, Aug. 16, 1612, Brown, ed., *Genesis*, II, 575; Digby to James I, Aug. 15, 1613, *ibid.*, II, 656; Digby to James I, Nov. 12, 1612, *ibid.*, II, 593-594.

[13] Philip III to Velasco, May 23, 1613, Brown, ed., *Genesis*, II, 631-632; Digby to James I, May 13, 1613, *ibid.*, II, 632.

however, that he must not attack the Spaniards nor go into any occupied parts of the Spanish "Indies." The Spanish ambassador protested against Raleigh's enterprise, on the ground that it could not fail to violate Spanish territory, but he was assured that Raleigh would be instructed under pain of death not to infringe upon Spanish interests.

The expedition set out for America in March of 1617. Its objective was the Orinoco River, but an exploration of the river failed to find the gold mine, and in fighting that broke out with the Spaniards a Spanish fort was taken and destroyed. Raleigh returned to England in June, 1618, and when the Spanish ambassador complained and demanded that Raleigh be punished, King James, to appease him, ordered the execution of the sentence of death that had been passed upon Raleigh in 1603.

The execution of Raleigh by James I was something more than a gesture of appeasement, however. James was committed to a policy of rapprochement between England and Spain that, he hoped, would be cemented by the marriage of his son, the future King Charles I, to the Infanta of Spain. This personal policy of James actually ran counter to the projects and objectives of the mercantile interests of England, which were directed toward further colonial expansion in America, further interloping in the commerce of the Spanish colonies, and a belligerent attitude that would presently lead England into an alliance with the Dutch against Spain.

More typical of English international interest, therefore, was the so-called Amazon Company, organized in London, which was given a royal patent in 1619 for the colonizing of the unoccupied territory, claimed by Portugal, between the Amazon and the Orinoco Rivers. King James, upon the complaint of the Spanish ambassador, tried to stop the company's first colonizing expedition, but it got away in 1620 and went out to locate the proposed colony on the banks of the Oyapoc River. This settlement, which never flourished, was followed by others on the Amazon River and elsewhere in the region.

Meanwhile, the Thirty Years War had begun in Europe, and the Dutch war of independence against Spain, which was renewed on the expiration of the Twelve-Years Truce in 1621, was merged with the larger war.

2. The Thirty Years War and the Anglo-Dutch Alliance of 1625

The Thirty Years War, which was really a series of wars over religious and dynastic questions among the major powers of Europe, began in 1618 and lasted until 1648. On one side, in this long struggle, was the Holy Roman Emperor, Ferdinand II, and a congeries of states of the Empire that were predominantly Catholic; with this group was allied Spain, another Catholic country. Opposed to the Imperial and Spanish group were certain Protestant states, led by Frederick, the Elector Palatine of the Rhenish Palatinate, and, at one time or another, other Protestant states, such as Denmark and Sweden; Holland, of course, was already at war with Spain, and when the Twelve-Years Truce ran out in 1621, the war was renewed with vigor on both sides. England entered the war on the side of Holland; but England's participation was brief. France, under Richelieu, entered the war against the Emperor in 1635; this intervention changed the character of the war and prolonged it until peace was made in two separate treaties, one at Münster and one at Osnabrück, in what was called the Peace of Westphalia.

The impulse to build colonial empires overseas was not limited to Spain, France, England, and Holland. Denmark and Sweden felt it and made the effort to found colonies, or, at least, to acquire for themselves shares of the rich profits to be derived from commerce with the "new world" overseas, as did, presently, Prussia and Austria. Thus, already, when the Thirty Years War began and the Dutch war for independence was renewed, Denmark and Prussia were not only interested in participating in the general European conflict but also in cutting in on the profits to be gained from intervention in the commercial and colonial aspects of it.

King Christian IV of Denmark had shown his interest in overseas expansion by founding, in 1616, the Danish East India Company, patterned after the Dutch East India Company, and asked the Dutch for trading privileges in the Dutch sphere in the East Indies. This curious request was promptly and naturally refused, but the Dutch recognized the right of the Danish company to explore, occupy, and exploit hitherto unoccupied territories in the "new world." They particularly directed the Danes' attention to the possibilities for colonization and trade in the unoccupied islands of the West Indies.

While the Danish overseas impulse was developing, the Protestant princes in Germany invited Denmark to join them against the Catholic powers. Denmark agreed, and to implement and strengthen Denmark's participation, Christian IV allied himself with the Dutch. The Danish-Dutch treaty, signed on May 14, 1621,[14] but never ratified by Denmark, provided, in rather general terms, for a military alliance of the two states, the detailed terms of which were to be determined at a joint conference. The last article (Article 8) provided that the anticipated conference should also discuss questions pertinent to the relations between the two countries in the East and West Indies. The conference was held at Bremen in August and September, 1621. It discussed the question of commercial relations in the East and West Indies, and the commissioners of the two countries signed an agreement [15] that recognized the right of the Danes

---

[14] Davenport, ed., *European Treaties*, I, 275-279.
[15] Davenport, ed., *European Treaties*, I, 280-284.

to occupy lands and to trade in both the East and the West Indies; it also recognized the principle of the closed national commercial and colonial sphere in the provision that the nationals of each should refrain from going into the sphere of the other.

This agreement also failed of ratification by either party. Its great significance lay in the fact that, despite the failure to ratify them, the Dutch-Danish Treaty of the Hague and the agreement of Bremen had the effect of establishing a rapport between the two countries that promoted the overseas activities of both.

In its search for allies against Spain, Holland next turned to France. France was cool to the Dutch overtures until Cardinal Richelieu became the chief French minister. Richelieu listened with interest to the Dutch request for an alliance and to the suggestion that France form a French West Indian Company to cooperate with the Dutch West India Company in the prosecution of war, trade, and colonization against Spain in America. Since the two countries were already commercial and colonial rivals, it was difficult to come to any agreement, but a treaty was finally signed,[16] which provided for mutual assistance against Spain. With regard to traffic to the East and West Indies the treaty provided merely that the French ambassador would negotiate the details with the Dutch government at the Hague. This part of the treaty never had any real effect.

The Dutch had turned to the English for an alliance against Spain as early as 1621, but so long as James I pursued his policy of rapprochement with Spain, Dutch requests for an alliance fell on deaf ears. It appears, also, that the creation of the Dutch West India Company, with its projects for colonies in Brazil, in the Caribbean, and in North America, caused the English mercantile and colonizing interests to fear such vigorous Dutch competition, especially with regard to the possibility of having Dutch colonies planted in the midst of the English plantations, in areas the English had staked out for themselves.

It was because of this that the English looked with distrust upon the activities of Henry Hudson under Dutch auspices, in the course of which the English government forbade him from working for the Dutch again. Then, when the Dutch began to build forts and trading posts in the Connecticut, Hudson, and Delaware valleys the English government made this penetration subject matter for diplomatic protest. Again, when the English government began to hear of the Dutch penetration of the area between New England and Virginia, it instructed Sir Dudley Carleton, English ambassador at the Hague, to protest the founding of Dutch colonies there and to demand the withdrawal of those already settled. The English had already effectively occupied those territories, the instructions

[16] Davenport, ed., *European Treaties*, I, 285-289.

said; let the Dutch withdraw.[17] Carleton inquired among the Dutch merchants of Amsterdam and reported that, though Dutch merchants were trading there and though they called the area New Netherland, he could not learn that they had planted any colony there.[18] He did protest, however, along the lines indicated by his instructions, asserting that England had prior title to all that territory ("*jure primal occupationis*") and, therefore, that the Dutch government should prohibit its people from going there for trade or for founding colonies.[19]

The Dutch States-General, in response to Carleton's protest, instigated an investigation of the situation in New Netherland,[20] but this question was soon lost in the more pressing problem of an alliance with England for the prosecution of the war against Spain. Meanwhile, the Dutch West India Company proceeded to found and strengthen its colonies on the Hudson, on the Connecticut, and on the Delaware rivers. It also proceeded to carry out its plans in the West Indies and in Brazil.

By 1624 James I had finally become convinced that the Spanish infanta would not marry his son Charles. Meanwhile, the Dutch had proposed a union of the Dutch West India Company with similar companies to be organized in France and England for the joint prosecution of warlike commercial and colonial projects against Spain.[21] Now, the Dutch ambassador in London proposed again an alliance between Holland and England against Spain and Portugal. James listened with interest, but he would go no further than to sign an alliance that was purely defensive. Such a treaty was signed on June 15, 1624. James died soon thereafter, on April 6, 1625, and Charles I, who succeeded him, had no tender feelings for Spanish sensibilities. Indeed, England now turned to the Dutch for aid, both in Germany, where Charles was interested in restoring his brother-in-law, Frederich V, to the throne of the Palatinate, which Spain had seized, and at sea. Thus, in view of the new English belligerency and because the defensive alliance already existed, it was easy to negotiate an alliance that was both defensive and offensive, which was consummated in the Treaty of Southampton, on September 17, 1625.[22]

Under the terms of this treaty, there was created an offensive and defensive alliance "for the purpose of attacking the King of Spain in open warfare, in all his realms, lands, subjects, and rights, both on this side of

[17] Privy Council to Sir Dudley Carleton, Whitehall, Dec. 15, 1621, N.Y.C.D., III, 6-7.
[18] Carleton to the Lords of the Council, The Hague, Feb. 5, 1621, N.Y.C.D., III, 7-8.
[19] Carleton's Memorial to the States-General, N.Y.C.D., III, 8.
[20] N.Y.C.D., III, 27.
[21] Secret Resolution of the States-General on a proposed Union of the West India Companies, Mar. 22, 1624, N.Y.C.D., I, 29-30.
[22] Davenport, ed., *European Treaties*, I, 290-299.

the line and beyond it." [23] The two allies promised mutually to protect each other's realms and subjects, and they would join forces in aggressions against the commerce of His Catholic Majesty, both in Europe and in the West Indies, but especially against the Spanish treasure ships returning from Spain. The treaty defined contraband of war (for the first time by treaty) and declared that ships trading with Spain in contraband articles would be "good prize," no matter to whom they belonged. Both parties promised not to make a separate peace.

A great joint naval expedition under this treaty was prepared, to proceed against Cadiz and the treasure fleet from America, but, though it sailed, it ended in inglorious and ignominious failure. This failure, added to quarrels between England and Holland over political issues, weakened the enthusiasm of both parties for the alliance. Worst of all, several Dutch merchant ships were seized by English warships on the ground that they were carrying contraband of war to the Spanish enemy. As the Dutch had always maintained the principle and the practice of the freedom of commerce, even of trade with the enemy—a practice that had netted them enormous profits—these seizures, even though the ships were violating the Treaty of Southampton, embittered the Dutch against the English.

In 1627 Holland attempted to patch up the disputes, nevertheless, by the negotiation of a new treaty of navigation. But the English were now in no mood for a rapprochement, and this negotiation failed. With them, indeed, failed the Anglo-Dutch alliance of 1625.[24]

3. The Failure of the Dutch Alliance and the Rapprochement of England with France

Dutch mariners and freebooters had long been active in the West Indies, as has been noted. Now, with the renewal of the Dutch war of independence and the creation of the Dutch West India Company, Dutch colonizing activity in the West Indies, in the Caribbean islands, and in mainland areas claimed by Spain redoubled. By the year 1623 it was reported that there were eight hundred Dutch ships in American waters, most of them engaged in trade and privateering, but other warships engaged in raiding Spanish mainland settlements. The Dutch also invaded Portuguese Brazil (the Portuguese and Spanish empires were still united under the crown of Spain) and occupied a huge fragment of it centering around Bahia, which fell to the Dutch in 1624, and Pernambuco, taken soon afterward. The most spectacular Dutch action against Spain in the

[23] Davenport, ed., *European Treaties*, I, 294.
[24] For Anglo-Dutch relations in these years see Edmundson, *Anglo-Dutch Rivalry during the First Half of the Seventeenth Century*.

West Indies, however, was the capture, in 1628, of a great Spanish treasure fleet, carrying gold, silver, and pearls to the value of some four million florins, by the Dutch admiral Pieter Heyn. Spanish power in the West Indies was shaken by this blow, and the Dutch took advantage of this fact to step up their destruction of shipping and raids on Spanish settlements. Spain made a series of weak efforts to retaliate, but they were ineffective; Spain's power and prestige had almost reached the *nadir* of their influence in America.

The result was a practical Dutch monopoly of trade in the Spanish Caribbean area. Incidentally, the Dutch established colonies at Berbice, in Guiana (1626), St. Eustatius and Curaçao (1634), and Saba (1640). Meanwhile, English commercial interests were also taking advantage of Spanish weakness to establish colonies on St. Christopher ("St. Kitts") (1624), Barbados (1627), and a number of other islands. Since England was at war with Spain, these islands were occupied, in effect, as wartime measures.

Meanwhile, the Alliance of Southampton had come into operation, but it had failed, and its effects upon the course of events were negligible. England's attention, in fact, began to be diverted, soon after the Treaty of Southampton, to other matters, both internal and external, to say nothing of the mounting anti-Dutch feeling in that country. Charles I was having trouble with his Parliament, which came to a bitter stalemate in the suspension of Parliament in 1629; more important for the history of international relations, in 1627 he became involved in the so-called "Huguenot War" with France.

Tensions between France and England had been mounting ever since the marriage of Charles I to the French princess Henrietta Maria in 1625. Henrietta Maria, being a Catholic, aroused enmity among the Protestant English; France's negotiation of a separate peace with Spain in 1626, followed by an alliance with that country against England in 1627, made war practically inevitable, while Richelieu's suppression of the Huguenots in France inspired an abortive English effort to aid them. Finally, Richelieu's new and expansive colonial and commercial policies, marked by the creation, in 1626, of the St. Christopher's Company (followed in 1635 by the Company of the West Indies), for the colonization of the vacant islands in the West Indies, and, in 1627, of the Company of New France (the Company of One Hundred Associates) for the development of Canada, excited the jealousy and the cupidity of the English mercantile and colonizing interests and made this war a commercial and colonial war as well as a religious one.

It thus came about that in the year 1628 David Kirke and his brothers took out letters of marque against the French and sent a fleet to Canada.

This expedition captured a rich fleet of French colonists and supplies in the Gulf of St. Lawrence, the first fleet sent out by Richelieu's Company of New France, and seized the French forts of Port Royal, St. John, and Pentagoët (which the English called Penobscot). Sir William Alexander, who had received a proprietary patent for Nova Scotia in 1621, then planted a colony at Port Royal, and, with the Kirkes, formed the Scottish and English Company, which received from Charles I a charter to colonize the region of the St. Lawrence with a monopoly of the trade of that region. Early in 1629 this company planted a colony on Cape Breton Island and succeeded in capturing the French settlement at Quebec. Unfortunately for the Scottish and English Company, the treaty ending this Anglo-French war, the Treaty of Susa, had been signed some three months earlier.

The Treaty of Susa, signed April 24, 1629,[25] provided, in addition to its European articles, only that "prizes" made during the war should not be returned; those made after the war were to be restored. No specific mention of America was made; presumably, the "prizes" made after the war would include Quebec.

After the Treaty of Susa efforts were made by the two signatories to negotiate a settlement of all the outstanding issues between them. Among these were the English seizure of Quebec and the destruction by a French fleet of the English colony on Cape Breton Island, both of which had taken place after the signature of the Treaty of Susa. But the negotiations dragged on, chiefly because the French were reluctant to pay the balance still due on Queen Henrietta Maria's dowry, and it was not until March 29, 1632, at St. Germain-en-Laye, that a final treaty of peace was signed.[26]

Under the terms of this treaty, all the places occupied by the English in New France, Acadia (including Alexander's colony), and "Canada" (the territory on the St. Lawrence in the neighborhood of Quebec) were to be restored to France; the furs seized at Quebec, which were the property of the French United Company (the predecessors of the Company of New France), or their value, were to be delivered to Guillaume de Caen for that company. Vessels seized since the Treaty of Susa were to be restored or paid for. France, on its side, promised to pay Charles I the remainder of Henrietta Maria's dowry.

In the summer of 1632 Samuel de Champlain reentered Quebec and again hoisted the Fleur-de-lis over New France, "Canada," and Acadia in the name of France. So far as Europe was concerned, the Treaty of St. Germain-en-Laye left Richelieu free to turn his whole attention to a prosecution of his war against the Hapsburgs in the Thirty Years War, which France entered in 1635.

[25] Davenport, ed., *European Treaties*, I, 300-304.
[26] Davenport, ed., *European Treaties*, I, 315-323.

4. *England's* Rapprochement *with Spain*

While the negotiations that led to the Anglo-French Treaty of St. Germain-en-Laye were going on, England had deserted its alliance with the Dutch and had come to terms with Spain.

Spain's attention had been diverted by a renewal of conflict with France over the ownership of northern Italy, so Philip IV, in 1629, sent the Flemish painter Peter Paul Rubens to England to try to make peace. Rubens, a skillful diplomat, found Charles I in need of money and willing to make peace if Spain would restore to his brother-in-law, the Elector Palatine of the Rhenish Palatinate, the throne and ownership of that little country. Spain was willing to pay this price, but the treaty, which closely followed the text of the Treaty of London of 1604, was actually signed in Madrid.

In the course of the negotiations the old question of the right of English ships to go to the West Indies came up again. Spain was still unwilling to admit in writing that the English had any right to go there, although the Spanish negotiators assured the English orally that Spain would not really question their right and even went so far as to promise a tacit recognition of the legality of the English colony of Virginia.

The Treaty of Madrid was signed on November 15, 1630.[27] Shortly thereafter Spain and England signed a secret alliance against the Dutch, who were, in fact, England's greatest rivals in the commercial and colonial world.

Under the provisions of the Treaty of Madrid "free commerce" between the two countries was restored, "in all their kingdoms, dominions, and islands . . . where there was commerce between the said kingdoms before the war between Philip II, King of the Spains, and Elizabeth, Queen of England . . ."[28] Curiously, this treaty abandoned the doctrine of the two spheres, which involved the idea that "there is no peace beyond the Line," for it provided that, since news of the peace would take some time to go around the world, peace between the two peoples would not officially be in effect "beyond the Line [until] after the space of nine months" from the date of the publication of the peace.

This treaty left the *status quo* in America unchanged. Spain was now free to pursue its interests in Italy; England, after its Treaty of St. Germain-en-Laye with France, could devote its full attention to the rapid expansion of its commerce and its colonial holdings in America.

[27] Davenport, ed., *European Treaties*, I, 305-314.
[28] Davenport, ed., *European Treaties*, I, 313.

5. The Portuguese-French and the Portuguese-Dutch Alliances

Portugal regained its *de facto* independence from Spain in December of 1640 and proclaimed the Duke of Braganza its king, calling him John IV. In need of allies in its war of independence, which was to continue many years, the tiny kingdom turned to France and arranged an alliance.

Portugal had lost colonies and commerce to France, Holland, and England during the union with Spain (1580–1640). Its most pressing concern now was to regain some of these and to protect itself from the expected efforts of Spain to restore the crown. It therefore turned to France, Holland, and England for help, despite their inroads into the Portuguese empire, chiefly because they were enemies of Spain but also because it was thought that association with them would be more effective in the rehabilitation of the Portuguese colonial empire than continuing to fight them. France, already at war with Spain, welcomed the Portuguese association and readily concluded an alliance with Portugal on June 1, 1641.[29]

Under the terms of the alliance the two countries agreed to help each other against Spain in Europe and to combine their fleets with that of the Dutch to capture the Spanish treasure fleets returning from America. The fleets were, in fact, united, but they accomplished little or nothing.

When Portugal turned for an alliance to the United Netherlands, it found the Dutch friendly but not very cooperative.

The Dutch had actually seized, during the Thirty Years War, while Portugal was united to Spain, a huge fragment of Brazil and many valuable parts of the Portuguese empire in the Far East and in Africa. What Portugal now proposed was a truce between them and Dutch naval aid against Spain, with a restoration to Portugal of the parts of Brazil taken by the Dutch West India Company.

The Dutch East India Company and West India Company were not prepared to make any compromises that would diminish either their profits or their colonial holdings. The treaty of alliance [30] that was finally achieved was, therefore, a good deal less ideal than the Portuguese had hoped it might be. The treaty was long and detailed, but it embodied many provisions of importance to Dutch-Portuguese relations in the East and West Indies and in Africa.

In the first place, the treaty provided for a truce for ten years between the two countries in all their territories "on both sides of the Line"; it was to go into effect immediately, but the areas covered by the charters

[29] Davenport, ed., *European Treaties*, I, 324-328.
[30] Davenport, ed., *European Treaties*, I, 329-346.

of the Dutch East India Company and West India Company were excepted; in those areas the truce was to go into effect only when the King of Portugal's ratification of the treaty should reach the Hague; within eight months of that day, negotiation was to begin for an agreement for permanent peace within the area of the Dutch West India Company. The Dutch West India Company and its "subjects" in the lands it had acquired (that is, in Brazil) were to have the same rights of commerce, exemptions, liberties, *et cetera*, that other Dutch citizens had in Portuguese territories, except that they would not bring Brazilian products to Portugal. Portuguese subjects would not bring Brazilian products to Holland. Limits between the territories held by the two parties were to be fixed by agreement, and each might thenceforth defend the territories assigned to it as its own. In all such territories in Brazil the principle of the closed colonial sphere was recognized; the nationals of one of the signatories might not enter the territories of the other. An exception to this provision was made in Portugal's agreement that, if that country needed foreign ships to carry on its commerce with Brazil, it would hire Dutch ships. Both signatories agreed not to trade in any way with the Spanish Indies or with Spain's allies. Furthermore, since the Dutch had acquired their holdings in Brazil at a time when they were ruled by Spain and the inhabitants were enemies of Holland, and since those people had now returned to the allegiance of Portugal and were now, therefore, friends of the Dutch, it was agreed that no claims for property acquired before this treaty should be presented on either side. It was also agreed, as to the continuing war with Spain, that, if the seat of the war should be transferred to the Spanish West Indies and conquests should be made there, such conquests were to be divided between them.

In their European territories, or anywhere else, "on this side of the Line," the subjects of both parties were to be permitted to visit and trade. All Christians, subjects of either of the parties, "whether on this or on the other side of the Line," were to enjoy liberty of conscience in their private homes and on their ships.

The States General of Holland were immediately to furnish a fleet of warships to the King of Portugal; King John would furnish fifteen of his own; the joint fleet was to be employed against the coasts of Spain.

This treaty, thus, specified many provisions with regard to the relations between their colonies and the treatment of their nationals within the colonies, but it neither resulted in any great achievement against Spain nor brought real peace or a settlement of the colonial *status quo* as between the signatories themselves. Portugal's ratification was long delayed, and the Dutch companies took advantage of the delay to extend their conquests in Africa and Brazil. While the Portuguese government protested vainly against this violation of the sense of the treaty, the natives in the conquered areas rose against the Dutch and expelled them. By 1649 the Portuguese had regained their African possessions seized by the Dutch and all the Dutch-held territories in Brazil except Pernambuco and three military stations. These last holdings of the Dutch in Brazil were recovered by the Portuguese in 1654. Thus it came about that Portuguese independence, which the Dutch had signed the Treaty of the Hague of 1641 to guarantee, very quickly brought with it such a reaction against the Dutch themselves as to drive them out of some of the Portuguese colonies they had occupied and contributed mightily to the ultimate failure of the Dutch West India Company.

6. The Anglo-Portuguese Alliance

While the newly independent Portuguese were making their alliances with the French and the Dutch, they were also turning for help to England. In this direction their diplomacy was rewarded with somewhat greater success, for in the Anglo-Portuguese alliance of January 29, 1642, the modern foundations were laid for the "oldest European alliance, the oldest alliance in the world." [31]

England and Portugal were drawn together by their common enmity toward Spain and the United Netherlands, and when Portugal achieved its independence in 1640 its best hope for aid lay in England. Actually, however, this hope was handicapped by the close friendship of the House of Braganza with the House of Stuart, which presently found itself at war with its own Parliament, and by the aid, mostly indirect, which Portugal gave the House of Stuart in that war.

In any case, Portugal sent an embassy to London in 1641 to negotiate a treaty of alliance. England, still ruled by Charles I, was willing, but it demanded the same concessions that Portugal had already granted the Dutch. A compromise resulted, and the treaty, as eventually signed, provided that English merchants living in Portugal should enjoy a measure of religious toleration and protection from the Inquisition, and a degree of extraterritoriality. The treaty did not mention the colonies of either country, and it alienated the English because Portugal backed the wrong side in the great civil war that started in the same year; it therefore had little effect. And yet, because it provided a solid basis for eventually improved commercial relations between England and Portugal, so much of whose commerce was derived from its colonies, the treaty occupies a significant place in the history of Anglo-Portuguese colonial diplomacy, a diplomacy that came to clearer and more tangible fruition in the Treaty of Westminster of 1654.[32]

[31] Jones, "Beginnings of the Oldest European Alliance: England and Portugal, 1640–1661," *Annual Report of the American Historical Association for the Year 1916*, I, 405-418. For the text of the treaty see Brazão, *The Anglo-Portuguese Alliance*, 34-36.
[32] See Chapter VII.

7. The End of the Monopoly: The Dutch-Spanish Treaty of Münster, 1648

The end of both the Thirty Years War and the Dutch war for independence came, at last, in the so-called Peace of Westphalia. This "peace" was actually the product of two international conferences, one at Osnabrück and one at Münster, in the province of Westphalia, in western Germany. These conferences, composed of representatives of the warring powers, began in 1643 and worked at the problems of peace for five years, while the war continued; the two treaties that composed the peace were signed in the year 1648. Even then, the peace was not complete, for France and Spain still found it impossible to compose their differences. Yet this fact worked in favor of the Dutch, for Spain, in order to separate France from Holland, offered the Dutch their independence and a recognition of their rights in the commercial and colonial world that was far more liberal than might otherwise have been expected. It thus fell out that the Spanish and the Dutch ended their long conflict in the treaty signed at Münster on January 30, 1648.[33]

This agreement was not arrived at without long and bitter debate. To begin with, the Dutch were divided among themselves. The Dutch West India and East India Companies were actually opposed to peace, since a continuation of the war against the now greatly enfeebled Spain would be far more profitable than peace. Another group strenuously opposed deserting France by making a separate peace with Spain. Since some sort of truce or peace had to be made, however, the companies proposed that the doctrine of the two spheres should be applied in a provision of the treaty that would make peace on "this side of the Line," but leave them free to carry on their profitable private hostilities beyond it; that their right to trade in all places in the world where the King of Spain had no settlements or forces should be specifically recognized; that Spanish subjects should be excluded from places and lands occupied by the Dutch West India Company; and that the Dutch title to all the places in the "new world" already occupied should be recognized. Most Dutchmen, probably, felt that the *sine qua non* for peace must be a full recognition by Spain of Dutch independence, and a similar recognition at least of the right of Dutch ships and merchants to go to any unoccupied territory in the world for trade or colonization, or both.

But Spain was in no mood, even now, to give explicit recognition to the right of Dutchmen, or of anyone else, to go into the Spanish colonial sphere as defined by the papal bulls and the Treaties of Tordesillas and Saragossa. Furthermore, Spain refused to include in the treaty anything

[33] Davenport, ed., *European Treaties*, I, 353-366.

that might be interpreted as recognizing the independence of Portugal. It was extremely difficult, therefore, to arrive at an agreement, especially with regard to the Indies, East and West.

It was only after strenuous and acrimonious negotiation, and a realization that France and Spain would never make peace between themselves,[34] that the Dutch-Spanish Treaty of Münster was finally signed. In it, as it emerged from the conferences, Spain explicitly recognized the independence and sovereignty of the United Provinces of the Low Countries, that is, the Netherlands. With regard to the "new world," the treaty provided specifically that the navigation and trade of the Dutch to the East and West Indies should continue, and this provision was extended to the rulers and states comprised in the charter bounds of the Dutch East and West India Companies. Both Spain and the Netherlands were to retain the places and territories that they possessed at the moment in both the East and the West Indies, as well as those possessed in Brazil or on the coasts of Africa, Asia, or North America, including the places that the Portuguese had taken from the Dutch since the year 1641. Also included were places and territories that the Dutch might take from the Portuguese in the future. The freedom of officials and employees of the Dutch East and West India Companies to voyage to and from the Dutch colonies was specifically recognized; each of the parties promised to keep its nationals out of the closed colonial sphere of the other. This provision was extended specifically to the West Indies and the Dutch-occupied portions of Brazil and those taken from the Dutch since the year 1641 by the Portuguese. The peace was to begin only after one year in the East Indies and after six months in the West Indies; it is to be noted that while this provision gave the two companies a substantial time in which to continue their profitable depradations in Spanish areas around the earth, it also abandoned the "doctrine of the two spheres" and its companion principle that "there is no peace beyond the Line."

So ended the Dutch war of independence. So ended, also, in final, complete success, the Dutch challenge to the Hispano-Portuguese claims to a monopoly of the "new world." The greatest significance of this treaty, indeed, lies in the fact that here, for the first time in a permanent treaty, Spain explicitly recognized the right of another nation to go into and acquire territory in the American hemisphere. It would not be long before Spain would be forced to recognize the same right of the other colonizing nations.

[34] See Chapter IX.

CHAPTER V

Anglo-Dutch Relations Bearing upon America, 1648-89

1. Anglo-Dutch Rivalry and the Treaty of Westminster, 1654

DURING THE YEARS between England's Treaties of Madrid with Spain (1630) and St. Germain-en-Laye with France (1632) and the Peace of Westphalia (1648), England was torn by political tensions and civil war. Such colonial activity as took place was carried on by private individuals and groups, and the government took relatively little active interest in them. English mercantile interests, too, were preoccupied with affairs pertinent to the civil war and to European matters. The most significant result of these facts, so far as international colonial affairs were involved, was that there was created a sort of commercial vacuum in the colonies, into which the ever-alert Dutch moved with alacrity and with considerable profit to themselves. At the end of the civil war, this condition was discovered, and the English Parliament took vigorous steps to correct it.

In Holland, itself, a political revolution took place in 1650 when the stadholder, William II, died. William had been the son-in-law of Charles I, and had given sympathy and encouragement to the Stuart royalists, thereby earning a bitter enmity among the English Parliamentarians. Now, when William died, the office of Stadholder was abolished and the government of the Netherlands was vested in the States-General, where the dominant power lay with the province of Holland and its Grand Pensionary.

This led the English to anticipate a more sympathetic attitude toward England in the Low Countries, and an effort was made to unite the two Protestant commonwealths. But the Dutch were not receptive to the idea, since they felt, perhaps rightly, that a union with England might mean the loss of their independence and an overshadowing of the Dutch republic by England. They did show a willingness, however, to negotiate an alliance, along with which they demanded the joint Anglo-Dutch sponsorship of the principle of the complete freedom of the seas (as against the English claim to complete and exclusive sovereignty over the seas surrounding Britain), a definition of contraband of war, a recognition of the right of neutrals, in time of war, to trade (except in contraband of war) with belligerents, that "free ships make free goods," and that the Dutch should have the same privileges as Englishmen in the commerce of the English colonies in America, "as hitherto they have sailed and traded thither. . . ." They suggested, further, that the Dutch and English colonies in North America maintain peaceful relations with each other and that the boundaries between them be defined. Finally, they proposed a complete boycott, by both of them, upon the carrying of Portuguese goods, either of American, African, Asian, or European origin, as an aid to the Dutch in their struggle with the Portuguese, particularly in Brazil.[1]

These proposals relative to the colonies were intended, of course, to protect the colonial and commercial position established by the Dutch in America during the Thirty Years War and the English civil war, particularly in English colonial commerce, which was now closed off to them by the English Navigation Act of 1650. But the English were in no mood to accede to these demands. Struggling, as it was, to rehabilitate its own economy, the Commonwealth was deliberately working toward a strict exclusion of the Dutch from the very American colonial commerce into which the Dutch had infiltrated during the civil war. The negotiations were suspended, and Parliament, far from showing the slightest disposition to compromise with Dutch ambitions, proceeded, in October of 1651, to pass a new and more explicit "Act of Navigation," which was directly aimed at the destruction of Dutch competition with English commerce, both in Europe and in the English colonies. This act required that all ships trading with the English colonies in America be English owned and manned; that goods imported into England must be carried in English ships or ships of the country producing the goods and must be brought directly from the place of their production; that in the case of goods produced in the Spanish and Portuguese colonies, such goods might be brought from ports in Spain or Portugal.[2]

The government of the Netherlands, reviving the negotiations for some sort of alliance, protested against the discriminatory nature of this law and asked that it be suspended. The English Council of State refused; and the English negotiators countered with demands for reparations for injuries done to Englishmen by Dutchmen in the East Indies and Brazil, on the basis of the principle of effective occupation. As for the Navigation Act, the English negotiators maintained that since the English had

[1] Davenport, ed., *European Treaties*, I, 7-8.
[2] Firth and Rait, eds., *Acts and Ordinances of the Interregnum*, II, 425-429.

always been prohibited by the Dutch from trading with Dutch colonies and places in Dutch possession, England would continue to acquiesce in that prohibition, but must insist upon maintaining the same exclusive policy toward the Dutch in the administration of their own possessions. To the Dutch proposal that the boundary between New Netherland and New England be fixed, the English negotiators maintained that all of North America north of 37° North Latitude (the southern boundary of Virginia) and as far northward as 52° North Latitude (the latitude of Newfoundland) belonged to England by reason of prior occupation; therefore, "not knowing of any plantation of the Netherlanders there, save a small number up in Hudson's River, Wee thinke it not necessary at present to settle the limits, which may be done hereafter in convenient tyme." [3]

England thus applied, in its negotiations with regard to its colonies, the principle of the closed sphere of colonial interest that had governed the administrative policies of the European colonizing nations from the beginning. It also reasserted the principle of effective occupation by insisting that its title to territory in North America rested upon the fact that it had actually occupied that territory with its colonies.

During the year 1652 tension mounted between England and Holland. The English became alarmed over the expansion of the Dutch navy; and when a Dutch fleet under the command of Admiral Tromp refused to strike its flag, in accord with an ancient custom imposed by the English, as it was passing an English fleet in the Channel on May 19, 1652, a fight ensued, and war became practically unavoidable. There followed the so-called First Dutch War, which was, in fact, a war for maritime, commercial, and colonial supremacy.

The government of the Netherlands and the Dutch West India Company hoped to avoid an extension of the Anglo-Dutch war to America. The Dutch colonies in America were therefore instructed to maintain friendly relations with the English colonies. This policy was successful for a time; some of the English colonies, at least, desired no part in the war.[4] But fighting broke out in New England in 1654, only to be ended soon thereafter by the conclusion of peace.

Oliver Cromwell, who had come to the supreme power in England in 1653, was anxious to make peace with Holland, as another Protestant country. But he was no more ready to permit the Dutch to participate in the trade of the English colonies than his predecessors had been. He was, however, disposed to accept a sort of "union" of the two countries that would eliminate rivalry by permitting free commercial intercourse of the citizens of both countries in the dominions of both, wherever located. Again the Dutch rejected the idea of a union of the two countries

[3] N.Y.C.D., I, 486-487.
[4] See Chapter X.

and proposed instead, a division of the overseas commerce of the world between them. Thus, according to the Dutch proposal, the Dutch would have a monopoly of the trade to the East Indies; the English would be given a monopoly of the trade with the American hemisphere, except Brazil; Brazil itself would be divided between them.

These proposals having failed of acceptance, the negotiations ended in an agreement to make peace and form an alliance. So far as the colonies and colonial commerce were involved, the treaty, finally signed at Westminster on April 15, 1654,[5] provided that the nationals of the two countries might trade and travel in the lands and cities of each other in Europe, "saving all the laws and ordinances of either commonwealth respectively." This meant, of course, the Navigation Act, which excluded the Dutch from English dominions overseas. The treaty further provided that a joint commission, to be composed of two commissioners from each signatory, should be created to adjudicate all claims, one against the other, between the years 1611 and 1651, "in the East Indies, and in Greenland, Muscovy, Brazil, or anywhere else"; in any case in which the commissioners could not agree, the dispute was to be submitted for arbitration to the "Protestant Cantons of Switzerland."

The Anglo-Dutch Treaty of Westminster of 1654 represented a substantial diplomatic victory, with regard to the colonies, for England, since the Dutch, in effect, recognized and accepted the English Navigation Act of 1651, which excluded them from Anglo-American colonial trade. It is also to be noted that it was probably the first international treaty providing for the settlement by arbitration of international disputes relative to America.

2. Anglo-Dutch Relations, 1656-67

Despite the legal exclusion of the Dutch from Angloamerican colonial commerce by the English Navigation Act of 1651 and the Treaty of Westminster, 1654, Dutch traders, both from the Netherlands and from the Dutch colonies in America, continued to trade with all the English colonies in America. Dutch interlopers and their ships were seized by the English, and the Dutch seized English ships trading in the East Indies, with the result that tension mounted rapidly between the two countries in the last years of the Protectorate. This tension was eased by an agreement, made in 1659, to adjust all claims and to maintain peace "in the East Indies as well as elsewhere within and outside of Europe."

After the restoration of Charles II to the English throne, the Dutch tried again to negotiate an alliance and a commercial treaty with England. Again, the Dutch asked for a commercial treaty to accompany

[5] Davenport, ed., *European Treaties*, II, 7-20.

the alliance, in which they hoped for provisions in effect repealing the Navigation Act, which had just been reenacted and strengthened by Parliament in October of 1660, and the delimitation of boundaries between Dutch and English colonies in America.[6]

In the East Indies, the Dutch East India Company and the English East India Company were quarreling over commerce and territories, and the English demanded a settlement of the English company's claims before making a treaty. In North America, on the other hand, friction had arisen between New Netherland, which had absorbed New Sweden on the Delaware in 1655, and Maryland, on the south, and between New Netherland and New England on the north. The Dutch asked that the boundary dispute with Maryland be referred to commissioners; they demanded the return to New Netherland of the Connecticut River, seized by the English settlers in that area; and, in view of the rapid spread of English settlement on Long Island, they requested a return of "a part of Long Island, unjustly usurped . . . by the English of the North." They asked that the boundary between New Netherland and New York be fixed, and that free trade between the Dutch and English colonies be restored as provided in the Treaty of Southampton.[7] The English, as was to be expected, stood firm in their refusal to modify the Navigation Act. They did, however, propose freedom of commerce between the two nations in all their possessions, including the colonies, but "saving the laws and statutes of both countries"—which would have meant, in effect, an acceptance by the Dutch of the Navigation Act of 1660. The Dutch were willing to accept this, but so great were the tensions and rivalry between the English East India Company and the Dutch East India Company in the East Indies that the impossibility of forming an alliance became clear. Nor were the English willing to recognize the existence or the legitimacy of New Netherland by fixing boundaries between it and the English colonies. They preferred to ignore the existence of the Dutch settlements, which would make it easier to seize them later on.

The result of the impasse was the signature, on September 14, 1662, at Whitehall, of a simple treaty of friendship.[8] By the terms of this treaty, the two signatories agreed upon peace in all parts of the world, with freedom of commerce and travel in their dominions in Europe. The island of Pulo Run, in the East Indies, was to be returned to the English, and claims of one signatory against the other in the East Indies or in the part of the world "on this side of the Cape [of Good Hope]" originating before 1654 were to be submitted to the adjudication of a joint claims commission. As for commerce outside of Europe, the nationals of one signatory were to be permitted to travel and trade in the dominions of

[6] Davenport, ed., *European Treaties*, II, 73-76.
[7] N.Y.C.D., II, 132.
[8] Davenport, ed., *European Treaties*, II, 73-85.

the other, "provided that they and every one of them do in their trade and merchandising yield obedience to the laws and statutes of either nation respectively." This meant, of course, that the Dutch recognized and accepted the English Navigation Act of 1660.

The ink on the Anglo-Dutch Treaty of Whitehall was hardly dry before new tensions arose between England and the Netherlands. The difficulties surrounding the settlement of claims under that treaty aroused bitterness, rivalries, and conflicts in the activities of the merchants and colonies of the two countries in Asia, Africa, and North America, with and without the secret support of their governments, and practically nullified the peace arranged by the treaty. In March of 1664, King Charles II granted the area between the Connecticut River and the Delaware River, then occupied by Dutch New Netherland, to the Duke of York, on the bland assumption that this was unoccupied territory, and an expedition was sent out by the Duke, under the command of Colonel Richard Nicolls, to occupy his colony. The "occupation" of the colony, then governed by Peter Stuyvesant but practically defenseless, was accomplished without difficulty; but this seizure of a Dutch colony in time of peace, coupled with other seizures and armed conflicts on the coast of Africa, made a new war inevitable.

Active fighting between the Dutch and the English began in the spring of 1665. Louis XIV of France, an ally of the Dutch since 1662,[9] tried to mediate between the belligerents, but the effort failed, and France was drawn into the war on the side of the Netherlands. The aid of France significantly strengthened the Dutch cause, and in the course of the war, French forces conquered several British colonies in the West Indies—St. Christopher, Antigua, and Montserrat. Meanwhile, the government of Charles II was having trouble, especially financial trouble, at home. Louis XIV, more interested in his projects for the seizure of territories in the Rhineland in his Spanish wife's name on the ground of what he called the principle of "devolution," was no less ready to end the war than was Charles II. Charles, therefore, invited the Dutch to make peace, and, after some haggling as to the locale, the Anglo-French-Dutch negotiations began at Breda, in the Netherlands. The negotiations proceeded on the basis of the principle of *uti possedetis*, or a general agreement that each side should keep what it had taken; but France and England, for reasons of their own, made some exceptions to the rule.

The Anglo-Dutch Treaty of Breda, signed on July 31, 1667,[10] provided, in the first place, that all claims of the English or the Dutch against each other should be dropped and forgotten; both parties were to keep all lands, forts, places, and colonies, as well as ships, they had taken during

[9] See Chapter IX.
[10] Davenport, ed., *European Treaties*, II, 119-131.

the war prior to May 20, 1667; anything seized or occupied since that date was to be restored. With regard to disputes in Africa and America, specifically, the treaty provided that all such differences should be forgotten, and that both parties should continue to "enjoy the same liberty of trade and navigation in Africa as well as in America, which they used and enjoyed, or of right might use and enjoy, at the time when the treaty of the year 1662 was subscribed." Offenders against the treaty, whether in Europe, Africa, Asia, or America, were to be punished.

Here, again, the principle of the two spheres, that there should be "no peace beyond the Line," was abandoned, and the treaty was made uniformly effective (except for allowances of time for communication with the more distant parts of the earth) all over the world.

3. The Dutch and the Spanish Succession

By the Franco-Imperial Treaty of Vienna, of 1668,[11] France and the Holy Roman Empire had agreed that, upon the death of the ailing King Carlos II of Spain, the vast dominions of Spain should be divided between Louis XIV, whose claim derived from Philip IV of Spain through Louis's wife, Maria Teresa, Philip IV's daughter, and the Emperor Leopold, whose mother, Maria, was a daughter of Philip III of Spain, as the most logical heirs to the Spanish inheritance.

This treaty was secret; but the rapid expansion of the power of Louis XIV in his War of Devolution against Spain aroused in England, Sweden, and the Netherlands the fear that Louis XIV might be upsetting the balance of power and that, on the death of Carlos II, he might unite his own worldwide dominions to those of Spain, thereby creating a colossus that could dominate the affairs of the whole of Europe.

It was for reasons such as these that Great Britain, Sweden, and the Netherlands joined together in a treaty of alliance, signed at the Hague on May 7, 1669,[12] which was intended to guarantee, with Spain's consent, the preservation of the Spanish dominions.[13] Spain and France had just ended the War of Devolution by the Treaty of Aix-la-Chapelle, signed May 2, 1668,[14] but Spain, nevertheless, did not trust France. Anticipating the possibility that Louis XIV might invoke the principle of devolution in the name of Maria Teresa as a basis for a claim upon additional Spanish territories, or even upon Spain itself and its empire,[15] the Spanish were moved by a lively fear of some future attack. While not a party to the

[11] See Chapter IX.
[12] Davenport, ed., European Treaties, II, 166-169.
[13] See Chapter X, for a history of the role of the Spanish inheritance in European diplomacy.
[14] Vast, ed., Les grands traités du règne de Louis XIV, II, 1-22.
[15] See Vast, ed., Grands traités, II, 1-10.

Triple Alliance of the Hague,[16] Spain nevertheless welcomed and even subsidized Sweden as a member of it.

The preamble of this treaty stated the purpose of the alliance as being the guarantee of the peace just made by France and Spain at Aix-la-Chapelle, "in order to prevent, thereby, similar inconveniences [conflicts] in the future and the consequences, so dreadful for all of Christianity, that might ensue [that is, the further increase and expansion of French power by the annexation of Spanish possessions to the French empire]." [17]

The treaty itself merely provided that "in case it should happen (which God forbid) that the most Christian King should some day fail in the execution or the punctual observation of what he has promised in the said Treaty [of Aix-la-Chapelle], and principally, if . . . he should attack . . . any of the realms, estates, countries, or subjects of His Catholic Majesty in whatever place, or in whatever part of the world," in that case, the allies would employ all their forces to block the attack and force him to make due reparation for the damage caused. Should the attack be made at such a distance (as, say, in America) as to make impossible immediate action on the spot, the allies would use their forces somewhere else (as, say, in Europe) in order to force him, thus indirectly, to abandon his attack.[18]

The formers of this alliance had good reason to fear the expansive ambitions of Louis XIV; the language of the treaty is a thinly veiled statement of the principle of the balance of power as it involved all of Spain's possessions, whether Spain itself, its other European territories, or its colonies in America and Asia.

4. The Third Anglo-Dutch War and After

The association of Great Britain with the Dutch in the Triple Alliance of 1669 did not end the bitter commercial and colonial rivalry between them.

Actually, even while the Treaty of the Hague was being negotiated, Charles II was drawing closer to Louis XIV. Charles's reasons were chiefly domestic concerns, while Louis XIV was anxious to separate England from its Dutch allies in order to move forward with the plans that culminated in his attack upon the Dutch in April of 1672. The result of this *rapprochement* was the secret Anglo-French Treaty of Dover of 1670, by which, in return for a secret subsidy from Louis, Charles took sides with France.[19] England, now the ally of France, also declared war

---

[16] Davenport, ed., *European Treaties*, II, 166-169.
[17] Davenport, ed., *European Treaties*, II, 168.
[18] Davenport, ed., *European Treaties*, II, 168-169.
[19] See Chapter IX.

on the Netherlands. The armies of Louis XIV invaded the Netherlands, and it appeared that the Low Countries might be completely destroyed. The Netherlands hurriedly made a treaty of friendship with Sweden,[20] to prevent that country from taking sides against them.

This treaty was in part a renewal of the Treaty of July 28, 1667, which had provided for the settlement of disputes between the Dutch West India Company and the Swedish-American Company in America arising from the seizure of New Sweden by Peter Stuyvesant in 1655. Since those disputes had not been settled, the present treaty provided that they should be settled within a year.[21]

Meanwhile, the Dutch had asked England and France for peace. France and England agreed between themselves that neither would make a separate peace, and that terms for peace would be presented jointly. England's terms for peace relative to America were rejected by the Dutch, who then had turned to Spain and asked for mediation, as provided in the Dutch-Spanish treaty of August 30, 1673.[22] This move had failed because of Spain's fear that England might turn upon the Spanish colonies. The Netherlands then turned to Sweden, which had already succeeded in bringing the belligerents together at Cologne.

The Dutch had improved their position in the war, but the factor that saved them was the unpopularity of the Anglo-Dutch war in England. On the other hand, the English people were strongly anti-French, and resented Charles II's rapprochement with France. Charles II was thus forced to make a fairly generous and separate peace with the Netherlands because Parliament had delayed making appropriations for the war pending the withdrawal of the King's Declaration of Indulgences and the signing of Parliament's Test Act, and had finally refused to make the appropriation altogether. When the Dutch directly asked for peace, therefore, and Sweden offered to mediate, Charles felt compelled to accept.

The Anglo-Dutch Treaty of Westminster, signed on February 19, 1674,[23] provided for peace between England and the Netherlands, a peace that would apply to the subjects of the two nations anywhere in the world. It was agreed that all territories and places taken by either party during the war should be returned, which meant that New York, seized by the Dutch on August 9, 1673, should be restored to England. The ninth article of the treaty stated that, in view of the vital importance of freedom of commerce to both signatories, especially that to the East Indies, a new treaty for the regulation of commerce should be drawn up

[20] See Chapter VIII.
[21] This provision had to do with damages incurred in 1655. But as the Dutch retook New York on August 9, 1673, shortly after this treaty was signed, this provision might have been of considerable material interest to them.
[22] Davenport, ed., *European Treaties*, II, 214-228.
[23] Davenport, ed., *European Treaties*, II, 229-240.

promptly by an Anglo-Dutch joint commission. Should this commission fail to agree upon all points, the disputed matters were to be submitted to the arbitration of the Queen Regent of Spain.

In the negotiations for the regulation of Anglo-Dutch commerce provided for in the Treaty of Westminster of 1674, the Dutch proposed that there be made two treaties, one to regulate trade and navigation in Europe, the other to be a special treaty with regard to the East Indies. According to the Dutch plan, the marine treaty for Europe would have permitted the nationals of each party to trade in the territories of the other. But this was, in effect, a restatement of the old Dutch demand for a relaxation of the English navigation acts in favor of Dutch nationals.

The English negotiators refused this proposal, as usual. They also demanded that the terms of the treaty be extended to the entire world.

In the treaty,[24] as finally made, the two signatories agreed, in general, upon the principle of the freedom of their nationals to trade with all the world, and, in particular, their right as neutrals freely to trade with belligerents in time of war.[25] Rules and regulations for the mutual treatment and behavior of their ships were laid down; a list of articles to be considered contraband was included. Articles to be considered noncontraband were also listed; among these appeared a number of products that were, or might be, products of colonies in the East Indies or America, such as silk, spices, tobacco, cotton, dried fish, masts and lumber, *et cetera*. As the English had insisted, the terms of this treaty were extended to all the world. Nothing was said about commerce between the nationals of one of the signatories and those of the other in the colonies.

The Treaty of Westminster of 1674 and its supplementary marine treaty of London, which together marked the end of the third Anglo-Dutch war, along with the Treaty of Nymwegen,[26] which ended the Franco-Dutch war, signaled the end of the period when the Netherlands played, in world affairs, the role of a major commercial and colonial power. From this time onward, for almost a century, the Dutch were to follow the lead of England; and it was to England that they looked for the protection of their colonial interests in America. The identification of Dutch colonial and commercial interests with those of England became closer with the rise of William of Orange as the Dutch national leader and his marriage to Mary, daughter of James, Duke of York, later to be King James II of England. It became a personal union when William himself ascended the throne of England at the time of the Glorious Revolution in 1688.

[24] Chalmers, ed., A *Collection of Treaties between Great Britain and Other Powers*, I, 177-191.
[25] This was a provision that came to be of extreme importance in Anglo-Dutch relations in the eighteenth century.
[26] For the Treaty of Nymwegen, see Vast, ed., *Grands traités*, II, 23-99.

France, under the leadership of Louis XIV, was now emerging as the great disturber of the balance of power in Europe, in America, and in the East Indies. Even Spain and Portugal felt their colonial empires to be threatened by the rise of France, and they, also, found it expedient, in the last decades of the seventeenth century, to look at the might of England to protect them against the new colossus.

CHAPTER VI

Anglo-Spanish Diplomacy Relative to America, 1648-89

1. The Protectorate

WHEN OLIVER CROMWELL became the Lord Protector of England in 1653, he came to power with certain well-formulated ideas as to the possibility of British colonial expansion in America. France and Spain were still at war, and Cromwell believed that he might acquire for England American territories claimed by both of them without, thereby, precipitating war. This thought, based partially, at least, upon the old idea that there is "no peace beyond the Line," led him to seize both French (Acadia, 1654) and Spanish (Jamaica, 1655) colonial lands.

Cromwell was still influenced by the religious thought that in fighting the Catholic powers he was advancing the cause of Protestantism, but he was on much firmer and up-to-date ground when he thought that the expansion of the English colonial empire at their expense would promote English commerce and, thereby, English wealth. Cromwell actually adopted a grandiose scheme, called the "Grand Design," outlined by Thomas Gage,[1] a renegade Catholic priest who had lived in Mexico, as a plan for action in the West Indies. The scheme envisaged the seizure of several West Indian islands and the conquest of Central America; these territories would be colonized by Englishmen, and England would assume control of the entire Caribbean area. Such an achievement would spell the breaking of Spanish power in America and a corresponding expansion of English power and wealth. Cromwell believed the project easily feasible. As soon as the Dutch War drew to a close, he sent a naval and military expedition, under the command of Admiral William Penn

[1] Gage, The English-American, his Travail by Sea and Land: or, A New Survey of the West-India's.

and General Robert Venables, to the West Indies to see what they could take. At the same time, Cromwell presented an ultimatum to the Spanish ambassador demanding religious freedom for Englishmen in Spanish territories and freedom of the English to trade in Spanish colonies. The Spanish ambassador replied with his famous remark that to demand these two things of the Spanish King was to demand his two eyes, and that, of course, Spain had not the slightest intention of granting either.

Spain, however, did not declare war, as Cromwell apparently had hoped it might, but the Penn-Venables expedition sailed anyway, with rather vague and flexible instructions which left to the discretion of the leaders the ultimate decision as to what they should do. "The design in general," said the instructions, "is to gain an interest in that part of the West Indies in the possession of the Spaniard, for the effecting whereof we shall not tie you up to a method by any particular instructions." [2] After a fiasco on the island of Santo Domingo the expedition did succeed in taking Jamaica, early in 1655.

The King of Spain, Philip IV, when he heard of the seizure of Jamaica, took the position that the act itself was a declaration of war. England then formed an alliance with France [3] and Portugal, which was still fighting for its independence against Spain, and in the course of the fighting that followed England took Dunkirk, in the Spanish Netherlands (Belgium). This war was ended by the Peace of the Pyrenees, signed at the "Isle of Pheasants," in the Pyrenees Mountains, on November 7, 1659.[4]

The Treaty of the Pyrenees was a very long one, which was concerned chiefly, after peace and the marriage of Louis XIV to the Infanta Maria Teresa of Spain, for which it provided, with the allocation of territories in Europe. The terms for mutual commerce in Europe were laid down, and great care was taken to define contraband of war and noncontraband. Portugal was not included in the peace and remained at war with Spain. But France, as Portugal's ally in the war just ended, reserved the right to try to bring about peace between them.

Nothing in America was mentioned, but by its omission Spain accepted the fact of English possession of Jamaica. Article 42 of the treaty, by which the crest of the Pyrenees was recognized as the dividing line between France and Spain,[5] also provided that if any of the territories on the two sides of the Pyrenees watershed should overlap the ridge, the section on the side of France should belong to France and the section on the side of Spain should belong to Spain.

[2] Watts, *Histoire des colonies anglaises aux Antilles, 1649–1660,* 466-469.
[3] See Chapter IX.
[4] Vast, ed., *Grands traités,* I, 93-175.
[5] Vast, ed., *Grands traités,* I, 115-116. This provision was sharply modified by a supplementary treaty signed on May 31, 1660 (*ibid.,* I, 116, fn. 1).

2. *The Treaty of Madrid, 1667*

Meanwhile, Charles II, recognized as King of England by Spain although not yet restored to his throne, had been engaged in a series of negotiations with the King of Spain that had produced in 1656 a treaty of friendship between the two monarchs. According to the terms of this treaty the Anglo-Spanish Treaty of 1630 was to be renewed. The treaty had also promised that England would collaborate with Spain, that Spain would assist Charles in the recovery of his crown, that England would assist Spain in the reannexation of Portugal; Charles would also prohibit his subjects from occupying any more islands claimed by Spain in the West Indies and would withdraw them from territories occupied while Charles was "abroad"; this would mean Jamaica.

This treaty never had any effect. Philip failed to assist Charles to re-occupy his throne. Charles did proclaim the end of Cromwell's war with Spain, but his interest was distracted by the enticing prospect of marriage with a Portuguese princess, and he listened with interest to the offers of Portugal to form a strong commercial and colonial union with England.[6]

Charles II and his Parliament were, in fact, greatly interested in commercial and colonial expansion. It was in this mood that the King granted Dutch New Netherland to his brother, the Duke of York, and Carolina, in territory claimed by Spain, to eight of his followers, among a series of other actions relative to colonies, while Parliament passed a series of laws calculated more effectively than before to exclude foreigners from the colonial trade. By his marriage to Catherine of Braganza of Portugal,[7] he had extended the British colonial empire and had acquired for England an additional share in the trade of the East Indies. In 1661 he made a treaty of commerce and colonial friendship with Sweden, and in 1662 he made an agreement as to commerce and friendship with the Dutch. After his marriage, he turned again to Spain.

England's interest in a treaty with Spain centered in several branches of commerce. One of these was the traffic in Negro slaves, which, because Spain had no African supply area of its own for Negroes, it had to entrust, under a contract called the *asiento*, to foreigners. Charles II issued a new charter to the company called the Royal Adventurers. Trading into Africa, in 1663, which gave the company a monopoly of the English slave trade. He hoped that this company might be given the *asiento* for supplying Negroes to the Spanish colonies, then held by two Genoese entrepreneurs.

Spain, in view of its uncomfortable position in European affairs and because of its fear of an attack by Louis XIV (which did eventually come

[6] See Chapter VII.
[7] See Chapter VII.

in the form of the "War of Devolution"), was not adverse to a *rapprochement* with England. At the same time, Spain was prepared to face the inevitable recognition of the independence of Portugal in order to be free from the burdens of the still continuing Portuguese war. Negotiations for English mediation of the Portuguese war and for a treaty of commercial and colonial friendship with England began in the spring of 1664.

The treaty with England was made first. In the course of the negotiations, Sir Richard Fanshawe, the English ambassador to Spain, tried to resolve still outstanding problems in the relationships between the two countries. With regard to America, he asked for freedom for English merchants to trade with the Spanish West Indies; he also asked for a share, for the English Royal Adventurers, of the *asiento*; better still, he suggested that the *asiento* be given directly to the English company. Spain, on its side, asked for a cessation of English illicit trade and piracy in the Spanish West Indies, the restoration of Jamaica, and a renewal of the Treaty of 1630. Fanshawe, however, asserted that that treaty had not, in any case, extended the peace it made to areas "beyond the Line" and insisted upon a new treaty.

The negotiations lagged during the years 1665 and 1666, largely because of the complex international situation arising from England's war with the Netherlands and France and France's "War of Devolution" against Spain. But the Portuguese forces in the war won a decisive victory over the Spanish army at Villaviciosa in June, 1665, and Philip IV died on September 17 of the same year. After Philip's death negotiations were renewed, both in London and in Madrid, and in May, 1666, Fanshawe was replaced as English ambassador by the Earl of Sandwich.

Sandwich's negotiations proceeded felicitously, since Spain was tired of the Portuguese war and distrustful of France. On May 23, 1667, England and Spain signed at Madrid two treaties, one a treaty of commerce, the other an agreement anticipating a truce between Portugal and Spain to be mediated by England.

In the Treaty of Friendship and Commerce [8] it was provided that trade should be permitted between the nationals of the two countries, "where hitherto trade and commerce hath been accustomed" (which meant, of course, *not* in the colonies of either signatory). English ships were to be permitted to bring into Spain the products of the East Indies. Both signatories were to see to it that their subjects observed the treaty and kept the peace. Most important of all, the crown of Spain "granted" to the subjects of the English king "all that is granted to the States of the United Provinces of the Netherlands and their subjects in their treaty of Münster, 1648 . . ." [9] which meant, in effect, that Spain thereby recog-

[8] Davenport, ed., *European Treaties*, II, 94-109; Chalmers, ed., *Treaties*, II, 1-34.
[9] Davenport, ed., *European Treaties*, II, 107.

nized England's right to trade in the entire world and to own territories anywhere, including America.

After this treaty, negotiations for a mediated peace between Spain and Portugal continued. Such a peace was eventually signed at Lisbon on February 13, 1668.[10]

3. The "American" Treaty of Madrid, 1670

The Anglo-Spanish Treaty of Madrid of 1667, although it acknowledged England's right to trade and to own colonies in the "new world," and although both crowns promised to keep the peace, had little or no effect upon the conflicts between Spaniards and Englishmen in America. English privateers and pirates continued their depredations upon Spanish commerce, and Sir Thomas Modyford, governor of Jamaica, who shared their profits, refused to stop them. The most spectacular of the pirates was Henry Morgan, who sacked Porto Bello on the Isthmus of Panama and then went on to sack Panama City in 1670, after a new treaty of peace had been made for America. The Queen Regent of Spain finally declared war upon England in the areas south of the Tropic of Cancer.

England's legitimate trade with Spanish America by way of Seville and Cadiz was a highly profitable one and suffered from Spanish retaliation in the form of discriminations against it in Spain. At the same time, England stood to gain certain commercial and territorial concessions in America if it could bring its unruly friends and subjects in the West Indies to order. England sent Sir William Godolphin to Madrid to try to negotiate a special treaty with regard to the American issues.

In his negotiations with the Count of Peñaranda, Godolphin took the position that the Treaty of Madrid of 1667 had established peace between the two nations only in Europe, and that the conflict in America, in perfect conformity with the principle of the two spheres, or that "might makes right beyond the Line," should not be thought of as a violation of that treaty and, therefore, punishable.[11]

Because of Spain's weakened position, both in Europe and in America, the Spanish crown, against the advice of the Council for the Indies, made a treaty with Godolphin that was highly favorable to England.[12] It confirmed, in the first place, the Treaty of Madrid of 1667. Peace, under the new treaty, was stated to be established "as well in America as in other parts of the world." All hostilities and conflicts were to end, "in whatever part of the world," but in the West Indies in particular; prisoners taken by one side or the other in America were to be released immediately upon

[10] See Chapter VII.
[11] See Haring, *Trade and Navigation between Spain and the Indies*.
[12] Davenport, ed., *European Treaties*, II, 187-196.

the publication of the treaty. The subjects of each of the signatories were to abstain from visiting the ports and colonies of the other in the West Indies; provision was made, however, for the possibility that one or the other of the signatories might at some future time license the subjects of the other to trade in its colonies under certain conditions (this was apparently included to anticipate the possibility that the *asiento* might be granted to an English company). However, it was also provided that the ships of one of the signatories might put into the ports of the other under dire necessity, such as storms, pursuit by pirates or enemies, and urgent need of repair. In such cases, however, the ships that took refuge under these conditions must strictly observe the limitations of the treaty relative to trade. The freedom of both nations to navigate in American waters was assured, "provided nothing be committed or done contrary to the genuine meaning of these articles." [13]

Of supreme importance to England was the provision that "the Most Serene King of Great Britain, his heirs and successors, shall have, hold, and possess forever, with full right of sovereignty, ownership, and possession, all the lands, regions, islands, colonies, and dominions, situated in the West Indies or in any part of America, that the said King of Great Britain and his subjects at present hold and possess." [14] For this was an explicit *de jure* recognition, the first Spain ever conceded to England, of the legitimacy of England's colonies in America, including Jamaica, seized by the English only as recently as 1655.

This was one of the few European treaties made during the colonial period to deal purely with international problems in America. As such it became a sort of basic charter for the relations of England and Spain in the western hemisphere for a century. It is particularly significant, however, as a special treaty for America springing from the old European doctrine of the two spheres, that is, that Europe is one sphere for international law and relations and that the "new world" is another.

4. The Anglo-Spanish Alliance of 1680 and the Truce of Ratisbon, 1684

After the nexus of treaties made at Nymwegen in 1678 and 1679, which brought a general peace to Western Europe, [15] Spain turned to England in the hope of making an alliance with that country against France for the protection of the Spanish Netherlands against further incursions of Louis XIV in that area. England, seeing in the Spanish gesture an opportunity to expand its colonial and commercial empire in America,

[13] Davenport, ed., *European Treaties*, II, 195.
[14] Davenport, ed., *European Treaties*, II, 194.
[15] See Chapter IX.

proposed that Spain, in return for an alliance, grant English merchants a share in the direct trade with the Spanish colonies. This would include a share in the *asiento*, permission for a few English ships to visit Buenos Aires each year for trade, a monopoly of the business of cutting logwood in Campeche, and the freedom to collect salt at Punta de Araya, on the coast of Venezuela.

When a treaty of alliance was signed at Windsor on June 20, 1680, none of these English demands was granted. Instead, while the treaty reaffirmed the peace between the two countries "both within and without Europe," and the Treaties of Madrid of 1667 and 1670 were reaffirmed, the "league of defense and union" was to be effective "only within the limits of Europe." However, should the possessions of one of the signatories be attacked, "even outside of Europe," the ally would endeavor to cause the attack to cease; failing which, should the attacked ally be compelled to use force against the aggressor in Europe, then the other ally would use his forces in assisting the first to stop the aggressor by joint pressure in Europe.

War broke out between France and Spain again in 1683, when Louis XIV again invaded the Spanish Netherlands and Catalonia and seized the city of Luxembourg. Unhappily for Spain, it found that its alliance of 1680 with England was worthless, since Charles II had renewed his *rapprochement* with Louis XIV. Since Spain could get no assistance from either the Emperor or the Dutch, it felt constrained to accept the mediation of the Dutch for the effecting of a twenty-year truce with France.

According to the terms of this truce, the so-called Truce of Ratisbon,[16] Spain accepted Louis XIV's extortions. The text of the treaty of truce provided that the truce should be in effect both "within Europe and without, both on this side of and beyond the Line. . . ."

The four decades between the Peace of Westphalia and the outbreak of the War of the Palatinate in 1689 constituted a period of steady decline in Spain's colonial power. When William of Orange formed the defensive League of Augsburg against the further expansion of France in 1686 and this league became the Grand Alliance of 1689, Spain became a member of the League and the Alliance. And with good reason; because Spain itself and Spain's colonial empire were very soon to become one of the great stakes in the international diplomacy of Europe.[17]

[16] Davenport, ed., *European Treaties*, II, 286-292.
[17] See Chapter X.

CHAPTER VII

Anglo-Portuguese Colonial Diplomacy, 1648-89

THE PEACE OF Westphalia (1648) left France and Spain still at war. England, under the government of Parliament, had just emerged from its civil war and was vigorously attempting to rehabilitate its economy and to reestablish its position in the international community. Its efforts brought it into commercial and colonial conflict with the Netherlands,[1] with France,[2] with Portugal, and with Spain.[3]

1. Cromwell's Rapprochement with Portugal

During the English civil war Portugal had sympathized with the Stuart cause and had allowed Prince Rupert's fleet to use Portuguese harbors as bases of naval operations. Because of this, English fleets had operated against Portuguese fleets, and one valuable Portuguese fleet, homeward-bound from Brazil, had been taken by the English admiral Blake.

After the execution of Charles I and the establishment of the English commonwealth, Portugal, still at war with Spain, asked that the relations between itself and England be stabilized. Negotiations went on for several years without result. After Cromwell came to power in 1653 there was some additional delay, but a treaty was finally signed at Westminster on July 20, 1654.[4]

This treaty was concerned chiefly with commercial and colonial questions. It provided for free commercial intercourse between England and Portugal, "saving nevertheless all the laws and statutes of each place"— that is, in particular, the English Navigation Act of 1651, which excluded

[1] See Chapter V.
[2] See Chapter IX.
[3] See Chapter VI.
[4] Davenport, ed., *European Treaties*, II, 31-35; Chalmers, ed., *Treaties*, II, 267-286.

all nations, including the Portuguese, from trade in the English colonies. The English, however, were to be free to trade between Portugal and Brazil and other Portuguese conquests and possessions in the West Indies, with the exception of certain goods that might be carried only by the Brazil Company, on terms of practical equality with the nationals of Portugal itself. The only condition was that English ships so trading must travel with Portuguese convoys. English trade with Portuguese colonies in the East Indies was to be free of any restriction, under "most-favored-nation" conditions. Should the Portuguese Brazil Company or any other Portuguese subjects need to hire ships for trade to Brazil or the West Indies, they promised (with certain exceptions) to hire English ships. Englishmen trading in Portuguese territories were to enjoy liberty of conscience and freedom from persecution by the Portuguese Inquisition, provided they did their worshiping in private houses and not in public. Violators of the treaty, whether in Europe, America, Africa, or the East Indies, were to be punished; conflicts between subjects of the two signatories, anywhere in the world, were not to be considered causes for war in Europe. Debts arising out of the seizure of English ships trading for Portugal to Brazil or the East by Prince Rupert or Prince Maurice, nephews of Charles I, were to be paid, after verification by a joint Anglo-Portuguese claims commission, by Portugal. The right of England to trade, as a neutral, with Spain, with which Portugal was still at war, was recognized.

This treaty was highly favorable to the merchants of England, for that country entered largely into the commerce of the Portuguese colonies while the Portuguese effectively acknowledged and accepted their exclusion from trade with the English colonies by the English Navigation Act of 1651. Indeed, from this moment in history onward, Portugal's commerce with its colonies was largely dominated by English participation in it. Henceforth, Portugal and its colonies were in considerable measure a commercial satellite of England.

2. The Anglo-Portuguese Alliance of 1661

The active and expansive colonial interest and activity manifested by Oliver Cromwell and the Protectorate were carried forward by Charles II after his restoration to the English throne in 1660. While Charles handed out princely colonial grants to his friends, including the one to New Netherland given his brother, the Duke of York, Parliament was busy passing a series of new laws more effectively excluding foreigners from the trade of the English colonies and channeling the profits of that trade into the coffers of English entrepreneurs.

In 1656 Charles, recognized as king of England by Spain, had made a treaty of friendship with that country, among the terms of which was Charles' promise to assist Spain in the reannexation of Portugal, despite Portugal's very valuable aid to him against his rebellious subjects in England.[5] Upon reascending his throne, however, Charles cooled in his friendship for Spain and allowed himself to be won over to the side of Portugal by the simple fact that Portugal outbid Spain for his support.

Portugal, indeed, was desperately fighting for its life and independence in a war that had begun with its separation from Spain in 1640. Spain had at last made peace with France in 1659,[6] and was now free to concentrate its efforts upon Portugal. That country had made a desperate effort to make peace and an alliance with the Dutch, but its proposals for peace were blocked by the Dutch East and West India Companies, which found the war against Portugal profitable and which anticipated making further conquests of Portuguese colonies in the East Indies and in America, particularly Brazil. In its desperation, therefore, Portugal, both in order to separate England from Spain and to win English aid for itself, prepared to make Charles II a handsome offer in return for an English alliance.

The Portuguese offer to Charles II included marriage with Catherine of Braganza, who would come with a dowry of over eight hundred thousand pounds, together with Bombay in India and Tangier in northern Africa. Portugal also offered England great concessions in the East Indian trade, a renewal of the Treaty of Westminster of 1654, which gave England a highly favored position in the trade of Brazil and the Portuguese West Indies. In return for all this, Portugal asked England's assistance in its war against Spain and the Netherlands. If possible, Portugal hoped England might mediate a peace; failing that, it proposed that England join it in its war against Spain.

Spain, in the meantime, was attempting to hold Charles II to his treaty of 1656 and to prevent him from forming an alliance with Portugal. The Dutch, also, attempted to prevent the English from making an alliance with Portugal. France, on the other hand, having just made peace with Spain, encouraged Charles in the hope that a *rapprochement* might be achieved between England and France, both in Europe and in America.

Charles accepted the Portuguese offer, and a treaty embodying it was signed in London on June 23, 1661.[7] Under the terms of this treaty, the Anglo-Portuguese treaties of 1642 and 1654, with all the privileges they granted to England in Portugal and in the Portuguese colonies, were reaffirmed. Tangier and Bombay were ceded to England. Most important of all, from the English point of view, English subjects were to be permitted to trade freely in all the dominions of the King of Portugal in

---

[5] See Chapter VI.
[6] See Chapter IX.
[7] Davenport, ed., *European Treaties*, II, 57-62; Brazão, *The Anglo-Portuguese Alliance*, 39-41.

the East Indies, in Brazil, and in the Portuguese West Indies, and were to have the privilege of having their agents reside there. Any former Portuguese colonial possessions that might be taken by the English from the Dutch were to be recognized as English. England promised never to make a peace with Spain that would hamper its assistance to Portugal and never to return Jamaica to that crown. By a secret article England promised to protect and defend all the conquests of the colonies belonging to Portugal, both then and in the future. The King of England was to mediate a peace between Portugal and the Netherlands and the Dutch commercial companies; should the mediation fail, England was to protect the Portuguese dominions everywhere from the Dutch; should the Dutch succeed in taking any Portuguese possession, the English were to assist Portugal in forcing the Dutch to give it up.

This was really a treaty of armed assistance; it did not necessarily involve war with any of Portugal's enemies. So far as the colonies and their commerce were concerned, it placed Portugal more than ever under English domination.

3. Portugal and Spain

England eventually succeeded in mediating a peace between Portugal and Spain. It was preoccupied, in the years from 1664 to 1667, with conflict with the Netherlands and with France; but in the latter year, when peace among them was made at Breda,[8] France, still at war over the annexation of Spanish territories in Europe by the principle of "devolution," immediately approached England with the idea of getting Charles II's support against Spain. On the other hand, Spain, still at war with Portugal, sought England's friendship.

Taking advantage of this mood, England made two proposals to Spain: the first was that Spain make peace with Portugal, thereby recognizing Portugal's independence; the second was a treaty of friendship. With regard to the latter, England and Spain came to terms in the Treaty of Madrid of 1667,[9] after which negotiations for a peace between Spain and Portugal went forward, negotiations that were made easier by a political revolution in Portugal which dethroned King Alfonso VI and placed Don Pedro, his brother, in the position of regent.

It thus fell out that, under the guidance of the Earl of Sandwich, the British ambassador in Lisbon, negotiations between Portugal and Spain quickly came to a successful conclusion in the Treaty of Lisbon, signed on February 13, 1668.[10] Under the terms of this treaty, Spain implicitly

[8] See Chapters V and IX.
[9] See Chapter VI.
[10] Davenport, ed., *European Treaties*, II, 157-165. See also, Temple, *The Works of Sir William Temple*, I, 344-360.

recognized the independence of Portugal. The subjects of both signatories were to be granted the same privileges extended England by the Anglo-Spanish Treaty of Madrid of May 23, 1667 insofar as this treaty was still in force. Since by the Treaty of Madrid in 1667 Spain had extended to the English the same rights overseas that were extended to the Dutch by the Treaty of Münster (1648), these rights were now also extended to the Portuguese. Spain had recognized Portugal's possessions in the "new world" ever since the Treaty of Alcaçovas of 1479; the present treaty, in effect, merely reiterated Spain's recognition of Portugal's title to its possessions in Asia, Africa, and America. But the treaty prohibited the nationals of both signatories from trading in each other's colonies in America.

By this treaty, while it ended Portugal's war of independence with Spain and clarified Portugal's colonial status *vis-à-vis* that country, Portugal, nevertheless, fell still more completely under the commercial and colonial domination of England. From now on, until the War of the Spanish Succession, when Portugal momentarily followed Louis XIV's lead against England, Portugal was generally to be found on England's side in diplomatic exchanges relative to America. By the so-called Methuen Treaty of 1703, Portugal once more cemented its commercial, military, and diplomatic subjection to England.[11]

[11] See Chapter X.

CHAPTER VIII

The Swedes, the Danes, and the Brandenburgers, 1648-89

1. The Anglo-Swedish Treaties of 1654

IN THE FIRST half of the seventeenth century Sweden, along with the other commercial nations on the western seaboard of Europe, became interested in establishing colonies in North America. The Swedish West India Company was formed in 1638, and this company sent a colony to the shores of Delaware Bay, which it named "New Sweden," and where the colonists built Fort Christina. Their trade with the Indians brought them into conflict with the Dutch, and after the Peace of Westphalia, in 1655, the colony of New Sweden was seized by the Dutch governor of New Netherland, Peter Stuyvesant.

Sweden, meanwhile, like the Netherlands, was highly interested in trade with the English colonies along the Atlantic seaboard. England, on its side, was interested in commerce with the Baltic countries, including Sweden, because of the dependence of the English navy and mercantile fleet upon that area for naval stores. The two countries were the more strongly drawn together, after the Peace of Westphalia, by the formation of a Dutch-Danish alliance which culminated, in the course of the first Anglo-Dutch war, in a Danish-Dutch treaty which promised to close the Sound (the narrow strait separating Denmark from Sweden) to English ships.

The result of these circumstances was a *rapprochement* between England and Sweden. Sweden proposed an alliance and a commercial treaty that would provide for freedom for the nationals of both countries to trade in each other's territories, not only in Europe, but also in the "islands and ports subject and belonging to the commonwealth of England in Virginia,

New England, Guiney, and elsewhere." But the English Council of State was no more disposed to open the colonies in America to Sweden than it was to admit the Dutch; it therefore replied that although it would welcome freedom of commerce in the territories of the two nations in Europe, it could not open to the Swedes the commerce of "The Barbadoes and such plantations, ports and places in America, belonging to the Commonwealth of England, whereunto trade and traffic is prohibited without special license, both sides observing the laws, customs and ordinances of each place respectively." [1] Thus, in terms almost identical with those used by the Commonwealth in dealing with the Dutch, England slammed the door to its colonies in the face of the Swedes.

The negotiations continued, however, and a general treaty of commerce and amity was signed by the two countries in Upsala on April 21, 1654.[2] This treaty was concerned chiefly with the freedom of commerce between the two nations "where commerce was carried on hitherto," and the regulations governing that commerce, which should be free, "provided . . . the laws and ordinances of the aforesaid Commonwealth and Kingdom . . . have been observed." Which, of course, meant, so far as England was concerned, the English Navigation Act of 1651. Specific questions relative to American and African trade and relations were postponed for later determination.

At the time of the Anglo-Swedish negotiations of 1654, Swedes and Englishmen had come into conflict in Africa and in North America. In Guinea, the English Company Trading to Guinea, or Guinea Company, found itself in a series of quarrels with the Swedish African Company over territory and trade along the Gold Coast. In America, New Sweden had come into conflict both with the English in Maryland and with the Dutch in New Netherland, and after the settlement of a trading post on Delaware Bay by a group of colonists from New Haven and the seizure of New Haven ships there by the Dutch, the three-way international tension in the area became acute. The Swedish government instructed Governor Johan C. Rising of New Sweden, in the spring of 1654, to keep peace with the Dutch and the English, which he did. The questions arising out of this situation came before the negotiators in Upsala, and an effort was made to adjust them in an agreement signed on May 18, 1654.[3]

This agreement provided that, with regard to the disputes of the two African companies in Guinea, those disputes should be submitted for adjudication to a joint Anglo-Swedish commission. The same sort of solution was applied to the disputes in North America, that is, the question of

[1] Quoted from Johnson, *The Swedish Settlements on the Delaware: Their History and Relation to the Indians, Dutch and English, 1638–1664,* II, 620–621, in Davenport, ed., *European Treaties,* II, 21.
[2] Davenport, ed., *European Treaties,* II, 21–26; Chalmers, ed., *Treaties,* II, 20–29.
[3] Davenport, ed., *European Treaties,* II, 27–30.

the boundaries between Swedish and English settlements in America was also to be submitted to a joint Anglo-Swedish commission.

This informal agreement, signed for England by Bulstrode Whitelocke, the English ambassador, did nothing to resolve the question of Swedish participation in the trade of the English colonies, beyond the exclusion implicit in the Treaty of Upsala. It simply provided for two joint commissions for the adjustment of the issues in the local quarrels in Africa and North America. In accepting this mode of settlement of the boundaries between New Sweden and the English colonies, however, England tacitly recognized the existence of a bona fide Swedish colony on the shores of Delaware Bay, a sort of recognition it had never officially given to Dutch New Netherland.

2. The Anglo-Swedish Treaty of Westminster, 1656

Since the tension between Sweden and the Dutch continued after the Anglo-Swedish treaty of alliance of Upsala of 1654, Sweden sought to strengthen its ties with England. At the same time, King Charles X was still interested in the possibility that Swedish merchants might acquire a share in the trade of the English American colonies in return for a privileged share for English merchants in the Baltic trade, upon which England was so dependent for naval stores. To this interest was added the long-standing question of boundaries between Swedish and English colonies in America, which still had not been settled.

The Swedish desire for a strong alliance with England failed of realization because of Oliver Cromwell's desire not to antagonize the Dutch, with whom he had just made peace. A commercial and colonial treaty was achieved, however, which dealt with the problem of colonial relations in North America. This treaty, signed at Westminster on July 27, 1656,[4] provided for commercial intercourse and the freedom of neutrals to trade with belligerents, and it defined contraband of war. With regard to America, the exclusion of Swedes from trade with the English colonies by the English Navigation Act of 1651 was again confirmed, but it relaxed that exclusion to the extent of a highly ambiguous proviso that if any of the subjects of the Swedish king, presenting letters of recommendation from him, should solicit licenses to go to the colonies, the Lord Protector would "not unwillingly . . . satisfy the desire of the Most Serene Royal Majesty of Sweden in this matter, so far as the state of affairs and of the Commonwealth may at the time permit." The Swedes had also wished to arrange for a definition of the boundary between Virginia and New Sweden, but the treaty was silent on that question.

[4] Davenport, ed., *European Treaties*, II, 48–52.

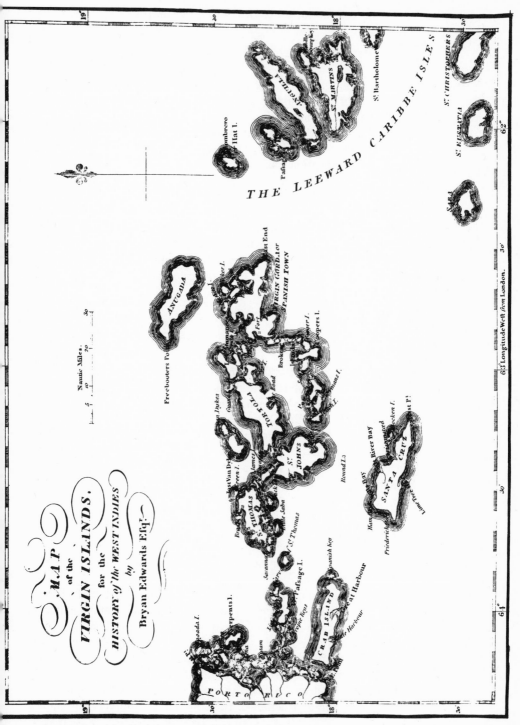

THE VIRGIN ISLANDS. (From Bryan Edwards, *The History, Civil and Commercial, of the British West Indies* [London, 1819].)

3. The Anglo-Swedish Treaty of Whitehall, 1661

After Charles II returned to the throne of England in 1660, he and his government sought all possible means to extend the commerce and the colonies of England. Among others, England negotiated with Sweden for a renewal of the commercial agreements of 1654 and 1656. The treaty that resulted from this negotiation was, thus, a restatement of the earlier treaties, with the exception that it omitted the provision for a possible licensing of Swedes desiring to go to the English colonies.

In the meantime, however, the Dutch had seized the Swedish colony on the Delaware, so that the question of boundaries between this colony and the English colonies was no longer an issue between the two countries. The Dutch, for their part, feared that the Swedes and English might act together, under their alliance, to retake the Swedish colony. These fears were irrelevant, however, since the English seized all of New Netherland, including New Sweden, in 1664.

4. The Anglo-Swedish Alliance of 1665

As already noted, colonial and commercial tensions between the Dutch and the English continued to mount through the year 1663, despite the treaty of friendship made between them in 1662. Among the issues in dispute was the claim of the Dutch to a monopoly of the slave trade on the African Gold Coast. In the effort to enforce this monopoly the Dutch came into conflict with Danes, Swedes, Englishmen, and others. At the same time, the Swedes were still resentful of Peter Stuyvesant's seizure of New Sweden in 1655, and persisted in demanding its return. When the Dutch declared a blockade of the entire Gold Coast of Guinea, under pretense of the necessities of war with the African natives, Charles II sent a naval expedition to break the blockade, which seized Cape Verde, Cabo Corso, and a number of Dutch ships. Following this, in February of 1664, the Duke of York sent the famous expedition which seized the Dutch colony of New Netherland.[5]

In view of the mounting tension and the apparent inevitability of war with the Dutch, Charles II sought alliances with Sweden and Denmark. These two countries, on their side, exasperated by the arrogance of the Dutch, hoped to fish some benefit out of the troubled Anglo-Dutch waters. But Sweden was not overly anxious for a treaty of alliance with England, so long as that country persisted in excluding Swedes from the trade of its American colonies. Indeed, in Swedish eyes, despite Sweden's grievances against the Dutch, the destruction of the commercial and colonial empire

[5] See Chapter V. See also Brodhead, *History of the State of New York*, II, 5–7.

of the Netherlands by England, with its consequent inflation of English power, would dangerously upset the fairly even balance between them.[6]

The negotiations continued, nevertheless, and a defensive treaty of alliance was signed at Stockholm on March 11, 1665,[7] several months after the English had seized New York, and, with it, New Sweden.

All reference to the colonial situation was omitted in the treaty, except the provision that the friendship envisaged should extend everywhere, including the "colonies of both signatories, both in Europe and outside it, especially in Africa and America . . ." and that friction between the nationals of both, in the colonies or elsewhere, should cease.

5. The Peace between Sweden and the United Netherlands, 1667

While the Anglo-Swedish alliance of 1665 was being negotiated, the Netherlands were also attempting to form an alliance with Sweden. Sweden replied to the Dutch advances with the demand for, among other things, a restoration of the places taken from Sweden in Africa and America. But, while the negotiations were going on, early in 1666, Louis XIV entered the Dutch war against England, and the Swedes modified their demands. Sweden was now prepared to accept a money payment for New Sweden, since England now possessed it in any case; and they were willing to settle, in the matter of colonial trade, for freedom to trade in the Dutch colonies, in America and elsewhere, that would equal that of the nationals of the other allies of the Netherlands. These proposals were rejected by the Dutch, but John Isbrandts, the Dutch negotiator, suggested that the Swedes and the Dutch combine forces to wrest New Sweden and New Netherland from the English. Louis XIV, as the Netherlands' ally, also intervened in the negotiations to urge Sweden to ally itself with the Dutch, on the grounds that a victory by England would upset the balance of colonial and commercial power.[8]

The negotiations lagged because of the persistence of self-interest and distrust on both sides, with the result that it was not until July 28, 1667, that a treaty of friendship and alliance between Sweden and Holland was signed at the Hague, only three days before the Netherlands made peace with England at Breda.[9]

The Swedish-Dutch treaty of alliance of the Hague provided that the claims that had arisen from conflicts between the Swedish African Company and the Dutch West India Company on the Guinea Coast should

[6] See d'Estrades, *Lettres, Mémoires, et Négociations*, III, 10, 22, 27, 43, 71, for this application of the balance of power.
[7] Davenport, ed., *European Treaties*, II, 86-93.
[8] *Recueil des Insts.*, II, Suède, 57 *et passim*.
[9] Davenport, ed., *European Treaties*, II, 110-118.

be mutually cancelled. Territory in Africa claimed by the Swedes was ceded to the Dutch West India Company. A money compensation was to be paid to the Swedish Company by the Dutch Company. With regard to the injuries committed or suffered by the two companies in America, it was provided that those injuries "ought to be examined as quickly as possible according to the rules of justice and equity with the envoy of his said Sacred Royal Majesty at The Hague. An agreement should be reached thereupon and satisfaction given forthwith and without delay to the injured party." [10]

6. The Dutch-Swedish Treaty of Commerce, 1673

When Louis XIV began his war against the Dutch in 1672, both France and the Netherlands turned to Sweden for an alliance. The Swedish-Dutch alliance of 1667 was still in effect, and in 1669 Sweden, the Netherlands, and England had formed a Triple Alliance for the preservation of the possessions of Spain, precisely against Louis XIV. Sweden, never enthusiastic with regard to alliances with the Dutch, allowed itself to be bought off by Louis XIV in an alliance with France made in 1672. In the war that followed, England sided with France, and the Dutch, under the leadership of William of Orange, were reduced to desperate straits. But Sweden could hardly afford to let the Netherlands be destroyed, nor could it, with equanimity, see England vastly increase its commercial and colonial power. Furthermore, Sweden's commerce, which involved so many articles considered to be contraband of war, was suffering by reason of seizures by the belligerents, especially the Dutch.

For all these reasons, Sweden was anxious to bring about a peace by mediation. The offer was accepted, and negotiations began in 1673, while to regularize relations between Sweden and Holland, those two states made a treaty of peace and commerce between them.[11] Aside from the usual commercial provisions and definitions of contraband and noncontraband this treaty provided that the claims of the Swedish American Company and the Dutch West India Company against each other relative to disputes and damages in America, the chief of which was the seizure of New Sweden by the Dutch in 1655, which had not been settled as provided in the Treaty of the Hague of 1667, should now be settled.

7. The Colonial Diplomacy of Denmark

While the other maritime nations of Western Europe were building up colonial empires in the seventeenth century, Denmark also found itself

[10] Davenport, ed., *European Treaties*, II, 118.
[11] Davenport, ed., *European Treaties*, II, 206–211.

interested in colonial and commercial expansion. Thus, during the reign of King Christian IV, at about the time when the Dutch West India Company was formed, Danish merchants and Dutch merchants resident in Denmark had aroused in the King an active interest in promoting Danish commerce to the "new world" and even in the acquisition of colonies. The King's chief interest, however, was in the struggles of the Thirty Years War; and so Denmark failed to found colonies in America, although the Danish Guinea Company built a number of posts on the Guinea coast of Africa. Danish interest in colonies and colonial commerce did not die, however, and the Danes shared with the Dutch the penetration of the trade of the English American colonies during the years of the Great Rebellion.

After the Peace of Westphalia, as a benevolently pro-Dutch neutral in the first Anglo-Dutch war, Denmark hoped to share with the Dutch the opening of the English colonial trade that was expected to be forced upon England at the end of that war. When peace negotiations began, the Dutch insisted that the Danes be included in the benefits of the treaty. This was agreed upon, and there followed direct negotiations between Denmark and England, negotiations which resulted in the English-Danish Treaty of Westminster, signed on September 25, 1654.[12]

The Danes, of course, like the Dutch, had asked that the anticipated freedom of commerce between the two countries include the trade in the English colonies. Like the Dutch, however, they were disappointed, for, with regard to the colonies the treaty provided only that there should be a mutual freedom of commerce, "except in those colonies, islands, harbors, and places under the dominion of either [signatory], to which it has been forbidden to sail or trade without special leave or license previously obtained from the other party, to whom such colonies . . . belong." Which meant, of course, that there was to be no relaxation of the English Navigation Act in their favor, any more than there was to be in favor of the Dutch.

Despite the collaboration of the Danes and the Dutch in the first Anglo-Dutch war, the Danes, as the Swedes, were in fact natural commercial competitors and enemies of the Dutch. When war broke out in 1658 between the Danes and the Swedes, the Dutch took advantage of the occasion to seize or destroy the Danish ports on the coast of Africa and practically to drive the Danes out of the slave trade. The enmity between the two countries led the Danes to turn to England for help, and there took place a series of negotiations that led to the Anglo-Danish commercial treaty of 1661.[13]

[12] Davenport, ed., European Treaties, II, 36–39.
[13] See Dumont, ed., Corps universel diplomatique du droit des gens . . . , VI, part 2, 346–348; Hertslet, ed., Treaties, I, 179–186.

The outbreak of the second Anglo-Dutch war led the Netherlands to seek a *rapprochement* with Denmark, and in 1666 the Dutch made with Denmark a treaty of peace and alliance against England.[14] This treaty provided for a settlement of the disputes between Dutchmen and Danes on the coast of Africa and permitted the reopening of the Danish slave trade to America. It also drew Denmark into the war against England. The Danes participated in the negotiations at Breda in 1667, and on July 21, 1667, a treaty of peace was signed between them.[15]

This treaty did little more than to restore peace between the two countries; it did, however, specifically provide that any territories seized, "in or out of Europe," were to be restored.

Shortly after the Anglo-Danish Treaty of Breda the King of Denmark, Frederick III, sought a further reconciliation with England. Denmark was not happy, in particular, with its exclusion from English colonial trade and sought to have that exclusion, under the English Navigation laws, relaxed in Denmark's favor. This was not granted, of course, but a treaty was signed at Copenhagen on July 11, 1670, nevertheless.[16]

This treaty provided for peace and commerce between their respective peoples and territories, "both within Europe and without Europe." The subjects of each king were to be free to visit and trade with the people and places of the other, but it was specified that the subjects of the King of Great Britain "shall in no wise come to the prohibited ports, mentioned in the earlier treaties, nor to the [Danish] colonies, without seeking and obtaining special license from the King of Denmark and Norway. . . . In like manner, the subjects of the Most Serene King of Denmark and Norway should not go to the British colonies without seeking and obtaining special license from the Most Serene King of Great Britain." [17]

This treaty was notable because in it Denmark followed the English example of excluding foreigners, including Englishmen, from its colonies. At the moment, Denmark's only colonies were in Africa; within a year or two, however, the Danes were to occupy the island of St. Thomas in the Virgin Islands.[18]

About 1670 a group of Dutch merchants resident in Denmark persuaded King Christian V that Denmark ought to expand Danish commerce to the Far East and the Danish Negro slave trade, based on the coast of Guinea, and to found Danish colonies in America to serve as bases for the use and the distribution of the Negroes. King Christian, therefore, chartered the

---

[14] Dumont, ed., *Corps universel diplomatique*, VI, part 3, 59–82.
[15] Chalmers, ed., *Treaties*, I, 73–78.
[16] Davenport, ed., *European Treaties*, II, 197–205.
[17] Davenport, ed., *European Treaties*, II, 204.
[18] See Westergaard, *The Danish West Indies under Company Rule, 1671–1754.*

Danish East India Company in 1670 and the Danish West India Company in 1671. The latter company, given a monopoly of the slave trade and of colonial possessions in America, was expected to reestablish the Danish possessions on the coast of Africa and to found colonies in the Caribbean.

For its first colony in America the Danes occupied the island of St. Thomas, in the group known as the Virgin Islands, where there were already living a scattering of Dutchmen and Englishmen. The English governor of the Leeward Islands, Sir Charles Wheeler, protested the Danish occupation on the ground that St. Thomas had already been colonized by Englishmen,[19] but upon complaint by the King of Denmark through diplomatic channels, the protest was dropped, and the colony prospered. This was the beginning of the Danish possession of the Virgin Islands, a possession that was to produce a series of exchanges of claims and counterclaims between Danish governors of the Virgin Islands and British governors of the Leeward Islands in the eighteenth century.[20]

8. Brandenburg

Another European power that entered the colonizing activity in the West Indies about this time was Brandenburg. This country, as Denmark, was inspired by the Dutch, and in 1672, at the time of the French and English attack upon the Netherlands, Fredrick William, "the Great Elector," was the only European ruler who aided the Dutch against the host of their enemies. Frederick William found it necessary to make his peace with Louis XIV, but he still sympathized with the Dutch cause. His attention was diverted from the Dutch struggle by the invasion of his possessions by Sweden in 1675, and other matters produced tensions between them.

Meanwhile, especially while Brandenburg was still a belligerent, when a considerable number of Dutchmen served under the Elector, these Dutchmen persuaded him that he should build up the electorate's power by engaging in maritime commerce, the slave trade, and the building of a colonial empire. A Dutch admiral, Benjamin Raule, was commissioned to organize trade and found colonies, and a profitable beginning was made in a series of raids on French commerce in the West Indies.

A new treaty of alliance was made with the Dutch at Cöln-am-Spree on March 8, 1678.[21] This was a defensive alliance, but it provided specifically that if either signatory should be attacked in his territories, "even outside Europe and in whatever parts of the world," the other would come to the aid of the one attacked; if one of the allies, attacked in a possession out-

---

[19] C.S.P., Col., A& W.I., 1674, 1675-76, with Addenda, No. 397, p. 151.
[20] See Chapter XIII.
[21] Davenport, ed., European Treaties, II, 247-255.

side of Europe, should find it necessary to use arms against the attacker in Europe, the other ally would assist the one attacked in his operations in Europe. The paragraph providing for commercial relations states that

Commerce and trade shall be carried on and advanced between the subjects of both parties without any hindering or interruption, and accordingly the ships of both parties or of their subjects shall be free to go in or out of each other's harbors, or to remain therein.

Nothing is said here of the colonies or of restrictions upon trade. It is probable that the Dutch proposed this provision in order to be able to call upon Brandenburg for help in Europe if some Dutch colony were attacked. But it seems probable, also, that Brandenburg accepted the provision because it expected soon to have colonies in America.

When the Netherlands and Spain made peace with France at Nymwegen early in 1679,[22] Brandenburg was left fighting France and Sweden with no ally other than Denmark. The Elector was forced to make peace, which he did in May.[23] As this peace was thought of as not extending to America, a special agreement was signed by the representatives of France and Brandenburg on May 16, 1679[24] This agreement referred specifically to two Brandenburg privateers destined to make war on French shipping and colonies in the West Indies and provided that if the Elector would order them to abstain from raiding French shipping Louis XIV would order the French West Indies fleet, under the command of the Compte d'Estrées, not to molest them. Once the agreement was signed, the Elector ordered all his captains to abstain from attacking French shipping in America, and Louis XIV ordered d'Estrées to permit all Brandenburger ships to navigate freely in the Caribbean, "provided, however, that they not do any trading in my islands in that region."

A definitive treaty of peace between France and Brandenburg was signed at St. Germain-en-Laye in June of 1679.[25] The Elector of Brandenburg asked, during the negotiations, that Brandenburger ships be allowed to trade in French ports, both in Europe and in the French colonies. But France was no more disposed to relax its closure of its colonies to foreigners than England was disposed to relax its navigation acts. The Elector's demand, therefore, was refused, and in the Treaty of Nymwegen it was provided only that there should be a freedom of commerce between the subjects of France and Brandenburg, "both by land and by sea and other waters." In another secret treaty, signed on October 25, 1679,[26] it was provided that there should be a freedom of commerce between the subjects

---

[22] See Chapter IX.
[23] Dumont, ed., *Corps universel diplomatique*, VI, pt. 1, 403–404.
[24] Davenport, ed., *European Treaties*, II, 261–265.
[25] Vast, ed., *Grands traités*, II, 117–125.
[26] Vast, ed., *Grands traités*, II, 126–134.

of the two signatories "in the lands, realms, and countries of His Most Christian Majesty, as also in the states of His Electoral Highness and in the harbors and ports which belong to them." The colonies were not mentioned; presumably it was the understanding of the signers of this treaty that this blanket provision for freedom of commerce did not extend to America.

After this peace Raule went ahead with his colonial schemes and organized the Brandenburg-African Company in 1680. Louis XIV, who now wished to be on friendly terms with Brandenburg for the forwarding of his schemes in Germany, entered into an alliance with Brandenburg against Spain and instructed his governors in the West Indies to assist the Brandenburgers in every possible way.

Meanwhile, the good relations between Brandenburg and France continued, and negotiations for a closer alliance went on through the year 1680. The Elector was surrounded by enemies—the Holy Roman Empire, Spain, the Netherlands—and urgently desired such a powerful ally as Louis XIV promised to be. Louis, for his part, still needed a friend among the imperial electors for the furtherance of his expansive schemes in the Germanies. So far as America was concerned, the Elector was determined to build a colonial and commercial empire there, and the benevolence of France would be of the utmost value.

Since Spain owed Brandenburg an old debt of which there was no prospect of payment, the Elector adopted a policy of paying himself by raids on Spain's American commerce. Thus, in 1680 a Brandenburger fleet was dispatched to the West Indies, where it collaborated with the French fleet of Admiral d'Estrées. Since Brandenburg had no colonies of its own in that area, other than the leased base on Danish St. Thomas, the Elector asked permission to send his fleet into the harbors of the French islands. Louis XIV refused this request but otherwise treated benevolently the Brandenburgers' enterprise. As Colbert de Croissy, Louis's secretary of state, expressed this principle, the principle of the closed colonial sphere in America:

everyone lived and acted only for himself, allowed no entrance to their harbors to others, not even to those with whom they were in close friendship in Europe. If this privilege were granted to the elector, it was to be feared that other friends and allies of France would also claim it.[27]

This was a clear and concise statement of the basic French mercantilistic colonial policy with regard to other powers, which was also common to all the colonizing powers of Western Europe.

With the approach of war, Louis XIV relaxed and permitted the Brandenburgers to use the ports of his colonies as bases for their fleet. The

[27] Quoted in Davenport, ed., *European Treaties*, II, 276.

Dutch, in particular, resented the colonial and commercial rivaly of Brandenburg and threatened war. This drove the Elector, in his need for aid, yet more urgently into the arms of France, and he asked Louis XIV for a strengthening of their alliance.

On January 11, 1681, France and Brandenburg signed a new treaty of alliance at Cöln-am-Spree.[28] By the terms of this treaty, apart from the arrangements for neutral military assistance, Louis XIV promised the Elector that if he should acquire Spanish territory [in America?] or seize Spanish ships, and if Spain should attack him therefor, France would aid the Elector, not only by the force of its arms, but, also, by giving Brandenburg's ships and forces "a free entry into its ports and an assured retreat in its states." This evidently meant an opening of French ports in the West Indies, since those ports had already been opened by the King's order.

When, after the Treaty of Cöln-am-Spree (1681) between France and Brandenburg, Louis went ahead with his seizures of territories in the Germanies based upon the principle of "reunions," he alienated his former ally, Sweden. This led Sweden to ally itself with its former enemy and rival, the Netherlands.[29] The Elector of Brandenburg was delighted, because his traditional enemy, Sweden, was now separated from France, and he had visions not only of recovering Pomerania, taken by Sweden, but also of receiving active French support in his plans for colonial and commercial expansion in Africa and the West Indies.

The Dutch, of course, violently resented Frederick William's colonial enterprises, complaining especially against the activities of the Brandenburg-African Company, and sought to recall Benjamin Raule, Brandenburg's colonizing Dutchman, from the Elector's service. The Elector, on his side, insisted that the Dutch West India Company did not have an exclusive monopolistic control of Africa or of the slave trade, and he knew that the Dutch themselves had been the most distinguished and consistent defenders of the principle of the freedom of the seas. These things being true, he proposed to continue sending his ships to Africa and trading in areas not actually occupied by any other European power.

When, in the face of the Swedish-Dutch Alliance of 1681, Louis XIV proposed a new alliance, Frederick William accepted, and on January 22, 1682, a new treaty of alliance was signed at Cöln-am-Spree.[30] It confirmed and strengthened the alliance of 1681. The chief difference from the former treaty, so far as America was concerned, was that the provision in the older treaty for French aid against Spain was now expanded to include any power (presumably the Dutch) that might attack the Brandenburgers in the course of their reprisals on Spanish shipping in the West Indies. Further-

---

[28] Davenport, ed., *European Treaties*, II, 275–279.
[29] Dumont, ed., *Corps universel diplomatique*, VII, pt. 2, 15–16.
[30] Davenport, ed., *European Treaties*, II, 280–285.

more, His Most Christian Majesty extended to the Brandenburger ships the same hospitality in his ports, "in Europe and elsewhere"; he specifically promised his benevolent protection to the Brandenburg-African Company on the coasts of Guinea.

In pursuance of his plans for colonial and commercial expansion, Frederick William and his Dutch admiral, Benjamin Raule, sought a colony in the West Indies to serve as a base for the Brandenburgers' slave trade with the Spanish colonies in America. This trade was already a near-monopoly of the Dutch West India Company, which had won from Spain the *asiento*, or contract for supplying the Spanish colonies with slaves.[31] Spain was unwilling to permit the Brandenburgers to take their Negroes directly into the Spanish colonies, but it was willing to have its colonials trade for the slaves at some non-Spanish depot. Frederick William sought to buy the island of Trinidad from Spain, which His Catholic Majesty indignantly refused. He then offered to buy the island of St. Croix from France, but this Louis XIV refused. Frederick William then turned to Denmark, which had occupied the island of St. Thomas, in the Virgin Islands, since 1672, with the idea of leasing an area to serve as a depot for slaves on that island. To this the King of Denmark agreed, and a treaty embodying such an arrangement was signed at Copenhagen on November 24, 1685.[32]

The treaty declared, first, that the King of Denmark had sovereignty over the island of St. Thomas, as well as over St. John, "and all the other neighboring and appertaining islands in West Virgin where the [Danish] Company is in actual possession. . . ." [33] This, in itself, is a recognition of a much more extensive Danish establishment in the Virgin Islands than had been hitherto acknowledged. The treaty also declared that nothing in it was to derogate the charter of the property of the Danish Company.

The Brandenburgers who planned to establish themselves in the leased area were to be assigned as much land as could be cultivated by two hundred slaves, and the lease was to run for thirty years, with the possibility of renewal. They undertook to enter their Negroes and other goods at the ports designated and to pay the required duties. Other regulations were stipulated as to the trade of the Brandenburgers. Goods imported from Denmark and Norway were to pay no import duties; but goods coming from other countries would be expected to pay the regular duties.

The treaty provided an extraterritorial administration of justice in the leased area, that is, misdemeanors and other infractions of order among Brandenburgers were to be tried before Brandenburger judges and according to Brandenburger law. Disputes or disturbances between Branden-

[31] Scelle, *La traite négrière aux Indes de Castille*, I, 523 ff.
[32] Davenport, ed., *European Treaties*, II, 293–308.
[33] Davenport, ed., *European Treaties*, II, 303.

burgers and Danes were to be tried before tribunals composed of equal numbers of judges (two each) from both sides.

The Brandenburgers dwelling in the island were to have the freedom to trade wherever the Danes had free trade, provided they paid the Danish Company the required duties. Rules were laid down for peaceful relations between ships of the two signatories on the slave coasts of Africa, and for the sale of slaves by one company to the other. Should war break out between Denmark and Brandenburg, the Brandenburgers were not to be disturbed in their concession. On the other hand, should they be attacked by any enemy the Danes would protect them. There was to be a freedom of religion to all faiths, but all religions except the Reformed (Calvinist) and the adherents of the Augsburg Confession (Lutheran) must be exercised only privately; no other faith was to be permitted to build a church or other public building.

This Treaty between Brandenburg and Denmark resulted in a great deal of friction. The success of the Brandenburgers in their slave trade aroused the jealously of the Danes, and the Danish Company failed to realize as high profits from the arrangement as had been anticipated. The Brandenburgers, through their new Elector, Frederick III, complained about the interpretation given the treaty by the Danish Company, and especially against the imposition, by the Danish governor, of a high land tax upon their concession and, upon their refusal to pay it, the seizure of their goods by the governor.

The dispute was not immediately settled, but the expediencies of the War of the League of Augsburg [34] forced the two disputants to settle, after a fashion, their American quarrel.[35] Thus, it came to pass that in 1692 a treaty between the two countries was signed at Cöln-am-Spree,[36] which provided, with regard to the West Indies, for a settlement of the claims of the Danish and Brandenburger companies against each other, for an indemnity to the Brandenburgers for their losses in goods, and for the payment of the taxes due the Danish government from the Brandenburgers. Two months later a supplementary agreement [37] was made which guaranteed the payment of the Danish indemnity if it should not be paid as provided in the original treaty.

[34] See Chapter IX.
[35] See Davenport, ed., *European Treaties*, II, 335.
[36] Davenport, ed., *European Treaties*, II, 334–345.
[37] Davenport, ed., *European Treaties*, II, 346–349.

CHAPTER IX

Anglo-French Diplomacy with Regard to America, 1648-1702

1. Oliver Cromwell's Colonial Diplomacy with France

IN THE PERIOD after the Treaty of Münster of 1648 the colonial and commercial competition between the English and the Dutch reached its peak with the first and second Anglo-Dutch wars. English relations with France were also hostile as the maritime competition between these two nations grew. The first Dutch war ended with the Treaty of Westminster of April, 1654, and the English government then determined to reach a settlement regarding its precarious relations with France and Spain. Each of these nations, having been at war with each other since 1635, desired an alliance with the English republic. Both, however, seemed dangerous to the English, Spain because of Philip IV's disapproval of Charles I's French marriage and sympathies; France because of Louis XIV's support of the exiled Stuarts during the English civil war.

For some time Cromwell's government had vacillated between an alliance with one of these countries or war with both. Relations with France were the more difficult: not only did Louis shelter the Stuarts, he also opened French ports to royalist privateers and allowed French ships to prey on English commerce, particularly that of the Levant Company. Ill treatment of the Huguenots irritated Cromwell, and by early 1654 his government favored a war against France. An expedition sent originally against the Dutch in Manhattan turned, on news of the Anglo-Dutch peace, against French Acadia, to which both England and New England had presented claims, and captured the forts of St. John, Port Royal, and Penobscot (Pentagoët). Cromwell refused the demands of Cardinal Mazarin that he restore these forts, but the French, anxious to win England's favor in view of the European situation, did not declare war. No attempt was then made by the English to settle this region, their interest being only to control the fisheries and timber trade of the coastline.

Cromwell was still trying to decide against which of the two nations to make war, and by the end of 1654 he favored an expedition against the Spanish Indies as less dangerous to England and to European peace and as justified by Spain's conquest in time of peace of Tortuga (1635) and of the Puritan colony of Providence (1641). Late in 1654, then, Cromwell decided on a reprisal raid in the Caribbean, which, under the "doctrine of the two spheres," [1] would not commit him to a war in Europe. Considering Spain's efforts to achieve an English alliance, Cromwell wrongly expected Spain to submit as France had to the Acadian conquests. At the same time, the English government presented its conditions for an alliance with France: France should not give financial or other aid to any of the English royal family except the Queen Mother; the rights of the Huguenots should be confirmed; losses by subjects of either country should be referred to commissioners. To force acceptance of these conditions the English threatened an alliance with Spain.

The adoption of a policy directed against the Spanish Indies gave the conferences with the French ambassador, Antoine de Bordeaux, a new direction. French offers to form a military alliance against Spain were refused because the English wished to limit hostilities to America and because Cromwell did not wish to make any agreement which would bind him to acquiesce in the oppression of the Huguenots in France. England desired that any Anglo-French treaty be limited to commercial matters. The problem of the restitution of the Acadian forts was reintroduced by Bordeaux, who alleged that Acadia had been illegally seized, since letters of reprisal, under which the English conquerors had operated, did not allow the seizure of fortified places. He advised submitting the question to arbitrators. Cromwell, however, was very reluctant to surrender conquests which he considered important and which the English justified on the grounds of possession based on prior discovery. They were, they claimed, the first discoverers of the entire Atlantic coast. Cromwell was unwilling to submit the matter to arbitrators, unless these were empowered to terminate all Anglo-French disputes involving Acadia and New France, disputes which involved large sums of money claimed by the English as reparation for damages to English subjects and property. The French refused this proposal.

When Philip IV learned of the English attack on Hispaniola and the capture of Jamaica in the spring of 1655, he held that this act constituted a declaration of war and so recalled his ambassador from England and detained English merchants and property in Spain. Cromwell was then forced to accept the French alliance, and in November of 1655, the two nations signed a treaty at Westminster.

[1] See Chapters III and XII.

The final treaty provided for peace between the two powers. Each promised to give no aid to rebels or enemies of the other, a promise which gave to Cromwell assurance that the Stuarts would be denied French support and to Louis freedom from interference in his anti-Huguenot policies. Most of the treaty was concerned with the regulation of Anglo-French commerce in Europe, and provided, among other things, reciprocal freedom for importation of certain goods. Article 24 provided for the appointment of three commissioners from each side "to consider, examine, estimate, and liquidate . . . captures and losses, and fix and determine the compensation, payment, and satisfaction for them." The commission was to meet in London within six weeks of the publication of the treaty and was to settle the controversies within five months. This failing, the controversies would then be referred to the arbitration of the republic of Hamburg. Article 25 provided that the disputed restitution of the Acadian forts captured by the English be referred to these commissioners and/or arbitrators for settlement.[2]

The commission never met. France was content that each side retain what it possessed, and so England kept Acadia until the Treaty of Breda.

In 1656 France and England made an alliance for the conquest of the Spanish Netherlands. In 1658 they captured Dunkirk and invaded the Spanish provinces. By the Treaty of the Pyrenees of 1659, which ended the war that had been going on between France and Spain since 1635 as well as this Anglo-French phase of it, England secured Dunkirk and France part of the Netherlands. It was arranged that Louis XIV should marry the Infanta Maria Teresa, who was to surrender her right of succession to the Spanish throne in return for a large dowry, a stipulation said by contemporaries to have been suggested by the French, who knew that Philip IV could never raise the sum and that thus the question of succession would remain open to Louis's ambitions.[3]

There was nothing in the Treaty of the Pyrenees that bore directly upon the colonies, but the provision in the treaty that the crest of the Pyrenees Mountains should be the boundary between France and Spain presently became a precedent for French claims to the St. Lawrence, Ohio, and Mississippi drainage basins in North America.[4]

2. The Peace of Breda

In 1665 England entered another war with the Dutch,[5] and France was brought into the conflict by the Franco-Dutch alliance concluded at Paris

---

[2] Dumont, ed., Corps universel diplomatique, VI, pt. 2, 121–124. Translated in Davenport, ed., European Treaties, II, 45–47.

[3] Petrie, Earlier Diplomatic History, 1492–1713, 157. See also, Vast, ed., Grands traités, I, 79–90, 115–116, and 116, fn. 1.

[4] See Chapter XIII.

[5] See Chapter V.

in 1662, which guaranteed mutual aid and defense.[6] Louis XIV was reluctant to undertake hostilities against England for fear of driving England into an alliance with Spain, a country with which he expected to be at war as soon as he asserted his wife's claim to the Spanish succession by invading the Spanish Netherlands. Pressed by the Dutch to come to their aid against England, Louis sent ambassadors to London to attempt mediation, but these efforts failed, and so, in January of 1666, France declared war on England, to be joined a month later by Denmark.

In order to offend England as little as possible, Louis XIV tried to confine the fighting to Europe; he also instructed his governors in the French West Indies and in Canada to maintain neutrality in America. The English, however, desired to relieve France of its colonies, and British colonial governors were instructed to attack the French in the West Indies and in Canada.

As a result of England's insistence upon fighting the war in America, England's West Indian colonies suffered gravely in the course of hostilities. In 1665 the Dutch attacked Barbados, Nevis, and Montserrat, and the following year the militia of the French part of St. Christopher captured the English part of that island. Later, the French captured English Antigua and Montserrat, which the English recovered in 1667. The French also retook the Dutch islands of St. Eustatius and Tobago, which the English had captured in the course of the war. Surinam, the English colony in Guiana, fell to the Dutch.

In the north, despite royal instructions and appeals by the English governors to the contrary, the English colonists limited their activities to defensive measures. The French sent expeditions against the Mohawks in the hope of opening the way for the capture of Albany, but there was little direct fighting between the two sides.

Domestic circumstances also made the war turn badly for England. Plague and the great London fire of September, 1666, weakened England's military capability, as did financial difficulties in the government. Charles II ended England's hostilities with France in a secret treaty of April, 1667,[7] the first of several secret agreements which he was to make with Louis XIV. By this treaty Charles agreed not to oppose a French invasion of the Spanish Netherlands on the understanding that the French would not help the Dutch in their war with England. It was also agreed that Louis would restore the English part of St. Christopher in return for the restoration of Acadia, which the English had held since 1654.

Prior to this agreement, efforts had been made by the Swedes and the French to arrange peace conferences. Breda was selected as the site and

[6] Davenport, ed., *European Treaties*, II, 69–72.
[7] Mignet, ed., *Négociations relatives à la Succession d'Espagne sous Louis XIV*, II, 43–45. See also, Davenport, ed., *European Treaties*, II, 132–133.

representatives of the belligerents assembled there in May of 1667. While the English and Dutch debated the settlement of disputed colonial territorial claims, including the fate of New Netherland, Louis's armies crossed the Flemish frontier as the beginning of his War of Devolution. The Dutch, fearful of repercussions on their own security, speedily concluded a treaty of peace with England.[8] On the same day, July 31, France and England concluded a public treaty of peace.

The Anglo-French treaty formalized the territorial agreements of the secret treaty of April. The English part of St. Christopher was restored to England, in return for which the English returned to the French "the country which is called Acadia, situated in North America." The treaty further provided for mutual restoration of all territories taken since 1665, a provision which returned Antigua and Montserrat to English possession. Slaves belonging to the English on the islands captured by the French who "shall wish to return again under the dominion of the English (but without any force or constraint)" were at liberty to do so. This settlement of the problem of captured slaves later caused much dispute, as few slaves were willing to return voluntarily to their former masters.[9]

The treaties of Breda marked a significant shift in the colonial competition for North America. The Dutch were effectively removed as a threat to British colonial expansion because, although they remained a formidable maritime power, the loss of New Netherland temporarily removed them from North America and confined their colonial activities to a few small islands in the West Indies and to Surinam, which they had just won from England. On the other hand, France and England now confronted each other as serious adversaries in America. While the war in Europe was primarily an Anglo-Dutch affair, with France giving as little support as possible to its Dutch ally, the fighting in the West Indies was chiefly between France and England and assumed proportions beyond those dictated by the European policies of the two governments, which were as yet only playing at war. Essentially, the fighting between England and France in America was another war entirely, motivated by conflicts and ambitions quite separate from those governing their European relations. The sugar trade of the West Indies had thrived to the point where it had become a valuable prize for the nation strong enough to win and/or hold it. Likewise, the territorial disputes in the northeastern part of continental North America, with their connected disputes over fisheries, the fur trade, and maritime trade routes, were a constant irritation to colonists whose feelings were little influenced by official policies. This war marked the real beginning of the confrontation of France and England over colonial mastery in America.

[8] See Chapter V.
[9] Davenport, ed., *European Treaties*, II, 132–142.

3. The Re-Cession of Acadia

The most pressing problem in the developing Anglo-French confrontation in North America to present itself at this time was that of Acadia, a
region highly prized for its fur trade and fishery. The Anglo-French Treaty
of Breda returned this territory to France, but exactly what Acadia was and
where it lay was an undefined matter which was to plague diplomats for
almost a century to come. Since its discovery the region had been claimed
by both the French and the English, but both sides were equally uncertain
as to the extent of the territory, that is, whether it comprised only the peninsula (the modern province of Nova Scotia), or all the land north and east
of the eastern boundary of New England up to the St. Lawrence. One problem lay with the uncertain cartography of the period, but by far the greater
problem was the unwillingness of both sides to agree upon any common
boundaries.

In 1603 the King of France had given a commission to one Sieur de
Monts to explore and settle the country between the St. Lawrence basin
and the English settlements to the south. The unsettled region was called,
on contemporary Italian maps, Acadia and was defined by the French
Royal Commission to comprise the territory between 40° and 46° North
Latitude, a definition employed by French maps of the period, which showed
46° to run through Cape Breton and 40° to run parallel to the coast of
Maine. These boundaries never came into use because they were totally
ignored by the English. De Monts' expedition, sent out under the command of Samuel de Champlain, made a settlement at the mouth of the
St. Croix River in 1604. The settlement failed, but it became well enough
known through Champlain's narrative to have the St. Croix River placed
on all contemporary maps of the region.

The charter of 1606 to the Plymouth Company of the Virginia Company allowed the company to form settlements in Virginia, the northern
boundary of which was placed at 45°. This overlapped the French claim,
which extended southward to 40°, and led to some conflicts between French
and English settlers. A new patent to the Council for New England in
1620 extended the northern boundary to 48°, an extension apparently
made to establish English claim to Acadia. In 1621 James I granted a
territory which he called Nova Scotia to Sir William Alexander, naming
the St. Croix River as the western boundary and the St. Lawrence as the
northern boundary.

In 1627, during the war between England and France, the English
seized Port Royal; in 1629 they seized Quebec. By the Treaty of St.
Germain-en-Laye, of 1632,[10] which formally ended the war, Britain re-

[10] See Chapter IV.

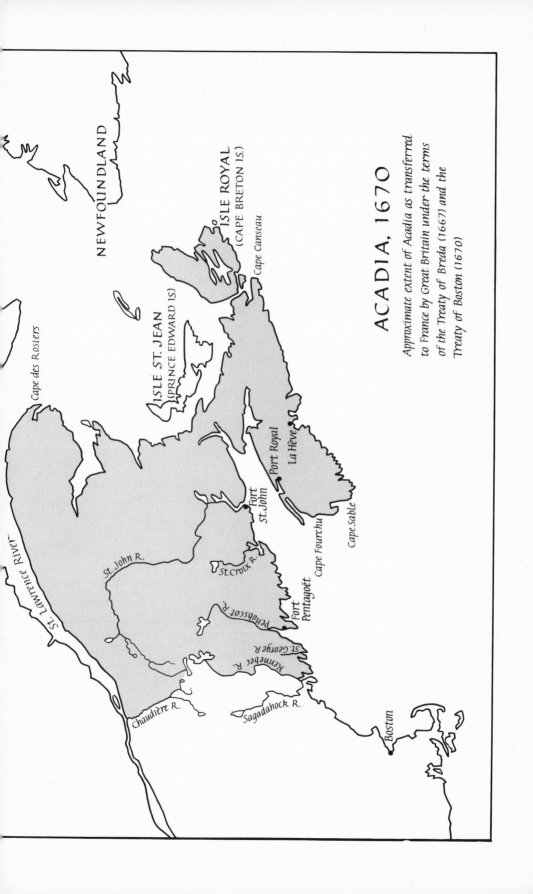

NEWFOUNDLAND

ISLE ROYAL
(CAPE BRETON IS.)

Cape Canseau

ISLE ST. JEAN
(PRINCE EDWARD IS.)

Cape des Rosiers

St. Lawrence River

St. John R.

Fort
St. John

St. Croix R.

Port Royal

La Hève

Cape Fourchu

Cape Sable

Penobscot R.

Fort
Pentagoët

St. George R.

Kennebec R.

Chaudière R.

Sagadahock R.

Boston

ACADIA, 1670

Approximate extent of Acadia as transferred
to France by Great Britain under the terms
of the Treaty of Breda (1667) and the
Treaty of Boston (1670)

stored to France "all the places in New France, L'Acadie and Canada, occupied by the subjects of his Majesty of Great Britain," but no mention was made regarding the possession of Acadia as a whole or of any boundaries for it. The Company of New France had been preparing, since the Convention of Susa of 1629, to exploit this region, particularly for its furs. Now, in 1632, the Sieur de Razilly was appointed governor of Acadia and was sent there to take possession of the forts held by the English and to promote French trade and settlement in Acadia.

King Charles I, however, did not understand the cession of places in Acadia to imply cession of the whole territory. In 1635 the Council for New England passed a patent in favor of Lord William Alexander, son of the founder of Nova Scotia, granting him all the territory between the St. Croix and Kennebec Rivers, although the Treaty of St. Germain-en-Laye had implied the cession of all territory from the Kennebec River eastward. Alexander's grant was never exploited, and it gradually lapsed and became extinct. New Englanders from Plymouth and Massachusetts Bay colonies had, in the meantime, established a number of trading posts in the area for the purpose of buying furs from the Indians and were much distressed at the prospect of losing this trade. The English expedition of 1654, undertaken in time of peace by Cromwell's order and with the help of New Englanders, which took possession of all the French posts in Acadia from Penobscot (Pentagoët) to Canseau, was apparently justified by Charles I's claim that his cession of places in Acadia did not mean Acadia itself.[11]

In 1656 Oliver Cromwell granted to Thomas Temple, William Crowne, and Charles de la Tour the greater part of Acadia, that is, the peninsula, together with both coasts of the Bay of Fundy and all the mainland to the St. George's River near the Kennebec to a distance of one hundred leagues inland. Charles de la Tour had been one of the lieutenants of the French governor of Acadia, de Razilly, until his death in 1635, whereupon de la Tour had come into conflict with d'Aulnay Charnisay, another of de Razilly's former lieutenants, over their territorial rights in Acadia. By 1645 d'Aulnay had made himself master of all Acadia, but upon his death de la Tour was, in 1651, appointed lieutenant general of Acadia. De la Tour's new relationship with the English was based upon a visit he made to England with his father, Claude de la Tour, in 1630, at which time his father was created a baronet of Nova Scotia by Sir William Alexander and was granted, with his son, two baronies in that territory. De la Tour's grant extended from modern Yarmouth along the south coast of Nova Scotia as far as Mirleguash and was the basis of the Cromwell grant of 1656.

In 1664 Charles II granted his brother, the Duke of York, a territory

[11] For a discussion of local, American disputes over Acadia between New Englanders and the French governors, see Chapter XI.

nearly identical in area with that granted to Lord William Alexander in 1635, a region which later became known as the Territory of Sagadahoc. This grant completely ignored the grant made by Cromwell to Thomas Temple and his associates in 1656. Temple's rights (he had purchased those of Crowne and de la Tour), as well as those of the Duke of York, were also ignored by the stipulation in the Treaty of Breda that Acadia be delivered to France.[12]

The actual restoration of Acadia did not, however, take place until 1670. There were several reasons for this delay. Thomas Temple resisted royal orders and spent considerable sums in defense of his rights to the territory. The boundaries of Acadia were disputed between the French and English, and part of the territory claimed by the French fell within the patent of the Duke of York to the territory called Sagadahoc. Moreover, the French procrastinated in the restoration of the English part of the Caribbean island of St. Christopher, which was also stipulated in the Treaty of Breda.

In order to facilitate the exchange of Acadia, Louis XIV sent the Marquis de Ruvigny to London as his envoy extraordinary. It was apparently at his request that the letters patent by which Charles II surrendered Acadia named the specific places which defined Acadia:

... in pursuance of the said Treaty, the King surrenders for himself, his Heirs and Successors for ever, all that Country call'd *Acadia*, lying in *North America*, which the said most Christian King *did formerly enjoy, as namely, The Forts and Habitations of Pentagoet, St. John, Port Royal, la Have and Cape de Sable, which his Subjects enjoy'd under his Authority till the English possess'd themselves of them in the year 1654* . . .[13]

The idea that the restoration was to be limited to certain places was repeated in Charles's royal order to Sir Thomas Temple, Governor of Nova Scotia, to surrender Acadia to France:

It is only the country of Acadie he is to restore; not any part of Nova Scotia or any other country or Province; or any part even of Acadie itself but what originally belonged to the most Christian King and was taken from him by the English. [14]

When Louis XIV's commissioner Mourillon du Bourg delivered Charles's order to Temple in Boston, Temple refused to surrender his lands on the grounds that only la Have and Cape de Sable, that is, the

---

[12] Ganong, "A Monograph of the Evolution of the Boundaries of the Province of New Brunswick," *Transactions of the Royal Society of Canada*, 2nd Series, VII (1901), 155-186.

[13] "A Memorial Concerning the Limits of Nova Scotia or Acadia, presented by His Majesty's Commissaries to the Commissioners of His Most Christian Majesty, dated January 11, 1751," *Mémoires des Commissaires*, II, 21.

[14] The King to Temple, Nov., 1667, *C.S.P., Col.*, A.& W.I., 1661–68, No. 1638, p. 520.

peninsula, belonged to Acadia, Pentagoët, St. John, and Port Royal being in Nova Scotia and bordering on New England.[15] This protest was based apparently on the wording of his own grant of 1656. Temple's efforts were to no avail, for in 1669 Charles II sent emphatic orders to Temple to surrender Acadia in accordance with the earlier orders. This order was delivered to Temple in Boston by the Sieur Grandfontaine, Louis XIV's new commissioner.

The surrender of Acadia was effected by an agreement, signed in Boston on July 17, 1670, between these two men regarding the conditions of surrender.[16] By this time the territory to be surrendered was understood by both sides to consist of the whole of the land and not merely the five forts, that is, "generally all the lands and rivers which are comprised in the extent of the said country of Acadia," although once again the exact extent of the territory was not defined. Immediately after the surrender Grandfontaine promised to give complete liberty to all of Temple's people in Acadia to withdraw along with their property, and to allow English fishermen along the coasts of Acadia to continue their work for three more months, but the following year they could not return without French permission. The same condition was extended to persons loading coal on Cape Breton. In August Pentagoët was surrendered to Grandfontaine and Port Royal and Jemseg to his lieutenant.

Thus, by the surrender of Acadia, the French gained undisputed possession of both the peninsula and the mainland, the understanding of the two governments being

That the Forts *Pentagoet, St. John, Port Royal, Cape Sable,* and *La Heve* having been, at the Desire of the Ambassador of *France,* inserted by Name in the Order for the Execution of the Treaty of *Breda,* as Descriptive of the whole Territory of *Acadia,* and these being the only Forts and Settlements which then existed in the Province and being situated in different Parts of it, two of them without the Peninsula, the Surrender of these Forts by one Power, and the Possession taken by the other, is a full Evidence of the Surrender and Possession of all *Acadia,* in Pursuance of the said Treaty, such as it had been ever possess'd by the Crown of *France* before it. [17]

Temple's efforts to resist the surrender were cited as the cause of the two nations coming to this agreement over the territorial concept of Acadia,[18] although it is more likely that the relations at this time between Charles II and Louis XIV were more influential in leading Charles to ignore English claims to the area and to accept French demands for the

[15] "A Memorial Concerning the Limits of Nova Scotia . . ." *Mémoires des Commissaires,* II, 23.

[16] Davenport, ed., *European Treaties,* II, 185–186.

[17] "A Memorial Concerning the Limits of Nova Scotia . . ." *Mémoires des Commissaires,* II, 25–27.

[18] *Mémoires des Commissaires,* II, 27.

surrender of the whole territory as far as Pentagoët. Charles, after all, had a somewhat personal interest in this region as part of the Territory of Sagadahoc, which he had granted to his brother, the Duke of York, in 1664. The complete reversal of his orders regarding the execution of the articles of the Treaty of Breda, from his letter to Temple of 1667 in which he said that only those parts of Acadia formerly occupied by the French were to be restored, to the orders of 1669, can be better understood when it is realized that during the interval Charles had become involved in negotiations with the French for an alliance against the Dutch and for support of unpopular domestic policies, negotiations which culminated in the secret Treaty of Dover of 1670. Apparently, Charles decided, during these negotiations, to sacrifice England's advantageous position in Acadia in order to win French support in matters closer to his own interests. Thus, by the surrender, it was understood by both the French and English governments that Acadia comprised all of the territory as far as the Pentagoët (Penebscot) River.

The surrender of Acadia, called Nova Scotia by the New Englanders, had been protested by them since the publication of the Treaty of Breda as obstructive to their fur trade and fishery and as a potential source of danger in time of war with France. When the surrender was finally effected by this agreement of 1670, the government of Massachusetts immediately set about determining its northeastern limits, found them in Penobscot (Pentagoët) Bay, and so notified the Governor of New France. The French, however, extended their claims farther southwest to the Kennebec River,[19] and so the problem of the Acadian boundaries continued as a source of future conflicts.

4. The Secret Treaty of Dover, 1670

The secret Treaty of Dover of 1670 was ultimately bound up in the complicated problem of the Spanish Succession and the ambition of Louis XIV to acquire the Spanish crown for his own family. Louis's War of Devolution, result of his first claim to the Spanish Succession, had alarmed the countries around Flanders, where the war was fought, sufficiently to bring them into an alliance. In January, 1668, England and the United Provinces united in an alliance to force France and Spain to make peace and to guarantee the peace after it had been concluded. They were joined in May, by Sweden, although the treaty of general guarantee was not signed until a year later, thus creating the first of the Triple Alliances formed in coalition against the territorial and dynastic ambitions of Louis XIV in the era of the contested Spanish Succession. Meanwhile, in April,

[19] *Mémoires des Commissaires*, II, 27.

1668, France and Spain signed a treaty of peace at Aix-la-Chapelle, a treaty which ceded to France all the parts of Flanders which had been conquered during the war.

As soon as Louis XIV had signed the treaty of Aix-la-Chapelle he began to work for the dissolution of the Triple Alliance and, most particularly, for the destruction of the United Provinces, which had opposed his claims to the Spanish Succession and, especially, his annexation of the Spanish Netherlands as a threat to their own territorial integrity. He began by attempting to lure England out of this alliance into a union with France against the Dutch. Since Charles II had always represented the Triple Alliance as a disinterested effort to preserve the peace of Europe rather than as an alliance against France, and since the conditions which had produced the alliance (the war between France and Spain) no longer existed, Louis claimed there was no longer any justification for the existence of the alliance and so there were no reasons preventing him from seeking an alliance with Charles. Louis's ambassador, Colbert de Croissy, on his arrival in London in August, 1668, found Charles II agreeable to an anti-Dutch alliance with France for both religious and economic reasons. Charles wished to declare himself a Catholic and to reestablish Catholicism in England, and he required French support and French money to suppress the probable rebellion which would result. Moreover, despite the fact that England had united with Holland in the Triple Alliance, there still existed an intense commercial rivalry between the two nations which was in no way ameliorated by their alliance. War against the Dutch furnished hope for seizing Dutch ships, colonies, and commerce. But Charles hesitated to take open steps against the Dutch for fear of opposition from his people and Parliament, many of whom believed that England would be powerless against French aggression if Holland were to fall and who felt tied to the Dutch by their common bond of Protestantism. Also, Charles's secretary of state, the Earl of Arlington, was an avowed friend of Holland and Spain. Therefore, preliminary conferences were carried on between Louis and two Catholic emissaries from Charles, Lord Henry Arundell and Sir Richard Billings, with the encouragement of Charles's sister Henrietta, who had married the Duc d'Orléans. Not until November of 1669 were Colbert or Arlington informed of the negotiations for French support of Charles.

In December, Billings presented a draft of a treaty to Colbert, which stipulated that Louis was to pay Charles two hundred thousand pounds before Charles declared himself a Catholic and was to aid him with money and troops should the English rebel. The two Kings were to ally themselves in war against the United Provinces and Hamburg. Louis was to pay Charles eight hundred thousand pounds a year as long as the war lasted, and Charles was to receive part of Zeeland as his share of the conquest. Moreover, in the event of the probable death of the Spanish king without heirs, Charles II would aid Louis in the acquisition of his rights to the Spanish monarchy (as accorded him by the secret Franco-Austrian Treaty of Partition of 1668) [20] on condition that Louis help him take possession of the island of Minorca, Ostend, and all the Spanish possessions in America. France had earlier offered to help Charles secure Spanish America on the condition that Charles not ally himself with the Dutch while France was at war with Spain, but this demand of 1669 was awkward for Louis because the Treaty of Partition promised Minorca and Spanish America to Austria. Therefore, Louis urged that the provision regarding the Spanish inheritance be limited to a general obligation to joint action, a limitation which Charles accepted on the condition that no treaty regarding the fate of Spain be made by France unless Charles and Louis mutually agreed to it.

The final treaty secretly concluded at Dover on June 1, 1670, provided for an alliance between the two nations.[21] Louis promised not to break the peace with Spain and to uphold the Treaty of Aix-la-Chapelle; Charles was permitted to maintain the Anglo-French treaty according to the terms of the Triple Alliance. With regard to the Spanish Succession, it was finally agreed and settled in this treaty that Charles would help Louis to acquire any "new rights" to the Spanish monarchy which might fall to him, that the particular provisions regarding joining the forces of the two kings and the recompensation of Charles would be settled after the death of the King of Spain, and that neither king would make any treaty regarding these "new rights" except by mutual consent. Charles was to declare himself a Catholic and would receive financial and military aid from Louis in case of a rebellion of his subjects. After his declaration, at his convenience, he would join France in a war against the Dutch; neither king could make peace without the other's consent.

Charles' motives for making this treaty cannot be found merely in his religious ideals, for he did not, in fact, become a Catholic until just before his death. Rather, one must look beyond such a narrow interpretation to Charles's ambitions for England as a whole. It had been clear for many years to the leaders of Europe that the Spanish empire would be broken up on the death of its moribund King Carlos II. Charles was determined that England should secure a place in the lucrative West Indian trade, either by achieving actual control of the Indies, as was suggested in the first draft of the treaty, or else by replacing the Dutch as chief traders and securing the friendship of the new masters of the Spanish empire. Since France rejected the first alternative because it had already, unbeknownst to Charles, promised Spanish America to Austria, Charles accepted the second, undoubtedly believing that his promise to help Louis XIV secure his "rights" to the Spanish monarchy would mean help for

[20] See Chapter X.
[21] Davenport, ed., *European Treaties*, II, 180–182.

Louis to secure control of Spanish America with a large part of the commerce thereof to fall to England. The alliance with France had, therefore, a double purpose: to destroy Dutch commercial and maritime competition, especially in the colonial trade, and to secure the friendship of France as potential ruler of Spanish America.

This treaty, with its startling provisions relating to Charles's public profession of Catholicism, could not be revealed to Charles's Protestant ministers. One of these ministers, the Duke of Buckingham, was directed to engage in negotiations for a sham Anglo-French treaty, which was concluded in December of 1671, with stipulations nearly identical with those of the Treaty of Dover but excluding the provisions relating to Catholicism and to the Spanish Succession. In February, 1672, a second sham treaty, closely similar to this, was concluded. Both these treaties were centered around arrangements for a new Dutch war. Charles's new pro-French foreign policy was supported either knowingly or through deception, by his chief ministers, five of whom (the Earl of Arlington, Sir Thomas Clifford, Baron Ashley, the Duke of Buckingham, and the Earl of Lauderdale) were to dominate English politics for the next three years as the infamous "Cabal."

5. England and the Franco-Dutch War

The war against the Dutch which had been envisaged by the secret Treaty of Dover was declared in 1672. During the two years between the signing of the Dover treaty and the declaration of war France had succeeded in isolating the Dutch from their Swedish allies with the conclusion of the Treaty of Stockholm of April, 1672; in securing its eastern flank by the occupation of the duchy of Lorraine; and in gaining the friendship of Bavaria and the neutrality of the Empire. Of the Imperial States only Brandenburg stood by the Dutch, and a defensive treaty between these two states was concluded at Cöln-am-Spree in February of 1678.[22]

By the Treaty of Dover it had been agreed that Charles would have the initiative in deciding when the Dutch war would begin: Louis would fix the date only after Charles announced his conversion to Catholicism. This announcement was never made, so the war was begun when Louis's preparations were complete. Justification for the English declaration of war was found in the ever-available maritime and commercial disputes, in this case a deliberately provoked insult to the British flag from the Dutch fleet. The negotiations regarding this incident and others were patently insincere on the part of the English; as one official said: "Our business is to break with them and yet to lay the breache at their door." [23] The insult

---

[22] See Chapter VIII.
[23] Quoted in Clark, *The Later Stuarts, 1660–1714*, 73–74.

to the flag was considered sufficient cause for war, which Charles declared on March 17, 1672, followed by Louis's declaration of war of April 6.

Despite the greater power of the French forces the Anglo-French alliance failed to conquer the Dutch as quickly as hoped. A rapid victory was essential, for Europe would not long accept without protest Louis's un-provoked invasion of the Dutch provinces. Victory, however, was not forthcoming. When the Dutch, at one point, made proposals for a peace settlement with France, Charles II sent his ministers to Louis to arrange jointly the terms of peace; from these negotiations emerged a new Anglo-French Treaty of Heeswijk (July 16, 1672), which engaged each king not to make peace except by mutual consent and on mutually accepted terms.[24] The terms which each nation demanded, however, were so severe as to make acceptance by the Dutch impossible. The intransigence of the English and the French also helped to precipitate a revolution in the United Provinces which brought Prince William of Orange to power as stadholder and, for the next thirty years, as the most determined and constant opponent to French aggression.

The war did not go as well for England as Charles had hoped when he made the treaty. In the first place, English hopes to gain Dutch territory were dashed by the inability of the combined French and English fleets to destroy the Dutch navy or even to maintain a blockade of Dutch ports. In America, the Dutch easily recaptured New York, which they had surrendered to England by the Treaty of Breda in 1667. This loss was little compensated by the English conquest of the Dutch West Indian islands of St. Eustatius, Saba, and Tortuga in 1672. Secondly, the war proved to be unpopular with Charles's subjects, who very soon guessed some of the implications of the secret treaty of alliance. Just before the opening of the war Charles had issued a declaration of religious indulgence which led to renewed domestic strife, and it was only after Charles had cancelled the indulgence that Parliament consented to vote money for the war. Moreover, Prince William of Orange, from the moment of his accession to power, had endeavored by several means to draw England out of the war: he secretly provided aid to the English anti-French and anti-Catholic party, and he encouraged the participation of Spain in an alliance to force England to make peace. Spain had for some time feared a new French attack on the Spanish Netherlands, and when the Anglo-French alliance attacked the Dutch, Spain feared an eventual attack on its West Indian holdings. Therefore, by a treaty signed at The Hague in 1673 [25] Spain allied itself with the Dutch and agreed to break with England and declare war if England would not consent to peace terms. This pre-sented a serious threat to English trade with Spanish America.

These factors were aggravated by tensions within the Anglo-French

24 Dumont, ed., *Corps universel diplomatique*, VII, pt. 1, 208.
25 Davenport, ed., *European Treaties*, II, 221–228.

alliance, and it proved very difficult for these two traditional rivals to achieve friendly accord or mutual confidence in the West Indies. The situation on St. Christopher was particularly difficult, for the English part of the island had not yet been restored by the French to its original owners in accordance with the terms of the Treaty of Breda. In January, 1671, Sir Charles Wheler had been appointed governor of the Leeward Islands and entered negotiations with the French to settle the terms of the transfer. By July terms had been reached and in August Wheler issued a proclamation setting out the conditions by which English planters could recover their lands. These conditions proved unacceptable to the English government, since they included, among other things, a time limit on English claims, and so, on the advice of his Privy Council, the King declared Wheler's proclamation void on the grounds that "nothing could have been more contrary to his commission and instructions, and to the just interest of the ancient planters." [26] Wheler was recalled and Colonel Sir William Stapleton was commissioned governor of the Leeward Islands. The French continued to insist that the conditions of surrender be those agreed to by Wheler, and it was not until Charles II made a direct approach to Louis XIV that the restitution was settled. The long delay embittered feeling between the French and English in the Leeward Islands for many years to come.

All of these problems coupled with the rising discontent of Parliament, plus the fact that William of Orange offered acceptable terms for peace, encouraged Charles II to enter peace negotiations. These were begun at Cologne under the mediation of Sweden in June of 1673 and resulted in a treaty of peace between England and the United Netherlands concluded at Westminster in February of 1674.[27]

The treaty marked the final divergence of English and French interests in their colonial involvements and policies. Henceforth, the English and Dutch moved together to block the ambitions of the French. Indeed, the assumption by the English of their role as opponents to French colonial expansion is evident even in the execution of the Treaty of Westminster: although the treaty provided for mutual restoration of all conquests, the Dutch did not wish the immediate return of St. Eustatius and Saba for fear they might then fall to the French, so the English agreed to hold them until a general peace should be made.

The defection of England left France alone in the war, which continued for more than four years despite Charles II's offer to act as mediator in peace negotiations. For England, neutrality meant a trade revival based on the wide definition of neutral rights recognized when it made peace with the Dutch. Louis XIV continued to woo Charles with cash, now in an effort to keep England from becoming his enemy. Despite the advent

[26] *C.S.P., Col.*, A.& W.I., 1669–74, No. 706, p. 308.
[27] Davenport, ed., *European Treaties*, II, 237–240. See also Chapter V.

of Lord Danby, a man of strong anti-French feelings, to power as Lord Treasurer, Charles continued to pursue his own personal pro-French policies, a practice which alienated him from Parliament. In November of 1675 Charles prorogued Parliament until February, 1677, after a demand from the opposition party that English troops serving as auxiliaries in the French army be recalled. Earlier, Charles had made a secret agreement with Louis XIV that if Parliament made the vote of money for Charles's support dependent on war with France, Charles would dissolve Parliament and receive a yearly income from Louis. The demand of the opposition party seemed sufficient cause for prorogation, and Charles received as a result his money from Louis. When Parliament did meet again the House of Commons demanded active measures against France and demanded a Dutch alliance before voting funds for Charles's support, but Charles refused to surrender the right of the crown to make war and peace.

Charles did, however, desire an end to the continuing Franco-Dutch war, for it was becoming impossible to carry on the government without abandoning neutrality. The peace congress had not yet made any progress. In the winter of 1677–78 Charles's niece, Mary of York, married Prince William of Orange. Louis then stopped his payments to Charles and Charles consequently summoned Parliament to meet in February of 1678. In Charles's speech from the throne, he demanded that Parliament vote money for an army and navy to save the Spanish Netherlands. In January, Lawrence Hyde, English ambassador to Holland, had signed a treaty of defensive alliance with the Dutch. But England, despite these appearances, did not join in the war, for Louis XIV, on his own terms, made peace with the Dutch and their allies at Nymwegen in the following summer.[28]

6. The Neutrality of America

Despite the official though uncertain friendship between France and England during the reign of Charles's successor, James II, relations between the colonials of these two nations grew ever worse. There were many points of long-standing friction in America which were unaffected by fluctuations in official policies. In Canada the French fur traders found their expansion blocked by English establishments at Hudson Bay and in the Great Lakes area, both of which regions were the subjects of rival and hotly disputed territorial claims.

In New York Governor Dongan claimed that the Iroquois Indians were under the protection of England, to the great displeasure of the French, with whom the Iroquois were at war and who had long claimed sole possession of the Iroquois lands. Dongan attempted to extend his jurisdiction over a vast amount of territory claimed by the French, in-

[28] Vast, ed., Grands traités, II, 23–99.

cluding the entire St. Lawrence and Ottawa Rivers and Lakes Frontenac and Champlain. The New Englanders claimed that their colony extended as far east as the St. Croix River, which lay well within the Acadian territory claimed by the French since the Treaty of Breda. In Acadia the French protested the encroachments of the New Englanders on their fishing and fur trade and charged them with piracy on the Acadian coasts. On Newfoundland the English protested French encroachments. In the West Indies relations between the two nations constantly deteriorated, particularly on St. Christopher, where the two nations continued to quarrel over the execution of the Treaty of Breda.[29]

To the mother countries, a war in America would at this time have been extremely disadvantageous. Louis XIV required peace with England in order to execute his schemes for securing the Spanish Succession. James II had several reasons for desiring the continuance of peace: in the first place his pro-Catholic domestic policies had disturbed many of his countrymen and an unpopular war might endanger his position; secondly, he desired to preserve amicable relations with Louis XIV as a Catholic ally and as a source of revenue which he tried to exploit as had his brother, Charles II; in the third place James wanted to maintain England's neutral status in the probable event of another European war so that his country could grow wealthy on its neutral trade as it had after it withdrew from the Franco-Dutch war in 1673.

In their desire to maintain peace the two monarchs were in a mood to consider negotiations for a treaty of neutrality in America. The idea of America as a separate sphere subject to rules and conditions different from those applicable in Europe was one of the oldest bases of European diplomacy with regard to America, and the subject of an Anglo-French treaty of American neutrality had been considered several times before.[30] Just such a treaty had, in fact, been made between the English and French residents of St. Christopher in 1678.[31] Although this treaty, called the Treaty of Sandy Point, was never ratified it served as a foundation for later negotiations between Louis XIV and James II.

It was Louis who first revived negotiations for an American treaty of neutrality. Louis's ambassador to London, Paul Barillon d'Amoncourt, Marquis de Branges, contacted Sir William Stapleton, Governor of the Leeward Islands, who had promoted the Sandy Point treaty of 1678 and had promised to try to win the consent of his King to a treaty of neutrality including all the West Indies and even New England, and asked Stapleton to promote consideration of such a treaty by his government. Stapleton, therefore, on December 14, 1685, petitioned the Lords of Trade to consider

---

[29] For a discussion of direct international relations between French and English colonies in America in the seventeenth century see Chapter XIII.

[30] Davenport, ed., *European Treaties*, II, 256.

[31] Davenport, ed., *European Treaties*, II, 256–260. See also Chapter XI.

a treaty of neutrality. At the same time Louis sent François d'Usson, the Marquis de Bonrepaus, as envoy to the English court with instructions to investigate England's commercial and colonial state and its mood regarding a treaty of neutrality. He soon learned that James II desired a general treaty for North America. Barillon was therefore empowered to treat with the English on this basis.

Formal conferences with the English commissioners began in March of 1686. Both sides had numerous matters in America to discuss beyond the terms of neutrality. France desired to prohibit English vessels from fishing or trading along its American coasts under penalty of confiscation of boats and merchandise, to restrain English governors from giving aid to Indians with whom the French were at war, as was done by Governor Dongan to the New York Iroquois, to regulate the rights of the French and English in the disputed Hudson Bay fur trade, particularly in the region of the Nelson River, where there had been much reciprocal depredation, to prevent the English from taking commissions from powers at war with France to carry on privateering against French vessels in American waters, to secure the observance of the treaties of Breda and Boston, both of which were still subject to dispute, to secure the right of the French to fish for turtles in the Cayman Islands, and to arrange the exchange of the English part of St. Christopher for some other French territory, possibly St. Croix.

The English presented their grievances in many of the same areas. They demanded satisfaction for the confiscation of their fishery vessels by the French Acadian fishing company, liberty for English ships to seek water and wood on the coasts of French America, and friendly treatment for English ships forced to seek shelter on French American coasts; they claimed their right to compensation for their losses at Port Nelson in Hudson Bay and desired security against further injury to the Hudson's Bay Company; they desired access to the salt pans on St. Christopher, which lay within the French portion of that island, and security against privateering by the French.

Although negotiations went slowly, most of the terms of the treaty had been settled by May and the treaty itself, the so-called Treaty of American Neutrality, was signed on November 16 and promptly ratified by both kings.[32] The treaty provided peace and friendship between the two nations in both North and South America and stipulated that no injury would be done by ships or soldiers of either nation to American possessions or subjects of the other. In order to guarantee that neutrality would not mean loss of position the treaty provided that "each king shall have and retain for himself all dominions, rights, and prerogatives in the seas, straits, or other waters of America, with the same amplitude which belongs to each

[32] Davenport, ed., *European Treaties*, II, 319–323.

by right and in the same manner in which he now enjoys them" (Article 2). Each side was to abstain from trade and fishing in the territories occupied by the other, but ships of either nation driven to seek shelter in rivers or coastal waters belonging to the other would be received with friendship. Arrangements were made for the French inhabitants of St. Christopher to draw water from rivers belonging to the English side, for English inhabitants to take salt from salt pans in the French territory, and for the French to hunt tortoises in the Cayman Islands. Measures were taken for the treaty to regulate ships carrying letters of marque and to suppress piracy. Any rupture occurring in Europe between the two nations was to have no effect in America, where subjects of both nations were to continue "in the same manner as if no such rupture had occurred in Europe." Similarly, conflicts between nationals of the two countries in America were not to be considered causes for war in Europe.

This treaty represents one of the most explicit expressions of the "doctrine of the two spheres," which had long played various roles in international relations regarding America. Many earlier treaties and "understandings" had acknowledged the fact that different conditions governed the policies of and relations between various nations in their American colonies; usually it was understood that peace settlements in Europe were not necessarily applicable in America.[33] In this case, however, necessity compelled the French and English governments explicitly to recognize America as a sphere formally acknowledged to be free from the vicissitudes of European politics, which would also, it was hoped, be free of intercolonial strife.

Unfortunately, the treaty left untouched or unsettled many controversies which were constant sources of intercolonial dispute. The problem of the rival claims to Hudson Bay and the regulation of its fur trade, for example, was not even mentioned. Moreover, other potentially explosive disputes arose shortly after the treaty was made. Just before the treaty was signed in November of 1686 word reached France that a French expedition had seized three English forts at Hudson Bay. When the English signed the treaty a few days later they were apparently unaware of this event, but when they learned of their loss shortly afterward they were infuriated. In the West Indies the English governor of Barbados, Edwyne Stede, was directed in 1686 by his king to establish English ownership of the islands of St. Lucia, St. Vincent, and Dominica, which were also claimed by the French. Stede sent ships at intervals to these islands, and their visits, which were regarded as raids or attacks by the French occupants, created tension in this area. Moreover, the problems on St. Christopher had not

[33] For instance, Louis XIV insisted that the Franco-Spanish Treaty of Peace of Nymwegen did not apply to America, and continued, long after that peace, warlike actions against Spanish trade and colonies there.

yet been fully settled, for the English there now demanded satisfaction for damages to their property and return of slaves and artillery taken by the French before the Treaty of Breda.

In order to settle these disputes, to establish the limits of the respective territories of the two nations, and to execute the general terms of the treaty of neutrality, both crowns appointed commissioners to meet in London in May of 1687. France was represented by Barillon and Bonrepaus, who had negotiated the treaty, and England by the earls of Sunderland and Middleton and Lord Godolphin.

The chief matter of discussion by the commissioners was the conflicting claims of the two nations to Hudson Bay. Since 1682 conflicts between subjects of the two crowns and particularly between the English Hudson's Bay Company and the French Company of the North had produced much reciprocal damage and ill feeling. The English company demanded indemnification for French destruction of its factory at Port Nelson, on the west side of the bay (1682), of its three forts and other establishments at the bottom of James Bay (1686), as well as for other seizures and damages committed against English subjects, ships, merchandise, and trade. The French, for their part, claimed that the English had destroyed the French fort at Port Nelson in 1683 and justified their capture of English forts in James Bay as reprisal for this damage. The English declared that in dispossessing the French of Port Nelson they were merely recovering what was rightfully theirs. Both sides tried to establish their own rights to the entire bay region on the basis of priority of discovery, possession, and occupation and denied the validity of claims made by the other side.[34]

Since no agreement about the ownership of the bay could be reached, the French commissioners proposed an "accommodation" by which the French would surrender the three English forts at the bottom of the bay, which they had taken in 1686, in return for the English surrender of Fort Nelson, which had been taken from the French in 1683. Limits were then to be fixed between the territories belonging to the two companies. The Hudson's Bay Company, to which the proposal was referred, absolutely rejected it, replying that "it cannot but seem strange and dissonant from all reason, that the French Comm[rs]. should now come to offer the said Company their own, which they took by violence, in exchange for another part of their own, which the French never had any Colour of Right to."[35] Perhaps most important to the Company than the supposed injustice of the French offer was the unwillingness of its directors to share any part of its lucrative fur trade with the French, and to this end they strove mightily to discourage any sort of compromise:

[34] *Mémoires des Commissaires*, II, 68–69.
[35] *Mémoires des Commissaires*, II, 70.

Most humbly Representing to his Maty., That in case the French be suffered to be Sharers in the Bay and Streights of Hudson or be permitted to Trade therein, the Company cannot any longer Subsist, but must inevitably be dissolved, and by the monopoly of the French, a Trade of so great importance to the Nation be utterly lost, having been hitherto wholly supported by his Maty's favour to them in the Enjoyment of the Sole Trade of the Bay.[36]

A proposal by members of the Hudson's Bay Company that either one of the two companies buy out the interest of the other was refused by the French, because their company was not financially able to do this. Finally, Bonrepaus suggested that the English divide the bay into two equal parts of which the French would choose one. But the English preferred to delay making a decision on this suggestion, and their king, James II, whose pro-Catholic and absolutist policies had already alienated many of his people, was reluctant to make any independent decisions regarding the bay settlement. He therefore only empowered his commissioners to treat for boundaries in America. An instrument instructing the governments of both kings in America to refrain from acts of hostility against subjects of the other in America was then signed by the commissioners, its purpose being to allow time for collecting information necessary for settlement of American boundaries.[37]

The meetings of the commissioners were then recessed until January of 1689, and orders were sent to the royal governors of each nation in America to furnish information regarding the extent of their American possessions. The North American territories in dispute, beside Hudson Bay, were the country of the Iroquois and the southern portion of Acadia between the Pentogoët and the Kennebec Rivers. It was understood that a certain degree of latitude regarding actual possession was possible; the instructions to the Marquis de Denonville, governor of New France, informed him that

As respects the countries not occupied, at present, by any European Nations His Majesty's intention is to appropriate unto himself those actually necessary for the maintenance of Trade and the preservation and increase of the Colony. [38]

The commissioners did not meet again, for the English Revolution of 1688, Louis's aggressive European policies, and the ensuing Anglo-French war ended all possibilities for any agreements concerning America.

7. America in the Diplomacy of King William's War

The accession of William of Orange to the English throne in 1688 brought to a head the diplomatic and colonial conflicts which had troubled Europe since the Franco-Dutch Treaty of Nymwegen of 1678.[39] After the

[36] *Mémoires des Commissaires*, II, 71.
[37] Davenport, ed., *European Treaties*, II, 329.
[38] N.Y.C.D., IX, 371–372.
[39] See Chapter V.

signing of this treaty, Louis XIV had embarked upon an aggressive policy designed to secure the territorial and economic security of France. French *chambres de réunion* (commissions of lawyers appointed for the purpose) presented legal claims to various imperial cities of vague status. By the Treaty of Westphalia France had gained control of Upper and Lower Alsace. Through his ties with the Spanish royal family, Louis had fully expected the Bourbons to be installed on the Spanish throne at the death of the childless Carlos II, and he had begun the annexation of Spanish territories in the War of Devolution (1667-68) and the Dutch War (1672-78), which gave him part of the Spanish Netherlands and Franche-Comté.[40] In 1681 the French seized Strasbourg, and in 1684 they bombarded Genoa and captured Luxembourg. The rest of Europe was powerless to oppose Louis: Spain, under its moribund King, was too weak to prevent French annexations of its territories; England was in a state of virtual civil war over the policies of the Stuarts; Austria was involved in a difficult war with the Turks. In 1684 French pressure persuaded the Dutch to conclude a treaty whereby the Dutch would persuade Spain to accept a truce in all dominions of France and Spain. Spain, unable to resist, empowered the Emperor to act on its behalf at the Diet of Ratisbon, which was to regulate the terms of the treaties. By the Franco-Austrian treaty of truce France was to hold for twenty years Strasbourg and all the places assigned it before August, 1681, by the French *chambres de réunion*.[41] The Franco-Spanish treaty compelled Spain to make large concessions of its European territories to France in return for a truce which was to be effective in both Europe and America.[42]

The colonial situation in America was also fraught with conflicts. The Franco-Spanish Truce of Ratisbon scarcely expressed France's real ambitions in Spain's American territories. Aware of Spain's weakness in the Gulf of Mexico Louis wished to drive the Spanish out of this region, and the occupation by the French of a part of Hispaniola provided a base for French encroachments into Spanish territories. La Salle's plan to establish a colony near he mouth of the Mississippi, although abortive, was another expression of France's ambitions in Spanish America.

Conflicts between the American colonies of France and England had long made maintenance of amicable relations between the two countries difficult. The French felt that the English Hudson's Bay Company and the New England colonies were encircling their own possessions on the bay and in the northeast. The English for the same reason opposed French advances along the Mississippi and in the Great Lakes basin. Disputed sovereignty over Indian tribes, notably those of the Five Nations, was another source of diplomatic and military conflicts. There was also con-

[40] Wolf, *The Emergence of the Great Powers, 1685–1715*, 17.
[41] Petrie, *Earlier Diplomatic History, 1492–1713*, 196.
[42] Davenport, ed., *European Treaties*, II, 287.

tinuous friction between these two nations in the Sugar Islands of the Caribbean. Attempts by the French and English to establish a state of neutrality in America were, on the whole, failures. The Treaty of Sandy Point, concluded in 1678 between the governors of the French and English parts of St. Christopher, which was intended to neutralize several of the West Indian islands in the event of war between the parent nations, was never ratified by the home governments.[43] The Treaty of American Neutrality concluded by James II and Louis XIV at Whitehall in 1686 was intended to prevent almost inevitable colonial warfare. However, that treaty in no way attempted to resolve the disputed American claims of the two nations, and the commissioners appointed in 1687 to execute the treaty had accomplished nothing, as has been noted.

Attempts to establish peace in Europe and America, ineffectual and generally insincere as they were, did nothing to resolve existing conflicts or to prevent the aggressive policies of France. The accession of William of Orange to the throne of England brought that nation under the direction of a man who had long been Louis's most determined opponent and changed England's policy with regard to France's activities from the indetermination of James II to the firm resistance of William. William III, with the resources of the most powerful nation in Europe, next to France, at his command, required only a suitable opportunity to begin a war with France.

Louis XIV did not long keep him waiting. In September of 1688 French armies invaded the Palatinate, occupied Mainz, Trier, and Cologne, and brought an end to the Truce of Ratisbon. In November William landed in England to assume the crown and in the same month France declared war against the Dutch. In May, 1689, William led Britain and the Netherlands into the League of Augsburg to form the so-called Grand Alliance against France. The chief war aim of the allies was the reestablishment of the territorial settlements of the Treaties of Westphalia and the Pyrenees in order to deprive Louis of all his gains since his assumption of personal power. Emperor Leopold desired and received support for his claims to the Spanish throne. To the English, the colonial situation was of great importance: in their declaration of war of May, 1689, they included French encroachments in Newfoundland and invasion of the West Indies and of the provinces of New York and Hudson Bay during the negotiations of the Anglo-French treaty of American neutrality among the reasons for their decision.[44]

The war in Europe, although spread over a wide area, was indecisive. Louis XIV's aggressions had made enemies of most of his neighbors—the Emperor, some German princes, the Dutch, English, Spanish, and Savoy-

[43] See Chapter XIV.
[44] *London Gazette*, No. 2452 (May 9–13, 1689) and *General Collection of Treatys*, I, 281.

ards—but his forces were strong enough to carry the war beyond the frontiers of France into the territories of his foes.

The most serious fighting of the war took place in America. There, even before hostilities broke out in Europe, frictions between French and English colonies were driving the inhabitants to disregard the Anglo-French Treaty of American Neutrality. Hudson Bay at once became the scene of active warfare, each side seeking to establish its rights of possession by driving the other from the area. Several of the five forts on the bay changed hands in the course of the fighting; when peace was declared the English held Fort Albany and had captured and razed Moose Fort and Fort Rupert. Both forts held by the English at the outbreak of the war had been captured by the French, New Severn in 1689 and Nelson, which, after several times changing hands, was secured by the French in 1697. Newfoundland, since the reign of Charles II, had been the scene of rivalry in the important fishery. During the war each side attacked the settlements of the other, but the French were, on the whole, the more successful, having destroyed most of the English settlements while defending unharmed their own principal fortified settlement at Placentia. Conflicts between French Acadia and New England had long since arisen over disputed sea lanes, privateers, and jurisdiction over Indian tribes. The New Englanders succeeded in capturing Port Royal and the rest of Acadia in 1690 but soon lost it again to the French. An attack against Quebec was planned in 1690, but the British lacked sufficient power to make it successful.

In the West Indies there was a great deal of fighting among the various islands. In 1689 the French captured the English part of St. Christopher only to lose the entire island to the English in 1690. The English destroyed the French settlements on Marie Galante, St. Barthélemy, and St. Martin. In 1689 the French captured St. Eustatius from the Dutch and lost it to the English the following year. Martinique was attacked by the English and Jamaica by the French, who also captured Spanish Cartagena. On Hispaniola the French and Spanish attacked each other's settlements; an Anglo-Spanish expedition against the French on this island was attempted in 1695 but failed.

By 1693 both sides realized that the war might be indicisive and were, for various reasons, anxious to make peace. Louis XIV needed peace in order to secure his claims to the Spanish throne, for if Carlos II were to die while Spain was at war with France the Bourbon claims would be ignored and the Spanish crown would pass to one of the two claimants put forth by Emperor Leopold—his second son, Charles, or his grandson, the electoral prince of Bavaria. Leopold, for his part, found it to his interest to encourage the continuation of the war by inducing his allies to insist upon the achievement of their original war aims—the surrender of all French conquests and *réunions* made since the middle of the century. William

III desired peace in order to secure his own position on the English throne and because of the severe financial difficulties which England and the United Netherlands were experiencing.

Louis's first move toward peace was in the form of an effort to draw a proposal of terms from the Dutch. When the Dutch showed themselves to be unwilling, Louis dispatched the Comte d'Avaux to Sweden as a special ambassador to establish Franco-Swedish relations and to persuade the Swedes to act as mediators in the peace negotiations. D'Avaux's first task was to prevent Sweden from renewing its treaty with the Emperor and to hold it to its policy of exact neutrality.[45] Once Sweden had consented to mediate, d'Avaux was sent the French conditions of peace, to be communicated by Sweden to the allies. As general conditions Louis required that the future peace be based upon the Treaties of Münster and Nymwegen and the Truce of Ratisbon.[46] To the Emperor, Louis offered to demolish certain French fortresses which threatened imperial territory, in exchange for the Emperor's cession to Louis of all territories presently possessed by France according to the terms of the Treaties of Nymwegen and Ratisbon.[47] To the Spanish Louis communicated his claim that, because Spain had acted as aggressor against him, France had a right to keep all its conquests in Spanish Flanders and in Catalonia as payment for injuries, but because he was anxious to make peace, he would return all French conquests in Catalonia. To the Dutch Louis offered to reestablish Franco-Dutch commerce on the terms of the Treaty of Nymwegen and to cede to Spain, as part of the barrier so anxiously desired by the Dutch, one of two strongly fortified French cities, Namur or Mons, as well as Charleroy. To the English Louis offered to renew all treaties of commerce having effect at the beginning of the war and demanded restoration of all French territories in America taken by the English during the war.[48]

The allies, for their part, had their own conditions for peace. Spain and the Empire desired to see the Treaty of the Pyrenees used as the basis of peace in order to prevent the Bourbons from inheriting the Spanish empire.[49] The Dutch desired a barrier in the Spanish Netherlands to protect

[45] "Mémoire du Roy pour servir d'instruction au Sr. Comte d'Avaux, Dec. 1, 1692," *Négociations de Monsieur le Comte d'Avaux, ambassadeur extraordinaire à la cour de Suède, pendant les années 1693, 1697, 1698 . . .* ed. Wijnne, (in *Werken van het Historisch Genootschap, Gevestigd te Utrecht,* N.S., Nos. 33–36), I, 4–5.

[46] Louis XIV to d'Avaux, May 27, 1693, *Négociations de M. le Comte d'Avaux,* I, 189–194.

[47] *Négociations de M. le Comte d'Avaux . . . ,* I, 189–194.

[48] Louis XIV to d'Avaux; Oct. 15, 1693, *Négociations de M. le Comte d'Avaux,* I, 409–413.

[49] By this treaty of 1659 Louis XIV's Spanish queen, Maria Teresa, older daughter of Philip IV, had renounced for herself and her descendents all rights to the Spanish Succession. Louis held the renunciation invalid because Philip IV had never paid his daughter's dowry.

them against French aggression. The English desired recognition of William III as king and the settlement of long-standing colonial disputes.[50]

In 1693, because no real foundation for negotiations had been reached, William III rejected all French offers.

Negotiations were begun again in Holland in 1696. Antonie Heinsius, Grand Pensionary of Holland, distrustful of Sweden, treated with Louis Hector de Callières-Bonnevue, the French negotiator, through Jacob Boreel, burgomaster of Amsterdam, for the settlement of the main points preliminary to a general congress to be mediated by Sweden. Heinsius presented a project for peace which included: (1) recognition of William III as king of England; (2) restoration of Strasbourg to the Emperor, and of Luxembourg and all territories taken by the *réunions* to Spain, (3) exemption for Dutch vessels of the duty of fifty sous per ton; (4) sureties for the protection of Protestant foreigners, consuls, and merchants residing in France; (5) a general congress which would base its efforts to settle all differences on the terms of the Treaties of Westphalia and Nymwegen.[51] Louis refused to recognize William III before the signing of the peace; he refused, also, to make all the territorial concessions demanded, but by the end of the year the preliminary points had been adjusted.[52]

By February of 1697 all the allies but Spain had accepted the mediation of Sweden. A manor house of William III in the village of Ryswick near Delft was chosen as the site of the congress, which opened on May 9, 1697. The Baron of Lillienroth represented Charles XI of Sweden as mediator. Present were the representatives of France, England, Spain, the Empire, and of some of the German princes of the Empire. The talks promptly bogged down in questions of protocol, and it seemed that no progress toward peace would ever be made.[53]

It was the intervention of William III which led to peace. William, concerned that he had not received a definite promise from Louis to recognize him as King, sent the Count of Portland to Delft to negotiate directly with Marshal Boufflers, who represented Louis XIV, under the mediation of the Lord of Dykvelt. William demanded satisfaction from Louis on three points: (1) that Louis no longer support the deposed James II and that James be invited to reside outside France; (2) that Louis no longer demand that James's supporters receive amnesty and return of their confiscated goods; and (3) that Louis not forbid William to receive in his realms Frenchmen who wished to dwell there.[54] Louis accepted these terms, and the removal of James to Avignon and the

---

[50] Davenport, ed., *European Treaties*, II, 354.

[51] Davenport, ed., *European Treaties*, II, 158.

[52] Matthew Prior to James Vernon, Jan. 8, 1697, in "The Prior Papers," *H.M.C.*, *Mss. of the Marquess of Bath*, III, 100–101.

[53] For a description of the Ryswick meetings, see Macauley, *History of England*, ed. Firth, VI, Chap. XXII.

[54] Vast, ed., *Grands traités*, II, 161.

payment by England of the jointure of James's wife Mary of Modena were settled.[55] William then persuaded Spain and the Emperor to agree to make peace, having promised Louis that, when his demands for recognition of his rule and disavowal by Louis of James's claims had been satisfied, he would oblige the Empire and Spain to make peace and that, in the event of their refusal, the English and Dutch would conclude peace without them.[56]

The only remaining differences to be settled between France and England concerned America, where long-standing colonial disputes had been compounded by various territorial conquests made during the war. First, the English and French plenipotentiaries agreed to base the settlement of American problems on the same terms as the Treaty of Breda—that is, restoration of all territories to their prewar ownership and status. Restoration of the *status quo* had been one of Louis XIV's earliest conditions for peace with England. The English were somewhat reluctant to accept this condition, having gained through the war some valuable French holdings, particularly the French part of St. Christopher and some forts on Hudson Bay, and feeling that restitution was not to their advantage.[57]

Matthew Prior, secretary of the English embassy of The Hague, had drawn up a project for a peace treaty with France and presented it to the Swedish mediator at Ryswick.[58] By the fourth article both sides promised satisfaction for all injuries done by subjects of each king to subjects of the other before the declaration of the war. This article referred especially to Hudson Bay. The seventh article provided for the restoration by the French and English of all conquered territories to their prewar possessors, with the exception of a clause which provided that "such places as belong to His Majesty of Great Britain, which the French seized during the peace preceding this present war,"[59] were to remain in British hands. The clause referred to three British forts on Hudson Bay that had been taken by the French in 1686 and retaken by the British during the war. Without this clause, Prior's seventh article would have been "of the greatest prejudice to the Hudson's Bay Company," for otherwise the forts would have been lost to the English.[60]

The French ambassadors, replying to Prior's project, recommended that the fifth article, which concerned mutual freedom of commerce, be extended to include the colonies. They also proposed having a treaty of neutrality in America like that made in 1686, but were willing to post-

[55] Macaulay, *History of England*, VI, 2714.
[56] Marshal Boufflers to Louis XIV, July 8, 1697, in Grimblot, ed., *Letters of William III and Louis XIV*, I, 8.
[57] William Blathwayt to Matthew Prior, June 27, 1697, "The Prior Papers," *H.M.C.*, *Mss. of the Marquess of Bath*, III, 156–157.
[58] *Actes et Mémoires des négociations de la Paix de Ryswick*, II, 183–191.
[59] *Actes et Mémoires des négociations de la Paix de Ryswick*, II, 186.
[60] William Blathwayt to Matthew Prior, June 27, 1697, "The Prior Papers," *H.M.C.*, *Mss. of the Marquess of Bath*, III, 123.

pone its consideration until after the making of peace.[61] King William did not think a neutrality in America "convenient" for the English but agreed to the French proposal because he believed that "the referring the consideration of such a treaty to commissioners may induce the French to give their concurrence in other things that may be desired by us." [62]

The English consented to the proposed extension of free commerce to the colonies and agreed to the proposal to neutralize America. Since the French had refused to accept the special clause of the seventh article, King William ordered his ambassadors to insist then on a clause which would provide that all disputed matters in Hudson Bay be determined by commissioners who would be appointed for the negotiation of the treaty of commerce.[63] The French for their part agreed that the right to the disputed Hudson Bay forts should be adjusted by commissioners.[64] On September 16 Matthew Prior drew up an eighth article of the treaty, providing for commissioners to settle the disputed titles to Hudson Bay.[65]

On September 20 the ambassadors of England, France, Spain, and the United Provinces met at Ryswick, where the French signed treaties of peace with the Dutch, Spain, and England, and a treaty of commerce with the Dutch. Later, on October 30, peace was concluded between France and the Empire.

By the Anglo-French treaty of peace France recognized William's title to the throne of England and promised to withhold all aid from the Jacobites. Free navigation and commerce between the two nations were restored to their prewar state. All territories were returned to their prewar possessors, and commissioners were to be appointed by each side to examine disputed claims to Hudson Bay.[66]

The Franco-Dutch treaty of peace also provided for the return of all conquests made during the war to their original owners, which meant that the West Indian islands of Saba and St. Eustatius were to be returned once more to the Dutch.[67]

A similar article was included in the Franco-Spanish treaty of peace. The treaty also provided for the restoration to Spain of all places in Europe occupied by the French since the Treaty of Nymwegen and for the return to Spain of all réunions except for those places specifically ceded to France by the treaties of Aix-la-Chapelle and Nymwegen.[68]

[61] Matthew Prior to William Blathwayt, Aug. 16, 1697, "The Prior Papers," H.M.C., Mss. of the Marquess of Bath, III, 146–147.

[62] William Blathwayt to Matthew Prior, Aug. 19, 1697, "The Prior Papers," H.M.C., Mss. of the Marquess of Bath, III, 148.

[63] Mss. of the Marquess of Bath, III, 346–7.

[64] Mss. of the Marquess of Bath, III, 155–58.

[65] Mss. of the Marquess of Bath, III, 532–33.

[66] Davenport, ed., European Treaties, II, 360–365.

[67] Vast, ed., Grands traités, II, 190–198.

[68] Vast, ed., Grands traités, II, 190–198.

For America, the articles in these various treaties providing for a return to the prewar territorial *status quo* meant a continuation of prewar territorial disputes. On the island of St. Christopher, which had formerly been uneasily shared by the French and English and which had been wholly occupied by the English since 1690, English colonists had settled on French lands and were reluctant to give up their new homes. When they were ordered in 1698 to restore the French part of the island to its original owners, the English settlers systematically destroyed everything around them. This led to a long-drawn-out dispute with the French which lasted until war broke out again in 1702.[69]

On Newfoundland, also, conflicts between French and English settlers were to continue. Lack of interest on the part of the English government prevented any steps to protect what was becoming an important fishing industry. The threat of French competition in the fishing apparently failed to impress itself on the minds of the diplomats, and the situation was left to fester until war broke out again.

Because the treaty also failed to provide any settlement for long-standing disputes between the colonies of New York and New France over conflicting territorial claims and, most particularly, jurisdiction over the Five Nations of Indians, negotiations were carried on by the governments of these two colonies in 1698. Both sides claimed to have "always" enjoyed jurisdiction over the Indians and presently to enjoy rights of trade and religious supervision.[70] Likewise, both sides interpreted the absence of mention of the Indians in the peace treaty to imply that jurisdiction was not disputed by the home governments. As the English representatives said, "It was not necessary to mention the Indians in the Articles of Peace because it is unnecessary to mention individually all subjects of each prince and these Indians are subjects of the King of England." [71]

The customary unwillingness to compromise on claims regarding America was characteristic also of these negotiations and they were, not unexpectedly, without result. The conflicts in the New York and Great Lakes area dragged on to provide grist for yet another war.

The Anglo-French joint commission provided for in the Anglo-French Treaty of Ryswick for the adjudication of American disputes met in London in 1699. The members for France were Comte Tallard, M. Darbos, and M. Davegou. England was represented by the Earls of Pembroke, Bridgewater, Portland, and Tankerville.[72]

The commission took up the problem of ownership of Hudson Bay and

[69] Burns, *History of the British West Indies*, 389–390.
[70] "Report of Messrs. Schuyler and Dellius' Negotiations in Canada, New York, July, 1698," in *N.Y.C.D.*, IV, 347–351.
[71] *N.Y.C.D.*, IV, 349.
[72] *C.S.P., Col., A.& W.I.*, 1699, No. 137, pp. 82–83.

the question of payment of claims for damages presented by French and English fur traders. Both sides presented claims to the whole of the bay, the English by right of discovery, the French by right of prior settlement.[73] Because a compromise seemed impossible, the French commissioners presented a modified version of their proposal of 1687 that the bay be divided between the two powers. They proposed that a line be drawn across the bay at Cape Henrietta-Maria and that the English choose either the northern or southern zone. As a counterproposal, the Hudson's Bay Company proposed a boundary at 53° North Latitude or from the Albany River on the West to the Rupert River on the East, the English taking all territory, which comprised most of the bay, north of these rivers. Urging from the English commissioners that the Hudson's Bay Company offer a more generous compromise produced only a slight movement of the eastern boundary northward to the Canuse River.

The commission also took up the matter of the boundaries of Acadia. The French commissioners claimed that the western boundary of Acadia was the Kennebec River; the English commissioners claimed that the St. George River was the "ancient boundary fixed in Sir Thomas Temple's patent." [74] Apparently, the French commissioners at one time proposed to exchange the part of St. Christopher occupied by the French for the territory between the St. George River and the Kennebec, but the English stuck to the St. George as a boundary and insisted upon the restoration of the *status quo ante* in St. Christopher.[75]

The commission's deliberations were still dragging on without any real settlement when they were interrupted by the outbreak of the War of the Spanish Succession in 1702.

King William's War was thus without real results or even effective settlement. In Europe the war produced a shuffling of alliances which were to remain effective for the next decade. England was drawn away from France and, under William III, into a union with the Dutch based upon their common need to protect their commerce against the French. The British alliance with the Empire continued, as England saw this as the most effective means of preserving the European balance of power against French preponderance. The question of the Spanish Succession was still unsettled and productive of uneasiness.

The failure of all efforts to settle American problems left these issues— disputes over boundaries, territorial claims and Indian jurisdiction—hang-

[73] "State of the Rights of his Majesty on Hudson Bay; 26 August, 1697," C.A.O., F113, 15–19; "Lettre de M. le Comte de Maurepas en lui envoyant les mémoires des observations et réponses aux anglais sur le mémoire donné de leur part à Messrs. les ambassadeurs aux Conférences de la Paix à Riswick," 7 September, 1697, C.A.O., F113, 20–23; "Second mémoire de la Compe. française pour servir de réponse à la réplique de la Compe. angloise," C.A.O., F113, 6–14.

[74] Copy of a letter from John Nelson to the Board of Trade Jan. 26, 1698, C.S.P., Col., A& W.I., 1697–98, No. 922 (III), p. 50.

[75] C.S.P., Col., A& W.I., 1700, Nos. 368 (I) and 368 (II), pp. 213–214.

ing. Actually, there was no real desire for settlement on the part of any of the governments involved. Neither the French nor the English were willing to compromise in the slightest; both nations apparently preferred to entrench their positions and await the next outbreak of hostilities to extend their control.

8. *The Partition of the Spanish-American Inheritance*

Shortly after the making of the Peace of Ryswick, the question of the disposition of the vast realms of Carlos II of Spain again became an acute issue in the international relations of England and France. As early as 1668, France had agreed to a division of the Spanish inheritance with the Emperor, and the problem of the division of that great empire in case of the expected early death of the sickly Carlos, who was without direct heirs, had been a constant theme in the diplomacy of the European states, especially France. Now that peace was made, Louis XIV broached the question with William III, early in 1698. William III was interested, since he greatly feared the further aggrandizement of France, whether in Europe or in America, but most especially in the West Indies. William had, indeed, promised Leopold I, King of Austria and Holy Roman Emperor, the entire Spanish inheritance in order to block the ambitions of Louis XIV; but he was now persuaded, both as King of England and as stadholder of Holland, that such an accession of power to the Emperor might be just as dangerous as it would be in the hands of Louis.

Negotiations between Louis and William eventuated in the "Treaty of Partition" [76] signed at The Hague in 1698 by France, England, and Holland. This treaty provided, in the name of the preservation of the balance of power, a complicated division of Spain's holdings in Europe among the various claimants. The crown of Spain, together with the Spanish empire in America, was assigned to the eldest son of the Elector of Bavaria.

In the specifications dividing the lands along the Pyrenees Mountains between France and Spain, it was provided that the provinces of Guipúzcoa, with Fuenterrabia and St. Sebastián, among other territories, should go to the Dauphin of France. It was stated, however, that

if there are some places dependent on the said province, which are beyond the Pyrenees, or other mountains of Navarre, Avala, or Vizcaya on the side of Spain, they will pertain to Spain, and if there are some places similarly

[76] Davenport, ed., *European Treaties*, III, 1–15. For a study of the part Spain's American possessions played in European diplomacy relative to the partition of the Spanish inheritance, see Margaret Anne Fisher, "America in European Diplomacy relative to the Spanish Succession, 1665–1713," unpublished Ph.D. dissertation in the University of Washington Library (1967).

dependent on the provinces submitted to Spain, which are on the side of the Pyrenees or other mountains of Navarre, Avala, or Vizcaya, on the coast of the province of Guipuzcoa, they will pertain to France, and the slopes of the said mountains and the mountains between the said province of Guipuzcoa, Navarre, Alava, and Vizcaya, to which they belong, shall be divided between France and Spain in such a way that there will remain as much of the said mountains to France as remains to Spain . . .[77]

While this use of the height of land of the Pyrenees Mountains between France and Spain as the boundary, which was an elaboration of a similar one in the Treaty of the Pyrenees of 1659, made no reference to America, it set a precedent in the matter of establishing territorial boundaries that was of considerable force in the Anglo-French disputes of the eighteenth century over the boundaries between the British and French empires in North America.[78]

The electoral prince of Bavaria died in 1699, which made it necessary for the signatories of the Partition Treaty of 1698 to reconsider the division of the Spanish inheritance. After considerable wrangling a new treaty was agreed upon at London in April of 1700. By this new partition Spain and the Spanish-American empire were assigned to the Archduke Charles of Austria, second son of the Emperor.[79]

Neither of the partition treaties ever took effect, because the King of Spain, just before he died, made a will leaving his entire empire to Philip of Anjou, grandson of Louis XIV. Long disturbed by the prospect that his empire would be divided on his death among foreigners, and long pushed by the supporters of the various candidates for his throne to decide in favor of one or the other, Carlos finally chose the Bourbon prince as his heir and successor in the hope that, under French protection, the territorial and religious integrity of the Spanish empire would be preserved.

Louis XIV, torn by the choice between the relatively small gains allowed to France by the Partition Treaty of 1700 and the vast empire left in its entirety to his grandson, chose to ignore his commitments under the Partition Treaty and to accept the terms of Carlos's will. This, of course, meant war, for it was a foregone conclusion that the other signatories would not permit such a monstrous upset of the balance of power by the effective union of the French and Spanish empires. It also meant that the terms of the Partition Treaty never had any practical effect in America, since that treaty was completely nullified by Louis XIV's action and by the war, the so-called War of the Spanish Succession, that immediately followed.

[77] Davenport, ed., *European Treaties*, III, 10.
[78] See Chapter XIII.
[79] Davenport, ed., *European Treaties*, III, 16–28.

CHAPTER X

Angloamerica in the Diplomacy of the War of the Spanish Succession and the Peace of Utrecht, 1702-13

1. Early Wartime Negotiations

DURING ALMOST ALL the duration of the War of the Spanish Succession negotiations were carried on among the various participants in view of defining the conditions of the eventual peace. After a series of French disasters, including the defection of Portugal and Savoy, the loss of Gibraltar, the arrival of the Archduke Charles (proclaimed King Carlos III of Spain by the allies in Vienna, September 19, 1703) in Spain to claim the Spanish throne, and the military defeat at Blenheim (1704),[1] Louis actively began to negotiate for an end to the war. His desire to make peace may have been intensified somewhat by the fact that a number of campaigns had been fought in America, the outcome of which had been generally unfavorable to the Franco-Spanish cause. Spanish Florida was attacked by forces from English Carolina, which, after years of hostilities in this area, seized upon the war as an occasion to eradicate the Spanish threat and opposition to English expansion, as well as to prevent French reinforcement of St. Augustine. An attack on St. Augustine in 1702 placed the city in English hands, but the fortress, the Castillo de San Marcos, remained impregnable and the Carolinians retreated without having broken the Spanish hold on Florida. Another attack by Carolinians, in 1703, in the Apalachee region, ended Spanish control north of the St. Johns River and placed that area with its lucrative fur trade in English hands. By 1708 the English, through their Indian allies, had secured a fairly firm possession of the entire southeast, from Charleston to Mobile Bay, with the exception of the Florida peninsula.[2]

[1] This defeat was to be followed at fairly regular intervals by the disasters at Ramillies (1706), Oudenaarde (1708), and Malplaquet (1709).
[2] Wright, "English-Spanish Rivalry in North America, 1432–1763," 125.

Meanwhile, in the Caribbean area, several changes had taken place. In 1702 the English captured the French part of St. Christopher; in 1706 the French captured the English island of Nevis. In South America the Portuguese captured the province of Maranhão, which lay south of the Amazon but was claimed by France.

In the face of France's generally unfavorable position, both in Europe and in America, Louis was confronted by a number of issues involved in the negotiating of peace, both with regard to matters that concerned the objectives of the individual dynastic and national participants in the war and with regard to the larger international issues that had helped to motivate it. Chief among these issues, both because of its own significance and because it involved so many other aspects of the war, was the disposition of the Spanish monarchy. Louis, desiring to profit from all opportunities, tried, largely unsuccessfully, to obtain the "full-powers" of his grandson, Philip of Anjou, whom he had recognized as king of Spain, in order for his own plenipotentiaries to negotiate for Spain, especially on the subject of commerce. Philip and his government do not seem to have accepted Louis's efforts, for the Court of Bergeyck appeared at all the early negotiations making proposals to the allies, especially the Dutch, on behalf of Spain.[3] Because of the military and diplomatic setbacks of 1703 and 1704, Louis lost hope of securing the entire Spanish monarchy for Philip, and, in October of 1705, proposed a partition in the hope of retaining at least a portion of the Spanish inheritance. By these terms, Philip would relinquish Naples, Sicily, and the Spanish Netherlands. The proposal was not accepted by the allies.

In June, 1706, the Archduke Charles was re-proclaimed King Carlos III of Spain and the Indies by the allies in Madrid. Louis, in view of this situation and with the hope of luring the Dutch into an alliance, informed Grand Pensionary Antonie Heinsius, in August, 1706, that he was willing to surrender Spain and the Indies if Philip retained Naples, Sicily, and Milan, with the title of king. The Duke of Marlborough,[4] when he learned of these overtures, refused to consider them, for he believed England obliged to preserve the Spanish monarchy entire. In truth, he thought Bourbon rule in Italy threatened England's Mediterranean trade by giving the French yet another base for competition.[5]

In 1707 Philip's forces regained most of Spain and "Carlos III" left Madrid for Barcelona. Louis's bargaining position was thus much stronger

---

[3] Dahlgren, *Les rélations commerciales et maritimes entre la France et les côtes de l'Océan Pacifique*, I, 579–580.

[4] The Duke of Marlborough played a decisive role in British military and diplomatic policies from 1701 until his fall from power in 1711. In 1701 King William III appointed him commander in chief of English forces and ambassador extraordinary with the task of framing the new Grand Alliance. Both roles he retained until his fall; as ambassador he directed the early negotiations for peace.

[5] Davenport, ed., *European Treaties*, III, 133.

and he exploited it in an attempt to draw the Dutch into a separate peace. Nicolas Mesnager was sent to Holland to confer. The Dutch at this time were disturbed by the exclusiveness of the commercial privileges granted to the English by "Carlos III" of Spain, and were concerned about the future of their own West Indian trade. Louis had long been aware of the divergencies of commercial interests among the allies of the Grand Alliance, and he now sought, by exploiting these differences, to sow discord among the allies. Mesnager was directed to persuade the Dutch of commercial advantages which would accrue to them if they supported Philip's rule in Spain. Officially, the Dutch held to the principles of the Grand Alliance and declared they would never consent to allow the Indies to fall into the hands of any prince other than "Carlos III." [6] But in secret they listened to the French proposals and offered their conditions. On the subject of commerce they were adamant: the status of the Dutch and the English in the trade of Spain and the Indies was to grow no worse; the status of the French must grow no better.[7]

The military campaigns of 1708 were disastrous for the French, and Louis again prepared to surrender Spain and the Indies to "Carlos III." Philip V, however, refused to relinquish his holdings, and Amelot de Chaillou, French ambassador to Spain, protested to Louis against the abandonment of Philip, believing that for Spain to fall into the hands of the Hapsburgs would be more disastrous for France than a continuation of the war. Louis, convinced, resolved to continue his defense of Spain and the Indies.[8] Meanwhile, Philip, independently of France, had sent the Comte de Bergeyck to the Dutch at the end of 1708 to make overtures on his behalf. Bergeyck was authorized to propose that Spain and the Indies be left to Philip V with the sacrifice of Spanish Italy to "Carlos III" and the Spanish Netherlands to the Dutch.[9] In return for their support of Philip, the allies were offered participation in the commerce of the Indies as members of a trading company which would give equal and perpetual interest to the Spanish, French, English, and Dutch. To the Dutch Bergeyck was authorized to grant all the accessory advantages they desired for their commerce in Spain and the Indies and promised that the *asiento* would be included in the commerce of the proposed company. The Dutch demanded that the French be excluded from the company, to which Bergeyck, pretending a break between France and Spain, seemed to consent. Then the Dutch, led by the English, demanded that Louis himself remove Philip from the throne of Spain, by force of arms if necessary. To this Louis could not consent and the negotiations collapsed.[10]

[6] Scelle, *La traite Négrière aux Indes de Castille*, II, 477.
[7] Dahlgren, *Les rélations commerciales et maritimes*, I, 564.
[8] Scelle, *La traite négrière*, 478.
[9] Davenport, ed., *European Treaties*, III, 134.
[10] Scelle, *La traite Négrière*, II, 478–481.

Despite his generous promises Philip's agent was unable to make the preliminary concessions first demanded by the Dutch of Mesnager. The Dutch agent, Van der Dussen, had asked for "Spain, the Indies, the Milanese and the Spanish Netherlands, together with what has been added, as also a favorable treaty of commerce." [11] Louis XIV, learning of Van der Dussen's memorial, accepted its terms as a basis for negotiation and sent Pierre Antoine Rouillé to the Netherlands in March, 1709, to treat for peace.

The English, hearing of these negotiations and fearing the defection of their Dutch allies, announced themselves willing to sign a barrier treaty which the Dutch had long desired as security against French aggression. In return, Marlborough demanded that no peace negotiations be concluded with France until England and the States-General had agreed on the preliminaries. These preliminaries were drawn up by both the English and the Dutch and expressed the deepest desires of each nation. The Dutch demanded a barrier against the French and the cession of certain cities which would enable them to dominate the Spanish Netherlands.[12] The English preliminaries required recognition of the Archduke Charles ("Carlos III") as king of the entire Spanish monarchy and evacuation of Spain by Philip V and his French troops and officers. If Philip did not leave Spain within the stipulated time Louis XIV was to help drive him out. France was to recognize the Protestant succession in England, conclude a treaty of commerce with that country, and raze the fortifications at Dunkirk; the Dutch were to be granted their barrier and terms of commerce with France such as were stipulated by the Treaty of Ryswick and the tariff of 1644.[13] In America France was to be excluded absolutely and perpetually from the Spanish Indies. It was to cede all its possessions on Newfoundland to England; the English later added the cession of Hudson Bay to these demands.[14]

In May of 1709 Marlborough and Viscount Charles Townshend were appointed ambassadors to the States-General, with whom they were to work for a renewal of the Grand Alliance and to work out the preliminaries of the peace. The French were informed that there would be no cessation of arms until the allies had agreed on the terms of the preliminaries. Included in the ambassadors' instructions from Queen Anne were directions to require the "restoration" of Hudson Bay and Newfoundland according to ancient British claims: [15] "We think our just right to New-

---

[11] Quoted in Davenport, ed., *European Treaties*, III, 135.

[12] Devenport, ed., *European Treaties*, III, 135.
Actes et Mémoires touchant la Paix d'Utrecht, I, 33–54.

[13] "Articles préliminaires arrêtés en 1709. Pour servir au Traité de la Paix générale,"

[14] Davenport, ed., *European Treaties*, III, 136.

[15] For a discussion of these claims contemporary to these negotiations, see Doc. 554: Council of Trade and Plantations to the Queen, June 2, 1709, in *C.S.P.*, *Col.*, *A.& W.I.*, 1708–09, pp. 323–340.

foundland and Hudson's Bay to be of so great and necessary importance to Us and Our Realms that We cannot give Our consent to a Peace unless the aforesaid countrys and places be agreed to be restored to us." [16] The ambassadors were especially directed to insist that the cession of Newfoundland and Hudson Bay be articles in the preliminaries.[17] The great concern for the protection of English interests displayed in the instructions to the British ambassadors reveals the cracks in the Grand Alliance. The British ministers saw clearly that if the Dutch continued to negotiate as before the interests of the allies would be lost by the impatience of the Dutch to conclude the peace when their own interests had been comprehended in the preliminaries.[18] When these demands were presented to the French, the Marquis de Torcy, who had recently joined Rouillé, protested but finally agreed to the cession of Newfoundland on the condition that the British restore French holdings in the West Indies which had been taken during the war. The fate of Hudson Bay, however, he wanted referred to the negotiations of the general treaty, it being "chiefly a matter of accounts" which could be taken up by the commissioners who, prior to the war, had been appointed to settle the intercolonial disputes in that area.[19] The English were adamant in their determination that the demanded territories be relinquished to them. Secretary of State Henry Boyle informed his ambassadors that the Queen was determined to have the whole of Newfoundland and especially desired to possess the French base at Placentia as soon as possible and without any compensatory restoration of French West Indian territories. Boyle moreover insisted that the matter of Hudson Bay was more than a mere matter of accounts and that "the Crown of England has an undoubted right of title to the whole Bay and Streights of Hudson, and therefore her Majesty can never relinquish that claim." [20]

Conferences between the English ambassadors, Heinsius, the French plenipotentiaries Torcy and Rouillé, and Prince Eugene and Graf Philipp von Sinzendorff, representing the Empire, began immediately upon the arrival of the English representatives. The allies felt confident that the distress in which France found itself would force Louis XIV to make sacrifices rather than open the spring military campaign.[21] After several days the allies drew up a project to serve as a basis for a general peace. It was somewhat modified by the observations of the French plenipoten-

[16] Instructions to Marlborough and Townshend, May 2, 1709, in Legg, ed., British Diplomatic Instructions, II, France, 1689–1721, 11.

[17] Legg, ed., British Diplomatic Instructions, II, France, 1689–1721, xvi–xvii.

[18] Doc. 2923: Marlborough and Townshend to Secretary Boyle, May 19, 1709, in Mss. of the House of Lords, N.S., IX, 264–265.

[19] Doc. 2923, Marlborough and Townshend to Secretary Boyle; May 21, 1709, in Mss. of the House of Lords, 1710–1717, N.S., IX, 266.

[20] Boyle to Marlborough and Townshend, May 18, 1709, in Legg, ed., British Diplomatic Instructions, France, II, 1689–1721, 12–13.

[21] Davenport, ed., European Treaties, III, 132.

tiaries and was signed by the representatives of the Grand Alliance on May 28. The project provided that Louis XIV recognize the Archduke Charles as king of the entire Spanish monarchy, that Philip retire from Spain along with all French troops there or elsewhere in Spanish dominions. France was to be absolutely excluded from the Spanish West Indies and was to cede its possessions on Newfoundland to Britain. The French plenipotentiaries objected unsuccessfully to the absolute exclusion of France from the Spanish Indies because the Spanish had always allowed an indirect trade in necessary French goods; they desired that their trade in the Indies be allowed on the same terms as during the reign of Carlos II. The cession of Newfoundland was agreed to by the French plenipotentiaries on the understanding that the conditions thereof be settled during the conclusion of the general treaty of peace. As for Hudson Bay, the English plenipotentiaries, contrary to their instructions, agreed to refer the whole matter, including the indemnification of injured English subjects, to commissioners.[22] Louis XIV, although he had agreed to the cession of Newfoundland to the British and of Alsace to the Empire and to the destruction of France's West Indian commerce, knew he could not bring about the cession of the Spanish monarchy to "Carlos III," and he was, in any case, unwilling to turn French arms against his grandson. So he refused to sign the project and revoked all his offers to the allies, thus breaking off the negotiations.

2. The Gertruydenberg Conferences, 1710

France's affairs continued badly, and the next year Louis again made efforts for peace. Conferences were held at Gertruydenberg, in the Netherlands, from March to July, 1710, between the French plenipotentiaries, Marshal d'Huxelles and the Abbé Polignac, and the Dutch deputies, Villem Buys and Van der Dussen. The Dutch demands were based upon a project of peace published in January of 1710, which in the matter of the West Indies and the disposition of the Spanish monarchy largely repeated the preliminaries of 1709. After stipulating that no part of the Spanish monarchy could ever belong to a French prince, the project added that "the Spanish Indies shall be comprised in everything that shall be said of the Kingdom of Spain, as composing a principle part of it, and the King will not permit any vessel belonging to his subjects to go to the said Indies, whether to carry on trade or under any other pretext." [23] Not only did the Dutch show themselves here to have come to follow the English policy with regard to the Indies, but their demands for French exclusion from the Caribbean trade shows the strength of this principle. After almost

---

[22] Davenport, ed., *European Treaties*, III, 137–139.
[23] Quoted in Scelle, *La traite négrière*, II, 482.

eight years of war, their own agitaiton for a barrier, and the English maneuver to exclude them from the Indies, the Dutch still stressed this, one of the principles for which the Grand Alliance had first undertaken the war.

Although the Spanish were, by Louis's command, represented by the French plenipotentiaries, the Comte de Bergeyck appeared at the Gertruydenberg conferences, making direct offers to the allies on the part of Philip V. Chief among these was the guarantee of "all the advantages and all the securities that the two powers [England and the Netherlands] may demand for their commerce" in exchange for retention of Philip on the Spanish throne.[24]

Louis was unable to resist the demand of the allies that France be excluded from the West Indian commerce and he even offered to pay subsidies to the allies to help them carry on their war against Philip V. But he would not consent to the Dutch demand that he either persuade Philip, his grandson, to renounce the whole Spanish monarchy or compel him by means of French forces to leave Spain and, within two months, place "Carlos III" on the throne.[25] Turning their resentment against the Dutch, Louis and his ministers refused to listen to further propositions from Holland, and so the conferences at Gertruydenberg came to an end.

By the latter part of 1710 several changes had occurred in the situations of the antagonists which somewhat strengthened the French bargaining position. In the European military arena, the allied victory at Malplaquet in 1709 proved a great disappointment: the allies suffered heavy financial losses and Marlborough failed to destroy the French army as he had intended or to march to Paris as the English had hoped. The British were growing weary of the war and had been disappointed by the allies' failure to make peace at Gertruydenberg. In Spain the forces of the allies lost ground until, by autumn of 1709, only Catalonia remained under the control of the Archduke Charles.[26]

In America, the English, in 1710, captured French Acadia. A great expedition was also sent against Quebec under the command of Sir Hovenden Walker, but this expedition ended in catastrophe. Fighting between these two powers in Hudson Bay and Newfoundland had been inconclusive, but the overall position of the English was stronger. During 1712, the French appeared to be preparing an invasion of St. Christopher in the West Indies. A raid of French privateers did take place, but it did not seriously affect the English tenure of the island.

English policy was changed by the fall of Marlborough and the rise of the Tories to power under the leadership of Robert Harley, the Count of

---

[24] Dahlgren, *Les rélations commerciales et maritimes*, I, 580. The role of Austria in these negotiations, especially in the disposition of the "new world" and of Spanish commerce, was rather small.

[25] Davenport, ed., *European Treaties*, III, 140.

[26] Trevelyan, *England under Queen Anne*, II, *passim*.

Oxford, and Edward Villiers, the Earl of Jersey. The new ministers, following the sentiments of their heavily taxed nation, desired peace. At the same time, the French victory at Villaviciosa and the later abandonment of Charles by the Allies assured Philip V of the throne of Spain. The fidelity of the Spanish people to Philip was assured, and the alliance between Spain and France was renewed. The departure of the Archduke Charles from the Spanish scene ended one of the major obstacles to peace. Because Charles was no longer able to procure for the English the commercial advantages stipulated in their treaty of 1707, the English turned to Philip V to seek equivalent concessions from him. English support the candidacy of Charles as "Carlos III" of Spain was abandoned with finality when the Holy Roman Emperor Joseph I died in April of 1711, placing the Archduke on the Austrian throne as Emperor Charles VI. Under these circumstances, Charles's sovereignty over Spain and its dominions would endanger the balance of power as much as their retention by the Bourbon Philip. The English claimed that since support of Charles's claim was not one of the original objectives of the Grand Alliance of 1701 they were able to drop it without betraying the terms of the alliance. At the same time the British were much disturbed by the apparent neglect by the Dutch, who were most concerned with European affairs, of British commercial and colonial interests. Henry St. John, writing to an English agent in Amsterdam, expressed the general English dissatisfaction with the course of the Gertruydenberg parlays:

Holland . . . gains a great barrier, daily extends her dominion, and keeps her trade uncramped by prohibitions. I doubt Britain, was this war to conclude tomorrow with the evacuation of Spain and the Indies, would have no particular advantage above the common one, except such as would be very precarious, since it would depend upon Austrian gratitude. [27]

3. The Preliminaries of Peace, 1710-11

As early as the end of 1710 the English ministry had made known to the French through Abbé Gautier, an agent of Torcy residing in London, that it desired peace with the assurance of sufficient commercial advantages and that the English court would no longer absolutely insist on the surrender of the entire Spanish monarchy to the Hapsburgs. Louis XIV was asked to renew negotiations with the Dutch and afterward enter separate and secret negotiations with the English. Resentful of his humiliation at Gertruydenberg, Louis refused to deal further with the Dutch, who nevertheless did not cease to make proposals, but he was willing to negotiate with England. The Tory leaders then demanded that France estab-

[27] Bolingbroke to Mr. Drummond, Nov. 17, 1710, in Parke, ed., *Letters of Bolingbroke*, I, 15.

lish the terms of peace to serve as bases for negotiation and to be communicated to the other allies, the English desiring to conceal their own overtures to France.[28] This secrecy was at first a matter of outbidding the Dutch, a not difficult task in view of that nation's obstinacy with regard to the disposition of the Spanish throne. It was also essential to prevent the breakup of the already strained Grand Alliance before a suspension of arms had been declared. Hence the need for secrecy and the illusion that France had submitted the "spontaneous" offers that were, in fact, dictated by the English.

The demands of the Tory ministers were not essentially different from those of their Whig predecessors. Repeated was the insistence on the recognition of the Protestant succession in England, the destruction of French fortifications at Dunkirk, the cession of Newfoundland, Hudson Bay, and St. Christopher, a grant of trading privileges in the West Indies, specifically in the form of the *asiento*, and a new commercial treaty with France. Different was the emphasis placed on these demands. The insistence that Philip V be ejected from Spain was laid aside on British acceptance of a promise that the crowns of France and Spain would never be united. The maintenance of the barrier, which had come first in the Whig demands and had been specified as to towns and areas to be included in the barrier, was demanded by the Tories only in principle and its details were left to be settled at the general congress. In contrast was the preciseness of British demands for the satisfaction of their own interests. These included the definite cession of Gibraltar and Port Mahon, and the grant of the *asiento* to Britain for a period of thirty years, together with the grant of certain places in America to Britain for the convenience of the *asiento* traders. The concern of the Tories who made the preliminaries was with English commercial interests in America and the Mediterranean rather than with European entanglements.

Six articles, closely conforming to the English proposals, were signed by Torcy on April 22, 1711. They provided for: (1) securities for British trade in Spain, the Indies, and the Mediterranean; (2) a barrier in the Low Countries and the security for Dutch commerce; (3) satisfaction for the other allies; (4) settlement of the Spanish monarchy, with security for the trade and interests of all belligerents; (5) immediate opening of peace conferences; (6) Aix-la-Chapelle or Liège as the site of the general peace conference.[29] These proposals were then communicated to the Dutch, who, like the English, desired elucidation of these general proposals. In July, Matthew Prior, the poet-statesman, was sent to Paris to discuss the preliminaries. His instructions stressed the commercial advantages which he was to secure for England: control of the Newfoundland fisheries, cession of Gibraltar and Port Mahon (to which the King and

[28] Parke, ed., *Letters of Bolingbroke*, III, 141.
[29] Davenport, ed., *European Treaties*, III, 141.

Queen of Spain had consented at the beginning of these negotiations), trade privileges in Spain equal to those granted the French (most-favored-nation status), and the concession of the *asiento*.[30]

In July, also, Secretary of State St. John went to France with Abbé Gautier to communicate England's precise demands which were to be settled by the peace. The first was for a guarantee that the crowns of France and Spain would never be united, now a greater possibility than before since the death of the Dauphin on April 14, 1711, which placed Philip of Anjou in direct line for succession to the throne of France. The other demands were repeated, but with greater precision: for Britain were demanded the recognition of the Protestant succession; a new treaty of commerce between Britain and France; demolition of Dunkirk; cession of Gibraltar and Port Mahon as permanent security for British Mediterranean commerce; concession of the *asiento* for the South Sea Company; and cession of certain American places, two in the north and two in the south, for the convenience of this commerce; most-favored-nation status in the Spanish trade; cession of places in Spanish America to protect England's trade there; cession of Newfoundland and Acadia and "restoration" of Hudson Bay; [31] and retention by both sides of all territories in North America which each nation would possess at the time of publication in America of the ratification of the peace treaty.[32] The English South Sea Company had by this time been chartered (June 23, 1711), and the demands for places in Spanish America were motivated by the desire to ensure the company's success. Despite French resistance to the granting of such places, Prior was adamant in his demands.

These conferences of the late summer of 1711, conducted in both Paris and London, brought forth the differences between French and English politics. The English desired only to speak of cessions in North America, but the French ministers Torcy and Mesnager were most concerned with the Dutch barrier. St. John was aware that England's future lay in its overseas trade and was determined to present his countrymen with a bounty of concessions. The privileges which he sought from France and Spain were therefore to be denied the Dutch, despite the terms of the Barrier Treaty of 1709 which had guaranteed equal commercial rights as between the English and Dutch. The interests of the Whig mercantile class and the bitter feelings of the Tories toward the Dutch were thus united in one program popular enough to bring the whole country to the support of the new ministry.[33]

Several factors supported the aggressiveness of the English demands for

[30] McLachlan, *Trade and Peace with Old Spain, 1667–1750*, 48.

[31] Acadia fell to an expedition of New Englanders and British marines in September, 1710. See Chapter IX.

[32] Legrelle, *La Succession d'Espagne*, IV, 594–595.

[33] Trevelyan, *England under Queen Anne*, III, 182.

cessions in America. The capture of Acadia placed this territory, with its strategic position at the mouth of the St. Lawrence, firmly in British hands. Pressure from the Hudson's Bay Company for a settlement of disputes over Hudson Bay and its surrounding territories had been strong since the highly unsatisfactory Treaty of Ryswick.[34] By 1711 British diplomats were much more conscious of the significance of Hudson Bay and were in a better position to argue their claims. For the French, retention of the bay was of critical importance because the whole economy and thus the very survival of New France depended upon the fur trade, in which Hudson Bay played a vital part. Despite this, Louis XIV instructed his envoys to agree to the cession of the bay. The English, however, were not satisfied with a mere cession. The Lords of Trade had conducted an inquiry into the disputed rights and claims to the bay and reported to Lord Dartmouth that the company had just title to the entire bay and straits. On these grounds the ministers insisted on a "restoration" of Hudson Bay, a change of language which would negate any future French claims or disputes about the terms of a cession.[35] There was similar pressure on the British envoys to obtain the cession of Newfoundland, and the fate of this island occupied most of the London conferences of 1711. The merchants of the West Country, jealous of French success in the Newfoundland fishery, pressed for the cession of the entire island to Britain and the debarment of the French from all commerce there. Both the French and the English were aware of the significant role which the Newfoundland fishery played in the development of French seamen and in the French economy, and both sides were finally obliged to compromise their original positions. The French firmly resisted English demands that they completely abandon Newfoundland; Louis XIV even consented to the cession of Hudson Bay in order to retain the rights of fishing and drying fish on Newfoundland and to affirm French claims to Cape Breton Island. The English, in the face of French determination, modified their demands for complete cession of Hudson Bay, Newfoundland, and Acadia, in which they included Cape Breton Island, to grant the French limited fishing rights on Newfoundland and the right to settle and fortify Cape Breton Island. Although aware of the potential difficulties of both these compromises, St. John nevertheless consented to them out of the necessity of hastening an agreement with the French in view of the weakness of his bargaining position after news of the failure of the British expedition against Quebec reached England. British demands for the cession of all of St. Christopher in the West Indies were strongly supported by the fact that the British had captured the French portion of the island in 1702 and had held it against French attacks since then.

[34] See Chapter IX.
[35] Rich, "The Hudson's Bay Company and the Treaty of Utrecht," *Cambridge Historical Journal*, XI (1954), 183–197.

The fate of the West Indies was another knotty problem which had to be resolved in these preliminary negotiations. Philip V absolutely refused to grant England's demand for "cautionary" towns in the Spanish West Indies, although Louis XIV, anxious for peace, was willing to compromise:

For myself I should wish that it might be possible to oblige them [the English] to desist from this demand for places in the Indies, because it is certain that if it be absolutely necessary to grant it, the commerce of my subjects will suffer no less than that of the Spaniards ... But if the peace depend upon it, peace is so necessary that we must purchase it at this price. And as I do not see that Spain is in condition to sustain the war without my help, it is necessary that the Catholic King have some regard for the needs of my kingdom. He would find himself too embarrassed if I were to withdraw the troops that I have sent him. [36]

The French took upon themselves the right to negotiate in the name of the Spanish, and Torcy warned Prior that England's demand for four places in the Indies would delay the peace and their cession would arouse the jealousy and opposition of the Dutch. Prior replied only that, since the terms of the settlement of the Indies were to be kept secret there was no reason to fear that the Dutch would demand similar concessions for themselves. Moreover, Prior declared that Britain would not protest if France were to demand places in the Indies for her own trade.[37] Spain, meanwhile, had been persuaded to relinquish its ownership of Gibraltar and Port Mahon, and to concede the *asiento* to England; the two Mediterranean ports were, after all, no longer in Spanish hands and since the Spanish themselves could not carry on the *asiento* it made little difference to them whether that trade was handled by the French or the English. The joint commercial company proposed in 1708 was offered again by Philip V's envoy, the Comte de Bergeyck, this time excluding the Dutch and giving the English a more preponderant position, but the English were adamant in their insistence on a monopoly of the Spanish West Indian trade. The Spanish then proposed to cede Gibraltar to the English in return for English abandonment of their demands for places in the Indies. Philip was anxious that the English receive no more extensive privileges with regard to the *asiento* than the French had enjoyed.

The desires of the Spanish somewhat modified the instructions given to the French envoy, Mesnager, when he went to London. When Mesnager informed the English of Spain's refusal to cede places in the Indies, Prior reduced the demand of four places to two, then demanded only permission for English agents to reside in the Indies to sell merchandise brought

---

[36] Louis XIV to Duc de Vendôme, June 22, 1711. Quoted in Scelle, *La traite Négrière*, II, 491.
[37] Legg, ed., "Torcy's Account of Matthew Prior's Negotiations," *Eng. Hist. Rev.*, xxix (1914), 530.

them by the Spanish and places where the agents of the South Sea Company could debark Negroes. Finally, St. John informed Mesnager that he would have to choose between protecting French or Spanish interests, because the English would be more demanding of cessions from the French in North America if they did not gain all they wanted from the Spanish. Mesnager chose to sacrifice Spanish interests and consented to the English demand that they be given the concession of the *asiento* for a period of thirty years, instead of the ten years granted the French, the only substitution the English would accept for the cession of definitely named places in America.

In the long run Spanish interests were better protected in these negotiations than were those of the French. England gained from Spain the *asiento*, cession of Gibraltar and Port Mahon, and guarantee of most-favored-nation status in the Spanish trade, but it relinquished its demand for places in the Indies and, since the English were not interested in forming the proposed joint commercial company, they did not gain the dominant position in the Spanish colonial trade through Cadiz which had been offered them. France, on the other hand, had lost Hudson Bay, Newfoundland, Acadia, and St. Christopher, had consented to demolish the fortifications at Dunkirk, to grant England a favorable treaty of commerce, and to recognize the Protestant succession in England.

In the beginning of September the Abbé *Gautier* carried the preliminary demands of Britain, which embodied the terms of the negotiations, to Versailles. A few weeks later he returned to London with the French replies to the English articles, authorization for Mesnager to sign the replies as conditions to be granted under a general treaty of peace, and a project of general proposals from France to her enemies. France agreed to the English demands for recognition of the Protestant succession: a favorable Anglo-French treaty of commerce; demolition of the fortifications at Dunkirk; cession of Gibraltar and Port Mahon in England; the concession of the *asiento* for thirty years; and most-favored-nation status in the commerce of Spain. With regard to the British demand for the cession of places in Spanish America to be named in the general treaty, the French were silent, although they agreed to assign the British a place on the Rio de la Plata for the refreshment and sale of slaves. The French consented to the cession of Hudson Bay and Newfoundland but reserved the right to fish and to dry fish on that island. French demands for the restoration of Acadia and renunciation of British claims to Cape Breton Island were referred to the general peace negotiations.

These preliminary articles were signed on October 8 by Mesnager, St. John, and Lord Dartmouth.[38] St. John told his Queen, "This agreement contains more advantages for your Majesty's Kingdom than were

---

[38] Text in Davenport, ed., *European Treaties*, III, 147–151.

ever, perhaps, stipulated for any nation at one time." [39] At the same time the general articles for the allies were signed.[40]

The French proposals to the allies for the general peace included replies to the English demands; cession of the Spanish Netherlands to Bavaria to serve as the barrier for Holland, augmented by certain French cities given in exchange for other cities which would form a barrier for France; the demolition of the fortifications at Dunkirk in exchange for possession of the cities of Lille and Tournai; the commerce of Spain and the Indies to be carried on as it was during the reign of Carlos II, with the French, like all other nations, holding to those laws; the renunciation by Philip V of all claims to the Kingdom of Naples, Sardinia, and the Duchy of Milan; the renunciation by the House of Austria of all claims to the Spanish monarchy and the withdrawal of all Austrian troops from Spanish territory immediately after the establishment of peace; and the permanent cession of certain territories to the Duke of Savoy.[41]

4. The Congress of Utrecht, 1712

The French preliminaries to the general peace, as accepted by Britain, were unsatisfactory to the other allies. The Dutch complained of the vagueness of these articles and accused the English of having advanced their own commercial interests contrary to the terms of the Barrier Treaty of 1709, which had promised the Dutch most-favored-nation status in Spanish dominions. The States-General sent Villem Buys to London in October of 1711 to obtain more specific preliminaries from France and a permanent alliance with Britain, but his mission was a failure because the English ministry was determined that no negotiations could take place with the Dutch until they agreed to enter the general peace conferences. An Anglo-Dutch treaty was, indeed, drafted, but it was not ratified by the States-General because it did not confirm earlier treaties. The English ministry had opposed such a provision of confirmation because it was determined that the Barrier Treaty of 1709 must be annuled in order to prevent the Dutch from using the terms of that treaty to claim an equal share in the *asiento* or in other hoped-for advantages in the Spanish trade. The Dutch finally yielded to British pressure and agreed to participate in a congress to treat for peace on the basis of the preliminary articles. The congress was scheduled to open at Utrecht in January, 1712.

The Austrians also objected to the preliminaries because they did not

[39] Trevelyan, *England under Queen Anne*, III, 185.
[40] Text in *Actes, Mémoires, et autres pièces authentiques concernant la Paix d'Utrecht*, I.
[41] *Actes. Mémoires, et autres pièces authentiques concernant la Paix d'Utrecht*, I, 308–313.

provide for the allotment of Spain and the Indies to an Austrian prince. But since the Dutch had consented to participate in the congress, Emperor Charles VI also consented. Portugal and Savoy protested the articles because they implied that Spain would remain in the hands of a Bourbon prince, an eventuality contrary to the Anglo-Portuguese and Anglo-Savoy treaties of alliance, which provided that no peace would be made while a Bourbon prince ruled Spain. But they, too, agreed to attend the congress.

The congress opened on January 29, 1712. The first task of the plenipotentiaries was to agree to a cessation of arms, possible only when the terms of the peace had been settled. The English representatives, the Bishop of Bristol and the Earl of Stratford, were instructed to demand, with regard to America, the same conditions agreed upon in the London preliminaries of October 8, 1711, with the additional request that they endeavor to fix the boundaries of English and French settlements in North America, that the Hudson's Bay Company be recompensed for damages inflicted by the French, and that the French cease interference with Indian allies of the British. In European matters the English demands repeated earlier ones for barriers between France, Holland, and the Empire, recognition of the Hanoverian succession in England, cession of Gibraltar, and an Anglo-French commercial treaty. The English plenipotentiaries were not informed of their government's tacit agreement that Philip V should be allowed to remain on the Spanish throne; they were instructed only to insist on the separation of the crowns of France and Spain, the desire of the government being to conceal from its allies the special advantages which Britain hoped to gain from Spain.[42]

France was represented by the Marquis d'Huxelles, the Abbé de Polignac, and Nicolas Mesnager, who had negotiated previously at Gertruydenberg and London. They were directed to ensure Philip V's control of the Spanish throne by accepting the partition of the Spanish monarchy and by commercial and territorial concessions from France. Essentially, their task was to reach an accord with the English; the demands of the Dutch and other belligerents were expected to be silenced by English pressure when the English felt that satisfactory conditions for peace had been achieved.[43] Terms regarding British interests had been settled by the London preliminaries with the exception of the fate of Newfoundland, the discussion concerning this island having been put off until the peace conferences. Specific instructions concerning Newfoundland were contained in a memoir from the Comte de Pontchartrain to the French plenipotentiaries.[44]

Pontchartrain's memoir defended French possession of Canada and re-

[42] Instructions of the Queen to the Bishop of Bristol and the Earl of Stratford; December 23, 1711, H.L.R.B., 78442, II, Pièces.
[43] Letter of Louis XIV to his plenipotentiaries; Jan. 30, 1712. Cited in Davenport, ed., European Treaties, III, 155n.
[44] A.E., Méms. et Docs.: Amérique, 22: fols. 13–42.

fused the justification of any English demands for cession. The only acceptable settlement regarding Canada would be one, based on the Treaty of Ryswick (Articles 7 and 8), adjusting boundaries between French and English colonies. The propriety of French titles to Newfoundland, Acadia, and Hudson Bay were defended. The plenipotentiaries were instructed to cede Newfoundland to English demands under the following conditions: (1) that the French be allowed to demolish their fortification at Placentia, removing all their arms and munitions, and that the English not rebuild there; (2) that the French have two years in which to retire with their effects; (3) that French fishing rights, including rights of drying and salting fish, be continued as before the war; (4) that Acadia, including Port Royal, be restored to the French and that Cape Breton Island remain their undisputed possession. If necessary for retention of the Newfoundland cod fishery, the French plenipotentiaries were directed to consent to the preservation of the fortifications at Placentia for the British. So important were Acadia and Cape Breton considered for the defense of the St. Lawrence River that as a last resort even the Newfoundland fishing rights might be given up to keep these places secure in French hands. Also, the English version of the boundary of Acadia, that is, the St. George River rather than the Kennebec River, would be accepted if this would preserve Acadia for the French. Hudson Bay would also be ceded in its entirety with the sole final condition that the French be given navigation rights there in case of the discovery of a northwest passage. With regard to the Caribbean, Pontchartrain directed the plenipotentiaries to cede St. Christopher if the English would give up their claims to Placentia and Newfoundland. The French Leeward Islands of St. Martin and St. Barthélemy might be offered for this purpose. Nevis, which had been captured by the French, was to remain in French hands until the exchange of prisoners and surrender of English slaves, agreed upon at the English surrender of the island, should be completed. St. Augustine, in Spanish Florida, was to be requested from the English, who were to be assured that the city would not be used by the French as a base for their claims against Carolina, but would be ceded to the Spanish, along with Louisiana, for the protection of Spanish holdings in the Caribbean, especially Havana and the Bahama channel. This would be in the nature of an exchange for the cession to the French of the Spanish part of Santo Domingo, a cession which Pontchartrain reminded the plenipotentiaries was the "greatest service" which Spain could render Louis XIV, since their joint possession of the island had long been a source of conflict. St. Croix, with its strategic location, could be used as a bargaining point, either to make Spain cede Santo Domingo or to trade with England for Newfoundland or Hudson Bay. Regarding Franco-Portuguese relations, the most important settlement was that of the boundary between Portuguese Brazil and French Guiana, a boundary which the plenipotentiaries were directed to have placed at the Amazon River, assuring a part in the river trade for France. Maranhão could be ceded to Portugal in exchange for the Amazon boundary. Regarding the *asiento* demanded by Britain, the French government was willing to allow this concession for the thirty-year period demanded by the English, provided that the French be allowed until 1715 to fulfill their own *asiento* contract. Otherwise, France would consider sharing the *asiento*, English participation then to commence immediately, or else would exchange the three years the French *asiento* was still supposed to run for England's surrender of its place in Buenos Aires.

Austria sent Graf von Sinzendorff, who was directed to insist on the preliminaries of 1709, which gave Spain and the Indies to Austria, and to offer the English all the advantages in Spanish territories which they might receive from France or Philip V.

The Dutch continued their objections to leaving Philip V on the Spanish throne, their chief interest being their own trade in the Spanish Indies and their fear of not securing it if Philip continued his rule. They continued to insist on an equal share with the British in the Spanish trade.

Portugal continued to support the claims of the Emperor Charles VI to the Spanish thrown. From France was demanded cession of the Brazilian Cap du Nord, which lay between the Amazon and Vincent Pinson (Oyapock) Rivers and was claimed by the Portuguese to belong to the province of Maranhão.[45]

As the negotiations proceeded the breach between Britain and her allies, which had been evident from the time of the preliminary discussions, continued to widen. The demands of the Dutch for equal trading rights were resented by the English, who felt they had borne a disproportionate share of the war and thus deserved special compensation. In February of 1712 the British House of Commons adopted resolutions denouncing the Barrier Treaty of 1709 as detrimental to English trade and interests. The next month the House declared that the Dutch and Austrians had failed to fulfill the terms of the Grand Alliance, which had forced Britain to assume an unequal share of the burden of the war. The Barrier Treaty was again denounced as having neglected English commercial interests in Spain and Spanish dominions and as having been made without either the crown of England being a party to it or the Spanish government having ever observed the terms of the treaty.

Attempts to reach a peace settlement continued. In March the representatives of the Grand Alliance presented their demands to France. The English repeated their earlier demands concerning North America. Then, to allow Britain and France opportunity to arrange a plan of a general peace, the official activities of the congress were suspended for several months beginning at the end of March. During this time the two govern-

[45] *Actes, Mémoires, et autres pièces authentiques concernant la Paix d'Utrecht,* I, 326–328.

ments attempted to settle disputes between them regarding: (1) prevention of a union of the French and Spanish crowns; (2) a suspension of arms; (3) commercial and colonial problems; (4) satisfaction of the demands of other participants in the war.

European fears of a union of the crowns of France and Spain had been aggravated by the death of the Dauphin, the Duc de Burgundy, in February of 1712. Then, a month later, his older son, the Duc de Bretagne, also died, leaving only a sickly child, the Duc de Berry, younger son of the Dauphin, between Philip V of Spain and the throne of France.[46] To assuage the fears of the allies and to enable peace talks to continue, Louis XIV proposed that Philip either renounce all his claims to the throne of France and content himself with possessions of Spain and the Indies or else yield Spain and the Indies to the Duke of Savoy and receive in exchange the crowns of Savoy and Sicily, thus making himself available to succeed his grandfather in case of the death of the young Dauphin.[47]

Philip chose to retain the crown of Spain and to surrender the place in the French succession promised him by Louis XIV's letters patent of 1700 on the Spanish succession.[48] The decision was later confirmed by a series of royal renunciations. Philip renounced all claim to the French throne and provided for the succession of the Spanish throne, in the event of the failure of his line, through the House of Savoy. The right to the French throne was transferred to the Duc de Berry and his descendents and in the event of the failure of this line, through the line of the Duc d'Orléans and, finally, the Duc de Bourbon.[49] The Duc de Berry and the Duc d'Orléans, for their part, renounced all rights to the throne of Spain and confirmed the succession of the House of Savoy in the event of the failure of Philip's line.[50]

The problem of the separation of the two crowns having been settled, Britain consented to a suspension of arms. A temporary cessation of fighting, signed by French and English ministers in June of 1712, limited the area of the truce to Flanders and had, as a condition, the surrender of Dunkirk to the English and the future acknowledgment by all parties of Philip V and his issue as successors to the throne of Spain. As conditions for a general suspension of arms Britain demanded the recognition of the right of succession to the throne of Spain of the Duke of Savoy in the event of the failure of Philip's line. When terms, including this condition, had

[46] The Duc de Berry later succeeded his great-grandfather to the throne of France as Louis XV.

[47] Torcy to Bolingbroke, May 13, 1712, *Letters of Bolingbroke*, I, 496–497.

[48] Included in *Lettres-patentes du Roy, du mois de Mars mil sept cens treize; par lesquelles Sa Majesté a admis la Renonciation faite à la Couronne de France par le Roy d'Espagne son Petit-fils*, (1713), 20–22.

[49] *Lettres-patentes du Roy*, 6–14. Dated Nov. 7, 1712 (N.S.).

[50] *Lettres-patentes du Roy*, 15–18 and 18–20. Dated Nov. 24 and Nov. 19, 1712, respectively.

been agreed upon, the general convention of a worldwide cessation of arms between Britain and France was signed in August of 1712, to last until December, and was ratified by Philip V in November, after the publication of the royal renunciations and acknowledgment of the rights of succession of the Duke of Savoy. After Philip's ratification the truce was prolonged until April of 1713.

5. The British Asiento, 1713, and the Anglo-Spanish Peace

After the suspension of arms Britain sent Robert Sutton, the Baron Lexington, to Spain as special ambassador. He was to effect Britain's formal recognition of Philip as King of Spain, to receive confirmation from Spain of French promises, especially to treat concerning the *asiento*, and to obtain satisfaction of the demands of English commercial houses in Cadiz. These merchants desired reestablishment of former treaties of commerce between England and Spain; enjoyment of all the commercial privileges in Spain which had been granted other nations, especially France and the Hansiatic cities, since the arrival of Philip V; restitution of all prizes and confiscations taken during the war; rights of free exportation of English manufactured goods to the Spanish Indies, paying only two per cent duties and receiving silver as payment, being restricted only to using Spanish vessels.[51] This direct negotiation was undertaken partly on the recommendation of France in response to England's demands for cessions of territory in the Indies from Spain, especially the demand for a post on the Rio de la Plata.[52]

Philip used this occasion to rid himself of the mediation of France and to bargain directly for Spain's role in the peace. Baron Lexington arrived in Madrid in October, 1712, and presented Britain's demands: (1) recognition of the Hanoverian succession in England; (2) Philip V's renunciation of all claims to the French throne; (3) renewal of former Anglo-Spanish treaties; (4) cession of Minorca and (5) Gibraltar to Britain; (6) cession of Sicily to Savoy; (7) Spanish commerce conducted on the same terms as during the reign of Carlos II; (8) the *asiento* granted to Britain for thirty years, with some land on the Rio de la Plata; (9) exemption from duties on British products and goods in Spanish and Spanish-American ports; (10) most-favored-nation status in the Spanish trade; (11) amnesty to Spanish supporters of the House of Austria.[53] The Spanish almost immediately granted articles 1, 2, 3, 7, 8, and 10. Articles 4, 5, 6, 9, and 11 were referred to the Marqués de Monteleon for discussion in London. Monteleon was also directed to receive assurance from the British

[51] Scelle, *La traite négrière*, II, 528–529.
[52] McLachlan, *Trade and Peace with Old Spain, 1667–1750*, 49.
[53] Davenport, ed., *European Treaties*, III, 167.

that the fishery of Newfoundland would remain open as previously to Guipúzcoans and other Spanish subjects. The demands for the *asiento* and cession of a district on the Rio de la Plata were granted with the restriction that the asientists build no fortifications in their plantation and that they submit to inspections by a Spanish official appointed by Philip.

British desire to exclude other nations, especially France, from the Indies motivated their abandonment of their demand for an exemption from Spanish duties. The Comte de Bergeyck succeeded in convincing Lexington that an exemption from the duties would be more embarrassing to Britain in its execution than its value was worth. Although Lexington continued to urge publicly the cession of this exemption, he privately admitted its disadvantages:

if they grant it [the exemption from the duty] to us, they must grant it to all the world, then the French and Dutch will carry their commoditys to the West Indies custom free, which will glut the market so that they will be of no value when they come. Therefore Y think we had better stick to our clandestine trade, wich [sic] by the Assiento we have entirely to ourselves exclusively to all the world . . . and make it as difficult to others as we can . . . [54]

After Lexington had witnessed Philip V's renunciation of the French succession in November he was joined by Manuel Manasses Gilligan, an expert on the Spanish-American slave trade, and negotiations for the *asiento* were begun. The project of the English *asiento* as presented by Gilligan was more complete and extensive than the commercial provisions of the Anglo-Austrian treaty of 1707 or the *asiento* of the French Guinea Company. The English agreed to relinquish their demand for exemption from the fifteen per cent duty on British manufactures in exchange for the favor of being permitted to send a ship of five hundred tons each year for thirty years to trade in the Spanish Indies, the only condition being that the English South Sea Company not engage in any contraband trade.

The treaty of the *asiento*, based on Gilligan's project, was finally signed at Madrid on March 26, 1713, to take effect on the following May 1.[55] The agreement was made between the two sovereigns, Queen Anne undertaking the agreement on behalf of the South Sea Company, and provided for the importation, during the thirty years of the contract, of 144,000 slaves of all ages and both sexes, at the rate of 4,800 per year. On each slave the asientists were to pay a duty of 33⅓ pieces-of-eight. Moreover, the asientists were to advance to the King of Spain, to replenish his depleted treasury, a loan of 200,000 pieces-of-eight, in two equal payments, the first to be due two months after Philip signed the *asiento*, the second two months later; the sum would be repaid during the final ten years of the thirty-year *asiento* by deductions from the duty which the English asientists were to

[54] Lexington to Lord Dartmouth, Oct. 20, 1712, in Scelle, *La traite négrière*, II, 531.
[55] Davenport, ed., *European Treaties*, III, 171–185.

pay on their slaves, at the rate of 20,000 pieces-of-eight per annum. The duties of the asientists were to be paid only on 4,000 Negroes each year; the duties on the remaining 800 were granted them in consideration of their risks and good faith. For the first twenty-five years of the contract the asientists were to be free to import more than the fixed number of 4,800 slaves, if they found a need and market for them, paying 16⅔ pieces-of-eight duty on each Negro imported above the fixed number. Moreover, the asientists were free to carry on this trade in British ships, the only restriction being that the crews give no offense to the Roman Catholic religion; these ships were free to carry their slaves to all ports of the Caribbean and to Buenos Aires, landing in ports where there were royal officers who could search the ships and certify the number of Negroes imported. The importers were free to sell their slaves at the best prices possible everywhere but at Santa Marta, Crimana, and Maracaibo, where the price was limited to 300 pieces-of-eight per slave so as to encourage the inhabitants to buy them.

Because the British claimed a need for slaves along the Rio de la Plata the asientists were allowed to bring into Buenos Aires some 1,200 of their annual importation of 4,800 slaves, to be sold at the best prices possible, to be carried in four ships, 800 to Buenos Aires, the remaining 400 to be "carried into, and serve for the provinces above, and kingdom of Chile, selling them to the inhabitants, if they will come to buy them in the said port of Buenos Aires." The asientists, moreover, were to be assigned some land on the Rio de la Plata sufficient to cultivate and breed cattle for their subsistence, where they could build wooden houses but no fortifications, and where they would be under the direction of a resident Spanish officer appointed by the King of Spain. Slaves could be introduced into the South Sea (Pacific) by means of Panamá and Perú, all other ports there being closed to the asientists; in return for this trade the merchants were allowed to export gold and silver duty-free. The merchants were likewise granted leave to bring into Panamá all stores and provisions necessary for the maintenance of the ships used in the Perú trade. The English directing the *asiento* in Spanish ports would be treated as Spanish subjects with the sole restriction that no more than "four or six" Englishmen could reside in any one port; as many of these as necessary could travel into the interior to carry out their trade. The asientists could appoint for each port they visited Spanish judges-conservators who alone would have jurisdiction over all matters relating to the *asiento*, all other Spanish officers being forbidden to meddle; appeal from the sentences of these judges-conservators would be to the Supreme Council of the Indies, of which the King would appoint a member to be protector of the *asiento* and the asientists could propose a member to be their judge-conservator (all this in the same manner as Article 8 of the Portuguese *asiento*).

Ships of the asientists could not be detained by Spanish officers for any reason whatsoever nor could they be obliged to pay excessive prices for food or other necessities; nor could the ships, goods, or buildings of the asientists be seized or searched by Spanish officers, except when there was evidence of fraudulent importation, when search could be made only in the presence of the judge-conservator and only illicit goods could be seized. From the day the English would take possession of the *asiento* it was forbidden to the French Guinea Company or any other person to import Negro slaves to Spanish America. The ships of the asientists, on entering any port, would be thoroughly searched for contraband merchandise, which, if found, would be confiscated and the guilty parties punished. Provisions put ashore in Spanish ports for the sustenance of Negroes would not pay duties, but if they were brought in or exported from Spanish ports or sold, as was allowed, as surplus provisions, they would have to pay duties. After the asientists had landed in a port, paid the duties, and sold part of their cargoes of slaves, they could carry the remainder to any other port and sell them there duty-free; they could receive in payment for their slaves gold, silver, or the produce of the country which they could carry away without paying duties. The ships of the asientists could sail freely from English or Spanish ports, but the asientists were obliged to give full account of their activities and cargoes to the King of Spain and they were restricted from carrying anything or anyone in their ships other than Negroes, supplies for the Negroes, and the gold, silver, and produce which they received in payment. For the refreshment of slaves after the voyage from Africa and for their sustenance, the asientists could hire parcels of land in the neighborhood of their factories as plantations, which were to be cultivated by slaves and by the inhabitants of the country where they were located.

The *asiento* was to be suspended in case of a declaration of war between Spain and Britain and the asientists removed from the Indies with all their effects. They were granted all privileges ever granted any other asientists, as long as they were not contrary to the articles of this present contract. On the condition that the South Sea Company abstain from any illicit trade, the King of Spain, in an additional article, allowed the company to send an annual ship of five hundred tons to trade in the Indies, from which the Spanish crown was to receive one-fourth of the profit as well as five per cent of the other three-fourths; the goods carried by these ships could be sold, free of all duties, but only at the time of the fair at the port visited by the annual Spanish merchant fleet.

Although the privilege of the annual ship was accorded the English asientists only on the condition that they engage in no contraband trade, the other provisions of the *asiento* contract offered many occasions for fraud. The direct communication between England and the Spanish colonies and access to all Spanish ports on the Atlantic and Caribbean where royal officers or their officials resided provided means of entry to a vast part of Spain's American domain. The number of slaves which the asientists were allowed to import led inevitably to fraud: the asientists claimed the right to introduce twelve hundred slaves per annum into Buenos Aires, although that city and the neighboring provinces could absorb only a fraction of that number. There remained the slave market of Chile, previously forbidden to all foreigners, and it is possible that the English intended in their conception of the *asiento* to use the trade in surplus slaves as a means to penetrate the Pacific. Possibilities for contraband existed in the provision allowing the English factors to advance into the interiors of the Spanish colonies, where they inevitably acted as merchants. The grant of a section of land along the Rio de la Plata to the asientists provided a base for smuggling activities.[56]

The day after the *asiento* was signed Baron Lexington concluded a preliminary treaty of peace with Spain. The eleven demands which he had first presented on his arrival in Madrid in October of 1712 were all granted except the ninth (concerning exemption from Spanish duties on British goods), from which Queen Anne had agreed to desist in exchange for the privilege of the annual ship for the asientists. Britain was forced to make several concessions to the Spanish in order to save the treaty, including British guarantee of the possession by the powerful and influential Princesse des Ursins of a principality in the Low Countries and maintenance of the Spanish in the Newfoundland fishery, which was conceded in exchange for a clause in the treaty which allowed Britain to keep all territories it then possessed in the Indies. Spain, for its part, promised to prohibit the trade of the Indies to all other nations.

The preliminary Anglo-Spanish treaty of peace was signed at Madrid on March 27, 1713.[57] It provided for the recognition of the Hanoverian succession in Britain and of the right of Philip V to the Spanish throne by providing for the renunciation of the claims of Emperor Charles VI to Spain in exchange for Philip's renunciation of his claims to Austrian states in Italy and Flanders. Former Anglo-Spanish treaties were renewed. Other articles guaranteed the *asiento*, affirmed Britain's surrender of its demand for the fifteen per cent exemption on duties payable on British products imported into Spain, guaranteed to Britain all privileges which it had enjoyed in Spanish dominions at the time of the death of Carlos II, especially by the Anglo-Spanish treaties of 1667 and 1670, and assured Britain of most-favored-nation status in Spanish trade. The Indies were absolutely closed to trade by all foreign nations (except the British asientists). Britain promised to maintain Spanish fishing rights in Newfoundland.

Britain, although it had acquired the coveted *asiento*, had failed to win the other prizes desired from Spain, the cessions of additional territory in

[56] Scelle, *La traite Négrière*, II, 554–557.
[57] Davenport, ed., *European Treaties*, III, 190–192.

Spanish America and new commercial advantages. On the other hand, it had succeeded in acquiring a commercial monopoly in the Spanish Indies by securing the prohibition of all other nations, including the French and Dutch, from those parts. But even the *asiento* did not grant as many privileges as the British ministers and merchants had hoped when they began negotiations for it with the French in 1711. The South Sea Company, which had been founded specifically in the hope of penetrating Spain's Pacific colonies, found itself limited in its activities to the Atlantic coast. The privilege of the annual ship, which had been thought an adequate equivalent for English abandonment of the claim to exemption from the fifteen per cent export duties at Cadiz, was far from satisfactory; instead of involving a right to carry on a general trade to all the ports of the Spanish Indies, as had been hoped, the provision for the annual ship limited the asientists to trading in one port in direct competition with the Spanish merchant fleet.[58]

The thwarting of English hopes for a general trade in English merchandise in the Spanish West Indies spurred interest in the advancement of contraband trade. The loopholes in the *asiento* which provided occasion for this trade were used. Hoping to gain further commercial concessions from Spain, and particularly to advance opportunities for clandestine trade, Lexington, in July of 1713, submitted a memorial to the King of Spain demanding special commercial privileges for England. He requested acknowledgment by treaty of the right of the English to cut logwood on the Yucatan coast at Campeche and Honduras, a practice which had long been disputed between the two governments and for which the English were determined to receive Spanish sanction. Permission to buy provisions and wood at Spanish Caribbean ports was requested for the inhabitants of the British Caribbean islands, these islands being claimed to be too small to produce for themselves adequate provisions and lying inconveniently far from Great Britain and North America. Protection of British trading ships was sought by a request that such ships found on the coasts of Spanish colonies not be seized as violating the provisions of the *asiento* unless they were taken in a port and actually engaged in illicit trade.[59] Each of these requests was rejected by the Spanish.

6. The Treaties of Utrecht

During the same period, the British succeeded at Utrecht in persuading the Dutch to sign a new barrier treaty, thereby nullifying the former treaty

[58] McLachlan, *Trade and Peace with Old Spain, 1667–1750*, 59.

[59] "Lord Lexington's Memorial to the King of Spain relating to Commerce with His Majesty's answer by the Marques de Bedmar, July 13, 1713." In Doc. 3144, "Papers Relating to the Spanish Trade; June 29, 1714." *Mss. of the House of Lords, 1712–14*, N.S. Vol. X, 376–392.

of 1709 and removing a major obstacle to peace. The two purposes of the new treaty were to guarantee the Hanoverian succcession in Britain and to guarantee and regulate the Dutch barrier. Significantly, this new treaty, signed at Utrecht on January 29, 1713, ignored the earlier demand of the Grand Alliance that the entire Spanish monarchy be surrendered to the House of Austria and the clause of the former treaty that a share in the Spanish-American trade be accorded the Dutch. By this treaty the British freed themselves from their responsibilities to the Grand Alliance and were able to proceed, conscience free, to achieve their intended goal—a monopoly in the Spanish-American trade facilitated by the most widely amicable settlement of the Spanish dynastic problem.

Meanwhile, the conferences between France and England, which had begun with the suspension of the activities of the general congress at Utrecht in March, 1712, continued. When the problem of the separation of the crowns of France and Spain had been solved by the formal renunciations of Philip and the Duc de Berry and Duc d'Orléans, the English and French representatives were free to concentrate on the discussion of their own interests, colonial and commercial.

Chief among the problems negotiated was the settlement of colonial differences, especially those in North America, where England pushed its advantage by exploiting territorial conquests and France's weakened situation, and where France endeavored to preserve its access to the mouth of the St. Lawrence and New France. The numerous proposals exchanged between the two nations reflected these interests. Finally, in August of 1712, the British plenipotentiaries presented a project which proved acceptable to both sides as a basis for peace. By the articles of the project which concerned America, Hudson Bay was given in its entirety to the English, together with all fortresses erected by the French, intact with their cannon and military stores. Boundaries between French and English territories in America were to be determined by commissioners appointed from both sides. The Hudson's Bay Company was to be indemnified by the French for all damages inflicted upon it by the French. France was also to cede to Britain the island of St. Christopher, Acadia *"limitibus suis antiquis comprehensam,"* and its holdings on Newfoundland, including Placentia with its cannon and military stores. The project established French possession of Cape Breton Island and French fishing rights on Newfoundland in the region called Petit Nord. British sovereignty over the Five Nations of Indians, a matter long disputed by the French, was demanded, and the French were to be prohibited from interfering with these tribes and all others allied to Britain. Moreover, British right to trade in the disputed Great Lakes basin was claimed.[60]

The project did not satisfy the French, and they proposed several amend-

[60] Davenport, ed., *European Treaties*, III, 196–198.

ments. The plenipotentiaries at Utrecht requested that the claims of the Hudson's Bay Company against the French be placed before the future commissioners; these commissioners were also to be charged with the adjustment of the capitulation of Nevis to the English. With regard to Newfoundland, the plenipotentiaries protested the British claim to the right of first possession there and in Cape Breton and their demand for the cannon and military stores at Placentia. The French also demanded clearer definition of the territorial limits of Newfoundland, so as to determine possession of the surrounding islands, and the exact location of Petit Nord, which was located variously on French and British maps. The article which established sovereignty over the Indians the French desired amended to allow Indian subjects or allies of the two crowns to trade reciprocally on each other's lands.

The Comte de Pontchartrain also made observations on the English project which were sent, with royal approval, to Torcy as instructions for the procedure of the French plenipotentiaries at Utrecht. While the cession of Hudson Bay was granted and the regulation of boundaries between French and English colonies approved, Pontchartrain demanded that the French be allowed to keep the guns and ammunition which they had there and that the boundary of Hudson Bay be drawn northward from the Atlantic coast of Quebec, rather than from the mouth of the St. Lawrence where the English had described the boundary in their project. He believed it essential that any agreement confirm French possession of all the banks of the St. Lawrence, the islands of the gulf and those adjacent to Acadia. The islands surrounding Newfoundland were desirable for their proximity to the fishing grounds, and Pontchartrain demanded that those beyond the half-league limit set by the English which were still in French possession be retained by the French. In the matter of the regulation of Indian tribes the French king disagreed with his plenipotentiaries; he desired that the tribes dependent on any particular colony, French or English, be allowed to trade only in that colony and be forbidden to cross any boundaries.[61]

The English, in their response to Pontchartrain's observations, granted French demands for retention and removal of the guns at Hudson Bay and for French possession of the gulf islands.[62] Negotiations were continued to adjust the remaining differences between the two nations. Compromises were reached regarding the limits of the Newfoundland and Acadian fisheries. British attempts to persuade the French to quit the Newfoundland fishery entirely, long encouraged by the English merchants and fishermen who resented French competition, failed, and Britain finally agreed to

---

[61] "Lettre de M. de Pontchartrain aux Plenipotentiares à Fontainebleau, 17 Aoust 1712," in *Extraits des Négotiations d'Utrecht Concernant l'Amérique Septentrionale,*" A. E., Méms. et Docs.: Amérique, 24: fols. 89–91.

[62] "Réponse aux observations sur le projet," in "Lettre du Roy aux P.P.; 6 Aoust 1712," in *Extraits des Négociations d'Utrecht, ibid.,* fols. 91–92 vo.

accept French fishing rights in the Petit Nord region. The limits of the Acadian fishery were fixed to exclude the French from fishing within thirty leagues of the Nova Scotian coasts, beginning from Sable Island, which came into British possession, and extending to the southwest. Limits to the north were not set so that the French would have free fishing around Cape Breton Island. French subjects in Acadia and Newfoundland were granted, on the behest of the French government, the right to remain on their lands or to sell them at will, as well as freedom, for those who chose to remain under British rule, to practice their Roman Catholic religion. France, in turn, yielded to British demands, made on behalf of Portugal, that France promise not to molest Portuguese dominions and that the French give up all claims to the navigation of the Amazon River.

As soon as the French and English had settled the differences between them all obstacles to peace had been removed and the general congress at Utrecht proceeded. On April 11, 1713, treaties of peace were concluded between France and Britain, France and Portugal, France and Prussia, France and Savoy, and France and the States-General; on the same day treaties of commerce were signed between France and Britain and France and the States-General.

The Anglo-French treaty of peace [63] formalized the agreements which the two nations had made during their conferences. France acknowledged the Proetstant Hanoverian succession in England, and promised to maintain the separation of the French and Spanish crowns. Louis XIV agreed to raze the fortifications at Dunkirk, to restore to Britain the Hudson Bay and Strait, and, now, to surrender all buildings and fortifications in that territory to the British intact with all artillery and munitions. Boundaries between Hudson Bay and the French colonies, and between other English and French colonies, were to be defined by commissioners. The same commissioners would regulate French reparations to the Hudson's Bay Company for damages inflicted upon them by the French and the settlement of French claims against the English for damages inflicted on Montserrat and on ships taken by the English during peace. France would cede St. Christopher, Acadia according to its *"anciennes limites,"* [64] along with Port Royal (Annapolis) and all dependent lands and islands, with French subjects in the future being forbidden to fish within thirty leagues of the south coast beginning at Sable Island. Newfoundland and its adjacent islands would belong in the future entirely to Great Britain and would be vacated by their French inhabitants within seven months of the exchange of ratifications of the treaty, except in those places where the French were allowed to fish (between Cape Bonavista north and west to Point Riche), where

---

[63] Davenport, ed., *European Treaties*, III, 193–214.

[64] Just what the *"anciens limites"* were was not defined, and the lack of a definition proved a source of future Anglo-French conflicts.

HUDSON
BAY

Ft. Severn

Ft. Albany
Moose Fort • Ft. Rupert

CANADA

St. Lawrence R.

NEWFOUNDLAND
St. Johns

CAPE BRETON
Louisbourg

Quebec
St. John's R.

L. Superior
Sault
Ste. Marie
Montreal
Ft. Frontenac
L. Huron
L. Michigan
Detroit
L. Ont.
L. Erie
Albany

Port Royal
NOVA SCOTIA
(ACADIA)

Boston

Philadelphia
New York

Ft. St. Louis
Ohio R.

Cahokia

Kaskaskia

BERMUDAS (British)

OUISIANA

Mississippi R.
Alabama R.
Apalachicola R.
Savannah R.
Charles Town

Biloxi Mobile
Pensacola
FLORIDA
St. Augustine

BAHAMAS
(British)

Havana
HISPANIOLA
PORTO
RICO
ST. EUSTATIUS (Dutch)
ST. BARTHÉLEMY
ST. MARTIN
VIRGIN IS. ANGUILLA
(Danish)
BARBUDA
ANTIGUA
(Brit.)

EXICO
CUBA
ST. CHRISTOPHER (Brit.)
NEVIS (Brit.)
MONTSERRAT (Brit.)
GUADELOUPE (Fr.)
DOMINICA (Fr.)
MARTINIQUE (Fr.)
ST. LUCIA
ST. VINCENT
BARBADOS
(Brit.)
GRENADA
TOBAGO

Vera Cruz
YUCATAN
JAMAICA

CURAÇAO (Dutch) TRINIDAD

HONDURAS

MOSQUITO
COAST

Cartagena
NEW GRANADA
Orinoco R.

Porto Bello
Panama
VENEZUELA

British

French

Spanish

Dutch

Danish

EUROPEAN POSSESSIONS IN NORTH AMERICA AND THE CARIBBEAN AREA
AFTER THE PEACE OF UTRECHT, 1713.

they were forbidden to build any fortifications or permanent residences. Cape Breton Island and all other islands in the mouth and gulf of the St. Lawrence River would remain French; French subjects in ceded territories would have liberty to leave within a year with all their movable effects, and those who chose to remain under British rule were to enjoy freedom to practice their Roman Catholic religion. The French promised not to interfere with the Five Nations or other Indian "subjects" [65] of Great Britain and the British not to interfere with those of France. All Indians would have liberty to trade freely among themselves and to visit both French and English colonies for commerce. Commissioners were to decide which tribes were allies of each of the two nations.

Of special interest to England, and a clear victory for the English policy of excluding France from direct participation in Spanish colonial trade, was Louis XIV's acceptance of the new status quo in Spanish America implicit in his promise:

not to try to obtain or even to accept in the future that anything be changed or modified for the benefit of his subjects in Spain or in Spanish America, whether in matters of commerce or in matters of navigation, from the usages practised during the reign of the late King of Spain Charles Second, nor to procure for his subjects any advantage not accorded equally and to the same extent to the other peoples and nations who trade there.[66]

The Anglo-French commercial treaty signed at Utrecht was the product of several years of negotiations between the two nations and expressed to a large extent the ambitions of British merchants who had long desired greater freedom to import their wares, especially colonial products such as tobacco, furs, sugar, and fish, into France. A commercial treaty had been drafted in 1709 but abandoned when the Gertruydenberg negotiations collapsed. Secretary St. John, in 1712, had submitted to the Board of Trade and Plantations a new draft, based upon that of 1709, and the Board had made revisions which further facilitated trade, particularly regarding the importation of tobacco and salt fish into France. In 1712 St. John proposed and Louis XIV accepted demands that commissioners from both nations meet in London to regulate the duties and impositions paid in each kingdom and that France and Britain give each other the commercial privileges of the most-favored nation. The English, like the Dutch, also endeavored to win the benefit of the low French tariff of 1664, but they won only a compromise with the French which gave the benefit of the tariff to the English at the price of lowering English duties in pro-

[65] The language of Article 15 of the treaty is to the effect that the French will not molest *"les Cinq Nations ou cantons des Indiens soumis à la Grande Bretagne."* The meaning of the word *"soumis"* was so vague that it made it possible for the French to question the meaning of the whole article later on. See Chapters XIII and XIX.

[66] Davenport, ed., *European Treaties*, III, 210.

portion to the French and of yielding to the French fishing rights in the part of Newfoundland known as the Petit Nord.

The treaty provided for free navigation and free entry into all European dominions of both nations and most-favored-nation status in mutual trade. The French tariff of 1664 was to be restored when the English had lowered duties on French goods to the level of those on goods from other countries and had repealed all laws prohibiting the importation of French goods. Commissioners were to meet to discuss the disputed trade in wood, sugar, salt fish, and whale products. French duties on tobacco would be the same for both English and French merchants, who would also have equal liberty of selling their products.

The final Anglo-Spanish treaty of peace and the treaty of the *asiento* were formally concluded at Utrecht. The terms of the *asiento* remained as they had been settled in Madrid with the exception of a sole "correction" regarding the method of payment of money by the asientists to the Spanish monarch.[67] The treaty of peace repeated most of the terms of its preliminary form. Moreover, it returned the rules of navigation and commerce in the Spanish Indies to the state in which they had existed under Carlos II. Both nations granted the other most-favored-nation status in all their continental dominions. Spain ceded Gibraltar and all of Minorca to Britain and Sicily to the House of Savoy. Of particular significance was the promise extracted from Philip V to the effect that:

neither the Catholic King, nor any of his heirs and successors whatsoever, shall sell, yield, pawn, transfer, or by any other means or under any name, alienate from them and from the crown of Spain, to the French or to any other nations whatever, any jurisdictions, dominions, or territories, or any part thereof, belonging to Spain in America. On the contrary, that the Spanish dominions in America may be preserved whole and entire, the Queen of Great Britain engages that she will endeavor and give assistance to the Spaniards, that the ancient limits of their dominions in America be restored and settled as they stood in the time of the aforesaid Catholic King Charles the Second, if it shall appear that they have in any manner or under any pretext, been broken into or lessened in any part, since the death of the aforesaid Catholic King Charles the Second.[68]

Thus was the territorial integrity of the Spanish American empire preserved as Carlos II would have wished. Thus, also, was the set English policy of blocking further French territorial expansion in America at the expense of Spain written into the final peace.

It was the Anglo-Spanish commercial treaty that underwent the greatest and most significant alterations between Madrid and Utrecht. The English

[67] Davenport, ed., *European Treaties*, III, 232–233.
[68] Davenport, ed., *European Treaties*, III, 229.

plenipotentiaries at Utrecht abandoned their claim for the right of English merchants in Spain to elect and pay a judge-conservator, thus removing a valuable protector of English commerce. The ratified treaty also doubled the duty on goods imported by British merchants from Africa to Spain.[69]

In sum, the British gained much less than they had hoped from their treaties with Spain. Trade with Old Spain did not grow as expected because of Spanish poverty and the competition of French manufactures, and the commercial treaty provided further impediments because it did not provide sufficient civil rights for English merchants living in Spain and because, although it did standardize duties payable by English merchants, these duties were too high and too inflexible. Indeed, the commercial treaty proved so harmful to English trade in Spain that within two years it had to be renegotiated. The shortcomings of this treaty were largely due to the preoccupation of the English statesmen negotiating the peace with gaining a share in the Spanish-American trade through the concession of the *asiento*. But the *asiento*, as granted to the English, was far too limited to provide as many opportunities for profit as the statesmen had expected. Moreover, although the French were officially excluded from the Spanish-American trade by the Anglo-Spanish and Anglo-French treaties of peace, the French trade continued, albeit illicitly, aided by strategic French locations in Hispaniola.

Treaties of peace and commerce were also made on the same date between France and the States-General. The treaty of peace granted the Dutch their barrier and was largely concerned with its location and regulation. France also promised not to seek advantages in the commerce of Spain and Spanish America which were not enjoyed during the reign of Carlos II.[70] The Franco-Dutch commercial treaty was solely concerned with regulation of their European commercial relations, no mention being made of their American territories or commerce.[71]

France also concluded a treaty of peace with Portugal. The treaty provided for regulation of Franco-Portuguese European trade and navigation, including reciprocal privileges and exemptions. With regard to America, France relinquished all claims to the disputed area in northern Brazil called Cap du Nord, lying between the Amazon and Vincent Pinson (Oyapock) Rivers. Portugal was allowed to rebuild the fortresses in this region which it had been obliged to demolish by the terms of the Treaty of Lisbon (March, 1700) and to build new ones. France relinquished also all pretense of any right to navigate the Amazon or to use its banks, as well as all claims to any other Portuguese domains in America or any other part of the world. French subjects from Cayenne or other French territories

[69] McLachlan, *Trade and Peace with Old Spain, 1667–1750*, 53.
[70] *Actes . . . concernant la Paix d'Utrecht*, III, 1–42.
[71] *Actes . . . concernant la Paix d'Utrecht*, III, 77–109.

were forbidden to enter Portuguese-American territories, and French missionaries were forbidden to undertake the conversion or spiritual direction of the inhabitants of Portuguese territories. The treaty was guaranteed by Great Britain.[72]

The other treaties signed by France on April 11, with Prussia and Savoy, settled their European differences and in no way concerned America.

The peace was completed by later treaties made between the other participants. Spain and the Netherlands concluded a treaty of peace at Utrecht on June 26, 1714. Based upon the Treaty of Münster (1648), the new Spanish-Dutch treaty included a provision for mutual freedom of trade in Europe and confirmed the Spanish-Dutch treaty of navigation made at the Hague in 1650. Navigation and commerce in all colonial territories were to remain "as they are carried on at the present," which stipulation continued the policy of closed trade. This article reenforced Spain's promise to close the trade of the Indies to all nations except the British farmers of the *asiento*, a policy reflecting pressure to exclude France from the Spanish-American trade. There was also an article guaranteeing the permanent separation of the French and Spanish crowns.[73]

Spain also concluded a treaty of peace with Portugal at Utrecht on February 6, 1715. The most important part of this treaty was the settlement of the Portuguese *asiento*. Spain agreed to pay to the Portuguese asientists the sum owed them, plus interest, although the original debt was somewhat reduced, and the manner of payment was regulated. Beyond this debt, Portugal agreed to renounce all sums due its *asiento* company. The two nations granted each other most-favored-nation status in their European trade, the colonial trade being closed. The treaty was guaranteed by Great Britain.[74]

The Anglo-Spanish commercial treaty of 1713, which proved disadvantageous to England, was renegotiated in Madrid and signed on December 14, 1715. The duties which the English paid on imports to, and exports from, Spain were adjudged too high, and a new article provided that British subjects would pay only the duties on goods they brought in or out of Spain which they had paid during the reign of Carlos II. Spain formally acknowledged the right of British subjects to gather salt on the island of Tortuga, permission to do so having been granted during the reign of Carlos II. This new treaty restored and confirmed the Anglo-Spanish Treaty of Madrid (1667) as the basis for the regulation of trade, and both nations promised to abolish any innovations in commerce made since then.[75]

[72] *Actes . . . concernant la Paix d'Utrecht*, II, 544–555.
[73] Davenport, ed., *European Treaties*, III, 239–244.
[74] Davenport, ed., *European Treaties*, III, 248–251.
[75] Davenport, ed., *European Treaties*, III, 253–255.

This group of treaties, known as the Peace of Utrecht, marked an end to the War of the Spanish Succession and a landmark in the long-continued national and colonial rivalries which had lasted many decades. For the nations of the Grand Alliance, the treaties brought a realization of many of the demands for which they had gone to war. For France and Spain, the peace represented a vast loss of territory and of commercial, colonial, and international power.

The settlement of the dynastic problem in Spain, which was the primary excuse for the war, was settled satisfactorily, although not as the Grand Alliance had originally demanded. Emperor Charles VI of Austria lost Spain and the Spanish Indies, but he was compensated with European territories, including possession of the Spanish Netherlands and territories along the Rhine as a barrier against France. To Britain and Holland, a Spain under Philip V, formally separated from France, was as satisfactory as a Spain under Charles VI—what mattered was that Spain remain navally weak, dependent upon and defenseless against the mercantile inroads of the maritime nations. Philip's renunciation of his place in the French succession and the concurrent renunciations by his Bourbon relations of their claims to the Spanish throne ended fears for the union of these two crowns. France's political influence in Spain also further diminished through the ascendancy of Philip's anti-French queen, Elizabeth Farnese.

The dynastic settlement also served to preserve the European balance of power. Permanent separation of the French and Spanish crowns ended fears of the creation of a populous and wealthy block in Western Europe and of a vast and powerful colonial empire in the "new world." The Spanish empire, although large and wealthy, remained, without French assistance, weak and without direction—ready prey for its jealous rivals.

France's commercial superiority in Spanish dominions was ended by the terms of the various treaties. Most significant was the loss of the coveted *asiento* to Britain, which gave the possessor not only a monopoly in the Spanish-American slave trade but also a generally acknowledged occasion for illicit traffic in manufactured goods. France was excluded from other exceptional privileges in the Spanish trade by articles in the various treaties of peace which returned France's commercial status in Spanish territories to what it had been during the reign of Carlos II. The desire of the victors to ensure their own advantage in the international trade, especially that with Spain, resulted in the number of most-favored-nation status articles in the treaties. Such status was mutually granted by the French and British in their commercial treaty and by the British and Spanish, the Dutch and Spanish, and the Spanish and Portuguese in their respective treaties of peace.

The Grand Alliance reaped from the peace many of the territorial settlements for which it had gone to war. The Dutch and the Austrians both gained barriers against France, and within these military buffer zones both nations gained a considerable amount of economic power. Of the two defeated nations France suffered by far the greatest territorial losses, Spanish territorial integrity having been preserved at the price of commercial concessions to the British. Besides the regions lost to the Dutch and Austrian barriers, France was forced to make considerable concessions in America to Portugal and Great Britain. By surrendering its claims in Brazil, France limited its holdings in South America to the tiny province of French Guiana. The surrender of Hudson Bay, Acadia, Newfoundland, and St. Christopher to Britain represented the loss of lucrative fur, sugar, and fishing areas and strategic military locations, losses which seriously weakened the power of France in North America.

The results of the Peace of Utrecht were not comprised alone in the articles of its treaties. For the victors the treaties and concessions which they won were far less satisfactory than they had expected. The deficiencies of the English *asiento* have been discussed above. The Anglo-Spanish commercial treaty also proved unsatisfactory. Although the British won political protection and territorial security, by the Spanish cession of Gibraltar and Minorca, for the advancement of their highly valued Spanish trade, the practical immunities which they had enjoyed under the Anglo-Spanish Treaty of Madrid (1667) were not secured in the new treaty. The Treaty of Utrecht of 1713, for all its seeming advantages, proved unworkable in practice. England's European trade with Spain, so profitable that the English merchants had supported the War of the Spanish Succession to win it back from France, was not regained by the treaty.

The Anglo-French commercial treaty, which was to open France to British colonial products, proved unacceptable to the British Parliament and was never ratified.

The Dutch-Spanish treaties of peace and commerce failed to provide the Dutch with any tangible benefits. Philip V promised the Dutch most-favored-nation status in the commerce of continental Spain, a promise which gave the Dutch theoretic equality with the English but actually provided no comparable advantages. The English, after all, had the *asiento*, and the Dutch found themselves exactly where they were after the Treaty of Münster—incapable of carrying on licit commerce in Spanish America. The English, while ostensibly promoting the commercial interests of their allies, had succeeded in securing for themselves a monopoly in the Spanish-American trade.

France's territorial cessions to Britain, ample though they were, seemed nevertheless insufficient to many Englishmen, and the terms of these cessions provided occasion for future conflicts. Those concerned with the Newfoundland fishery were strongly resentful of the "disgraceful" surrender of a share in that fishery to the French. The directors of England's naval power realized the dependence of France upon the North American fishery for the training of sailors and saw the French Newfoundland fishery as a military as well as an economic threat to England. The lack of definition of the boundaries of ceded areas also caused conflict. The much-disputed boundaries of Acadia were reserved by the Anglo-French treaty of peace for future adjustment by commissioners, whose futile attempts a few years later did nothing to end the almost continual intercolonial bickerings. Likewise, the treaties did not determine which Indian tribes were to be considered allies or subjects of France or England, preserving this decision for the commissioners and providing a seed for future wars. The New Englanders, their appetites for French territories whetted by the capture of Acadia, hungered for the rest of New France and so provided stimulus for its capture half a century later.

For all its individual significance, the Peace of Utrecht is even more interesting as a single point in the long international rivalry for America and the rise of British imperialism. In the course of the War of the Spanish Succession Britain succeeded in removing both the French and Dutch from competition in the Spanish-American trade, the former by military victory, the latter by a somewhat nefarious betrayal of the interests of the Grand Alliance. The American territories which France ceded to Britain marked a greater victory over France than the dissatisfied British of the time realized. Not only had these areas become untenable to France by reason of England's growing naval ascendancy, but, by their cession, provided England with bases from which still further to weaken France's control over its remaining North American holdings. From 1713, although France was still powerful, it was only a matter of time before England's colonial ambitions, implemented by its rising naval superiority, would drive the French from Canada.

For Spain, too, the year 1713 was a significant point in a pattern of national and imperial decline. Although Spanish-American territorial integrity was guaranteed both by England and by the promise of Philip V as King of Spain never to alienate any part of his American dominions to another nation, much control over Spain's American trade passed into the hands of Britain with the *asiento*. With its commerce so largely in the hands of foreigners, the territorial integrity of the Spanish empire lost much of its significance, and its growing decline continued unimpeded.

CHAPTER XI

Direct Intercolonial Relations in America during the Seventeenth Century

THE INTERNATIONAL HISTORY of the European colonies in America in the seventeenth and eighteenth centuries was predominantly a history of the interrelations of European states with regard to their colonies. From the very beginnings of settlement, however, the colonies of the European powers in America came into contact with each other in ways that led them into direct exchanges and relationships that were calculated to promote or defend their own respective self-interests. The geographic circumstances of the colonies—their remoteness from Europe, the threats to their survival from wilderness and from hostile aborigines, the sentiments of the colonists with regard to their European governments and their American homes, their commercial exchanges and territorial rivalries with each other—all served to create needs and desires that arose out of their own experiences in the areas where they were located.

These colonial self-interests did not always coincide exactly with those of the mother countries; on the contrary, they often ran counter to the diplomatic policies of the metropoli. It is to be noted, also, that out of these more or less direct international—or intercolonial—relationships in America, based, as they were, upon colonial self-interest, there were born certain attitudes, policies, and principles that were to lay the foundations for the established diplomatic policies of the American nations in later centuries.[1]

[1] See Savelle, "Colonial Origins of American Diplomatic Principles," *Pacific Historical Review*, III, No. 3 (Sept. 1934), 334–350.

1. *Anglo-Dutch Intercolonial Relations*

The Plymouth-New Netherland Trade Agreement of 1627

The Dutch and English claims to territory on continental North America overlapped considerably. The Dutch West India Company, chartered in 1621, colonized the area granted the defunct New Netherland Company by its charter of 1614, that is, the unoccupied territory between the fortieth and the forty-fifth degrees of North Latitude. In 1620 James I of England granted to the Council for New England absolute ownership of all lands between the fortieth and the forty-eighth degrees of North Latitude, from the Atlantic to the Pacific. When the colony of Massachusetts obtained its royal charter in 1628 its domain was extended westward across the already established colony of New Netherland to the Pacific.

These conflicting claims were the source of much dispute, both in Europe and in America, where the rivalry was based less upon abstract political claims than upon competition for the fur trade and fertile farming areas and upon disputed boundary lines. The English were particularly adamant about refusing to recognize not only Dutch claims but even the very existence of New Netherland. One of the earliest of many expressions of this attitude occurred in 1620, when the New England Captain Thomas Dermer warned Dutch traders on the Hudson not to continue their occupation of "English" territory. In 1622 England officially protested to the Hague against the intrusion of the Dutch into what it considered English territory and asked that the sending of ships and colonists from the Low Countries to the colony be stopped. The exigencies of the European situation, however, led the two countries, despite their colonial and commercial rivalries in America, to unite in an alliance against Spain in the Treaty of Southampton in 1625.[2]

This treaty had the effect, for a few months, of ameliorating the tensions between the two countries in America. Thus, when the Dutch West India Company appealed to King Charles I of England to send out orders to English warships and privateers to let the company's ships pass to and from America without molestation, whether for trade or for the common military purposes of the two allies, Charles complied by issuing an Order-in-Council, on September 5, 1627, decreeing that the Dutch West India Company's ships, with their cargoes or their prizes, "shall have free ingress, egress, and regress into and out of all his Majestie's ports, havens, roads, and creekes, as by the articles of the treaty, made at Southampton, the 7th of September, 1625, more at large appeareth." [3]

It was in conformity with the Treaty of Southampton, then, and in the

[2] See Chapter IV.
[3] Davenport, ed., *European Treaties*, I, 292; N.Y.C.D., III, 12–13.

spirit of this short-lived cooperative English mood, that the Dutch governor of New Amsterdam, Peter Minuit, wrote to the governor of New Plymouth in March, 1627, proposing the establishment of a mutual trade between the two colonies. Governor William Bradford replied that the offer of trade was acceptable, so Dutch Director Peter Minuit sent Isaac de Razière to Plymouth as New Netherland's first ambassador. De Razière arrived in Plymouth bearing goods, which the English bought, and offering trade and assistance against the French, which, as Bradford wrote "though we know it was with an eye to their own profit, yet we had reason both kindly to accept it and make use of it." [4] The negotiations were somewhat hampered by the demands of the New Englanders that the Dutch justify their title to their colony, which the English claimed belonged to them. Another complaint which the English had against the Dutch was that they came to America "not with intent to plant, but to forage the country, and the fishermen leave their fishing and do nothing but trade, to the great detriment of this country and the state of England." [5]

Nevertheless, the convenience of an intercolonial trade encouraged the English to accept the Dutch proposal, and an informal alliance for mutual defense and trade was established.

The New England-New Netherland Treaty of Hartford, 1650

Dutch commerce with New England continued with varying degrees of success as long as the Dutch held New Netherland, despite almost constant disputes between the two colonies over territory and boundaries. It was a trade based on necessity and convenience, rather than friendship: local products were exchanged for difficult-to-obtain European goods or sold when local prices were better than those offered by the mother countries or where it was desirable to escape payment of European import duties. This intercolonial trade was not always accepted by the mother countries, particularly by England, where the sense of rivalry with Dutch maritime enterprise was strong, but it continued to exist despite censure from Europe because the American colonists found that their situation sometimes dictated economic practices contrary to those expected by the mother countries.

Most of the Anglo-Dutch diplomatic relations in North America were concerned, however, with aspects of their territorial rivalry. This first became a major issue in 1632, when the English detained in Plymouth a Dutch vessel, the *Eendract*, returning from New Netherland, on the pretense that its cargo was procured in the English colonies and that the Dutch West India Company had appropriated some territory belonging

[4] "Correspondence between . . . the Colonies of New Netherland and New Plymouth, 1627." *Collections of the New York Historical Society*, 2nd Series, I, 360–368.
[5] "Correspondence between . . . New Netherland and New Plymouth," *lou. cit.*, 2nd Series, I, 366.

to the English.[6] The situation gave occasion for both governments to assert their claims to the region between Plymouth and Virginia. The Dutch based their claim on first possession of unoccupied land and purchase from the Indians; [7] the English claimed that their charters included the territory occupied by the Dutch and denied that the Indians could be considered true possessors of the land they "sold," being nomads and holding the land in common.[8]

While the home countries were trying to settle these claims the colonists in America pressed forward to occupy the unsettled territory between them along the Connecticut River. The Dutch, who had long traded in the area, sought to strengthen their claim by purchasing land from the Indians and erecting a fort. The English, with their expanding population, began to settle in the region. The Dutch protested this intrusion, but in vain; the English were determined to crowd the Dutch out of their lands and the Dutch, with their smaller population, were unable to resist. The English followers of Thomas Hooker moved into the area in 1636 and founded the towns which became the nucleus of the colony of Connecticut.

While the two groups of colonists were thus competing for the lands between them, an Indian war in the early 1640s brought them together. New Netherland bore the brunt of the Indian attack, and the government of this colony demanded that the Englishmen who lived in Dutch territory be enlisted to assist in the war. An English captain, John Underhill, offered his services to the Dutch and ultimately led several expeditions against the Indians.[9] Once again, the exigencies of frontier life and the fact that survival against the Indians and other dangers from the wilderness was possible only by cooperation, drew the colonists together.

Such cooperation was usually only temporary. Englishmen living in territory claimed by the Dutch willingly recognized Dutch jurisdiction when they desired Dutch protection. Such was the case of these settlers during the Indian war. In another instance, the English settlers of Rhode Island, when they were at odds with the government of Massachusetts Bay, solicited permission to take shelter under the Dutch and to be subject to their rule. The Dutch recognized clearly the expediency motivating English recognition of their territorial jurisdiction:

'tis thus far with the English, that they are very willing to recognize the Netherlanders, and make use of them as a cloak in time of need, but again when this is past, they regard them not and make fools of them.[10]

In 1646 Governor Eaton of New Haven proposed an adjudication of

[6] Mr. Van Arnhem to the States-General, Apr. 5, 1632, N.Y C.D., I, 45.
[7] West India Company to States-General, May 5, 1632, N.Y.C.D., I, 50–52.
[8] Answer to the Remonstrance of the Dutch Ambassadors, Apr., 1632, N.Y.C.D., I, 57–59.
[9] Journal of New Netherland, 1641–46, N.Y.C.D., I, 181–188.
[10] "Remonstrance of New Netherland," July, 1649, N.Y.C.D., I, 285.

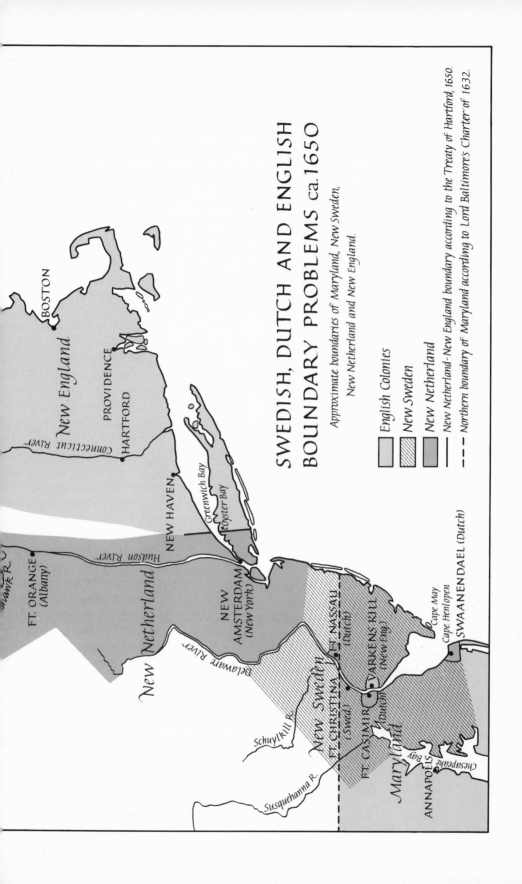

SWEDISH, DUTCH AND ENGLISH
BOUNDARY PROBLEMS ca.1650

Approximate boundaries of Maryland, New Sweden,
New Netherland and New England.

	English Colonies
	New Sweden
	New Netherland
——	New Netherland–New England boundary according to the Treaty of Hartford, 1650.
– – –	Northern boundary of Maryland according to Lord Baltimore's Charter of 1632.

BOSTON

New England

PROVIDENCE

HARTFORD

Connecticut River

NEW HAVEN

Greenwich Bay
Oyster Bay

FT. ORANGE
(Albany)

Hudson River

New Netherland

NEW
AMSTERDAM
(New York)

Delaware River

Mohawk R.

Schuylkill R.

New Sweden
FT. CHRISTINA
(Swed)

FT. NASSAU
(Dutch)

VARKENS KILL
(New Eng)

Cape May
Cape Henlopen

SWAANENDAEL (Dutch)

FT. CASIMIR
(Dutch)

Susquehanna R.

Maryland

Chesapeake Bay

ANNAPOLIS

territorial disputes between the English and Dutch colonies. The Dutch West India Company postponed its decision until after the fall of Charles I, but later advised Peter Stuyvesant, governor of New Netherland, to "fix upon a provisional boundary, to be approved of by each principal." [11] It was hoped that the settlement of the boundary, besides preventing future difficulties with the English colonies, would encourage the settlement of a secure New Netherland. Stuyvesant went to Hartford in September, 1650, to meet with the commissioners of the United Colonies of the New England Confederation. The issues which he wanted settled were the settlement of a boundary between the Dutch and English colonies, the "usurpation" of the Connecticut Valley by the English, the detention of Dutch fugitives by New Haven authorities, and the repeal of an act passed by the commissioners prohibiting the Dutch from trading with Indians within English jurisdiction.

During the conferences the English brought forth their own grievances. They complained that William Kieft, Stuyvesant's predecessor as governor of New Netherland, had challenged the English settlement at Stamford, Connecticut, had directed the destruction of an English fort on Delaware Bay, and had seized the English settlement at Greenwich in 1642. In 1642 an English trader was forced to pay duty on beaver pelts which he was carrying from Delaware to Connecticut; the following year this same trader was seized and imprisoned by the Dutch and Swedes on the Delaware. Stuyvesant asserted Dutch territorial rights to the area and denounced the New Haven colony as a trespass on Dutch territory. He claimed that the Dutch possessed all the land between Cape Henlopen and Cape Cod.[12] Finally, it was decided that two representatives should be chosen by each party to treat for a settlement. The English commissioners gave power to Simon Bradstreet and Thomas Prence; Stuyvesant chose George Baxter, his English secretary, and Thomas Willet, a Plymouth merchant trading in New Amsterdam.

An agreement was concluded at Hartford on September 19, 1650. Reparation for injuries done against the English was delayed until Stuyvesant, who was adjudged innocent of having directed any of them, could consult the States-General and the West India Company. Disputed possession of the Delaware Bay region was not settled because Stuyvesant would not relinquish the Dutch claim of sole title to that territory, although he had no commission to make any settlement in that area; for this reason both parties were left in *statu quo prius* there to develop their interests in trading or planting. A boundary was settled between New England and New Netherland. It divided Long Island from Oyster Bay

[11] N.Y.C.D., XIV, 85.
[12] Shurtleff and Pulsifer, eds., *Acts of the Commissioners of the United Colonies of New England, 1643–1679*, II (*Records of the Colony of New Plymouth, in New England, X*), 17.

south to the sea, giving the eastern part to the English and the western part to the Dutch; on the mainland, the boundary began on the west side of Greenwich Bay and ran north for twenty miles. Its further course was to be determined by the governments of New Netherland and New Haven, provided that it did not come within twenty miles of the Hudson River. The Dutch were forbidden to build within six miles of the line, but they were allowed to hold all lands in Hartford of which they were previously in actual possession. Provisions were made for the return of fugitives and for the creation of a defensive alliance.[13]

Many New Netherlanders were displeased with the agreement, feeling that Stuyvesant had surrendered too much. They felt

as if everything would shortly be English, for experience shows that the boundary line four leagues west of Greenwich encroaches as it goes into the interior of the country and that the English will in a short time be in the neighborhood of Fort Orange and the [Indian] trade. The Dutch governor is absolutely stripped of the Fresh River and New Haven . . . on which he declares he has not, nor ever had, any pretensions. And then his former various protests and menaces were read to him . . . which he denied . . .[14]

Stuyvesant's choice of Englishmen to represent him was also protested:

All the arbitrators were English and friends of the English; and in this affair they pulled the wool over the Director's eyes . . .[15]

Nevertheless, the West India Company found the provisional agreement acceptable and directed its envoys in London to reach an agreement about it with the English government. But the beginning of the first Anglo-Dutch war delayed further action on the treaty.

During the war, which lasted until 1654, the Dutch and English colonies in America were left largely to their own devices in conducting their intercolonial relations. On the basis of the agreement of 1650 they attempted to regulate the boundary and the settlement of the area between them. Each side made complaints against the other: the Dutch protested English encroachment on their lands, while the English accused the Dutch of inciting the Indians against them. In May, 1653, Director Stuyvesant proposed a treaty of neutrality between the colonies and shortly thereafter the General Court of Massachusetts adopted a policy of neutrality toward the Dutch in the war between England and the Netherlands.[16] Although neutrality was maintained, intercolonial disputes continued.

[13] Davenport, ed., *European Treaties*, II, 4–6.
[14] Translation of the News from New England, 1650, N.Y.C.D., I, 460–461.
[15] "Memoir on the Boundaries of New Netherland," by Adriaen van der Donck; Feb. 16, 1652, N.Y.C.D., I, 457–459.
[16] Shurtleff and Pulsifer, eds., *Acts of the Commissioners of the United Colonies of New England*, II (*Records of the Colony of New Plymouth*, X), 56–57.

In February, 1656, the States-General ratified the Treaty of Hartford.[17] England failed to ratify it, even after a Dutch embassy was sent to England in 1660 to try to arrange a settlement of the boundaries in America. The reason for English reluctance to agree to a boundary was a new colonial policy adopted after the Restoration in 1660: the government hoped to bring its American colonies under a unified and systematic administration, and absorption of New Netherland would give England control of the whole Atlantic coast of North America.

As part of this new policy Connecticut obtained, in 1622, a royal charter granting it all lands westward to the sea, including New Netherland. Henceforth Connecticut advanced claims to jurisdiction over Greenwich, West Chester, and Long Island, where many Englishmen had settled under Dutch jurisdiction, and officers and soldiers were dispatched to enforce this claim.

Director Stuyvesant protested Connecticut's action, and in September, 1663, went personally to Boston to remonstrate to the commissioners of the United Colonies against these violations of the Treaty of Hartford. In October he appointed three commissioners, Cornelius van Ruyven, Olaff Stevensz van Cortlandt, and John Lawrence, to go to Hartford to seek redress for injuries against the Dutch. The Dutch commissioners desired to bring the Connecticut government to agree to accept the boundaries of 1650, which the English refused to do, saying they regarded the provisional boundary "absolutely as a nullity and of no force, as his Majesty had now settled the limits for them." [18] Moreover, the English claimed "that they did not know any Province of New Netherland, but that there was a Dutch Governor over the Dutch Plantation on the Manhatans." [19] Although the Dutch protested that their right to the territory claimed by Connecticut was indisputable, based upon first discovery, purchase from the Indians, and first possession, the English replied that the Dutch could keep only as much as they actually held and that the English had a right to occupy the rest. The Dutch protested, in vain, that possession of part meant possession of the whole. No agreement could be made and the Dutch commissioners returned to New Netherland.

The rest of the history of New Netherland, until its seizure by England in 1664, reveals the continuing efforts of the Dutch to halt English encroachments on their land. It was a futile effort, for the Dutch colony never had a large population, and most of those who did settle were more interested in trade than farming, while the English population was constantly growing and moving into empty areas, including those claimed by the Dutch.

[17] N.Y.C.D., I, 611–612.
[18] "Journal kept by Cornelius van Ruyven, Burgomaster Cortlandt and John Lawrence," N.Y.C.D., II, 385–393.
[19] "Journal kept by Cornelius van Ruyven . . . ," N.Y.C.D., II, 385–393.

Relations between New Netherland and Virginia, 1619-64

The Dutch very early established amicable trade relations with the English in Virginia. Although the earliest contacts were hampered by the fear of the Virginians that the Dutch were inciting the Indians against them, by 1617 relations were established on a more friendly basis. Several of the early leaders of the colony, such as Thomas Dale and Thomas Gates, were hired by the Dutch to promote their trade. The Dutch never opposed England's title to Virginia and only maintained that its northern limit lay south of New Netherland. Indeed, in 1610, Noel Caron, the Dutch ambassador to London, proposed that the Dutch join the English in settling Virginia as a bulwark against their common enemy, Spain.[20]

Trade between Virginia and the Dutch was based upon Virginia's expanding tobacco crop. The Virginia Company defended its right to carry on this trade on the basis of the Royal Proclamation of 1610, which granted to the company the right to trade outside the British realm. The English government, however, did not wish to accept this interference of the Dutch in the economic life of its empire, and there were several debates in Parliament concerning the possible regulation of colonial trade, for the time being without result.

Virginia wished to continue its trade with the Dutch, who offered better prices for its tobacco than did the English and who sold European goods more cheaply. Many furs from New Netherland were smuggled into Virginia for shipment to England, where they received high prices. In July of 1620 a committee of the Virginia Company was appointed to negotiate with the Dutch to arrange for the sale of Virginia tobacco in the United Provinces. Within a year the company had factories in Holland to handle its trade there. Dutch traders were also conducting business in Virginia.

The merchants and the Privy Council of England strongly objected to such commercial relations between Virginia and the Netherlands, and in 1621 the Privy Council ordered that all Virginia tobacco had to be first landed in England; then, in a series of later orders, the Privy Council instructed the governors that Virginia must be closed to Dutch ships.[21] The protests of the Virginia Company, deprived of the right to seek the best market for its only product, went unheard, so the Virginians continued to sell their tobacco directly and illegally to the Dutch who visited the colony.

In the 1630s trade between Virginia and the Dutch colony on the South (Delaware) River developed, following a visit, in 1633, to Virginia of David DeVries, promoter of the Dutch colony, Virginia, with its one-crop economy, was an excellent market for Dutch foodstuffs. Moreover,

---

[20] John More to Sir Ralph Winwood, Dec. 15, 1610, Brown, *Genesis*, I, 440.
[21] *C.S.P., Col., A.& W.I., 1574–1660*, p. 26; Beer, *Origins of the British Colonial System*, 233–234.

the economic opportunities of New Netherland, with its concentration on trade rather than agriculture, attracted many enterprising Virginians, whose presence there strengthened the bonds between Virginia and the Dutch colonies.[22] When the Dutch colonies, during the 1630s, began to cultivate their own tobacco, some Virginians moved to the Dutch plantations where the tobacco they grew could be sold for a better price than in Virginia.

During the English civil war and for some twenty years thereafter, Virginia's trade with the Dutch grew. In July, 1649, the Commonality of New Netherland petitioned the States-General that peace between their country and England be preserved in the interest of the profitable Dutch trade in Virginia.[23] But Parliament, largely directed by Oliver Cromwell, initiated, in 1650, a program of commercial reforms and restrictions, one of the most severe of which forbade Englishmen and foreigners to trade with Virginia, a royalist stronghold, and other rebellious colonies.[24] During this period of interdict the Dutch trade assumed even greater significance in Virginia, for it became the chief outlet for Virginia's tobacco crop and the chief source of imports of food and manufactured goods. Indeed, this trade assumed such volume that the West India Company complained to Governor Stuyvesant in New Netherland that many Dutch ships bearing goods intended for New Netherland were going instead to Virginia.[25]

In March, 1651, Virginia surrendered to a Commonwealth fleet. Among the articles of surrender was one providing "That the people of Virginia have free trade as the people of England do enjoy to all places and with all nations according to the lawes of that commonwealth. And that Virginia shall enjoy all privileges equall with any English plantation in America." [26] The Virginians interpreted this article as freeing them from the restrictions of the trade act of 1650 and, after it was enacted, from the Navigation Act of October, 1651, which was intended to end the dominance of the Dutch in the English colonial carrying trade.

The Dutch were concerned that the Navigation Act meant that Dutch ships found in Virginia would be considered as prizes. Dutch merchants requested that they be freed from the rigors of the act and that their trade with the English colonies be allowed to continue.[27] In November of 1651 the Dutch ambassadors to England, Jacob Cats, Gerard Schaap, and Paúlus van de Perre, were instructed to negotiate a liberal trade treaty with England that would have included trade with the English colonies, but the consummation of these negotiations was prevented by the outbreak

[22] Flick, ed., *History of the State of New York*, II, 58.
[23] *N.Y.C.D.*, I, 269.
[24] *C.S.P.*, *Col.*, *A&W.I.*, 1574–1660, p. 343.
[25] *N.Y.C.D*, XIV, 77.
[26] Hening, ed., *Statutes at Large*, I, 363–365.
[27] *N.Y.C.D.*, I, 436–437. For the Anglo-Dutch negotiations of 1651, see Chapter V.

of the Anglo-Dutch war in 1652. Friendly trade relations between the Dutch and English in Virginia continued, nevertheless.

Acting under instructions similar to those given the Dutch ambassadors in 1651, Peter Stuyvesant, in May, 1653, sent an embassy to Virginia to propose "a close and firm alliance, correspondence and commerce, without regard to the undesired and unexpected bloody differences between their and our nation in Europe." [28] The concept of the colonies as a separate sphere of interest was implied here. The government of Virginia merely referred the proposal to the English government. Other overtures made by Stuyvesant during the war and for several years thereafter were also unproductive, although the Anglo-Dutch trade in America, particularly the export of Virginia tobacco to Holland by way of New Netherland, continued.

In January, 1660, following the death of Virginia's Governor Matthews, Stuyvesant sent Nicholas Varleth and Captain Bryan Newton to that colony as envoys to present the condolences of New Netherland and to propose an alliance against the Indians. They were also directed to "propose with all possible persuasive reasons a mutual correspondence and unmolested commerce and traffic, back and forwards, of the yachts, as both nations enjoy them in the Fatherland, with goods and wares from their own countries and places." [29]

Negotiations with the assembly and new governor of Virginia, Sir William Berkeley, produced a treaty "of amitie and commerce" which was signed at Jamestown in April, 1660. The treaty provided for the Dutch to enjoy free trade in Virginia, on condition that they pay the usual duties on the tobacco which they exported. Trade by either party with Indians dependent on the other was prohibited. Inhabitants of either colony trading with the other would enjoy the same rights in courts of law that natives of the colony enjoyed. Runaway servants from either colony found living in the other would be apprehended and returned to their masters. Debtors from either colony fleeing to the other could be sued by their creditors in the colony to which they had fled. [30] Ratifications of the treaty were exchanged at New Amsterdam in June, 1660.

Officially, the treaty had little effect. The Navigation Act of 1660 barred the Dutch from the Virginia trade, and Governor Berkeley, in 1662, was instructed to forbid shipment of tobacco from Virginia in any but English vessels. Unofficially, however, the trade between Virginia and the Dutch flourished for the next four years. Because of rising tobacco production, prices in England were too low to provide the Virginia planters with sufficient profit, and the Dutch furnished a ready outlet for surpluses. The conflict between the English Navigation Acts and Virginia's desire and

[28] N.Y.C.D., XIV, 241–242.
[29] N.Y.C.D., XIII, 145–147.
[30] Davenport, ed., *European Treaties*, II, 55–56.

need to trade with the Dutch was resolved by the Virginia assembly by an act passed in March, 1660, which provided that

Whereas the restriction of trade hath appeared to be the greatest impediment to the advance of the estimation and value of our present only commodity tobacco, *Be it enacted and confirmed,* That the Dutch and all strangers of what Xtian nation soever in amity with the people of England shall have free liberty to trade with us, for all allowable commodities, And receive protection from us to our utmost powers while they are in our jurisdiction, and shall have equall right and justice with our own nation in all courts of judicature, *Provided* they give bond and pay the impost of ten shillings per hogshead laid upon all tobacco exported to any fforreigne dominions . . .[31]

With the surrender of New Netherland to England in 1664, Dutch trade with Virginia declined and stricter enforcement of the Navigation Acts became possible. That this trade should have flourished as it did was evidence of the great disparity between the economic needs and ambitions of England and Virginia: to England, a monopoly over the economic life of its colony promised profits to English merchants and to the coffers of the English government; to the colony, desiring to enrich and develop itself, freedom of trade promised the most desirable course. The Dutch, in this case, served as the vehicle for Virginia's economic survival and growth. Virginia's adherence to a policy of free trade was the earliest expression of what was to become a strong theme in colonial protests against the economic domination of England.

Relations between New Netherland and Maryland

The territorial limits of New Netherland extended southward into Delaware Bay, where the Dutch quite early established forts and trading posts. Their title to the area was not, however, uncontested. Besides the rival settlement of the Swedes, begun in 1638,[32] the English, also, had a desire to control the Delaware country. Ships from New England and New Haven appeared in the region after 1640 and frequently tried to sail up the Delaware River to trade with the Indians, over whom the Dutch wished to maintain a commercial monopoly.

The greatest challenge to Dutch control in the area north of Virginia came with the establishment of Lord Baltimore's colony of Maryland, chartered in 1632 and first settled in 1635. As early as 1638 Governor Calvert officially encouraged trade with the Dutch, and a profitable and friendly commerce continued for several years. But relations were embittered by disputes over boundaries and territorial claims: Governor

---

[31] Hening, ed., *Statutes at Large,* I, 540.
[32] See Section 2 of this Chapter.

Fendall, Calvert's successor, claimed the region between the thirty-eighth and fortieth parallels and refused to recognize the right of the Dutch to the Delaware region.

During the 1650s English pressure on the Dutch became stronger. Governor Fendall sent Colonel Nathaniel Utie to the Dutch settlement at New Amstel to state that it lay within Lord Baltimore's province and that the Dutch must leave.[33] The New Amstel government protested the English claim and defended its own grant. Director Stuyvesant of New Netherland then dispatched two representatives to Maryland to defend the Dutch title to the Delaware region. The claim of New Netherland to the Delaware River was justified and Dutch title to American territories demonstrated as having descended from Spanish titles. The claims put forth by Utie were protested as contrary to the law of nations and the Anglo-Dutch treaty of 1654. The Dutch demanded the return of all Dutch and Swedish fugitives hiding in Maryland, with the promise that English fugitives would be likewise returned.[34] The Dutch mission was unsuccessful in settling the conflicting claims, and the West India Company finally presented a defense of its title to the States-General and offered to accept settlement of the boundary by arbitration between the Dutch and English governments.

Following the offer of arbitration friendlier relations between Maryland and the Dutch colonies developed. In August of 1663 the government of Maryland and the Dutch at New Amstel signed a treaty with the chiefs of the Delaware Bay Indians which provided for peace and justice between the English and the Indians and included as a final article "That the s^d Indian Kings & their Subjects shall inviolably observe these selfe same Articles towards the Dutch in Delaware Bay, as well as to the English of the Province of Maryland." [35] Trade also improved, with the Marylanders exchanging their tobacco for Dutch merchandise and slaves.

But persistent rumors that the English planned to take over the Delaware region, plus frequent English threats, caused many of the Dutch inhabitants of New Amstel to flee. Others fled from or were lost in an epidemic during the winter of 1658–59. In 1663 Stuyvesant, under instruction from the West India Company, transferred administration of the whole Delaware Valley to Alexander d'Hinoyossa. This virtually severed the connection of the New Amsterdam government with the remaining Dutch settlements in the Delaware region, and the area was gradually absorbed by the English.

[33] Vice-Director and Council of New Amstel to Colonel Nathaniel Utie, Sept. 9, 1659, N.Y.C.D., II, 73–75.

[34] "Vindication of the Dutch Title to the Delaware River," Oct. 6, 1659, N.Y.C.D., II, 80–84.

[35] Browne, ed., Proceedings of the Council of Maryland, 1636–67, in Archives of Maryland, III, 486.

2. New Sweden and Its Neighbors

The Delaware River region had been claimed and partly explored before the Swedes established their colony there in 1638. Sweden at this time had become an important power in Northern European politics, and this colonial project was part of an effort to acquire a share in the riches of the "new world" enjoyed by Sweden's western neighbors. In March, 1638, two small Swedish ships arrived in Delaware Bay, led by Peter Minuit, former director of New Netherland. Immediately after their arrival, Minuit purchased from local Indian chiefs for the New Sweden Company lands from Duck Creek to the Schuylkill, a distance of about sixty-seven miles along the west bank of the Delaware River and extending indefinitely westward.

Shortly thereafter, Minuit sent a ship to Jamestown to exchange its cargo for tobacco. Governor Berkeley was not allowed to permit such trade but proposed that the Swedes apply to England for permission to trade with Virginia. The Dutch became aware of the presence of the Swedes on the Delaware when Minuit attempted to sail above Fort Nassau. Violent protests were made to this intrusion in territory claimed by the Dutch, but the Dutch were at this time not strong enough to take any more effective action against the Swedes, and so Minuit was able to continue his work unmolested as long as he avoided Fort Nassau.

However, the prospect of profitable trade with the little Swedish colony was strong despite protests against its existence, and the English and Dutch very early, perhaps even in 1638, began to trade with the Swedes.[36] In 1640 Dutch settlers from Utrecht arrived at Fort Christina to settle within the limits of New Sweden. In April of the same year Peter Ridder, the new director of the colony, sailed above Fort Nassau and bought from the Indians lands from the Schuylkill to the falls at Trenton. The land lying south of Duck Creek to Cape Henlopen was also purchased, and the following year some land on the east bank of the Delaware River was added to this territory.

Dutch protests against the presence of the Swedes were somewhat stilled by the arrival of English ships from New Haven in 1641. The merchants of New Haven had found their colony badly located for trade with the Indians and therefore sent their agents to the Delaware region to purchase unoccupied lands there. The land which they did purchase was, however, claimed by the Swedes as having been already bought from the Indians, and so vigorous protests against the English presence followed. Protests became even stronger when the English settlement proved successful and English trade attracted most of the Indians away from the Swedes and Dutch.

[36] Johnson, *The Swedish Settlements on the Delaware* . . . , I, 198.

During the 1640s the colony of New Sweden became firmly established. Its agriculture developed, and trade, largely based upon the export of beaver skins purchased from the Indians, was carried on with the Dutch colonies as well as with Europe. But lack of support from the mother country and the inclination of the settlers for farming turned New Sweden into an agricultural rather than a commercial colony. In the later years of the 1640s and the early 1650s no ships came from Sweden, and much of the Indian fur trade was lost to the Dutch and English because the Swedes had little to sell. Repeated requests were sent to Sweden for supplies and additional settlers, and when these were not forthcoming the inhabitants of New Sweden were forced to rely upon the English and Dutch to furnish necessary Indian goods at exhorbitant prices. Even this trade diminished when war erupted between Britain and the Netherlands and when the Swedish fur trade was ruined by war among the Indian tribes.

In 1643 the Swedes arrested a group of Englishmen from New England who were trading with the Indians near Fort Christina. The Swedes had received rumors that the leader of the English trading party was bribing the Indians to murder the Swedes and Dutch and to destroy their settlements. The Englishmen were required to appear before a court of inquiry, consisting of Swedish, English, and Dutch commissaries, which was held in Fort Christina on July 10, 1643. The main objective of Swedish Governor Johan Printz was apparently to disprove the English claim to the Delaware River region, for discussion of these claims occupied most of the attention of the court. The decision of the court of inquiry was that the English traders were guilty of bribing the Indians and that they had no rights or possessions around the Delaware River; the penalty, however, was lenient: the traders were only obliged to pay double duty on the beaver skins in their possession.[37] Communications then ensued between New Sweden and New England in which each party tried to defend its title to the Delaware region. But the English for the time avoided the area, although they did not give up their hopes of settling there.

Relations with the Dutch during the 1640s were occasionally somewhat friendlier because both the Swedes and the Dutch needed support against the intrusions of the English on the Delaware. But the Dutch trade along the river at Fort Nassau and on the Schuylkill disturbed the Swedes, and Printz, who had no instructions to prevent it, could not hinder it. In his report of February, 1647, Printz told his government that the Dutch must be removed from the river, "for they oppose us on every side, they destroy our trade everywhere . . . they stir up the Indians against us . . . they begin to buy land from the savages within our boundaries, which we have purchased already eight years ago, they give New Sweden the name of New

---

[37] Johnson, *The Swedish Settlements on the Delaware*, I, 383–387.

Netherland and dare to build their houses there."[38] There followed several years of intermittent disturbances dependent upon the degree of activity of the Dutch in the area and aggravated by rumors of evildoing which each side was suspected of planning for the other.

By 1654 relations between the Swedes and the Dutch had become bitter. The Swedes captured the Dutch Fort Casimir and the Dutch soon planned not only to recapture that fort but to drive the Swedes entirely out of the Delaware region. During the following year preparations were made in Holland and New Netherland for an expedition against the Swedish colony, which was launched in September, 1655. The Dutch recaptured Fort Casimir, took the Swedish Fort Christina, and forced the surrender of Swedish Governor Johan Rising. The articles of capitulation, signed on September 15, provided for the evacuation of all Swedes who desired to leave, while those who elected to remain on the Delaware were obliged to take an oath of fidelity to the Dutch.[39]

Thus ended the existence of New Sweden as an independent colony. The New Sweden Company, reorganized as the American Tobacco Company, continued to operate as factors for the sale of American tobacco in Sweden and Finland. The business of the company was very large and successful, involving, as it did, a virtual monopoly on tobacco imports which drew protests from many Swedes. Finally, in 1660, the King of Sweden abolished the company as harmful to his other subjects.

Relations between New Sweden and England's North American colonies during the 1650s were more amicable than those with the Dutch. Partly responsible was a treaty of alliance and commerce signed by Great Britain and Sweden at Upsala in April, 1654, which provided for free passage and commerce in all dominions of both nations.[40] This agreement was adopted because England was as unwilling to agree to the specific opening of its American colonies to Swedish trade as it was to open them to the Dutch. A month later special articles were concluded between the plenipotentiaries of Britain and Sweden which provided for the establishment of peaceful relations in their respective African and American colonies. The American colonies were directed to "labor for their mutual preservation until the question of the boundaries of the colonies and other regulations for amity, if there be any, together with the remaining business of individuals, shall be decided before the commissioners duly appointed by both sides.[41]

The commissioners were never appointed, but when the commissioners of the United Colonies learned of the Anglo-Swedish alliance they wrote

---

[38] Quoted in Johnson, *The Swedish Settlements on the Delaware*, I, 415.
[39] N.Y.C.D., I, 607–609.
[40] Davenport, ed., *European Treaties*, II, 25–26. See Chapter VIII.
[41] Davenport, ed., *European Treaties*, II 29–30.

to Swedish Governor Rising expressing their hope that amicable relations between their colonies would be established.[42]

3. The English and French Colonies in America

The most widely dispersed, the most powerful, the most persistent, and the most troublesome rivals of the English colonies in the American hemisphere were those of France. Everywhere the English went to plant colonies, it seemed, the French went also. About the time when Virginia was founded, the French appeared in Acadia; while the New England colonies were being planted, the French appeared in Canada; as the English colonized certain unoccupied islands in the Caribbean, the French planted colonies on others nearby; as the English were occupying New York and Pennsylvania, the French from Canada were exploring the Great Lakes basin and exploring and occupying the valleys of the Ohio and the Mississippi Rivers; shortly after the settlement of the Carolinas, the French occupied the lower Mississippi Valley. Wherever English and French colonies were established in proximity with each other, direct contacts took place between them, often as warlike enemies, often as traders with each other, often as rivals for the fur trade and the good will of the Indians, and almost always as rival claimants to territory, whether on the mainland or among the islands of the Caribbean; once, at least, their proximity to each other led to an agreement between a French and an English colony in America to remain neutral in the case of a war between their mother countries in Europe. In these relationships, also, the pursuit of their own self-interests often led them into activities and policies that ran counter to the interests and the diplomacy of their mother countries.

Acadia and New England

The French province of Acadia, founded by Samuel Champlain in 1604, had a strategic and thus highly desirable location. It guarded the mouth of the St. Lawrence and thus its possession to a large extent determined the welfare of New France. Its maritime importance was increased by the fact that it bordered on the rich fisheries of the Grand Banks and on shipping lanes used by ships traveling by the northern route to and from Europe. Moreover, Acadia was for many years a rich source of furs, which were one of the principal economic resources of the northern colonies.

The first contacts between Frenchmen and Englishmen in the northeast

[42] Shurtleff and Pulsifer eds., *Acts of the Commissioners of the United Colonies*, II (*Records of the Colony of New Plymouth*, X), 127–128.

were those of fishermen, who began exploiting the fishing grounds in the sixteenth century. In the early years of the seventeenth century both nations established colonies on continental North America and consequently possessed permanent bases from which to pursue their rivalries.

Virginia, the first of England's American colonies, was granted by its charter of 1606 the whole area of the continent lying between 34° and 45° North Latitude. This overlapped French claims, and the northern boundary lay very close to the French colony at Port Royal, established in 1604. The northern part of Virginia was granted to a company of Plymouth merchants who sent an expedition in 1606 to the mouth of the Sagadahoc River in what is now the state of Maine. This colony was a failure and was abandoned in 1608, and for the next decade the Plymouth Company devoted itself solely to the exploitation of the fisheries and fur trade in "North Virginia," coming into close competition with the French who were active in the same area.

It was almost inevitable that the French and English should come into conflict over this region which they both claimed. In 1613 an armed man-of-war, under command of Captain Samuel Argall of Jamestown, was sent out against the French on the northern limits of Virginia. The French had been gradually extending themselves southward, and Argall's expedition was intended to check this movement and rescue North Virginia from French encroachment. Argall landed in Acadia and destroyed Port Royal and a Jesuit colony on Mount Desert Island, killing some of its inhabitants and carrying others back to Virginia. The French protested, demanding restitution of their losses and that the English define the boundaries of Virginia, "inasmuch as we thought the difficulty might have come on account of the neighborhood of the two colonies." [43] Although the French defended their long possession of the region, the English ambassador, in speaking with a representative of the French government in Paris, replied that "the interest which they [the French] pretended to have in the discoveries which we had made with great perill and charge . . . was contrarie to the received custome and practise of all nations, wherewith he was so well satisfied, as he said, that he would no more dispute that matter with me." [44]

In 1620 King James I of England granted to the Council for New England all the land on the continent of North America lying between 40° and 48° North Latitude, "throughout the Maine Land, from Sea to Sea," without taking the slightest notice of the fact that the French had already effectively occupied that territory in two areas, the colony of Acadia, centering about Port Royal, and the colony of Canada, or New France, on the St. Lawrence, centering about the town of Quebec. The next year, 1621, James granted to William Alexander the area, carved, as it were, out

[43] Montmorency to James I, Oct. 28, 1613. Brown, *Genesis*, II, 664–665.
[44] Sir Thomas Edmondes to James I, Jan. 2, 1613/4. Brown, *Genesis*, II, 677–678.

of the domain of the Council, that Alexander named Nova Scotia, which coincided roughly with the same area that the French called Acadia.[45] For several years Alexander did little to colonize his domain, but in 1628 David Kirke seized the three French settlements at Port Royal, St. John, on the St. John River, and Pentagoët, on the Penobscot (Pentagoët) River. It was during that same summer that Alexander finally sent a group of settlers to build a colony at the site of the former French Port Royal.

Acadia and Canada were restored to France by the Treaty of St. Germain-en-Laye (1632),[46] and Louis XIII appointed Isaac de Razilly governor of Acadia. The treaty did not define the boundaries of Acadia, and the French government instructed de Razilly to drive the English settlers out of the area as far as Pemaquid, near the mouth of the Kennebec. Accordingly, Charles de la Tour, one of de Razilly's lieutenants, seized the colony of Plymouth's trading post at Machias, and in 1635 the Sieur d'Aulnay Charnisay, de Razilly's other lieutenant, drove the English from Plymouth out of the former French post at Pentagoët, on the Penobscot River, which had been taken over by settlers from Plymouth after David Kirke had taken it from the French. Plymouth sought help from Massachusetts for the defense of this post, but it was refused.

When Isaac de Razilly died in 1635, de la Tour, in control of Port Royal, and d'Aulnay, settled at Pentagoët, or Penobscot, quarreled over the governorship and over the fur trade of Acadia. Meanwhile, a flourishing trade in Acadian furs and English manufactured goods had sprung up between the merchants of Boston and the "subjects" of de la Tour.

This intercolonial trade with Acadia led Massachusetts into direct involvement in Acadian affairs. Charles de la Tour, whose claim to Acadia was based upon the Nova Scotian baronetcy which he had inherited from his father as well as upon French royal authority, made several attempts to form an alliance with Massachusetts Bay. In 1641 he sent an envoy to Boston to propose a treaty based upon free intercolonial commerce, assistance for de la Tour against d'Aulnay, and the right for de la Tour to purchase English goods from Boston merchants. The Bostonians declined to make a treaty on the grounds that the envoy carried no letters or commission from his master.[47] In actuality Governor Winthrop was anxious to avoid involvement in Acadian affairs for fear of reprisal from the French government and consequent interference from England in New England's relations with adjacent French and Dutch colonies.

In 1642 de la Tour again sent emissaries to Boston, this time armed with letters from him requesting aid against d'Aulnay. The Bostonians entertained the Acadians respectfully but took no action toward creating

[45] For a discussion of the Anglo-French diplomatic disputes over the ownership and the boundaries of Acadia-Nova Scotia in the seventeenth century, see above, Chapter IX.

[46] See Chapter IV.

[47] Winthrop's Journal, "History of New England," 1630–49, Hosmer, ed., II, 43.

an alliance or granting aid. In 1643 de la Tour himself appeared in Boston, having come from France and finding his way into Acadia blocked by d'Aulnay. He requested aid against his rival and showed the magistrates his commission from the vice-admiral of France, which convinced the Bostonians that despite reports from d'Aulnay to the contrary de la Tour was on good terms with the French government. Convinced that the wrath of France would not be aroused against the colony, Governor John Winthrop offered him unofficial aid:

Whereupon, though we could not grant him aid without advice of the other commissioners of our confederacy, yet we thought it not fit or just to hinder any that would be willing to be hired to aid him; and accordingly we answered him that we would allow him a free mercate [market], that he might hire any ships which lay in our harbor.[48]

A month later de la Tour sailed for Acadia accompanied by four Bostonian ships and seventy volunteer soldiers. During their sojourn in Acadia the New Englanders accompanied de la Tour on an attack upon a fortified mill belonging to d'Aulnay. The mill and some adjacent grain fields were burned. Within a month of their departure the ships and men hired by de la Tour returned to Boston. De la Tour himself returned to Boston in the winter of 1644–45 and spent several months petitioning the court for aid against d'Aulnay, without success.

De la Tour's failure to win further aid from Massachusetts lay less in a change of feeling against him than in the refusal of the other citizens of the colony to become involved in French affairs. He retained the favor of the government of Boston: his claim to Acadia, which had been in English hands from 1627 to 1632, was based partly upon an English grant, and he was, moreover, clever enough to lead the Protestant New Englanders into believing him a Huguenot, surrounding himself as he did with French Protestants. Governor Winthrop defended his support of de la Tour on the grounds of charity and commercial freedom:

I will shew that this strife betweene La Tour and Daulnay doth nicely conserne us; and first in point of duty, in that our distressed neighbour calls to us for help; a speciall providence of God and his owne good opinion of our charitableness, brought him to us . . . nor were we in this case to stand upon the justice of the quarrell betweene them, no more than any man would doe, if he saw his neighbour under foote and in danger to be killed, he would first rescue him from danger, ere he enquire of the cause. . . .[49]

Even during de la Tour's final visit to Boston, although he was refused further aid, the government of the colony sought justification for helping

[48] Winthrop's Journal, Hosmer, ed., II, 107.
[49] The Governor's Answer to the Ipswich letter about De la Tour, Hutchinson Papers, eds. Whitmore and Appleton, I, 136–147.

him from the government of Scotland, which had formerly had authority over the settlement of Acadia or Nova Scotia.[50] The loss of Acadia with its fishery and fur trade had fallen hard upon New England, and it is possible that the Bostonians hoped that a victorious de la Tour would restore their privileges.

Other circumstances, however, negated this local sympathy for de la Tour. In the first place, the other members of the New England Confederation were reluctant to offer support to a Frenchman. John Endicott, in a letter to Governor Winthrop, expressed the prevalent New England distrust of the Acadian:

as long as La Tour and Dony [d'Aulnay] are opposites they will weaken on [sic] another. If La Tour should prevaile against him we shall undoubtedly have an ill neighbour. His Father and himselfe as I ame informed, have shed the blood of some English already . . . I must needs say that I feare we shall have little comfort in having any thing to doe with theise Idolatrous French.[51]

There were also fears of retribution from d'Aulnay, who was believed to be much stronger than de la Tour.[52] Other New Englanders objected that aid to de la Tour was ethically wrong and politically dangerous.[53]

Alarmed at the possible consequences of their participation in the attack upon d'Aulnay the Massachusetts authorities issued an order forbidding their people "to use any act of hostility otherwise than in their own defense, towards French or Dutch." [54] In May, 1644, they wrote to d'Aulnay, enclosing a copy of this order, denying having given commission to the colonists who had attacked him and offering to make satisfaction. At the same time they complained of d'Aulnay's action in capturing the English trading post at Penobscot (Pentagoët), in refusing their trade at Port Royal and threatening their trade with de la Tour, and in issuing commissions to d'Aulnay's captains to take English vessels and goods. The Massachusetts authorities especially desired to know from d'Aulnay whether he was inclined to make peace or war with them so that they might make their own preparations accordingly.

D'Aulnay had by this time succeeded in deposing de la Tour and having himself appointed governor and lieutenant general of Acadia. In the autumn of 1644 d'Aulnay sent his envoy, a Monsieur Marie, to Boston with a commission from the King of France condemning de la Tour as a rebel and with authority to negotiate an alliance of peace and amity with Massachusetts. On October 8 the magistrates signed an agreement with

[50] John Winthrop, Jr., to Lord Forbes, Dec. 23, 1644, in *Winthrop Papers*, IV, 501.
[51] Apr. 19, 1643, in *Winthrop Papers*, IV, 394-395.
[52] Thomas Gorges to John Winthrop, June 28, 1643, *Winthrop Papers*, IV, 396.
[53] Richard Saltonstall and others to the governor, deputy governor, assistants, and elders, May 14, 1643, *Winthrop Papers*, IV, 397-401.
[54] Quoted in Davenport, ed., *European Treaties*, I, 348.

Marie, on condition of ratification by the commissioners of the United Colonies. The agreement provided for peace between the inhabitants of Massachusetts and Acadia, for mutual freedom of trade, and for freedom from reprisals for offenses unless satisfaction was not made. It was also provided "that the governor and majestrates aforesaid bee not bound to restrayne their merchantes from tradeing with the ships with what people soever, whether French or others, in what place soever inhabiting," a provision which left the people of Massachusetts free to continue their trade with de la Tour.

D'Aulnay refused to ratify the Treaty of Boston until he had received satisfaction for injuries which he claimed to have sustained from New Englanders who participated in de la Tour's attack against him. He demanded that New England send commissioners to treat with him on this matter. The General Court at Boston protested its innocence of complicity in de la Tour's expedition and presented d'Aulnay with its own complaints of injuries sustained from Acadians.[55] Commissioners were appointed but were unable to settle the differences. Finally, in September, the government of Massachusetts tried a more direct method of appeasing d'Aulnay. It presented his commissioners with a sedan chair as a gift for d'Aulnay in satisfaction of his injuries.[56] The chair was accepted and d'Aulnay signed the agreement on September 28, 1646. The commissioners of the United Colonies had previously ratified it on September 2, 1645.

In 1654 Acadia again fell into British hands as the result of a raid launched by the Cromwellian government, but by the Treaty of Breda in 1667 it was restored to France. The English recaptured the province in 1690, during King William's War, but soon after lost it again to the French. Thus during the first century of its existence Acadia was the scene of almost constant strife between the British and French for control of the territory, its fishery and furs. Both sides seized each other's trading posts, ships, and furs, and each endeavored to incite the Indians against the other. The situation was in no way alleviated by the mother countries, which not only both presented strong and uncompromising claims to Acadia but were never able to determine the exact extent of the province.

When the War of the Spanish Succession broke out in 1702 the inhabitants of New England and Acadia were fully ready to participate. During the 1690s their relations had become particularly bitter. Seizures of fishing boats were practiced by both sides, particularly the French, who were attempting to establish absolute control over the fishing grounds. Encroachments over the frontier and disputed jurisdiction over Indian tribes made observance of the treaty of American Neutrality (Treaty of

[55] May 22, 1646, *Records of the Governor and Company of the Massachusetts Bay in New England*, Shurtleff, ed., II, 157–158.
[56] *Winthrop's Journal*, ed., Hosmer, II, 284–285.

Whitehall) of 1686 and the peace Treaty of Ryswyck (1697) nearly impossible.[57]

The War of the Spanish Succession fell particularly hard on New England. Because New York adopted a policy of neutrality,[58] the French in Canada were freed from the need to defend themselves against that colony or to attack it, and so were able to concentrate their forces on New England. In 1704 a party of French and Indians surprised the village of Deerfield, Massachusetts, and carried out one of the bloodiest massacres in American history. French privateers devastated the New England fisheries. In 1705 Governor Dudley of Massachusetts made overtures for the negotiation of a treaty of neutrality with New France, and in October the Governor of Canada, the Marquis de Vaudreuil, submitted a draft treaty. The draft provided for peace between the two colonies and complete neutrality, with no aid to be given to the war in any way. Peaceful passage was to be allowed between the two colonies, but no trade in any form was to be allowed. The treaty was not to become effective until Dudley had brought the other northern colonies to ratify it.[59] Dudley did not find the draft acceptable, but he nevertheless submitted it to New York, no doubt hoping to gain further respite for his ravaged colony by prolonging the truce which had accompanied the negotiations. Vaudreuil suspected him of stalling and so resumed the attacks on New England.

By the Treaty of Utrecht, signed in 1713, France ceded Acadia to Britain, placing that province, with the exception of Cape Breton Island, permanently in English hands. Cape Breton was recognized as belonging to France.

The New York Frontier

The area which witnessed the most constant and long-enduring colonial rivalry in North America was the region which now comprises upper New York state and which was, in the seventeenth and eighteenth centuries, the scene of many disputes between the French on the north and the Dutch and English in the south for control of land, jurisdiction over Indians, and, most importantly, access to and domination of the route to the Great Lakes basin and its lucrative fur trade.

Relations between New France and the Dutch of New Netherland were peaceful despite their disputed territorial claims. In the first place, their actual settlements were so far apart that there was never any need to adjust boundaries. Explorations by Champlain in the northern and western parts of New Netherland were unchallenged by the Dutch, and only when the French attempted to take possession of the Delaware in 1622

[57] For the treaty of American neutrality and the Peace of Ryswick, see Chapter IX.
[58] See Chapter XIII.
[59] N.Y.C.D., IX, 770–772.

and of the Hudson in 1623 were they driven away. The activities of French Jesuit missionaries within Dutch territory made the Dutch uneasy about the possible loss of influence over the Indians but they did not protest, being more interested in the present fur trade than in the future welfare of the souls of the Indians, while they relied to a great extent upon the Iroquois to protect their interests. Trade in goods and furs was carried on by the Dutch and French along the frontier, and Dutch ships fished off Newfoundland.

Although conflict never erupted between the French and the Dutch, there were in their colonial situations many seeds for future intercolonial warfare. The boundaries between New Netherland and New France were never defined; jurisdiction over Indian tribes was never settled; the activity of French missionaries in Dutch territory and the influence of these missionaries over the Indians was ominous; competition for the fur trade would grow as local pelt-bearing animals grew scarce and it became necessary for merchants to seek out new and more distant sources.

It was these seeds of conflict which the English inherited when they took possession of New Netherland in 1664. Being more numerous and having greater resources at their disposal, the English pressed the development of their new colony, particularly its fur trade, and very soon the seeds of dispute germinated into intercolonial warfare.

At this point the Iroquois confederacy, known as the "Five Nations" of Indians, assumed its role as the principal disturbing factor in Anglo-French intercolonial relations, which it was to hold until 1713, when the French, by the Treaty of Utrecht, recognized the Iroquois as British subjects. The Dutch had originally gained the friendship of the Iroquois, buying their furs and selling them European weapons with which they established supremacy over their Indian neighbors. By their relatively kind and fair usage the Dutch had won the alliance of the Iroquois and were able to keep the confederation either friendly or neutral throughout their rule of New Netherland. The French, on the other hand, very early incurred the hostility of the Iroquois by giving support to their enemies, the Hurons and Algonquins, against them. Between 1609 and 1615 these Indians and their French allies inflicted several severe defeats upon the Iroquois and drove them into friendship with the Dutch who could provide them with arms.

The English continued the friendly commercial relations with the Iroquois which the Dutch had enjoyed. They also attempted to strengthen their relations with the Five Nations by taking the position that, since the territory inhabited by the Iroquois was part of the province of New York, the Indians were therefore British subjects. Moreover, although the French had a strategic advantage in the fur trade by reason of the many trading posts they had established in the interior and around the Great Lakes, the English, because of lower manufacturing costs in England, were able to sell their trade goods at much lower prices to the Indians and thus attracted many of them to Albany, the center of the British fur trade. The Iroquois played their most significant role in the English fur trade as middlemen between the English merchants and other Indian tribes to the west: their own country had few beavers so they traded English goods with other Indians for pelts which they then sold to the English for more goods and the European arms and rum which had become necessary for their own survival. Thus the Iroquois interfered in the French fur trade by trading with tribes allied with the French.

Trade came to assume a political significance even greater than its economic importance, for it became the chief means of alliance with Indian tribes and thus a vital weapon in intercolonial and international warfare. Even when furs were not needed they were purchased at the highest possible prices. The French Canadian Company was required, during the late seventeenth century, to buy all beaver furs offered and to destroy the ones not needed by French hat makers by burning them in the presence of a government officer. Toward the end of the century the French began to buy cheap English goods in Manhattan, a policy which allowed them to undersell the Iroquois in their trade with the western Indians, which, in the eighteenth century, assumed large and troublesome proportions.

French efforts to subdue the Iroquois continued. The power which the Iroquois gained with their European weapons over other tribes made the French fear the loss of their Indian allies and the divergence of the fur trade to Albany. As an effort to end the depredations of the Five Nations the French, during the 1660s, several times violated the territory of New York in campaigns against them. The English protested not only French trespassing in their territory but the violation of the then-prevailing Anglo-French peace.[60] The Iroquois were finally frightened into making a brief peace with the French during 1666–67 by news of an Anglo-French treaty which brought the Iroquois temporarily under French domination and thus out of British protection.[61]

Another factor in the Anglo-French conflict along the New York frontier was geography. New York was, of the English North American colonies, in closest geographical relation to Canada. It possessed, moreover, the only practical approach by land from the English colonies to the centers of French power at Quebec and Montreal, and it alone was located so as to block French expansion and communications to the west. As an ice-free outlet to the sea New York was long coveted by the French Canadians.

A third factor contributing to conflict along the frontier was the undefined state of the frontier itself. The English claimed that their territory

[60] Colonel Nicholls to Governor Tracy, Aug. 20, 1666, N.Y.C.D., III, 133.
[61] Colonel Nicholls to Governor Tracy, Aug. 20, 1666, N.Y.C.D., III, 121–122.

extended northward and westward to the "Lake (or River) of Canada" [62]
and would recognize no French claims or conquests south of the
St. Lawrence or east of the Great Lakes. But no actual boundary had ever
been defined or settled, so the French could justify their settlements along
the edges of this territory as logically as the English could protest them.

The first significant conflict between New France and New York lasted
from 1684 to 1688 and was precipitated by a punitive expedition launched
by the French against the Iroquois, who had been making war on French
Indian allies around the Great Lakes. Governor Dongan of New York,
feeling himself obliged to protect the Iroquois and to challenge French influence in the west, but instructed not to give French governor La Barre
"just cause of complaint" [63] against him, met the French challenge by
making a bold claim of British rights to jurisdiction over the Iroquois and
their territory. He protested French encroachment on English territory,
which he defined as extending to the St. Lawrence and the Great Lakes.[64]
Dongan also warned the Iroquois of French preparations against them and
in return received their request for a protective alliance, which he accepted.
The French expeditions against the Iroquois failed through the weakness of
the French, and in 1685 La Barre was recalled to France and the Marquis
de Denonville was appointed in his stead.

Denonville's instructions warned him of the efforts of Governor Dongan
to assist the Iroquois and "to extend British domination up to the Banks
of the River St. Lawrence, and over the entire territory inhabited by these
Indians," and directed him to treat the British as enemies when found in
Indian territory.[65] At the same time the French ambassador in London,
Paul Barillon d'Amoncourt, was directed to protest Dongan's assistance to
the Iroquois "notwithstanding those Nations have always been subject to
France, since their country was discovered by the French, without any ob-
jection on the part of the English." [66]

A correspondence then developed between Dongan and Denonville in
which each protested the policies of the other—British trade with the
western tribes and French efforts to establish themselves on the Niagara.
So bitter did the dispute become that Louis XIV was prompted to send
a special ambassador, the Comte d'Avoux, to London to bring about a
settlement of disputed boundaries in America, which to the French
meant Hudson Bay in the North and Niagara and the Great Lakes region
in the South. A settlement was not possible, for neither side would compromise its claims. Finally, fearing that an Anglo-French war would erupt
on account of this and other American intercolonial disputes, James II pro-

[62] Sir John Werden to Governor Andros, May 7, 1677, N.Y.C.D., III, 247.
[63] Sir John Werden to Governor Dongan, Dec. 4, 1684, N.Y.C.D., III, 353.
[64] Dongan to La Barre, June 24, 1684, N.Y.C.D., III, 448.
[65] Royal Instruction to M. de Denonville, Mar. 10, 1685, N.Y.C.D., IX, 271.
[66] M. Seignelay to M. Barillon, Mar. 10, 1685, N.Y.C.D., IX, 269.

posed a treaty of American neutrality *vis-à-vis* Europe, which was signed at Whitehall in November, 1686.[67] The treaty pledged Britain and France to maintain peace between their subjects in America and the French and British subjects in America to maintain peace regardless of relations between the mother countries. It did not, however, attempt to settle any of the disputes threatening the maintenance of peace, although it provided for the appointment of commissioners to do so, so that conditions in America were not essentially altered and the French and English governors continued their policies of competition along the New York frontier. Dongan continued to assist the Iroquois against the French, inciting the protests of the French commissioners against this interference in their claimed jurisdiction over the Five Nations, and the French continued to construct forts around the Great Lakes.

In the face of French expansion, Dongan sought authority and material assistance from his government to pursue the same policies as the French— to establish forts and trading posts in the interior and to send missionaries to live among the Indians as the Jesuits did.[68] Since such aid was not given, Dongan pursued the only means he could of preventing French expansion: he furnished arms to the Iroquois against protests from Canada and the terms of the Treaty of American Neutrality. By 1688 Dongan had secured the firm friendship of the Iroquois and their agreement not to make peace with the French until the French had complied with their demands (which were actually the demands of the English): the destruction of the forts at Onijaro and Cadaracqui and the return of goods taken from the Indians. Protests continued to be sent back and forth between Canada and New York. The French imprisoned several English traders and seized their possessions for trespassing in French territory, which claim Dongan denied as insubstantial. " 'Tis a very hard thing," he wrote, "that all the Countryes a Frenchman walks over in America must belong to Canada." [69] The French were also accused of capturing and cruelly treating Iroquois who traded in French territory and of invading the country of the Senecas, one of the Five Nations. Denonville, on his side, protested Dongan's alliance with the Iroquois as contrary to the Treaty of Neutrality.

In 1687 Dongan and Denonville agreed to attempt the peaceful settlement of disputes between them. French agents, the Jesuit Father Valliant and a Monsieur du Mont, were sent to New York to treat with Dongan. To them Dongan presented his demands: that the goods and arms taken from British traders be restored to them, that French forts built in the Iroquois country be demolished, that Iroquois captured by the French be released.[70] The French agents first demanded satisfaction for ill-treatment

[67] See Chapter IX.
[68] Dongan to the Lord President, Feb. 19, 1688, *N.Y.C.D.*, III, 510–511.
[69] Dongan to Denonville, Oct. 25, 1687, *N.Y.C.D.*, III, 514.
[70] Dongan to the French agents, Feb. 3, 1688, *N.Y.C.D.*, III, 520–521.

which they had received traveling through Mohican territory to New York. They also demanded satisfaction for injuries done by the Senecas in Canada.[71] They protested British trade in territories claimed by France and they defended their right to seize goods of such traders.[72] They suggested that controversies concerning boundaries, destruction of French forts, and the restoration of captured goods be referred to the English and French kings "as it is commanded in the treaty of neutrality," a fruitless gesture since it was because the kings, through their commissioners, had been unable to settle these disputes that the Americans were obliged to seek their own settlements. They also proposed a meeting of all the Indian tribes involved in order to effect a peace among them and a cessation of arms on both sides. They demanded that the British prevent the Senecas and other tribes from molesting Indians allied with the French, and that Indian prisoners of both sides be released. The meetings came to nothing, for neither side was willing to compromise in any way.

Anglo-French relations in Europe had meanwhile degenerated to the point of war, and in May, 1689, Britain declared war on France, citing as one of the causes French encroachments on British-American territories, including New York.[73] The colonies, which had maintained peace only precariously, immediately abandoned the Treaty of Neutrality and entered into war among themselves. Both France and England were so occupied with the conduct of the European war (the War of the League of Augsburg) that they could give little attention or support to their North American colonies, which were thus thrown largely upon their own resources. The British colonies suffered most as a result of this situation: lacking a central authority and divided by many separate interests, they were unable to develop enough combined military power to injure the French or even effectively to defend themselves. Each side developed schemes for the conquest of the other, but since neither the French nor the English government could spare the necessary soldiers and arms few formal intercolonial military campaigns were launched. The sort of military activity possible was surprise raids, in which the French, accustomed to life in the woods with their Indian allies, were far more active and successful than the English. The frontier areas of New York and New England suffered severely under the French raids.

King William's War, as it was called in the colonies, ended with treaties of peace signed at Ryswyck in the Netherlands in September of 1697. Because the Anglo-French treaty provided for a return to the *status quo ante bellum* in the American possessions of the belligerents, it did little to end intercolonial disputes in America. Commissioners were appointed

[71] French agents to Dongan, Feb. 4, 1688, *N.Y.C.D.*, III, 521.
[72] French agents to Dongan, Feb. 4, 1688, *N.Y.C.D.*, III, 522.
[73] For a discussion of America in the European phase of this war, called in America King William's War, see Chapter IX.

to discuss disputed colonial questions, but they were unable to reach any agreements before war again broke out in Europe in 1702.

The brief interwar period in America was marked by a renewed struggle over the status of the Iroquois and over control of the west. Governor Bellomont of New York and the French government in Canada both claimed sovereignty over the Iroquois. The English claim was based upon alliances and friendships with the Iroquois which they had inherited from the Dutch; [74] the French argument rested upon the claim that the French had been first to live among the Iroquois. Because the French held many Iroquois prisoners, Bellomont was most anxious to establish the Five Nations as British subjects who were thus included in the peace and must be released. The French protested that they were rebellious French subjects who had to make a separate peace with France. This separate peace was concluded in 1701, and was a diplomatic victory for the French, for it seemed to establish a basis for French claims of sovereignty over the Five Nations.

French expansion to the west and the memory of injuries suffered in the war prompted Bellomont to seek means of establishing the security of his colony. He requested assistance from England to repair frontier forts, increase the militia, and gain the firm support of the Iroquois who, through English weakness, were being seduced by the French. He also requested that Church of England ministers be sent among the Iroquois to counteract the influence of French Jesuit missionaries.[75]

Concern in New York grew as the French became ever more firmly established in the west. The English had done little to extend their own influence into the interior, although they were ideally located to do so. Because the Albany traders enjoyed a legal monopoly of the New York fur trade they had traditionally had the pelts brought to Albany and opposed the establishments of forts and settlements to the west for fear of interception of this trade. Governor Bellomont's proposals that the English establish forts in the Indian country and on the Great Lakes came to nothing, partly because of opposition from Albany, partly because means to do so were not forthcoming from the British government.

During this same period friendly trade relations developed between Albany and Montreal. In 1701, aware that another war was imminent, the Montreal merchants suggested that a policy of neutrality be maintained between Canada and New York. In this way both colonies would be spared the expense of defending their frontiers, and the profitable trade between Montreal and Albany could be continued. The French King,

[74] Bayard to Earl of Bellomont, New York, July 6, 1698, "English Right to the Sovereignty over the Five Nations," B.M., Lansdowne Mss. 849: fols. 73–73v.

[75] Earl of Bellomont's propositions concerning the security of the British plantations in North America, in his letter to the Board of Trade, July 15, 1700, B.M., Lansdowne Mss. 849: fols. 29–43.

during the same year, instructed his governor in Canada to maintain peace with the Iroquois, who, for their part, were willing to remain neutral as long as Albany was not attacked.

Thus, when the War of the Spanish Succession broke out in 1702, New York did not become involved in it. Many factors were involved in the policy of neutrality adopted by the colonial government. The Albany traders desired neutrality in order to continue their trade with Canada, and their influence on the colonial council and assembly was strong enough to force acceptance of their wishes. The assembly, for its part, welcomed neutrality so as to be spared the expense of defending the frontiers. Moreover, the Iroquois, who in the past had been the force which the English used against the French, were less attached to the English cause, having suffered badly from the French during the preceding war. The Indian confederacy became divided into French and English factions. New York's policy of neutrality was strongly condemned by its neighbors, particularly New England, which suffered severely from the French and their Indian allies during the war.

New York's neutrality was ended in 1709, when the English government turned its attention to the war in America and plans were developed for a massive land and sea attack upon Canada. When orders to prepare for the expedition were received, and a clear possibility of permanently destroying New France was offered, New York readily abandoned its policy of neutrality, with opposition only from the Albany traders, and the assembly voted men and money for the campaign. The attack, however, was abandoned when the English goverment diverted elsewhere the forces which it had intended to send against Canada. A similar expedition was planned for 1711, and again New York unhesitantly contributed its share. This expedition also was a total failure, and New York resumed its neutrality, refusing to engage in the war except at the command of the British government.

The war was ended in 1713 with the Peace of Utrecht. By the terms of the Anglo-French treaty the Iroquois were recognized as British subjects, but many of the factors which in the past had contributed to disturbances along the frontier remained to create conflicts in the eighteenth century.[76]

St. Christopher, 1624-78: The Treaty of Sandy Point (1678)

The English and French inhabitants of the Caribbean island of St. Christopher ("St. Kitts") were very early forced into relations with one another. The first English colonists arrived in 1624 and established their settlement in the middle of the island. The date of the arrival of the French on the island is uncertain: Captain John Smith wrote that three Frenchmen were living there when Captain Thomas Warner arrived with

[76] See Chapters X and XIII.

his party of colonists, and a few more French settlers may have arrived at the beginning of 1625. It is certain that in the same year a French privateer, commanded by Pierre Belain, Sieur d'Esnambúc, put into St. Christopher to repair damages inflicted by a Spanish warship. The English offered no objection to its presence; rather, they welcomed d'Esnambúc's proposal that a French colony be established on the same island, no doubt because of their fears of the increasing hostility of the Caribs.

An attack by the Caribs in November of 1625 brought the French and English on St. Christopher together to repulse them. The Caribs were driven off, but the general precariousness of the position of the European settlers on the island forced the French and English into an attitude of cooperativeness. In 1626 the Caribs threatened another attack, and the French and English joined to forestall them with a surprise massacre. Shortly afterward, when the French were attacked by the Caribs, the English went to their assistance and together they drove most of the Caribs from the island.

With the departure of the Caribs the common Indian danger to the French and English was removed and the need for cooperation between them was lessened. Friction between them grew. In 1627 a treaty was signed by Warner and d'Esnambúc which formally divided the island, alloting to the French the two ends of the island and giving the English the middle section which they had already settled. Each governor was to have sole jurisdiction over subjects of his own nation and over ships of his nation which visited the island. The treaty also provided for mutual assistance against the Caribs and the Spaniards. In case of disputes between French and English residents, the delinquents were to be judged by French and English magistrates. In the event of war in Europe between France and England the islanders would maintain local neutrality unless expressly commanded by their kings to enter the war, and in such event they would give warning before any act of hostility.[77] This treaty was renewed many times (in 1638, 1644, 1649, 1655, 1662, and 1666) but it did not prevent hostilities or bitterness between the rival settlements.

One source of hostility was that the division of the island did not prevent communication between the two nations. The English section in the middle of the island was divided by a rugged range of mountains, and traffic between the two English sections thus divided usually passed through French territory. The salt ponds which were regarded as mutual property lay on a peninsula at the southeastern extremity of the island, and visits by the English sometimes involved trespass on French lands. Moreover, the most reliable sources of fresh water were in the Eng-

---

[77] The text of this treaty is in Burns, *History of the British West Indies*, 743–744.

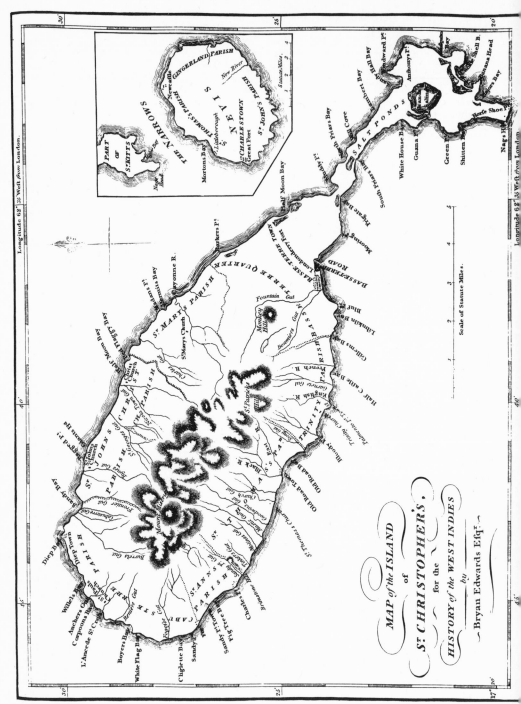

THE ISLAND OF ST. CHRISTOPHER. THE ENGLISH AND FRENCH ZONES, CIRCA 1678. (From Bryan Edwards, *History of the British West Indies* [London, 1819].)

lish section. The English population grew much faster than the French and landhungry English settlers frequently encroached upon the fertile and relatively empty lands belonging to the French.

Only problems of mutual survival were sufficient to draw the English and French into cooperation. From the time of its settlement, St. Christopher was critically short of food because tobacco was grown to the exclusion of other crops. In 1639 the English and French governors, Sir Thomas Warner and the Chevalier de Poincy, agreed to limit the amount of tobacco grown on the island.

When the island agreement of neutrality was renewed in 1666 the French officials on St. Christopher in accordance with instructions from the French West India Company, proposed that the treaty be extended to include the islands neighboring St. Christopher and the island of Jamaica. The English governor of the Leeward Islands, Lord Willoughby, did not accept. Instead, when news arrived in the West Indies of the outbreak of war between England and France in Europe, Governor Watts of St. Christopher gave the French three days in which to submit to England. The French then fell on the English and made themselves masters of the island. By the Treaty of Breda, which ended this war, the English portion of St. Christopher, like all other captured colonial territory, was restored to its original owners, although this restoration was long delayed by the French.

Relations between the English and French in the West Indies continued with uneasiness on both sides which was hardly mitigated by the official peace between their two nations. For the English in the Leeward Islands the situation was particularly precarious because they were numerically fewer than the French and their defenses were extremely inadequate.

Toward the end of 1677 the Comte de Blénac, Governor-in-Chief of the French Antilles, offered to make a new treaty of neutrality for the Leeward Islands, based upon the precedents of St. Christopher. Sir William Stapleton, Governor of the Leeward Islands, welcomed the proposal as a relief to the weak English position. The two governors of St. Christopher, Colonel Abednego Matthew and Monsieur de St. Laurens, were empowered to negotiate the treaty, which they signed in May, 1678, at Sandy Point, a small town on the island.

The treaty provided for peace and neutrality between the islands governed by Stapleton and de Blénac. In the event of war between England and France no act of hostility would be committed by any subjects on ships of these two governments in the islands. Ships of either nation could travel safely near the islands of the other. Differences between subjects of the two nations would be judged jointly by the French and English generals or their appointees. For the assurance of the treaty it was agreed that each party would give hostages to the other and that two of these hostages should be sent to Europe to petition the Kings of France and England to ratify the treaty.[78]

Stapleton and de Blénac ratified the treaty soon after it was signed, but the French King refused to sign it unless Jamiaca and Barbados, the strongest British islands, were included in the neutral area.[79] The Lords of Trade consented to this on condition that the clause in the treaty which provided that the terms of the Treaty of Breda be observed were changed to protect English interests,[80] and commissioners were appointed who introduced new provisions. France, however, refused to accept any alterations in the original treaty other than the neutralization of Jamaica and Barbados.

The Treaty of Sandy Point never was ratified by the mother countries and so never came into operation. It was, however, of significance as a step toward the Treaty of American Neutrality concluded by the governments of England and France at Whitehall in 1686. The series of neutrality agreements on St. Christopher which concluded with the Treaty of Sandy Point are of significance also as an early expression of the concept of the "two spheres" and of a nascent American attitude of noninvolvement in European affairs. Like many intellectual concepts, these had their roots in practical problems: the vicissitudes of political relations between England and France fell heavily upon their Caribbean colonies where difficulties of survival and development and the peaceful maintenance of local relations were severe enough without the added burden of participation in European wars.

The direct relations carried on by Europe's American colonies were in so many ways different from those of the mother countries that it can be said that America was a new world not only in its geography but also in the psychology of the Europeans who settled there and made it their home. The whole situation of the colonies was so different from that of the mother countries, and, often, from the conceptions which the mother countries had of the colonies, that intelligible communication was sometimes not possible. The colonists, regardless of the amount of support provided by their mother countries, were essentially on their own: it was they who had to push back the forest, to fight off or conciliate the Indians, to force a living out of the soil, sea, and forests around them, and to deal with the neighboring colonies of other nations.

Because of these conditions, the colonies developed diplomatic policies in many ways so different from those directed by the mother countries that they present an entirely different perspective. The colonies were almost all

---

[78] Davenport, ed., *European Treaties*, II, 258–260.

[79] *C.S.P., Col., A.& W.I.*, 1677–80, No. 1007, p. 367.

[80] "Journal of Lords of Trade and Plantations," June 12, 1679, *C.S.P., Col., A.& W.I.*, 1677–80, No. 1019, p. 374.

established to aid the mother countries in a variety of ways: for trade or exploitation of natural resources, or for military strategy, or to receive surplus population. But the colonists, once established, developed their own interests, often at variance with those of their mother countries. Intercolonial trade, for example, was carried on to some extent between all the European colonies in America, often contrary to the regulations of the mother countries, particularly England, and often in times of war between them. The European policies of the metropoli were not nearly as strong or effective in the colonies as the immediate and natural desire of the colonists to reap a ready profit wherever it was offered, regardless of the consequences to imperial plans. Thus developed the trade in Virginia tobacco with the Dutch, or the sale of arms by Albany merchants to Indians who used them against New England during the War of the Spanish Succession, or the trade of the Albany merchants with Montreal. Similarly, too, there had already begun, well before 1700, direct trade among English, Dutch, French, and Spanish colonies in the West Indies and between the northern English colonies on the continent of North America and all of the European colonies in the Caribbean area. This became notably true in the War of the Spanish Succession.

Evidence of independent action is to be seen in the political as well as in the economic relations of the colonies. Most particularly, one observes the several treaties or agreements of American neutrality arranged during the seventeenth century. During these early years of their existence the colonies were far less able to bear the costs and damages of war than were their mother countries, yet the frequent European wars of this century almost inevitably spread to America. Treaties of neutrality, like those accepted by the French and English residents of St. Christopher or that negotiated by Governor Dudley of Massachusetts and Governor Vaudreuil of Canada in 1705, or a policy of neutrality and noninvolvement, such as that adopted by New York during the War of the Spanish Succession or as exemplified by the Treaty of Sandy Point, were largely efforts to avoid the extremely precarious situation of a colony at war. To these colonists the business of survival and building their homes was of more importance than carrying out the military policies of distant European governments.

On the other hand, there were many occasions when, although mother countries were at peace, the colonies found it to their interest to engage in wars that might well have involved the mother countries in war in Europe. Such, for example, were the bitter, seesaw conflicts between the French and the English fur traders in the Hudson Bay area, in the littoral of the Bay of Fundy and along the New York-Great Lakes frontier, or in the West Indies, which led the governments of James II and Louis XIV to arrange the Treaty of American Neutrality signed at Whitehall in 1686. Such, also, were the English raids upon Spanish colonies around the Caribbean that had led to the Anglo-Spanish "American" Treaty of Madrid in 1670.[81]

During the eighteenth century England was to become master of eastern North America, and at the end of the century its colonies sought their independence. There were many factors leading to this rebellion, one of which was certainly the growing consciousness of the differentness of the American settlements from England and their need to pursue policies to the benefit of thier own and not English interest. The seeds of this attitude lay in the intercolonial relations of the seventeenth century.

[81] See Chapter VI.

CHAPTER XII

The Impact of the New World of the Colonies upon the Evolution of the Theory and the Practice of International Law

THE AGE OF Discovery, the overseas expansion of European civilization, the foundation of colonial empires, and the international rivalries among European powers for commercial and colonial empire that accompanied these other phenomena were, by-products of the so-called commercial revolution and the rise of modern capitalism. So, also, in many ways, was the appearance of the modern integral state out of the ruins of feudalism. The appearance of an "international law" was a necessary consequence of the creation of modern national states. For as these states took form and achieved a mutual international recognition of their national identities and their sovereignty, it became necessary to formulate a dependable set of rules, conventions, and institutions for the conduct of their relations with each other.

Thus, it was in the course of the sixteenth century that, beginning with the Italian states, the national states of Western Europe adopted the custom of sending permanent embassies to each other and that there grew up a body of rules, or "protocol," governing the behavior and the privileges of ambassadors, their staffs, and other diplomatic agents, while resident in foreign lands. Of much greater importance was the growth and general acceptance of a body of principles and conventions regulating the behavior of the states themselves that has come to be known as "international law."

It is to be noted, of course, that there is not, and that there never has been, a code of law as between states that the states must obey, in the same sense in which the citizen must obey the municipal law of his country, since there is no sanction provided for in "international law" that can coerce any national state in the interest of the international community as a whole, yet, despite the fact that any sovereign state may ignore "international law" almost with impunity, it is possible to speak of international law as "a body of obligations which is, in a sense, independent of and superior to [the positive legislation of independent states]." [1] This body of obligations is thought of as

binding upon nations, not merely as something to which they may be tacitly assumed to have agreed, but also as a fundamental condition of their admission to the full and equal participation in the intercourse of civilized states.[2]

For its authority or influence over the actions of states, this set of obligations appeals to the authority of the great writers on the relations between states, of whom Hugo Grotius (1583–1645) is the best known, to the terms of treaties, which are regarded as contracts between states, to the decisions of international tribunals or joint international commissions, to boards of arbitration, and to the judgments of prize courts.

The overseas expansion of European commerce, with its correlative growth of colonial empires and of commercial and imperial rivalries, contributed significantly to the body of concepts and obligations known as international law. From the very beginning of the Age of Discovery, for example, there arose such questions as these: how does a European state establish title of ownership over a hitherto unknown non-European territory? What were the rights, if any, of the aboriginal inhabitants of the "new world" in the face of European occupation? What should be the policy of a colonizing power vis-à-vis its empire that must be respected by the other colonizing powers? What should be the international law or custom relative to the seas or the highways of commerce? Should the European system of municipal or international law and relations be thought of as extending to the "new world," or were the overseas areas of colonies and empires to be regarded as constituting a separate "sphere," with its own code of international law and conduct?

These and many other questions bearing upon the "legal" relationships between the colonial powers and their empires arose out of the experiences of the European nations in the "new world." The international discussion of such questions resulted in the formulation of a number of the basic principles in international law.

1. The Right of Title by Discovery and by Papal Donation

When the Portuguese sea captains, directed by Prince Henry the Navigator and his successors, explored the coast of Africa they took possession of those lands in the name of the King of Portugal on the basis of the idea that first discovery gave the discoverer a right of possession, despite

---

[1] Moore, A Digest of International Law, I, 2.
[2] Moore, A Digest of International Law, I, 2.

the fact that the land was already inhabited. But a title to the sovereignty over a newly discovered land that was based upon discovery alone was generally recognized as being inchoate, or incomplete. Both Portugal and Castille, therefore, turned to the Pope for a supernational confirmation and completion of their titles based upon discovery alone.

The supernational authority of the Pope in international affairs was widely recognized in the fifteenth century. It did not command the almost universal respect and acceptance it had enjoyed in the feudal era, to be sure, and it was to be dramatically and effectively challenged in the course of the Protestant revolt of the sixteenth century at the time of the exploration of Africa and the discovery of America. However, at this time, the Pope was recognized as having a decisive authority, both as an arbiter of international disputes and, most emphatically, as having authority to dispose of heathen, non-Christian peoples and their territories in the interest of bringing them to Christianity.

The first grant of the Canary Islands to a European, in fact, had been made in 1345, to Luis de Cerda by Pope Clement VI.[3] This grant was the basis of Castile's claim to the islands in the fifteenth century, a claim recognized by Portugal in the Treaty of Alcaçovas (1479).

It was entirely in conformity with international practice, and with a reasonable expectation that the Pope's pronouncements might be respected as having the force of international law by the Western colonizing nations, therefore, that Portugal appealed to the Pope in 1455 for a confirmation and completion of its title to the lands its explorers had discovered in Africa, as well as to the mission to teach the peoples there the Christian religion, that Spain appealed in 1493 to papal authority for completion of its title to the lands in America discovered by Columbus, and that both countries invited and received papal sanction for the Treaty of Alcaçovas, the Treaty of Tordesillas, and other secular treaties bearing upon the "new world" made between themselves.

The principle of national titles to ownership of new colonial lands derived from first discovery, papal confirmation, or international treaties was, in fact, generally accepted and respected by other nations, about the end of the fifteenth century and the beginning of the sixteenth. It was for this reason that John Cabot was instructed by King Henry VII to "navigate in any seas to the east, north and west, and to occupy and possess any new found lands hitherto unvisited by Christians." [4] It was for the same reason, too, that similar clauses were included in the charters issued by the English government to the colonies of Virginia (1606), the Council for New England (1620), and others.

Title of ownership, then, was generally thought to derive, in the first

[3] Roncière, *Histoire de la marine française*, II, 104–106.
[4] Quoted in *Camb. Hist. Brit. Emp.*, ed., Rose *et al.*, I, 184.

place, from first discovery, which was usually accompanied by a formal act of taking possession, raising the national emblem over the land, and similar ceremonies. But title by mere discovery alone was soon found to be insufficient, and had to be completed by some other title, such as occupation, while the authority of the Pope to dispose of non-European lands and peoples was challenged, both by Protestant countries such as England and by Catholic countries such as France, and both in theory and in practice. Thus, by the end of the sixteenth century there existed a consensus, among the states other than Spain and Portugal, that national title to new lands, whether derived from prior discovery or from some other principle, would be recognized and accepted by the international community only in areas actually occupied and administered by the claiming power.

The first great theorist on international law to examine these questions relative to national ownership of newly discovered lands was Francisco de Vittoria (1468?–1546), one of the great Spanish jurists of the sixteenth century. Thus, in his *De Indis et de Iure Belli* (1532) [5] Vittoria explained that dominion over one state or people by another must be founded on natural, divine, or human law. Under natural law, the first discovery of a deserted land may, indeed, be thought of as giving the discovering state title to the ownership of that land. America, however, was inhabited by the Indians, who as Vittoria demonstrated, were the true owners of it; therefore, Spanish title to America could not be established under natural law.

Nor could Spain's title to dominion over America be derived from human law, on the ground, say, that the Emperor (Charles V) was the ruler of the world, since there is no ruler of the world under natural, divine, or human law. The Indians, said Vittoria, have no overlord of any kind. Similarly, Vittoria dismissed the validity of any title to ownership of America derived from a papal pronouncement, since the Pope's authority is limited to spiritual affairs. No temporal or civil power is given the Pope by natural, human, or divine law. Even in spiritual things, the fact that the Indians live outside Christianity, and may be guilty of all the sins of disbelief and idolatry, does not authorize the Pope to empower the Emperor to employ force to establish a Christian dominion over them. The most that can be demanded of them is that they listen to the doctrines of the Christian faith when it is preached to them, while the Christians are bound to demonstrate the validity of their faith by exemplary living, something scandalously lacking among the conquering Europeans. Even though the Christian faith were adequately presented to the Indians and they were to refuse to accept it, this would not be a reason to justify making war upon them. War is no argument for the truth of a faith and

[5] Francisco de Vittoria, *De Indis et de Iure Belli Relectiones*, Being Parts of *Relectiones Theologicae XII*. Translated by John Paisley Bate; ed. Ernest Nys (Scott, ed., *The Classics of International Law*, No. 7).

can only induce the Indians to feign belief. As for the nonreligious sins of the aborigines, Christian princes cannot, even by the authorization of the Pope, restrain the Indians from sins against the law of nature, since the Christian princes have no authority over them.

The only valid title to dominion over aboriginal peoples that Vittoria recognized as being possible was one that might be established by the voluntary choice of the native peoples involved. Such a choice could be exercised, he said, only with the consent of the majority, in any case. But the Indians had never made any such voluntary choice of the Spanish King as their ruler. This sort of title to America, therefore, did not exist for Spain or any other country.

Vittoria did recognize that, under the law of nations (a part of human law), the Spaniards had a right to travel peaceably in Indian lands and to trade with them, and he anticipated the "most-favored-nation" clause that was to become common to most commercial treaties of the ensuing cen-turies when he said that Spaniards in the American lands should have the same rights to dig for gold, to fish for pearls, or to trade, that other na-tions might have. Furthermore, he recognized that the Christians had a responsibility to try to convert the Indians to Christianity, and that the Pope might delegate this responsibility exclusively to the Spaniards if he thought that desirable. Vittoria even went so far as to acknowledge that the Spaniards might use force to compel the Indians to allow them to build facilities for preaching, to preach without molestation, to protect their converts from forcible reconversion to idolatry, or to prevent human can-nibalism in the name of idolatry.

Curiously, Vittoria anticipated the later doctrine of trusteeship:

Although, as we have said before, the Indian aborigines are not entirely wit-less, they are certainly not far from it, and for that reason are not qualified to found or govern a proper state according to human and political standards. . . . It could therefore be argued that for their own benefit the Kings of Spain might "take over the government of the country, nominating prefects and governors for their cities, and even giving them new rulers, if it were clearly necessary for their well-being." My opinion is that there might be something in this argument; for if they were all quite unintelligent this action would certainly not only be lawful but also strongly to be recommended: one might almost say that our Kings would be obliged to do it, as they would if the Indians were children." [6]

However, such a seizure could be justified only if everything were done for the good of the natives and not just for the profit of the Spanish con-querors.

The net conclusion of Vittoria's thought was, in effect, that Spain's title, by right of discovery alone, was insufficient; title by right of conquest was not justified. The only possible valid titles must be either (1) by

[6] Quoted in Hamilton, *Political Thought in Sixteenth-Century Spain*, 133.

voluntary action of the majority of the Indians, (2) by military action undertaken in defense of religious missions, or (3) occupation under the terms of a sort of trusteeship undertaken for the Indians' own good. Vittoria did recognize, however, that Spain should be accorded the same privileges in the Indian lands accorded to other European nations, and that the Pope might delegate to Spain and its missionaries an exclusive monopoly of the work of converting the Indians to Christianity.

2. Religion, the Church, and the Right
of Colonial Occupation

Another of the great Spanish jurists who examined the bases of Spain's title to America was Francisco Suarez (1548–1617). Suarez took the Bible (as had Vittoria) as his basic statement of the guiding principles in divine international law, and he concentrated his discussion upon the power of the Pope to grant heathen lands to Christian princes. Since the Pope is the supreme authority in Christendom, with the power to coerce even secular rulers, and since the church has the right and the duty to preach the gospel everywhere, the Pope has the sole responsibility for sending missionaries to convert the people in newly found lands to the one true faith. But he may also delegate this responsibility to a Christian prince. Thus, as Suarez says,

> The Pope can distribute among temporal princes and kings the provinces and realms of the unbelievers; not in order that the former may take possession of these regimes according to their own will, for that would be tyranny . . . but in order that they may make provision for the sending of preachers of the Gospel to those infidels, and may protect such preachers by their power, even through the declaration of just war, if reason and a rightful cause should require it. For this purpose, then, the Pope may mark off specific boundaries for each prince, which that prince may not later transgress without committing an injustice. This, as we read, was done by Alexander VI in the case of the kings of Portugal and Castile.[7]

According to this doctrine the assignment of exclusive spheres of ownership and missionary enterprise to Portugal and Spain in the papal bulls of 1455, 1481, and 1493, and in others, was in entire conformity with divine law, as found in the Bible, and in harmony with the *ius gentium* based upon "natural reason." The Pope had delegated his authority to send missionaries to the new lands exclusively to the secular rulers of these two states. And, since the Church had the power to defend its missionaries, it delegated this power, also, to the rulers, according to the principle recognized in both the civil and the canon law, that "when jurisdiction is

[7] Francisco Suarez, *Selections from Three Works of Francisco Suarez, S.J.* (Scott, ed., *The Classics of International Law*, No. 20), II, 746.

granted, everything morally necessary for the exercise thereof is granted as well." [8] Suarez distinguished between pagans who were the subjects of the missionary sovereigns and those who were not. Over the latter the missionary states had no power, since even the Church has no spiritual power or temporal jurisdiction over pagans not subject to any Christian state. In the lands over which they now had sovereignty, however, the delegate states might use force, if necessary, to protect their missionaries and to bring the pagans to hear the preaching of the gospel.

Suarez was emphatic in his caution against giving the secular rulers unlimited authority to seize pagan lands in the name of religion, since this would inevitably lead to an abuse of both religion and power.

Still, for Suarez, the chief ground for justification of the occupation of pagan lands by Christians was, apparently, the religious argument, based upon Christ's charge upon His disciples to go unto all the world and preach the gospel. It was only natural that Suarez should have recognized the Pope as the supreme international authority in matters pertinent to colonial expansion and that he should have accepted the papal bulls as literally international law, fully binding upon the parties involved.

With all the Spanish jurists, in fact, religion, and the propagation of the true Christian faith, lay at the very heart of international law relative to colonial expanson. They all shared the contemporary sixteenth-century assumption that there should be a complete unity of religion in any state, old or new; it was for this reason that they all accepted the idea that a single colonizing or missionary state should be given an exclusive monopoly of missionary work in any given area. All of them, however, although they accepted the logic of the position that the true religion must go into a newly discovered pagan land, had difficulty justifying the use of force in the support of missionary work. All of them accepted the necessity, however, in the long run.

3. The Principle of Effective Occupation

The theories of Francisco de Vittoria and Francisco Suarez relative to Spain's title to its American possessions were only theories, and they were almost completely ignored by the Spanish government in its colonial policy. They also had little or no effect upon the practice of international relations relative to colonial possessions. They are of great significance, however, as a systematic, logical effort to arrive at a rational set of basic principles to explain the nature of national titles of ownership of territories in the "new world" and the relations between colonizing states based upon what they conceived to be their titles to the lands they claimed.

In practice, the majority of the colonizing states did give a certain recog-

[8] Suarez, *Selections from Three Works of Francisco Suarez, S.J.*, II, 743.

nition to the title to new lands, however inchoate, achieved by a discovering state simply by reason of its discovery. But the non-Iberian powers rejected Portuguese and Spanish claims to exclusive possession of lands in the "new world" based upon papal donations, although Spain and Portugal persistently invoked the authority of such donations until well into the eighteenth century. Even the papal donations, themselves, in granting to Spain or Portugal lands discovered or to be discovered by their nationals, usually did so "provided however they at no time have been in the actual temporal possession of any Christian owner. . . ." [9]

It was the pragmatic principle of "effective occupation" that eventually came to govern the actual practice of the colonizing states in their relations with each other having to do with the ownership of colonial territories. This principle was generally invoked, especially, by the challengers to the self-created Hispano-Portuguese monopoly of the "new world," France, England, and the Netherlands; and the Spanish and Portuguese crowns were eventually compelled to accept it. Queen Elizabeth I of England put it bluntly and formally in her reply to the Duke of Mendoza, the Spanish ambassador to London, when he protested the invasion of Spain's *Mare Nostrum* in the eastern Pacific by the famous around-the-world expedition of Sir Francis Drake. Mendoza had based his protest upon Spain's claim to an exclusive possession of America derived from Spain's prior discovery of the continent. Elizabeth replied,

For that their [the Spaniards'] having touched only here and there upon a coast, and given names to a few rivers or capes, were such insignificant things as could in no ways entitle them to a propriety further than in the parts where they actually settled and continued to inhabit.[10]

This principle was consistently followed by England through the next century. It was invoked, for example, when Spain protested the settlement of Virginia, and King James I replied that the area occupied by the colony was not Spanish, since Spain had never effectively occupied it.[11] It was finally recognized by Spain in the Spanish-Dutch Treaty of Münster, according to which Spain admitted Dutch ownership of the places in the "new world" actually occupied by Dutch nationals.[12] The validity of England's title to the lands it actually occupied in America was recognized by Spain in the "American" Anglo-Spanish Treaty of Madrid of 1670.[13]

From the Peace of Westphalia (1648) onward, in fact, the principle of effective occupation was generally respected and observed in the inter-

[9] The papal bull, *Inter Caetera*, May 3, 1493, Davenport, ed., *European Treaties*, I, 62.
[10] Quoted in *Camb. Hist. Emp.*, I, 185.
[11] Brown, *Genesis*, I, 120–121. See Chapter IV.
[12] See Chapter IV.
[13] See Chapter VI.

national relations of the colonizing powers dealing with their colonies. As with so many "principles" of international law and custom in the colonial period, however, it was easily and unscrupulously violated by the colonizing powers when it was to their interest to do so. Thus, England, which had so vigorously and, as a rule, consistently, supported the principle in the sixteenth and early seventeenth centuries, flagrantly violated it in 1664, when, assuming that the Dutch colony of New Netherland, in an area which had never been effectively settled by the English was a violation of English territorial ownership, based merely upon prior claim, arbitrarily seized that colony in time of peace, despite the fact that the area had been effectively occupied by the Dutch since about 1625.

4. The Rights of Native Populations

The Portuguese occupation of territories in Africa and Brazil, the Spanish occupation of Hispaniola, and the ruthless conquests of Mexico and Peru by Cortez and Pizzaro raised, in the minds of many European theorists in the field of international law, the question of whether native peoples in the "new world" had any rights of which their treatment by European colonizing powers was a violation. This question was one of major interest to the Spanish theologian-jurists of the sixteenth century.

Luis Molina (1535–1600), for example, reasoned that the natives were the rightful possessors of their lands according to natural law: "infidelity does not destroy natural or human law, on which ownership and dominion are founded, therefore it does not destroy the latter either." There is nothing, he says,

to hinder infidels being masters of their own things and possessing things as private persons. For rule, jurisdiction and ownership are things common to the entire human race, being based not on faith and charity, but arising directly or indirectly from the very nature of things and their first foundations.[14]

Francisco de Vittoria and Domingo de Soto, Vittoria's disciple, took the position that the Indians in America were independent, sovereign peoples, and that they had exactly the same rights, as peoples, as the European states, since international law should be recognized as applying equally to all nations, just as municipal law applies equally to all citizens. But while they have the rights of sovereign peoples, according to Vittoria, since foreigners have a natural right to trade with them, and since Christians have a divinely ordained right, even duty, to teach them Christianity, the natives must not try to prevent the Christians from doing so.

Molina, however, limited the right of foreigners to trade with the native peoples:

[14] Quoted in Hamilton, *Political Thought in Sixteenth-Century Spain*, 120.

On the other hand the state or its governor can rightfully forbid, to all foreigners the use of the country's possessions which are the joint property of all the citizens, provided that foreigners have no urgent or serious need of them. . . . *The country's common possessions over which the entire community has control are just as much its own belongings as the personal possessions of the individual citizens are their own belongings.* The state can rightfully refuse any commercial dealings with foreigners without doing them an injury which would justify war, and we do in fact see that this is the common practice of many countries. All the more may a country refuse trade, harbour facilities and residence to foreigners when it sees that such will add to their power, for it may rightly fear (human nature being what it is) that they will conquer the country or that it will suffer some other disadvantage for their trade and their presence.[15]

This is a clearer statement of the rights of the native peoples than was Vittoria's, and it is by implication a repudiation of Spain's conquests of the American Indian nations. Indeed, for all the Spanish jurists, although with varying degrees of clarity, the only justification for the use of force against an aboriginal, non-Christian people derives from the necessity for protecting missionaries in the propagation of the Christian faith.

Hugo Grotius (1583–1645), in his brief defending the right of the Dutch to trade with the peoples of the East, took much the same position as that of the Spanish jurists with regard to the right to trade. One of his chief theses was that

Infidels cannot be divested of public or private rights of ownership merely because they are infidels, whether on the ground of discovery, or in virtue of a papal grant, or on grounds of war.[16]

The Portuguese, he said, had not acquired any legal rights over the East Indians,

since the property and sovereign powers of the East Indians ought not to be regarded as things that had no owner prior to the advent of the Portuguese, and since that property and those powers—belonging as they did to the peoples of the Indies—could not rightly be acquired by other persons, it follows that the said peoples are not Portuguese chattels, but free men possessed of full social and civil rights [*sui iuris iuris*].[17]

The Portuguese had, to be sure, acquired certain rights to trade with the East Indian rulers, said Grotius, but these had been acquired by agreements and treaties which, by the very fact of their having been made, constituted a recognition of the sovereignty of those peoples and their rulers.

By the time of the founding of the French, Dutch, and English em-

[15] Quoted in Hamilton, *Political Thought in Sixteenth-Century Spain*, 103.
[16] Grotius, *De Jure Praedae* (Scott, ed., *The Classics of International Law*, No. 22), I, 216.
[17] Grotius, *De Jure Praedae*, I, 226.

pires in America, the idea that native peoples in the "new world" had the rights of sovereign states was generally given lip service by the European imperial states. In practice, however, this concept was more often than not ignored by the actual colonizers, who, as a matter of actual fact, often had never heard of it.

Among the original English colonists in America the idea that the Indian tribes were the sovereign owners of the land was strong, and it became stronger in the eighteenth century. To be sure, the original settlers in Virginia, Plymouth, the British West Indies, and Massachusetts occupied the land without asking the Indians' permission. Indeed, the Puritans attributed the smallpox epidemic that wiped out so many Indians in New England, just before the English came, to God's desire to clear the way for them, and their victory in the Pequot War to a similar divine intention to ease the way for His chosen people.

But one of Roger Williams' quarrels with Massachusetts arose out of his criticism of the Bay Colony for illegally—as he thought—occupying the land that rightfully belonged to the Indians, and when he needed land on which to build his own settlements at Providence, he carefully purchased it from the Indians as the rightful owners. The custom of purchase by formal treaties, with its implicit recognition of the original ownership of and sovereignty of the Indian tribes over their lands eventually became well-nigh universal in the relations of the English colonial governments with the natives.

Until the time of the Peace of Utrecht, however, English thought and policy with regard to the Indians was highly equivocal. Late in the seventeenth century, Governor Thomas Dongan, in his correspondence with the governor of French Canada, insisted that the Iroquois were "subjects" of the King of England and that their lands south of the St. Lawrence River, by the voluntary submission of the Iroquois themselves, were British territory.[18] In actual fact, however, as the French were to insist throughout the eighteenth century, the Indians had no concept of the ownership of land as "property" or as national domain of the sort held by Europeans.

The Indian tribes consistently denied that they were "subjects" of either the English or the French,[19] and both European nations found themselves forced to respect the Indians' position. The native tribes were encouraged in this attitude, of course, by the French, who negotiated with them on this basis. Thus, in 1701, Governor Callières made with the Iroquois the so-called Treaty of Montreal, by which the independence of the Iroquois was recognized and the Indians promised to maintain an

---

[18] See N.Y.C.D., III, 438, 439, 503, 515–517, et passim. See also Chapter XIII.
[19] See, for eample, the "Declaration of Neutrality by Three of the Iroquois Nations," N.Y.C.D., IX, 384–386.

attitude of neutrality between the French and the English.[20] Typical, also, was the attitude of the Abenaki Indians of the region of Maine, who similarly insisted upon their independence, a recognition of which was conceded by the English in a treaty with those Indians made at Casco Bay (Portland) in 1727,[21] by which it was agreed that the King of England was not the king of the Abenaki lands. As the Chief Panaouamskeyen explained it, "God hath willed that I have no King, and that I be master of my lands in common." [22] The English also recognized orally the right of the Abenakis, in case of war between the English and the French, to ally themselves with the French against the English. Eventually, when the question of attributing the Iroquois to England or France arose at Utrecht, the Anglo-French treaty of peace finally provided (Article XV) that French Canadians would not molest "The Five Nations or tribes of Indians subject to Great Britain, nor the other nations of America [that are] friends of that crown." Similarly, the subjects of Great Britain would behave peaceably toward "the American subjects or friends of France;" [23] yet the treaty provided, further, that an international commission was to decide which Indians were to be counted as "subjects" of France and which the "subjects" of Great Britain.

Despite the theoretical exposition of the rights of native populations by the great European jurists and the general assumption of the Europeans, both diplomats and colonists, that they were dealing with quasi-sovereign nations that had certain rights that must be respected, the practices of the European colonizing nations in their relations with the populations of the "new world" fell in reality far short of the actual recognition of the full sovereignty of the native peoples. Spain and Portugal reduced the native Americans to complete subjection by military force, while the practices of the English, the French, and the Dutch, notwithstanding the many "treaties" made with the Indians, were equivocal, and resulted, in the cases of the Dutch and the English, at least, in the slow acquisition of Indian lands and in pushing the Indians back into the interior of the continent. It was only in the East Indies, where there already existed a high level of civilization and *de facto* sovereignty of princes, that the practices of the Europeans had the form and the appearance of dealings between fully sovereign peoples. Even there, in many cases, "treaties" between the Easterners and the Westerners were products of forceful coercion.

So far as relations between the European states and the Indians of North America are concerned, the treaties made with the native tribes had, at best, only a very doubtful status in international law. The Indians hadn't

---

[20] See also, Wrong, *The Rise and Fall of New France*, II, 557–560.

[21] N.Y.C.D., IX, 955, 966–967, 990–993. See also, Garneau, *Histoire du Canada*, IV, 190 ff.

[22] N.Y.C.D., IX, 967.

[23] Davenport, ed., *European Treaties*, III, 213.

the slightest conception of the state, in the European sense of the word, as a responsible body-politic, nor of contractual relationships between such states. Similarly, they had no sense of the national or private ownership of land or of national boundaries. The "treaties," themselves, were generally oral, written down only in the reports made by the interpreters. Based heavily upon expediency, they were considered binding only so long as it suited the interests of the contracting parties to observe them. They were, in fact, ephemeral agreements made by representatives of two widely disparate cultures. Far from really reaching agreements, the treaties dealt in European concepts and legal traditions that the Indians never clearly understood. No Indian treaty ever had the status, either in law or in diplomacy, that any treaty between two European powers was recognized as having.

Nevertheless, the universality of the practice of arranging relationships with the Indians constituted, in itself, a sort of consensus among both the Europeans and the Indian tribes, that the native peoples did have certain rights that the Europeans were bound to respect. As such, the practice may well be called an implementation of a sort of "customary law," or theory, in this area of quasi-international relations.

Indeed, the theory of the rights of native peoples, as first laid down by the Spanish jurists, developed by treaties, and applied in the rudimentary form of the treaties made with the Indians of North America, may probably be said to be the earliest chapters in the history of an attitude toward native peoples which, after many vicissitudes, would flower in the abandonment of "colonialism" in the twentieth century and the full acceptance of political states formed by formerly "colonial" native peoples into the world community of states.

5. Closed Spheres of Colonial Exploitation

In the early documents defining the relations between European states with regard to their colonies, it was practically always recognized that within colonial territories the proprietary state enjoyed a complete and exclusive monopoly of control and exploitation, whether in government, religion, commerce, immigration, or any other matter. Thus, in the bull *Romanus Pontifex*, of January 8, 1455, the Pope not only gave to King Alfonso, "and not to any others," the new territories discovered and to be discovered by the Portuguese "as far as the Indians who are said to worship Christ," for the purposes of government, commerce, and the work of converting the natives to Christianity, but also provided that "whosoever shall infringe these orders" should be punished by excommunication. Later, in the Treaty of Alcaçovas, Castile and Portugal agreed to a division of colonial territories between them, and both signatories promised that "they will not . . . order or consent, but rather forbid, that any of their people, native or subject . . . or any other foreign people who might be within their kingdoms and dominions . . . go to traffic in the said trade or in the islands or lands of Guinea [or the Canaries]." Anyone doing so without special license was to be punished.[24]

Similarly, in the bull *Inter Caetera of* May 3, 1493, Pope Alexander VI gave the lands discovered by Columbus to the King of Castile with the specific proviso that "we strictly forbid all persons of no matter what rank, estate, degree, order, or condition, to dare, without your special permit . . . to go for the sake of trade or any other reason whatever to the said islands and countries . . ." [25] Similarly, too, in the Treaty of Tordesillas (1494), Spain and Portugal promised to keep their ships and citizens out of each other's colonial spheres.[26] Thereafter, throughout the colonial period, the colonizing powers maintained, in their colonies, the principle and the practice of the "closed door," and each state insisted that other nations recognize and observe the principle.

This question was one of the major issues, for example, in the first Anglo-Dutch war (1652–54), and it was a bitter defeat for the Dutch when they were compelled to sign the Anglo-Dutch Treaty of Westminster (1654) containing the clause providing for freedom of commerce between the two countries, but "saving all the laws and ordinances of either commonwealth respectively," [27] which meant that the Dutch by international agreement recognized and promised to respect the English Navigation Act of 1651. The same sort of international recognition of the principle of the "closed door" was provided in the Anglo-Spanish "American" Treaty of Madrid (1670)[28] and the Anglo-French Treaty of Whitehall (the Treaty of American Neutrality (1686).[29]

6. The Doctrine of Natural Boundaries in the Colonies

Another set of concepts that powerfully affected the international relations between European states relative to their colonies in America grew up around the idea that international boundaries should follow lines marked by clearly discernible natural features of the terrain, such as rivers, lakes, the watersheds of mountain ranges, shorelines, or scientifically fixed and unalterable lines such as lines of latitude and longitude. This general concept was put into effect by the Franco-Spanish Treaty of the Pyrenees (1659), which made the summit of the Pyrenees mountains the boundary

[24] Davenport, ed., *European Treaties*, I, 44.
[25] Davenport, ed., *European Treaties*, I, 63.
[26] Davenport, ed., *European Treaties*, I, 97.
[27] Davenport, ed., *European Treaties*, II, 17.
[28] Davenport, ed., *European Treaties*, II, 194–195.
[29] Davenport, ed., *European Treaties*, II, 320.

between Spain and France.[30] This same provision, somewhat elaborated, was repeated in the Partition Treaty of 1700 between France and England and Holland.[31]

In the disputes between France and England over boundaries in North America, France consistently took the position that the nation which discovered a river automatically came into possession of the entire drainage basin of that river, and that the proper boundary between that colonial possession and the next was the height of land between the drainage basins. Thus, as early as 1645, when the Sieur Huault de Montmagny was commissioned to be the governor of Quebec, that territory was defined as "the provinces watered by the St. Laurence River and the other rivers that flow into it and the places that depend upon them in New France." [32] This same definition was repeated again and again, and the boundary between Quebec and Acadia was thought to be the height of land between the St. Lawrence drainage basin and the rivers that flowed into the Atlantic, which was vaguely thought to be some ten leagues to the south of the St. Lawrence.[33] Upon the basis of the same idea, the boundary between the French possessions and those of the English on the interior of the continent was thought by the French to be the height of land between the St. Lawrence-Great Lakes basin and the drainage basins of the Hudson and the Susquehanna. As for the Ohio and the Mississippi, since those great rivers had first been discovered, explored, and occupied by Frenchmen, France held title to the entire basin drained by each one of them and its tributaries. As Governor Denonville of Canada put it in 1688,

All the foregoing demonstrates sufficiently the incontestable right the French have to the Iroquois lands . . . and others whereof possession has also been taken in his Majesty's name, along the River St. Laurence, the lakes it forms and the Rivers discharging therein, which constitute the continuation of the waters of said River St. Laurence . . . and it demonstrates their possession of the great River Mississipi which they have discovered as far as the South Sea, on which river also they have divers establishments as well as on that of Oyo, Ouabache, etc., which flow into the said River Mississipi, and of the countries and lands in the vicinity of said rivers, where they actually carry on trade . . .[34]

Apparently, the French negotiators at Utrecht in 1712 were prepared to apply this doctrine in regard to the boundaries of Hudson Bay, since they were instructed that

[30] Vast, ed., *Grands traités*, I, 79–175 (Articles 42 and 43).

[31] Davenport, ed., *European Treaties*, III, 16–28.

[32] "Prolongation de la Commission de Gouverneur et Lieutenant-Général à Quebec, au Sieur Huault de Montmagny," June 6, 1645. *Mémoires de Commissaries du Roi* . . . , II, 715.

[33] See Ganong, "A Monograph of the Evolution of the Boundaries of the Province of New Brunswick," *Trans. Roy. Soc. of Can.*, 2nd Series, VII (1901), pt. 2, 183–184.

[34] "Memoir of M. de Denonville on the French Limits in North America," Mar. 8, 1688, N.Y.C.D., IX, 377–384.

[His Majesty, Louis XIV] consents . . . to cede Hudson Bay, with the rivers that fall into it; those which fall into the St. Lawrence River, with the lands adjacent to them should belong to New France, of which the French have been in possession more than 150 years.[35]

This general principle was invoked by the French again and again, throughout the eighteenth century, to justify their claim to the entire Mississippi Valley, which meant that, in that direction, the boundary between the French possessions and the English must be the Allegheny watershed. Thus, as late 1761, the French "experts" were recommending that, in the treaty of peace to be made at the end of the Seven Years War, the boundary between the English possessions and the French be that divide.[36]

The English, on their side, generally disregarded watersheds as natural boundaries and more often claimed as boundaries either such easily visible physical features as rivers and lakes or the less visible but scientifically verifiable lines of latitude and longitude. This general practice was based upon historical arguments, as with regard to New York and Acadia, or, somewhat more effectively, by a sort of extension of their old principle of "effective occupation" which rested upon the occupation of the land by themselves or their Indian allies. Thus, in their argument with the French over the ownership of the lands south of Lakes Ontario and Erie, they based their claim on the fact that this land originally belonged to the Iroquois Indians, and that, since the Iroquois were "subjects" of the British king, the Iroquois lands, which were clearly bounded on the north by the St. Lawrence River and the lakes, belonged to England.[37] As early as 1676, Sir John Werden wrote to Governor Andros in New York the following explanation of New York's boundaries based upon Dutch precedent:

As to yo[r] thoughts of bounding the Dukes Territoryes Northwards by Canada [that is, as bounded by the northern shore of Lake Ontario and the St. Lawrence River], you will doubtless doe well to looke upon them as being soe bounded, the Dutch having ever claymed & never lost the possession of the same. . . .[38]

In 1700 William Penn, in his "Suggestions respecting the Plantations" (ca. 1700) also expressed the same idea:

Wee take the South side of the River and Lakes of Canada to be our just and

---

[35] "Mémoire sur les Pays de l'Amérique, que la France doit céder aux Anglais par la paix prochaine," endorsed "Joint à la lettre du S. de Quierin [sic?] du 13 Jan.[r] 1713," A.N., Cols. C11E: 210–11.

[36] "Memoir on the Boundaries of Canada. By M. Dumas." Apr. 15, 1761, N.Y.C.D., X, 1134–1138. See Chapter XIII.

[37] "Memorial of the Right of the British Crown over the New York Indians," 1709, N.Y.C.D., V, 75–77; ibid., passim, Vols. III, IV, and V.

[38] "Sir John Werden to Governor Andros, Jan. 28, 1675/6," Report of the Regents of the University on the Boundaries of the State of New York, I, 26.

reasonable boundarys, saile and trade with the Indians being much concerned therein.[39]

As for the ownership of the parts of the continent lying between the 34° and 45° North Latitude, the English habitually cited the original charter to the Virginia Company (1606) and the actual occupation of the continent that followed it. With regard to the boundaries of Acadia, the English rested their claims upon Sir William Alexander's charter of 1621, which named the St. Croix River as the western boundary of Nova Scotia, actual occupation of the coast of Maine by the men from Plymouth and Massachusetts, and, eventually, the charter to the Duke of York in 1664, which named the St. Croix River as the eastern boundary of the Duke's grant in that area and the Penobscot (Pentagoët) River as the western boundary. At other times, however, as in the Treaty of Boston (1670)[40] and in the negotiations of the Anglo-French joint commission of 1749,[41] the English recognized the Penobscot River as the western boundary of Acadia. However inconsistent the English may have been relative to which river they thought was the boundary, it was almost always a river that marked the boundary.

Even the French, themselves, when expediency seemed to suggest another principle, fell back on rivers, rather than mountains, as the best boundaries. Thus, in 1718, when an effort was about to be made by the Anglo-French joint commission of 1719[42] to define the boundaries between the English and French colonies in America, one of the memoirs provided the French commissioners for their guidance rejected the idea of the height of land as a boundary between the Atlantic plain and the St. Lawrence Valley, "because this high ground is very close to the St. Laurence, which would be the same as giving New France to the English."[43] Instead, this memoir proposed that Acadia be limited to a part of the peninsula, that the area along the coast between the peninsula and the Penobscot be recognized as part of New France, and that the boundary between New England and New France be the St. George's River and a line drawn from [the source of that river?] along the height of land to the source of the Orange [Hudson] River, from whence it would follow the crest of the Appalachian divide to the south-westward through the continent.[44] Actually, however, there appeared a difficulty in the fact that the Appalachian Highland did not reach the sea; the French "experts,"

---

[39] 'Mr. Penn's Suggestions respecting the Plantations" (ca. 1700), N.Y.C.D., IV, 757.

[40] See Chapter IX.

[41] See Chapter XVIII.

[42] See Chapter XVI.

[43] "Mémoire pour servir à régler les limites, entre la Nouvelle France, La Nouvelle Angleterre, et l'Acadie, autrement Nouvelle Ecosse," C.A.O., F113, 2 Acadie: fol. 25.

[44] "Mémoire pour servir à régler les limites entre la Nouvelle France, La Nouvelle Angleterre, et l'Acadie . . . ," C.A.O., F113, 2 Acadie: fols. 27–28.

therefore, recommended that the boundary across the Coastal Plain from the Appalachians to the Gulf of Mexico be the Apalachicola River.[45] Thus, while the French generally followed the "height-of-land" theory as to natural boundaries, they were willing to accept rivers as boundaries when it was to their interest to do so.

Generally speaking, in fact, the chief base of the English argument at any given time was expediency; and, as rivers and lakes, in the English view, were the most easily identifiable natural boundaries, the English tended to fix upon them as the best markers. As Dr. William Douglass was to say, about the middle of the eighteenth century:

The natural and most effectual boundaries of countries or territories seem to be large rivers (thus the upper Rhine divides the French acquisitions from sundry German sovereignties) and mountains impracticable (the Pyrenean mountains in general divide France from Spain, the Dafforn Hills divide Sweden from Norway, the Carpach, or Carpathian mountains divide Poland from Hungary, and Transylvania). The great river of St. Laurence, the lakes Ontario and Erie, and the Apalatian mountains may answer the intended British and French boundary, without any advantage or acquisition, disadvantage or loss on either side; but merely for peace and good neighborhood.[46]

Whether he knew it or not, Dr. Douglass had the support, as a principle of international law, of such an eminent jurist as Emmerich de Vattel, whose *Law of Nations* was published just a few years after Douglass's *Summary*. For Vattel, in his classic statement of the principles of international law, had this to say about rivers as international boundaries:

In case of doubt, every territory terminating at a river is presumed to have no other boundary than the river itself; because nothing is more natural than to take it as a boundary when one establishes oneself on its banks; and when in doubt one always presumes that which is the most natural and most probable.[47]

7. The Doctrine of the Two Spheres

Throughout the colonial period, the essentially mercantilistic principle of the closed national colonial empire was accepted and respected in international law. This meant, in effect, that the colonizing states mutually and tacitly agreed that a state might, and generally did, govern its colonies, in respect to its relations with other states, under a set of municipal laws that was different from the laws governing the direct relations among the same states in Europe. Thus, the English Navigation Acts, which were internationally recognized in a series of treaties, were acts prohibiting colonial

[45] "Mémoire au suject de l'Etablissement de la Colonie de la Louisiane [envoyé?] par ordre de Monseigneur le duc de Noailles" [1723?], A.N. Col., C13A, 7: fols. 228–233 vo.
[46] Douglass, A *Summary, Historical and Political* . . . I, 8.
[47] Vattel, *Le Droit des Gens*, I, 235–236.

trade with the citizens of foreign states, which commerce among the metropoli might be mutually free and open. Similar exclusions of foreigners from colonial commerce were enforced by all of the colonizing powers, and these exclusions were all recognized, confirmed, and respected under the terms of many treaties.

Logically, this meant that all the colonizing nations accepted the idea that, while in Europe there might prevail one system of law and international relations, another, separate and distinct set of laws and international conventions prevailed in the relations between those same European states having to do with the colonies. This is the essential idea in the "doctrine of the two spheres."

This doctrine had its origin in the division of the "new world" by the papal bulls of 1455, 1493, and 1506, and others, and by the Hispano-Portuguese Treaties of Alcaçovas (1479), Tordesillas (1494), and Saragossa (1529).[48] It is to be noted, however, that, while an effort was made by these acts to distinguish and define national spheres of exclusive interest in the colonial world, there also appeared the idea that the entire colonial world "beyond the lines of amity" was a sphere distinct from Europe, with its own set of international laws, conventions, and institutions.

There had been no actual line of demarcation between the new world and the old drawn in the papal bulls and the treaties made prior to 1493. A definition of national colonial spheres was achieved in the Treaty of Alcaçovas (1479) simply by attributing the Canary Islands to Spain and all the rest of the new lands in Guinea and beyond to Portugal. In the papal bull *Inter Caetera*, dated May 4, 1493, however, a line was drawn by the Pope through the Atlantic Ocean from pole to pole one hundred leagues west of the Azores, as already noted. This was the first of the "lines of amity." This line was moved westward at the request of Portugal by the Treaty of Tordesillas (1494).[49] But this line was a north-south line only. It soon became apparent that there was a need for another line, drawn east and west, to demarcate the spheres of amity and/or anarchy to the southward.

One of the earliest and clearest statements of this principle that "there is no peace beyond the Line," or that "might makes right beyond the Line" is to be found in the oral agreement that accompanied the Franco-Spanish Treaty of Cateau-Cambrésis (1559). In that case, the French negotiators, appealing to the principle of the freedom of the seas, demanded that Spain recognize the right of Frenchmen to sail to the Indies, at least to the lands which, although discovered, did not belong to either the Spanish or the Portuguese. The Spanish negotiators refused to admit of any compromise of their claim to exclusive ownership of the entire American hemisphere, including the seas, based upon prior discovery and the papal bulls of

[48] See Chapters I and II.
[49] See Chapter II.

Alexander VI and Julius VI; and they demanded, in their turn, that France accept the Spanish exclusion of Frenchmen and all other foreigners from the seas of the "new world." As neither of the two countries could accept the demands of the other, an oral agreement was finally arrived at, to the effect that beyond the "line of demarcation,"

they [the French] would not go to the lands possessed by your Majesty [Philip II of Spain] and by the King of Portugal, or that one would abide by the terms of past treaties, according to which the Indies are not mentioned, and if they [the French] were found doing anything there that they should not be doing, they would be punished. . . . We [the Spanish negotiators] declared to them [the French] that if they went there in time of peace, one [the Spaniards] would throw them into the sea, with the understanding that this action would not be thought a contravention of the treaties of friendship between us. . . .[50]

It is to be noted that, in this negotiation, the area to be prohibited to the French was the "Indies" that lay beyond the "lines of amity." These lines were there understood to be the line of demarcation defined in the Treaty of Tordesillas, as a north-south "line of amity," and the parallel of latitude in which lay the "Capes of Bojador and of Não" as an east-west line. The two countries, thus, accepted the principle that "there is no peace beyond the Line" or that "might makes right beyond the Line."

This principle of the two spheres was a basic principle in French international relations relative to colonies for well over a century. In 1604, for example, King Henry IV commented upon the Anglo-Spanish Treaty of London [51] as follows:

I think that they will make use of this treaty as my subjects and the Spaniards have done since the peace [of Coteau-Cambrésis] of 1559, that is, that the French have continued their voyages [to the West Indies], although they are not mentioned in the treaty, but if the Spaniards found them beyond the line they have treated them [the French] as enemies, while the French have treated them [the Spaniards] in the same manner, without having it thought, because of such actions, that the peace has been violated.[52]

In the course of the seventeenth century, the doctrine of the two spheres underwent a mixed and irregular set of modifications. On the one side, for example, under the terms of the Dutch-Spanish truce of 1609 it was provided that the truce should have effect all over the world except that, as a matter of expediency on account of distance, it would not apply in the areas "outside of Europe" before the expiration of one year.[53] In the Anglo-Spanish Treaty of Madrid of 1630, the peace was to take effect "beyond the Line" after nine months from the date of ratification; and in

---

[50] Davenport, ed., European Treaties, I, 220–221, fn. 9.
[51] See Chapter III.
[52] Quoted in Davenport, ed., European Treaties, I, 221 fn.
[53] Davenport, ed., European Treaties, I, 267.

the Dutch-Spanish Treaty of Münster (1648), it was provided that the peace between the two countries should be established everywhere, "without exception as to places nor as to persons." However, because of the time required for news of the peace to reach the other parts of the world, it was agreed that the peace would not be regarded as fully effective before the expiration of one year within the limits of the charter of the Dutch East India Company (the East Indies) and before the expiration of six months within the area assigned to the Dutch West India Company (roughly, the Atlantic basin).[54] Increasingly, during the rest of the century, treaties came to be regarded as applying to the entire world.

On the other hand, however, there were numerous later occasions when the doctrine of the two spheres was invoked to advance or protect the interests of the colonizing powers. Thus, when Oliver Cromwell seized Acadia from the French in 1654 and Jamaica from Spain in 1655, he hoped and expected that these acts of violence in the "new world" might not cause war between England and these two countries in Europe. His expectations were justified in the case of France, for Cardinal Mazarin, willing, for reasons of state, to sacrifice Acadia to French interests in Europe, accepted the English seizure in the Anglo-French Treaty of Westminster of 1654. Spain, on the other hand, scorned Cromwell's interpretation of the doctrine of the two spheres and declared the seizure of Jamaica to be an act of war.[55]

In 1666, when Louis XIV reluctantly entered the Second Dutch War with England, he instructed his colonial governors in America to maintain a strict neutrality relative to the Anglo-Dutch war. The English and Dutch, however, for reasons of their own, both carried the war to America. Thus, Louis's effort to apply the doctrine of the two spheres to this war failed.[56]

Again, when, after the Anglo-Spanish Treaty of Madrid of 1667, Spain protested the continuance of English raids upon Spanish commerce and colonies in America, England replied that that treaty was made for Europe only, since it made no effort to solve the many questions at issue between the two countries in the western hemisphere. Spain actually proclaimed a local, regional war against England south of the Tropic of Cancer, while England, wishing to avoid war, proposed that a new and separate treaty relative to American questions be made. The result was the so-called "American" Treaty of Madrid of 1670.[57] The practical effect of this arrangement was a tacit new recognition of the doctrine of the two spheres, according to which the treaty of 1667 was thought of as generally limited to Europe and that of 1670 was specifically made for affairs in the American hemisphere.

---

[54] Davenport, ed., *European Treaties*, I, 363–364.
[55] See Davenport, ed., *European Treaties*, II, and Chapter VI.
[56] See Chapter IX.
[57] See Chapter VI.

Similarly, Louis XIV, in his treaty of peace with the Dutch, made at Nymwegen in 1679, accepted a provision that the treaty should apply to all the world. But he insisted that the Franco-Dutch commercial treaty, signed on the same day, should apply only to Europe. More particularly, although he made peace with Spain at Nymwegen in 1678, he made it very clear that he did not consider this peace as applying in America, and he encouraged his governors in the West Indies to continue an active buccaneering warfare against Spanish commerce and colonies. His objective, of course, was to bully Spain into granting him a favored position in the trade of the Spanish colonies, but the underlying principle was clear. As Jean Baptiste Colbert, Louis's great mercantilist minister, wrote to the Sieur de Gabaret, governor of one of the French islands,

The King [Louis XIV] ordered me to write to you these lines on a very important matter which must be kept very secret. Peace being made with Spain in Europe, but not in other parts of the world, it may be that some day his Majesty will take the resolution to trouble the great and free commerce that the Spaniards have in the West Indies.[58]

He also instructed the governor to keep him well informed as to the movements of the Spanish *flotas* and other shipping in the Caribbean area.

The most outstanding example of the explicit application of this doctrine of the two spheres in an international treaty took place in 1686, when England and France, in order to prevent the conflicts of their nationals in America from precipitating war in Europe, agreed upon the Treaty of Whitehall, also called the Treaty of American Neutrality. By this treaty the two signatories agreed that the American disputes should not be considered a cause of war in Europe and that, *per contra*, a war between them in Europe should not be taken as a reason for conflict in America.[59]

The doctrine of the two spheres, resting upon the idea that Europe was one political and international sphere, with its own system of laws, institutions, and international conventions, and that the "new world" was another, continued to be a basic principle in European international relations for another century, at least, although with diminishing force. What may have been its last notable statement in an international treaty appeared in the Hispano-Portuguese "American" treaty of Madrid of 1750. In this treaty it was explicitly stated that (Article 2):

Since war is the principle cause for abusing or altering established arrangements, His Catholic Majesty [of Spain] and his Most Faithful Majesty [of Portugal] wish that if (which may God forfend) a break should take place between the two crowns, the peace between the subjects of both powers in South America shall be maintained, and they shall live at peace with each other just as if there were no such war between their sovereigns. [Violators of this provision will be

[58] Quoted in Newton, *European Nations in the West Indies*, 308–309.
[59] See Chapter IX.

punished.] Similarly, neither of the two nations will permit the use of its ports in America . . . by the enemies of the other . . . The said continuation of perpetual peace and good neighborliness shall have effect not only in the lands and islands of South America . . . but also in the rivers, ports and coasts in the Atlantic from the latitude of the southern tip of the Island of San Antonio, one of the Cape Verde islands, southward, and from the meridian [of longitude] that passes through in western extremity, toward the west.[60]

That is to say, the colonial peace established by the treaty was to be effective as between all the Spanish and Portuguese colonial possessions beyond the particular "lines of amity" fixed by the treaty itself.

The "doctrine of the two spheres" was a reality in international law and relations throughout the colonial era, despite the fact that, as the colonies became more and more integrated with the mother countries in Europe, it came to have less and less force among them. On the other hand, it was to have its own development and expression in the colonies, as, for example, when Governor Peter Stuyvesant of New Netherland in 1651 proposed a treaty of neutrality between New Netherland and New England, or when Massachusetts blocked a declaration of war against the Dutch because, as the Massachusetts General Court put it, "it was most agreeable to the gospel of peace which we profess, and safest for these colonies at this season, to forbeare the use of the sword." [61] Commercial benefits to be derived from continued peace between the two groups of colonies were of importance, also, although they were not explicitly emphasized. Similarly, the French and English colonists of St. Christopher put into effect the same idea in their own treaty of neutrality, made at Sandy Point in 1678.[62]

The "doctrine of the two spheres" was, thus, of great importance to the Euro-American colonists, and it provided abundant colonial precedents for the later classic expression of the same doctrine by James Monroe in his famous presidential message of 1823.[63]

8. Freedom of Commerce and Freedom of the Seas

When, by the bull *Romanus Pontifex* (1455) Pope Nicholas V donated to Portugal all the lands "discovered and to be discovered" in Africa and beyond, "as far as the Indians who are said to worship Christ," he included

[60] Cantillo, ed., *Tratados*, 406–407.
[61] Shurtleff and Pulsifer, eds., *Acts of the Commissioners of the United Colonies of New England* (*Records of the Colony of New Plymouth*, Vols. IX and X), II, 41, 64; Hutchinson, *History of Massachusetts*, I, appendix X, 452–453. See also, Savelle, "Colonial Origins of American Diplomatic Principles," *Pac. Hist. Rev.*, III, No. 3 (Sept., 1934), 333–350.
[62] Davenport, ed., *European Treaties*, II, 256–260. See Chapter IX.
[63] See Barcia-Trelles, "La Doctrine de Monroë dans son Développement Historique . . . ," Hague Academy of International Law, *Receuil des Cours*, XXXII (1930), Part 2, 391–405.

all "the provinces, islands, harbors, places, and seas whatsoever" already acquired and yet to be acquired. He thus gave to Portugal the sea covering an immense portion of the earth's surface as well as the land. The bulls of 1493 did not mention the seas as part of the papal donation, but the Iberian powers assumed that the seas were included, and, in the Treaty of Tordesillas they agreed that, inasmuch as Spanish ships on their way to and from America "must cross the seas on this side of the line, pertaining to the said King of Portugal," they might sail "over the said seas of the said King of Portugal," provided they followed the most direct routes to and from the Spanish zone west of the line of demarcation. Thus, since the seas in the two great spheres were owned by the two Iberian powers along with the lands there, the seas were regarded as closed to foreign interlopers in exactly the same sense as were the colonial lands.

It was hardly to be expected that the other commercial states of Western Europe might mildly accept this assumption of the ownership of the seas of the "new world" and their arbitrary closure by the Iberian powers to the ships and citizens of other nations. Indeed, the ships of other nations, especially the French and the English, swarmed out over the newly discovered seas to reap the profits to be derived both from attacking or trading with the new lands and from raiding the commerce of the Iberian powers with them.[64] Francis I, King of France, when Carlos I of Spain sent a caravel to trail and observe Jacques Cartier on his expedition to Canada in 1541, expostulated to the Spanish ambassador:

Is the mere sending of my ships there [to America] a declaration of war and a contravention of my treaties with His Majesty [Carlos I]? The sun shines for me as well as for others; I should like to see the clause in Adam's will that excludes me from the division of the world.[65]

The principle of the freedom of the seas remained one of the bases of French international policy pertinent to colonial expansion. It was the basic argument in the demands of the French negotiators at the Treaty of Cateau-Cambrésis (1559), as already noted, and King Henry IV often cited it in justification of the many French voyages to the "new world" during his reign.

The attitude of Queen Elizabeth I of England was similar to that of Francis I. To be sure, England had long claimed sovereignty over the seas surrounding the British Isles, and would do so again. Furthermore, because England, in the feudal era, had owned both shores of the English Channel, it had claimed ownership of the Channel as a sort of English internal waterway. It had required foreign ships passing through the Channel to recognize English sovereignty over "the narrow seas" by dipping their flags; the failure of a Dutch fleet to do this was one of the causes of the Anglo-Dutch war of 1652–54.

[64] See Chapter III.
[65] Quoted in Roncière, *Histoire de la marine française*, III, 300.

With the worldwide expansion of English commercial and colonial interests in the sixteenth century, however, and in the face of the Hispano-Portuguese claim to an exclusive ownership of the seas in a large part of the world, Queen Elizabeth took the position that there was no such thing as national ownership of the oceans, and that they were free and open to all. Thus, when Bernadino de Mendoza, the Spanish ambassador, complained of Drake's expedition into the Pacific, she replied that Spain's effort to prohibit the English from sailing to the Caribbean or elsewhere was a violation of the law of nations and that English ships would continue to sail wherever they wished, "since the use of the sea is common to all." [66]

A little later, in the course of a dispute with Denmark over the fisheries off Iceland, Elizabeth took the position that international law guaranteed a freedom to all nations, not only to traverse the seas, but, also, to fish in all the seas, everywhere. A property-title to the sea, she said, was unthinkable, and she even repudiated, apparently, the English claim to sovereignty over the English Channel; she was prepared to insist upon sovereignty over what might strictly be called "territorial waters. [67]

The theory of the international law governing the principle of the freedom of the seas was another of the topics touched upon by the famous Spanish jurists of the sixteenth century. Thus, Fernando Vasquez Manchaea (1512–69), like Francisco Suarez, conceived of an international community of states governed by what he called the "*jus naturale et gentium*," that is, natural and international law, under which each state enjoyed a freedom of navigation everywhere, since the sea is common to all nations.

Another early writer on international law who wrote on the freedom of the seas was Albericus Gentilis (1552–1608), an Italian scholar who moved to England to become a professor of jurisprudence at Oxford. In Gentilis' famous *Hispanae advocationis libri duo (Spain's Advocate)* and *De Jure Belli Libri Tres (Three books on the Law of War)* he argued for a very broad concept of territorial waters under the restrictive government of the state to which they appertained.[68] But it was Hugo Grotius, a Dutchman, who provided the classic expression of the doctrine of the freedom of the seas, early in the seventeenth century.

The penetration of the Indian Ocean and American waters by Dutch ships in the course of the Dutch war of independence against Spain and Portugal inevitably brought conflicts between them and the ships of the Iberian powers, especially those of Portugal in the Indian Ocean. In 1603, for example, the Portuguese ship *Catherine* was taken by Captain Jacob

[66] Quoted in *Camb. Hist. of the Brit. Emp.*, I, 199.
[67] Elizabeth's liberal position relative to the seas around Britain was reversed by her successors, James I and Charles I.
[68] See *Camb. Hist. Brit. Emp.*, ed. Rose *et al.*, I, 195–205.

Heemskerck in the name of an Amsterdam firm. It was awarded to the Dutch East India Company in prize court in 1604. There was some criticism of the company and the government because of the Dutch policy of seizing merchant ships at sea, so the company apparently engaged young Hugo Grotius to write a defense of the policy. The result was Grotius's famous essay, *De Jure Praedae Commentarius (Commentary on the Law of Prize)* [69] one chapter of which was published separately as *Mare Liberum (The Freedom of the Seas)* in 1608. In this famous essay Grotius formulated the classic expression of the doctrine of the freedom of the seas.

Grotius's chief concern in the larger work, of course, was a study of the law of prize. Thus, given the justness of a war, the seizure of enemy property is justifiable: "The essential characteristic of just wars consists above all in the fact that the things captured in such wars become the property of the captors." [70] Furthermore, one belligerent is justified in seizing the property of the enemy as a recompense, or reprisal, for the property the enemy has seized from him. The seizure of a Portuguese ship by a Dutch ship in time of war, therefore, was legally justifiable.

Grotius noted that during the war then going on peaceful commerce had been carried on between the Netherlands and Spain, and that Dutch merchants, for several years after the annexation of Portugal by Spain, had exempted Portuguese merchants from attack or seizure and permitted them to bring Portuguese and Brazilian products to the Low Countries. But Dutch ships were seized in Spanish and Portuguese ports, and the Dutch had to pay extremely high ransoms for them, while Dutch citizens were abused. When Dutch ships began to go to the East Indies, the Portuguese, claiming the Dutch had no right to sail there, since to sail upon the Indian Ocean was to trespass upon Portuguese property, seized a number of Dutch ships, thus forcing the Dutch into a policy of reprisal. The seizure of the *Catherine* by the Dutch was such a case. The ship was taken, the crew was put ashore in Brazil, and the ship was adjudged good prize in a Dutch prize court.

With regard to the right of the Dutch to go to the Indies, Grotius adduced the following arguments:

In the first place, he said, "we hold that, by the authority of that primary law of nations whose essential principles are universal and immutable [natural law], it is permissible for the Dutch to carry on trade with any nation whatsoever." [71] For, since no nation produces all the things necessary for its existence and welfare, and since, therefore, all nations must buy from others the things they cannot produce, giving in exchange their own products, "according to the law of nations, the privilege of barter must be

---

[69] Grotius, *De Jure Praedae*, (Scott, ed., *The Classics of International Law*, No. 22), I, Chapter XII.

[70] Grotius, *De Jure Praedae*, I, 43.

[71] Grotius, *De Jure Praedae*, I, 218.

common to all, not only in a negative . . . sense, but also positively . . ." [72]
And, in another place, "Freedom of trade, then, springs from the primary
law of nations, which has a natural and permanent cause, so that it cannot
be abrogated. Moreover, even if its abrogation were possible, such a result
could be achieved only with the consent of all nations. Accordingly, it is
not remotely conceivable that one nation may justly impose any hindrance
whatsoever upon two other nations that wish to enter into a contract with
each other." [73] The Portuguese claim to the right of exclusion is specious,
therefore, and the Dutch have the right to trade with the nations of all
the world, under both natural law and the law of nations.

As for the sea, since, in the first place, it cannot be occupied, it cannot
become the private or national property of any owner, "since all ownership
has its origin in such occupancy." Furthermore, the sea, as the air, is the
"common possession of all men and the private possession of none." It is
clear, therefore, that "the Portuguese have not established a private right
over that part of the sea which one traverses in sailing to the East Indies." [74]
If, indeed, the share of the Spaniards, who share in the same claim to
jurisdiction over the oceans, be added to the share claimed by the Portuguese, "very nearly the entire Ocean will have been delivered into the hands
of two peoples, while all the remaining nations will find themselves restricted to the narrow waters of the north." [75]

As for the donation of Pope Alexander VI, it is revealed by the foregoing
argument, says Grotius, as a "vain and empty text." For, "since neither the
sea nor the right of navigation thereon can be the private property of any
man, it follows that such gifts could not have been bestowed by the Pope
nor received by the Portuguese." Moreover, since the Pope is not the
temporal lord of the whole earth, he is not the temporal lord of the sea.
Even if he were, he could not transfer his title to any king or nation. The
Pope's authority, in any case, is spiritual only; the sea and the navigation
upon it are not spiritual matters. Again, the Pope has no authority to commit acts repugnant to the law of nature; since it is repugnant to the law of
nature for any person to possess the sea, the Pope cannot possibly possess
it. Finally, since the Pope has no power to deprive any man of his rights,
he surely never had any power to deprive all the nations of the world except Spain and Portugal of their natural right to navigate on the sea. For
all these reasons, the papal donation of the oceans of the world is utterly
without force or effect.[76]

As a final refutation of Portugal's claim to ownership of the sea, Grotius
rejected that part of Portugal's argument that was based upon prescription,
or custom. For since, he said, ownership by prescription or custom is rooted

[72] Grotius, *De Jure Praedae,* I, 255.
[73] Grotius, *De Jure Praedae,* I, 257.
[74] Grotius, *De Jure Praedae,* I, 230, 231, 238.
[75] Grotius, *De Jure Praedae,* I, 239.
[76] Grotius, *De Jure Praedae,* I, 244 ff.

in civil law, it is not applicable in relations between states or peoples. Even in civil law, "prescription . . . is not applicable in regard to those things which have been assigned to all mankind for its common use." And Grotius cited the great Spanish jurist Fernando Vasquicas to show that this was true, even in Spanish civil law.[77]

Grotius's final conclusion, then, based upon natural law, the law of nations, and the civil law, is that Portugal's claim to exclusive ownership of the oceans traversed on the way to India, and by inference, Spain's similar claim to a prescriptive and exclusive sovereignty over the oceans traversed on the way to America, were utterly specious, and that "the Portuguese do not possess any right in virtue whereof they may forbid any other nation whatsoever to navigate the oceanic tract extending to the East Indies." [78]

It has been noted that Queen Elizabeth of England took a very liberal position relative to the problem of freedom of the seas and that she was prepared even to relax the old exclusive English position relative to the seas adjacent to England itself. With the accession of James I, this liberal attitude was reversed, and the old exclusive attitude was maintained by England throughout the seventeenth century. Since the English position ran counter to the arguments of Grotius, many books were written to refute him and to justify the English policies. The greatest of Grotius's English antagonists was John Selden, whose book, *Mare Clausum (Closed Sea)* was published in 1635. Selden claimed, not on the basis of theory but on history and the records of actual cases, that England had always exercised the right to control navigation in the "English" seas and the authority to license fishing in them. Selden was not concerned with the worldwide or colonial aspects of the problem, however; and his work is significant chiefly as showing why a nation should have authority over its own territorial waters.

The interrelated doctrines of freedom of commerce and of freedom of the seas were highly congenial to the English and Dutch colonists in America in the seventeenth century. Indeed, their experiences as new societies led them to grow naturally in that direction. Thus, the normal economic development of the colonies induced in each of them an impulse to trade with their foreign neighbors, English, Dutch, French, or Spanish, as the case might be, whether permitted or prohibited by the respective mother countries. The English colony at Plymouth very early entered into commercial relations with Dutch New Netherland; Massachusetts found it profitable to trade both with the French in Acadia and with New Netherland; Virginia developed a strong trade with New Netherland; and all the northern colonies presently engaged in an active and highly profitable trade

[77] Grotius, *De Jure Praedae*, I, 248, 249–250.
[78] Grotius, *De Jure Praedae*, I, 255.

with the Dutch, French, Danish, and Spanish West Indies, while the British West Indies, and particularly Jamaica, became bases of active trade with the colonies of the other powers in the Caribbean area. It was obviously to the interest of all of the English colonies to trade as freely as possible with their non-English colonial neighbors. This brought them squarely into conflict with the mercantilistic policy of the closed colonial door practiced by all the European nations; it also brought them into conflict with the English Navigation Acts.[79]

The earliest colonial statement of the principles of the freedom of commerce and of the freedom of the seas was formulated by the magistrates of Massachusetts in 1644. This statement grew out of the relations of Massachusetts with the French in Acadia.

When Acadia had been returned to France under the terms of the Treaty of St. Germain-en-Laye (1632), Charles de la Tour, one of the French contestants for hegemony in Acadia, had sought trade relations and an alliance with Massachusetts, and had actually hired a number of Massachusetts ships to assist him in his fight with his rival, the Sieur d'Aulnay Charnisay.[80] This episode raised a number of questions relative to international law and custom, both with regard to intervention in a civil conflict in a neighboring colony and with regard to freedom of trade.[81] There was a popular protest against intervention, represented by the famous "Ipswich Letter," [82] which was signed by a group of leading Massachusetts citizens. Moreover, d'Aulnay threatened to seize any Massachusetts ships that he might find serving de la Tour. The governor and council of Massachusetts informed d'Aulnay that they had "expressly prohibited all our people to exercise any act of hostility either by Sea or Land against you, unless it be in their own defence, until such time, as they shall have further commission." They requested that d'Aulnay recall the commissions he had issued,

forasmuch as our merchants are entered into a way and form of commerce with said De la Tour, which firstly, they tendered to yourself, but according as we have been informed, you refused; nevertheless, we see not just reason . . . to hinder them in their just and lawful callings, nor to hinder their own defence, in case they shall be assaulted, either by you or yours, during their trade with the said Sir.[83]

In his reply to the "Ipswich letter," the governor had explained that it was entirely within the rights of Massachusetts citizens to trade with de la Tour, and even to hire their ships out to him, provided they did not allow

[79] See Chapter XIII.
[80] See Chapter XI.
[81] *Winthrop's Journal*, ed., Hosmer, II, 43.
[82] *The Hutchinson Papers*, eds., Whitmore and Appleton, I, 131–132.
[83] Governour and Council's Letter to Mons. d'Aulnay, from Salem (n.d.; probably late 1644) *Colls. of the Mass. Hist. Soc.*, 3rd Series, VII, 99–102.

themselves to be drawn into the civil war between de la Tour and d'Aulnay. When engaged in such trade, or as hired carriers, they must, under international law, be free from molestation:

It is lawful [he said], for the owners and masters of shipps, and is in the way of their calling, to be hyred by la Tour . . . But if our shipps shall be opposed in their lawfull course, the justice of their cause will lye in that: as for example: a man travailing in a wagon in England, and carrying his goods with him, his creditor sets upon the wagon to take his debtors goods from him by force, the wagoner may defend him [the traveler] and his goods, being now in his charge without any respect to the former engagement; for the justice of his cause ariseth upon another ground.[84]

This is, in effect, a statement of the principle of the right of neutrals to trade with belligerents, and that "free ships make free goods."

Later on, when de la Tour was recalled to France and Massachusetts made a treaty of commerce with d'Aulnay,[85] it was agreed that there should be a mutual freedom of trade between the English colony and d'Aulnay; but it was also specifically provided that "the governor and majestrates [of Massachusetts] aforesaid bee not bound to restrayne their merchants from trading with the[ir] ships with what people soever, whether French or others, in what place soever inhabiting." [86] This was, in effect, a recognition by d'Aulnay of the right of the Massachusetts merchants to trade with de la Tour. In a larger sense, however, it was an explicit statement of the principle of the freedom of commerce in general.

Similar American expressions of these principles were frequent, in the relations between the English colonies and their non-English neighbors. Both principles, that of the freedom of commerce and that of the freedom of the seas, would eventually enter into the discussion of the relations between the colonies and the mother country itself, and would become important bases for the formulation of the later foreign policies of the United States.

Another aspect of the history of the principles of freedom of commerce and the freedom of the seas centered about a set of ideas and agreements relative to the rights of neutrals to trade with belligerents in time of war, in goods not "contraband," and to the definition of contraband. This aspect of international law and custom had been evolving in the development of European maritime international relations since the late feudal era. As early as 1225, for example, Venice had adopted the famous *Consulato del Mare* as a code of legal principles to govern its own shipping, and this code

---

[84] *Hutchinson Papers*, I, 143.

[85] Davenport, ed., *European Treaties*, I, 347–352. For a narrative of the relations between Massachusetts and Acadia in this period see Chapter XI.

[86] Davenport, ed., *European Treaties*, I, 351–352; Shurtleff and Pulsifer, eds., *Acts of the Commissioners of the United Colonies*, I, 59–60.

had gradually been accepted by the other Mediterranean cities.[87] Under this code, all enemy goods were contraband, even on neutral ships. It was only later that a distinction began to be made between "contraband goods" or goods useful in war, and "noncontraband goods," which were regarded as having no warlike use. In the course of the seventeenth century, this distinction was explicitly made in most commercial treaties, and the principle that "free [neutral] ships make free goods," indicating the basic freedom of neutrals to trade with belligerents in "noncontraband" goods came to be generally (but not universally) accepted among the states of Western Europe.

So far as the colonies were concerned, they played no active part in the evolution of this doctrine, although, as already noted, they were very much interested in it. The contribution of the colonies is to be noted only in the fact that certain products that originated in the colonies appeared on lists of goods that were regarded as "noncontraband." At the beginning, the list of noncontraband goods was limited to foodstuffs, but gradually the list was extended to include many other commodities. Thus, for example, in the Anglo-Dutch Treaty of Commerce made at London on December 1, 1674,[88] there appears an extensive list of "noncontraband" goods, which includes a number of products that were either peculiarly American, such as tobacco, or that were highly important in the colonial economies, such as sugar, textiles (presumably such as cotton fabrics from India), clothing and vestments, "together with the materials whereof they use to be made" (presumably including North American furs), spices (which came chiefly from the East Indies), and so on.

Again, in the abortive Anglo-French Treaty of Commerce made at Utrecht in 1713,[89] it is specifically stated (Article XVII), that in the trade of either, as a neutral, with enemies of the other, "it is now stipulated concerning ships and goods, that free ships shall also give a freedom to goods . . . contraband goods being always excepted. . . ."[90] The definition of "contraband" goods includes the usual list of warlike commodities, and the list of "noncontraband" goods includes cloth, clothing and materials for making it, tobacco, spices, fish, sugar, salt, cotton, hemp and naval stores, lumber and ships, all of which were produced in the colonies of one or the other of the signatories.

During the imperialistic wars of the eighteenth century the principle that "free ships make free goods" became a matter of bitter debate between England, as a belligerent, and the neutrals. The reason was that the Dutch, the Danes, the Portuguese, and the Spaniards, when neutrals, took advantage of the principle that "free ships make free goods" to carry the trade,

[87] Hill, *History of Diplomacy*, I, 362.
[88] Chalmers, ed., *Collection of Treaties*, I, 177–191.
[89] Chalmers, ed., *Collection of Treaties*, I, 390–424.
[90] Chalmers, ed., *Collection of Treaties*, I, 403.

especially the colonial trade, of the belligerents with the objective of assisting the belligerents in the evasion of the effects of the British control of
sea lanes, and, in the Seven Years War, the British blockade of the French
colonies. The Dutch, for example, insisted that the principle of "free ships
make free goods" contained in the Anglo-Dutch maritime treaty of 1674
made Dutch ships immune to seizure in wartime when carrying French
colonial commerce, even though that commerce were closed to them in
time of peace. The British response to the Dutch claim was the so-called
"Rule of the War of 1756," which declared that a trade closed in peacetime could not, in time of war, be opened to neutrals to be carried on between belligerents and their colonies. It was the trade of the French colonies, in this case, which was the prime consideration in the pronouncement
of this new British doctrine in international law.[91]

9. The Peaceful Settlement of Colonial Disputes

Although there appears to be no record of a single international dispute
among European powers relative to America that was settled by peaceful
means, both the idea and efforts to effectuate it in practice were customary
throughout the colonial period. Thus the Treaty of Tordesillas (1494) had
in it a provision for an Hispano-Portuguese joint commission of geographers to agree upon, and survey, the line of demarcation agreed upon in
that treaty. Similarly, the Hispano-Portuguese Treaty of Vittoria (1524)
provided for a joint commission of "astrologers" and pilots to meet and
determine the line of demarcation in the Pacific provided by that treaty.
In this case, the commission actually met at Badajoz, in the famous "junta
of Badajoz," in April and May of 1524. It failed to accomplish anything;
but a similar provision was included in the Treaty of Saragossa (1529),
which stipulated (Article 2) that the Pacific line of demarcation should lie
17° east of the Moluccas, that a joint commission of six geographers
should be named to draw a map of the new line. Again, nothing came of
the provision; but the idea and the practice of attempting to settle disputes
relative to the colonies persevered, especially after the Peace of Westphalia
of 1648.

Thus, in the Anglo-Dutch Treaty of Westminster (1654), which brought
to an end the first Anglo-Dutch war, it was provided that a joint commission was to meet in London to adjudicate claims and counterclaims
arising between 1611 and 1651, in the East Indies, America, or elsewhere.
Should the commission not be able to agree, the cases involved were to
be submitted to the arbitration of the Protestant cantons of Switzerland.
The commission apparently met in London, but it achieved nothing.[92]

[91] See Chapter XX.
[92] Thurloe, "Review of Negotiations," *Eng. Hist. Rev.*, XXI (1906), 324.

The Anglo-French Treaty of Whitehall (Treaty of American Neutrality) of 1686 [93] provided for an Anglo-French joint commission to settle
the Anglo-French disputes in America. The commission met in 1687, but
its labors were interrupted by the outbreak of the War of the League of
Augsburg. Again, a joint Anglo-French commission for the settlement of
American disputes was provided for in the Anglo-French Treaty of
Ryswick (1697). This commission also met, but its discussions were interrupted by the outbreak of the War of the Spanish Succession. The
Anglo-French Treaty of Utrecht provided for another commission, for the
same purpose. This commission did not meet until 1719; but it, too,
failed.[94] The Treaty of Seville (1729), of which France, Spain, and England were the principle signatories, provided for a Franco-Spanish joint
claims commission and an Anglo-Spanish commission. Apparently, the
Franco-Spanish commission never met, but the Anglo-Spanish commission
did meet in 1732. This commission labored for over a year but could agree
on nothing.[95] Again, after the Peace of Aix-la-Chapelle, in 1750 England
and France created a joint commission to try to settle the American
issues between them. Again, the conferences were unable to agree on
anything, and the issues were placed in the hands of the diplomats for
direct court-to-court negotiation. This, too, failed, and the Anglo-French
issues in America were left to the final arbitrament of the Seven Years
War.[96]

The idea of peaceful settlement of American disputes, then, whether by
joint commission or by arbitration, was an accepted principle among the
great colonizing states of Western Europe, throughout the colonial period.
It was an idea, however, which never succeeded in settling any international dispute between European powers relative to Angloamerica.

10. Colonial Empires and the Balance of Power

One of the major principles in the theory and practice of international
relations which emerged in the course of the seventeenth century was
the principle of the balance of international power. This principle, although not entirely new and although it had force as international law
only (if then) when written into actual treaties, was, in a sense, a sort of
substitute for the supernational power of the Pope, which had practically
(if not totally) disappeared from international relations by the end of the

[93] See Chapter IX.
[94] See Chapter XVI. See also, Savelle, "The Forty-ninth Degree of North Latitude
as an International Boundary, 1719: The Origin of an Idea," *Canadian Historical
Review*, XXXVIII, No. 3 (Sept., 1957), 183–201.
[95] See Chapter XVII.
[96] See Chapter XIX.

sixteenth century.[97] It never 'achieved a status of authority comparable to the former authority of the Pope, to be sure, but it was constantly invoked, from about 1600 onward, to check a dangerous growth of power in the hands of any nation. Furthermore, since colonies were coming to be thought of as constituting one of the major bases of a nation's wealth and power in the international community, the principle was applied in international relations relative to colonies to prevent any nation from acquiring a dangerous excess of power by the acquisition of too extensive colonial possessions.

Thus it was that implicit in the Peace of Westphalia there ran the intent of the non-Hapsburg powers to reduce and limit the power of the Hapsburgs. Similarly, with the inflation of French power under Louis XIV, the other nations of Europe drew together in a sort of concert to put a curb upon the danger of a French domination of the whole Continent, a concert that finally broke Louis's power in the War of the Spanish Succession. It was the question of the Spanish Succession, in fact, including the Spanish colonial empire in America, and the fear of a union of the two empires, that brought on that great war.

Thus, the Treaty of the Hague, of 1701, by which the "Second Grand Alliance" against Louis XIV was formed, specifically invoked the principle: that, whereas Louis XIV had seized the entire Spanish inheritance in the name of the Duke of Anjou and had, among other things, sent many ships of war to the Spanish Indies to take possession of them,

and in this and very many other ways the kingdoms of France and Spain are so closely united and grown together that . . . the French and Spaniards being thus joined will in a short time become so formidable to all that they may easily arrogate to themselves empires over all Europe . . . and since France and Spain are taking advantage of this state of affairs to unite more and more closely for suppressing the liberty of Europe and destroying trade . . . ,[98]

the signatories were thus forced to take military action and to form a close alliance to prevent any such upset in the balance of power, whether in Europe or in the "new world".

King William III of England, in announcing to Parliament the outbreak of the War of the Spanish Succession, expressed the same idea:

By the French king's placing his Grandson on the throne of Spain, he is in a condition to oppress the rest of Europe, unless speedy and effectual measures be taken. Under this pretence, he is become the real Master of the whole Spanish monarchy; he has made it entirely depending on France, and disposes of it, as of his own dominions, and by that means he has surrounded his neigh-

[97] See Hill, A History of Diplomacy, III, 361; Dupuis, Le Principle d'équilibre et le concert européen de la Paix de Westphalie à l'acte d'Algéciras, 9–21.

[98] Davenport, ed., European Treaties, III, 84. See also, Bourgeois, Manual historique, I, 245.

bours in such a manner, that, though the name of peace may be said to continue, yet they are put to the expense and inconveniences of war.—This must affect England in the nearest and most sensible manner, in respect to our trade, which will soon become precarious in all the variable branches of it; in respect to our peace and safety at home, which we cannot hope should long continue; and in respect to that part, which England ought to take in the preservation of the liberty of Europe. . . .

I will only add this: if you do in good earnest desire to see England hold the balance of Europe, and to be indeed at the head of the Protestant interest, it will appear by your right improving the present opportunity.[99]

The practical realities of a system of international relations operating upon the basis of a balance of power were recognized by the theorists early in the seventeenth century. Henri de Rohan made the following comment upon it in 1638, in the midst of the Thirty Years War:

The chief interest of all the other states is to maintain the balance so equal between these two great monarchies [Austria and France] that neither one, whether by force of arms or by negotiation, may even come overwhelmingly to prevail, and to achieve an assurance that the repose and the security of all the others may be secured by this equilibrium.[100]

Later in the century, other theorists, such as François-Paul de Lisola and Archbishop Fénelon of Cambrai, elaborated upon the principle. Fénelon, for example, based his analysis of the principle upon the idea that the community of states constitutes a sort of international society, in which every member must be constantly on guard to prevent an excessive aggrandizement of any one of its neighbors. It had been necessary in the sixteenth century, he said, for the other nations to oppose the establishment of Philip II of Spain on the throne of England by his marriage to England's queen, since this would have meant the annexation of a powerful England to the Spanish empire, including not only Spain, but also Spanish kingdoms in Italy, in the Low Countries, and in the East and West Indies, and would, thereby, have placed Philip in a position to "lay down the law" to all the other states of Christendom. The national laws of dynastic succession and inheritance, in such cases, must cede to the natural law governing the security of all the nations:

In a word, anything that upsets the equilibrium, and which significantly advances the establishment of an universal monarchy, cannot be just, even though founded upon the written laws of any particular country.[101]

It was for such reasons that Fénelon, in 1710, advised Philip V of Spain

---

[99] Cobbett, *Parliamentary History*, V, 1,220, 1,331.
[100] Quoted in Nys, "La théorie de l'équilibre européen," *loc. cit.*, XXV, 50. See also, Dupuis, *Le Principe d'équilibre et le concert européen*.
[101] Fénelon, *Ouevres choisies*, IV, 361.

(Philip of Anjou), who would presently be heir to the throne of France, to abdicate his Spanish throne. He warned Philip that if he insisted on holding on to the Spanish throne, he must face a long, long war, during which the states combined against him would destroy Spain's commerce and colonies in America, and his Spanish subjects would hold him responsible. Should Philip refuse to abdicate, Fénelon advised Louis XIV to make a separate peace; in that case the allies would move with all their combined power against both Spain and Spanish America.[102]

With the victory of the allies in the War of the Spanish Succession, the principle of the balance of power was written into practically all the peace treaties made at Utrecht in 1713, in the form of an absolute renunciation, by Philip V, of any and all claims he might have to the throne of France. At the same time, the principle was applied to the American colonies of Spain in the provision, for example, in the Anglo-Spanish treaty of peace, that the Spanish kings would never alienate any of their possessions in America, to France or to any other nation.[103] Not only did Spain promise not to alienate its American possessions to France or any other nation; England promised to guarantee the preservation of the territorial *status quo* of the Spanish colonies against any and all infringements. Incidentally, this British guarantee of the colonial *status quo* in Spanish America already anticipated the comparable paragraphs of the Monroe Doctrine of the next century.

It is to be noted that, within the then prevailing mercantilistic theory of national economy, the position of any state in the international power structure was thought ultimately to rest upon its commerce; and the prosperity of the national commerce was thought to derive largely, if not chiefly, from the nationally owned and controlled colonies. Thus, Geronimo de Uztariz, a Spanish economic and political theorist, explained that a nation cannot have a large population, strong armies, and international prestige without having a great commerce; its commerce cannot be great without great industries producing exportable goods. Uztariz then went on to mention France, Holland, and England as examples, citing the importance of colonial trade for all of them; and he urged his own government both to regulate and protect its colonial commerce more effectively and to encourage manufactures with the aim of restoring Spain's former position of grandeur in the international power scale.[104] A similar position was taken by Bernardo de Ulloa, who lamented the fact that such a great proportion of the wealth coming to Spain from America immediately flowed out again to France, Holland, and England for the

---

[102] Fénelon, *Ouevres choisies*, IV, 389–395.
[103] Davenport, ed., *European Treaties*, III, 229. See Chapter X.
[104] Geronimo de Uztariz, *Theorias y practica de comercio*, 2, 17–18, 141, 234, 324, *et passim*.

purchase of manufactures to be shipped to the Spanish colonies. He urged that Spain build up its own manufactures and, thereby, retain a greater proportion of the American wealth in Spain itself, thereby providing an economic base for a restoration of Spain's former predominant position in the international balance of power.[105]

Emmerich de Vattel, the greatest eighteenth-century theorist on international law, confirmed the general conviction that national power derived from national "external" commerce; he, too, cited England and Holland as the great examples. Europe, he said, constitutes an integral political system, or body, in which all the nations are bound together by their mutual self-interests. Constant international relations make of Europe a sort of federal republic of which the members, which are independent, but bound together by common interests, form themselves into alliances to preserve order and liberty.

It is this which has given birth to this famous idea of the Political Balance, or of the Equilibrium of Power. One understands by that a disposition of things by means of which no power may ever find itself in a position to exercise an absolute predominance over, or to lay down the law for, the others.[106]

England, of course, was, for Vattel, the perfect example of the state whose position of power in the international scale derived from its external commerce, including that with its colonies. "Today [he was writing about 1750] it is chiefly commerce which places in its [England's] hand the balance of Europe," [107] and he continues:

England, whose wealth and whose fleets have a very great influence, without alarming any state with regard to its liberty, because this power appears to be cured of the spirit of conquest [sic!]; England, I say, has the glory of having in her hands the Political Balance. She is careful to keep it in a state of equilibrium.[108]

For a half-century before the Peace of Utrecht, France, with Louis XIV at its head, was thought of as being the greatest menace to the international equilibrium. After that peace, in which England played the role of the chief guarantor of the commercial and colonial equilibrium, Great Britain came to be looked upon as the chief threat to it, especially in America. With its dominant role in the trade of Spanish America by reason of the *asiento* and the illicit trade that went on under it, coupled with the vast wealth now deriving to it from its own colonies, England was increasingly thought of as being a threat, not only to the balance of power in America, but also to that in Europe. French policy, about the

[105] Bernardo de Ulloa, *Rétablissement des manufactures et du commerce d'Espagne*, Part I, 2–7; Part II, 24–32.
[106] Emmerich de Vattel, *Le Droit de Gens . . .* , II, 40.
[107] Emmerich de Vattel, *Le Droit de Gens . . .* , I, 81.
[108] Emmerich de Vattel, *Le Droit de Gens . . .* , II, 40.

time of the Treaty of Seville (1729), was strongly influenced by this consideration, and it was largely on the basis of this that France turned to a serious effort to establish a permanent alliance of French and Spanish interests, both in Europe and in America.[109]

After the beginning of the War of Jenkins' Ear in 1739, France's Cardinal Fleury repeatedly warned England that it must not take any territory belonging to Spain in America. Such seizures, he said, could only be regarded by France as dangerous expansions of English colonial possessions and power, and must force France to enter the war on Spain's side.[110] France sent a fleet to America in 1740, and the cardinal explained to Lord Waldegrave, the British ambassador, that France did not intend war to take any of the English possessions, but only to protect French commerce and prevent England from seizing possession of the entire West Indies and from, thereby, becoming more powerful in that area than it was already.[111]

Many of the leaders of England itself recognized that by its aggressive expansionism Great Britain was now exciting the fears of the other states of Europe. The Duke of Newcastle faced this fact frankly in 1738, at the time of the debate over the Convention of the Pardo.[112] He warned the members of the House of Lords against precipitately entering upon a war with Spain. Should England not allow Spain an opportunity to make reparation for its depredations in America, the other nations

might look on our proceedings as the effect of a design, either to seize upon some part of the Spanish dominions in America, and to annex it to our own crown. . . . Did any of our European neighbors, My Lords, suspect that we had formed a design to dismember any part of the Spanish monarchy from that Crown, there is not the least doubt but they would look upon us with a very jealous eye; because, as your lordships know, the further alienation of any part of that monarchy is strictly guarded against in a separate article of the treaty of Utrecht, and for the observance of this article both we and the French are guaranters. If it were suspected, that we designed to force the Spaniards to allow us a free trade in all its branches to their settlements in America, the French would not fail to oppose us in such a design, the king of Spain, in the same treaty of Utrecht, having laid himself under an engagement, not to grant it to the subjects of any nation of Europe except his own. . . . This, my Lords, has always been looked upon as a necessary step towards preventing any one nation in Europe from becoming too rich and too powerful for the rest . . .[113]

[109] See, for example, 'Mémoire . . . du Commerce général" (1728–29), B.N., Ff., n.a., 23085. See Chapters XV and XVII.

[110] "Extracts of Letters from Ld Waldegrave, relating to any Declaration, made to Him by the Cardinal—and of the Answers sent to Ld. Waldegrave," P.R.O., S.P. 78/221: fols. 276–279.

[111] Waldegrave to Newcastle, Sept. 11, 1740, P.R.O., S.P., 78/223: 385–387.

[112] For the Convention of the Pardo see Chapter XVII.

[113] Cobbett, *Parliamentary History*, X, 771–772.

Newcastle went on to say that if no one nation had a monopoly, all Europe would benefit equally from trade with Spanish America,

whereas, should too large a share of them come into the hands of any other nation in Europe . . . they might be employed to purposes inconsistent with the peace of Europe, and which might one day prove fatal to the balance of power, that ought to subsist amongst her several princes.[114]

Many English leaders, however, defied both Spain and the possibility of European combinations in the name of the balance of power. Such, for example, was William Pulteney, afterward the Earl of Bath, and the Earl of Carteret. The latter, for example, was quoted as saying to the Swedish ambassador one evening after dinner—perhaps a little *en vin*,— "what is the good of taking ships? We shall take from Spain some countries in America, and we shall keep them in spite of the whole world." [115] At another time, Carteret gave to the House of Lords his opinion as to how the operations against Spanish America should proceed:

I hope they will be chiefly directed towards seizing such lands and cities belonging to the Spanish dominions in the Indies, as may contribute towards the benefit and enlargement of our navigation and commerce, which we now have a right to in those parts of the world. We have met with such provocations from Spain, as must render this war just on our part, in the eyes of every impartial judge; and, in the persecution of a just war, no power in Europe has a right, few of them can have an inclination to direct us, or to restrain us from making such conquests as may be sufficient for answering the charge of the war, as well as such as may be necessary for preventing our meeting with any injustice for the future.[116]

The inconclusive outcome of the War of the Austrian Succession did not allay European fears that England designed to upset the balance of power by an unlimited expansion of its American empire. The fear persisted; and, when war became imminent again in 1755, Rouillé, the French foreign minister, expressed to Mirepoix, the French ambassador in London, his opinion that "the English, in order to satisfy their unjust aims of ambition and conquest, wish to destroy in the new world the balance of power that it is essential to maintain there for the security and the interests of all the commercial nations." [117]

[114] Cobbett, *Parliamentary History*, X, 771–772.
[115] Quoted in Pares, *War and Trade in the West Indies*, 66.
[116] Cobbett, *Parliamentary History*, XI, 71.
[117] Rouillé to Mirepoix, Mar. 17, 1755, A.E., Corr. Pol., Ang., 438:280–283. For the War of Jenkins' Ear and the War of the Austrian Succession, see Chapter XVII.

CHAPTER XIII

International Relations on the "Great Frontier" in America, 1713-54

THE PEACE OF UTRECHT, far from bringing a clear and definitive peace among the English, French, Dutch, Spanish, and Portuguese colonies in America, created many new and more congenial conditions for strife. Thus, in the decades following the peace, new local friction areas appeared, and old ones became more inflamed, between the French and the English colonies, all the way from Hudson Bay to the Caribbean. Similar areas of friction appeared, or became newly exacerbated, between the English colonies and the Spanish. Similarly, too, but with less drama and international fireworks, both frictions and correspondences developed between French and Spanish colonies, French and Dutch, and Dutch and Spanish. Negotiations, in all these cases, took place directly between resident governors of the colonies. In most instances it was these direct negotiations which defined the issues in the local areas, and the recommendations of the governors, derived from the local conflicts, which provided the bases for the diplomatic demands of the mother countries against each other in Europe. The correspondence between English governors and French governors, for example, was a direct correspondence arising out of actual situations along the frontiers. While it had to do chiefly with rival territorial claims, it touched upon many other issues, such as exchanges of prisoners, treatment of trades and settlers, the privileges of missionaries, Indians and Indian trade, intercolonial commerce, and so on. On a very few occasions, as in the case of the Treaty of Frederica (Georgia), between the English governor Oglethorpe, of Georgia, and the Spanish governor Moral Sanchez, of Florida, the correspondence resulted in actual local treaties or agreements between colonies. In the majority of cases, however, the issues that arose in the course of this governor-to-governor correspondence were referred back to the home governments and became the subject matter of court-to-court correspondence in Europe.

Since the local issues arose out of local situations, the governors, through their reports to their home governments, exercised a powerful, perhaps decisive influence upon the diplomatic policies and the specific diplomatic demands of the mother countries relative to the colonial situation, in their correspondence with each other in Europe.

International relations among the European colonies in America did not involve only disputes, however. For, next in importance to the intercolonial disputes over territorial possessions was the existence of a vast, relatively peaceful and mutually profitable intercolonial commerce. However, while this commerce constituted bonds of friendship among the European colonies in America, it tended, in general, to run counter to the mercantilistic colonial and international policies of the mother countries and to complicate their relationships with each other with regard to America. In the colonies themselves the colonial governors conducted the colony-to-colony exchanges relative to commerce, on the one hand, and performed the functions, as it were, of agents in the field for the imperial and international policies of the mother countries, on the other. Eventually, a number of British colonial governors in the northern colonies found themselves in the position of justifying the intercolonial trade to the British government in the face of their instructions to suppress it, and of even going so far as to suggest changes in British international policy and practice that might accommodate them to the needs and interests of the colonies.

1. *The Frontier Diplomacy of Anglo-French Imperial Rivalry in North America*

The general lines of French intercolonial diplomacy in North America were laid down by the Marquis de Vaudreuil, Governor of New France, in a memoir relative to Anglo-French relations which he wrote to the Duc d'Orléans, regent of France, in 1716. While he would preserve the outward appearance of good relations with the English colonies, Vaudreuil was chiefly concerned with the defense of Canada, "should a new war break out with the English." For, he said, "it cannot be, for an instant, doubted but the English, on the first rupture between France and England, would employ all their efforts to seize the whole of Canada, and consequently the entirety of North America, whence might follow the loss of Mexico, from which they would expel the Spaniards in a few years without any resistance. . . . It is impossible to express how much the power of England would increase should she seize the remainder of North America, and how formidable that power would become in Europe." [1]

[1] M. de Vaudreuil to the Duc d'Orléans, Feb., 1716, N.Y.C.D., IX, 868–872.

Vaudreuil displayed a remarkable prescience relative to the historical probability that the Anglo-Saxons might come in time to dominate the whole continent, and he shared the mercantilist view of many of his contemporaries that, since the position of one of the maritime states in the balance of international power in Europe depended largely upon large colonial possessions and the commercial profits derived from them, such an accretion of colonies to the British empire would place that power in a position to "lay down the law" to all the others in the European community.

To meet the English threat, which to him was very real, Vaudreuil proposed that more soldiers be sent from France to America, that the fortifications of Louisbourg and Quebec be perfected, that posts be erected in the Indian country, and that the friendship of the Indians be preserved by the provision of plentiful supplies of presents and brandy at such posts as Forts Frontenac, Detroit, and Michilimackinac and at such others as should be constructed. The friendship of the Indians, including the Iroquois, was essential, both for the sake of the Indian trade and for blocking English expansion. The English traders were already going into the Indian country; Vaudreuil proposed to persuade the Indians to expel them. As for Acadia and the disputed territory of the Abenaki Indians,[2] Vaudreuil reported that

They [the English] have . . . wished to seize the territory occupied by the Abenakis and the Indians of the River St. John, on the ground that it depends on Acadia which has been ceded to them by the French.

But the Indians made answer to them, that this territory has always belonged to them; that they were not subjects of the French, but only their allies and friends; that the French could not give the English a territory that belonged to them, and which they would not quit.

In order to cultivate the friendship of the Abenakis and stiffen their resistance to the English, Vaudreuil proposed to build two churches, where the Indians could be converted to Catholicism and won over to the French cause, one on the St. John River, and one on the Piscataway River.[3] The French Council of Maritime Affairs approved Vaudreuil's policy of "preserving a good understanding, externally, with the Governors of the English Colonies" while he carefully watched the English "intrigues" among the Indians and did everything possible to win the natives' friendship and to encourage them to block English expansion into the Indian lands.[4]

Thus was French policy for facing the threat of English expansion in North America outlined by a colonial governor familiar with the practical

[2] See Chapter IX.
[3] N.Y.C.D., IX, 868–872.
[4] The Council of Marine to M. de Vaudreuil, June 26, 1717, N.Y.C.D., IX, 873–874.

exigencies of the situation and with imagination enough to anticipate the course that English expansion was likely to follow; thus, also, was the governor's proposed policy approved by the French home government. The policy outlined by Vaudreuil was to be consistently followed by the French, everywhere in America, from this time until the Seven Years War.

On the English side, Governor Robert Hunter of New York in 1715 called the attention of Secretary of State James Stanhope to the strategic position of New York for the protection of all the English colonies against the French in Canada. He urged the increase in the number of English soldiers in the province, and the building of a fort "up Hudson's River upon the entry to the Lakes." [5] He also reported the activities of the French in subverting the Indians, especially the Five Nations, from their friendship with the English, and he urged that everything possible be done to hold the friendship of those Indians.[6] Hunter's fears and his proposed policy of friendship with the Indians and fortification of the frontiers were supported by private commentaries upon the New York situation, such as the report that the French were seeking the Indians' permission to "build a house (as they call it) in the Onondago country," [7] and by such persons as Colonel Caleb Heathcote, who urged Governor Hunter to call a congress of English colonial governors to devise a common defense against the French threat.[8] Hunter, himself, looked upon French activities south of the Lakes as "an open infraction of [Article 15 of] the peace lately concluded," and he made it his policy to urge the Iroquois to refuse to allow the French to build forts in their country.[9] Governor Hunter, as Governor Vaudreuil, sensed the impending struggle for the control of the continent; his suggestions, based upon the *de facto* situation, and his diplomatic arguments against the French, were in general adopted by the British government as bases for English diplomatic policy.[10] He and his successors also followed the lines he laid down in their correspondence with the French governors of Canada relative to the frontier, to relations with the Indians, and to the Indian trade.

These two contemporary colonial governors, their thinking and policies, and their influence upon the diplomatic relations of their respective mother countries, were typical. It was the colonial governors, or their lieutenants, who gathered the data and formulated the arguments advanced in the chancelleries of Europe.

[5] "Extract of a letter from Col. Hunter, Governor of New York, to Mˢ Secʳʸ Stanhope dated New York, the 29 Septʳ 1715," N.Y.C.D., V, 456.
[6] N.Y.C.D., V, 456; also, "Memorial of Mr. Champaute to the Lords of Trade," n.d., *ibid.*, V, 456–457.
[7] "Mr. Ludwick to the Lords of Trade," Aug. 23, 1715, N.Y.C.D., V, 422–423.
[8] Caleb Heathcote to Robert Hunter, July 8, 1715, N.Y.C.D., V, 430–431.
[9] "His Excellency Brigadier Hunter's reply to the Five Nations . . . ," June 13, 1717, N.Y.C.D., V, 485–486.
[10] See, for example, "Lords of Trade to Secretary Stanhope," Nov. 18, 1715, N.Y.C.D., V, 467–469.

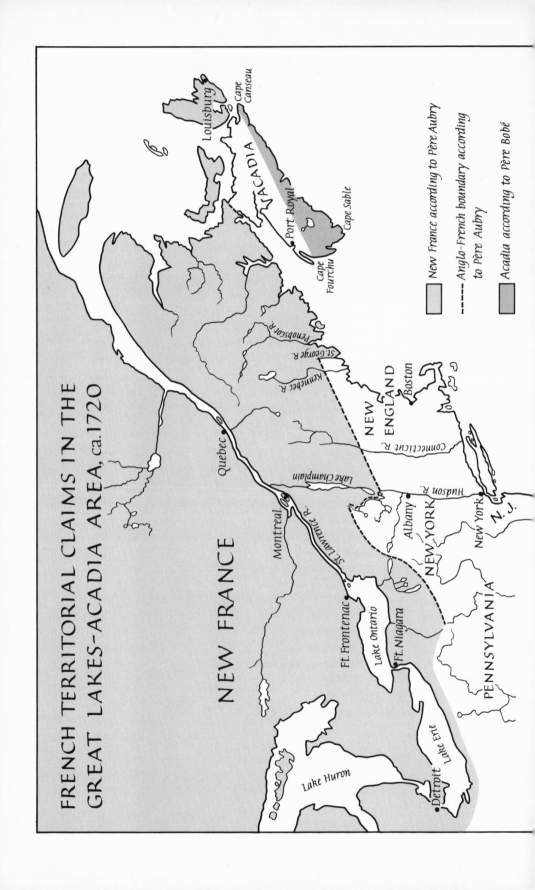

FRENCH TERRITORIAL CLAIMS IN THE
GREAT LAKES–ACADIA AREA, ca. 1720

NEW FRANCE

Lake Huron

Detroit

Lake Erie

Ft. Niagara

Lake Ontario

Ft. Frontenac

St. Lawrence R.

Montreal

Quebec

Lake Champlain

PENNSYLVANIA

NEW YORK

Albany

New York

N.J.

Hudson R.

Connecticut R.

NEW
ENGLAND

Boston

St. George R.

Kennebec R.

Penobscot R.

Cape
Fourchu

Cape Sable

Port Royal

ACADIA

Louisburg

Cape
Canseau

New France according to Père Aubry

Anglo-French boundary according
to Père Aubry

Acadia according to Père Bobé

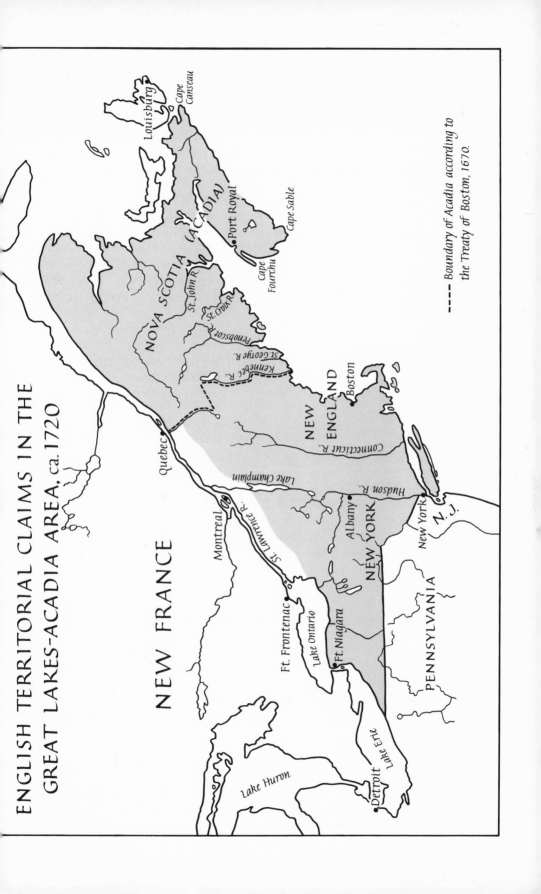

ENGLISH TERRITORIAL CLAIMS IN THE
GREAT LAKES-ACADIA AREA, ca.1720

- - - - Boundary of Acadia according to
the Treaty of Boston, 1670.

Louisburg
Cape Canseau
Port Royal
Cape Sable
Cape Fourchu
NOVA SCOTIA (ACADIA)
St. John R.
St. Croix R.
Penobscot R.
St. George R.
Kennebec R.
NEW ENGLAND
Boston
Connecticut R.
Quebec
Montreal
St. Lawrence R.
Lake Champlain
NEW FRANCE
Ft. Frontenac
Lake Ontario
Ft. Niagara
Albany
Hudson R.
New York
N. J.
NEW YORK
PENNSYLVANIA
Detroit
Lake Erie
Lake Huron

2. The Diplomatic History of Acadia, 1713-54

When news of the signing of the Anglo-French Treaty of Utrecht reached America, the English governor of Acadia and the French governors of Cape Breton Island and of Canada very soon found it necessary to correspond directly with each other over the interpretation and the execution of the provisions of that treaty.

The first of the provisions that called for intercolonial cooperation was that which provided (Article 14) that the French inhabitants of all the American territories "ceded or restored" to England were to have the right to remove within a year, with their movable possessions, to French territory. The French government expected that many Acadians would move to Cape Breton Island, and arrangements were made in 1714 between Governors St. Ovide de Brouillon, of Cape Breton, and Francis Nicholson, of Nova Scotia, to effect the transfer. St. Ovide sent representatives to Nova Scotia to assist the *habitants* who might choose to move, and a few families did actually emigrate. But the one-year term expired, the Acadians lost interest, and the English Board of Trade, convinced that, in any case, the emigration of the Acadians would weaken the economy of the colony and would strengthen the French, recommended that the movement be stopped, and it was."

In 1718 Lieutenant Governor Doucett, of Nova Scotia, revived the issue. He wrote to Governor St. Ovide that, although the time for emigration allowed the French *habitants* by the treaty of peace had expired, it was still possible for them to leave Nova Scotia if they wished. He suggested that St. Ovide make the necessary arrangements. At the same time he wrote to the Governor of Canada, the Marquis de Vaudreuil, within whose overall jurisdiction Acadia fell, asking him to advise the *habitants* in Acadia that they were free either to leave or to become subjects of the British King, and to order those who chose to leave Nova Scotia to retire to Canada.[12] Vaudreuil replied that he had been informed that the English were not permitting the Acadians to leave.[13] He did, however, write what seems to have been an open letter to one Louis Allain, at Port Royal, telling him that he might take the loyalty oath to the British King if he wished; Allain must remember, however, that if he chose to remain a British subject he would not enjoy the free exercise of his *Catholic religion* (this statement, of course, was false). More important, Vaudreuil told Allain that he might move across the Bay of Fundy to the area about the St. John River, since this territory was not in Acadia, or English Nova

[11] Brebner, *New England's Outpost*, 66–67; Gipson, *British Empire*, V, 171–173.
[12] Doucett to St. Ovide, May 15, 1718, *C.S.P., Col., A.& W.I.*, 1717–18, No. 565 (IV), pp. 269–270; Doucett to Vaudreuil, May 15, 1718, *Ibid.*, No. 565, (V), p. 270.
[13] Vaudreuil to Doucett, Sept. 27, 1718, *C.S.P., Col., A.& W.I.*, 1717–18, No. 789 (I), pp. 406–407.

Scotia, but belonged to France.[14] The Acadians showed little interest, however, and no significant movement of Acadians took place. The problem presented by the choice facing the Acadians, however, to take the oath of loyalty to Britain or to emigrate, as originally provided by the Anglo-French Treaty of Utrecht, remained a bitter question between French and English governors until the mass deportation of the Acadians in 1754 and the final cession of most of French North America to England by the Treaty of Paris in 1763.

Closely related to the business of removal of the Acadians was the provision, in the same Article 14 of the Treaty of Utrecht, that all the French subjects in the colonies "ceded or restored" to England, who chose to remain in those territories and under the sovereignty of Great Britain, should "enjoy the exercise of the Catholic and Roman religion, conformally to the laws of Great Britain." The French governors of Cape Breton and the governors-general of Quebec, as well as the bishop of Quebec, understood this to mean that the bishop of Quebec and the governor of Canada should have the right to name priests to minister to the French Canadians and missionaries to serve the Catholic Indians in Acadia. This, too, became a matter of some bitterness in the correspondence between the French and English governors, since the French priests sent to the Acadians, especially those in the lands west of the Bay of Fundy, which the French regarded as being outside of Acadia, taught the Acadians that they were still subjects of the King of France. Similarly, the missionaries among the Indians in this area taught the savages that their country had not been ceded to England and encouraged them to resist English "encroachments" upon the Indian lands.[15] The complaints of the English governors evoked the response that the right of the Acadians to worship according to their Catholic religion was guaranteed by the Treaty of Utrecht, which was true; Governor Armstrong, in 1732, protested that the French priests, in the name of their religion, were subverting the Acadian subjects of the English king. He expelled two of them, and requested St. Ovide to send two "of known probity" who would administer their religion and leave politics alone. As for the treaty right of the Acadians to their religion, he reminded St. Ovide that, although the Treaty of Utrecht did, indeed, guarantee the right of the Acadians to their religion, it specified that this right was granted "only so far as the laws of Great Britain allow." Thus, the priests, if they were to administer the Catholic religion, must, in doing so, also obey the laws of England.[16]

[14] Vaudreuil to Louis Allain, Sept. 22, 1718, C.S.P., Col., A.& W.I., 1717–18, No. 789 (IV), p. 406.

[15] Governor Philipps of Nova Scotia to Governor St. Ovide de Brouillon, of Cape Breton. May 14, 1720, Nova Scotia Archives, I, 26–28; same to same, Aug. 10, 1720, same, July 26, 1736, ibid., II, 107–108.

[16] Armstrong to St. Ovide June 17, 1732, Nova Scotia Archives, I, 96–97; same to ibid., I, 38–39.

The problem of Roman Catholicism in Acadia, like the problem of the oath of allegiance, remained a source of dispute in the correspondence of the governors until the Seven Years War.

The assumption by Governor-General Vaudreuil in 1718 that the western shore of the Bay of Fundy was not English, since it was not a part of the Acadia ceded to England by the Treaty of Utrecht, but was a part of Canada, raised again the old question of what the *"anciennes limites"* of Acadia were.[17] Vaudreuil had, in fact, in the letter he wrote to Doucett in April, 1718, requested Doucett "not to permit your English boats to go in the River St. John, which is still part of the French dominion."[18] Doucett replied to the French governor in the same friendly terms, but he expressed surprise at Vaudreuil's assumption that the lands along the Bay of Fundy were French, and he insisted that they were part of Acadia and, therefore, English.[19]

Vaudreuil's claim of 1718 that the western shore of the Bay of Fundy was not a part of Acadia, or Nova Scotia, and was still, therefore, French, appears to have been arrived at after the Treaty of Utrecht. Vaudreuil had been in Paris at the time of the peace; he brought news of it with him to Canada immediately afterward. He was instructed, among other things, to arrange to move all the Abenaki Indians, allies of France, from that region to Cape Breton Island, an instruction apparently based upon the then determination of the French court in good faith to restore Acadia, with its *"anciennes limites,"* to England. Apparently, the French Ministry of Marine at that time understood the boundary of Acadia toward New England to be the St. George River, fixed by England and France about 1700 under the terms of the Treaty of Ryswick. The Jesuit Père de la Chasse, for twenty years a missionary among the Abenakis, was asked to convey to the Indians the news of the peace and of the plans for their removal to Cape Breton.[20]

Meanwhile, the English had already brought the news of the peace to the Abenakis and had pointed out to them that France, in ceding Acadia, had ceded to the English the Abenaki lands. The Indians were deeply disturbed and, on the ground that they were independent nations and that their land was their own and, therefore, not to be disposed of by any foreign nation, protested the action of France, and flatly refused to abandon their lands.[21] The Père de la Chasse was convinced that were France to insist upon removing the Abenakis, they would not go, but would

[17] See Chapter IX.

[18] Vaudreuil to Doucett, Apr. 15, 1718, C.S.P., *Col.*, A.& W.I., 1717–18, No. 789 (I), pp. 406–407.

[19] Doucett to Vaudreuil, May 15, 1718 C.S.P., *Col.*, A.& W.I., 1717–18, No. 565 (V), p. 270.

[20] "Memoir respecting the Abenaquis of Acadia," 1718, N.Y.C.D., IX, 878–881.

[21] N.Y.C.D., IX, 879.

become implacable enemies. Instead, advised the father, it should be the policy of France to defend the Indians in the possession of their lands and to protect them by force of arms if necessary.[22] This advice was adopted, and the missionaries were instructed to pacify the Indians and to assure them that France would protect them and their lands in every way possible. Vaudreuil himself said to them, "I shall secretly send you some hatchets, some powder and lead"; he finally went so far as to assure the Indians that "rather than abandon them to the mercy of the English, he would himself march at their head." [23]

It was thus, apparently in view of the local situation, especially the refusal of the Indians to move, that the French willingness to release to England the greater Acadia was revised. The Père de la Chasse and the French missionaries among the Abenakis strongly advised against conceding the Indians' lands to the English, and it became the official French policy not only to claim the territory for France, but also actively to back the Indians in their resistance to the English. Once the French had repented of their cession of the greater Acadia, Vaudreuil and other French policy makers argued that this policy was "the only means we possess to prevent the English establishing themselves throughout that entire country up to the height of land—that is, very near Quebec and Montreal." Indeed, it was argued, if matters were allowed to proceed as they had begun, "New France will be bounded on the South by the River St. Lawrence; it will be necessary to abandon all our posts and settlements on that side, and nothing will prevent the English and the Iroquois making irruptions into the very heart of the Colony." All the more reason, as Père de la Chasse advised, to come to some arrangement "with the Governor of Boston" fixing the boundaries between New England and Canada in the neighborhood of the Bay of Fundy. This recommendation was also "incessantly urged" by Michel Bégon, the Intendant of Canada.[24]

A number of proposals were made to Vaudreuil and the French Ministry of Marine as to what the boundary should be. A typical proposal, embodying the basic French fear of English expansion, was that proposed by Père Joseph Aubry, long a missionary among the Abenakis. According to Aubry's memorial, it would be a grave mistake on the part of France to cede to the English, as part of Acadia, the lands lying along the Bay of Fundy. Acadia, he said, was only the peninsula that the English called Nova Scotia. The land along the coast from the Isthmus of Beaubassin to Casco Bay, not being a part of Acadia, had not been ceded to England by the treaty, and, therefore, still remained French. This non-Acadian territory should be considered as extending at least as far westward as the St. George River (east of Casco Bay) where "by mutual agreement the arms of England

[22] N.Y.C.D., IX, 879–880.
[23] N.Y.C.D., IX, 880.
[24] N.Y.C.D., IX, 878, 879, 880.

and France were set up as Boundary marks at the preceding peace [of Ryswick, 1697]. . . ." The proposed boundary between French and English colonies in that part of the world, therefore, should run from this point on the St. George River where the boundary was fixed straight to the Hudson River and thence along the height of land between the waters flowing southward and those flowing into the Great Lakes basin.[25]

Père Aubry's suggestion represents approximately the French concepts of Acadia and of the part of "New France" that lay along the Bay of Fundy upon which were to rest the French claims for the next half century; with the significant exception, apparently based upon the thinking of another missionary, Père Bobé.[26] This view held that the "ancient" Acadia included only the portion of the Peninsula of Nova Scotia that lay to the southeastward of a straight line drawn across the peninsula from Cape Sable or Forked Cape to Cape Canso. Port Royal, which lay outside the line, was accepted as part of the Utrecht cession only because it was specifically mentioned in the Treaty of Utrecht.[27]

It seems clear, then, that French diplomatic policy with regard to Acadia was sharply revised, after the Treaty of Utrecht, in the light of the recommendations of the men actually on the scene, especially the missionaries and the intendant, channeled through the governor of Canada, the Marquis of Vaudreuil. The new policy appeared just before the creation of the Anglo-French American boundary commission in 1719, and it was the basis of the negotiations of that commission with regard to Acadia.[28] At the same time, it became the position supported by the governors of Canada both in their relations with the Indians and in their correspondence with the British governors of Nova Scotia and of Massachusetts.

Thus it was that when, on September 22, 1718, Governor Vaudreuil again wrote to Governor Doucett of Nova Scotia, referring to the formation of the Anglo-French alliance of 1717 [29] and bespeaking good relations between themselves, he warned the English governor to keep English ships away from the St. John River, since that was French territory.[30] During that same summer, he began to activate a program among the Indians in the course of which the missionaries encouraged the Abenakis to resist the British settlement that had been taking place, on the ground

[25] "Reverend Father Aubery on the Boundary of New France and New England," Jan., 1720, N.Y.C.D., IX, 894–896.

[26] "Mémoire by M. Bobé respecting the Boundaries," N.Y.C.D., IX, 913–917.

[27] "Mémoir by M. Bobé respecting the Boundaries," Mar., 1723, N.Y.C.D., IX, 913–917.

[28] See Chapter XVI.

[29] See Chapter XVI.

[30] Vaudreuil to Doucett, Sept. 22, 1718, Dec. 13, 1718, C.S.P., Col., A.& W.I., 1717–18, No. 789 (I), pp. 405–406.

that those lands were the Indians' own, as those of an independent nation, and could never have been ceded by France to England, since France did not own them, while the governor and the intendant furnished them with arms and ammunition.[31]

In the summer of 1719, at about the time when the Anglo-French joint commission for settling American boundaries was being created, the English Board of Trade instructed Governor Philips, of Massachusetts, to propose to the governor of Canada the creation of a joint commission for the on-the-ground location of the boundary between New England and Canada.[32] This he did, in June, 1720, but Vaudreuil replied that he had no orders to appoint any such commissioners; perhaps they would arrive on the King's ship in August.[33]

Meanwhile, the tension between the Abenakis and the English increased, encouraged and supported by the French, and in 1722 the tension reached the point of war. Governor Samuel Shute of Massachusetts wrote to Vaudreuil protesting the French aid to the Indians as a violation of Article 15 of the Treaty of Utrecht, since the lands involved were part of Acadia and the Indians, therefore, were "English Indians.[34]

Vaudreuil flatly contradicted Shute's contention. These Indians, he said, were the allies and friends of France, on land that was an integral part of New France. He frankly avowed his support for the Abenakis and said he proposed to continue, since he had orders from his court to do so.[35]

In 1723 Vaudreuil sent one Denis de la Ronde to Boston to deliver a sort of ultimatum relative to the English-Abenaki war. De la Ronde was instructed to say to the English that the Abenakis would not stop fighting until the English abandoned their lands. The Indians, said Vaudreuil, having allies (that is, presumably, the French), would henceforth be more successful in their war against the English. The English post on the east side of the St. George River, since it was in the territories of the Abenakis under the protection of New France, must be demolished. Since the Treaty of Utrecht forbade the English from molesting the Indian allies of France, the English must cease doing so; since the Abenakis were Catholics, they could never be friends of the English; they were under the protection of France, and they had every right to defend their lands as

[31] "Extrait de la réponse en datte du 26. 8. 1719 faite par M.ʳˢ de Vaudreuil et Bégon cydevant Gouverneur général et Intendant en Canada au Mémoire du Roy en datte du 23 May de ladᵉᵗ année. A.E., Méms. et Docs., Amér.: fols. 61–61vo.

[32] "Draft of H. M. Instructions to Governor Philips," C.S.P., Col., A.& W.I., 1719–20, No. 255 (II), p. 131. See also, Chamorel (French ambassador in London) to Abbe Dubois, June 13, 1719, A.E., Corr. Pol., Ang., 324: fols. 113–114 vo.

[33] Vaudreuil to Philips, July 9, 1720, C.S.P., Col., A.& W.I., 1720–21, No. 241 (XVI), p. 157.

[34] Shute to Vaudreuil, Apr. 15, 1722, C.S.P., Col., A.& W.I., 1722–23, No. 805 (V), pp. 418–420.

[35] Shute to the Board of Trade, July 27, 1722, C.S.P., Col., A.& W.I., 1722–23, No. 242, p. 117.

they were doing (Vaudreuil clearly implied that they were receiving aid from the French and would continue to do so).[36] In a letter to Governor Shute, Vaudreuil repeated that the Abenakis would not end the war "until you [the English] entirely abandon all their rivers and . . . things be set on the same foot, as they were before the Treaty of Utrecht." The treaty said nothing about the Abenaki lands; it was the English, therefore, who were violating Article 15 of the treaty, since they were oppressing and fighting these Indians who were allies of France, on French territory. Thus, it was the English who were violating the Treaty of Utrecht, not the French.[37]

These arguments were repeated in the correspondence between Governor William Dummer of Massachusetts and Governor Vaudreuil in 1724. Dummer protested that the Abenakis were subjects of the King of Great Britain and were living on British territory, a part of Nova Scotia (Acadia); French meddling with them, especially through the activities of the Jesuit missionary, the Père Rasle, was a flagrant violation of the Treaty of Utrecht. Disputes between the English and the Indians were none of Vaudreuil's concern; Dummer hinted that, if French meddling did not stop, he might loose the English Indians upon the French in Canada.[38] To which, of course, Vaudreuil acidulously replied that Dummer was ignorant of the facts—that the boundary between New France (not Acadia) and New England had been jointly fixed at the St. George River in 1700; that although certain individual Indians had "submitted" the Indian lands to the English, the whole nation repudiated the cession; that the lands in question were not part of Acadia, but part of New France, and that, under the terms of the Anglo-French Treaty of Utrecht, the Abenakis must be considered allies of France; and that the trouble with the Indians was due to English violations of the treaty. Vaudreuil even offered to mediate the quarrel, should Dummer ask it. As for Dummer's hint that he might set the English Indians upon the French,

"I am less terrified [he wrote] by your threat to launch the [English] Indians upon me than you should be of those Indian nations which, by your own fault, you have aroused against you." [39]

Vaudreuil also protested the death, at the hands of the English, of Père Rasle.

The dispute was continued by Dummer's reiteration of the English claims, supported by a reference to the submission to the English of the

---

[36] "Instructions of Vaudreuil to Denis de la Ronde, going to Boston . . . ," Canada, Public Archives, *Report 1923*, Appendix D, Miscellaneous, 22.

[37] Vaudreuil to Shute, Oct. 23, 1723, *C.S.P., Col., A.& W.I., 1722–23*, No. 805 (VIII), pp. 420–421.

[38] Dummer to Vaudreuil, Sept. 15, 1724, *Collections of Maine Historical Society: Documentary History of Maine*, X, 223–224.

[39] Vaudreuil to Dummer, Oct. 30, 1724, A.N., Cols., c11/46:fols. 136–141 vo.

Penobscot and Norridgewock Indians, together with their lands, in a treaty with Sir William Phipps, a Boston adventurer, in 1693.[40] The boundary of 1700, he said, was superceded by the Treaty of Utrecht (he did not specify how). His letter was to be delivered by Samuel Thatch and William Dudley, sent as commissioners to confer with Vaudreuil "pursuant to such instructions as they have received from me." [41]

The Massachusetts commissioners apparently discussed with Vaudreuil the question of the entire Anglo-French boundary from Acadia to the Great Lakes, for they wrote to the New York Commissioners of Indian Affairs at Albany that Vaudreuil had informed them that he would look upon the building of any fortifications on the Onondaga (Oswego) River by the English as a violation of the Treaty of Utrecht, and that he would demolish them; he could, he said, set the Five Nations of Indians against the English at any time. Representatives of the Abenaki Indians, present at the conference, claimed "all of Acadia except Port Royal," and asserted there could be no peace until their sovereignty was recognized.[42]

Peace was made between the Indians and the English by the Treaty of Casco Bay in 1727. Without surrendering their claim to sovereignty over their lands, the Indians tacitly permitted the English to remain and agreed to assist them in keeping peace.[43] The governor of Canada, now the Marquis de Beauharnais, reluctantly reported the peace to his master, and Louis XV expressed surprise and distress at hearing of it; but he approved the governor's plan to continue his policy of holding the Indians' friendship by gifts and through the activities of missionaries, and of continuing to maintain, in his relations with the English, that the land was French under the terms of the Treaty of Utrecht. Beauharnais was also encouraged to send French settlers into the area.[44]

It was shortly after this that Beauharnais decided to build a fort at Crown Point on Lake Champlain. At the same time he reported that the English were building new forts along the coast of the Bay of Fundy from the St. George River eastward. He still maintained, however, that Acadia was only the part of the Peninsula of Nova Scotia east of a line drawn from Forked Cape (northwest of Cape Sable) to Cape Canso, and that all the land from that line (except Port Royal) to the St. George River was part of New France, under the terms of the Treaty of Utrecht. It could be seen, he said, by the activities of the English, "how they seek every possible means to extend their hold upon this land farther and

[40] See Colls. of the N.H. Hist. Soc., II, 235–236.

[41] Dummer to Vaudreuil, Jan. 30, 1725, C.S.P., Col., A.& W.I., 1724–25, No. 740 (XXV), pp. 437–438.

[42] Commissioners from Massachusetts Bay to the Commissioners of Indian Affairs at Albany, 1725, C.S.P., Col., A.& W.I., 1724–25, No. 740 (XXX), pp. 439–440.

[43] Colls. of the N.H. Hist. Soc., II, 260–263; see also, "Indian Explanation of the Treaty of Casco Bay," N.Y.C.D., IX, 966–967.

[44] Louis XV to Messrs. Beauharnais and Dupuys, N.Y.C.D., IX, 1,002–1,006.

farther [eastward]." He again urged his government to name commissioners to fix the boundaries "between them and us." [45] Nothing, however, was done. In fact, the Anglo-French *entente* of 1717 had come to the end of its effectiveness, and there was beginning an era of coolness between the two crowns in Europe that was to open the door for further conflict in America.[46]

While the correspondence between the governors of Canada and Massachusetts over the Abenakis and the Bay of Fundy littoral was going on, there was taking place a parallel, but less bitter correspondence between the English governor of Nova Scotia and the French governor of Cape Breton. At the beginning, this correspondence was concerned, as already noted, with the removal of Acadian *habitants* to Cape Breton Island. The two governors had also had occasion to correspond about other matters, such as the fisheries, the seizure of ships, the privileges of French missionaries among the Acadians, and so on.

The question of boundaries was involved, for example, in the problem raised by the presence of French fishermen in the Gut of Canso, between Nova Scotia and Cape Breton Island, a problem that became acute in 1718. In the summer of that year Lieutenant Governor Doucett wrote Governor St. Ovide de Brouillon, of Cape Breton Island, calling his attention to the fact that the French fishermen were active in that area and that they had made a settlement on the island of Canso, which, he said, was in effect a part of the mainland of Nova Scotia. St. Ovide replied that the fishermen were fully entitled to fish in the gut and on the islands of Canso, since this gut was "the small entrance of the Gulph of St. Lawrence, otherwise called the River of Canada," recognized as belonging to France by the Treaty of Utrecht. As for the settlement on the "mainland" of Nova Scotia, the land at that place was not English, since the *"anciennes limites"* of Acadia, which was ceded to England, touched the Gulf of St. Lawrence in the neighborhood of the St. Mary's River, and this settlement was located outside the Acadian boundary. He suggested that the whole matter be left to the judgment of the two courts in Europe.[47]

The English governors of Nova Scotia were not satisfied with St. Ovide's explanation of the Treaty of Utrecht relative to the fisheries and the Acadian boundary, and Governor Shute, of Massachusetts, sent Captain Smart, of H.M.S. *Squirrel*, to Louisbourg to confer with St. Ovide with regard to boundaries and to request him to order the French "interlopers" out of English waters and lands. St. Ovide refused the English

[45] "Reply of Oct. 10, 1731, by Messrs. Beauharnais and Hocquart to the King's Memoir of May 8, 1731," A.N. Cols., C11A/54: fols. 136–167 vo.

[46] See Chapter XVI.

[47] St. Ovide to Doucett, July 21, 1718, C.S.P., Col., A&W.I., 1717–18, No. 635 (I), pp. 325–326.

request. He wrote to Shute that he had conferred with Smart, but that they disagreed as to the interpretation of the Treaty of Utrecht, especially with regard to the fisheries and the question what the *"anciennes limites"* of Acadia were. St. Ovide agreed, however, to withdraw all the French "after the fishing was over," provided the English, also, were evacuated, thus leaving the area vacant until ownership of it should be decided by the home governments.[48]

Captain Smart, apparently unwilling to wait, proceeded to fall upon the French fishing fleet, dispersing it and taking three prizes.[49] In the summer of 1720 the French retaliated, whereupon Governor Philipps of Nova Scotia demanded restitution, but got no result.[50]

Correspondence between the English governors of Nova Scotia and the French governors of Cape Breton continued intermittently until about 1740. The general tenor of the English correspondence was one of complaint against French anti-English propaganda among the Indians, especially that of the missionaries, as already noted.

Basically, the exchange of ideas between Cape Breton and Nova Scotia rested upon the same conflicting interpretation of the Treaty of Utrecht as that between the governors of New France and the governors of Massachusetts: the English rested all their arguments upon the conviction that the *"anciennes limites"* of Acadia (or Nova Scotia) as ceded to England by the Treaty of Utrecht included all the land between the Atlantic, the St. Lawrence River, and the eastern boundary of New England. The French, on the other hand, insisted (after the first preliminary discussions of policy by the French ministry immediately following the Peace of Utrecht) that the *"anciennes limites"* of Acadia included only a strip of the Peninsula of Nova Scotia along the Atlantic Ocean. All other contentions, whether relative to the *habitants*, the Indians, the missionaries and religion, trade, or settlement, stemmed from these conflicting presuppositions.

The Peace of Aix-la-Chapelle left the local boundary and other questions relative to Anglo-French relations in America still unsettled. In Acadia, as elsewhere, with Cape Breton returned to France by the peace, the situation stood just where it had stood before the War of the Austrian Succession (King George's War) began.

Governor William Shirley of Massachusetts had corresponded during

---

[48] Captain Southard's Journal [on mission from Governor Shute and the Council of Massachusetts to Governor St. Ovide], *C.S.P., Col., A.& W.I.,* 1719–20, No. 137 (VI), p. 69; St. Ovide to Governor Shute, Sept. 23, 1718, *ibid,* 1719–20, No. 213, VIII, pp. 105–106.

[49] Nathaniel Shannon to George Vaughan, Oct. 22, 1718, *C.S.P., Col., A.& W.I.,* 1717–18, No. 782, (II), p. 403.

[50] Governor Philipps to the governor of Cape Breton, Aug. 8, 1720, *C.S.P., Col., A.& W.I.,* 1720–21, No. 241 (IX), pp. 154–155.

the war just ended with both Governor Duquesnel of Cape Breton, and Governor Beauharnais of Canada relative to exchanges of prisoners.[51] This correspondence became more active in 1747, when Governor Beauharnais sent a letter to Shirley under a flag of truce proposing an exchange of prisoners.[52] This exchange was soon followed, in the summer of 1748 (before the treaty of peace was signed) by a letter from the new governor of Canada, the Marquis de la Galissonière, suggesting peaceful relations between them. Shirley replied by telling de la Galissonière that the Five Nations of Indians were complaining that members of those tribes, held prisoner in Canada, were being "kept in Irons." These Indians, he reminded de la Galissonière, were vassals of England and must be treated as such. He proposed an exchange of these Indians for French prisoners of war in English hands; he also asked de la Galissonière to stop demanding of the Iroquois that they go to Canada to negotiate their own exchange of prisoners. Now that the preliminaries of peace had been signed, he said, it ought to be possible for the two governors to iron out their local differences.[53]

But the old tensions flared up in Acadia again, for de la Galissonière wrote to Governor Mascarene of Nova Scotia, early in 1749, complaining of the new effort to exact oaths of allegiance from the *habitants*, even in the lands around the St. John's River, which, he said, repeating the old French argument, lay entirely within New France. He also demanded that the Abenaki Indians of that area be included in the peace.[54] To which Mascarene replied that the English troops on the western shore of the Bay of Fundy were within Acadia, and, therefore, in English territory. The *habitants* punished by the English Captain Gorham were punished for treason against the King of England in assisting the French activity in this area during the war. As for the Indians, they, too, had sided with the French, and, since they were in English territory, they must make their peace with the English governor at Annapolis before they could expect to enjoy the benefits of peace.[55]

At about this same time, de la Galissonière sent a detachment of soldiers to build a fort at the mouth of the St. John River to buttress the

[51] Shirley to Duquesnel, Sept. 22, 1744, Canada, Public Archives, *Report 1894*, 102–103; Duquesnel to Shirley, n.d., *ibid.*, 1894, 103.

[52] Shirley to Gideon Wanton, Aug. 20, 1747, *Shirley Correspondence*, I, 395; see also, Governor Benning Wentworth's Message to the New Hampshire Assembly, Aug. 27, 1747, Bouton *et al*; eds., *Docs. and Recs. rel. to the Prov. of New Hampshire*, 1738–49, V, 526. See also, *Board of Trade Journals*, 1741/2–49, 348, 355.

[53] Shirley to the Marquis de la Galissonière, July 29, 1748, *Shirley Correspondence*, I, 437–440.

[54] De la Galissonière to Mascarene, Jan. 15, 1749, Canada, Public Archives, *Report*, 1894, 133.

[55] Mascarene to de la Galissonière, Apr. 25, 1749, Canada, Public Archives, *Report*, 1894, 137–138.

French claim; [56] Governor Cornwallis, who succeeded Mascarene, protested his action to de la Galissonière's successor, the Marquis de la Jonquière, who became governor of Canada in the fall of 1749, on the ground, as usual, that this was English territory.[57]

Cornwallis also had to face the question of religious jurisdiction, for the bishop of Quebec wrote to him proposing to make an official ecclesiastical visit to Nova Scotia, as his predecessors had done. He recognized that the Acadians in Nova Scotia were British subjects, and he promised not to do anything contrary to their British allegiance.[58] Cornwallis refused to allow him to enter Nova Scotia, since he could not recognize the bishop's jurisdiction in British territory where the King of England was the ultimate authority in all religious affairs. He would, however, permit the continued religious functioning of French priests, so long as they acquired the necessary permission from him.[59]

On the matter of jurisdiction, Governor Shirley had earlier entered the correspondence with the by now standardized English argument that the Abenaki Indians on the St. John River were settled "within the heart of Nova Scotia" and, consequently, in British territory. Both the Abenakis and the Frenchmen living in that area, he said, were British subjects. If they had not taken the oath of allegiance to the British King they were traitors; "so far as it depends on me," he wrote, "they shall not be admitted, Sir, to terms of Peace, till they have made a proper submission for their treachery. . . ." He answered de la Galissonière's threat of making trouble on the Massachusetts frontiers by a threat of reprisal. Whatever happened in the region of the St. John River, he said, since it was an integral part of Nova Scotia, was of no concern to the French governor, whether it pertained to the Indians or to missionaries or to anything else; he took particular exception to the claim of the bishop of Quebec to religious jurisdiction over Nova Scotia. He expressed surprise at de la Galissonière's claim to the St. John's River region as French territory under the Treaty of Utrecht (renewed by that of Aix-la-Chapelle); incidentally, he also expressed the opinion that "we look upon Fort St. Frederick at Crown Point as an Encroachment upon His [Britannic] Majesty's territories," unless specifically granted to France by the Treaty of Aix-la-Chapelle (which, of course, it was not).[60]

[56] Mascarene to the Duke of Bedford, June 2, 1749, N.Y.C.D., X, 190.

[57] Cornwallis to de la Jonquière, Nov. 1, 1749, Canada, Public Archives, Report, 1894, 148.

[58] Bishop Pontbriand to Cornwallis, Oct. 28, 1749, Canada, Public Archives, Report, 1894, 148.

[59] Cornwallis to the bishop of Quebec, Nov. 1, 1749, Canada, Public Archives, Report, 1894, 148.

[60] Shirley to the Marquis de la Galissonière, May 9, 1749. Shirley Correspondence, I, 481–485.

Thus was the "cold war" between the English and the French colonies in North America reopened. Thus, too, did the colonial governors hammer out the issues in the local conflicts. Both Shirley and de la Galissonière were called to Europe at the end of 1749 to serve on the Anglo-French joint commission for the defining of the boundary between English and French colonies in America which began its work in 1750. The local international debates were carried on by their successors, without, however, adding anything to the argument on either side. Meanwhile, the claims and counterclaims of the governors had found their way into the negotiations of the commissioners and the diplomats in Europe.[61]

3. The Great Lakes Frontier

The Anglo-French Treaty of Utrecht had not defined a boundary between the French and the English colonies in the Great Lakes area. It did include the vague provision (Article 15) that the French inhabitants of Canada were not to molest the Five Nations of Indians "subjects of Great Britain" [62] or the other Indians "friends of that Crown," and that the subjects of Great Britain would conduct themselves, similarly, in a peaceful manner toward "the American subjects or friends of France." As for the actual boundaries between the English and the French possessions in North America, it was agreed (Article 10) that a joint Anglo-French Commission of experts should be appointed to determine them.[63]

Before the proposed joint commission eventually met in Paris in 1719, the French, particularly, began a series of actions to establish their "effective occupation" of the territories they were to claim, as well as to block English expansion. As early as 1715 they were reported to be building a fort in the Onondaga country. When, in 1720, the Governor of Canada, the Marquis de Vaudreuil, sent Chabert de Joncaire to Niagara to build a "house" there, "to prevent the English introducing themselves into the Upper country and to increase the trade at Fort Frontenac," [64] Governor Burnet, of New York, wrote to the French governor protesting both the erection of the fort and the rumored activities of the French traders and missionaries among the Iroquois Indians seeking to subvert them from their friendship with the English. All these activities, he said, were infractions of the Anglo-French Treaty of Utrecht, "by which the Five Nations have been conceded to the English." That treaty, he reminded

---

[61] See Chapter XVI.

[62] "*Soumis à la Grande Bretagne.*" See page 342n.

[63] For the history of this commission, which met in Paris in 1719, see Chapter XVI, and Savelle, "The Forty-ninth Degree of North Latitude . . . ," *Can. Hist. Rev.*, XXXVIII, No. 3 (Sept. 1957), 183–201.

[64] "Abstract of Messers. de Vaudreuil and Bégon's Report on Niagara," Oct. 26, 1720, *N.Y.C.D.*, IX, 898–899.

Vaudreuil, had provided that all the Indians were to be free to trade with both the French and the English; the fort at Niagara would put it in the power of the French to stop the "Far Indians" from going to Albany to trade. Furthermore, since the fort was built "on territory belonging to our Indians," it was a further infraction of the treaty. Vaudreuil himself, wrote Burnet, in a letter to Colonel Peter Schuyler (acting governor before Burnet's arrival in New York), had cited his own orders, as well as those of the governor of New York, as prohibiting both governors from "undertaking anything" until England and France should make a treaty defining the boundaries between their colonies. Surely, Burnet said, the construction of this fort was a violation of Vaudreuil's own orders! [65]

To which Vaudreuil expostulated that Governor Burnet was "the first English Governor-General who has questioned the right of the French, from time immemorial, to the post of Niagara." That area had been occupied, he said, by the Sieur de la Salle, who had also built vessels on Lake Erie; the French had built a fort there "thirty-four years ago [1686]" and had used it for trade ever since then. Since the territory, thus, was indisputably French, the Treaty of Utrecht and the proposed boundary commission had nothing to do with that particular spot. While the treaty did, indeed, recognize the Iroquois or any other Indians as "the subjects of France or England," the fact was, he said, that the Indians were independent, the "subjects" of no European nation, and were most properly to be treated as allies rather than subjects. As for the fear that the post at Niagara might close the routes of trade to the Indians, Vaudreuil assured Burnet that the Indians would always enjoy the liberty they had always had to come and go through that area. For the rest, Vaudreuil assured his English colleague that the reports he had received of French subversive activities among the Iroquois were unfounded rumors and should not be taken seriously. He had, he said, promised the Indians some missionaries and a blacksmith, since the Indians had requested them, and he closed his letter in a gentle, diplomatic reminder to the English governor of the dangers that might threaten New York should the governor feel so brash as to resort to violence against the French in the Indian country.[66]

In July, 1726, Governor Burnet wrote M. de Longueuil, commander in chief in Canada,[67] complaining of the rebuilding of Fort Niagara "with the design of shutting in the Five Nations, and preventing the free passage of the other Indians at that point to trade with us as they have been in the habit of doing." His protest repeated the argument that such an occupation of Iroquois territory was a violation of the Treaty of Utrecht, in which, he said, it is provided that "the 5 Nations shall be left to the

---

[65] Burnet to Vaudreuil, July 11, 1721, N.Y.C.D., IX, 899–900.
[66] Vaudreuil to Burnet, July 11, 1721, N.Y.C.D., IX, 900–903.
[67] Governor Vaudreuil had died on Oct. 10, 1725.

English, and that the French shall not molest them in any manner, and that all the Indians in America shall enjoy full liberty of resorting to each of the two Nations to make their trade without any hindrance." Since, he said, "the 5 Nations have been ceded to us by the French at that last peace," they could make no claims to the Indian lands. Burnet then requested Longueuil, in the name of the treaty and in the spirit of the existing Anglo-French *entente*, to stop the building of the fort. If it were not stopped he would have to refer the matter to his home government for a direct protest to the King of France.[68]

Longueuil replied to Burnet that there was no intention, in the rebuilding of Fort Niagara, to "shut in" the Indians in any way. Far from being a hindrance, the fort would actually facilitate the movement of the Indians going in any direction. As for the Treaty of Utrecht, he felt sure that there was no contravention of the treaty in rebuilding Fort Niagara, in conformity with the orders of his court, on land that France had always possessed. The Five Nations, Longueuil said, were "neither your subjects or ours," and they did not feel the "uneasiness" the English felt about the building of the fort, since they had given the French their "unanimous consent" for its building.[69]

Burnet reported to the Duke of Newcastle, secretary of state, the activity of the French at Niagara and his exchange with Longueuil. He reported that only the Onondagas, of the now Six Nations (since the Tuscaroras from South Carolina had joined the former five), had consented to the building of the fort, and that all the others, especially the Senecas, who actually owned the land on which the fort stood, had bitterly protested the French action. All the tribes, he said, now begged the King of England to demand of the French King that the fort be torn down. Burnet reported that he planned to build a fort as Oswego, at the mouth of the Onondaga River, to counterbalance the French fort at Niagara. He called Newcastle's attention to the nature of the French action as a violation of the Treaty of Utrecht and to Longueuil's explicit denial that the Iroquois were subjects of the King of England; and he sent the secretary of state a reconfirmation, by the sachems of the Onondaga, Seneca, and Cayuga tribes, of the Five Nations' "deed" of their land to England made in 1701, a reconfirmation that specifically defined the land on which Fort Niagara was built and that on which Fort Oswego was to be erected.[70]

Burnet concluded his letter with the following appeal:

This is a matter of such consequence to His Majty's Dominions in North America that I humbly rely on Your Grace's obtaining such a redress, as the

[68] Governor Burnet to M. de Longueuil, July 5, 1726, *N.Y.C.D.*, V, 802.

[69] M. de Longueuil to Governor Burnet, Aug. 16, 1726, *N.Y.C.D.*, V, 802–803.

[70] Governor Burnet to the Duke of Newcastle, Dec. 4, 1726, *N.Y.C.D.*, V, 803–804; the deed is in *ibid.*, V, 800–801; see also, *ibid.*, IV, 908–911.

Treaty entitles this Province and the Six Nations to, from the French, which can be [no] less, than a demolition of this fort at Niagara.[71]

As soon as the new French governor of Canada, the Marquis de Beauharnais, received word of the building of Fort Oswego, he sent a peremptory summons to Captain Evert Bancker, English commandant at the fort, to demolish and abandon it within fifteen days. At the same time, he sent M. de la Chassaigne, Governor of Three Rivers, as an emissary to Governor Burnet with a letter protesting the building of the fort.[72]

In his message to Burnet, Governor Beauharnais protested the permission the New York governor had given to the English merchants, chiefly from Albany, to open a trading post on the shore of Lake Ontario, at Oswego. Since this land belonged to France, he said, trade with the Indians in that place was the exclusive privilege of the French traders; the presence of English merchants there was an intrusion. As for the fort the English had built, it constituted a trespass upon the lands of Canada, "of which those of Lake Ontario and the adjacent lands make a part," and which the French had effectively occupied for so long a time. He then protested the occupation of the land along the lakes as a violation of that part of the Anglo-French Treaty of Utrecht that provided that neither nation would encroach upon the other before the joint commission envisaged by the treaty should decide what the boundaries should be.[73]

In his reply to the French governor, Burnet repeated the already established English position. The English, he said, had traded at Oswego for more than five years, in full conformity with the fifteenth article of the Treaty of Utrecht, which provided for full liberty of the subjects of both crowns to go and come in the territories of the Indians for the purposes of trade. This, he said, covered "all the Lakes and all the Continent"; and this liberty was shared by the Indians, who were entirely free to go into the territories of both the French and the English colonies for the purposes of trade. Even the definition of boundaries between those colonies would not change the nature of this freedom of trade provided by the treaty.

As for the fort at Oswego, Burnet bluntly told the French governor that the idea was first suggested to him by the French fort at Niagara, "upon the lands of the Five Nations," as confessed by Longueuil. In fact, he said, the lands on both sides of Lake Ontario belonged to the Iroquois, and the Indians had never ceded them to the French. He complained of Beauharnais' interpretation of the Treaty of Utrecht and insisted that,

[71] N.Y.C.D., V, 804. For a discussion of Anglo-French court-to-court correspondence relative to this matter, see Chapter XVI.

[72] Summons of the governor of Canada to demolish Fort Oswego, July 15, 1727, N.Y.C.D., V, 828; Burnet to Newcastle, Aug. 24, 1727, ibid., V, 824–825.

[73] The Marquis de Beauharnais to Governor Burnet, July 20, 1727, N.Y.C.D., V, 827–828. His argument was somewhat inconsistent, since he protested, first, that the land in question was manifestly French and then admitted, by implication, that it might possibly be awarded to the English by the proposed joint commission.

whereas the French fort at Niagara was an infraction of that treaty, since it stood on the lands of the Iroquois and, therefore, of England, the fort at Oswego was not such an infraction, since it stood on English (Iroquois) soil, and it would be maintained.[74]

Thus, in the correspondence between the colonial governors, the conflicting French and English arguments developed. Basically, the French rested their claim to the land south of the lakes on the ground of prior discovery and effective occupation. The English case was grounded upon the contention that those lands had always belonged to the Iroquois and that when the Iroquois submitted themselves to the King of England and ceded their lands to him, the ownership of those lands became English. It was these rival positions, formulated by the colonial governments, which became the bases of the diplomatic exchanges between the French and English courts in Europe.[75]

In 1730 the governor of Canada, then the Marquis de Beauharnais, having heard that the English merchants from Albany were going to Lake Champlain to trade with the Indians, sent a detachment of soldiers to that area to drive them out. Having found no English, the soldiers returned to Canada. But the governor, convinced that the reports were true, proposed to build a fort at Crown Point, at the upper end of the lake, to stop them:

The English [he wrote], bent on augmenting their possessions in America, profit by the peace to advance into the country of Canada, and use every means to gain over the Indians. 'Tis known that with a crew to establish himself on Lake Champlain, the King of England granted it to the children of M. Peter Schul [Schuyler], a famous citizen of Orange [Albany], and there is every reason to fear that, if not provided against, they will seize on it, and in such case it will be necessary to oblige them to retire.[76]

The governor's proposal to build a fort at Crown Point was approved by the French King; the governor was instructed, also, to send as many farmers as possible to that area in order to build up a French settlement around the fort.[77] The fort was accordingly built in the summer of 1731.

When the New York provincial government heard of the French action at Crown Point, Rip Van Dam, president of the council, in the absence of a governor, informed the Board of Trade, whereupon this French "encroachment" was made the subject of a diplomatic protest to France by

[74] Burnet to Beauharnais, Aug. 8, 1727, N.Y.C.D., V, 829–832.
[75] See Chapter XVI.
[76] "Abstract of M. de Beauharnais' despatches relative to Crown Point, with the King's Approval," Feb. 5, 1731, N.Y.C.D., IX, 1,021–1,022, et seq.
[77] "Louis XV to Messrs. de Beauharnais and Hocquarl," May 8, 1731, N.Y.C.D., X, 1,024–1,026.

the Earl of Waldegrave, British ambassador to Paris, on the ground that Crown Point lay within the province of New York, in the country of the Iroquois, subjects of England. This action, said the ambassador, was in "absolute opposition" to Article 15 of the Treaty of Utrecht, and he demanded that the fort be razed—which, of course, was not done.[78] When Governor William Cosby arrived in New York after the fort at Crown Point was built, he recognized it as a *fait accompli*. But in 1733 he recommended to the ministry that, in view of the rapid expansion of the colony northward, a line of forts be built across northern New York facing the French, beginning with a post on the Hudson River at the location nearest Crown Point and extending to Oswego.[79] This policy was adopted only in principle by the British crown; the actual building of forts along the frontier was left to the colonies, with expenses to be paid by appropriations by the colonial legislatures.

Crown Point, however, remained an irritant to the English governors of New York; after the Peace of Aix-la-Chapelle it became a subject for discussion in the direct correspondence between the English governors and the governors of Canada.

In the years following the Peace of Aix-la-Chapelle, the governors of New York and Canada again engaged in a local diplomatic duel over the frontier between their two provinces. By this time the arguments on the two sides were set, and little that was new was added, except that now the English began to challenge the French right to the Ohio Valley as well as that to the lands south of the Great Lakes.

The correspondence began in 1748 over the exchange of prisoners. Governor Clinton, of New York, wrote to the Marquis de la Galissonière, the governor of Canada, asking that certain Mohawk [80] Indians, "subjects of Great Britain," then prisoners of the French, be returned, since peace had been signed. De la Galissonière replied by refusing to return the Mohawks, and demanded, in turn, the return of French prisoners in the hands of the Mohawks. He denied that the Mohawks were subjects of Great Britain and insisted that the Mohawks send delegates to Quebec to negotiate an exchange of Indian prisoners directly with him.[81] He did, however, send a deputy, a M. Designers, to New York to arrange an exchange of English and French prisoners. Designers reiterated de la Galissonière's refusal to treat with Clinton with regard to the Mohawks, since all the Indians were independent. He did suggest that Colonel William Johnson, a New

[78] "Declaration of the British Ambassador respecting a French Fort at Crown Point," June 13, 1752, N.Y.C.D., IX, 1,034. See Chapter XVI.
[79] Governor Cosby to the Duke of Newcastle, Dec. 15, 1733, N.Y.C.D., V, 972.
[80] The Mohawks were one of the Five Nations of the Iroquois.
[81] De la Galissonière to Governor Clinton, Aug. 25, 1748, N.Y.C.D., X, 190; De la Galissonière to Comte de Maurepas, Oct. 26, 1748, ibid., X, 185–186.

York gentleman who was a close friend of the Mohawks, procure the release of Frenchmen who were prisoners of the Mohawks.[82] There followed a long and difficult exchange of correspondence and of conferences, in the course of which little real progress was made, an impasse that was eventually resolved only by orders sent directly from the English and French courts to the governors requiring them to release all prisoners in America, Indian and white alike.[83] In the meantime, Clinton had challenged de la Galissonière's flat refusal to recognize the Iroquois as "subjects" of Great Britain. This, Clinton believed (wrongly), was an entirely new turn in French policy that had never before been taken by any French governor, all of whom, he said, had accepted Article 15 of the Anglo-French Treaty of Utrecht as declaring that they were such subjects.[84]

De la Galissonière's repudiation of Article 15 of the Anglo-French Treaty of Utrecht was important for the negotiations between England and France that were to follow immediately, since de la Galissonière himself became a member of the Anglo-French joint commission to define the boundaries between the English and the French colonies in America that began its work in 1750.[85]

4. The Ohio Valley

The question of the ownership of the Ohio Valley became a critical and pressing subject for discussion and contention in the correspondence of French governors with English governors only after the Peace of Aix-la-Chapelle. Since the area was of vital concern to New York, Pennsylvania, and Virginia, the governors of all these provinces were involved in the dispute at one time or another, and each of these colonies had a part in the correspondence. The bulk of the interchange, however, took place between Canada and New York, at least until Governor Dinwiddie of Virginia sent George Washington on his mission to assert Virginia's claim to the valley in 1753.

The origins of this particular chapter in international diplomacy relative to the imperial conflict went back, of course, to the years just following the Peace of Utrecht. The French had established a string of posts and forts along the Great Lakes and in the Wabash and Mississippi Valleys, stretching from Fort Frontenac to Biloxi, Mobile, and New Orleans, and this line of establishments had been strengthened at numerous points during the War of the Spanish Succession and in the years immediately following. There was a limited amount of intercommunication, northward

---

[82] M. Desligners to Governor Clinton, Oct. 15, 1748, N.Y.C.D., X, 190–191.
[83] Duke of Bedford to Governor Clinton, Dec. 7, 1749, N.Y.C.D., X, 197; Louis XV to the Marquis de la Jonquière, Feb. 28, 1750, ibid., X, 199.
[84] Clinton to de la Galissonière, Oct. 10, 1748, N.Y.C.D., X, 191.
[85] See Chapter XIX.

and southward, between Canada and Louisiana, the importance of which the French habitually exaggerated in their correspondence with the English governors. The result of the establishment of the French "iron curtain" was that the French were fairly firmly established all along the line, and they were completely satisfied that all the rivers and lakes involved, together with their entire drainage basins, belonged to France.

The English, on the other hand, had hardly penetrated the lands lying along the western watershed of the Alleghenies before the Peace of Utrecht. As early as 1715, however, the French governors had, in fact, reported the presence of English traders in the area of the Wabash River, and their presence in that area was reported again and again in the 1720s and 1730s.[86] The French governors saw this penetration in the framework of a larger perspective, and interpreted the English expansion in the Ohio Valley, as everywhere else, as part of a larger imperialistic surge that would drive the French out and place the English in complete domination of the continent. As Governor Beauharnais wrote in 1730, commenting upon the presence of the English in the Wabash area,

It is with sorrow that I see the maneuvres of the English throughout the continent and the intention they have to make themselves the dominant power there. The Mississippi region has already felt the effects of their insinuations on the minds of the savages in the unhappy blow they struck against the French of that region by the Natchez and the Yazoos; they await only, I think, an occasion to do the same sort of thing in this area [i.e., the Wabash].[87]

Bienville, Governor of Louisiana, reported in 1735 that the English were actually established on the upper Ohio and had won the allegiance of the Miamies and the Quatinons.[88] He also warned against the Spaniards of the Southwest: although they were less enterprising, he said, they could be expected, on the occasion of the first war, to seize the Illinois country; they had already attempted, as early as 1723, to establish themselves on the Missouri River; they would still be there if the Kansas Indians had not driven them away.[89]

The Ohio Valley saw little or no Anglo-French activity during King George's War (the War of the Austrian Succession). But the organization of and grant to the Ohio Company of Virginia, and the vigorous increase in the activities in the valley of English traders from the Eastern

[86] Ramezay and Bégon to M. de Pontchartrain, Sept. 13, 1715, N.Y.C.D., IX, 931; "Extract from a despatch from Vaudreuil and Bégon," Jan. 6, 1717, A.N. Cols., C11A/37: fol. 06; Beauharnais to "Monseigneur" (Maurepas?), Sept. 28, 1726, Ibid., C11A/48: fols. 142–142 vo.; Beauharnais and Hocquart, Mémoire sur les sauvages du Canada, Dec. 20, 1735, ibid., C11A/63: fols. 218–222.

[87] Beauharnais to "Monseigneur" (Maurepas?), Oct. 10, 1730, A.N. Cols., C11A/52: fols. 196–200 vo.

[88] Mémoire sur res sauvages du Canada, Dec. 20, 1735, A.N. Cols., C11A/63: fols. 218–222.

[89] Mémoire sur les sauvages du Canara, Dec. 20, 1735, A.N. Cols., C11A/63: fols. 218–222.

seaboard, about the end of the war, excited the fears of Governor de la Galissonière of Canada and caused him to take vigorous measures to block the English advance.

It was the settlements in the Illinois country that constituted the economic and strategic heart of the French settlements in the Ohio drainage basin, and de la Galissonière was fully conscious of their importance. Their economic value, he reported in 1748, had been greatly exaggerated, and they would be an economic liability upon the French crown for a long time to come. But they should be maintained, because they constituted the best existing barrier in that area against the penetration of the French trading area by the English, or even their expansion toward Mexico. Further, he said,

We must not flatter ourselves that our Continental colonies; that is to say, this and Louisiana, can ever compete in wealth with the adjoining English colonies, nor even carry on any very lucrative trade; for, except pelting, the amount of which is limited, and whose profits are and will be always diminishing, we shall scarcely ever have it in our power to furnish any but similar commodities to those of Europe; we shall not be able to supply them at the same price, though mostly of inferior quality, and though ours is an immense country, we have no outlet except by two rivers equally out of the way, whose navigation is inconvenient and perilous.[90]

The Illinois country could be easily seized by the British if not more adequately defended. In that case, the French would lose the Mississippi, and the Spanish colonies, even Mexico, would be gravely threatened.

It was upon the basis of such convictions that de la Galissonière sent Pierre Joseph Céloron de Blainville to the Ohio Valley in 1749 to proclaim French ownership, to impress the Indians, and to warn the English to stay out.[91] And the policy that de la Galissonière initiated, his successors continued. He himself, when he returned to France in 1749, wrote a long and penetrating memoir on the American colonies of France *vis-à-vis* the expanding English colonies, in the course of which he pointed out the absolute necessity to France, for the preservation of its colonies in North America, of the maintenance of the line of communications between Canada and Mississippi through the Ohio Valley. France had owned and occupied the valley, he said, since the discovery by La Salle. The English had not "come to that quarter to trade, except clandestinely, until the last war"; since the peace of Aix-la-Chapelle they have been summoned to retire from the valley; if they do not do so, the governor of Canada should constrain them to do so by force. Their presence there would be more dangerous to French interests than it was at Oswego: they would

[90] De la Galissonière to the Comte de Maurepas, Sept. 1, 1748, N.Y.C.D., X, 134-136.
[91] "Minute of the taking possession of the Ohio River and its tributaries by the French," N.Y.C.D., X, 189.

be in a better position to seduce the Indian nations; they would be free to interrupt communication between Canada and Louisiana; were the English ever to attack Mexico, it would be by way of the Ohio River; by the same route they might easily destroy the French posts in the Mississippi Valley; they could certainly destroy the French post among the Miamies and, thereby, seriously threaten Detroit. For all these reasons, de la Galissonière urged the construction of a line of forts upon the upper waters of the Ohio.[92]

The Marquis de la Jonquière, who succeeded de la Galissonière as governor of Canada, prepared, on the basis of de la Galissonière's line of reasoning, a plan to drive the English out of the Ohio Valley and to chastise the Indians who had befriended them. The plan was not executed before de la Jonquière was recalled, but two English traders among the Miamies were arrested and sent to France as a warning to others.[93]

The Marquis Duquesne, who succeeded de la Jonquière in 1752, was therefore given a set of instructions that clearly echoed the language and the thoughts in de la Galissonière's memoir. The English, he was told, had begun actively to penetrate the Ohio Valley since the Peace of Aix-la-Chapelle; "now they pretend to exclude us from it." They do not pretend, said the instructions, that the Ohio and its tributaries belong to them. They merely maintain that the Iroquois are masters of these lands, and, since the Iroquois are under the sovereignty of the English King, the lands belong to England. Yet the lands of the Ohio Valley undisputably belong to France, since the Sieur de la Salle discovered them, since the French have effectively occupied it by building posts there, and since this has always been the route of communication between Canada and Louisiana. The Iroquois do not have any authority over the Indians of the valley or their lands; "besides, the sovereignty of the English over them is a chimera." [94]

The English advance must be stopped. Since complaints to the King of Great Britain against English governors would be futile, it was necessary to act on the spot. The English must be driven out, not, as de la Jonquière had proposed, by military force, but by prevailing upon the Indians to do it. Meanwhile, as a necessary means to this end, every effort must be made to satisfy the Indians' need for trade and to preserve their amity and alliance otherwise.[95]

Acting under these instructions and de la Galissonière's recommendations, Duquesne proceeded to erect forts on the shore of Lake Erie, at Presqu'isle (Erie, Pa.), on the Rivíere aux Boeufs (Fort le Boeuf), and at the confluence of the Allegheny and Monongahela Rivers (Fort Du-

[92] Memoir on the French colonies in North America (1750), N.Y.C.D., X, 220–232.
[93] Minute of Instructions given to M. Duquesne, N.Y.C.D., X, 242–245.
[94] N.Y.C.D., X, 242–243.
[95] N.Y.C.D., X, 243–244.

quesne), in the years between 1752 and 1754. It was an "iron curtain" that failed.

Pennsylvania played a relatively small part in the intercolonial negotiations relative to the Ohio Valley. The Pennsylvanians had paid little attention to the growth of French settlements in the Illinois country in the decades following the Peace of Utrecht, although the French themselves reported a few English traders with the Indians in that area soon after that peace. The proprietors of Pennsylvania had sought to win the friendship and trade of the Indians west of the mountains, at least as early as 1734, however, when they deplored the apparent tendency of the Shawnees to desert their friendship with the English and attach themselves to the French.[96]

After the Peace of Aix-la-Chapelle, when Governor de la Galissonière of Canada sent Céloron de Blainville into the Ohio Valley to publicize France's claim to that region, Céloron wrote to Governor Hamilton of Pennsylvania warning him to keep English traders out of the valley:

I was surprized [Céloron wrote] to find traders from your government [Pennsylvania] in this country, to which England has never had any pretension. I treated them as politely as possible, although it was my right to regard them as interlopers and vagabonds, since their activities were contrary to the Preliminaries of peace signed more than fifteen months ago.[97]

Hamilton seems to have ignored Céloron's warning. In any case, the English initiative in the intercolonial correspondence relative to the Ohio Valley was quickly seized by Virginia.

The French activities in the Ohio Valley after the Peace of Aix-la-Chapelle, undertaken to block the expansion of the English, provoked a protest by Governor Robert Dinwiddie in the name of Virginia. That colony claimed the Ohio Valley under the terms of its charter of 1609. The charter had been cancelled in 1624, but Virginia still claimed the area, and Virginian interest in it took practical form with the organization of the Ohio Company of Virginia in 1748. It was to block this company, in fact, that the French governors, from de la Galissonière onward, took active steps to exclude English traders and settlers, to keep the Indians of the valley antagonistic toward the English, and to build a string of forts across the line of the English advance.

Governor Robert Dinwiddie, of Virginia, a confirmed British imperialist, wishing to serve his Virginia constituents in the Ohio Company, formulated a plan to build a series of forts in the Ohio Valley to block the French, just as the French were attempting to block the English. He sub-

[96] John Penn to a messenger from the Six Nations, Oct. 16, 1734, *Colonial Records of Pennsylvania*, III, 580.
[97] Céloron to the governor of Pennsylvania (n.d.), Margry, ed., *Découvertes*, VI, 686–687.

mitted his scheme to the Board of Trade, and it was approved in a set of instructions sent to him on August 28, 1753. According to these instructions, Dinwiddie was authorized to call out the Virginia militia for checking the French fort-building on the Ohio. But he was first to explain to the French commander in the valley the "undoubted right" of the British King to "such parts of the River Ohio as are within the limits of our province of Virginia or any other province or provinces in America, and to require the peaceable departure of any such Europeans or Indians offering to molest or hinder you [Dinwiddie] from carrying on the forts." But if the French refused to depart, and continued building their forts, Dinwiddie was authorized to resort to force.[98]

It was in these circumstances, and armed with the instructions, that Governor Dinwiddie sent George Washington to the Ohio Valley in 1753 to summon the French to stop their fort-building and get out of the valley. Washington bore a letter from Dinwiddie to the French commander, Legardeur de St. Pierre, in which Dinwiddie explained to the Frenchman that "the Lands upon the River *Ohio*, in the Western Parts of the Colony of *Virginia*, are so notoriously known to be the property of the Crown of Great Britain; that it is a Matter of equal Concern and Surprize to me, to hear that a Body of *French* Forces are erecting Fortresses, and making Settlements upon that River within his Majesty's Dominion." [99] Dinwiddie protested the French occupation as a violation of "the Law of Nations" and the treaties in effect between France and England, and summoned the French to withdraw from English soil and to "forbear prosecuting a Purpose so interruptive of the Harmony and good Understanding, which his [Britannic] Majesty is most desirous to continue and cultivate with the most Christian King." [100]

St. Pierre, of course, could not accede to the English governor's demands. He explained to Washington that the entire Ohio Valley belonged to France by reason of La Salle's discovery and of the effective occupation of the region by the French. The French officers, flushed with wine at the dinner at which they entertained Washington, swore that "it was their absolute Design to take Possession of the *Ohio*, and by G— they would do it. . . ." They bluntly informed the Virginian that the purpose of the fort-building was unequivocally to block the English advance. The commandant, more diplomatic, politely repeated the French claim to the valley and to authority over its Indians. Englishmen had no right to go there, he said, and he would be compelled to arrest any who did so. In any case, as a military officer, he explained, he could only obey his orders and build the fort.[101] In his letter to Dinwiddie, which Washington carried

[98] Quoted in Freeman, *Washington*, I, 275n.
[99] Dinwiddie to the commandant of the French forces on the Ohio, Oct. 31, 1753, in Cleland, *George Washington in the Ohio Valley*, 29.
[100] Cleland, *George Washington in the Ohio Valley*, 30.
[101] Washington's Journal, in Cleland, *George Washington in the Ohio Valley*, 17–22.

back to Williamsburg with him, St. Pierre lamented the fact that the governor had not addressed himself to the governor of Canada in the first place; he promised to send Dinwiddie's letter to Governor Duquesne. As for the summons to depart, he politely refused either to retire or to enter into a discussion of the merits of the case.[102]

Both governors sent expeditions into the valley in 1754 to seize and fortify the forks of the Ohio, but the French got there first, and Washington, commanding the Virginia expedition, was beaten by the French at Great Meadows and left the possession of the Ohio Valley in the hands of the French. Needless to say, the governors of Canada and of Virginia reported all these incidents to their European governments, and they fell into the stream of discussions between France and England relative to America then going on in London and Paris.[103]

Again, it was the reports of the colonial governors, and their recommendations, which gave the factual bases and the directions of policy to the diplomatic negotiations of the mother countries in Europe.

5. The Mississippi Frontier and Carolina's Relations With the Spanish Colonies

While the northern English and French colonies were conducting their own brand of international relations relative to the boundaries between them, to the Indians, to trade, and to prisoners of war, a parallel set of problems had presented themselves to the French and English governors of the South, with "Mississippi" or Louisiana on the one side and the Carolinas and, presently, Georgia on the other.

The English had established themselves in the Carolinas in the second half of the seventeenth century; the French had planted their settlements on the lower Mississippi and the Alabama River systems in the first decade of the eighteenth. By the time of the Peace of Utrecht (1713), both sides realized that they were in each other's way in the lands lying roughly between the southern end of the Allegheny massif and the Mississippi and between the Tennessee River and the Gulf of Mexico.[104]

The French had staked their claim to this region by the founding of Biloxi in 1699, and of Mobile in 1702. After the Peace of Utrecht the French staking of claims continued with the building of Fort Rosalie (Natchez) on the Mississippi River (1716), Fort Toulouse, on the Alabama River facing South Carolina (1717), and of New Orleans (1718).

[102] St. Pierre to Dinwiddie, Dec. 15, 1753, in McDowell, ed., *Documents Relative to Indian Affairs* [in South Carolina], 472.
[103] See Chapter XIX.
[104] For the history of English expansion and conflict with the French and Spanish in this region, see Crane, *The Southern Frontier, 1670–1732*.

English traders from Charleston had penetrated the southern mountains and the Gulf Coastal Plain before 1700; as the French moved into
"Mississippi" they found the English already trading in that area, and
they were disturbed over the influence the English had among the
Indians.[105] Jean Baptiste le Moyne de Bienville, presently to be named
governor of Louisiana, who was responsible for building, among others,
Fort Toulouse in 1717, had written, in 1716, that it was urgently necessary
to build this fort "in order to prevent the English from reestablishing their
alliance [of the war just ended] with the Indians "of that area." [106]

Reports from the governors of Louisiana, after the organization of that
colony in 1723, indicated that the eastward boundary of the colony "ought
to be" the Apalachicola River, assuming that this river "be taken from
the English of Carolina and from the Spaniards of Florida." Pensacola,
which lay within this boundary, should also be taken from Spain and
incorporated into Louisiana as a base for French trade with the Indians.[107]

Similar warnings of the French governors and other agents against the
expansiveness of both the English and the Spanish were sent in throughout
the 1720s and 1730s. Such a report, for example, called attention to the
"jealousy" of the English over the French occupation of Louisiana, their
efforts to subvert the Indians in the Gulf area from the French to the
English interest, and their efforts to cut communications between Canada
and Louisiana by establishing themselves on the Wabash.[108]

Again, when the War of the Polish Succession broke out in Europe in
1733, Governor Bienville, anticipating the involvement of England in the
war against France, expressed the fear that Louisiana's commerce might
be cut off by English privateers out of Jamaica, and that the Carolinas
might invade Louisiana through the Indian country. The only way to
protect Louisiana from the English from Carolina, he said, was by building up an Indian bulwark against them; this could be achieved by a
plentiful trade with the tribe, conducted in the same way as the English
conducted theirs.[109]

On the English side, such Carolina imperialists as Captain Thomas
Nairne, the provincial Indian agent, John Barnwell, and Governor Robert
Johnson called attention to the French "menace" and proposed ways and
means to meet it.

Nairne claimed, as early as 1708, that the English owned the area in

[105] Bienville to M. Hubert, Sept. 1717, A.N. Cols., C13A/5: fols. 63–63 vo.
[106] Bienville to "Monseigneur," Jan. 2, 1716, A.N. Cols., C13A/4: fols. 759–772.
[107] "Mémoire au sujet de l'Etablissement de la Collonie de la Louisiane envoyé par
ordre de Monseigneur le Duc de Noailles," 1723, A.N. Cols., C13A/7: fols. 228–
233 vo.
[108] Memoir on Louisiana and Illinois by Messrs. Perier and Salmon, Dec. 5, 1730,
A.N. Cols., C13A/13: lols. 28–30.
[109] Bienville to 'Monseigneur," Apr. 30, 1735, A.N. Cols., C13A/20: fols. 150–151.

which Mobile was founded by reason of a prior Indian "submission" to the government of Carolina. The French, he said, must be stopped; only South Carolina, " 'by trading and other Management,' could put a check to French aggrandizement at the expense of the English colonies on the one hand, and of New Mexico on the other." [110] He therefore suggested that the frontier be fortified, especially along the trade routes.

After the Peace of Utrecht the fort-building activities of the French, coupled with their penetration of the Indian country, had aroused the alarm of the South Carolinians to fever heat. It was this threat, at least in part, which caused the council and assembly of South Carolina to repudiate the proprietary government, which had provided no adequate protection for the colony, and to ask the crown to make it a royal province. In the words of the council and assembly,

The powerful settlement the French are now making within the limits of the Lords Proprietors [sea-to-sea] charter, and their building Forts within the territories of this Province . . . has already had this very ill effect that almost all the Nations of Indians to the S.W. of this Settlement have withdrawn their obedience from the British Government and depend wholy on the Crown of France. Whereby under God nothing can save this Settlement from falling into the hands of France upon the first Warr with that Crown, and even Virginia and other H. M. Dominions will thereby be in very great Danger.[111]

There was very little direct correspondence between the French governors of "Mississippi" or Louisiana and the English governors of South Carolina. What there was was directed chiefly to the problem of trade with the Indians and efforts of one side or the other to subvert the friendship, the trade, and the military alliance of the tribes from one side to the other. Thus, for example, in June, 1735, Governor Dinon d'Artaquette, of Mobile, wrote to Lieutenant Governor Broughton, of South Carolina, reporting the presence among the Indians of the Alabama area of Englishmen seeking to turn the natives against the French. He requested the governors of South Carolina and Georgia to forbid such activities among the French Indians, "without which our Governor will be obliged to send some troops to the Alibamons for to suppress and seize the most culpable." Even such communications were rare, however.

On the other hand, both the French governors of Louisiana and the Spanish governors of Pensacola recognized the threat contained in the expansion of English trade and influence among the Indians, and they drew together with the idea of presenting a common front to the common enemy. D'Artaquette reported to his government in 1734 that the Spanish governor of Pensacola had written to him suggesting this idea, warning

[110] Crane, *Southern Frontier*, 93.
[111] The "new pretended" council and assembly of S. Carolina to the Board of Trade, Dec. 24, 1719, *C.S.P., Col., A.& W.I.,* 1719–20, No. 493, pp. 287–289.

"that these advances ought to be suspected by us [the French] as much as they are by them [the Spanish]." [112]

The same fears arose after the Peace of Aix-la-Chapelle, although there was still little direct correspondence among the English, French, and Spanish governors on this subject.[113]

The international interests of the governors of South Carolina, in the period following the Peace of Utrecht, were more actively and intensely concerned with that colony's relations with the Spanish colonies to the southward than they were with affairs pertinent to the interior of the continent.

Correspondence with the Spanish governors began in connection with the "Yamassee War" that ravaged the Carolina frontier in 1715 and 1716. The Yamassees were thought to be receiving aid and encouragement from the Spaniards of St. Augustine, and Governor Robert Daniel, on the motion of the South Carolina assembly, sent Major James Cochran to St. Augustine to request, in the name of the first article of the Anglo-Spanish Treaty of Utrecht, which provided that neither signatory would give aid or encouragement to the enemies of the other, that the governor and his people refrain from assisting the Indians in their war against the English. Cochran was also instructed to request the return of prisoners taken by the Indians and of slaves taken by them and sold to the Spaniards.[114] The Spanish governor replied that he considered the Yamassee Indians Spanish subjects whom he was obliged to protect against the English. As for the prisoners and the slaves, he said he had no orders from his government on the subject; he must submit the question to the Spanish ministry and receive its instructions before he could release the prisoners or the slaves.[115]

War between England and Spain in Europe broke out again in 1718.[116] The causes of this war were chiefly European in nature, but it was extended to America, and both Virginia and South Carolina lived in fear of Spanish attack from Havana. The attack never materialized, but there was some privateering along the coasts of these colonies, which continued after peace was made in Europe. It was in these circumstances that in 1721 Governor Spotswood of Virginia sent a message under a flag of truce to the governor of Havana protesting against the continuance of privateering

[112] D'Artaquette to Maurepas, Sept. 1734, Rowland and Sanders, ed., *Miss. Prov. Archives*, I, 252–253.

[113] See, however, Governor Vaudreuil of Louisiana to Rouillé, Sept. 22, 1749, Pease and Jenison, eds., *Illinois on the Eve of the Seven Years War*, 116.

[114] Committee of the assembly of Carolina to Messrs. Boone and Beresford (agents for the assembly in London) Aug. 6, 1716, C.S.P., *Col.*, A.& W.I., 1716–17, No. 413 (I), p. 220; certificate of Robert Darnel, Aug. 13, 1716, *ibid.*, 1716–17, No. 413 (IV), p. 225.

[115] C.S.P., *Col.*, A.& W.I., 1716–17, No. 413 (IV), p. 225. See also, Governor Johnson to the Board of Trade, June 18, 1718, C.S.P., *Col.*, A.& W.I., 1717–18, No. 556, p. 266.

[116] See Chapter XIV.

and the seizure of British ships by the Spanish privateers. The governor of South Carolina, Spotswood reported, had notified the governor of Havana of the cessation of hostilities in 1720, but the Spanish governor had continued to issue commissions to privateers. One of these had seized three British ships, one from Philadelphia and two from London. When Spotswood's protest was presented to the Spaniard, he agreed to return two of the ships. One, however, he kept in custody because her cargo included "red wood" (probably mahogany) which could only have come from Spanish colonies (Spotswood had claimed that the wood was from Africa).[117]

On February 11, 1722, Don Antonio de Benavides, governor of St. Augustine, sent Don Francisco Menendes Marques to Charleston to negotiate with Governor Nicholson an agreement relative to Indian hostilities, the exchange of prisoners and the purchase of provisions, to protest the building of a fort "near the Islands of St. Catherine's" (Fort King George, near the mouth of the Altamaha River), and to remind the governor that Spanish colonial ports were closed to British traders.[118]

In his meeting with Menendes Marques, Nicholson evaded a commitment, saying he would gladly negotiate an agreement but that, unfortunately, he had no orders to do so; he would ask his home government for instructions. In the meantime, he replied to the questions raised by the Spanish envoy in the following ways:

With regard to trade, Nicholson felt forced to deny the governor of St. Augustine's request that Menendes Marques be permitted to buy provisions in the British colony. The Spanish governor, he said, had warned that the Spanish colonies were closed to British traders; it would be highly inconsistent for him to permit to the Spaniards a privilege of trading that they denied to the British, "especially as it is contrary to the treatys of Commerce between the two Crowns"; Nicholson would be glad "if their Majesties should grant a reciprocall and free trade between the subjects of both governments." [119]

Nicholson complained of the Spanish governor's failure to make restitution of British ships seized by Spanish privateers since the cessation of hostilities. He also asked the Spanish governor to indicate which Indian nations he considered Spanish subjects and which British, and to specify where, when, and by whom the Indian subjects of either crown had been "stirred up" against the other in time of peace. He expressed a willingness

[117] Lieutenant Governor Spotswood to the Board of Trade, May 31, 1721, C.S.P., Col., A.& W.I., 1720–21, No. 513, pp. 326–327.

[118] Benavides to Nicholson, Feb. 11, 1722, C.S.P., Col., A.& W.I., 1722–23, No. 427 (XXIV), p. 212; Instructions to Francisco Menendes Marques, ibid., 1722–23, No. 427 (XXIII), p. 212; Nicholson to Menendes Marques, Mar. 9, 1722, Ibid., 1722–23, No. 427 (XXI), pp. 209–212.

[119] Nicholson to Menendes Marques, Mar. 9, 1722, C.S.P., Col., A& W.I., 1722–23, No. 427 (XXI), p. 210. The "treatys" referred to were the Anglo-Spanish Treaty of Madrid of 1670 and the treaties of Utrecht of 1713. See Chapters VI and X.

to return any Spanish slaves then in Carolina as soon as the governor of St. Augustine should be willing to return British-owned slaves in Spanish hands. As for the fort then being constructed by the British, Nicholson expressed surprise that the Spanish governor should protest; he could only reply, he said, that it will be maintained "as long as H. M. shall think it for his service." [120]

This exchange seems to have had no practical result except that it was reported to the ministries of the two mother countries and became part of the substance of the diplomatic exchanges between them in Europe.[121] Later in the same year, however, Governor Benavides sent a second mission to Governor Nicholson, this time to request the restitution of Spanish ships taken by the British since the end of hostilities, and he asked Nicholson to communicate his request to the governors of the Bahamas and Virginia. He, for his part, promised that English ships taken by the Spaniards in the same period would be restored; at the same time, he asked Nicholson to send to him the "Spanish" Indians, some of whom were from Caracas and Campeche, who had been enslaved in Carolina.[122] Nicholson's reply was evasive; the governor promised only to "inquire" about any Indian captives; but this would take time, and he asked the Spanish governor to make similar inquiries relative to "English" Indians.[123]

In 1725 the governor of St. Augustine sent another mission to South Carolina. This mission had several objectives, the chief of which was to arrange an on-the-spot agreement as to the boundaries between Florida and South Carolina. The Spanish governor sent council president Arthur Middleton, as acting governor, a copy of a letter from the Duke of Newcastle to the Spanish ambassador in London which promised that His Britannic Majesty would instruct his governor of South Carolina to make such an agreement, "and that in case the fort erected on the Altamahan River [Fort King George] should be found within the Spanish territoryes the same should be demolished, or an equivalent given for the same." [124] But Middleton strongly protested to Newcastle that neither the Altamaha River nor Fort King George was in Spanish territory. He also pointed out to Newcastle the danger to South Carolina that would result from demolishing the fort. He reported, too, that in the powers sent to the Spanish governor, he was directed to settle the boundary beween Florida and South Carolina pursuant to the Anglo-Spanish Treaty of Madrid of 1670, at

---

[120] Nicholson to Menendes Marques, Mar. 9, 1723, C.S.P., Col., A.& W.I., 1722–23, No. 427 (XXI), pp. 209–212.

[121] Seete Paske, The Governorship of Spanish Florida, 1700–63, 126.

[122] Benavides to Nicholson, July 27, 1722, C.S.P., Col., A.& W.I., 1722–23, No. 373 (I), p. 180; Instructions to Captain Sebastian Lopez de Toledo, Aug. 3, 1722, ibid., 1722–23, No. 373 (VI), p. 181.

[123] Nicholson to Benavides, Aug. 7, 1722, C.S.P., Col., A.& W.I., 1722–23, No. 373 (IX), p. 182.

[124] Middleton to Newcastle, Sept. 10, 1725, C.S.P., Col., A.& W.I., 1724–25, No. 722, pp. 422–423.

which time the English actually possessed no land south of Charleston; if the English accepted such instruction as the basis for negotiation, they could not possibly claim any land south of the neighborhood of Charleston itself.[125] To the new governor of South Carolina, Francis Nicholson, Middleton also reported that the Spaniards had requested to buy a sloop and engage the services of a surgeon, both of which he had refused, "considering they might make an ill use of the same." He was the more impelled to this decision, he said, because the Spanish governor was instructed to "admit of noe equivalent, but upon refusal to have the fort demolished, that then he use proper methods to doe his [Catholic] Majestie justice." [126]

Nothing came, therefore, of this proposed boundary negotiation between the two governors. Then, as tension mounted between Spain and England, both in America and in Europe, the governor-to-governor correspondence became more strained. In March of 1728 President Middleton of the South Carolina council wrote to Don Domingo Martinez de la Vega, governor of Havana, protesting against the "piracies" being committed by Spanish ships along the Carolina coasts, under commissions from the governor, in time of peace. He had sent out a ship that had recaptured from the "pirates" an English prize; he was returning to Havana the Spanish crew, and he demanded that the "pirate" be punished. He informed the Spanish governor that he was assured that a treaty had been signed between their respective sovereigns.[127]

But the Spanish governor was in no mood to cooperate with the British acting governor. The ships bearing commissions from him, he said, were legitimate privateers, and the British must expect the Spanish to make reprisals, especially after the warlike behavior of Admiral Hosier, sent to cruise in the West Indies after the Austro-Spanish Alliance of 1725.[128] A little later de la Vega wrote Middleton to protest the fact that the Spanish fort at Apalachee (on the Apalachicola River) was being besieged by Englishmen and "English" Indians, and demanded that the British governor order the besiegers to retire.[129]

With the signing of the Treaty of Seville in 1729, there ensued a period of relative calm along the Carolina-Florida coast. There was some

[125] Middleton to Newcastle, Sept. 10, 1725, C.S.P., Col., A.& W.I., 1724–25, No. 722, pp. 422–423.
[126] Middleton to Nicholson, Sept. 10, 1725, C.S.P., Col., A.& W.I., 1724–25, No. 723, p. 423.
[127] Middleton to the governor of Havana, Mar. 23, 1728, C.S.P., Col., A.& W.I., 1728–29, No. 281 (VII), pp. 135–136. Middleton was wrong about the treaty. The Congress of Soissons was engaged in negotiations of American and European issues, and did draw up a set of preliminary agreements. Spain did not accede, however, until the Treaty of Seville was made in 1729. See Chapter XIV.
[128] See Chapter XIV.
[129] De la Vega to Middleton, May 25, 1728, C.S.P., Col., A.& W.I., 1728–29, No. 281 (VIII), p. 136.

correspondence between the governors of the two provinces, nevertheless, as when Governor Johnson arrested a crew of Spanish pirates who entered Charleston in 1734 and sent them to London for trial, while sending the non-English victims of the piracy to Havana.[130] Or as when the governor of St. Augustine protested, in 1735, against the action of Carolina traders in stirring up the Indians against the Spanish in the Apalachicola region.[131]

All of these exchanges were faithfully reported to the home governments, and entered into the negotiations between the two crowns relative to America then going on.[132] The English settlement of Georgia, however, soon aroused the attention and resentment of the Spanish governors, and the governor of Georgia took the place of the governor of Carolina, as it were, as the British representative in the international correspondence across the frontiers of the English and Spanish empires in that area.

6. The Diplomatic History of Georgia

Almost from the very beginning of Georgia's history, Governor James Oglethorpe was in correspondence with the Spanish governor of St. Augutine, Don Francisco del Moral Sanchez. This correspondence arose out of Oglethorpe's desire to have his colony of Georgia maintain a peaceful relationship with Spanish Florida. But this pious wish ran head-on into the Spanish conviction that this area, lying between South Carolina and St. Augustine, was Spanish and had been recognized as such under the terms of the Anglo-Spanish Treaty of Madrid of 1670.[133]

Spain had had, in fact, a string of posts and missions along this coast, by the Spaniards called "Guale," from about 1566 to about 1670. Upon the basis of this "effective occupation," therefore, Spain insisted that it was a part of America recognized as belonging to Spain by Treaty of Madrid.

On the other hand, Charles II of England had granted to the proprietors of "Carolina," with no more consideration for the presence there of Spanish settlements than he had in granting to his brother, the Duke of York, at about the same time, the Dutch colony of New Netherland, the territory along the coast as far south as the St. John's River (in the Charter of 1663) and (in the Charter of 1665) to the line of 29° North Latitude,

[130] Governor Johnson to the Duke of Newcastle, Aug. 4, 1734, C.S.P., Col., A.& W.I., 1734–35, No. 264, p. 182.
[131] Governor of St. Augustine to Governor Johnson, May 13, 1735, C.S.P., Col., A.& W.I., 1735–36, No. 157 (III), pp. 103–104.
[132] See Chapter XVI.
[133] For a detailed history of the Georgia-Florida disputes, see Lanning, The Diplomatic History of Georgia: A Study of the Epoch of Jenkins' Ear. See also, Reese, Colonial Georgia: A Study in British Imperial Policy in the Eighteenth Century, Chapter V.

south of St. Augustine. But the actual colony of Carolina, or the part of it called South Carolina, extended only as far south as Port Royal, just north of the Savannah River.

In the decades that followed the establishment of South Carolina, English traders had penetrated the Indian country to the southward and had succeeded in antagonizing both the Spaniards of Florida and many of the Indians in the territory. South Carolina's sense of insecurity was intensified by the appearance of the French in the southwest and the alliance of Indians and Spaniards toward the south.[134]

Shortly after the Peace of Utrecht Sir Robert Montgomery proposed (in 1717) to found a colony in the southern parts of South Carolina, a colony that was to be known as "Azilia," a sort of feudal margravate under the proprietors of Carolina. This colony was expected to be a buffer between South Carolina and the French and the Spaniards, but the project collapsed.

In 1720 Sir Francis Nicholson, provincial governor of the newly formed royal colony of South Carolina, suggested to the Board of Trade the desirability of fortifying the area between South Carolina and St. Augustine for the protection of South Carolina from Spanish attacks, as well as from the French of Louisiana, who were claiming the Altamaha as part of "Mississippi." The result was that a fort, Fort King George, was actually built at the mouth of the Altamaha. The Spanish government complained of this fort in 1724, on the ground that it stood on Spanish soil, but the tension was relieved when, in 1726, it burned down. It was rebuilt by South Carolina in 1727, but was abandoned about 1729.

Thus, a number of diplomatic exchanges between the Spanish and the English courts relative to the ownership of the Georgia area had taken place in the two decades between the Peace of Utrecht and the founding of Georgia. Curiously enough, when Georgia was actually founded, it was nearly two years before the new colony became a subject for active international dispute.[135]

The Spaniards, of course, resented the very existence of the colony. When the Duke of Newcastle, the secretary of state, sent Charles Dempsey to St. Augustine to try to pacify the Spanish and to open the way for negotiation with Oglethorpe, the Spanish governor, Francisco del Moral Sanchez, complained bitterly against the settlement of an English colony in territory he claimed belonged to Spain, and, especially, the expansion of the colony southward.[136] In April, 1736, Governor Oglethorpe wrote to Moral Sanchez suggesting that they maintain peace between them and informing the Spanish governor that he had forbidden the English settlers

---

[134] Crane, *The Southern Frontier*, Chapters I, II, III.
[135] See Chapter XV.
[136] Lanning, *Dip. Hist. Ga.*, 36–37; Reese, *Colonial Georgia*, 55–56; see also, Bolton and Ross, *The Debatable Land*, 73.

from crossing the St. John's River into Spanish territory. At the same time he expressed to Dempsey the opinion that it was a good thing that Spain was in possession of Florida:

"The Spanish and the English interests are naturally the same," he wrote. "We furnish them with provisions, they us with silver. They have more lands in America than they can use, the King of Great Britain also has more lands than sufficient, therefore he is not desirous of increasing by injustice his dominions, but of cultivating and peopling with regular towns and establishing good laws in those which he already possesses." [137]

Oglethorpe's claim, which was a bold extension of the terms of the Georgia charter, that the southern boundary of Georgia was the St. John's River, and his building of a fort on San Juan Island, in the mouth of that river, infuriated the Spanish governor of St. Augustine and, in his mind, gave the lie to Oglethorpe's pious wish for peaceful relations between them. He, therefore, bitterly complained not only that the English had built a fort only twenty-five leagues north of St. Augustine, on the north bank of the Altamaha River, on land clearly inside the Spanish colony, but also that the English were inciting the Indians to attack the Spaniards. Oglethorpe had no desire for war—as yet—and he assured Moral Sanchez that the Indian disturbances on the frontier were not due to English meddling.

Meanwhile, the Spanish Captain General of Havana, Juan Fernando de Guemes y Horcasitas, hearing of this extension of Georgia, dispatched Antonio de Arredondo to Frederica to demand that the fort be demolished and that the English withdraw at least as far as Port Royal.

After considerable wrangling, the two sides reached an agreement and drew up a treaty, which was later confirmed by Governor Moral Sanchez at St. Augustine. By the terms of this treaty, Oglethorpe agreed to evacuate Fort St. George, on condition that the Spanish not occupy the area, but without prejudice to the Spanish claim to that territory, at least until the home governments should agree as to where the boundary between Georgia and Florida really should be. It was also agreed that both parties should restrain their subjects and their Indian allies from crossing the frontier and harassing their neighbors.[138]

The English fondly expected that this treaty would guarantee peace between the two colonies, but such was not to be the case. It was accepted by the Georgia Board of Trustees, but it was repudiated by Spain, and Governor Moral Sanchez was called home and prosecuted for countenancing the occupation of Spanish territory by the English. When Benjamin Keene, the British ambassador to Madrid, in 1737 asked the Spanish

---

[137] Quoted in Reese, Colonial Georgia, 56.
[138] The treaty is calendared in C.S.P., Col., A.& W.I., 1737, No. 68 (I), p. 33.

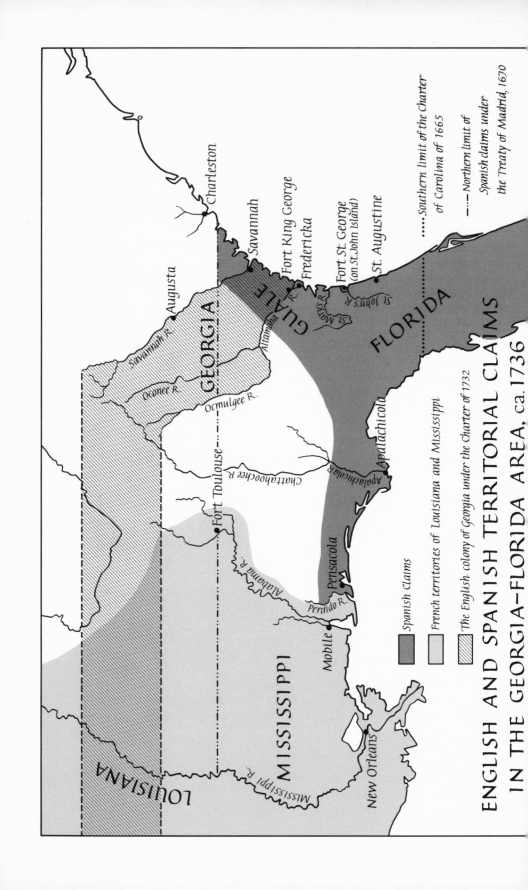

ENGLISH AND SPANISH TERRITORIAL CLAIMS
IN THE GEORGIA–FLORIDA AREA, ca. 1736

Charleston

Savannah

Fort King George

Fredericka

Fort St. George
(on St. John Island)

St. Augustine

Augusta

GEORGIA

GUALE

FLORIDA

Savannah R.

Oconee R.

Ocmulgee R.

Altamaha R.

St. Mary's R.

St. John's R.

St. John's R.

Apalachicola

Apalachicola R.

Chattahoochee R.

Fort Toulouse

Alabama R.

MISSISSIPPI

Pensacola

Perdido R.

Mobile

Mississippi R.

LOUISIANA

New Orleans

.... Southern limit of the Charter
of Carolina of 1665

——— Northern limit of Spanish claims under
the Treaty of Madrid, 1670

Spanish Claims

French territories of Louisiana and Mississippi

The English colony of Georgia under the Charter of 1732

ministers about the treaty, they told him that the King rejected it as a recognition of an English occupation of Spanish territory.[139]

Despite his friendly overtures to the Spanish governor of St. Augustine, James Oglethorpe shared the North American mood of colonial imperialism that characterized the recommendations of most of the English governors of that period. Not only was Georgia situated beside the Bahama channel, he said, through which Spanish treasure fleets must pass on their way home from the Spanish Indies; it might very well, in time of war, become an important military base for the conquest of Florida, Cuba, or even Mexico.[140] It was in this mood that he and his colony faced the prospect of war during 1738, and when the War of Jenkins' Ear broke out in 1739, he welcomed it.[141]

Meanwhile, the existence of Georgia had become an inflamed issue in the diplomacy of the two courts in Europe. Needless to say, English policy in the dispute rested solidly upon the recommendations of Governor James Oglethorpe.

7. The West Indies

The Anglo-French Treaty of Utrecht [142] recognized Great Britain's title to the island of St. Christopher in its entirety, thus ending the century-long joint occupation of that island. The treaty also provided that the joint Anglo-French commission, which was established by the treaty for the settlement of disputes in America, should take cognizance of French complaints derived from the surrender of Nevis to the French in 1706. Otherwise, the Anglo-French treaty of peace left the territorial *status quo* in the Caribbean as it had been, leaving the possessions of Spain, the Netherlands, France, England, Denmark, and Portugal, legally, at least, much as they had been before the War of the Spanish Succession. There were also several sizeable islands which, although still theoretically claimed by Spain, remained unoccupied. Such, in particular, were the islands of St. Lucia, Dominica, St. Vincent, and Tobago, to all of which both France and England had been asserting certain shadowy claims. These islands, and others, became subjects of intercolonial correspondence, claims, and counterclaims, in the three decades following the Peace of Utrecht, among the English, French, Spanish, Dutch, and Danish governors in the area.

But territorial ownership of the West Indies was by no means the only subject of these intercolonial exchanges. Quite the contrary, in fact; they were primarily concerned, at least at the beginning, with carrying into

---

[139] Reese, *Colonial Georgia*, 59.
[140] Reese, *Colonial Georgia*, 56.
[141] See Chapter XVII.
[142] See Chapter X.

effect the terms of the peace, the exchange of prisoners of war, the restitution of prizes taken after the dates of the treaties of peace, piracy, contraband or illicit trade, and so on.

Correspondence between English and Spanish governors in the West Indies area began, after the Peace of Utrecht, in a conciliatory mood. In 1713, Governor Archibald Lord Hamilton of Jamaica reported that the Spanish governor had written to him demanding reparation for a Spanish ship destroyed by one Captain Jackson, a demand that Hamilton recommended be granted, since the trade of Jamaica with the Spanish coast might probably be affected by the way in which the case was handled.[143] Again, in 1715, when the Spanish governor of Havana was reported to be preparing a brigantine to be sent against the nest of pirates in the Bahamas, Deputy Governor Thomas Walker of that colony seized eight of the pirates and sent them to Jamaica for trial. He informed the Spanish governor, the Marquis of Casatorres, of his action, and then went so far as to visit the governor in person, with the result that cordial relations were established between them.[144]

It was not long before this era of intercolonial good feeling in the Caribbean began to turn sour. Early in 1716, Governor Casatorres sent Don Juan Francisco del Valle to Jamaica to complain to Governor Hamilton of continued depredations on Spanish shipping commited by English subjects operating out of Jamaica, and to demand the vigorous suppression of these activities.[145] Hamilton replied that he deplored the English violations of the treaty of peace and that he would do everything he could do to stop them.[146] However, he said, the Spanish, "being the first aggressors I conceive they should be the first to give satisfaction. . . ." [147] Hamilton apparently corresponded with other Spanish governors, also, complaining of Spanish depredations upon English shipping.[148]

Peter Heywood, who replaced Hamilton when he was recalled, continued the correspondence by assuring the governor of Havana that he

[143] Hamilton to the Board of Trade, July 11, 1713, C.S.P., Col., A.& W.I., 1712–14, No. 388, pp. 195–196.
[144] Walker to the Board of Trade, Mar. 14, 1715, C.S.P., Col., A.& W.I., 1714–15, No. 276. p. 119; Marquis of Casatorres to Thomas Walker, Feb. 15, 1715, ibid., 1714–15, No. 276 (III), p. 119; "An Information, May, 1715," ibid., 1714–15, No. 459 (I), pp. 204–205.
[145] Casatorres to Hamilton, Jan. 3, 1716, C.S.P., Col., A.& W.I., 1716–17, No. 375(b), p. 189; del Valle to the Marquis de Monteleón, Mar. 18, 1716, ibid., 1716–17, No. 158, pp. 78–79.
[146] Apparently Hamilton was financially interested in them. See ibid., 1716–17, No. 158, pp. 77–78. Hamilton was removed and arrested for "prejudicing the treaty between Spain and Great Britain."
[147] Hamilton to Casatorres, Feb. 27, 1716, C.S.P., Col., A.& W.I., 1716–17, No. 357(b), pp. 189–191.
[148] Hamilton to the Board of Trade, June 12, 1716, C.S.P., Col., A.& W.I., 1716–17, No. 203, pp. 109–110.

would prosecute the English pirates. But he accused the Spaniards of stealing Negroes from Jamaica and of seizing British vessels "going on their lawful occasions." His most emphatic complaint was against the activities of the Spanish *guarda costas*, private "coast guard" boats which operated under commissions from the Spanish colonial governors and which were often in partnership with them, seizing British and other foreign ships on the high seas, often far outside Spanish territorial waters, on the ground that they were engaged in contraband trade with the Spanish colonies. Heywood claimed that the *guarda costas* were seizing British ships "under pretense of securing their own trade," and taking them to Trinidad, where they were "unjustly condemned [as smugglers], so that their Majestyes subjects here in the Indies seem to be at open warrs, whilst there is so perfect understanding between them at home." [149] Heywood also wrote a similar letter to the governor of Santiago de Cuba.[150]

The governor of Cuba, now Don Vicente de Baxa, replied to Heywood's complaint in a conciliatory vein. He expressed satisfaction at Heywood's promise to prosecute the English pirates, and promised, on his side, to investigate the activities of the Spanish *guarda costas*. He had also issued orders, he said, prohibiting the fitting out of vessels for privateering, either at Trinidad or in Cuba.[151]

But the piracy on both sides continued. So did the correspondence between the governors. So much so that Sir Nicholas Lawes, the new governor of Jamaica, reported in 1718 that Don Juan del Valle was still in Jamaica as representative of the governor of Havana, soliciting reparations for Spanish ships taken by English pirates. The governor and council of Jamaica promised del Valle that everything possible would be done to stop the piracy; at the same time, they expressed the hope that reparation might be made by the Spanish to the English shipowners "for their losses which are equall if not superior to those sustained by the Spaniards." Don Juan himself they invited to leave Jamaica, since he was suspected of spying.[152]

Meanwhile, Governor Walter Hamilton, of the Leeward Islands, had gotten into a dispute with the Spanish governor of Puerto Rico. For the Spanish governor of that island had sent an expedition, in time of peace,

[149] Heywood to the governor of Havana, Aug. 16, 1716, C.S.P., Col., A.& W.I., 1716–17, No. 339(I), pp. 179–180.
[150] Heywood to Don Mateo Lopez de Congas, Aug. 24, 1716, C.S.P., Col., A.& W.I., 1716–17, No. 339 (II), p. 180.
[151] Baxa to Heywood, Nov. 8, 1716, C.S.P., Col., A.& W.I., 1716–17, No. 409 (I), p. 211.
[152] Lawes to the Board of Trade, Sept. 1, 1718, C.S.P., Col., A.& W.I., 1717–18, No. 681, pp. 345–346; Reply of governor and council of Jamaica to del Valle, (n.d.), ibid., 1717–18, No. 681 (IX), p. 347. See also, Lawes to the governor of Havana, (n.d.), enclosed with Lawes to the Board of Trade, Jan. 31, 1719, ibid., 1719–20, No. 34 (I), pp. 20–21.

to Crab Island, just east of Puerto Rico and adjoining the British Leeward Islands as well as the Danish Virgin Islands, and the expedition had carried off the British settlers who had occupied land on Crab Island, along with their Negroes and other movable possessions, to Puerto Rico. This was a violation of British territory, wrote Hamilton, for "you cannot doubt but that Crab Island is unquestionably the right and title of the King my Master. . . ." [153]

The warship sent by Governor Hamilton to present his demand for a return of the English prisoners and their goods was not permitted to enter San Juan harbor, and the Spanish governor failed to answer Hamilton's letter. Apparently, he never paid the slightest attention to Hamilton's communication. The English seem to have returned to Crab Island, however. [154]

Piracy, "illicit" English trade with the Spanish colonies in the islands and on the mainland, and the activities of the Spanish *guarda costas* continued to be chief subjects of dispute between the English and Spanish colonial governors. Despite the excesses of the *guarda costas*, the claims of the Spanish that they were operating against illicit British commerce was well justified. By the *asiento* which they had won from Spain in 1713, the British acquired legal means to penetrate Spain's American territories. They used the sanction of the *asiento* as a cover for an illicit commerce in a wide range of goods, a commerce which thrived under semi-official encouragement from the British government and the cooperation of Spanish colonial officials, who were amenable to bribes and who found the goods brought by the English to be cheaper, better, and more plentiful than those legally imported from Spain.

The governor-to-governor correspondence continued until the two mother countries drifted into war in Europe in 1718, and piracy, as between English and Spanish subjects in America, was replaced by legal privateering and other forms of active warfare.

As peace approached, in 1720, [155] Governor Lawes of Jamaica reported that he had recalled all English privateers and had written the governors of the Spanish colonies in the area asking them to do the same. But the Spanish governors did not respond, and the activities of Spanish privateers and *guarda costas* continued. [156] The Spanish governor of Cuba, however, did complain to Governor Lawes, in 1722, of the English governor's hanging of Spanish marauders arrested off the Jamaican coasts. [157] To which

[153] "Walter Hamilton to the governor of Porto Rico," Apr. 5, 1718, *C.S.P.*, *Col.*, *A.& W.I.*, 1717–18, No. 494 (III), p. 235.

[154] Hamilton to the Board of Trade, May, 1719, *C.S.P.*, *Col.*, *A.& W.I.*, 1719–20, No. 173, p. 86.

[155] See Chapter XIV.

[156] Lawes to the Board of Trade, Aug. 24, 1720, *C.S.P.*, *Col.*, *A.& W.I.*, 1720–21, No. 213, p. 127.

[157] Governor of Cuba to Lawes, (n.d.), *C.S.P.*, *Col.*, *A.& W.I.*, 1722–23, No. 215 (I), p. 107.

Lawes replied that the Spaniards hanged were pirates, destroying and plundering English shipping on the high seas in time of peace, and had been given the internationally accepted punishment they deserved. At the same time he again complained to the Spanish governors about what he considered the excessive and unreasonable activities of the Spanish *guarda costas*.[158]

The issue of the *guarda costas* was continuous and bitter, and the complaints of the English governors in the West Indies about their depredations were almost constant. The presence on board an English or North American ship found on the high seas of Spanish money or dyewood, or other commodities that might have been produced in the Spanish colonies was considered *prima facie* evidence that the ship had visited a Spanish colony and was legal prey for the *guarda costas*. If a ship were found off the "direct" routes among the British possessions or between them and the mother country, it was considered to be violating the Spanish title to the American seas still claimed by Spain under the papal bulls of 1493.[159] In any such case, the ship would be taken to a Spanish colonial port and condemned as a legitimate prize, and the proceeds of the sale of ship and cargo would be divided among the crew and owners of the *guarda costas* and the governor.[160] It was such a case, for example, in which Captain Jenkins claimed he had lost an ear and which became a *cause célèbre* leading to the so-called War of Jenkins' Ear between England and Spain in 1739.[161] When the British governors protested the *guarda costas* they received only evasive answers. The Spanish governors, for their part, asserted that British traders, whether from the British West Indies, from Britain, or from the English colonies in North America, were violating the Spanish laws prohibiting foreign commerce with Spanish colonies by trading with them in defiance of all Spain's diplomatic and political efforts to prevent it.

Correspondence between British and Spanish governors during the 1720s was highly unsatisfactory from the British point of view. A demand of Governor Phenney, of the Bahamas, to the governor of Havana asking a return of deserters received only the response that "deserters are always

[158] Lawes to the Board of Trade, July 9, 1722, C.S.P., Col., A.& W.I., 1722–23, No. 215, pp. 106-107.

[159] See Chapter XV.

[160] See, for example, Governor Fitzwilliam, of the Bahamas, to the governor of Maracaibo, Sept. 17, 1735, C.S.P., Col., A.& W.I., 1735–36, No. 221 (IV), p. 146; and the governor of Maracaibo to Governor Fitzwilliam, Nov. 28, 1735, ibid., 1735–36, No. 221 (V), p. 146. See also, Governor Mathew of the Leeward Islands to John Yeamans, Jan. 17, 1737, ibid., 1737, No. 159, p. 83. Wrote Governor Mathew, "I am grown so great a man amongst my neighbours that the Marquis de San Felipe, Governor of Caracas, restores a sloop well-laden and taken by his *gard-cote [sic]* at my request, sends me a present of a tiger and fine words, etc."

[161] See Chapter XVI. For a history of the War of Jenkins' Ear and the issues involved see Pares, *War and Trade in the West Indies, 1739–63*.

protected in time of war, and ought much more in time of peace." In this case, the conversion of the deserters to Catholicism was alone sufficient to justify the Spaniards in allowing them to remain.[162] The Duke of Portland, governor of Jamaica, in 1724 wrote the governor of Panamá requesting the extradition of the English pirate ship *Cassandra*, which had accepted pardon and protection from Panamá. The Spanish governor refused to return the ship, saying he had taken it under His Catholic Majesty's protection, "for the security of commerce." Anyone interested, he said, might appeal to the King of Spain! [163]

As tension mounted again between England and Spain in 1726 and 1727, both in America and in Europe, the correspondence between the governors increased, and their failure to achieve any results with the Spanish colonial governors aroused a strong opinion among colonial and English merchants and public officials that England should authorize reprisals. As one petition of London merchants complained,

notwithstanding applications have been made from time to time to the Spanish Governors, and other Officers in America not only by the unhappy sufferers, but also by the Governors of your Majestie's Colonies; yet they have not been attended with any manner of satisfaction or redress.[164]

By 1727 things had gotten so bad that Governor John Hart of the Leeward Islands, for example, expressed the belief that the Spaniards were determined upon war, and asked the Board of Trade whether he should issue letters of reprisal against them. He sent an "express" to the governor of Santo Domingo to demand the restitution of seven British vessels seized by Captain Juan de Messa at the island of St. Croix in the Virgin Islands, under a commission from the Spanish governor. He received a reply, with a copy of the proceedings of the prize court that condemned the British ships, but since there was no one on the Leeward Islands who could translate these Spanish documents, Hart sent them to the Dutch island of St. Eustatius for translation. Hart believed the Spanish governor was playing for time in the hope that he might receive word that war was declared and feel justified in keeping the English prizes.[165]

The Treaty of Seville, signed in 1729, provided that all the American disputes between England and Spain were to be resolved by an Anglo-

[162] Governor Phenney to Lord Cartaret, July 6, 1724, C.S.P., Col., A.& W.I., 1724–25, No. 245, p. 131; M. Nicholson and J. Calder (South Sea Co. factors in Havana), to Governor Phenney, Apr. 2, 1724, *ibid.*

[163] The Duke of Portland to the governor of Panamá, Aug. 1, 1724, C.S.P., Col., A.& W.I., 1724–25, No. 74 (II), p. 49; Governor Badillo to Governor Portland, Oct. 5, 1724, *ibid.*, 1724–25, No. 74 (II), p. 49.

[164] Petition of the merchants of London and others trading to and interested in the British colonies in America, C.S.P., Col., A.& W.I., 1726–27, No. 152, pp. 74–75.

[165] Governor Hart to Governor Francisco la Roca Ferrer, Mar. 6, 1727, C.S.P., Col., A.& W.I., 1726–27, No. 503 (I), p. 249; Hart to the Board of Trade, Apr. 10, 1727, *ibid.*, 1726–27, No. 503, pp. 245–246; Hart to the Board of Trade, Mar. 5, 1727, *ibid.*, 1725–26, No. 464, pp. 229–230.

Spanish joint commission, which eventually met in 1732. But the local governor-to-governor protests over illicit trade, runaway slaves, freedom of the seas, and the *guarda costas* continued throughout the 1730s, until the outbreak of the War of Jenkins' Ear in 1739. Correspondence between British and Spanish governors continued even during the war years, 1739–48, but it was concerned mostly with exchanges of prisoners, the ransoming of ships, runaway slaves, etc.[166]

After the Peace of Aix-la-Chapelle (1748) the same old disputes recurred, and the same sort of intercolonial correspondence. Even the Anglo-Spanish commercial treaty of 1750 did not end the incidents and disputes in the Caribbean area, and these were presently exacerbated by the expansion of the English dyewood-cutting operations on the coasts of Spanish Central America.[167] When the Seven Years War began, and after England pronounced the "Rule of the War of 1756" and the "Doctrine of Continuous Voyage," [168] Spain eventually entered the war on the side of France. At this point the correspondence between British and Spanish governors effectually ended; and the governors were charged with the enforcement of the wartime prohibition of intercolonial trade. The trade itself, despite all that could be done to stop it, continued, however, even during the war.[169]

The correspondence between English and French colonial governors in the West Indies also opened amicably, in the years just following the Peace of Utrecht.

Thus, Governor Hamilton of Jamaica, in the late summer of 1712, after the cessation of hostilities in the War of the Spanish Succession but before the Peace of Utrecht, sent to the Comte d'Arguyan, French governor of Petit Goâve,[170] under a flag of truce, one hundred French prisoners of war, with an invitation to collaborate with him in the return of prisoners and prizes and the suppression of further hostilities. The French governor received Governor Hamilton's mission cordially and sent one of his own to Jamaica.[171] The exchange of missions, at least superficially, was successful, and Hamilton reported that

We have found the advantage of the agreement and good correspondence with the French Governor on the Coast of St. Domingo since the Treaty of Cessa-

---

[166] See, for example, *Board of Trade Journals*, 1741/2–49, entry for June 22, 1743, referring to a letter from Governor Tinker, of the Bahamas, dated Mar. 21, 1742, relative to an exchange of prisoners with the governor of Havana in the spring of 1743.

[167] See Chapter XIX.

[168] See Chapters XVIII and XIX.

[169] For the history of this wartime trade, see Beer, *British Colonial Policy, 1754–65*, Chapters V, VI, VII.

[170] On the west coast of Santo Domingo, in what is now Haiti.

[171] Hamilton to the Lord High Treasurer, Nov. 22, 1712, *C.S.P., Col., A.& W.I.*, 1712–14, No. 277, XVIII, pp. 145–146; Hamilton to the Board of Trade, Dec. 18, 1712, *ibid.*, 1712–14, No. 176, pp. 111–112.

tion, the privateers from Petit Guavas [sic] having usually most infested this coast, whereas there has not been the least infriengement [sic] on the Treaty on either side, that has not been effectually redress't and adjusted between us.[172]

But the English piracy continued, and in 1716 the Comte de Blénac, then governor of French Hispaniola, sent a mission to Jamaica to complain that English pirates from Jamaica were still preying upon French shipping and to demand that this piracy be stopped and that reparations be made for the French ships that had been seized.[173] The English reply was again conciliatory, but there was little abatement in the piracy. In view of this fact, the English and French governors followed, for a time, a policy of close communication and cooperation for the suppression of the pirates.

It thus happened that, early in 1721, Governor Feuquières of the French West Indies wrote to Samuel Cox, Acting Governor of Barbados, urgently requesting him to send a British warship to the French islands to assist in suppressing the pirates, since he had no French warship at his disposal. Cox complied and sent a frigate to join with the French forces.[174] A little later, he sent another.[175]

Feuquières also wrote to Governor Walter Hamilton, of the English Leeward Islands, asking his cooperation in joint action against the pirates. He proposed an agreement of fifteen articles, which Hamilton apparently signed, for he sent a ship to Martinique to cooperate with the French against the pirates.[176] By March, 1721, however, Feuquières wrote that the pirate danger had disappeared. He had received information from France that two French frigates were being sent out to the West Indies to cruise off Santo Domingo, so he had demobilized the forces he had been gathering.[177]

Meanwhile, on another front, Anglo-French intercolonial correspondence in the West Indies had begun to be concerned with territorial claims. Thus, Acting Governor William Sharpe, president of the council in Barbados, had reported, in 1715, that Governor Duquesne, of the French West Indies, had complained of the English woodcutters working on the island of St. Lucia, taking wood belonging to French subjects on

[172] Governor Hamilton to [the earl of Dartmouth?], Mar. 5, 1713, C.S.P., Col., A.& W.I., 1712–14, No. 291, p. 153.
[173] Michon to Hamilton, June 18, 1716, C.S.P., Col., A.& W.I., 1716–17, No. 308I, p. 165; Blénac to Hamilton, July 18, 1716, ibid., No. 308 (II), pp. 165–166.
[174] Samuel Cox to the Board of Trade, Feb. 4, 1721, C.S.P., Col., A.& W.I., 1720–21, No. 374, pp. 252–253.
[175] Samuel Cox to the Board of Trade (n.d.), C.S.P., Col., A.& W.I., 1720–21, No. 713, pp. 486–487.
[176] Feuquières to Walter Hamilton, Feb. 21, 1721, C.S.P., Col., A.& W.I., 1720–21, No. 501 (VII), p. 320. See also, ibid. 1720–21, Nos. 501 (IX), 501 (XIV), p. 320; Hamilton to the Board of Trade, May 19, 1721, ibid., 1720–21, No. 501, p. 316.
[177] Feuquières to Walter Hamilton, Mar. 13, 1721, C.S.P., Col., A.& W.I., 1720–21, No. 501 (XVIII), p. 321.

that island, and of others cutting wood on Tobago. English ships should stay away from both these islands, said Duquesne, since both belonged to France.[178] To which Sharpe replied that both these islands belonged to England; therefore, it was the French woodcutters and settlers who were trespassers and should get out.[179]

Besides St. Lucia, the French were reported in 1715 also to have occupied Grenada.[180] George Lillington, Chief Justice of Barbados, reported, in 1719, that the French were not only claiming St. Lucia as having been ceded to them in exchange for the French portion of St. Christopher ceded to England by the Treaty of Utrecht, but were also raiding St. Vincent, whose Negro inhabitants claimed to be British subjects.[181]

From about 1719 on, the question of ownership of unoccupied islands in the Caribbean area became the chief theme in the diplomatic exchanges relative to the West Indies between France and England in Europe, a theme that was rivaled in importance only by the problem of "illicit" commerce between the northern English colonies and the French West Indian islands. So far as St. Lucia was involved (it was the most vigorously contested of all the disputed Caribbean lands), this island was reported by the English governors and officials, from Governor Sharpe on, as being of great importance to England. It was said to have a fine soil and was thought to be capable of producing cacao, sugar, and wood; more important, however, were its fine harbor and its strategic position. As one informant wrote, if the French were to get possession of St. Lucia, and a war were to occur between France and England, "They'll be masters of all the Sugar Plantations." [182] St. Lucia had always been English, the governors asserted, and they maintained that in 1699 King William had issued an order to the governor of Barbados not to allow foreigners to settle on St. Lucia, Tobago, St. Vincent or Dominica, and "to assert our right to the said islands exclusive of all others . . ." [183]

In 1719, while the Anglo-French commission for the definition of American boundaries was sitting, the Marshal d'Estrées, one of the French nego-

[178] Sharpe to the Board of Trade, Feb. 28, 1714 (O.S.), C.S.P., Col., A.& W.I., 1714-15, No. 244, p. 108; Duquesne to the governor of Barbados, Feb. 24, 1715, ibid., 1714-15, No. 244 (I), p. 109. Actually, France had recognized the Dutch ownership of Tobago in the Treaty of Nymwegen, but, although the Dutch and the English had made sporadic efforts to place colonies there, it still remained, after the Peace of Utrecht, to all intents and purposes vacant.

[179] Sharpe to the Board of Trade, Feb. 28, 1715, C.S.P., Col., A.& W.I., 1714-15, No. 244, p. 108; Sharpe to Duquesne, Feb. 21, 1715 (O.S.), ibid., 1714-15, No. 244 (II), pp. 109-110.

[180] Remarks on French settlements in North America, Mar. 11, 1715, C.S.P., Col., A.& W.I., 1714-15, No. 271, pp. 115-116.

[181] Lillington to the Board of Trade, Oct. 31, 1719, C.S.P., Col., A.& W.I., 1719-20, No. 439, p. 247.

[182] Thomas Weir to the Board of Trade, Sept. 12, 1719, C.S.P., Col., A.& W.I., 1719-20, No. 384, pp. 221-222.

[183] Board of Trade to the Lords Justices, Oct. 2, 1719, C.S.P., Col., A.& W.I., 1719-20, No. 404, pp. 229-230.

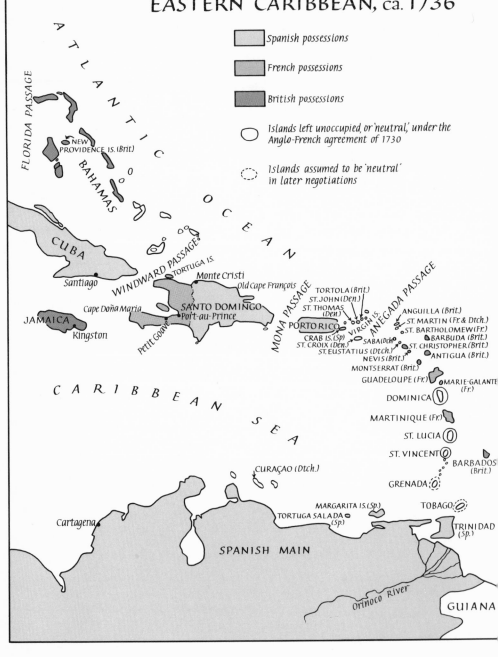

EUROPEAN POSSESSIONS IN THE
EASTERN CARIBBEAN, ca. 1736

- Spanish possessions
- French possessions
- British possessions

○ Islands left unoccupied, or 'neutral,' under the Anglo-French agreement of 1730

⬭ Islands assumed to be 'neutral' in later negotiations

ATLANTIC

FLORIDA PASSAGE

NEW PROVIDENCE IS. (Brit.)

BAHAMAS

OCEAN

CUBA

Santiago

WINDWARD PASSAGE

TORTUGA IS.

Monte Cristi

Old Cape François

Cape Doña Maria

SANTO DOMINGO

Port-au-Prince

JAMAICA

Kingston

Petit Goave

MONA PASSAGE

PORTO RICO

CRAB IS. (Sp.)

ST. CROIX (Den.)

TORTOLA (Brit.)
ST. JOHN (Den.)
ST. THOMAS (Den.)

VIRGIN IS.

ANEGADA PASSAGE

ANGUILLA (Brit.)
ST. MARTIN (Fr. & Dtch.)
ST. BARTHOLOMEW (Fr.)
BARBUDA (Brit.)
ST. CHRISTOPHER (Brit.)
ANTIGUA (Brit.)

SABA (Dtch.)
ST. EUSTATIUS (Dtch.)
NEVIS (Brit.)
MONTSERRAT (Brit.)

GUADELOUPE (Fr.)
MARIE-GALANTE (Fr.)

DOMINICA ○

MARTINIQUE (Fr.)

ST. LUCIA ○

ST. VINCENT ○

BARBADOS (Brit.)

GRENADA ⬭

CARIBBEAN

SEA

CURAÇAO (Dtch.)

Cartagena

MARGARITA IS. (Sp.)
TORTUGA SALADA (Sp.)

TOBAGO ⬭

TRINIDAD (Sp.)

SPANISH MAIN

Orinoco River

GUIANA

tiators, was authorized by his government to send a colony of French-men to St. Lucia. This he did, and Governor Robert Lowther of Barbados reported the event to the Earl of Stanhope, secretary of state, while writing Governor Feuquières, at Martinique, that this action was a trespass upon English territory and that the French settlers must be withdrawn.[184]

On the basis of Lowther's reports, the French occupation of St. Lucia was protested by the English ambassador and the English members of the joint commission in Paris and the d'Estrées expedition was withdrawn.[185]

No sooner had the French occupation of St. Lucia been quashed, how-ever, than the English proceeded to occupy the island. The Scottish Duke of Montagu was given a charter for the island by King George I in 1722, and Montagu promptly sent his own expedition, the main body of which went to St. Lucia but a part of which also went to St. Vincent.

The French governor, Feuquières, under orders from France, promptly challenged the English expedition. St. Vincent and St. Lucia did not belong to England, Feuquières argued, and he sent a military expedition to block the English project. Captain Nathaniel Uring, in command of the English, was compelled to sign a treaty of capitulation by which he agreed to withdraw his colonists, who then went to Antigua.[186]

Meanwhile, the English governors had begun to report that the French were settling on the islands of Dominica, St. Vincent, and Tobago. St. Vincent had been included in the Duke of Montagu's grant of 1722, but Gov-ernor Feuquières had insisted that the English abandon that island,[187] also, when they abandoned St. Lucia. St. Vincent did not belong to either France or England, wrote Feuquières, but to the Carib Indians. These Indians were under the protection of France, he said, and he would protect them.[188] The island was evacuated, and it remained so, technically at least, until it was declared "neutral" by the Anglo-French agreement of 1730.

Tobago, also, was coming to the attention of the English and French colonial governors and entering into their correspondence. As early as 1715

---

[184] [Lowther?] to Stanhope, Oct. 22, 1719, C.S.P., Col., A.& W.I., 1719-20, No. 422 (II, III), pp. 240-241; see also, George Lillington to the Board of Trade, Oct. 31, 1719, ibid., 1791-20, No. 439, pp. 247-248.

[185] See Chapter XVI.

[186] Captain Orme to [Mr. Burchett?] Mar. 25, 1723, C.S.P., Col., A.& W.I., 1722-23, No. 483, pp. 231-234; see also, "Account of the Duke of Montagu's intended set-tlement at St. Lucia; and of his being repulsed from thence by the French," ibid., 1722-23, No. 820, pp. 428-429; Governor James Hart to the Board of Trade, Jan. 26, 1723, ibid., 1722-23, No. 419, pp. 201-205.

[187] "Account of the Duke of Montagu's intended settlement at St. Lucia; and of his being repulsed from thence by the French," C.S.P., Col., A.& W.I., 1722-23, No. 820, pp. 428-429.

[188] Governor John Hart to the Board of Trade, Jan. 26, 1723, C.S.P., Col., A.& W.I., 1722-23, No. 419, p. 201; Feuquières to Hart, Jan. 21, 1723, ibid., No. 419 (VI), p. 205; see also, Newcastle to the Board of Trade, Nov. 13 1730, ibid., 1730, Nos. 532 and 532 (II), pp. 342-343.

Acting Governor William Sharpe of Barbados had warned the French governor of Martinique that Tobago belonged to England and that French subjects should not be allowed to go there.[189] Sparring between French and English governors went on for a decade, with little result, until, after the Duke of Montagu was compelled to give up St. Lucia in 1723, he asked, in 1728, for Tobago by way of compensation. The Board of Trade recommended that Montagu's application for Tobago be granted,[190] but France protested and this project, too, was abandoned.

Meanwhile, again, the French had protested the English occupation of St. Croix, in the Virgin Islands, and demanded the evacuation of that island, but without result.[191]

Thus, on the basis of the reports from the French and English governors in the West Indies, St. Lucia, Dominica, and St. Vincent had now become the subject of an emphatic exchange of protests and demands between the French and English courts in Europe. The controversy was settled temporarily by an exchange of letters between them in 1730, by which both nations agreed to retire from St. Lucia, Dominica, and St. Vincent and to leave them all "neutral" until some further determination should be made.[192] It was also proposed to neutralize Tobago and St. Croix; this was not formally done, but these two islands were apparently tacitly placed in the same category.[193]

After the Anglo-French neutralization agreement of 1730 the correspondence between the colonial governors relative to unoccupied islands was revived. The governor of the French West Indies, now the Marquis de Champigny, complained that the English had proclaimed their possession of the islands despite the evacuation agreement. Governor Viscount Howe of Barbados replied that he had only published his commission in St. Lucia; he had not taken possession. He, in his turn, complained to the French of the continued settlement of Frenchmen in St. Lucia.[194] Champigny then requested more time to complete the French evacuation, which Howe refused to grant.[195]

[189] William Sharpe to the governor of Martinique, Feb. 21, 1715, *C.S.P., Col., A.& W.I.,* 1714–15, No. 244 (II), pp. 109–110.

[190] Board of Trade to the King, Feb. 27, 1728, *C.S.P., Col., A.& W.I.,* 1728–29, No. 68 (I), pp. 40–41.

[191] Waldegrave to Newcastle, Nov. 16, 1730, *P.R.O., C.O.,* 28/21; French statement on St. Croix enclosed to Newcastle, Nov. 16, 1730, *ibid.*

[192] The Duke of Newcastle to the Board of Trade, Nov. 13, 1730 (with enclosures), *C.S.P., Col., A.& W.I.,* 1730, No. 532, pp. 342–343.

[193] Board of Trade to the King, Nov. 26, 1730, *C.S.P., Col., A.& W.I.,* 1730, No. 561 (I), p. 366.

[194] Howe to the Duke of Newcastle, Aug. 18, 1733, *C.S.P., Col., A.& W.I.,* 1733, No. 313, pp. 164–165; Champigny to Howe, July 12, 1733, *ibid.,* No. 313 (II), pp. 166–167.

[195] Champigny to Howe; Aug. 13, 1733, *C.S.P., Col., A.& W.I.,* 1733, No. 313 (V), pp. 167–168; Howe to Champigny, Aug. 15, 1733, *ibid.,* 1733, No. 313 (VI), pp. 168–169.

Recriminations between the French and English governors over St. Lucia and the other islands continued throughout the decade. The French, wrote Acting Governor Dottin of Barbados, to the Marquis de Champigny, in 1735, "only for form sake lock'd up their doors, but moved none of their effects and went over to Montinico, and in a few days afterward return'd back again to St. Lucia, where they still abide [and], are more numerous than ever." [196] But the French governors insisted that the French were evacuated. In December Champigny wrote Acting Governor Dottin that he had sent a French warship to St. Lucia to check on the evacuation, only to find two English warships there; the English and French officers then signed an agreement that the subjects of both nations in the island might remain until May 31, 1736, in order that they might be able to harvest their cotton.[197]

Meanwhile, tension between French and English governors was steadily increasing over the seizure of ships. In 1730, Governor Mathew of the Leeward Islands reported three English sloops burned by French men-of-war, for which Mathew wrote the Marquis de Champigny demanding compensation.[198] There followed a series of seizures of English ships by French garde-côtes, on the ground that they were violating French territorial waters and were suspected of contraband trade with the French colonies. A climax was reached in the rising Anglo-French tension in the West Indies in 1738, in the case of the ship Elizabeth, seized by the French off Doña Maria Bay, on the west coast of French Santo Domingo. This seizure came at a moment when tension was also rising in Europe between England and France and England and Spain, and it became a sort of cause célèbre in the worsening diplomatic relations between England and France.[199]

Both the French and the English empires in the Caribbean, as elsewhere in America, were expanding during these years. The colonial governors on both sides played important roles in the imperialistic race, each encouraging the expansion of his own empire with one hand while protesting and trying to block the expansion of the national rivals with the other.

Correspondence between English and French governors in the West Indies continued, even during the war years from 1739 to 1748, but this

[196] Dottin to Champigny, Dec. 4, 1735, C.S.P., Col., A.& W.I., 1735-36, No. 183 (V), pp. 122-123.
[197] Champigny to Dottin, Dec. 23 and 29, 1735, C.S.P., Col., A.& W.I., 1735-36, No. 208, p. 137.
[198] Mathew to Newcastle, Apr. 29, 1730, C.S.P., Col., A.& W.I., 1730, No. 110, p. 52.
[199] Newcastle to Waldegrave, Nov. 13, 1738, in Legg, ed., Brit. Dip. Insts., 1689-1789, VI, France, 1727-44, 210-211; same to same, Jan. 5, 1739, ibid., VI, France, 1727-44, 212-213. See also Chapter XVI.

correspondence was concerned chiefly with exchanges of prisoners and condemnations of prizes.[200] After the Peace of Aix-la-Chapelle, all the old Anglo-French imperial disputes in the West Indies, as elsewhere in the American hemisphere, reappeared in, if anything, a more ruthlessly imperialistic mood and with more virulence than ever before.

The treaty itself did not specifically mention the West Indies, otherwise than by providing that all conquests made there, as in the rest of the world, by either side during the war were to be restored, and that "otherwise everything [in the East and West Indies] shall be restored to the condition they were in or should have been in before the present war." [201] This was assumed to mean, at least by the British, that the Anglo-French agreement of 1730 to leave St. Lucia, Dominica, St. Vincent, and Tobago "neutral" and unoccupied was still in force. When the Anglo-French joint commission for the settlement of American boundaries and ownership met in 1750, the question of the ownership of these islands became one of the problems that it took up and tried to settle.[202]

But the colonial governors did not wait upon the deliberations of the commission. Already, in 1748, the Marquis de Caylus, Governor of Martinique (that is, of all the French West Indies), published in Tobago a proclamation to the effect that that island was the property of the French king; English ships were warned away from the island, and Caylus sent settlers to found a colony there. These goings-on were duly reported to the Board of Trade by Governor Henry Grenville of Barbados, whereupon the Duke of Bedford, secretary of state, instructed the Earl of Albemarle, British ambassador to France, to protest Caylus's actions to the French ministry and to request that strong instructions be sent to Caylus to desist from his "triffling chicaneries" and rigorously to carry out the terms of present and former Anglo-French agreements to evacuate all the "Neutral Islands" and leave them vacant until their ownership might be decided. Should the French ministry not agree to send out such orders, jointly with the British crown, the ambassador was to indicate that it would be necessary for the King of Great Britain to instruct his governors and officers in the West Indies to use force, if necessary, to drive the French settlers out of all the disputed islands.[203]

The French ministry disavowed Caylus' actions, but the occupation continued, and in 1754 an English ship drove away from the island a French ship supplying the colony there.

[200] See for example Board of Trade Journals, 1741/2–49, 167, entry for June 12, 1745, referring to a letter from Sir Thomas Robinson, Governor of Barbados, dated March 24, 1745, reporting a "cartel" between the British governor and the governor of Martinique for the exchange of prisoners.
[201] Davenport, ed., European Treaties, IV, 74.
[202] See Chapter XIX.
[203] Bedford to Albemarle, May 8, 1749, in Legg, ed., Brit. Dip. Insts., 1689–1789, VII, France, Part IV, 1745–89, 2–3; same to same, April 11, 1751, ibid., 14–16.

Actually French settlers had been moving into these islands, especially St. Lucia and Dominica, since before the war just ended. This fact came to the attention of Governor Henry Grenville, who not only reported it to his superiors in England but protested to Governor Caylus of Martinique. Caylus replied to Grenville that, although he would read to the public the proclamation of his court calling for the evacuation of the islands, he could not "hunt them out like wild boars." To which Commodore Holbourne, sent by England to supervise the evacuation replied, "Then I must, for I can only look upon them at present as so many banditti or outlaws and by no means as subjects of His Most Christian Majesty." [204]

This local dispute was referred back to England, and a protest was again lodged with the French court. The French ministry promised to execute the evacuations, but it failed to do so. Once again the governors and naval officers in the West Indies had to report, in 1753, that both St. Lucia and Dominica were occupied by Frenchmen and that Governor Bompar, who had succeeded Caylus, had organized a government and a militia in Dominica.[205]

It was, in fact, Caylus's action of 1749 that inspired the British proposal to France that a special convention be made between the two countries "to ascertain the neutrality for the time to come of the four islands now in question" and the creation of the Anglo-French commission to try to settle all the American disputes between the two countries, in 1750. The proposed convention was not made, and the commission wasted about four years in futile debate while the two empires drifted into war. As for the colonial governors, they continued to protest to each other, to fail to carry out the evacuation agreements in good faith and to take military action up to the brink of war,[206] which finally became official in 1756.

The Danes and the Dutch were also involved in the race for island possessions in the Caribbean after the Peace of Utrecht, and the governors of the English, Spanish, and French colonies were vigorous in the prosecution of the claims of their respective sovereigns against the expansiveness of these lesser powers as well as against each other.

In 1718, for example, when Governor Walter Hamilton of the British Leeward Islands heard that the Danes were cutting timber and planning to build settlements on the island of St. John, in the Virgin Islands, he sent a message to the Danish governor Bredal, of St. Thomas, to inform

[204] Bedford to Albemarle, Apr. 21, 1751, in Legg, ed., Brit. Dip. Insts., 1689–1789, VII, France, 1745–89, 14–16. Quoted in Gipson, British Empire, V, 313–314.

[205] Legg, ed., Brit. Dip. Insts., 1689–1789, VII, France, 1745–1789, 34–36. See also, Gipson, British Empire, V, 314, fn. 50.

[206] Bedford to Albemarle, May 8, 1749, in Legg, ed., Brit. Dip. Insts., 1689–1789, VII, France, Part IV, 1745–89, 3–4.

him that the island of St. John, as all the Virgins, belonged to the King of Great Britain. Indeed, he said, "The King of Denmark has no good title even to St. Thomas itself." He requested the Danish governor to recall his settlers from St. John and to abstain from occupying the island in the future. Should the Danes try to colonize the island, he declared, he would feel compelled to "take such other measures as are agreeable to my instructions" to preserve British sovereignty.[207] To which Governor Bredal replied that he could not "abate in any degree the claims of H. M. [the King of Denmark] upon the island of St. Johns." He asserted the validity of Denmark's title to St. Thomas, besides which, he said, "the legitimate occupation of a deserted island, and peaceful possession of it for so many years evidently justify it." [208]

This reaffirmation of the doctrine of effective occupation did not resolve the argument. But the English took no steps to drive the Danes out of the Virgin Islands, so they remained in possession.[209]

Governor Hart of the British Leeward Islands reopened the question of the ownership of the island of St. John in 1722. On May 1 of that year he wrote the Danish governor of St. Thomas demanding the "instant" withdrawal from that island of all the Danish subjects who had settled there, since the said island "undoubtedly appertains to the Crown of Great Britain." He wrote that he was sending to St. John Commander Ellis Brand, of H.M.S. *Hector*, to whom the island was to be restored. "In case of your refusall, I am not to be answerable for the consequences." The King of Denmark, he said, had no right even to the island of St. Thomas itself.[210]

At about the same time Hart sent a small expedition under Alexander Langdon to occupy Crab Island, just off the eastern end of Puerto Rico. It was now the Danish governor's turn to protest, which he promptly did. He wrote to Hart that he had protested to Langdon "in the strongest manner, because of "the pretension wch. my most gracious King [the King of Denmark] has, from the first settlement of St. Thomas, to Crab Island and other Islands adjacent to St. Thomas." But Langdon had persisted, and had planted "the flag of England, contrary to all the rights which my King has granted to my Lords and Masters, the Danish Company." He

[207] Walter Hamilton to the governor of St. Thomas, Apr. 5, 1718, *C.S.P., Col.,* A.& W.I., 1717–18, No. 494 (II), pp. 234–235; Hamilton to the Board of Trade, Jan. 6, 1718 [sic?], *ibid.,* 1717–18, No. 298, p. 147.

[208] Governor Bredal of St. Thomas to Governor Hamilton [of the Leeward Islands], Apr. 23, 1718, *C.S.P., Col.,* A.& W.I., 1717–18, No. 526 (III), p. 248.

[209] Hamilton to the Board of Trade, *C.S.P., Col.,* A.& W.I., 1720–21, No. 500, p. 313. For earlier diplomatic exchanges relative to the Virgin Islands, see above, Chapter VIII.

[210] Hart to the governor of St. Thomas, May 1, 1722, *C.S.P., Col.,* A.& W.I., 1724–25, No. 260 (II), p. 147.

requested Hart to recall Langdon and drop any British pretension to the ownership of Crab Island.[211]

Hart reported to Lord Carteret his investigation of the Danish settlements on St. Thomas and St. John, undertaken "pursuant to my 84th Instruction for asserting H.M. right to the Virgin Islands," and his dispute with the Danish governor. He assured Lord Carteret that the Danes could easily be driven out by force, and that he was eager to do it, if the King were willing.[212] He also reported to the Board of Trade, describing St. John and St. Thomas as fertile, as possessing fine harbors, and as having been occupied by the Danes; "this," he said, "in my humble opinion is an incroachment upon H. M. Dominions. . . ." [213] Hart again protested the Danish occupation of St. John to Governor Thombsen in June, 1724, and again demanded the island's evacuation,[214] only to receive a reply from the Danish governor that the King of Denmark possessed both St. Thomas and St. John, and that he was "ordered to defend the same to the utmost of my power." [215]

The English failed to act against the Danes, however, and they remained in possession of St. John and St. Thomas. France sold its claim to St. Croix to the Danes in 1733, on condition that it never be sold to a third power without France's permission, thus adding the third of the major islands in the Virgins group to the Danish empire.[216]

Correspondence between English and Dutch governors in the West Indies began, after the Peace of Utrecht, over the effort of the British governors to recover deserters who had fled to St. Eustatius.[217] Thereafter, correspondence between governors had to do chiefly with illicit commerce, in which the Dutch West Indian colonies, especially St. Eustatius, served as exchange points for English, French, Spanish, and Danish traders. In 1729 a flurry of excitement was caused by the flight of John Lindesay, one-time governor of St. Eustatius, to the Leeward Islands to escape his

[211] Governor of St. Thomas to Governor Hart, May 23, 1722, C.S.P., Col. A.& W.I., 1724-25, No. 260 (IV), pp. 147-148.
[212] Hart to Lord Carteret, May 24, 1722, C.S.P., Col., A.& W.I., 1724-25, No. 260 (I), pp. 145-146.
[213] Hart to the Board of Trade, July 12, 1724, C.S.P., Col., A.& W.I., 1724-25, No. 260, p. 144. Since the Danish Governor Thombsen had written in Danish, which no one in the Leeward Islands could translate, Hart sent Thombsen's letter on to the Board without knowing precisely what the Dane had said!
[214] Hart to Governor Otto Jacob Thombsen, June 6, 1724, C.S.P., Col., A.& W.I., 1724-25, No. 260 (III), p. 147.
[215] Thombsen to Hart, June 24, 1724, C.S.P., Col., A.& W.I., 1724-25, No. 260 (VI), p. 148.
[216] When the United States became interested in the Virgin Islands in 1868, permission for the sale was obtained by Denmark from France. The sale, however, was not consummated until 1917.
[217] Governor Hamilton, of the Leeward Islands, to the Board of Trade, Dec. 19, 1718, C.S.P., Col., A.& W.I., 1717-18, No. 797, p. 410.

debts to the Dutch Company, and the request of Governor Everard Roecx for the extradition of Lindesay. The English governor, Lord Londonderry, sent Lindesay to England for disposition, however, with the comment that "this Gentleman, whilst he was Governour, lived always very friendly with the inhabitants of this island." [218] Another flurry of interest was stirred up in 1734, when Governor Mathew of the Leeward Islands reported to the Duke of Newcastle in some alarm that the French and the Dutch inhabitants of the islands of St. Martin and St. Barthélemy, which were jointly occupied, had signed a treaty of neutrality between themselves which provided that, in case of war between France and Holland the two islands would remain neutral. This treaty was dangerous to British interests, Governor Mathew believed, since in case of war it would cut off communication between the British Leeward Islands and Great Britain and Ireland. The governor's reasoning is not clear, but he sent to Newcastle a copy of the treaty which he received from the governor of St. Eustatius at his own request.[219]

Otherwise relations between Dutch and English governors were cordial. After the outbreak of the War of the Austrian Succession and, especially, of the Seven Years War, during which the Dutch became involved in a neutral carrying trade that tended to nullify British military and naval effectiveness, the Anglo-Dutch governor-to-governor correspondence again became active and increasingly unfriendly.[220]

8. Intercolonial Relations Relative to Intercolonial Commerce

Commerce between the English colonies in America and those of other European states began almost immediately after their founding, and a number of treaties were made by the colonies during the seventeenth century aimed at promoting and regulating this commerce.[221] By the end of the seventeenth century these treaties had ceased, for one reason or another, to be useful, but the commerce, "licit" and "illicit," between Angloamerica and the French, Spanish, and Dutch colonies had substantially increased.

The parts of this trade with non-British colonies that violated the English navigation laws were, of course, illegal; but this did not prevent the Angloamericans from engaging in them. Other parts of it, such as the

[218] Governor Lord Londonderry to the duke of Newcastle, May 1, 1729, C.S.P., Col., A.& W.I., 1728–29, No. 684, p. 361.

[219] Mathew to Newcastle, Sept. 14, 1734, C.S.P., Col., A.& W.I., 1734–35, No. 313, p. 205; Copy of French-Dutch Treaty of Neutrality, July 14, 1734, ibid., 1734–35, No. 313 (I), p. 205.

[220] See Chapter XIX.

[221] See Chapter XI.

trade for sugar and molasses with the French West Indies or for hides or silver coin in the Spanish colonies, violated no English law, and were not, therefore, illegal from the British point of view.[222] Angloamerican trade with French or Spanish colonies, however, was always prohibited by the governments of France and Spain, and from their points of view it was "illicit." It was generally considered by them as smuggling and, therefore, punishable as such.

So far as English interests were concerned, the North American trade with the French, Spanish, Dutch, and Danish colonies, while not illegal, did often run counter to the economic interests of England; this was particularly true of the effect of this trade upon the economy of the British West Indies. The trade was, however, of enormous importance to the economic life of the northern colonies. This meant that the international economic orientation of the northern colonies, by its very nature, markedly diverged from that of the mother country as well as that of the Caribbean segment of the British empire.

The efforts of England to stop, to regulate, or otherwise to hamper this trade placed the colonial governors in the northern colonies in an anomalous position, since they recognized that it was of great importance, if not essential, to the economic prosperity of the colonies they governed. Thus, whereas the English governors in the West Indies could cooperate with French or Spanish governors, for the suppression of the trade with the hearty support of most of the colonists they governed, the governors of the northern continental colonies found themselves required by their instructions to try to suppress a commerce that was beneficial not only to the colonies but to the mother country as well. Since they did not have the

[222] Many efforts were made by the Board of Trade to stop the trade of the North American merchants with the foreign colonies (cf. Beer, *British Colonial Policy, 1754–65*, pp. 75–76, *et passim*). The Board found that there was no English law prohibiting it, except insofar as the "Staple Act" of 1663 prohibited the importation of European manufactured goods into the colonies unless they had first passed through England. The Anglo-French Treaty of Whitehall of 1686 did prohibit the trade of the nationals of either France or of England from trading with the nationals of the other (see Chapter IX); the Anglo-Spanish Treaty of Madrid did the same for trade between the subjects of those two states (see Chapter VI).

But neither of these treaties had been implemented in English law. In 1728 the Board requested an opinion on this commerce from the attorney general and solicitor general, who ruled that Articles Five and Six of the Treaty of 1686 intended to recognize the right of France to punish English subjects trading in French colonies and of England to punish French subjects trading in English colonies. "But we apprehend that it was not the intent of this Treaty to provide that either of the contracting powers should seize and confiscate the ships or goods of their own subjects for contravening the said Articles." Since there was no act of Parliament prohibiting Englishmen from engaging in this trade, it was not contrary to English law (Mr. Attorney and Mr. Solicitor General to the Board of Trade, June 3, 1728, *C.S.P., Col., A.& W.I.,* 1728, No. 230, pp. 107–108. See also, Ira W. Taylor, "Massachusetts Trade with the French West Indies, 1686–1733," unpublished Master of Arts thesis (1959) in the University of Washington Library.) The so-called Molasses Act of 1733 was a tacit recognition of the legality of the trade, since the law sought only to regulate it, not to prohibit it.

support of their "constituents," they could not with enthusiasm either suppress the trade with the foreigners or sincerely endorse their own instructions from home. Some of them, such as Lieutenant Governor Cadwallader Colden of New York actually argued with the mother country for a greater freedom of commerce for the colonies, even in time of war.

The cockpit of intercolonial trade in the American hemisphere lay in the islands and lands in and about the Caribbean Sea.[223] This commerce had been relatively free during the War of the Spanish Succession, and English and Dutch traders, particularly Angloamericans from the English continental colonies, had flourished on it, chiefly because of British and Dutch domination of the seas and the inability of France to prevent Anglo-Dutch trade, even with its own colonies.

After the Peace of Utrecht, France and Spain both attempted to stop the trade of English and Dutch ships with their colonies. Both countries legally excluded foreign ships and traders from their colonies, and France, having lost the *asiento* to England, had a direct interest in encouraging Spain to prohibit direct foreign trade with its colonies and rigorously to maintain its monopolistic system of channeling European trade with Spanish America through the *Casa de Contratación* in Cadiz, a trade in which French merchants had the largest single foreign interest.[224] By the terms of the Anglo-Spanish *asiento* treaty, English trade with Spain's American colonies was limited to the sale of Negro slaves at ports on the Atlantic and Caribbean coasts and to the privilege of sending a single shipload of English goods to be sold at the same time and in the same ports visited by the annual Spanish fleet supplying Spanish America. Moreover, the Anglo-French Treaty of Whitehall of 1686 had provided that English subjects should not trade with French colonies, and vice versa; the Anglo-Spanish Treaty of Madrid of 1670, renewed by the Anglo-Spanish commercial treaty of Utrecht, contained the same provisions with regard to English and Spanish subjects. But the English traders defied both the French and the Spanish regulations excluding them; it was in the course of this "illicit" trade that many English ships were seized by Spanish *guarda costas* or French *garde-côtes*, often on the high seas, on the mere suspicion that they had been trading in prohibited Spanish or French colonies. It is to be noted that, while the French and Spanish governors were under the strictest orders to enforce the law, and shared in the profits derived from the seizure of English prizes, many of the inhabitants of both the Spanish and

[223] For an analysis of this trade see Richard Pares, *War and Trade in the West Indies, 1739–1763* and *Yankees and Creoles: The Trade between North America and the West Indies before the American Revolution.*

[224] See, for example, "Mémoire au Sujet du Commerce illicite et très préjudicial à la France que les Anglais font à la Nouvelle Espagne" (1723), A.É., Méms. et Docs., Amérique, 7: fols. 161–169 vo.; and "Mémoire sur le Commerce des Anglais et des Français en Eopagne" (1724?), A.É., Méms. et Docs., Espagne, 32: fols 106–110 vo.

the French colonies engaged in the trade gladly, since it brought them provisions from North America and Ireland that they found it difficult or impossible to procure from their home countries. On the other hand, the English governors, under instructions to discourage the trade because it prospered at the expense of the economies of the British West Indies, did what they could to discourage it, but they were not always averse to sharing in the profits derived from it.

In general, therefore, the mood of the extensive governor-to-governor correspondence relative to this "illicit" trade, in the months immediately following the Peace of Utrecht, was, superficially, at least, one of cooperation in the suppression of piracy and illicit commerce. It was in such a mood, for example, that Governor Archibald, Lord Hamilton of Jamaica, received a communication from the governor of Cartagena written in July, 1713, asking for reparation for a Spanish vessel seized by the English Captain Jackson after the cessation of arms. Hamilton reported the Spanish governor's communication to the Board of Trade and recommended that the reparation be made, "the reputation of the service, and the trade of this Island to the Spanish coast being in some measure effected by it." [225] Again, Richard Harris, a colonial agent, warned Secretary Popple of the Board of Trade that France desired the suppression of the English clandestine trade with the Spanish colonies and had offered to suppress its own illicit trade there only because, on account of Louis XIV's influence at the Spanish court during the early years of the reign of his nephew Philip V, France had been able (as he believed) to get Spanish licenses to trade with the Spanish colonies legitimately. France, said Harris, desired the elimination of British trade with the Spanish colonies. But that would be catastrophic: the English dye industry would be paralyzed for lack of dye if the English could not get dyewood; furthermore, the supply of silver going to England from the Spanish colonies would be so reduced as to make English trade with the East Indies difficult. Therefore, he said, it would be greatly to England's interest to encourage and support its trade with the Spanish West Indies, even though it were clandestine.[226]

Governor Lowther of Barbados went even further. In 1715, he wrote to the governor of Havana implying the desirability of a trade between British and Spanish colonies, saying that he would "take all occasions of giving them [the Spaniards] marks of His Royal [Britannic Majesty's] favor as often as any Spanish ships or vessels shall find it necessary or convenient to touch at this place." [227] To the Board of Trade he wrote explaining his letter to the Spanish governor as having been written in the hope of open-

[225] "Lord A. Hamilton to the Board of Trade," July 11, 1713, C.S.P., Col., A.& W.I., 1712–14, No. 388, p. 195.

[226] Richard Harris to Mr. Popple, Dec. 27, 1714, C.S.P., Col., A.& W.I., 1714–15, No. 129, pp. 58–60.

[227] Lowther to the governor of Havana, Dec. 15, 1715, C.S.P., Col., A.& W.I., 1714–15, No. 715 (I), p. 360.

ing a trade with the Spanish colony. Lowther believed that the restrictions placed upon foreign trade with the Spanish colonies had sprung from Spain's fear of the French King Louis XIV; now that Louis XIV was dead, Lowther felt sure the Spanish colonies would welcome trade with the English.[228] This suggestion of Governor Lowther represented a widespread idea in the islands, and it was considered seriously even by the Board of Trade itself, for the Board went so far as to suggest, as late as 1720, that a "controlled trade" with the Spanish colonies might be desirable, since the British ships trading there procured commodities not produced in the British plantations.[229]

The proposals of British colonial governors and agents for the encouragement of Anglo-Spanish intercolonial trade were not destined to receive official sanction by either the crown of Spain or that of England. Spanish cloture of the English trade with Spanish America that had flourished during the War of the Spanish Succession was practically automatic after the restoration of peace, while, on the English side, any relaxation of the navigation laws that might have permitted Spanish sloops to visit the British islands was opposed by merchants in England, especially those concerned with the West Indies interests, and, most vociferously, by some British West Indian planters, who feared the trade of the northern British colonies with all foreign colonies as building up those colonies and encouraging their trade, which stood in a position of direct rivalry with that of the British islands. Thus, the British government was prevailed upon to follow a policy of discouragement of the trade, and the British governors were instructed to try to suppress it.

The trade continued, of course, and ships were seized on both sides, with the result that after about 1724 the Anglo-Spanish governor-to-governor correspondence became increasingly devoted to claims and recriminations relative to the seizure of ships that supposedly had either violated territorial waters or engaged in trade prohibited by the navigation laws of one or the other of the two empires. The seizure by Spanish *guarda costas* of British ships suspected of engaging in this clandestine trade quickly became, in fact, one of the main themes in the course of Anglo-Spanish diplomacy in Europe.[230]

Of even greater importance for the British colonies, especially those on the continent of North America, was the trade with the French islands. The correspondence between British and French colonial governors was largely concerned with this trade.

As early as 1714 the Board of Trade, having received reports of trade

[228] Lowther to the Board of Trade, n.d., *C.S.P.*, *Col.*, *A.& W.I.*, 1714–15, No. 715 (I), p. 359; Lowther to the Board of Trade, Oct. 25, 1715, *ibid.*, 1714–15, No. 654, p. 323.

[229] Board of Trade to Secretary Craggs, Feb. 25, 1720, *C.S.P.*, *Col.*, *A.& W.I.*, 1719–20, No. 575, pp. 363–364.

[230] See Chapter XV.

between Barbados and the French islands, instructed Colonel Sharpe, president of the council of Barbados, as acting governor, to make sure that British ships of war stationed at Barbados or other British ships did not trade with the French islands, since such a trade would be a violation of the Treaty of Whitehall of 1686; he was also, and for the same reason, not to permit French subjects to come to Barbados for trade.[231] A little later the French government sent strict orders to its colonial government in the Caribbean to stop the English trade, which persisted despite the orders sent to the British governors. The French governors were instructed to seize and confiscate all foreign ships engaged in the clandestine trade.[232]

It was in these circumstances, therefore, that Governor Lowther of Barbados wrote Lieutenant Governor Duquesne of the French West Indies in August, 1715, complaining of the French seizure of the sloop *Martha* and the refusal of the French to restore the sloop and its cargo to the owner. The French governor replied that he had strict orders from his court to stop the English trade. He, in his turn, complained that English ships were constantly coming to the French islands; this, he said, he must stringently forbid.[233] Similarly, in 1717 Governor Walter Hamilton, of the British Leeward Islands, wrote to the marquis de la Varenne, then governor of the French West Indies, complaining of a British ship belonging to a Mr. Roe and a Mr. Sooby that had been seized and confiscated at Martinique. As in the former case, the French governor replied that the ship had anchored at Martinique without permission and had attempted to trade.[234]

There were many such instances, and many such governor-to-governor exchanges. This commerce was of great importance to the northern English colonies, to the French colonists, and even to certain mercantile interests in the British islands, since the French sugar could be reexported at a profit. So the trade continued, despite all efforts, French and British, to suppress it. But it was competitive with the economic interests of the sugar planters in the British islands who depended for their profits on their monopoly to supply England and the British Empire with sugar. There were many complaints,[235] and Governor Lowther himself was accused of

[231] Board of Trade to Colonel Sharpe, Aug. 19, 1714, *C.S.P., Col.*, A.& W.I., 1714-15, No. 31, p. 14. For the Treaty of Whitehall, see Chapter IX.
[232] The Count de Pontchartrain to M. d'Iberville, May 8, 1715, enclosed with Secretary Stanhope to the Board of Trade, May 24, 1715, *C.S.P., Col.* A.& W.I., 1714-15, No. 439 (VI), p. 195.
[233] Governor Lowther to Lieutenant Governor Duquesne, Aug. 22, 1715, *C.S.P., Col.*, A.& W.I., 1714-15, No. 654 (II), p. 326; Duquesne to Lowther, *ibid.*, 1714-15, No. 654 (III), p. 326.
[234] Hamilton to the Marquis de la Varenne, Apr. 19, 1717, *C.S.P., Col.*, A.& W.I., 1716-17, No. 568 (I), p. 302; Verenne to Hamilton, May 6, 1717, *ibid.*, 1716-17, No. 568 (II), p. 302.
[235] See, for example, *C.S.P., Col.*, A.& W.I., 1719-20, pp. 198, 199-201, 353, *et passim*.

being interested in the trade with the French islands, an accusation which led to his recall.[236] Lowther and his supposed partner, George Newport, denied involvement in the trade, but the agents of Barbados in London admitted its existence and justified it on the ground that the governor (Lowther) thought it would be advantageous to the colony and knew of no act of Parliament prohibiting it.[237] The legislature of Barbados, however, prompted by the planters, passed a law laying a prohibitive duty upon the products of foreign islands, since, it was argued, foreign imports lowered the price of sugar and thereby hurt the British producers.[238]

It thus came about that the British colonies were divided within themselves as to the desirability and the permissibility of the trade with the foreign islands. In 1723 the Board of Trade undertook an inquiry among the colonial governors as to its extent and its importance to the economies of the colonies.

All of the governors reported that the trade was active and important. Governor Worsley of Barbados had already reported a trade between his island and Martinique, which, he said, was encouraged by the French government. French ships, he said, visited Barbados under a variety of excuses, and he cited, as an example, a French warship sent to the island by Governor Champigny of Martinique (that is, of the French West Indies). The ship came under pretense of seeing the island, but Worsley seized the ship and found that the commanding officer had an order from Champigny to purchase eight thousand barrels of flour. At the same time, however, he complained of the trade between the "Northern Colonys" and Martinique; "the consequences of this," he wrote, "must be the ruin of this Colony." [239] A few months later he complained again of this "illegal" trade and the part the North Americans had in it. Ships from Barbados went to Martinique, he said, and brought back "cacao, brandys, French silks, gloves, stockings, etc." for which the English gave money, beef, flour, and other provisions, although not so frequently as formerly, "since from the Northern Colonys, they [the French] are supplyed with those commodities, as well as with horses, cattle and timber, which they exchange chiefly [sic] with sugars and molasses." [240] The importation of such French manufactured goods as Worsley mentioned was, indeed, a violation of the British "Staple Act" of 1663. The worst aspect of this trade, in Worsley's eyes, was that "the English themselves have contributed towards the enriching the French

[236] Deposition of William Gordon, Feb. 12, 1720, *C.S.P., Col., A.& W.I.,* 1719–20, No, 558, p. 353; *ibid.,* 1719–20, No. 436 (II), p. 245.

[237] Agents of Barbados to the Board of Trade, Feb. 3, 1720, *C.S.P., Col., A.& W.I.,* 1719–20, No. 543, p. 343.

[238] Board of Trade to the King, Oct. 14, 1717, *C.S.P., Col., A.& W.I.,* 1717–18, No. 148, pp. 67–68.

[239] Worsley to the Board of Trade, Mar. 26, 1723, *C.S.P., Col., A.& W.I.,* 1722–23, No. 486, pp. 234–236.

[240] Worsley to the Board of Trade, Sept. 24, 1723, *C.S.P., Col., A.& W.I.,* 1722–23, No. 715, pp. 344–345.

settlements, by supplying them from the Northern Collonies, with lumber and horses, for which they carry back their suggar and molasses." The French would not be able to carry on the sugar industry, he said, without the lumber and horses from the north and the provisions from Barbados that the English traders carried to them.[241]

Governor John Hart, of the Leeward Islands, made a similar report. He complained of French seizures of British ships in the neighborhood of St. Lucia, with regard to which he had written to Governor Feuquières. But the French governor had replied that matters pertaining to trade fell in the province of the French admiralty, an area in which "he has no cognizance." Hart urged that the British government arrange through diplomatic channels for orders from the French court to the governors of Martinique and Guadelupe not to interfere with "lawfull" trade.[242] A little later, Hart reported to the Board of Trade that the inhabitants of the Leeward Islands carried on "a considerable trade" to Dutch Curaçao and Spanish La Guayra, as well as to French Martinique and Guadelupe. They carried provisions (as well as the horses, mules, and lumber mentioned by other reporters), in return for which they received sugars that were actually transported to England and delivered as products of the British plantations.[243]

St. Lucia, which was claimed by both France and England, seems to have been a center of a quite active Anglo-French trade. According to Governor Hope of the Bermudas, English and French ships met at St. Lucia, where commodities of all sorts were exchanged. Even if it were possible to base a free and legal trade with the French (which he seemed to favor), this clandestine sort of exchange was undesirable, because when enumerated commodities were imported in this manner there was no way of knowing whether they were stolen, bought, or taken from an uninhabited place. This sort of contact, therefore, should be suppressed.[244]

Not all the English colonial governors were not convinced, however, that all trade with the French should be discouraged. Governor Hope, for example, answered the Board of Trade's inquiries by reporting that the Bermuda Islands had no trade with Europe except that with Great Britain. Their best non-English trade was with the foreign plantations in America, whence they brought in sugar, rum, molasses, cacao, indigo, and logwood and brazilwood from the Bay of Honduras. It had always been customary for the governments of the foreign islands to "wink" at this trade, a policy

[241] Worsley's replies to queries from the Board of Trade, Oct. 18, 1724, C.S.P., Col., A.& W.I., 1724-25, No. 382 (V), p. 240.
[242] Hart to the Board of Trade, Apr. 9, 1723, C.S.P., Col., A.& W.I., 1722-23, No. 496, pp. 258-259.
[243] Hart to the Board of Trade, July 10, 1724, C.S.P., Col., A.& W.I., 1724-25, No. 260 (VIII), p. 149.
[244] Hope to the duke of Newcastle, Nov. 25, 1724, C.S.P., Col., A.& W.I., 1724-25, No. 418, pp. 247-275.

strongly supported by the inhabitants, since "if such things were not allowed, they could not subsist." [245]

Governor Francis Nicholson of South Carolina was caught in a paradoxical situation, for, while he was reporting that trade with the French colonies existed, the South Carolina Commons House of Assembly passed a law encouraging trade with the foreign colonies.[246] The governments of other northern continental colonies were in a similar quandary. While the governor of New York and his party reported the existence of illegal New York trade both with the French West Indies and French Canada, the assembly party, composed in part of persons engaged in this trade, favored it. It was the trade with Canada that had inspired the move to keep New York neutral in the War of the Spanish Succession;[247] now, in the decades following the Peace of Utrecht, New York's trade with Canada flourished; the resultant debate over whether it should be discouraged, conformably with royal instructions from England, or encouraged in the interest of the economic prosperity of the colony, became one of the issues in the party decisions in New York's provincial politics.

New England, of course, was the region that was most deeply involved in the trade with the French colonies, whether to Louisbourg to the north, to Canada to the west, or to the French West Indies to the south. Here, again, the English governors were in an anomalous position, bound by their instructions to discourage the intercolonial trade, while recognizing that this foreign commerce was of vital importance to the economic prosperity of their colonies. Jeremiah Dummer, agent for Massachusetts and Connecticut in England, represented, therefore, a general and experience-based set of convictions in New England when he wrote,

Why then should not Great-Britain form the same Judgment, and proceed by the like Measures in regard to her American Dominions, from whence she receives the greatest Advantages? It were no difficult Task to prove that London has risen out of the Plantations, and not out of England. Tis to them we [England] owe our vast Fleets of Merchant Ships, and consequently the Increase of our Seamen, and Improvement of our Navigation. Tis their Tobacco, Sugar, Fish, Oil, Logwood and other Commodities, which have enabled us to support our [English] Trade in Europe, to bring the Ballance of some Countries in our Favour, which would otherwise be against us, and to make the Figure we do at present, and have done for near a Century past, in all Parts of the Commercial World.

The Mother Kingdom must therefore needs rejoice in the Prosperity of every one of her Colonies, because it is her own Prosperity. . . .

[245] Governor John Hope to the Board of Trade, n.d., *C.S.P., Col.*, A.& W.I., 1724–25, No. 13 (I), pp. 12–13.

[246] Salley, ed., *Journals of the Commons House of Assembly of South Carolina* (1692–1726/7); see also, Hope to Newcastle, Nov. 25, 1724, *C.S.P., Col.*, A.& W.I., 1724–25, No. 418, pp. 247–275.

[247] See Chapter IX.

The only Interest of the People [of the colonies] is to thrive and flourish in their Trade, which is the true Interest of the Crown and Nation, because they reap the Profit of it. . . . The Trade of a young Plantation is like a tender Plant, & should be cherish'd with the fondest Care; but if instead of that, it meets with the rough Hand of Oppression, it will soon die.

As this is evident, so is it that whatever injures the Trade of the Plantations, must in Proportion affect Great-Britain, the Source and Center of their Commerce; from whence they have their Manufactures, whither they make their Returns, and where all their Superlucration is lodg'd. The Blow then may strike the Colonies first, but it comes Home at last, and falls heaviest on our selves.[248]

Thus, a thoroughly anomalous international situation existed, relative to this intercolonial commerce. Thomas Crawford, English resident at the French court, reported that the French ministers were "very jealous of their West Indies trade," and intended by all means to enforce the exclusion of the foreigners. The ministers, he wrote, were "far from being well satisfied with their own Governors, because they connive too much at the smuggling trade." [249] Actually, the French governors were seizing British ships, in accord with their instructions, while they "winked," as Governor Worsley put it, at the English trade, "especially from our Northern Colonys." The English governors, especially those in the northern continental colonies, stood in a similar anomalous position, although those in the British West Indies had a much stronger popular and legislative support in their efforts to discourage the trade than did those in the north. The West Indies opponents were also supported by a strong mercantile lobby in England. Thus, for example, the "Merchants trading to Jamaica" presented to the Board of Trade, in May of 1724, a memorial in answer to the Board's inquiries, strongly opposing the trade. "There having been lately French sugars introduced into Jamaica and thence into Great Britain," they said, "the importation thereof is not only contrary to the intent of our Act of Navigation, but also tends to the great encouragement of the French Colonys, and to the prejudice of our own." [250]

The Board of Trade recognized the importance of the intercolonial trade, and it went so far, in 1724, in a report to the King, as to "submit to your Majesty's great wisdom whether it may not be advisable to connive at this trade and carry the French sugars for them to foreign markets rather than let them be the carriers themselves; and so much the rather by this trade the Northern Colonies upon the Continent are probably enabled to pay the ballance which they yearly owe to Great Britain, not having com-

---

[248] Jeremiah Dummer, A Defense of the New-England Charters, 38–40.
[249] Thomas Crawford to Charles Delafaye, Aug. 23, 1723, C.S.P., Col., A.& W.I., 1722–23, No. 189 (I), pp. 332–333.
[250] British Merchants trading to Jamaica and the Board of Trade, May 31, 1724, C.S.P., Col., A.& W.I., 1724–25, No. 195, p. 105.

modities of their own produce to exchange against those they receive from us." [251]

One of the considerations invoked in 1727 by the Duke of Montagu in his plea for an Anglo-French agreement providing for the division of the island of St. Lucia between him and the French Marshal d'Estrées was the prospect that the clandestine trade at St. Lucia would be suppressed by effective occupation of the island.[252]

After the Anglo-French agreement of 1730 to leave St. Lucia, Dominica, and St. Vincent neutral, these islands continued to be bases of exchange in the clandestine trade, and the Anglo-French governor-to-governor correspondence was in large part devoted to the efforts to control this "smuggling." But the seizures of ships brought protests, and the English governors' protests against French seizures became increasingly bitter. President Dottin of the Barbados Council, as acting governor of Barbados, in 1736 complained to the Marquis de Champigny that English ships were seized and condemned without proof; "many prizes made by French guard sloops are owing not so much to illegal trading as to the unjustifiable methods those guard sloops take in chasing vessels which have no intention of going to those [French] islands, and carrying them into Martinique." [253]

As relations between France and England cooled, after 1731, the relations between British and French governors in America also cooled. More and more seizures took place; the letters of protest took on more and more of an exasperated, acidulous tone.

Parallel to the English colonial trade with the Spanish and French colonies there was a continuous development, in the decades following the Peace of Utrecht, of the same sort of trade with the Dutch and Danish colonies in the Caribbean area, with the usually consequent seizures of ships and an international correspondence of protest between colonial governors. Since the British and the Dutch were allies, however, and since Dutch policy with regard to intercolonial commerce closely approached a complete freedom of trade, the problems raised by the Dutch trade were less weighty and pressing than those which sprang with Anglo-French or Anglo-Spanish commerce.

[251] Board of Trade to the King, July 24, 1724, C.S.P., Col., A.& W.I., 1724–25, No. 291 (I), p. 175.
[252] Montagu to [Newcastle?] [May, 1727?], C.S.P., Col., A.& W.I., 1726–27, No. 574, pp. 294–295; Montagu to the King, ibid., 1726–27, No. 574 (II), p. 295.
[253] President Dottin to the marquis de Champigny, Jan. 28, 1736, C.S.P., Col., A.& W.I., 1735–36, No. 290 (II), pp. 190–191.

One of the earliest problems arising from the trade of British colonies with the Dutch colonies had to do with the importation of Negro slaves. Thus, Governor Walter Hamilton of Barbados reported to the Board of Trade in 1717 that the Dutch were importing slaves from Africa and transferring them to British vessels at St. Eustatius, whence they were delivered to the English colonies. Hamilton believed this trade to be illegal, since, he said, the King of England was deprived of his duty on slaves while the Dutch were taking the sugar given in payment for the slaves by the English, and were carrying it to foreign markets.[254] This trade infringed upon the privileges of the Royal African Company, also. The company protested, but the attorney general, at the request of the Board of Trade, ruled that there was no law prohibiting the importation of Negroes into the British colonies from the Dutch West Indies.[255] A little later, Lieutenant Governor Benjamin Bennett of Bermuda reported that the Dutch were "interloping" in the free-for-all trade at St. Lucia, "the place for tradeing [sic] on such occasions with the interloper." [256]

This trade with the Dutch resulted in the importation into the British colonies of Dutch manufactured goods, which was a violation of the Staple Act of 1663, and in the direct exportation of sugar, one of the enumerated articles, which was a violation of the "enumerated articles" clause of the English Navigation Act of 1660. English ships which went to St. Eustatius or Curacao for trade were, apparently, not prosecuted. Dutch ships, however, which visited the British colonies were seized. Thus, for example, Governor Mathew, of the Leeward Islands, in 1736 caused to be seized the Dutch ship *Two Sisters* and other Dutch ships thought to be trading with the British colonies. The Council of St. Eustatius wrote to him, asking for an explanation of the seizures, to which Governor Mathew replied that he was instructed to prevent illegal trade and that to prevent "chicane" by false passports he would cause to be examined every vessel that appeared in the area of the Leeward Islands.[257]

This Dutch trade, and a similar one with the Danes at St. Thomas, continued through the War of Jenkins' Ear and the War of the Austrian Succession. These trades, especially as they were carried on as trades of neutrals during the Seven Years War, would eventually come to trouble

[254] Hamilton to the Board of Trade, May 15, 1717, C.S.P., Col., A.& W.I., 1716–17, No. 568, pp. 301–302.
[255] Carkesse to Popple, Sept. 11, 1719, C.S.P., Col., A.&W.I., 1719–20, No. 383, p. 221.
[256] "News from Barbadoes, Antiqua, and Jamaica" (n.d.) enclosed with Bennett to the Board of Trade, Apr. 25, 1721, C.S.P., Col., A.& W.I., 1720–21, No. 463 (III), p. 294.
[257] Papers relating to complaint, Feb. 11/22, 1736/37 from an envoy extraordinary from the States-General of the Netherlands to the Duke of Newcastle, regarding seizure of Dutch ships by Governor Mathew, C.S.P., Col., A.& W.I., 1737, No. 93, 93(III) and 93(IV), p. 46.

the diplomatic relations between England and Holland and Denmark and contribute to the pronouncement, by England, of the famous "Rule of the War of 1756" and the "Doctrine of Continuous Voyage." [258]

In the years of armed peace that followed the Peace of Aix-la-Chapelle, the problem of intercolonial trade and its place in the international history of the English colonies in America reappeared with renewed insistence and significance for the British empire as a whole. As early as 1750 Governor Trelawney of Jamaica was complaining of the "clandestine trade carried on between the English northern colonies and the French Sugar islands." [259] Representatives of English merchants in the trade of the British West Indies presented to the Board of Trade a memorial asking for an act of Parliament that would totally prohibit the trade of the northern colonies with the foreign islands. The split between the economic interests of the West Indian planters and those of the northern colonies over this trade with foreign colonies became clear again, as it had in the arguments over the Molasses Act of 1733, when the colonial agents of the northern provinces appeared before the Board to oppose the memorial.[260] A little later, the lieutenant governor, council, and assembly of Antigua also presented a memorial against the trade, in which were included the French, the Dutch, and the Danes.[261] The lieutenant governor, council, and assembly of St. Christopher did the same.[262] The Board was troubled by the debate, but no action was taken at that time, either by the Board of Trade or Parliament.

As war between France and England approached in 1755, the British government and the colonial governors recognized the danger to British interests inherent in the trade of the British northern colonies, especially the trade in provisions, with the French colonies. [263] Governor Dinwiddie of Virginia complained in 1755 that Cape Breton and Canada were provisioned by Angloamerican traders, who took in return for provisions rum, sugar, and molasses from the French West Indies. He recommended that flour, beef, pork, peas, and bread be "enumerated" and that shippers be required to post bonds to land such provisions in some part of the British

[258] See Chapters XVIII and XIX.
[259] Journals, Board of Trade, 1750–53, 49.
[260] Journals, Board of Trade, 1750–53, 128, 138.
[261] Journals, Board of Trade, 1750–53, 168.
[262] Journals, Board of Trade, 1750–53, 155.
[263] For accounts of the wartime trade between the British American colonies and those of France and of the efforts of the British and colonial governments to suppress it, see Pares, War and Trade in the West Indies, Chapter IX, and Beer, British Colonial Policy, 1754–65, Chapters VI and VII.

empire.[264] Other governors recognized the "pernicious" character of this trade with the enemy, and the legislatures of several of the colonies enacted legislation intended to stop it. But the impossibility of achieving any unified action and enforcement among the colonies made effective restriction next to impossible. In the interest of providing a uniform law controlling the trade, Parliament did pass, in 1757 at the urging of the Board of Trade, a law that required that "all kinds of victual" shipped out of the colonies be landed in British territory, and bonds were required by shippers to guarantee the faithful observance of the law.[265]

This law, which, in effect, placed provisions on the list of enumerated articles, would have prevented trade in provisions with all other countries. It was interpreted loosely, however, by the Americans and even by some British officials. There were some exceptional cases, also. Lieutenant-Governor James De Lancey of New York wrote the Board of Trade in June, 1757, supporting a memorial of William Walton asking for permission to continue to send provisions to St. Augustine, for which he had a contract with the Spanish governor. Since Spain was a neutral, and since it was England's policy to keep it that way, the matter was referred to Secretary of State William Pitt for decision. Pitt, to please Spain, then issued an order-in-council authorizing the inhabitants of New York, "during his Majesty's pleasure, to export to St. Augustine such quantity of corn, etc., as may be necessary for the subsistence of the Spanish garrison there only." [266]

De Lancey, himself, interpreted the law rather loosely, in the interest of his constituents, holding it to mean that it did not apply to all neutral ports but only "such neutral Ports or Settlements from whence the enemy have actually drawn supplies or from whence they might be obtained." [267]

As pressures upon direct trade with the enemy mounted, the traders of the northern colonies turned more and more to trade through intermediary neutral ports, such as Spanish Monte Cristi, on the north coast of Santo Domingo or Dutch St. Eustatius or Danish St. Thomas. At such neutral ports the cargoes of the British ships would be transferred to French ships, and the trade went merrily on.[268]

The British government itself was in a quandary, for since Spain, Holland, and Denmark were all neutrals, and since England was desperately endeavoring to keep them so, the problem was especially difficult to handle in such a way as not to offend these states. Secretary of State Pitt concentrated upon eradicating the direct trade, and issued a strong circular letter

[264] Dinwiddie to Sir Thomas Robinson, Jan. 20, 1755, *Official Records of Robert Dinwiddie (Collections of the Virginia Historical Society*, n.s., III), 472–473; *Journals, Board of Trade 1754–58*, 131.
[265] Pares, *War and Trade in the West Indies*, 437–438.
[266] *Journals, Board of Trade, 1757*, 225, 331, 333, 421.
[267] James D. Lancey to the Board of Trade, June 3, 1757, N.Y.C.D., VII, 225.
[268] Pares, *War and Trade in the West Indies*, Chapter IX.

of instructions to the colonial governors on August 23, 1760, enjoining them to suppress it. Since, he said, British subjects in North America were trading with the French colonies in the West Indies, at Mobile, and in the Mississippi area, the governors must ascertain the facts and prosecute the offenders in this trade with the enemy.[269]

The governors of the northern colonies were, of course, bound to do their best to enforce these instructions. But a number of the governors demurred, nonetheless. They pointed out the danger to both the American and the English economies inherent in this policy of suppression, and they made positive suggestions as to how this aspect of the international relations of the colonies should be handled.

Governor Horatio Sharpe, of Maryland, for example, had already privately expressed to his brother, William Sharpe, in England, his opinions on the subject in July, 1760, before Pitt's circular was issued. While he criticized the notorious practice of Governor Denny of Pennsylvania in "selling" so many "flag-of-truce" commissions to Philadelphia merchants for the prosecution of the provision trade, he said,

"I do not entertain so ill an opinion of those who engaged in that trade as you seem to do, for I cannot help thinking that it was for the Interest of Great Britain in general since the Profits to those that carried it on amounted to much more than the French Planters got for their Sugar, which were mostly purchased with manufactures brought to N. America from Great Britain & being sent to Europe in English Bottoms were sold at Leghorn, Geneva, Amsterdam, & other foreign Ports as I have been told for Cash which was remitted from those Places to G. Britain to purchase more Goods there for the Same Trade, & the Consumption of N. America." [270]

From this plea for a greater freedom of trade for the American colonies, even in wartime, Sharpe went on to point out that the self-interest of the British "sugar islands" in desperately trying to maintain a monopoly of the sugar trade of the empire, was impoverishing both the northern colonies and England by forcing an increase in the price of sugar while forcing down the prices received by the northern producers for lumber and other products sold to the British islands. He deprecated the importance of the provision trade with Hispaniola, since, as he believed, the act of Parliament (the Flour Act of 1757) prohibiting the export of flour to any neutral ports had effectively "put an End to the greatest Branch of Business which had been before carried on here, I mean in the Northern Colonies[;] the merchants were at a loss how to employ their Vessels & themselves till they fell into the Trade you condemn." [271]

[269] Pitt to the British colonial governors in North America and the West Indies, Aug. 23, 1760, Correspondence of William Pitt, ed., Kimball, I, 320–321.
[270] Governor Sharpe to William Sharpe, July 8, 1760, in Browne, et al., eds., Archives of Maryland, IX, 442.
[271] Governor Sharpe to William Sharpe, July 8, 1760, in Browne et al., eds., Archives of Maryland, IX, 442.

James Hamilton, who succeeded Denny as governor of Pennsylvania, replied to Pitt's circular by blaming the Pennsylvania trade with the French islands upon his predecessor. But the trade was difficult to stop, he reported; "the most eminent Lawyers of this place [Philadelphia]" and the vice-admiralty court were in favor of it, "as there is not any Act of Parliament that immediately relates to, or prohibits this kind of Commerce. . . ." [272]

Similarly, Lieutenant Governor Cadwallader Colden of New York, while assuring Pitt that the instructions of August 23, 1760, would be carried out, made bold, nevertheless, to inform the prime minister, with evident approval "what has been said in excuse":

It is aver'd that this trade has been highly advantageous to Great Britain, by the great quantities of British Manufactures, in value far exceeding the value of the Provisions, & by the large returns in Sugars; & some pretend they can demonstrate this against the force of all contradiction.[273]

Colden recognized the importance of the trade with foreign colonies to the economies of the British colonies and he showed how the prosperity of the empire in this matter was bound up with the generally prevalent and growing idea of freedom of commerce as against the restrictions imposed by the mother country. Further, he recognized the conflict between the economic interests of the West Indies and those of the continental colonies, and he took it upon himself, as the official representative of a colony, to point out to the British ministry that the economic interest of Britain itself was bound up with a greater freedom of trade for the northern colonies. Finally, he suggested, as he and other colonial governors were doing in other areas, policies and procedures that might be followed by the mother country in its diplomatic relations relative to America with other countries in Europe. His suggestions reached the British ministry at a time when it was trying desperately to keep Spain neutral, vis-à-vis Britain's war with France. While there was little likelihood that Spain might have made any such treaty as Colden suggested, given the mood of the Spanish court at that time, the fact that he felt free to make it throws a good deal of light upon the position of colonial governors in the total international outlook of the British empire.

It is clear that much of the international policy of Britain relative to America was actually made in America. The colonial governor was a sort of advance diplomatic agent for the empire, and it was his reports and his recommendations relative to specific intercolonial situations that furnished

[272] Governor James Hamilton to William Pitt, Nov. 1, 1760, *Correspondence of William Pitt*, ed., Kimball, II, 351–355.
[273] Colden to Pitt, Oct. 27, 1760, *Colden Letter Books*, I (*Collections of the New York Historical Society*, 1876, IX), 26–28. See Chapter XX.

the basic materials for British correspondence with other powers. There were, of course, instances such as the return of Cape Breton to France by the Treaty of Aix-la-Chapelle, of sacrifice of colonial interests and recommendations to the European interests of the empire, but such instances were rare; usually the British ministry followed the prompting of the colonial governors.

The two basic international interests of the British colonies, as expressed by the colonial governors in their capacity as representatives of the will of the people of their colonies, were in imperialistic westward expansion and freedom of international commerce. Because these interests frequently ran counter to the policies of the imperial government, the colonial governors often found themselves in an anomalous position. The colonists had great enthusiasm for expansion, and the steady growth of their populations pushed them steadily westward into unoccupied territories, even when such movement conflicted with the treaties or other international agreements of the British government. The colonial governors, even when instructed to discourage the occupation of Indian or French-claimed lands, became some of the most vociferous colonial promoters of imperial expansion. In the matter of freedom of trade, the governor often stood in a Janus-like position between the interests of the colony he governed and those of the mother country. Where the international trade of the colonies conflicted with the imperial policy of monopoly in colonial commerce, the governor acted in a double capacity. He became a diplomatic agent for his colony *vis-à-vis* the Spanish, Dutch, French and Danish colonies with which it traded and also a quasi-diplomatic agent for his colony *vis-à-vis* the mother country, defending its economic interests while attempting to conciliate those of the imperial government.

CHAPTER XIV

The "Concert of Europe" and the Colonial Problem, 1715-29

1. The Quadruple Alliance and the Pacification of Europe

THE PEACE OF UTRECHT had attempted to reestablish—or preserve—the balance of power in Europe against the threat of overweighting, either on the side of a union of France and Spain and their emperors in the person of Philip of Anjou, the grandson of Louis XIV, or on the side of a union of the Holy Roman Empire with Spain in the person of Charles VI of Austria.

In its provisions with regard to America, the peace had given England the lion's share of the territory that changed hands, as well as a prospectively profitable special participation in the commerce of the Spanish empire, whether by way of Cadiz and the galleons or under the provision of the *asiento*. The Peace of Utrecht had also sought to preserve the balance of colonial power in America, since the balance in Europe was thought to depend, in large measure, upon the balance of colonial empires.[1]

But the pacification of Europe was not completed at Utrecht. Neither was the settlement of the international issues in America. Nor could these two aspects of the international situation after Utrecht be really separated, either.

In Europe, the Holy Roman Emperor, who was also king of Austria, did not consider his title to the formerly Spanish Netherlands (Belgium) sufficiently secure. At the same time, he was determined to extend his ownership and authority over as many as possible of the small principalities and kingdoms of Italy. The peace, as confirmed in the Treaty of Rastadt of March 7, 1714, between France and Austria, had left Austria in possession of Milan, Sardinia, Naples, Mantua, and the former Spanish ports in Tuscany; Sicily was given to Savoy, newly recognized as a kingdom. But

[1] See Chapter X.

Austria was not yet satisfied, and Charles VI of Austria refused to sign the treaty of peace, for this and other reasons. Charles then went on to expand his holdings in Italy and, especially, to acquire Sicily, by a variety of methods.

Spain, on the other hand, found itself completely excluded from Italy, and Spain's foreign policy was now concentrated on recovering Spain's territories and powers in that peninsula. This concentration of interest was sharply intensified by the marriage, in 1714, of Elizabeth Farnese, the only heiress of the Duke of Parma, to Philip V of Spain (she was his second wife). Elizabeth, indeed "The Termagant of Spain," devoted much of her very active life to promoting Spanish interests in Italy and, in particular, to seating her eldest son, Carlos, upon the ducal thrones of Parma and Tuscany, which Spain also claimed, and even, as eventually happened, upon the royal throne of Naples, or the Kingdom of the Two Sicilies.

As for England and France, these two former antagonists in the great war of the Spanish Succession drew together. Because of internal politics and dynastic problems as well as objectives of broader national interest, France, under the leadership of the regent, the Duc d'Orléans, and England, whose director of foreign relations was the Earl of Stanhope, in August, 1716, agreed to an alliance for the maintenance of the balance of power in Europe. The Netherlands then acceded to this agreement, to form what became known as the Triple Alliance. Austria acceded to the alliance and the proposed terms for a general peace laid down in the treaty, on August 2, 1718, thereby making the alliance quadruple; and the King of Sardinia acceded on November 8, to make it actually quintuple. But Spain refused to accept the cessions demanded of it by the terms of the proposed settlement.[2] Under the aggressive leadership of Cardinal Giulio Alberoni, an Italian prelate who had accompanied Queen Elizabeth Farnese to Spain, that country reopened its war with Austria and seized the island of Sardinia in the summer of 1717. The members of the Quadruple Alliance attempted to mediate between Austria and Spain for the avoidance of a new general conflict, but Spain refused to accept the proffered mediation, and in 1718 sent a naval expedition to seize Sicily. At this point, the allies decided to back their good offices with force, and

[2] The Quadruple Alliance, signed originally by Holland, England, and France on August 2, 1718, included three parts. The first was a proposed treaty between Spain and Austria by which the Emperor conceded to Don Carlos the succession to the duchies of Parma, Placentia, and Tuscany, while Spain conceded to the Emperor Sicily and the former Spanish Netherlands (Belgium). The second was a project for a treaty between the Emperor and King Victor-Amadeus, King of Sicily and Duke of Savoy (soon to be recognized as King of Sardinia) for the exchange of the island of Sardinia for Sicily. The third was a mediation convention among the four signatories which, beyond the agreement to arrange a peace between Spain and Austria, was also, in fact, an agreement to force Spain and Savoy to cede Sicily to the Emperor (Chalmers, ed., *Treaties*, I, 257–310).

England sent Admiral George Byng with a fleet to the Mediterranean to stop the Spaniards, which he did by destroying the Spanish fleet off Cape Passaro in Sicily and by assisting the Austrians in driving the Spanish army from that island. Meanwhile, a French army invaded Spain from the north.

In the face of these and other difficulties, Philip and Elizabeth had to give in and were forced to accede to the demand of the allies that Alberoni be dismissed. Finally, by the Treaties of Madrid of 1720, Spain agreed to the Anglo-French scheme for the settlement of the Italian question and acceded to the Quadruple Alliance on February 17, 1720.

By the terms of the general treaty, details of the general peace settlement were left to be arranged at a congress of all the signatories (this congress was eventually held at Cambrai, in France). In the articles covering the Spanish accession, Spain agreed to cede to the Emperor the island of Sardinia and to abrogate all Spain's claims to that kingdom. In the name of the European balance of power, Philip V renounced anew any and all claims that he might have upon the throne of France. Charles VI made a similar renunciation of any claim to the throne of Spain or its American empire and recognized Philip V as the legitimate King of Spain. Philip also abrogated all his claims to territories or places in Italy and Sicily possessed by the Emperor; Charles, in his turn, recognized the sons of Elizabeth Farnese, the Queen of Spain, as the legitimate heirs to the ducal thrones of Tuscany, Parma, and Placentia.

By the annexes to this treaty of accession [3] the signatories agreed upon conditions for the mutual and joint maintenance of the peace. They jointly agreed to give no countenance, encouragement, or refuge to the Stuart pretenders to the British throne; they jointly agreed to restrict the activities of corsairs upon the commerce of all the allies; they also agreed to protect each other's territories from invasion. Although the colonies were not specifically mentioned, presumably these guarantees applied to territories in America and other colonial areas as well as Europe. Provision was made for the accession of other powers to the collective agreement for peace in the western world, Portugal in particular.

In general, this treaty, with its annexes, embodying Spain's accession to the Quadruple Alliance and making peace between Spain and the Emperor, finally completed the pacification of Western Europe, the foundations of which had been laid at Utrecht in 1713. In it was included, at least indirectly, the pacification of the colonies of the signatory powers in America.

The apparent peace settlement achieved by the accession of Spain to the Quadruple Alliance was followed by a drawing together of Spain, France, and England. France signed a treaty of alliance with Spain on March 27, 1721; England signed with Spain a "private" treaty of peace and friendship

---

[3] Cantillo, ed., *Tratados*, 178–187. Actually, the basis of the settlement was the text of the Triple Alliance of August 2, 1718.

on June 13, 1721; the three of them signed a "treaty of defensive alliance" on the same day.

The Franco-Spanish treaty of alliance [4] provided for the mutual guarantee of the existing possessions of France and Spain "in whatever part of the world they may be situated in"; it particularly guaranteed the possessions of the Duke of Parma. It also provided most-favored-nation treatment for the citizens of France in Spain and a restoration to France of all the commercial and other privileges granted to the citizens of France by former treaties, which would include trade with Spanish America by way of Cadiz, and it provided for the restoration to Spain of Fuenterrabia and San Sebastián in Spain and of Pensacola, in Florida, seized by France in the hostilities of 1718–19. The King of France also promised to assist His Catholic Majesty in persuading England to return Gibraltar to Spain and to support Spain in its efforts to seat one of the sons of Elizabeth Farnese on the ducal thrones of Parma and Tuscany, together with those of Castro and Ronciglione, at that time held by the Pope. Finally, it was agreed that England would be invited to join in, and ratify, this alliance.

The importance of American territory in the international policies of France is revealed in the negotiation that preceded this treaty. The Marquis de Maulevrier, French ambassador to Spain, was instructed,[5] in the first place, to reestablish a "close union" with Spain through an accent upon the close family relationships existing between the two thrones. He was to press the matter of an extension of commercial privileges to the French merchants in Spain, and he was to demand something for France roughly equivalent to the *asiento,* now in the hands of the English, which France had enjoyed during the War of the Spanish Succession. He was to remind Philip V and his court that France, in its war to place Philip on the throne of Spain, had lost, among other territories, Hudson Bay, Acadia, Newfoundland, and the French part of St. Christopher. Surely the debt of Spain to France was incalculably great; surely Philip would wish to compensate France by placing its citizens in a position to benefit from the profits of Spanish commerce with the Spanish colonies. As for the cession of Pensacola, Maulevrier was to insist upon the retention of this place by France. Since it was so far to the west of St. Augustine, it was argued, it could be of no utility to Spain. For France, on the other hand, this port was and would be of immense importance, for the use that France might make of it in order to prevent the English from South Carolina from encroaching further upon Louisiana and from using it as a base for troubling the commerce of Louisiana. Let Spain cede Pensacola to France in partial payment of the vast sums Spain owed France on account of the late war!

[4] Cantillo, ed., *Tratados,* 194–198.
[5] *Recueil des Insts. . . . ,* XII, *Espagne,* II, 364–379.

If he was successful in this argument, Maulevrier was to set the eastern limits of the territory surrounding Pensacola at the Apalachicola Bay and River. Maulevrier was also to ask Spain, again as compensation for France's losses by the Peace of Utrecht, for the Spanish portion of the island of Santo Domingo.

Philip refused to countenance any cession of land in America; he insisted upon the return of Pensacola; Santo Domingo was not mentioned in the treaty. He did consent to name commissioners to meet with French commissioners relative to commercial privileges. It was agreed that Spain would demand the restoration of the territories mentioned in the treaty at the Congress of Cambrai, and that France would restore them, as though it had not been previously arranged!

In the negotiations of 1718 that had eventually led to the accession of Spain to the Quadruple Alliance, the Regent of France, negotiating for England, had been authorized to offer Spain Gibraltar as a price for its accession. Philip V refused the offer at that time, but when in 1720 he felt compelled to accede, he reminded England of the offer. Now, however, George I, realizing the certainty of opposition in Parliament, refused to make the offer again. William Stanhope, the British negotiator, did suggest that the Parliament might be appeased by the cession of Florida or the Spanish part of the island of Santo Domingo to England in return for Gibraltar, but it was now Philip who refused, saying he would not surrender any part of his Amercian possessions. Indeed, when Stanhope sought to reopen the discussions, King Philip and his ministers took a much firmer stand than before, and presented Stanhope with an ultimatum to the effect that if Gibraltar were not returned the *asiento* would be cancelled.

This stiffening of the Spanish attitude was due, in large part, to French encouragement. For France, despite the good will between France and England represented by the Anglo-French alliance, was now the greatest single non-Spanish participant in the commerce of Spanish America through Cadiz, while England was in a position to bypass the Cadiz trade, more or less fraudulently, under the privileges provided by the *asiento*. It was a matter of vital importance to France to build up its own position in the Cadiz trade while weakening the English position in the direct trade with Spanish America and discouraging the possibility that England might acquire further territories in America at Spain's expense.

By now (1720), the continued suspension of English trade with Spanish America under the *asiento* because of the war just ended had, indeed, tempted the English government to consider using Gibraltar as the price for a restitution of England's commercial privileges in America. Thus the English ministry again considered a proposal that Spain be offered an exchange of Gibraltar for a liberal revision of the situation in America. Spain was to abandon all claim to a share of the Newfoundland fisheries and was to recognize England's right to cut logwood at Campeche; if Spain agreed to these conditions and reopened the English commerce in its colonies, England would give Gibraltar back to Spain.[6] The bursting of the South Sea Bubble late in 1720, however, prevented this proposal from being presented to Spain.

By the terms of the "private treaty of peace and friendship" signed by Spain and England on June 13, 1721,[7] all former treaties between the two countries were reinstated, including the Treaty of the *Asiento* of 1716. The King of Spain promised promptly to notify the Council of the Indies of the renewal of the latter treaty and to send orders to his American governors and officials to the effect that no impediment be placed in the way of the freedom of movement of the slave ships of the South Seas Company. At the same time, King George I of England promised to send corresponding orders to his own governors and officials in America for the execution of the present and former treaties, particularly the provisions of Articles 8, 9, and 15 of the Anglo-Spanish Treaty of Utrecht,[8] which had provided for freedom of commerce between the subjects of the two countries in Europe, had left the commerce of the Spanish Indies in general as it had been conducted in the time of Carlos II, and had promised, on the part of Spain, that no special privileges in the American trade would be granted to France. Article 8 of that treaty had promised that the *asiento* for the slave trade to the Spanish colonies, formerly held by France, should be granted to an English company (which had been done); it also had provided that no Spanish territory in America would ever be transferred to France or the French. By the new treaty England again promised forever to guarantee the territorial integrity of Spain's empire in America as it existed in the time of Carlos II. By Article 9 all Englishmen were to enjoy each and every privilege granted by Spain to Frenchmen.

The Anglo-Spanish treaty of peace of 1721 thus reiterated the above-mentioned articles 8, 9, and 15 of the Anglo-Spanish Treaty of Utrecht of 1713, with specific mention of the English guarantee of Spanish territories in America and the right of the Spanish Basques to fish at Newfoundland. By Article 3 of the Treaty of 1721 England promised to send orders to its colonial governors and officials to return Spanish goods, ships, and properties seized during the war; England agreed to return, also, all the ships, crews, and effects of the Spanish fleet taken by Admiral Byng off Sicily in August of 1718.

This treaty effectively quieted all outstanding disputes between England and Spain in America as well as in Europe; but it was agreed not to

[6] Conn, *Gibraltar in British Diplomacy in the Eighteenth Century*, 55–56.
[7] Cantillo, ed., *Tratados*, 198–201.
[8] Cantillo, ed., *Tratados*, 75–86. See also Chapter X.

publish it until the coming Congress of Cambrai. It was also agreed, separately, that this treaty would not have any validity unless the King of England should write a letter to His Catholic Majesty promising to place the question of the restitution of Gibraltar before Parliament. This provision was never carried out, but the treaty was considered by the English to be in effect, nevertheless.

The text of the Anglo-French-Spanish treaty of alliance, also signed on June 13, 1721, was practically identical with that of the Franco-Spanish alliance signed on March 27. A new article was substituted for Article 6 of the Franco-Spanish alliance, however, to the effect that all commercial privileges extended to French or English subjects by Philip V's predecessors would be restored to the subjects of those two nations.

2. The Congress of Cambrai

With the formation of the Anglo-French-Spanish alliance of 1721 and the agreements to support each other at Cambrai, the three signatories were ready to enter the congress provided for by the Treaty of the Quadruple Alliance.[9] The purpose of this congress, as originally planned, was the negotiation of a thoroughgoing peace between Spain and the Empire and between the kingdom of Sardinia, or Savoy, and the Empire. At the congress, England, France, and the United Netherlands were to act as mediators.

This congress was eventually held, but it did not actually begin its deliberations until 1724, largely because England vacillated between supporting the interests of the Emperor and supporting the claims of Elizabeth Farnese and her son, Don Carlos, with regard to the Italian affairs. When it did meet, the congress spent most of its time arguing over protocol.

Spain's chief interest in the Congress of Cambrai centered about the problem of gaining the cooperation or at least the acquiescence of the Emperor in the seating of Don Carlos upon the ducal thrones of Parma and Tuscany, and much of the discussion at the congress revolved about this and other Italian problems. But the inability of Spain and Austria to compromise their difficulties gave England an opportunity to exploit the occasion to try to get the Emperor to abolish the Ostend Company.

The Ostend Company, with its headquarters at Ostend, in the Austrian Netherlands (the former Spanish Netherlands, now Belgium, acquired by Austria in the Peace of Utrecht), had been granted a charter by the Emperor in 1723. Actually founded by a group of English capitalists as a rival of the English East India Company, the Ostend Company was

[9] Chalmers, ed., *Treaties*, I, 257–310.

originally created for the purpose of trading with the Far East. English observers reported that it was underselling the English in the European market for Indian and Chinese goods and that East India goods brought by this company to Ostend were smuggled into England. Of even greater importance to England was the not-unjustified fear that the Ostend Company would send a colony of Flemings to the West Indies, enter into the Newfoundland fisheries, and seize upon a share of the woolens trade to Portugal and its American colonies, at that time practically an English monopoly.[10] The commerce of Holland would be similarly affected, and "The Commerce and Riches of one of the Bulwarks of the Protestant Interest would be thereby transferred to augment the strength of a *Roman Catholic* State." [11] The interests of Holland, with its own East India trade, were recognized as being identical with those of England. As for Britain, "While Britain preserves her Trade free from Encroachments, her Independency on the rest of *Europe* is indisputable: But should her Ministry, or any private considerations, or through . . . Reasons of State, permit or connive at any Establishments amongst her neighbours, which may interfere with, or diminish her own commerce, she may from that Moment conclude herself lost." [12]

It was argued by one commentator that the Ostend Company, if allowed to prosper, might ruin the economic life of England or Holland, which were inseparably bound together, and would thereby upset the balance of power and leave the preponderance of international power vested in Austria. Were Holland to fall from its commercial position, it would fatally affect England. Were England to fall,

Our Colonies on the Continent of *America*, would undoubtedly set up for *Free* and *Independent States*; and would soon flourish with all sorts of Manufactures (they now have from us) by means of the Workmen fled to them; and, by degrees, would bring our *Caribee Islands* to shake off their Subjection to us; and, by inter-trafficking with one another, entirely deprive *Great Britain* of those profitable returns she now annually receives from those Islands; and which, by being re-exported to *Holland*, enable the *Dutch* to trade advantageously with other Nations; and, consequently, the want of the Products of those Islands, would very sensibly affect their Commerce to other Parts of Europe.[13]

Here, indeed, may well have been the ideological key to most of England's international policy concerning America in the eighteenth century.

[10] Forman, *Mr. Forman's Letter to the Right Honourable William Pulteney, Esq., Shewing how Pernicious, the Imperial Company of Commerce and Navigation, lately established in the Austrian Netherlands, is likely to prove to Great Britain, as well as to Holland.*
[11] Forman, *Mr. Forman's Letter,* 39.
[12] Forman, *Mr. Forman's Letter,* 50.
[13] *The Importance of the Ostend Company Considered,* 27–28.

In any case, it was upon the basis of some such fears as these that England insisted upon bringing the matter of the existence of the Ostend Company into the Congress of Cambrai, with the support of Holland and France.[14]

The support even of Spain was sought in this protest, and as late as the spring of 1724 Spain mildly voiced its opposition to the existence of the company, which seemed to threaten Spain's own overseas commercial arrangements, on the ground that since all Spanish subjects except the Castilians—which would include the Belgians—were prohibited from sharing in Spain's overseas trade before the Low Countries were ceded to Austria, and since the treaties of Utrecht and Baden envisaged a maintenance of the *status quo* as of the time of Carlos II of Spain, the creation of the Ostend Company, as a change in the commercial *status quo* of that former time, was a violation of those treaties and therefore a violation of international law! [15]

Despite all these protests against the existence of the Ostend Company, however, the Emperor remained unmoved, and the congress made no headway in this matter, or in any other.

In the meantime, in the mood of good will, following the formation of the Franco-Spanish Alliance of 1721, France and Spain had made arrangements in 1721 for the marriage of Mlle. de Montpensier, daughter of the French regent, the Duc d'Orléans, to the Crown Prince of Spain, and of the Infanta Maria-Anna Victoria, daughter of Philip V (she was six years old), to Louis XV (who was twelve). The marriage of Don Louis to Mlle. de Montpensier was solemnized on January 22, 1722; but the little Infanta, after having gone to France in the expectation that she would be educated there against the day when she would marry the young king, because of a sudden shift in French policy, was abruptly returned to Spain in 1725, to the great humiliation of the Spanish monarchs.[16]

It was the extreme fury of the Spanish rulers over the insult to the Infanta by France, coupled with Spanish impatience over the dalliance and delay of the Congress of Cambrai, that prompted them to turn away from France, drop all efforts to make peace at the congress, and open a direct negotiation with the Emperor, Charles VI of Austria, for a settlement of the disputes between Spain and the Empire. The Spanish representatives at the Congress of Cambrai announced that they would no longer accept the mediation of France, and those of England refused to act alone. The result was that the representatives of all the powers were recalled, and the congress dissolved.

---

[14] Newcastle to Horace Walpole, May 7, 1724, in Legg, ed., *Brit. Dip. Insts.*, 1689–1789, IV, *France, 1721–27*, 66–69.

[15] Newcastle to Horace Walpole, April 6, 1724, in Legg, ed., *Brit. Dip. Insts.*, 1689–1789, IV, *France, 1720–27*, 60–61.

[16] Baudrillart, *Philippe V et la Cour de France*, III, 143 ff.

3. The Austro-Spanish Alliance of 1725

Spain's *rapprochement* with the Empire, inspired and carried through by the Baron (later Duke) Ripperdá, produced three treaties that shocked and thoroughly frightened the other powers of Western Europe.

The first of these, signed April 30, 1725, was a treaty of friendship and alliance between Spain and the Empire.[17] It provided, in addition to mutual help in case of attack upon either by a third power in Europe, that the Emperor would use his good offices to bring England to restore to Spain Gibraltar and Minorca, as, according to Ripperdá, England had promised to do. In return, Spain extended to subjects of the Emperor freedom of commerce in all His Catholic Majesty's *"reinos,"* with most-favored-nation treatment such as was then enjoyed by the subjects of England, and promised that if the ships of the subjects of the Emperor should be attacked, "whether on this or the other side of the line," Spain would make common cause with the Emperor to defend the Emperor's commerce. The Emperor, on his side, promised to do the same for the ships of Spain.[18]

The second treaty was a long treaty of forty-seven articles relative to commerce and navigation.[19] In general a commercial treaty, with definitions of contraband, the commercial rights of neutrals in time of war, and so on, certain of its provisions were extended to the East Indies; it also provided that the subjects of each should enjoy, in the territories of the other "existing in whatever region of the world," the privileges of the most-favored-nation; in the Spanish territories in particular, the subjects of the Emperor were to enjoy all the privileges extended to the subjects of England and Holland. Of especial potential interest to the maritime powers was the provision (Article 36) that the ships of the subjects of the Emperor, and of the Ostend Company in particular, might bring East Indian goods into the ports of Spain and dispose of them in such a way that the Ostend Company should enjoy the privileges extended to the Dutch by the royal *cedula* of June 15 and July 3, 1663. Furthermore, everything with regard to the overseas parts of the world, including America, that was conceded to the Dutch by the Treaty of Münster (1648) was also conceded to the subjects of the Emperor by the present treaty. Similarly (Article 47), everything conceded to the English by the Treaties of Madrid of 1667 and 1670 and by the Anglo-Spanish Treaty of Utrecht of 1713, insofar as these treaties were applicable to the needs of the subjects of the Emperor, was conceded to them.

---

[17] Cantillo, ed., *Tratados,* 206–208.

[18] This provision was inspired by the threats against the Ostend Company apparently implicit in the Anglo-Dutch attitude toward that company.

[19] Cantillo, ed., *Tratados,* 218–228.

The third of the treaties signed at Vienna by Spain and Austria was a "Treaty of Peace," signed June 7, 1725.[20] The chief concern of this treaty, which was probably for Spain the most important of the three, was the settlement of the situation in Italy. By this treaty the Emperor recognized the right of succession of Don Carlos and the other sons of Elizabeth Farnese, Queen of Spain, to the ducal thrones of Tuscany, Parma, and Placentia, and to the Island of Elba.

4. The Congress of Soissons

The news of the *rapprochement* of Spain with the Empire fell upon the chancelleries of Western Europe like a bombshell. Since the provisions of the settlement were not known, it was feared that the alliance might be a signal for a general war. England and Holland were especially apprehensive that the Ostend Company might have received special privileges in the trade of the Spanish Indies, East and West. This, at all costs, must be prevented.

This threat, coupled with a crisis in the international situation in Northern Europe, led England, France, and Prussia [21] to form a new alliance, called the Alliance of Hanover, in the summer of 1725. The Treaty of Hanover [22] was first of all a defensive military alliance; it also guaranteed the mutual defense of the territories of all the signatories, wherever they were in the world, along with their trading privileges. The latter provision, of course, was aimed at the Ostend Company. Meanwhile, England's prime minister, Robert Walpole, fearful for Gibraltar and English privileges in the Spanish Indies, demanded and received a declaration by France of French support of England in these matters, and England, in return, issued a declaration that any attack upon France would be regarded as cause of war by England.

The response of Spain and Austria to the formation of the Hanover Alliance was a new and more belligerent "very secret" treaty of alliance between them, signed on November 5, 1725.[23] This curious treaty provided for the marriage of two of the daughters of the Emperor with two of the princes of Spain, and it specified the support each was to give the other in case of war. Should the alliance of the two countries provoke a war with France, Spain promised to aid the Emperor in the recovery of Belgian lands held by France, of Alsace, and of other French territories. Should war break out with England, Austria would aid Spain in the recovery of Gibraltar and Minorca. The emperor's ships would protect Spanish ships

[20] Cantillo, ed., *Tratados*, 228–231.
[21] Holland acceded to the alliance on August 4, 1726.
[22] Paullin, ed., *European Treaties*, IV, 37.
[23] Cantillo, ed., *Tratados*, 231–235.

in the West Indies, and Spanish ships would protect the ships of the Emperor's subjects and, in particular, the ships of the Ostend Company.

For the next two years Western Europe balanced on the brink of war between the two rival combinations of power. For the Austrian-Spanish axis, the main considerations were the settlement of the Italian problem, the recognition of the Emperor's Pragmatic Sanction providing for the succession of his daughter, Maria Theresa, to his throne in case of a lack of direct male heirs, the promotion and the protection of the Emperor's commercial and colonial ambitions centering in the Ostend Company, and the checking of the commercial abuses committed by Englishmen and, in particular, the South Sea Company, in Spanish America. For the maritime powers and France the chief *desiderata* were the protection of Anglo-Dutch commercial supremacy, especially in overseas areas, the maintenance of English ownership of Gibraltar and Minorca, and the protection of France from just such a partition of its European territories as was envisaged by the secret treaty of Vienna of November 5, 1725.

Both sides took warlike actions. England, to prevent Spain from receiving the treasure from the Indies that would be used to support military action and pay the subsidies that Spain had promised Austria, sent Vice-Admiral Hosier to cruise off Porto Bello and Cartagena and warn the Spanish governors not to let the *flota* sail out. He was to assure them that his mission was entirely peaceful, but that if the treasure ships should sail he must take them to an English port. This must be done in order that the goods and money in the fleet belonging to Frenchmen, Dutchmen, and Englishmen might not be seized by the Spanish government and used for warlike purposes. Even in that case, he was to assure the Spanish officials, all the goods and treasure actually belonging to Spain or Spaniards would be faithfully accounted for and returned to their owners.[24]

Hosier's expedition was taken by Spain as a justification for hostilities. In retaliation, Spanish officials at Vera Cruz seized the South Sea Company ship the *Prince Frederick*, at the moment in that port; Spain called home its ambassador to England and proceeded to lay siege to Gibraltar. The Emperor, however, was not prepared to go to war for Spain, especially since he had not received all the subsidies Spain had promised him, and he even considered the possibility of appeasing the English and Dutch by suspending the Ostend Company for a period of years. England, on its part, was prepared to fight Spain, but France's prime minister, Cardinal Fleury, refused to commit his nation to a war over colonial affairs when the Emperor was showing a willingness to negotiate.[25] Actually, too, the

---

[24] *Newcastle to Horatio Walpole*, April 11, 1726, in Legg, ed., *Brit. Dip. Insts.*, 1689–1789, IV, *France, 1721–27*, 150–155.

[25] Legg, ed., *Brit. Dip. Insts.*, 1689–1789, IV, *France, 1721–27*, Introduction, xxxvi–xxxvii.

flota eluded Hosier and arrived safely in Spain; an Anglo-French declaration of war on Spain would now almost certainly cause the confiscation of all the Anglo-Dutch-French property in the treasure ships. In April, 1727, the Emperor replied to the demands of the maritime powers by announcing his willingness to suspend the Ostend Company for seven years.

In the light of these developments Cardinal Fleury proposed that one more effort be made to relieve the tensions between the two alliances by negotiation. The Emperor responded favorably, and the "preliminaries" for a general peace were signed at Paris on May 31, 1727—without Spain, of course. This action released the major tensions, although Spain still held out, and laid the groundwork for a new general congress.

The "preliminaries" [26] had provided, first, that the charter of the Ostend Company, along with "all the commerce of the Austrian Netherlands to the Indies," should be suspended by the Emperor for a period of seven years. All commercial privileges of the French, English, and Dutch were to be restored in the condition in which they had stood in 1725, both in Europe and in America. All hostilities were to cease; ships of the Ostend Company and of the Spanish *flota* already at sea were to be allowed to return to Europe without molestation. Consequently, the English fleet stationed off Porto Bello should be removed by the English and Vice-Admiral Hosier would be ordered to return to England. English commerce in Spanish America was to be restored according to existing treaties (which meant the *asiento*). It was agreed that there should be held a new congress of all the signatories at Aix-la-Chapelle (the place was later changed to Soissons because of the health of Cardinal Fleury) to adjust the details of all outstanding disputes among them.

Spain, now standing alone, presently acceded to the "Preliminaries" in what was called the "Declaration of the Pardo," [27] on March 6, 1728. However, according to this declaration, because certain events since the signing of the Preliminaries of a warlike nature had taken place in America, notably the seizure of the *Prince Frederick*, because the King of England had promised explicitly to order Vice-Admiral Hosier to withdraw from the waters of the West Indies, and because His Britannic Majesty had agreed that questions relative to the *Prince Frederick* and to contraband trade by the English in the Spanish colonies should be discussed by the Congress, this convention specifically provided that Spain, on its side, would raise the siege of Gibraltar, order the restitution of the *Prince Frederick* to the South Sea Company, and reestablish the trade of the company under the terms of the *asiento*. His Catholic Majesty promised also to release the "effects" of the *flota* belonging to the subjects of Eng-

[26] Cantillo, ed., *Tratados*, 241–244.
[27] Cantillo, ed., *Tratados*, 243–244.

land, France, and Holland. He further promised to be governed by the decisions of the proposed congress relative to contraband trade and to prizes made in America in suppression of this trade.

The Congress of Soissons began its deliberations on June 18, 1728. Each of the participants came to the conference with its own particular interests but with little inclination to make any compromises with the demands of the others.

For the Emperor, the great *desideratum* was a recognition of the Pragmatic Sanction and the protection of his power among the states of the Empire against the growing influence of France and England. He was therefore not adamant on the subject of the Ostend Company.

The British most desired the restoration of the commercial privileges enjoyed by the English in America prior to 1725, especially those provided for by the Treaty of the *Asiento*. This would involve the restoration of all the ships of the South Sea Company taken in America, particularly the *Prince Frederick*, which had been seized at Vera Cruz in retaliation for the English blockade. (This seizure was claimed by the British to be illegal since the Treaty of the *Asiento* had provided that in case of hostilities the South Sea Company should have eighteen months in which to withdraw its ships, goods, and personnel from America.) Should the Spaniards now have any complaints against the South Sea Company or claims against the English for supposed illicit trade with the Spanish colonies, those complaints and claims might be discussed by the congress. However, since the adjudication of all such claims would take much time, England proposed that the complaints on both sides should be referred, in the final treaty to be made by the congress, to a joint Anglo-Spanish commission. The British representatives at the congress were instructed to demand compensation for seizures of British ships by Spanish *guarda costas* in America. They were also to demand for British subjects the same privileges in the commerce of European Spain that the subjects of the Emperor enjoyed under the Austro-Spanish commercial treaty of May 1, 1725.[28]

If the English wished the congress to confine itself to the satisfaction of the Preliminaries, the Dutch were concerned not only with the liquidation of the Ostend Company, but also with the question of the Austrian succession and the establishment of the Spanish Infante Don Carlos on his Italian ducal thrones. But Britain feared a general discussion of European problems and France opposed a guarantee of the Pragmatic Sanction because of its interest in certain male heirs to the Austrian throne.

---

[28] Instruction for William Stanhope, Horace Walpole, and Stephen Poyntz, plenipotentiaries to the congress to be held at Soissons, April 30, 1728, in Legg, ed., *Brit. Dip. Insts., 1698–1789*, VI, *France, 1727–44*, 31–32.

For France, the chief objective of the congress was to split the alliance of Spain and Austria, represented by the Treaties of Vienna of 1725 and 1727, and, if possible, to draw Spain to the side of the allies of Hanover. Fleury even thought of the possibility of an alliance between France and Spain, but he dismissed it because of the strongly anti-French sentiments of Spanish Queen Elizabeth Farnese. It was because of this outlook that Fleury exerted his chief efforts to bringing about a reconciliation between England and Spain.

Cardinal Fleury, therefore, proposed that Spain agree to the restoration of the *Prince Frederick*, but only in return for some definite commitments by the English relative to contraband trade in the Spanish colonies. At the same time, the cardinal had a very lively interest in achieving a restoration of the commercial privileges formerly enjoyed by Frenchmen in Spain, particularly in the trade with the Spanish colonies in America via Cadiz.[29] To promote this end, Germain-Louis de Chauvelin, the new French foreign minister, advised the Comte de Rottembourg, French ambassador to Madrid, to warn Spain that Spanish discriminatory practices against French merchants engaged in the Cadiz trade, far from separating France from England, would only draw the two countries together.[30]

As for Gibraltar, Fleury took a noncommital position, since to favor either Spain or England must antagonize the other. With regard to the Italian question, Fleury hesitated to take a position until he might be sure that the Austro-Spanish alliance was broken. Time, he thought, was on the side of this eventuality.

As might have been expected, Spain was the chief obstructor of the work of the congress. For their Catholic Majesties, there were two major objectives. On the one hand, the Queen of Spain was still determined to get international approval for the occupation of the ducal thrones of Placentia, Parma, and Tuscany, as provided by the Quadruple Alliance, by her son Don Carlos, and, as a preliminary step, the garrisoning of these places by Spanish troops. On the other hand, the Spanish plenipotentiaries brought to the congress a long list of grievances against England, centering chiefly in the relations of the two empires in America. Thus, the Spanish representatives were to raise before the congress the question of British territorial expansion in the American hemisphere on the ground that the Treaties of Madrid of 1721 and of Utrecht of 1713 had provided that the territorial situation in America should remain as it had been in

[29] Sée and Vignols, eds., "Mémoires sur le commerce rédigés en vue due Congrèss de Soissons (1728), etc." in *Notices, Inventoires & Documents*, XII, *Études et Documents divers* (1926), 1–33.

[30] Baudrillart, *Philippe V et la cour de Franc*, III, 578; see also "État des Privilèges du commerce Étranger en Espagne," A.É., *Divers*, 55261, *Espagne*, 398: fols. 311–328.

the time of Carlos II, or, specifically, the Treaty of Madrid of 1670. The
English, they argued, since the Peace of Utrecht had seized the island of
Providence, in the Bahamas, and had given protection to the swarms of
pirates who used that island as a base. The English had also built the
fort called Tamaya (Fort King George, at the mouth of the Altamaha
River) which the Spaniards claimed was in Florida.[31] The Spaniards had
often requested the English to evacuate the fort and to order the governor of South Carolina to come to an agreement with the governor of
Florida as to where exactly the boundary between South Carolina and
Florida lay. But this had never been done. Similarly, the English had continued their illegal practice of cutting logwood on the coasts of Honduras
and had actually made settlements there. These activities were supported
from Jamaica. In addition to these territorial "usurpations," the Spanish
delegates raised the question of Spanish Guipuzcoan right to fish off Newfoundland, guaranteed, as they understood it, by the Treaties of Utrecht
(1713) and Madrid (1721). Finally, the Spanish plenipotentiaries were
instructed to bring into the congress a relation of all the abuses of commerce committed by the English, especially the South Sea Company,
under cover of the *asiento* treaty, and to submit to the congress the question whether the South Sea Company ship, the *Prince Frederick*, seized
by Spanish officials at Vera Cruz in 1727, on suspicion of smuggling (but
probably, in reality, in retaliation for the English blockade established by
the English Vice-Admiral Hosier) should be restored to the English. As
for the British complaints against seizures by Spanish *guarda costas* of
British ships found sailing close to the coasts of Spanish colonies, the
Spanish plenipotentiaries were to justify all such seizures on the ground
of the remarkable doctrine that Spanish dominion over all the seas in
America was undeniable; that ships going to or returning from English,
French, or Dutch colonies in the West Indies must sail strictly along the
most direct and universally recognized routes. It followed from this that
any ship straying from those routes would be assumed by Spain, as a
matter of fundamental right, to be trespassing in Spanish waters and, in
all probability, trading with the Spanish colonies, and that they were,
therefore, rightly subject to seizure and confiscation.

As for European matters, the Spanish emissaries to the congress were
to demand the restoration of the Spanish ships captured by Admiral Byng
off Cape Passero in 1718, or their value, as provided in the Treaty of
Madrid of 1721. Finally, they were to remind the British delegates of
George I's promise, made at the time of the Treaty of Madrid of 1721, to
bring the matter of the restoration of Gibraltar to the attention of Parliament, which had never been done, and demand that the claim of Spain
for a restoration of Gibraltar be considered by the congress—a proposal

[31] For a discussion of this and other Anglo-Spanish conflicts in America, see Chapter XIII.

from which they were discouraged by Cardinal Fleury, who was otherwise sympathetic with the Spanish grievances.[32]

In all the negotiations, Cardinal Fleury acted as a sort of mediator. In fact, it can almost be said that Cardinal Fleury *was* the Congress of Soissons. But for all his sagacity and skill, Fleury was unable to prevent the congress from arriving at a stalemate in its negotiations in the summer of 1728, a stalemate that was not broken until the summer of 1729, when the cardinal submitted a "provisional" treaty to the members of the congress. This treaty proposed to extend the suspension of the Ostend Company and to refer the settlement of the most difficult questions between Spain and England to an Anglo-Spanish joint commission. Spain still refused to collaborate, so Fleury turned to the Emperor; but the Emperor likewise refused to sign; his real reason for refusing was the absence of any compensation for the sacrifice of the Ostend Company.

The situation was again a sort of stalemate, and England urged France to join it in action against Spain. Fleury again temporized, and the death of the Austro-Spanish alliance finally took place when the Emperor definitely refused to marry his daughter Maria-Teresa to Don Carlos as provided in the Alliance of 1727 and then refused to acquiesce in the introduction of Spanish garrisons into the Italian duchies. These refusals infuriated Elizabeth Farnese, who now quickly repudiated the alliance with Austria and signified her willingness to make peace with France and England. The result was the Treaty of Seville, signed by England, France, and Spain on November 9, 1729.

5. The Treaty of Seville, 1729

Actually, the successful negotiation of the Treaty of Seville turned upon the Italian problem and the introduction of Spanish garrisons into Tuscany and Parma to guarantee Don Carlos's succession. This, of course, was the question dearest to Elizabeth Farnese's heart; but France was not prepared to sanction the introduction of Spanish troops into the duchies, at the risk of war with the Emperor, without a *quid pro quo* in the form of commercial privileges in Spain, while England would support the Spanish garrisons only if the *asiento* were restored and if Spain would abandon its clamor for the restoration of Gibraltar.

The Treaty of Seville [33] was thus, in the first place, a treaty of alliance which included a mutual guarantee of territories, "in whatever parts of the world they may be situated in," along with a restoration of commerce and commercial privileges according to the treaties existing among them

[32] Copy of Articles to Spanish delegates to Soissons touching limits and commerce in America, A.G.S., Estado, 6896; Joaquin de Barrenecher to the Marquis de la Paz, Soissons, Aug. 10, 1728, A.H.N., Estado, 3375.

[33] Cantillo, ed., *Tratados*, 247–260.

before 1725, with specifications as to the aid to be furnished by each ally in case either were attacked by a fourth state. The commercial privileges of France and England in Spain and in the Indies were specifically renewed. As for damages done to French and English subjects in America, His Catholic Majesty promised to make reparation for all damages done since the arrival of his orders for a suspension of hostilities at Cartagena on June 22, 1728; the French and British Kings promised, on their sides, to make reparations done to Spanish subjects in America in the same period.

For the adjudication of the claims and counterclaims of the English and Spanish nations, it was provided that an Anglo-Spanish joint commission should be named, which would consider all the points at issue between them, both in Europe and in America, whether as to commerce, boundaries, or other matters, as well as England's responsibility to restore to Spain the ships destroyed by Byng at Cape Passaro in 1718 (or their value). Similarly, a Franco-Spanish commission was to be named to adjudicate questions at issue between France and Spain.[34] Both commissions were to meet within four months of the ratification of the treaty and were to terminate their labor within three years; all the signatories agreed to abide by the commissions' decisions.

Of supreme importance to Spain, of course, was the provision of the treaty that Spain should introduce Spanish troops into Liorna, Puerto-Ferrayo, Parma, and Placentia to guarantee the possession of these places to Don Carlos, and that France and England would actively assist Spain in the achievement of this end. These two powers also undertook to guarantee Don Carlos in the possession of his ducal thrones. Holland was to be invited to join in the alliance, under the same terms as those accorded to France and England.

In a separate article it was provided that

Although conformably with the "Preliminary articles . . . it is agreed in Article 4 of the treaty signed today that the commerce of the English nation in America shall be reestablished as it was according to the treaties and conventions existing before 1725, nevertheless, for greater clarity it is declared by their Catholic and Britannic Majesties, still more strongly in the present article . . . that under this general convention are included the treaties of peace and commerce concluded at Utrecht July 13 and December 9 of the year 1713, in which are comprehended the treaty of 1667 made in Madrid . . . the treaty made in Madrid on December 14, 1715, as also the private contract commonly called the *Asiento* for the introduction of Negro slaves into the Spanish Indies, which was made March 26 of the said year . . . and equally the treaty of "*declaration touching that of the Asiento,*" made May 26, 1716. All of which treaties . . . from today, and even during the investigation of the commissioners, shall have all their force and vigor; and for their full observance His Catholic Majesty

---

[34] This commission never came into existence.

will immediately dispatch . . . the necessary orders and *cedulas* to his vice-roys, governors, and other ministers to whom they may pertain. . . .

Similarly His Britannic Majesty promises the same and obliges himself to send the necessary orders . . . to reestablish the commerce of Spanish subjects in all the countries under his rule upon the basis provided in the treaties referred to, and for their exact observance and fulfillment.[35]

In consequence of this separate article, it was also agreed that all ships and goods that had been seized by either party, if not for carrying on contraband trade, and in particular, the *Prince Frederick*, should be immediately returned. As for other claims of the two nations against each other, they, with their documentation, were to be submitted to the joint commission provided for in Article 6 of the Treaty.

In other separate and secret articles France and England gave Spain strong assurances that they would support His Catholic Majesty in his relations with the Emperor, and, in particular, in establishing Spanish garrisons in the Italian duchies claimed by Spain for Don Carlos, and in seating Don Carlos on his ducal thrones, even to the point of employing their forces against the Emperor if he should attempt to block these actions. Leghorn was declared to remain a free port.

Holland acceded to the Treaty of Seville on November 21, 1729. To this country's accession there was appended a separate and secret article providing that Spain, France, and Britain should bring pressure to bear upon the Emperor to bring him to dissolve the Ostend Company completely; should they not succeed, they promised they would "concert whatever measures might be necessary" to stop completely the trade of that company. Holland, on its side, accepted full participation in the obligations of the other signatories relative to support of Spain in the seating of Don Carlos on the thrones of his Italian duchies.

With the completion of the Treaty of Seville, Spain returned to association and alliance with the maritime powers against the Emperor. The emperor was isolated, the old balance—or imbalance—of power had been restored, and the Queen of Spain was now assured that she would have the positive force of England, France, and Holland in the seating of her son upon thrones of the Italian duchies. As for America, the intentions of Spain and England to settle their difficulties and to make peace had been written into a formal treaty, and a mechanism had been created for the peaceful adjustment of all the outstanding disputes between them in the "new world". It remained, now, only to make the mechanism function effectively.

[35] Cantillo, ed., *Tratados*, 250–251.

CHAPTER XV

Anglo-Spanish Colonial Diplomacy from the Treaty of Seville (1729) to the Convention of the Pardo (1739)

1. The Anglo-Spanish Joint Claims Commission of 1732

THE TREATY OF SEVILLE had provided that the signatories would assist in the garrisoning of the duchies of Tuscany and Parma and Placentia by the Spanish troops that would support Don Carlos de Borbon when he undertook to occupy the thrones of those duchies under Article 5 of the Quadruple Alliance,[1] and that the occupation by the Spanish troops would take place within six months after the signing of the treaty. If the Emperor should oppose the occupation, France and England were to employ their naval and military forces to overcome the Emperor's opposition and to assist Spain in introducing the Spanish garrisons despite the imperial opposition.

Negotiations between Spain, on the one side, and France and England, on the other, for completing arrangements for the introduction of the Spanish garrisons went on for a year or more after the signing of the Treaty of Seville. But the Emperor had made it clear, especially after the signing of the Treaty of Seville, that he would oppose, by force, if necessary, the introduction of the Spanish garrisons into the Italian duchies, and France and England, especially the latter, unwilling to risk an almost certain war with Austria, delayed the negotiations beyond the limits of the patience of the Spanish Queen. The Marqués de Castelar, Spain's special ambassador in Paris, therefore announced, in a formal and angry declaration, on January 28, 1731, that because France and England had demonstrated their unwillingness to carry out the provisions of the Treaty of Seville, their Catholic Majesties repudiated that treaty and that, thence-

[1] See Chapter XIV.

forward, Spain would consider the treaty and all its provisions void and of no effect.[2]

Meanwhile, England and the Low Countries, to forestall imperial opposition to Don Carlos, as well as for reasons more closely concerned with their commercial and colonial interests, had undertaken to come to an agreement with the Emperor on the outstanding European issues. The negotiations, conducted by Thomas Robinson, the British ambassador at Vienna, were difficult, and the price of imperial concessions was high, nothing less than the acceptance by the maritime powers of the Pragmatic Sanction.

But the price was paid—for a *quid pro quo* in the form of the final dissolution, by the Emperor, of the Ostend Company, which the Dutch and English had so greatly feared as a threat to their Asian and American commerce. Thus, by the Treaty of Vienna, signed on March 16, 1731, the Pragmatic Sanction was recognized by England and the Low Countries and the Emperor agreed to dissolve the Ostend Company. So far as Italy was concerned, the treaty promised that the Emperor would not oppose the introduction of the Spanish garrisons into the forts of Tuscany, Parma, and Placentia.[3]

Just as soon as the signatories of this, the so-called "second" Treaty of Vienna had ratified it, Benjamin Keene, the English ambassador in Madrid, showed it to the Spanish sovereigns and invited them to accede to it. In view of this demonstration of England's good faith and success in clearing the way for Don Carlos in Italy, he also invited the Spanish rulers to cancel the Castelar statement of January 28. This was done in a joint Anglo-Spanish statement of June 6. In this new declaration, signed by the Marquée de la Paz and José Patiño for Spain and by Keene for England,[4] Spain formally announced that the Castelar declaration notwithstanding, the Treaty of Seville was now considered to be in full force as between England and Spain. The two kings declared themselves ready punctually to execute that treaty's provisions, once the Spanish garrisons were landed in Italy. His Catholic Majesty, on his part, specifically declared that all the "privileges, concessions and exemptions" enjoyed by Great Britain under the Treaty of Seville and earlier treaties should continue in full force. A little over a month later, on July 22, Spain acceded to the Treaty of Vienna.

Preparations went on rapidly, now, to move Don Carlos to Italy. Meanwhile, the Duke of Parma conveniently died without male issue and the Duke of Tuscany signed a Family Compact with Spain[5] naming Don Carlos as his heir and inviting him to take up his residence in that duchy

[2] Cantillo, ed., *Tratados*, 257–258.
[3] Chalmers, ed., *Treaties*, I, 310–327.
[4] Cantillo, ed., *Tratados*, 258–259; A.H.N., Estado, 3375/1.
[5] Cantillo, ed., *Tratados*, 271–274.

immediately. Don Carlos, nothing loathe, accepted the invitation with alacrity and sailed from Barcelona in company with the troops for the garrisons and escorted by a British fleet, on October 17, 1731. He made his triumphal entry into Leghorn late in October. At long last, Elizabeth Farnese had the joy of seeing her son installed as the Grand Duke of Tuscany and of Parma.

The English star was definitely in the ascendant in Madrid, at least for the time being. To be sure, France, isolated by the English *rapprochement* with Austria and feeling an increasing need for the support of Spain against the Emperor, was making an intense effort to form an alliance with Spain, an effort which eventuated in the Bourbon Family Compact any conflict on the European continent, particularly if the conflict in- of 1733. It was the double objective of France to win Spain's support in volved Austria, and to achieve a restoration of France's "most-favored-nation" position in the trade with Spain's American empire that funneled through Cadiz. England, on the other hand, ardently wished to achieve a restoration of England's privileged position in the trade with the Spanish colonies that derived from the *asiento* and the illicit trade that surrounded it.

The result was a sort of diplomatic duel between the Comte de Rottembourg, the French ambassador at Madrid, and Benjamin Keene, the English minister there, for the favor of the Spanish rulers.

For the moment, at least, the English had the best of it, and Benjamin Keene exerted all his powers, to say nothing of those of the British purse, to make the most of the situation. He recognized, of course, that the joint declaration of June 6 was both too tentative and too vague to serve as a basis for the actual adjudication of the many disputes and claims of the two empires in America. He needed a more specific commitment of the King of Spain to the obligations assumed in the Treaty of Seville; most of all, he wished to bring into being the joint commission envisaged by that treaty. A constant stream of complaints against Spanish interference with English ships and trade in America was flowing into England, and Keene, under pressure from both his government and the South Sea Company, whose agent he was, took advantage of the prevailing Spanish good will to press for a declaration that would clear the way for the practical adjustment of the claims and complaints of the two countries against each other in America. On November 15, 1731, therefore, before conclusive news of the settlement of Don Carlos in his duties had arrived in Madrid, Keene submitted a proposed text for such a declaration to the Spanish ministry.[6] But it was not until February 8, 1732, that a joint Anglo-Spanish declaration of commitment and interest was issued.[7]

In this declaration the Spanish monarch promised to make reparation

[6] A.G.S., Estado, 6882.
[7] A.H.N., Estado, 3365/1; Cantillo, ed., *Tratados*, 259–260.

to the English for all damages done to their trade and shipping in America since 1728 and, in particular, since the signing of the Treaty of Seville; he also promised to see to it that all unjustified seizures of British ships and goods in America should be stopped; the strictest orders would be sent to the King's governors and officials in America to this effect. His Catholic Majesty promised still further that the *guarda costas* in America would be required to post bonds not to seize any British ships engaged in lawful commerce. His Britannic Majesty promised, on his part, that British warships would be ordered not to protect British ships engaged in trade prohibited by the Spanish crown, and that orders would be sent to British governors in America neither to encourage nor to protect invasions of Spanish territory in America by British colonists. Once he had this commitment in hand, Keene felt justified in driving for the beginning of actual negotiation of the disputes between the two empires.

The Treaty of Seville had provided (Articles 4, 5, 6, 7, 8)[8] that French and English commerce with Spain and its colonies was to be restored to the *status quo* existing before 1725. With regard to English trade in America, orders to this effect were to be sent by both governments to their governors and officials in America; Spain promised to pay reparations for damages inflicted upon British commerce and shipping in America since 1728, and the French and British crowns promised to pay reparations for any damages inflicted upon the subjects of Spain.

Commissioners were to be appointed by the Spanish and British crowns to adjust the public and private claims of their respective nations against each other, both in America and in Europe, as well as questions arising out of disputes over colonial boundaries. The commissioners were also to adjudicate the amount due the crown of Spain from England by reason of the seizure of Spanish warships by the English fleet off Sicily in 1718, under the Anglo-Spanish treaty of 1721 (renewed by the Treaty of Seville).[9] The commissioners were to finish their work within three years, and were to make a report of their decisions, which were to be paid or carried out by both nations within six months after the termination of the work of the commissioners.

The wave of good feeling in Spain toward England in the summer and fall of 1731 had given Benjamin Keene a favorable occasion to urge that the commission provided for by the Treaty of Seville be brought into being, and this he had proposed soon after the Anglo-Spanish declaration of June 6, 1731. By the time of the joint declaration of June 6, 1731, therefore, the English government had already appointed, as its commissioners, Arthur Stert, John Goddard, and Keene.[10] On September 7,

---

[8] Cantillo, ed., *Tratados*, 248–249.
[9] Article 5 of the treaty of 1721; Cantillo, ed., *Tratados*, 200.
[10] P.R.O., S.P., 94:106.

Keene had reported that the Spanish crown had appointed as its commissioners [11] Matheo Pablo Diaz del Ahandero, Marqués of Torrenueva, of the *Consejo de Hacienda*, Francisco Manuel de Herrera, of the *Casa de Contratación*, in Seville, and José de Quintana, of the Court of *Contadura*.[12] Thus, by the time of the joint declaration of February 8, 1732, all the commissioners were named and were ready to go to work.

The joint commission met for the first time in Seville on February 23, 1732.[13] This meeting was devoted to an exchange of powers and other formalities. The business of the commission was concerned, in general, with four sorts of problems. In logical order they were: (1) questions of a political, territorial, or military nature as between the two crowns. (2) questions of commercial relations in general in Spain and America, (3) the claims of private citizens of one nation against the other, and (4) the affairs of the South Sea Company, which was a private English company but in which, under the terms of the *asiento* treaty, the Spanish government was in several ways directly interested.

At the second meeting, held on March 3, the Spanish commissioners introduced a condition that almost paralyzed the commission's work and practically ensured that it would accomplish nothing. They demanded, first, that the South Sea Company immediately pay the duties due on Negroes introduced into the Spanish colonies since the Treaty of Seville and, second, that the company render to the King of Spain, as a one-fourth stockholder in the company, an accounting of its commerce to Spanish America according to the terms of the *asiento* contract.[14] There ensued an interminable series of wranglings over the date of the actual reopening of the slave trade, delays and losses to the company occasioned by the refusal of the Spanish colonial officials to obey their King's *cedulas*, mistreatment of the company's factors, and so on. It was finally agreed on March 28 that the reckoning of the duties due on Negroes should begin as of January 1, 1731. As for the company's accounts, it was agreed that they should be furnished within four months of that date—a promise that was not fulfilled.

On the other hand, the company insisted that before anything else be settled, the King of Spain must pay the company for its losses by seizure of its ships by Spanish officials in America and by Spanish *guarda costas*

[11] Keene to Newcastle, Sept. 7, 1731, P.R.O., S.P., 106.

[12] Commission of the Spanish commissioners, A.G.S., Estado, 6883.

[13] Keene to Newcastle, Feb. 23, 1732: P.R.O., S.P., 94–106; "Proceedings of the Commissioners at Seville," *ibid.*; Commissioners to Newcastle, Mar. 14, 1732, L.C., H.L. Mss., 209–139: fols. 38–41.

[14] "Proceedings of the Commissairies," P.R.O., S.P., 94–106; José de Quintana to Patiño, Jan. 8, 1735, A.G.S., Estado 6888. Articles 29 and 30 of the *asiento* had provided that at the end of every five years during the life of the contract the South Sea Company was to render to the King of Spain an account of its profits and pay to him his share as a stockholder (Cantillo, ed., *Tratados,* 66). See Chapter X for the *asiento* treaty.

operating in American waters under commissions from the Spanish King. This the Spanish commissioners refused to consider until the company's accounts should be in the Spanish King's hands. Because of the delay relative to the South Sea Company's affairs, the commission now turned its attention to other things.

One of the duties of the commission was to consider the complaints of English merchants resident in Spain. The English commissioners, therefore, soon after their arrival wrote to the English consuls in the country asking for information and formal documents. The claims sent in were numerous. The English merchants of Bilbao complained against an order of the Spanish crown that all imports into Bilbao be carried only in Biscayan ships; [15] other restrictions were reported by English merchants in La Caruña and Alicante; a group of English ships was detained in the Bay of Cadiz.[16] The English merchants in the Canaries complained that all non-Catholics were ordered to leave the islands; duties on English imports were arbitrarily increased; all ships for all ports in the Canaries were forced first to clear through the port of Santa Cruz.[17] Most of the restrictions and embarrassments upon English commerce in European Spain were removed or ameliorated.[18]

Moreover, the commission was charged with the settlement of claims arising out of the seizure of merchant ships in Europe and America since the cessation of hostilities in 1728. It was not until May, 1732, however, that the English commissioners presented their first claims for ships, six taken by the Spanish in Europe and fourteen in America, and these were followed by many others.[19]

The Earl of Newcastle had instructed the Board of Trade on April 9, 1731,[20] to invite those having claims against Spain to present them. But there were presented such an extraordinary number of claims, many of them of a ridiculous or incredible nature, that the commissioners in Seville were aghast. Many of these claims were submitted by North American merchants whose ships had been seized by the Spanish *guarda costas*; such, for example, was that of Benjamin Browne, of Boston, whose brigantine, *Two Sisters*, had loaded salt for the New England fisheries at the island of Tortuga.[21] Another case was that of the English captain Robert

---

[15] Keene to la Paz, Seville, Jan. 15, 1732, P.R.O., S.P., 94–111.

[16] A.G.S., Estado, 6887, *passim.*

[17] Spanish ministry to the English merchants in the Canaries, Seville, Feb. 1, 1732; P.R.O., S.P., 94:111.

[18] Keene to la Paz, Jan., 17, 1732, A.G.S., Estado, 6883.

[19] "Proceedings of the commissaries in Seville," P.R.O., S.P., 94:106; L.C., B.M., Add. Mss., 32766, 32769, *passim.*

[20] Newcastle to the Board of Trade, Apr. 9, 1731, P.R.O., S.P., 94:102.

[21] A.G.S., Estado, 6887.

Jenkins, who lost his ear in a fracas off Havana with the chief officer of a Spanish *guarda costa* on the deck of Jenkins' ship, the *Rebecca*, loaded, as he said, with sugar from Jamaica for London.[22] And there were literally hundreds of such claims. So many, and so unreasonable, that Keene was moved to protest to Charles Delafaye, secretary to the Duke of Newcastle,

I am almost blind with poking into old autos; one's understanding ought to suffer as well as one's eyesight in reading such stuff; besides the greatest part of them are imperfect, and I defy Doctor's Commons in the lump to comprehend and set them in a proper light. . . . In short, never was there such a heap of mangled confusion. We shall be laughed at by our adversaries. . . . But we shall have this advantage, that merchants and Parliament men will see with their own eyes here how loud the drum has been beat in England by passion and malicious representation. I don't excuse Spain, but *Fiat Justitia et ruat Mundus*. The Spaniards have been silent, but you will soon see that it is not for want of matter to produce against us.[23]

Actually, despite the fact that the Spanish King had repeatedly sent orders to his officials in America to end the seizures of British ships not flagrantly engaged in illicit trade, the seizures had persisted, and they continued, in fact, even while the commission was engaged in its negotiations.

The British admiralty, in desperation, on September 25, 1730, had issued orders to Rear Admiral Charles Stewart, on the Jamaica station, to protect British ships and trade in the Caribbean area, to seize piratical vessels, to demand restitution of seized English ships, and, if this were refused, to make reprisals upon Spanish shipping. Thus, after official news was received that an English ship, the *Woolball*, was seized by a Spanish privateer on June 2, 1731, an English warship seized the Spanish dispatch ship, *La Dichosa*, as reprisal for the seizure of the *Woolball*.[24] So great was the tension created by these incidents, now involving the British navy instead of private ships, that Benjamin Keene, on order from Newcastle, warned Patiño that if Spain did not stop the seizures of British vessels, the British navy would do so.[25]

Keene was instructed to demand that privateering, under the guise of the legitimate work of *guarda costas*, be stopped, that seizures and condemnation of British ships carrying small quantities of Spanish-American coins or silver cease, that British ships not be seized merely for sailing close to Spanish colonial lands, since this was unavoidable, and that immediate restitution be made for "unjust seizures" of British ships.[26] To

[22] A.G.S., Estado, 6882.
[23] Keene to Delafaye, Apr. 11, 1732, quoted in Armstrong, *Elizabeth Farnese*, 284–285.
[24] C.S.P., *Col.*, A.& W.I., 1732, Nos. 415, 417, pp. 234–235, 236.
[25] L.C., B.M., Add Mss., 32779, *passim*.
[26] Newcastle to Keene, Oct. 30, 1732, P.R.O., S.P., 94: fol. 113.

Montijo, Spanish ambassador in London, Newcastle reiterated his strong conviction that the basic problem in the matter of seizures was the necessity for formulating a clear definition of contraband.[27]

Patiño, although apparently genuinely desirous of a peaceful resolution of the tensions in America, expressed anger that the British should have resorted to force while the negotiations were going on,[28] but new orders were sent to Spanish-American officials for the restitution of British ships, including the *Woolball*, and the British government sent orders for the restitution of the *Dichosa*.[29] Tension eased, and the commission continued its work.

Of all the matters dealt with by the commission, the problems that had arisen out of the affairs of the South Sea Company were the most nearly impossible of resolution. As already noted, one of the very first actions of the Spanish commissioners had been to demand, as a non-negotiable *sine qua non* for further conversations, that the asientists pay the past-due duties on Negroes imported into the Spanish colonies since the Treaty of Seville and render to the King, as a one-fourth stockholder in the South Sea Company, an accounting of the company's business and a payment to His Catholic Majesty of his share of the profits.[30] The English commissioners had replied that because certain Spanish officials in America had refused to honor the king's *cedulas* reopening the importation of slaves it would be highly inequitable to require the company to pay duties on the maximum legal number provided for in the *asiento*, especially since the obstructions placed in the way resulted in substantial losses to the company in slaves and money.

Indeed, the British commissioners argued, on instruction from the company, that the Spanish King had amply "overpaid" himself by the value of the two British ships seized as reprisals.[31] As soon as the British commissioners had accepted the dates agreed upon, the Spanish commissioners assured them that His Catholic Majesty would give the company credit for every amount that it could show was a loss caused by interruptions of, or interferences with its trade in America since those dates.[32] It

---

[27] Montijo to la Paz, Oct. 16, 1732, A.G.S., Estado, 6884.

[28] Keene to Harrington, Sept. 19, 1732, P.R.O., S.P., 94: fol. 114; Crookshanks to Delafaye, Sept. 7, 1732, P.R.O., S.P., 94: fol. 106.

[29] Crookshanks to Delafaye, Seville, Sept. 2, 1732, P.R.O., S.P., 94: fol. 106; C.S.P., Col., A.& W.I., 1732, No. 417, p. 236.

[30] British commissioners to the South Sea Co., Mar. 21, 1732, P.R.O., S.P., 94: fol. 106; Translation of the Spanish paper delivered to the English commissaries on Mar. 3, 1732, *ibid.*

[31] South Sea Company to the British commissioners, London, Apr. 20, 1732, B.M., Add. Mss., 36806, Newcastle Papers; British commissioners to the South Sea Company, June 6, 1732, P.R.O., S.P., 94: fol. 106.

[32] British commissioners to the South Sea Company, June 6, 1732, P.R.O., S.P., 94: fol. 106.

was finally agreed, on March 28, 1732, that the company should pay duties on the actual number of slaves imported down to January 1, 1731, and that duties on the full legal number should be made for every year after that date.[33]

As for the South Sea Company's accounts, the English commissioners, in the name of the company, pleaded confusion in the company's affairs caused by war and peacetime violence that had plagued the company's business ever since the beginning of its history as an excuse for the company's failure to give an accounting.[34] They promised to have the necessary accounts for the Spanish commissioners within four months,[35] and they urgently wrote the company to prepare the accounts and send them to the commissioners immediately.[36] This the company promised to do.[37]

The South Sea Company was, of course, hardly disposed to pay out any money to His Catholic Majesty on any account. On the contrary, the company proceeded to present an enormous set of claims for ships seized by Spanish warships and *guarda costas*, damages done by Spanish agents, and losses incurred by interference with the company's factors in the conduct of their work in America.

Other irritating circumstances relative to the South Sea Company arose out of the problem of resuming the voyages of the "annual ships." According to the Anglo-Spanish *asiento* treaty the South Sea Company was allowed to send one ship of five hundred tons a year to sell English manufactured goods at the annual fair for the Spanish colonies held at Porto Bello. Particularly troublesome for the British was the necessity for getting a special *cedula* from the Spanish crown in each case, permitting the ship to sail, and the requirement that a Spanish agent be named to measure the ship to see that it conformed to the specification provided in the treaty.[38] Moreover, the date of the annual fair at Porto Bello was a movable one, and the South Sea Company was often caught off-balance by the setting of the fair at unexpected and inconvenient times.[39]

[33] "Proceedings of the commissaries," P.R.O., S.P., 94: fol. 106; British commissioners to the South Sea Co., Mar, 21, 1732, *ibid;* Commissioners to Newcastle, Mar. 28, 1732, P.R.O., S.P., 94: fol. 106.

[34] South Sea Company to the British commissioners, Apr. 20, 1732, B.M., Add. Mss., 36806, Newcastle Papers.

[35] British commissioners to the South Sea Company, June 6, 1732, P.R.O., S.P., 94: fol. 106.

[36] British commissioners to the South Sea Company, June 6, 1732, P.R.O., S.P., 94: fol. 106.

[37] South Sea Company to the British commissioners, Apr. 20, 1732, B.M., Add. Mss., 36806, Newcastle Papers.

[38] Newcastle to Keene, July 25, 1730, L.C., B.M., Add. Mss., 32770; Keene to Patiño, Mar. 18, 1732, A.G.S., Estado, 6883.

[39] La Paz to Keene, Nov. 14, 1730, L.C., B.M., Add. Mss., 32770.

Still another sore point for the company at this moment lay in the fact that the viceroy of Perú had held up the shipment of silver to Panamá and Buenos Aires. Such a stoppage made it impossible—or so the company claimed—for the South Sea Company's factors to collect what was due for the slaves delivered at these places. Keene protested this action directly to Patiño, pointing out that such a paralysis of the company's business was prejudicial to both the company and Spain, since His Catholic Majesty was a shareholder in the company.[40] All of these points of friction, and others, were argued by the English commissioners as circumstances making difficult an accurate accounting of the company's indebtedness—if, indeed, it should come to that.

Early in the course of the negotiations the joint commission had agreed to meet twice a week and that the claims of the two nations would be presented at alternate meetings.[41] It was in the course of the meetings devoted to Spanish claims that the whole list of Spanish complaints against the English in America appeared. They were, indeed, many and significant.

The most pressing and troublesome claims of Spain against England were those that pertained to the affairs of the South Sea Company, already described. Of no less importance, however, were the Spanish claims that pertained to territory in America.[42]

At the conference on April 17, 1732, the Spanish commissioners presented a set of claims relative to territorial disputes in America. Apart from the question of Spanish fishing rights at Newfoundland and Spain's demand that English logwood cutters withdraw from Honduras and Campeche, both of which were mentioned, the Spanish demands included the evacuation by the English of a number of territories which, the Spanish claimed, England had occupied since the "American" Treaty of Madrid of 1670 in violation of its terms.[43] This list was presented again, in more detailed form, on May 29.[44]

In the first place, the Spanish memorandum demanded that the fort erected in "Florida" (that is, south of South Carolina) be demolished. The island of New Providence, in the Bahamas (this was later rephrased to include all the Bahamas), must be evacuated; the islands of St. Catherine (Old Providence) and St. Andrew, off the Mosquito Coast, must be

---

[40] Keene to Patiño, Mar. 28, 1732, A.G.S., Estado, 6883.
[41] Proceedings of the commissioners, P.R.O., S.P., 94: fol. 106.
[42] "Proceedings of the commissaries", P.R.O., S.P., 94: fol. 106.
[43] Spanish claims delivered to the British commissioners, Apr. 17, 1732, P.R.O., S.P., 94:106.
[44] "Translation of the paper delivered by the Spanish commissaries in their conference of May 29," P.R.O., S.P., 94: fol. 106.

returned to Spain, as must, also, Puerto Real, Panistron (Virgin Gorda), and Tortola, in the Virgin Islands.[45]

In their argument the Spanish commissioners renewed the centuries-old Spanish claim to ownership of the entire continent, or all the lands west of the north-and-south line one hundred leagues west of the Azores proclaimed by the papal bull of May 4, 1493,[46] by right of first discovery, conquest, and settlement,[47] at least from the line of 40° North Latitude to the South Pole.[48]

In reply to these claims, Newcastle told the commissioners to say that they were not instructed to discuss these territories, since the Treaty of Seville spoke only of "borders." [49] The English commissioners, therefore, asked for time in which to request instructions from London. The Spanish commissioners agreed, but intimated that they would discuss nothing more until this set of questions had been discussed.[50]

Again on January 12, 1733, the Spanish commissioners asked if the English commissioners had received instructions relative to these territorial claims, whereupon the English postponed the question again by saying they would reply to the Spanish claims in writing.[51] They did submit a paper on territorial questions in March and demanded that the Spanish commissioners present documents to support their claims to the territories listed, before giving a final answer. These the Spanish commissioners promised to supply.[52]

With regard to the fisheries, meanwhile, the Spanish commissioners referred to Article 15 of the Anglo-Spanish Treaty of Utrecht, which vaguely confirmed to the Biscayan fishermen "all the privileges [of fishing at Newfoundland] that they can of right claim," [53] and to other treaties renewed by the Treaty of Seville.[54] They demanded, in the name of the

[45] *Ibid*. The fort in Florida referred to was Fort King George, at the mouth of the Altamaha River. See Chapter XIII.

[46] "Translation of the paper delivered by the Spanish commissaries in their conference of May 29," P.R.O., S.P., 94: fol. 106; Spanish complaints on lands occupied by the British, P.R.O., S.P., 94: fol. 114

[47] "From the Spanish commissaries," July, 1732, P.R.O., S.P., 94: fol. 106.

[48] [Spanish] paper relating to Spanish limits in America with translation, sent to Newcastle July 25, 1732, L.C., H.L., Mss., 209–139: fols. 285–192; "Proceedings of the Commissaries," P.R.O., S.P., 94: fol. 106.

[49] This was not literally true. The treaty (Article 6) said that the commissioners should treat of "all the respective pretensions in America, based on former treaties, whether relative to boundaries [*limites*], or in any other form" (Cantillo, ed., *Tratados*, 249).

[50] Keene to Newcastle, Sept. 26, 1732, P.R.O., S.P., 94:106; Newcastle to the commissioners, Kensington, Oct. 12, 1732, L.C., H.L. Mss., 209–139: fols. 565–568.

[51] Commissioners to Newcastle, Jan. 16, 1733, L.C., H.L. Mss., 209–139: fols. 669–671.

[52] "Proceedings of the Commissaries," P.R.O., S.P., 94: fol. 106.

[53] Cantillo, ed., *Tratados*, 80.

[54] "Paper delivered by the Spanish commissaries relating to the rights of fishing for Bacalao at Newfoundland," P.R.O., S.P., 94: fol. 106.

Spanish Basque fishing interests, that the rights of the Spanish fishermen, confirmed by the treaties, be defined, and that damages be paid by England for the numerous cases of denial of rights since the Treaty of Utrecht.[55]

The Spanish commissioners later withdrew their demand for a definition of the rights of Spanish fishermen at Newfoundland, on the ground that they had no instructions to negotiate on this subject and that, in any case, since it was a right provided for by treaties, it was not subject to discussion by the commission. They reserved the right, however, to bring it up again for discussion if they should be so instructed. The English commissioners, although empowered to discuss this matter, suggested that, since it was, in fact, a matter of interpretation of treaties, the Spanish court take it up through the usual diplomatic channels.[56]

One of the most troublesome territorial issues presented to the commission by the Spanish commissioners in their list of April 17, 1732, was the Spanish complaint over the English custom of cutting logwood on the Bay of Campeche, the Gulf of Honduras, and other parts of Central America.[57] This practice, said the Spaniards, had never been authorized by treaty; much violence had taken place in the course of Spanish efforts to suppress it; and the English had enslaved and otherwise abused the Indians, whom it was the duty of the Spanish crown to protect. The Spanish commissioners demanded that the English government issue orders to stop the practice, withdraw the cutters, and destroy the *rancherias* (cutters' settlements).[58]

On November 27, the English commissioners replied to the Spanish memorandum on Honduras in mollifying terms. The purpose of the commission, they said, was to improve relations between the two crowns; it seemed strange to them that Spain should refuse to debate the logwood question because they believed an English right did not exist, whereas the English considered it an undisputed right, ratified by long practice. As for Spanish ownership of Yucatán, the English appealed to the doctrine of "effective occupation," saying that the Spanish occupation of the Yucatán peninsula was hardly effective; therefore, the English title to the coast of Honduras (Belize) was better than that of Spain, since the

[55] "Claims delivered to the British Commissaries," Apr. 17, 1732, P.R.O., S.P., 94: fol. 106; "An Answer to the Biscayan demands to fish off Newfoundland," P.R.O., S.P., 94: fol. 114. In 1715 the Basques had sent an armed ship, the *San Nicolas*, to the fishing grounds to seize English fishing ships to compensate themselves for ships seized by the English.

[56] An Answer to the Biscayan demands to fish off Newfoundland," P.R.O., S.P., 94: fol. 114.

[57] Copy of letter from the Spanish commissaries to the Duke of Newcastle; enclosed with Keene to Newcastle, May 30, 1732, P.R.O., S.P., 94: fol. 114.

[58] *Ibid.*; A.G.S., Estado 6886, *passim*; Commissioners to Newcastle, Oct. 24, 1732, L.C., H.L., Mss., 209–139: fols. 573–576, 578–581; "Paper delivered by the Spanish relating to the cutting of log wood," P.R.O., S.P., 94: fol. 106.

English woodcutters had occupied that coast for so long. Furthermore, since the English already occupied this territory at the time of the Treaty of Madrid of 1670, this coast should be recognized as belonging to England.[59] Finally, the English commissioners stated, all rights, privileges, and practices in existence at the time of the Treaty of Madrid or before were confirmed by the Anglo-Spanish Treaty of Peace of Utrecht.[60]

The Spanish commissioners and the Spanish court were not satisfied; indeed, they found the English claims specious. The Spanish commissioners therefore refused to discuss the matter further and informed the English commissioners that they could not be responsible for the consequences of the refusal of the English to accept the Spanish demands.[61] Despite the Spanish refusal to discuss the matter further, however, the English delivered one more paper on the subject of logwood on January 22, 1733, in which they denied the "absolute" title of Spain to islands and/or continents in America and affirmed the right of all European princes to make conquests and settlements in the hemisphere in areas not already effectively occupied. Consequently, they maintained, it was up to Spain to prove its right and title and to show specific cases of infraction of existing treaties. The English thus had the last word; and there the matter rested, for the time being.[62]

Newcastle instructed the English commissioners to say that if Spain should now attempt to stop the logwood cutting, any such orders must be strongly protested as an extraordinary means of proceeding in a dispute in the midst of negotiation.[63] But the Spanish commissioners insisted that the Spanish king's sovereignty in his own territory was undoubtable and that if the logwood cutters were not withdrawn, Spain would feel compelled to drive them out by force.[64]

Early in 1733, the commission ceased to meet. First Goddard, then Stert, requested permission to return home, and both requests were granted. The commission continued, in theory, to exist, and negotiations

[59] British paper on logwood, delivered to the Spanish commissioners Nov. 27, 1732, L.C., H.L., Mss., 209–139: fols. 609–632.

[60] L.C., H.L., Mss., 209–139: fols. 609–632. The latter claim apparently refers to Article 15 of the Anglo-Spanish Treaty of Utrecht.

[61] Commissioners to Newcastle, Dec. 23, 1732, L.C., H.L., Mss., 209–139: fols. 649–652; Spanish paper on logwood delivered to the Commissioners Dec. 11, 1732, ibid., 209–139: fols. 652–660; "Proceedings of the Commissaries," P.R.O., S.P., 94: fol. 106.

[62] Paper delivered by British commissioners on logwood and British possessions, Jan. 22, 1733, L.C., H.L., Mss., 209–139: fol. 750 ff.

[63] Newcastle to commissioners, Whitehall, Nov. 9, 1732, L.C., H.L., Mss., 209–139: fols. 590–592.

[64] "Spanish paper relating to logwood sent to Newcastle, Dec. 12, 1732, L.C., H.L., Mss., 209–139: fol. 596.

of a desultory sort were presently resumed in London. But to all intents and purposes it was dead, and its death certificate was sealed by the outbreak of the War of the Polish Succession.

2. Problems in Direct Anglo-Spanish Diplomacy

Outside the debates of the Anglo-Spanish commission, in the levels of direct international exchange, the problem of American and overseas commerce presented itself, in the same months in which the commission was meeting, in the form of the Spanish project for a commercial company for overseas trade, particularly with the Philippines.

Benjamin Keene had gotten wind of the project for a company for Philippine trade as early as June, 1731. Now, in March, 1732, it was revealed that the Spanish crown had issued a *cedula* granting Isidoro de Massay, of Lamadriz, and his associates, of Seville, a group that soon came to be called the Philippine Company, the right to establish a direct trade between Spain and the Philippines.[65] Curiously enough, in view of English opposition to the project, Massay went to London to seek capital for the enterprise.[66] There apparently was some interest among London investors in procuring stock in the new company.[67]

The maritime powers immediately protested the creation of the company. The Dutch ambassador, Baron van der Meer, joined Benjamin Keene in a vigorous protest, arguing that the creation of the company was a violation of the Treaty of Münster, of 1648, since it was clearly aimed at changing the *status quo* of overseas commerce then existing. These ambassadors of the Protestant powers, England and Holland, even maintained that Pope Alexander VI's bull of 1493 clearly denied to Spain the right to go to the East by way of the Cape of Good Hope, and that Spain, having failed to find a westward passage to the East, had sold its trading rights in the Far East to the Portuguese. Spanish trade with the Philippines was carried on by way of Acapulco; any expansion of this trade by the Spanish, therefore, would be both a violation of the Treaty of Münster, as confirmed by the Treaty of Utrecht and the Treaty of Seville, as well as of the papal bull of 1493![68] The Dutch suggested to the French government that France also protest; but France, now engaged in an effort to form an alliance with Spain, refrained from doing so; indeed, Keene

[65] Keene to Newcastle, Mar. 14, 1732, P.R.O., S.P., 94: fol. 111; Keene to Newcastle, May 23, 1732, *ibid*. The Charter of the Compania de las Filipinas is in A.G.S., Estado, 7006.
[66] Keene to Newcastle, Mar. 14, 1732, P.R.O., S.P., 94: fol. 111.
[67] Montijo to Patiño, London, June 12, 1733, A.G.S., Estado, 6887.
[68] Joint Memorial of English and Dutch ambassadors on the Philippine Company, Aug. 16, 1732, P.R.O., S.P., 94: fol. 114.

reported that the Comte de Rottembourg ridiculed the idea that the Spanish company might succeed and suggested that the whole thing be ignored.[69]

From the English point of view, since English trade in the West Indies was so much more important than that of the Dutch, Newcastle reasoned to Keene that it was more important for England to avoid a rupture with Spain over the Philippine Company than it was for the Dutch. England was therefore prepared to leave its Dutch friends in the lurch if necessary. Keene was instructed to get the private ear of the Queen of Spain and to appeal to her gratitude for English aid to Don Carlos for a suppression of the Philippine Company and, by citing the fate of the Ostend Company, to point out how prejudical the Philippine Company, by antagonizing England, would be to the interests of Don Carlos. He was not, however, to use this argument with King Philip! [70] But Keene found it impossible to talk to the Queen alone and had to satisfy himself with vigorous protests to the minister Patiño.[71]

The Spanish minister replied that neither the Treaty of Münster nor any other prohibited Spain from trading as it wished with the Philippines; it was a "notorious right" of any prince to trade with his own colonies in any way he might choose. The Anglo-Dutch protest was, therefore, rejected.[72]

The negotiations of the Anglo-Spanish joint claims commission reached a stalemate early in 1733, and the by now halfhearted effort to adjust Anglo-Spanish disputes in America was transferred to London. There were several reasons for this move, however, other than the stubborn intransigence of the two contestants; chief among these was the fact that the attention of both of disputants, but especially that of Spain, was diverted by the outbreak of the War of the Polish Succession between rival candidates for the elective throne of Poland and their international supporters. Spain now found itself at war against Austria as an ally of France, bound to that country by the terms of the so-called Bourbon Family Compact of 1733.

3. The Bourbon Family Compact

The War of the Polish Succession broke upon Europe almost immediately after the death on February 1, 1733, of Augustus II, "the Strong,"

[69] Keene to Lord Harrington, Aug. 1, 1732, P.R.O., S.P., 94: fol. 114.
[70] Newcastle to Keene, July 14, 1732, P.R.O., S.P., 94: fol. 113.
[71] Keene to Newcastle, Aug. 19, 1732, P.R.O., S.P., 94: fol. 112.
[72] La Paz to Keene and Van der Meer, Sept. 4, 1732, P.R.O., S.P., 94: fol. 112; Keene to Newcastle, Aug. 19, 1732, ibid.; A.G.S., Estado, 6887, passim.

elective King of Poland (who was also Elector of Saxony). It was this event that crystallized the signature of the Bourbon Family Compact (Treaty of the Escorial) on November 7, 1733.

This famous treaty was the product of a line of thought that had played in the minds of French and Spanish kings and their ministers from the last years of Louis XIV onward. Although Philip of Anjou (Philip V of Spain) had renounced his claim to the throne of France in the Treaties of Utrecht, he always cherished a more or less secret hope that something might happen to make it possible for him to claim it, nevertheless. Failing that, he and his French kinsmen recurrently toyed with the idea of a close union between the thrones of France and Spain that would be based upon and bolstered by a formal recognition of the blood relationship that existed between the two branches of the Bourbon family. It was this thought, for example, that underlay the so-called "Spanish marriages" proposed (one of them was consummated) after the Franco-Spanish alliance of 1721.[73]

Now, when France discovered itself to be isolated by the *rapprochement* of England and Austria in the Treaty of Vienna of 1731, to which Spain speedily acceded, Cardinal Fleury and his foreign minister, Germain-Louis de Chauvelin, revived the idea in proposing a close alliance with Spain that might be highly beneficial to both countries.

France, of course, was, as usual, intensely interested in rebuilding French privileges and prestige in the commerce of Spain, especially that which flowed to Spanish America through Cadiz. In addition to this, France was concerned with the growth of Austrian power and the dangers inherent in the Emperor's determination to win universal acceptance of his Pragmatic Sanction. France was willing to support the interests of Don Carlos in Italy as the price of an alliance, and both France and Spain shared a distrust and resentment toward English "abuses" and expansion in America.

The Comte de Rottembourg, French ambassador in Madrid, was therefore instructed in 1731 to propose a family alliance to the Spanish monarchs. Rottembourg's negotiations were highly secret and were actually going on while the Anglo-Spanish joint claims commission was at work, throughout the year 1732. The recalcitrance and inflexibility of the Spanish commissioners, in fact, may have been due to Rottembourg's constant reminding of the Spanish monarchs of British arrogance and abuses in America. Indeed, Benjamin Keene noted this to Delafaye, who complained of the continued aggressions of Englishmen in America while the work of the joint Anglo-Spanish claims commission was going on,

For God's sake, Mr. Delafaye, as long as we have a mind to be at peace with this country, let us avoid doing the business of France as much as we can.

[73] See Chapter XIV.

They [and particularly Rottembourg] are here *aux écoutes,* and are always ready with a *vous avez raison, nous vous soutiendrons.*[74]

Negotiations for the Family Compact were delayed by Elizabeth Farnese's distrust of Cardinal Fleury and by the mental instability of Philip V. Even after the death of the King of Poland and the obvious threat to Spanish interests in Italy presented by an aggressive Emperor, Elizabeth Farnese refused to agree to the treaty, fearing a betrayal by France, until France should actually embark upon belligerent operations. Once France acted, the Treaty of the Escorial, as it was called, was finally signed on November 7, 1733.[75]

While the immediate objective of the Treaty of the Escorial was to combine the military forces of France and Spain against the Emperor, his Pragmatic Sanction, and his candidate for the throne of Poland, and for the protection of the interests of Don Carlos in Italy, the agreement also represented an accord upon some very profound ambitions, on both sides, directed at England.

For France, one of the reasons for a *rapprochement* with Spain was the hope of commercial advantages. Ever since the Peace of Utrecht France had resented its exclusion from the direct trade with the Spanish colonies that it had enjoyed at the end of the seventeenth century and the beginning of the eighteenth. Because of this exclusion, it had been forced to fall back on its trade with Spanish America through the *flotas* and *galeones* of the official Spanish merchant fleets centered in Cadiz and Seville. An alliance with Spain could, therefore, establish France as the most favored nation in this commerce with the Spanish colonies.

France also hoped that the treaty would provide Spanish support and cooperation in its imperial rivalry with England. In America, where the Anglo-French frontiers were in a highly flammable state, the French hoped that the Spanish alliance would provide the impetus needed to contain the English and even, perhaps, to eliminate them altogether.

By this device France demonstrated its consciousness of the fact that the great rival of French expansion in the colonial world was now England, and there had begun to dawn, among Frenchmen, a prophetic realization that the local conflicts that had been taking place along the frontiers in America were only parts of a larger, worldwide rivalry between the two empires that must eventually come to a showdown. Thus, the treaty represented, for France, a two-fold interest in Spanish cooperation against England in affairs pertaining to America.

Spain, on its side, was deeply annoyed by the abuses of the *asiento* practiced by the South Sea Company, by the illicit trade carried on in the

[74] Keene to Delafaye, Sept. 6, 1732, quoted in Armstrong, *Elizabeth Farnese,* 286.
[75] Cantillo, ed., *Tratados,* 277–278.

Spanish colonies by Englishmen and Angloamericans, and by the territorial expansiveness of the English in Honduras, "Florida," the Bahamas, and the West Indies generally. The alliance with France would provide the strength which Spain lacked to control the obstreperous English.

In the treaty, as it was finally drawn, it was provided that the two crowns would mutually guarantee the integrity of the two empires, both in Europe and in the outside world. France undertook to guarantee to Don Carlos his ducal thrones in Parma, Placentia, and Tuscany; should England or the Emperor or any other power do anything to threaten the peace or security of Don Carlos, France promised to come immediately to the aid of Spain in sustaining him. Should Spain, by reason of English actions relative to Italy or in America, see fit to suspend the commercial privileges in America enjoyed by England, and should England therefore begin hostilities against Spain or its colonies, France would make common cause with Spain against England. France also promised to employ its good offices with England to bring about the restoration of Gibraltar to Spain. The two crowns engaged themselves to oppose with all their forces the execution of the Pragmatic Sanction of the Emperor and to prevent him from disturbing Don Carlos in Italy, and to join their naval forces against England should that country enter the war on the side of the Emperor. With regard to Spanish colonial commerce, France was accorded a "most-favored-nation" position. Spain agreed that French complaints should be heard and ameliorated, whether pertaining to ships seized, the regulation of commerce at Cadiz, territorial conflicts in America, or anything else pertaining to the commerce or colonies of the two nations; to this end there was to be made a special secret commercial treaty between the two countries.[76] Article 13 was directed particularly at the English:

His Catholic Majesty recognizes all the abuses introduced into commerce contrary to the letter of existing treaties, especially by the English nation, in whose extirpation [from that commerce?] the Spanish and French nations are equally interested, has determined to make sure that all these things shall be brought into order and legality according to the letter of existing treaties. And if in antagonism to His Majesty's actions in this direction the English fail to observe any of their responsibilities to the Crown of Spain, or perpetrate any hostilities or insult to the Crown of Spain within Europe or outside of it, His Most Christian Majesty shall make common cause with His Catholic Majesty against England as explained in Article 4, employing to this end all his forces by land and by sea.

The treaty was thus also a defensive alliance against England relative to commerce and colonies.

[76] This treaty was never made.

4. The War of the Polish Succession and the Debate over Georgia

In the power struggle that ensued upon the death of Augustus the Strong, King of Poland, early in 1733, Stanislaus Leszczynski, the French candidate for the Polish throne (he was father-in-law of Louis XV of France) had been proclaimed King by the Polish Diet on September 12, and France and Spain now declared war upon Austria and Russia, who opposed Leszczynski and supported the candidacy of Augustus III, son of Augustus the Strong. But the war was more than a fight for the throne of Poland; for the participation of Charles VI of Austria involved his pet project, the Pragmatic Sanction, which France bitterly opposed. France, indeed, hoped for the destruction of Austrian power, with the aid of Spain. Actually, most of the fighting took place in Italy.

Though the Bourbon Family Compact of 1733 was also designed, in addition to its character as a military alliance, especially as a guarantee against England in case that country should come into the war, both France and Spain were sincerely anxious to keep England neutral, a sentiment that was reciprocated by Robert Walpole, who, as Chancellor of the Exchequer and First Lord of the Treasury, was the *de facto* leader of the English government. The result was that England remained neutral during the war, which lasted until 1735. Preliminary articles for peace were signed in Vienna on October 3, 1735, and these "Preliminaries" became the so-called Third Treaty of Vienna, by which Augustus III was recognized as King of Poland and France accepted the Pragmatic Sanction. Leszczynski was "compensated" by being made Duke of Lorraine; Don Carlos exchanged Parma and Tuscany with the Emperor and his heirs in return for the throne of Naples and Sicily (the "Kingdom of the Two Sicilies").

During these two years, 1733–35, the negotiations between Spain and England over affairs in America continued, but they were relatively quiescent. Spain was represented in England by the Conde de Montijo, as ambassador, and by Don Tomas Geraldino, who was Philip V's representative in the government of the South Sea Company.

Montijo, the ambassador, had arrived in London in the fall of 1732. Of him, Keene had written that his good will toward England was to be won by providing him with women. "He is the most amorous excellency I have met with. Lay but a fair lass in his way, you may mould him to what you please." [77] He was a successful ambassador, nevertheless; it was

[77] Quoted in Armstrong, *Elizabeth Farnese*, 291.

he who, in the fall of 1732, achieved an easing of tension by the exchange of the *Woolball* and the *Dichosa*.

Stert and Goddard, Keene's colleagues as the English members of the joint commission, arrived in London in the summer of 1733, complaining that further negotiations of the joint commission would be useless because of the limited powers of the Spanish representatives.[78] Nevertheless, they continued to work with Montijo and Geraldino toward the resolution of the Anglo-Spanish American disputes. The joint commission had never been discharged, and on November 5, 1734, Stert and Goddard discussed with Geraldino the desirability of formally transferring its activities to London. Geraldino was particularly impatient over the long delay in adjusting the affairs of King Philip V with the South Sea Company—the major task with which he was charged—and, since these affairs were a part of the work of the joint commission, he complained bitterly over the long delay in Stert's and Goddard's return to Spain. But Stert and Goddard replied that all the important matters between the two crowns had already been laid before the commission, and that, since the Spanish commissioners had shown little disposition to do the English "justice," there could be little use in returning. Geraldino argued that the effort to settle the disputes between the two countries, both the court-to-court issues and those concerning the affairs of merchants—on both sides—should be continued at all costs, since a continuation of the tensions might lead to war. If, he said, it were thought advisable to transfer the activities of the commission to London, he felt sure the King of Spain would be willing.[79]

In summarizing their arguments for transferring the work of the joint commission to London, Stert and Goddard explained that the two sides stood in a sort of stalemate with regard to America. England was insisting that no settlement could be made until Spanish "depredations," seizures of ships, and unreasonable "hardships" imposed upon English commerce in America should be stopped by the Spanish government and its American officials; Spain, on its side, would make no concessions until a stop should be put to the illicit commerce being carried on in the Spanish colonies by British subjects and until the affairs of the South Sea Company should be "precisely adjusted" in such a way that the King of Spain should have a reckoning of what was due him and the activities of the company itself should be strictly confined to the legal terms of the *asiento*.

The King of England, they said, had sent commissioners to Spain, and they had remained there three years, during which time they had presented a host of British complaints against the Spanish abuses and suppressions of English commerce in American waters. These complaints and claims had been fruitless, chiefly because of the failure to clarify the

[78] Montijo to Patiño, London, June 26, 1733, A.G.S., *Estado*, 6887.
[79] Goddard to Newcastle, London, Nov. 5, 1734, P.R.O., S.P., 94: fol. 106.

South Sea Company accounts.[80] In view, they said, of the fact that the South Sea Company's headquarters were in London, and especially in view of the confusion into which the affairs of the company had been thrown by the repeated interruptions caused by war, the negotiation of the company's disputes with Spain and with Philip V's representative, Geraldino, which, according to the Treaty of Seville, were to be referred to the joint commission, could be most effectively carried on in London.[81]

Moreover, they argued, in view of Minister José Patiño's known desire for a peaceful solution of the American problem, they felt sure that the wishes of the company and the work of the commission might be effectively coordinated if the commission were sitting in London. Englishmen having claims against Spain might appear personally before the commission if it were meeting in London, and it would be easy to report to Parliament and to command its continued support, whereas the return of the commission to Spain would be almost certain to precipitate an outcry of criticism in that body.

Montijo and Geraldino reported to Patiño the British insistence upon transferring the commission to London, especially Goddard's argument that it would be easier to settle the company's accounts in London than in Spain. But it all boiled down. Montijo said, to the desire of the English commissioners to excuse their own inaction and to be in a postiion to forestall criticism in Parliament.[83] Apparently, the idea of transferring the commission originated with Robert Walpole himself, and it appeared to Montijo that his reasons were basically political.[84]

Patiño refused to countenance the transfer of the commission to London. He instructed Montijo to remind the British ministry that His Catholic Majesty had the right to cancel the *asiento* contract and the annual ship, since the South Sea Company had failed in so many ways to live up to their conditions. The King of Spain's restraint, said Patiño, was the clearest proof of his desire for a peaceful settlement of all the matters at issue, whether with the company or with England.[85]

Meanwhile, Geraldino had proposed to the South Sea Company that it sell its interest in the annual ship to the King of Spain, in return for two per cent of the returns of the *flotas* and *galeones*.[86] But the company was in no mood to give up its legal privileges in the trade with the Spanish

[80] Actually, the South Sea Company deliberately hid its activities and its profits from the scrutiny of the Spanish King and his agents. It had no idea of letting him or them know the full extent either of its illicit activity or of its profits.

[81] Goddard and Stert to Newcastle, Dec. 6, 1734, P.R.O., S.P., 94: fol. 106.

[82] Goddard and Stert to Newcastle, Dec. 6, 1734, P.R.O., S.P., 94: fol. 106.

[83] Montijo to Patiño, Nov. 17, 1734, A.G.S., *Estado*, 6888. Stert and Goddard were members of Parliament, and were among the supporters of Robert Walpole (Geraldino to Patiño, Nov. 18, 1734, A.G.S., *Estado*, 6888).

[84] Montijo to Patiño, Nov. 17,1734, A.G.S., *Estado*, 6888.

[85] Patiño to Montijo, Jan. 24, 1735, A.G.S., *Estado*, 6888.

[86] Proposal of Geraldino to the South Sea Company (n.d.) A.G.S., *Estado*, 7006.

colonies—or all the opportunities for illegal activity and profit that went with them.

Meanwhile, also, the *voies de fait* in America had continued to trouble the relations between the two empires. Early in 1733, for example, a fleet of ships loaded with salt from the Tortugas bound for Boston was attacked by two Spanish ships of war and four of them were taken as prizes.[87] Keene entered a violent protest against this warlike action at the Spanish court and demanded severe punishment for the commanders of the Spanish vessels. He went so far as to say that, if satisfaction were not immediately forthcoming, the British King would be compelled to take new military action.[88] Spain desired no war with England, in view of the situations existing in Poland and Italy, and Patiño took a conciliatory position with regard to this incident. Similarly, he promised to give England some sort of satisfaction relative to the arbitrary action of the governor of Santiago de Cuba in seizing properties of the South Sea Company. Upon Keene's insistence he promised that the commanders of the Spanish warships would be suspended and that the governor of Santiago would be severely chastised.[89]

The greatest shock to Anglo-Spanish relations relative to America came with the establishment of the colony of Georgia.[90]

The part of North America in which Georgia was located, that is, roughly, between the Savannah River and the St. John's, had long entered into the diplomatic disputes between the two countries, and Spanish claims to the area had been presented to the Anglo-Spanish joint commission of 1732, as has been noted. Now, with the creation of the new colony, the Spanish protest was loud and vigorous.

The first reports of the creation of Georgia reached Spain early in 1733.[91] At the moment, Spain was so preoccupied with the imminent war over the Polish Succession and the position of Don Carlos in Italy that, as Keene wrote, it "desired nothing more" than that England remain neutral.[92] Little, therefore, was said about Georgia. Geraldino, the Spanish agent in London, was instructed, however, to ascertain whether the new colony was in territory that was rightfully Spain's, and, if it was, to protest this trespass upon Spanish territory and violation of the Treaties of

[87] Affidavit of Benjamin Browne, Apr. 25, 1733, A.G.S., *Estado*, 6887; Keene to Newcastle, Aug. 5, 1733, P.R.O., S.P., 94: fol. 117.
[88] Keene to Newcastle, Aug. 5, 1733, P.R.O., S.P., 94: fol. 117.
[89] Keene to Newcastle, Aug. 5, 1733, P.R.O., S.P., 94: fol. 117.
[90] For full discussions of the diplomatic exchanges that took place between England and Spain over Georgia, see Lanning, *The Diplomatic History of Georgia: A Study of the Epoch of Jenkins' Ear* and Reese, *Colonial Georgia: A Study in British Imperial Policy in the Eighteenth Century*.
[91] News from London, Aug. 27, 1733, A.G.S., *Estado*, 6887.
[92] Keene to Newcastle, Madrid, Nov. 4, 1733, P.R.O., S.P., 94: fol. 117; same to same, Dec. 14, 1733, *ibid.*

Madrid (1670) and Utrecht (1713). He reported on October 20, 1735,[93] that Georgia was, indeed, south of Carolina, between Carolina and Florida, but that Oglethorpe had been instructed to maintain good relations with the governor of Florida.[94]

Spain's moderation toward England is probably to be accounted for by the fact that Spain was anxious to have England guarantee the possession of the throne of the kingdom of Naples by Don Carlos, a guarantee which Montijo proposed to Walpole. Walpole assured Spain that England would guarantee to Don Carlos his throne, but that it could not make any public pronouncement on the subject until Spain had acceded to the Treaty of Vienna, which ended the War of the Polish Succession.[95]

It was, thus, only after the Peace of Vienna and the establishment of Don Carlos as the King of Naples (or King of the Two Sicilies), that Spain again took up the question of Georgia. Even then, Patiño was aroused to vigorous action only by the news that, in 1736, the Spanish governor of Florida, Don Francisco del Moral Sanchez, had made a treaty with Charles Dempsey, for Georgia, providing that Fort St. George, on the St. John's River, should be dismantled, that there should be no fighting until the home government should authorize it. But the treaty recognized the St. John's River as the southern boundary of Georgia,[96] and this, in Patiño eyes, represented an actual acceptance of a deep cut into Spanish territory by the English. The treaty was, therefore, repudiated, and Moral Sanchez was called home to Spain, tried for treason, and, reputedly, executed.[97]

5. The Convention of the Pardo and After

Upon the restoration of peace in Europe after the end of the War of the Polish Succession, more active negotiations between Spain and England relative to America were resumed.

Thomas Geraldino proposed to the English ministry a convention between Spain and England that promised, in the name of His Catholic Majesty, to indemnify all English merchants who had claims against Spain in the amount of £140,000 Sterling, and the English were disposed to accept. But the Spanish cabinet refused to ratify the convention, not so much on account of the amount as because of righteous indignation over

[93] Geraldino(?) to Patiño, London, Sept. 29, 1735, A.H.N., Estado, Libro 704, p. 25.
[94] Same to same, Oct. 20, 1735, A.H.N., Estado, Libro 704, pp. 34–36.
[95] Geraldino (?) to Patiño, Jan. 13, 1736, A.H.N., Estado, Libro 704, pp. 74–77.
[96] Lanning, The Diplomatic History of Georgia, 47; Reese, Colonial Georgia, Geraldino to the Marques de Torrenuevo, London, Jan. 31, 1737, A.H.N., Estado, Libro 706.
[97] Lanning, The Diplomatic History of Georgia, 48; Reese, Colonial Georgia, 58. For relations between Georgia and Florida, see above, Chapter XIII.

the insults and the menaces that were being heard daily in Parliament against Spain and the Spaniards.

A motion was introduced into Parliament that instructed the Walpole government to demand of Spain that it desist immediately from the right of search on the high seas. The resolution was approved in the House of Lords by one vote, but the House of Commons rejected it by a very narrow margin. The Walpole ministry then took advantage of the occasion, despite the opposition of Newcastle, who favored war, to instruct Keene to try to conclude a convention to settle outstanding disputes between the two countries. This Keene did, and the Convention of the Pardo was signed by Sebastian de la Cuadra and Keene on January 14, 1739.[98] The convention was still to be ratified by the governments of Spain and Britain.

By the terms of this convention the King of Spain promised to pay to the King of England £95,000 Sterling to indemnify all outstanding English claims against the King of Spain. The other questions in dispute, those relative to the right of visit and search on the high seas, the boundaries of Florida and Carolina (that is, Georgia), the privileges claimed by English commerce in America, and, finally, the adjudication of prize cases in America, were left to the decision of a new joint commission, which was to meet in Madrid.

Spain named as its commissioners Don José de Quintana and Don Esteban José de Abaría (Quintana had been a member of the commission of 1731-32); the King of England named Benjamin Keene and Abraham Castres, the latter the English consul general in Madrid.

While the commission began its meetings in fruitless conferences, the text of the convention of the Pardo, when published in England, was received by a storm of disapprobation. The South Sea Company, which had hoped to be excused from the debts it owed the King of Spain on account of the *asiento*, found itself faced with the following declaration of the Spanish court:

Don Sebastian de la Cuadra . . . declares formally that His Catholic Majesty reserves wholly to himself the right to suspend the *Asiento de Negros* and send the necessary orders for its suspension in America, in case the Company does not obligate itself promptly to pay the £78,000 sterling that it has admitted it owes on the account of duties due on slaves [imported into the ports of the Spanish colonies] . . . and he equally declares . . . that he will sign the aforementioned Convention under no other circumstances; . . .[99]

Spanish ratification of the convention was thus made conditional upon an action by the South Sea Company that it was hardly prepared to take, while mounting public opposition in Britain to the convention greatly lessened its chances of getting through Parliament.

[98] Paullin, ed., *European Treaties*, IV, 57–60.
[99] Cantillo, ed., *Tratados*, 345.

Because of the desperate efforts of Walpole, the convention was finally approved, but only by the narrowest of margins, by Parliament. At the same time, the Parliament provided substantial subsidies to the government for the purposes of war with Spain, in case that country should refuse to accede to the demands made upon it. Preparation for war was set in motion, and the squadron of Admiral Haddock was sent to Gibraltar to lend force to the British demands.

The behavior of the English offended the pride of the Spaniards and closed the door to further negotiations. The Spanish court replied to the British demands with demands of its own. Far from conceding the suspension of the right of search, it demanded categorically that the British government recognize that right; it suspended the execution of the convention and the payment of the £95,000 promised in the convention until the South Sea Company should cancel its obligations to the Spanish crown, and it even threatened to suspend the *asiento* and take other hostile steps if the British squadron did not retire immediately from the waters around Gibraltar.[100]

England finally issued a declaration of reprisal on August 20, 1739, and declared war on Spain on October 30 following. Spain responded with its own declaration on November 28, a declaration that recapitulated the long series of British abuses in America and the "unjust" and arbitrary acts of the British government. Thus began the so-called War of Jenkins' Ear.

6. *France and the War of Jenkins' Ear*

The sudden stiffening of Spain's attitude toward England following the negotiation of the Convention of the Pardo was apparently due, in part at least, to the influence of France.

The Anglo-French alliance, which had been severely weakened by England's negotiation of the Treaty of Vienna with Austria in 1731, had never really recovered from that blow. England had remained neutral during the War of the Polish Succession, and although lip service was paid to the alliance in the years following that war, France was not really disposed to renew it and turned instead to the idea of strengthening its family alliance with Spain.

Partly because of its isolation in the balance of Europe, partly because of the growing tension in the relations between England and Spain in America, and partly because of a new flare-up in the West Indies of commercial and navigational "incidents" between French and English ships and officials, England sought, in the year 1738, to renew the old Anglo-French alliance of 1716–31 and to make an Anglo-French convention relative to America that might both smooth Anglo-French colonial disputes

[100] Cantillo, ed., *Tratados*, 345.

in that hemisphere and keep France neutral in the threatening Anglo-Spanish conflict.

Fleury, of course, however willing he might be to compromise Anglo-French disputes in and with regard to America, was not at all interested in pulling England's chestnuts out of the fire in that country's disputes with Spain. On the contrary, he and his foreign minister, Jean Jacques Amelot de Chaillou, were at that very moment beginning a negotiation with Spain for a renewal of the Bourbon Family Compact of 1733, which was in part an alliance against England, and were instructing their ambassador in Madrid, Louis Pierre Engilbert, Comte de la Marck, to go to almost any lengths to stiffen Spain's resistance to England.[101]

The proposal for a new Franco-Spanish alliance had come first from the Spanish ambassador to France, the Marqués de la Mina, in April, 1738, before British ambassador Waldegrave's return to Paris after a visit to England. Fleury had temporized, but Amelot had suggested that the Spanish court prepare a "project" for the proposed alliance. The Spanish court, however, was less anxious to ask for French aid than was its ambassador. The Spanish monarchs still resented France's arbitrary conduct in the War of the Polish Succession and were determined to show France that Spain could get along without its help. Most of all, the Spanish court realized that France, in exchange for an alliance, would certainly demand for itself commercial privileges in Spain and whatever Spain might retrieve from England of the commercial privileges that nation enjoyed in America.[102]

But French policy was definitely swinging toward a new *rapprochement* with Spain, in part, at least, against England. From June, 1738, onward, Cardinal Fleury and Amelot pressed for both an alliance and a treaty of commerce—almost exactly as La Cuadra had foreseen. Spain, too, as tension with the English over American affairs mounted, became more and more receptive to the prospect of French diplomatic backing and, possibly, eventual military support. La Cuadra favored a defensive alliance, but without a commercial treaty; he also hoped that, in case of war, a common effort with France might lead to the restoration of Gibraltar, Minorca, and Georgia to Spain.[102a]

Negotiations for a new Franco-Spanish alliance thus proceeded through the summer of 1738 and into 1739, just at the time when Thomas Geraldino, now Spanish ambassador to London, was succeeding in making an agreement with the Walpole government for a settlement of the Anglo-Spanish disputes in America. The Spanish court refused to ratify the Geraldino agreement because of "insults" to Spain in the British Parliament, as has been noted; but the haughtiness and the firmness of the

---

[101] *Recueil des Inst., Espagne*, III, 191; Baudrillart, *Philippe V et la Cour de France*, V, Book IV, Chapters 1–3.

[102] Baudrillart, *Philippe V et la cour de France*, IV, 467–468.

[102a] Baudrillart, *Philippe V et la cour de France*, IV, 469.

Spanish rejection was undoubtedly strengthened by the French ambassador's assurances of French support in Spain's quarrel with England over the American issues.

Meanwhile, in Paris, the negotiations for a Franco-Spanish alliance continued, and it appeared by midsummer that the proposed alliance was on the point of realization. A general plan for the proposed treaty was drawn up, and the King of the Two Sicilies (the former Don Carlos) was included, in order to guarantee support for him in his struggle with the Emperor for a clearer recognition of his title to lands in Italy. Orders were given by Comte Maurepas, the French minister of marine, to prepare all French naval forces for action.

But the alliance was not made—yet. The French were insistent that there could be no alliance without the treaty of commerce, and a project embodying France's desires in the matter was given to the Comte de la Marck to take to Spain.[103] La Marck was instructed to demand certain concessions for France relative to maritime commerce and navigation, to the privileges of Frenchmen in Spain, especially merchants interested in consigned to foreigners coming from America in the *flota*. He was not, the Cadiz trade with America, and to the imports placed by Spain on goods however, to make any rash promises relative to Gibraltar and Minorca for fear of engaging France in a general war—which was the last thing Cardinal Fleury desired.[104]

For the treaty of commerce France demanded, in the first place, a reiteration of former most-favored-nation treaties. Amelot was shocked to learn that Spain, in planning to leave the new treaty silent on this point, expected to start from the famous Castelar statement of 1731, which cancelled all preceding treaties; if Spain could cancel all formerly existing treaties by a simple, unilateral declaration, it would be able to cancel the new treaty, if made, by the same procedure. Spain also proposed to deprive France of all trade to Africa.

The point of greatest disagreement, however, was Article 2, which embodied two major proposals. The first was a provision that the products of French colonies might be imported freely into Spain. The second was concerned with the Spanish King's freedom to increase the imposts upon French goods taken into Spain, including those shipped to America or from America to France, by way of Cadiz. France demanded a limitation upon this faculty, in the form of a fixed and invariable tariff, but la Mina reported that the King of Spain would prefer to renounce any alliance with France, rather than surrender or limit his sovereign right to raise or lower the tariff at will.

With regard to the right of visit and search on the high seas, claimed by Spain, France was willing to compromise, but insisted that the Spanish

[103] *Recueil des Inst., Espagne*, III, 191, 202.
[104] Baudrillart, *Philippe V et la cour de France*, IV, 471.

guarda costas must be of a certain size, to avoid abuses by small and inconsequential operators.

Spain still hesitated to accept the treaty of commerce, even though France expressed a willingness to make some slight concessions. When England declared war on Spain the treaty of commerce was not signed, nor, as a consequence, the alliance; France remained neutral.

In addition to his other two missions, the alliance and the treaty of commerce, and as a matter of cementing the family connection underlying the proposed treaties, de la Marck was instructed to bring to realization a proposal to arrange marriages between a prince of the Spanish royal family, Don Felipe, with the French "Madame Royale," Princess Louise-Elizabeth, and of the Spanish princess Maria Teresa, with the French Dauphin, still only nine years old. Don Felipe was married to "Madame" on August 26, 1738; the marriage of the Dauphin with Maria Teresa did not take place, because of their ages, until December 18, 1744.

The French court was greatly surprised by the signature, on January 14, 1739, of the Convention of the Pardo by England and Spain, an agreement that was expected to settle the disputes between the two countries in America. "It was not," as Amelot wrote, "that we should desire that war might break out between England and France, but it would have been of extreme importance to stop the excess of fraud [in America] that the English practice with impunity." [105] But Spain had its reasons, and hoped, in any case, soon to bring an end to the *asiento*. With the *asiento* and the abuse of the South Sea Company out of the way, it ought to be possible to settle the other questions at issue between the two empires without war.

La Marck's negotiations continued while he attempted to do all in his power to stiffen the Spanish attitude toward England, which he did with considerable success. At the same time, the Marqués de la Mina, the Spanish ambassador in Paris, continued the negotiation there to such a point that it appeared, in April, 1739, that the two treaties were on the point of being signed. But the Spaniards deliberately delayed the culmination because of La Cuadra's feeling against the commercial treaty, particularly by raising the question whether, since Holland and England had "most-favored-nation" treaties with Spain, those nations would automatically be entitled to any privileges accorded France. The negotiations were transferred back to Madrid in June, and La Marck was instructed to say to the Spanish court that if the Spanish rulers wished the assistance of France, they must consider the treaty of commerce a *sine qua non*. He was also to urge them to do something to appease the Dutch, for fear Holland might join England and thereby transform the Anglo-Spanish conflict into a general war.

---

[105] Quoted in Baudrillart, *Philippe V et la cour de France*, IV, 520.

The Convention of the Pardo, in fact, was proving to be unworkable, partly because of the stiffening Spanish attitude and partly because of the rising clamor for war in England, and when George II issued orders for general reprisals against Spain in August, 1739—an obvious cover for an attack upon the Spanish treasure fleets returning from America—Spain retaliated in kind, and it was only a matter of a few weeks before England declared war upon Spain at the end of October, as has been noted.

During all these months the negotiations between France and Spain continued. France persisted in its demand that the signature of the treaty of commerce be a *sine qua non* for the alliance, and la Mina reported that Fleury declared to him that even after a declaration of war against Spain by England, France would not announce its support of Spain except after the signature of the treaty of commerce—a remark that threw the Queen of Spain into a fury against France.

Thus matters stood in 1739 between France and Spain, when, relative to the Anglo-Spanish conflict over America, the War of Jenkins' Ear began. The Comte de la Marck's negotiation for a new Bourbon family alliance had not borne tangible fruit, and would not, until, in 1743, after the outbreak of the War of the Austrian Succession, France felt so desperately in need of allies that it found itself willing to accept an alliance with Spain without the accompanying treaty of commerce which was a *sine qua non* in 1738. But the consummation of the marriage of Don Felipe and "Madame" of France, together with French encouragement of Spain in Spain's disputes with England, did have the effect of building up a friendly mood on both sides. And although France did not go to war on Spain's side when the War of Jenkins' Ear broke out in 1739, France's moral support was worth a good deal to Spain during that conflict.

CHAPTER XVI

Anglo-French Diplomacy with Regard to America, 1716-39

T HE ANGLO-FRENCH TREATY OF PEACE made at Utrecht in 1713 had given England a vast aggregation of territories in America.[1] But the treaty had hardly been ratified before the two empires resumed their rival expansions and their bickerings over their respective possessions, even those that had been ceded by the treaty.

Yet the relations between France and England in Europe were cordial, and the Earl of Stanhope for England and the Abbé Dubois for France succeeded in negotiating at Hanover, in the summer of 1716, a treaty of alliance (to which Holland acceded in January, 1717) that gave these states a preponderance in the European balance of power that lasted for a decade and a half.[2]

This treaty was arranged primarily for the preservation of the terms of the international settlement arranged at Utrecht in 1713. It therefore provided for an alliance guaranteeing the enforcement of the Treaties of Utrecht, the possessions of the three signatories in Europe, and the established dynastic successions in France and England. America was not mentioned by name, but the treaty did provide (Article 1) that the signatories mutually guaranteed their "lands, countries, and towns . . . as well within as out of Europe."

The situations that were developing in America were overshadowed by the European interests of the alliance, and American disputes were several times compromised or postponed for the sake of not disturbing the harmonious cooperation of the two states in Europe. That is not to say, however, that disputes between these two powers in America did not occur, that they were not bitter, or that any of them were permanently settled.

The colonial expansion of both nations during these years greatly in-

[1] See Chapter X.
[2] Douglas, gen. ed., *English Historical Documents*, X: 1714–83, 913–916.

creased the opportunities for dispute along ill-defined frontiers and the vague boundaries mentioned in the treaties. For example, the cession of Acadia to England did nothing to end Anglo-French conflicts on the northeastern seaboard. Quite the contrary. When the French began, in the years following the Peace of Utrecht, to build a supposedly impregnable fortress at Louisbourg, on Cape Breton, which was to be the center of French military, maritime and fishing activity on the Atlantic coast of North America, a whole new series of disputes arose over the limits of English and French territorial waters. Just such disagreement over the control of the sea lay behind the attack, in the summer of 1718, of the English Captain Smart, commanding H.M.S. *Squirrel*, on a French fishing fleet which was found just off the mainland of Nova Scotia, in the "Gulf of Canso," the water passage between the islands of Canso and the mainland of Nova Scotia. Smart claimed the fleet was trespassing on English territorial waters.[3]

The French government immediately protested Smart's action, on the ground that the island of Canso lay in the Gulf of St. Lawrence, which was recognized by the Treaty of Utrecht as being French, that the fishermen were, therefore, in French waters, and that Captain Smart's action was a gross violation of the treaty and of international law. In 1719, a French warship was sent to seize an equal number of British ships by way of reprisal for Smart's action. This matter was brought before the joint commission then meeting in Paris and was discussed there; but the boundary question raised by the seizures was not resolved.

Meanwhile, in the southern parts of the Mississippi Valley, the French built Fort Toulouse, "among the Alabamas" (Indians), at the junction of the Coosa and the Tallapoosa Rivers, uncomfortably close to the frontiers of Carolina; New Orleans was founded in 1718 (Biloxi had been founded in 1699, Mobile in 1702); in 1721 the French agent, La Joncaire, rebuilt the old fort at Niagara. In the West Indies active rivalry for the possession of the disputed islands in the Caribbean area had begun almost immediately after the treaty of peace.

1. *The Anglo-French Joint Commission of 1719*

The Anglo-French Treaty of Utrecht (Article 11) had provided that outstanding disputes between the French and the English in America were to be settled by a joint commission.[4] Because of shifting political and

[3] For the local, governor-to-governor exchanges relative to this and other international incidents, see Chapter XIII.

[4] See Chapter X. For a discussion of the history of this commission, see Max Savelle, "The Forty-ninth Degree of North Latitude as an International Boundary, 1719: The Origin of an Idea," *Canadian Historical Review*, XXXVIII, No. 3 (Sept., 1957), 183–201.

dynastic events in Europe, however, it was not until after the formation of
the Anglo-French alliance that steps were taken to carry out the provisions
of the treaty.

It was apparently England that made the first move. The continued
friction in America prompted the Board of Trade, as early as the fall of
1717, to urge the government to reopen with France the possibility of
implementing Article 11 of the Treaty of Utrecht. Even so, it was not until
the summer of 1719 that this was done.[5]

The French, too, were now beginning to be worried over America. For
it appeared to them, according to the Marshal d'Estrées, President of the
Council of the Marine, that if the English claims in Acadia and the Hudson Bay area were admitted, France would have to get out of Canada
entirely. Therefore, in the spring of 1719, d'Estrées urged upon the Council of the Marine the necessity of proceeding at once to the naming of
commissioners.[6] That council, reviewing the friction that had arisen in
America during 1718 and 1719, and especially that at Canso, followed
d'Estrées' lead in urging upon the Abbé Dubois the necessity, from
France's point of view, of settling the American disputes and, in addition
to preventing the disputes from spreading into war, to block the imperialistic expansion of the English.[7]

At last, then, in the summer of 1719, it was agreed on both sides that the
joint commission envisioned by the Treaty of Utrecht should be created
and set to work. In England, the Lords Justices appointed Martin Bladen,
of the Board of Trade, the Earl of Stair, English ambassador to Paris, and
William Pulteney to be the negotiators for England. On the French side
of the Channel, Dubois named as his negotiators the Marshal d'Estrées
and himself. D'Estrées, as the active member of the French negotiating
team, turned to those old North American hands, La Mothe Cadillac, the
explorer, le Père Charlevoix, the historian, and the Sieur d'Auteuil, former
royal procurator-general in Canada, for assistance with the French case.

The first meeting of the joint commission took place on Saturday, October 31, 1719. Bladen, Pulteney, and Stair were present for England;
Dubois and d'Estrées represented France.[8] At this first meeting the time
was spent discussing procedure, and it was agreed to take up the American
problems in the order in which they were mentioned in the Treaty of
Utrecht. Accordingly, at the next meeting, questions pertaining to Hudson

[5] *C.S.P., Col., A.& W.I.,* 1717–18, No. 230, p. 116; *ibid,* 1719–20, No. 310, p. 162;
No. 360, p. 210.

[6] A.E., Corr. Pol., Ang. 328, fols. 82–82 vo.

[7] "Son A. de Bourbon et Le Mare d'Estrées à l'Abbé Dubois," Apr. 10, 1719, A.E.,
Corr. Pol., Ang., 328: fols. 123–123 vo; Mémoire cur Canseau, *ibid.,* 328: fols. 127–
129, *et passim.*

[8] *C.S.P., Col., A.& W.I.,* 1719–20, No. 420, p. 240; A.E., Corr. Pol., Ang., 379:
fols. 231–233 vo; G.B., P.C., Jud. Cee. *In the Matter of the Boundary between
Canada and Labrador* . . . , VIII, 4078. (Hereafter cited as *Labrador Boundary.*)

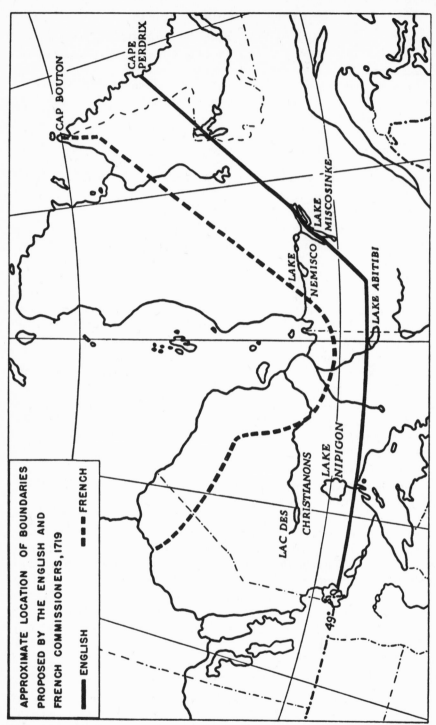

APPROXIMATE LOCATION OF BOUNDARIES PROPOSED BY THE ENGLISH AND FRENCH COMMISSIONERS, 1719. (Reprinted by permission of the *Canadian Historical Review*.)

Bay would be discussed.[9] At this second gathering, on November 4, the time was spent in a discussion of the method of determining the boundary of Hudson Bay;[10] at the third meeting, held November 7, the English commissioners presented to d'Estrées (Dubois being absent because of illness) a memorial setting forth the English proposal for a boundary, which closely followed their instructions.[11]

Unfortunately for the prospects of success of this commission, news had reached Paris just a few days before its first meeting that a French expedition—sent out by none other than the Marshal d'Estrées himself—had seized the island of St. Lucia. Dubois at first denied the reports and then avowed the seizure, on the ground that the island belonged as of right to France.[12] The attention of the commissioners on both sides was diverted by the St. Lucia incident, and after the third meeting and the presentation of the English memorial on Hudson Bay much time was lost in somewhat heated exchanges over the ownership of St. Lucia and the sudden French seizure.[13]

Because of the English protest, the French withdrew their new colonists from St. Lucia. But the infrequent subsequent meetings of the commission, beginning with the one held on January 15, 1720, were devoted to the St. Lucia incident and other points of tension in America, and the Hudson Bay question was postponed indefinitely.[14] Eventually, with the achievement of peace with Spain in 1721, the whole set of American questions was relegated to the discussions that were expected to take place at the proposed general peace conference to be held at Cambrai.[15] This, of course, meant the end of the Anglo-French joint commission of 1719–20, which to all intents and purposes had ceased to function early in 1720 in any case.[16] The complete futility of the joint commission, however, did not prevent a substantial exchange of ideas; and, though nothing definite resulted from the commission's labors, this exchange throws a clear light

[9] C.S.P., Col., A.& W.I., 1719–20, No. 420, p. 240; Labrador Boundary, VIII, 4078.
[10] C.S.P., Col., A.& W.I., 1719–20, No. 432, p. 244; Stair to Craggs, Nov. 4, 1719, P.R.O., S.P., 78: fol. 165.
[11] C.S.P., Col., A.& W.I., 1719–20, No. 438, p. 246; Labrador Boundary, VIII, 4081; A.E., Corr. Pol., Ang., 328: fols 493–493 vo.
[12] C.S.P., Col., A.& W.I., 1719–20, No. 432, p. 244; Stair to Craggs, Nov. 5, 1719, P.R.O., S.P., 78: fol. 165.
[13] Stair to Craggs, Dec. 27, 1719 (n.s.), P.R.O., S.P., 78: fol. 165; Bladen to l'Abbé Dubois, Nov. 8, 1719, A.E., Corr., Pol., Ang., 327: fols. 10–10 vo; Craggs to Dubois, Nov. 5, 1719 ibid.: fols. 11–11 vo.
[14] "Mémoire de M. Waldegrave envoyé à Chauvigny," Mar. 13, 1733, A.E., Corr. Pol., Ang., 379: fols. 231–233 vo.
[15] Mémoire sur les points qui doivent être examinés et décidés par des Comm^res du Roy de la g^de Bret^e," May 28, 1724, A.E., Corr. Pol., Ang., 347: fols. 342–350; "Mémoire pour servir d'Instruction au S. Comte de Broglie Lieutenant Général des Armées du Roy allant en Angleterre en qualité d'Ambassadeur . . . ," May 18, 1724, ibid.: fols. 266–329. See also Chapter XIV.
[16] Ibid.; C.S.P., Col., A. & W.I., 1720–21, No. 656, p. 436.

upon the thinking and the policies of the English and French empire-builders.

In the course of the meetings of the Anglo-French joint commission, both sides presented their ideas as to what the boundaries of the Hudson Bay area ought to be. The English commissioners were instructed to demand of the French the boundary defined by the Hudson's Bay Company in 1718: this was a line beginning at Grimington's Island, or Cape Perdrix, on Davis Strait, running southwestwardly through Lake Miscosinke, to the junction of this line with the line of 49° North Latitude, and thence along that parallel westward. It was now explicitly stipulated, however, that the said boundary must be understood "to regard the Trade of the Hudsons-Bay Company only," and that it was not to be considered as recognizing any claims to territory to the south or southwest of that line. The commissioners were also instructed to require of the French that they abandon their fort on the upper Albany River and that they promise to build no more upon the rivers that flowed into Hudson Bay.[17]

The line proposed by the French commissioners, beginning at Cape Benton, on Hudson Strait, would have roughly followed the shoreline of Hudson Bay around the bottom of the bay and toward the northwest as far as Churchill River. Curiously enough, although the French negotiators at Utrecht, on the basis of the general idea that the boundary between Hudson Bay and Canada ought to be the natural line provided by the height of land between the rivers that flowed into Hudson Bay and those which flowed into the St. Lawrence, had been willing to cede to England the entire Hudson Bay Basin,[18] the line now proposed would have left the English only a broad *lisière* along the coast of Hudson Bay and would have removed the English from their supposed encroachment upon New France. On the other hand, it would have left the French in an admirable position to stop the flow of furs to the bay, whether down the Rupert, the Moose, or the Albany, merely by building forts upon the upper reaches of these rivers on the French side of the line.

Obviously, the English were in no mood to permit any such thing. Equally obviously, the French government was not now to be expected to accede to the English demands, least of all to demolish French forts on the French side of the proposed line, in what they were deeply convinced was New France itself. Both the English and the French were now casting speculative glances at the vast hinterland of the bay and the Great Lakes. The next new chapter in the expansive rivalry for the control of North America would take place in that area.

[17] Legg, ed., *Brit. Dip. Insts., I, France, 1689–1721,* 197–198.

[18] "On consent pareillement de céder la Baye de Hudson avec les rivières qui y tombent, celles qui y tombent dans la rivière St. Laurent, avec les Terres adjacentes devant appartenir à la Nouvelle France, dont les Français sont en possession depuis plus de 150: ans." ("Mémoire sur les Pays de l'Amérique, que la France doit céder sux Anglais par la paix prochaine," Jan. 13, 1713, A.N., Cols., C 11E/2: fols. 10–11.)

Nothing was achieved, of course, by the Anglo-French joint commission of 1719–20 on American disputes and boundaries. While the arguments were going on, the war with Spain came to an end, and the American disputes, which now also involved Spain's interests, were put by for discussion at the proposed congress at Cambrai.[19] But the positions of the two countries in America were fairly clear. Both were determined to have the maximum extent of the lands claimed by them anywhere in the American hemisphere. Neither was disposed to compromise its claims in the slightest degree. Each one professed to believe that the other was pursuing a policy of expansion in America that was deliberately aimed at the limitation or even the liquidation of its own possessions there.

2. The "Neutral Islands"

When the English government had received a report of the d'Estrées colony on St. Lucia in 1719, it had ordered its commissioners in Paris to protest the French colonization of the island, on the ground that it belonged to England. Actually, both nations had made feints at the island of St. Lucia during the seventeenth century, and both had claimed it; but neither had colonized it permanently. Now, when the English commissioners protested d'Estrées' action, the Abbé Dubois, for the sake of peace, suspended the charter that had been issued to d'Estrées until the ownership of the island could be determined, and the marshal ordered his colony home.

Whereupon the English government, to the astonishment and chagrin of the French, on May 4, 1722, issued a charter for the same island to the Duke of Montagu, who promptly sent his own colony to the island.

This was too much for France, even at a moment of such good will, and the governor of the French West Indies at Martinique, the marquis de Champigny, sent an armed force to St. Lucia which compelled the English commander to surrender. The English colonists were then transported to Antigua, as has been noted.[20]

After the loss of his colony on St. Lucia, John, Duke of Montagu, proposed that that island be divided between him and the Marshal d'Estrées. But the French government was determined to assert its claim to the entire island and instructed its delegates to the Congress of Soissons to submit the question of the ownership of St. Lucia to the decision of the congress.[21]

[19] See Chapter XIV.

[20] For local governor-to-governor exchanges relative to this episode, see above, Chapter XIII.

[21] Memoir of French merchants regarding the extraordinary *indulto* of 1728 on goods returning from Spanish America, enclosed with Stanhope and Walpole to Newcastle, Nov. 18, 1728 (Part IV), L.C., B.M., Add. Mss. 32759; "Mémoire concernant le propriété de la France sur l'Ilse de Ste. Lucie ou Ste. Alonzie en Amérique, pour servir à M. le Cardinal de Fleury, et à Mrs. le Marquis de Fénélon et le Comte de Brancas cerest [sic] Plenipoteniaires du Roy au Congrès de Soissons," A.N., Cols., C 10c/1.

Nor was the Marshal d'Estrées disposed to take Montagu's proposal seriously. Failing there, in January, 1728, the Duke applied to the King of England for a grant of the island of Tobago as a sort of compensation for his loss of St. Lucia. But this island, also, was claimed by France, and Montagu's appeal came to nothing.

Meanwhile, the islands of Dominica and St. Vincent had attracted the attention of colonizing interests in both countries. England claimed both these islands, but France maintained it had a better title to Dominica and that, since the island of St. Vincent belonged to the Carib Indians, it should be left in their possession.

As a result of all these claims and counterclaims, France and England agreed in 1730, by an exchange of letters and of orders to their respective governors in America, to evacuate St. Lucia, St. Vincent, and Dominica, and to leave them "neutral" and unoccupied until their proper ownership might be determined.[22] Tobago and St. Croix were informally included. Technically, they remained in this status until their ownership was finally determined by the Treaty of Paris of 1763. This merely meant, in 1730, that the fate of these islands was left to the final arbitrament of some future war, and they continued to trouble the relations of the two countries in America for nearly a century longer.[23]

3. North America

On the continent of North America the race for empire continued, and this race, as elsewhere, had its reverberations in the diplomatic correspondence between the two countries.[24]

Thus, with regard to the area of Acadia, the French continued to maintain, as they had in the joint commission of 1719, that the Acadia ceded to the English by the Treaty of Utrecht included only the peninsula, or even less than that.[25] All the territory east of the St. George River and north and west of the height of land between the St. Lawrence-Great Lakes basin, they claimed, belonged to New France.[26] Incidentally, when war

---

[22] C.S.P., Col., A. & W.I., 1730, No. 561 (I), pp. 364–366; No. 561 (II),pp. 366–367; ibid., 1733, No. 235, pp. 135–136.

[23] Dominica and St. Vincent were confirmed to Great Britain by the Treaty of Versailles of 1783; St. Lucia and Tobago by the Treaty of Paris of 1814.

[24] For the international exchanges in North America, see Chapter XIII.

[25] "Extrait de la réponse datée 10 Octobre 1731 faite par Mrs. Beauharnais et Hocquart au Mémoire du Roi daté 8 Mai de la même année," A.N. Cols., C 11A/54:134–135 vo. This document even claimed that the true boundary of Acadia should be a line drawn from Cape Canso, on the northeast, to Cape Fourché to the southwest, to which the Treaty of Utrecht had specifically added Port Royal, which lay outside this line.

[26] "Mémoire pour servir à régler les limites entre la Nouvelle Angleterre et l'Acadie, Autrement Nouvelle Écosse," Nov. 8, 1718, C.A.O., F113:2 Acadie.

broke out between the Abenaki Indians of Maine and the "Bostonnais" or New Englanders, over the occupation by the English of certain Abenaki lands in 1722, the French supported the Abenakis as "Indians friendly to the French" under Article 15 of the Treaty of Utrecht and in land that was actually part of New France. The French King protested to George I the occupation of the Abenaki lands, therefore, and demanded that the English withdraw and leave the Abenakis in peace.[27]

It was on the basis of the French "river basin" doctrine of ownership, as well as to forestall the English, who were rumored to have designs on the same spot, that the French, in 1731, built a stone fort, Fort Frederick, at Crown Point, on Lake Champlain.[28]

The establishment of this fort called forth an immediate protest from the English government. The Earl of Waldegrave, English ambassador in Paris, wrote the French ministry on June 13, 1732, that the new fort, since it was built upon land owned by the Iroquois Indians and within the province of New York, was upon English territory and, therefore, that its creation was a violation of Article 15 of the Treaty of Utrecht. This being the case, Waldegrave demanded that the fort be razed immediately.[29]

On similar grounds the English protested the rebuilding of the fort at Niagara, which, in order to control the fur trade and to forestall the expansion of the English, was rebuilt by the French in 1721 and 1727. The English, not to be outdone, built a fort at the trading post at Oswego, at the mouth of the Oswego River, in 1727. This race for possession and the local colony-to-colony disputes that accompanied it were referred to the two home governments, and became the subject matter of an increasingly strained correspondence between the two crowns. Thus, the British ministry wrote to Cardinal Fleury pointing out that Article 15 of the Treaty of Utrecht recognized the Iroquois as subjects of England. Since Fort Oswego stood in Iroquois territory, therefore, the King of England was entirely within his rights in building it there.[30]

At the same time the English government protested the building of the fort at Niagara by the French. This protest was essentially the same as that against Crown Point, that is, that, since Article 15 of the Treaty of Utrecht

[27] Copie du Mémoire du Roy à Mrs. Vandreuil et Bégon, Meudon, June 9, 1723, A.N. Cols., C 11 A 45: fols. 118–120.

[28] N.Y.C.D., IX, 1,021 ff. See also Chapter XIII.

[29] N.Y.C.D., IX, 1034. The French, in defining the boundaries of their territories in North America, followed the doctrine that the nation that owned the main stream of a river owned all the land drained by the rivers and creeks that flowed into it. Thus Canada would include all the land drained by the rivers that flowed into the St. Lawrence and the Great Lakes on both the north and the south sides. The southern boundary of Canada in the Iroquois region, therefore, would theoretically follow the watershed between the St. Lawrence Valley and the Hudson and Susquehanna Valleys.

[30] Walpole to the court of France, Mar. 9, 1728, N.Y.C.D., IX, 996–997.

recognized the Iroquois Indians as subjects of England, and since the fort at Niagara stood upon Iroquois land, it represented a violation of that treaty.[31]

It was in these same decades that the French refortified Vincennes and built Fort Chartres at Kaskaskia, in the Ohio Valley, and Fort Natchez on the Mississippi. The eastern bounds of Louisiana were thought to be the Apalachicola River and the Alleghenies, and Louisiana was regarded as "a sort of advance guard against the English colonies." [32] In general, Louisiana was thought of as part of a chain of critical areas that included Acadia, the lands between the Great Lakes and Hudson Bay, and the West Indies. There was a real fear among French colonial thinkers that in view of the power of the English in New England, Nova Scotia, and the West Indies, "It is not difficult to guess that their plan is to drive us entirely out of the continent of North America." [33]

4. The Decline of the Anglo-French Alliance

With the signing of the Anglo-Austrian Treaty of Vienna in 1731, France felt itself to be isolated in Europe, as has been seen, and sought to bolster its strength by a *rapprochement* with Spain, an effort that produced the Bourbon Family Compact of 1733. So far as England was concerned, also, the alliance of 1716 was definitely weakened. The effect of this fact upon Anglo-French relations relative to America was that from this moment on neither of the two great imperial rivals in the American hemisphere was as disposed to a compromise of their disputes there as they both had been in the years between the Peace of Utrecht and the Treaty of Seville.

When the War of the Polish Succession broke out in 1733, France and Spain went to war against Austria and its allies. It was feared that England might enter the war, in which case the provisions of the Bourbon Family Compact of November of that year would come into play. But England and the Dutch proposed to mediate between the belligerents, and Cardinal Fleury, after some vacillation, showed an inclination to encourage them. The Anglo-Dutch mediation failed, however, and peace was achieved on October 3, 1735, as a result of the secret negotiations of France with the Emperor, in the "Preliminaries" of Vienna, which became a treaty of peace on November, 1738, a treaty to which Spain reluctantly acceded in April,

[31] "Memoir respecting Fort Niagara, presented to his Eminence, Cardinal de Fleury," May 9, 1727, N.Y.C.D., IX, 997–998.
[32] "Mémoire sur la Colonie de la Louisiane porté au Conseil de Régence le 11 Febrier 1716," A.N. Cols., C 13 A/4: fols. 49–80.
[33] *Ibid.*

1739.[34] This treaty concerned itself entirely with European problems; America was not mentioned.

In the years following the end of the War of the Polish Succession, French policy vacillated between friendship for England and a renewal of the alliance with Spain. In 1736 Cardinal Fleury proposed to England that the Anglo-French alliance of 1716 be renewed, but England doubted France's sincerity because of the anti-English bias of Germain-Louis de Chauvelin, Fleury's *Garde des Sceaux* and chief assistant in the conduct of foreign affairs. Chauvelin, however, was dismissed and was succeeded by Jean Jacques Amelot de Chaillou, and there ensued a period of relative cordiality between the two countries. It was not until January, 1738, that Fleury's proposal for a renewal of the alliance was put in writing.

The Earl of Waldegrave, British ambassador in Paris, was instructed to suggest an alliance between the two countries which would also provide mutual recognition of territories owned by them in America, the mutual guarantee of the existing status relative to them in Europe and American commerce, and the maintenance of the prevailing system of alliances and balance of power, and to invite Cardinal Fleury to submit a project embodying these points. England also asked that Holland be included in the treaty.[35]

Unfortunately for England, Fleury vacillated, and new incidents in America prolonged the delay. Several English ships passing too close to the coasts of the French West Indian islands recently had been seized under an ordinance of Louis XV issued in 1727 against illicit English trade with the French islands, which empowered the governors of the French islands to seize foreign (that is, English or Dutch) ships engaged in this prohibited trade. The legislature of the English island of Montserrat had thereupon passed an ordinance providing for the seizure of French ships passing within one league of its coasts, under which several French ships had been seized. Both sets of actions were recognized by England as violations of the Anglo-French Treaty of American Neutrality of 1686,[36] and Waldegrave was instructed to ask that the tensions be eased and the problem resolved by the inclusion in the proposed treaty of some provision strengthening the treaty of 1686.[37] However, since the negotiations of such an arrangement would take time, the British ministry proposed the immediate restitution of the English ship *Scipio*, seized by the French, and the French ship *Fleuron*, seized in retaliation by the British.[38]

Of greater importance to the British, however, was their desire to acquire French collaboration in protest against the activities of the Spanish *guarda*

[34] Cantillo, ed., *Tratados*, 303–317.
[35] Legg, ed., *Brit. Dip. Insts.*, VI, *France, 1727–44*, xxxiii, 193–196.
[36] See Chapter IX.
[37] Instructions for Waldegrave, Apr. 10, 1738, in Legg, ed., *Brit. Dip. Insts.*, VI, *France, 1727–44*, 196–200.
[38] Legg, ed., *Brit. Dip. Insts.*, VI, *France, 1727–44*, 198.

costas in America. Fleury had already expressed sympathy for the English position, and it was hoped he might be willing to put it in writing.[39] Fleury did submit a "project" for an alliance, but it was worded in such a way as to cast doubt upon the English title to some of England's possessions in America, such as Georgia.[40] Fleury indicated that he had Georgia in mind, and was loathe to guarantee to England a territory which might turn out to be, in justice, Spanish. Matters went from bad to worse when news arrived in England that the French had seized an English ship, the *Elizabeth*, near Doña Maria Bay, in French Santo Domingo, claiming that she was engaged in illicit trade. The English protested bitterly, on the ground that all the ships trading with English Jamaica used the Windward Passage, on which Doña Maria Bay was located, that the passage was very difficult, and that ships must stop at Doña Maria Bay for water and refreshment.[41] To prohibit them from doing this would be tantamount to stopping all British trade with Jamaica. The French then proposed that English ships use other bays, but required such conditions as to make their use utterly impracticable. Since the French ministers were so stubborn about it, the ministry and the ambassador came to the conclusion that the French were deliberately attempting to paralyze English trade with Jamaica.[42]

By this time Fleury was busily engaged in negotiating an alliance with Spain and encouraging that country to make a firm stand against England. The cardinal even went so far as to voice a threat that if the British should make themselves "masters of anything considerable there [in America], he could not then help taking the necessary measures on such an occasion." [43]

Despite this threatening attitude on the part of France toward England, the proposed Franco-Spanish alliance was not yet made, chiefly because France still insisted upon a commercial treaty, and France did not enter the war against England—yet.

5. *The Ideologies of English and French Imperialism*

The *voies de fait* which characterized the rival expansions of the French and the English colonial empires in America in the first half of the eighteenth century were not accidental or random skirmishes; nor did they spring entirely from expediency. On the contrary, they were the manifestations in the realm of actuality of fairly clear and widely accepted ideas and deliberate policies on both sides.

[39] Legg, ed., *Brit. Dip. Insts.*, VI, *France, 1727–44,* 198–199.

[40] Legg. ed., *Brit. Dip. Insts.*, VI, *France, 1727–44,* xxxiii. Fleury proposed a guarantee of territory the possession of which was *"libre et non contestée."*

[41] Legg, ed., *Brit. Dip. Insts.*, VI, *France, 1727–44,* 211, 212.

[42] Legg. ed., *Brit. Dip. Insts.*, VI, *France, 1727–44,* 212.

[43] Quoted in Legg, ed., *Brit. Dip. Insts.*, VI, *France, 1727–44,* xxxvii; see also, *ibid.,* 231–232.

Both sides professed to fear the imperialistic "designs" of the other. Each side explained its expansion in America on the ground that it was merely occupying territory that was its own and justified its new forts and Indian alliances on the ground that they were purely defensive. But both also had positive visions of profits from expansion, whether from the Indian trade of the interior of North America or an expanded area for the cultivation of sugar in the West Indies. The archives of both countries are full of memoranda pointing out to the ministers of each the national advantages to be derived from the blocking of the expansion of the other by forts at strategic points, by the occupation of territory, and by the economic exploitation of the Indian trade and the natural resources of the lands to be occupied.

For example, on the French side, as early as 1720 it was frankly stated in a "Memoir on the present state of the Province of Louisiana" that one of the prime purposes for the establishment of Louisiana was "to prevent the English from establishing themselves there, which would render them too powerful, for it is certain that, once in Louisiana, they would soon go on to seize both new and old Mexico." [44] On the other hand, with the French in Louisiana, the Spanish, "in the fear of losing Mexico, would be very careful not to form against France any foreign alliance." In fact,

it will be easy for the French to seize Old and New Mexico from Louisiana, at some moment when they find themselves not to fear the jealousy of the other powers, it being well known that although the Spaniards seized the New World some two hundred years ago they have not, for that, become more formidable since this easy wealth threw them into such a softness as to cause us to regard them in much the same way as they once regarded their American Indians.[45]

As another French summary of January, 1720, put it, the English and the French were each claiming territory claimed by the other, all up and down the continent of America. Evidently, if there was to be peace, the respective holdings of the two must be defined. But

If anything should occur to prevent the definition of boundaries in America, it would be of great consequence not to suffer the English to locate themselves in any part of the French territories that they claim belong to them, because if these places did not [eventually] fall to them by an agreement upon the boundaries, one would have great difficulty in dislodging them; and this would be for them the basis of a pretense to ownership afterwards. Their behavior in the past is a sure guarantee of what we may expect of them in the future.[46]

The French experts were convinced that the English had imperialistic designs on all of North America:

[44] "Mémoire sur l'Estat présent de la Province de la Louisiane en l'année 1720," A.N. Cols., C 13A/6: fols. 99–110.
[45] "Mémoire sur l'Estat présent de la Province de la Louisiane en l'année 1720," A.N. Cols., C. 13A/6: fols. 99–110.
[46] "Extrait d'une liasse de papiers concernant les limites du Canada et de l'Acadie," endorsed "sans lieu Janvier 1720," C.A.O., F113A, II, fols. 95–107.

They [the English] will never agree to anything that may stand in the way of their intention to make themselves masters of the whole of North America, in order to achieve eventually the possession of the entirety of that part of the world.[47]

The writer concluded by observing that the only way to prevent this sort of English expansion, if the government did not wish to use overt force, was to employ the savages to prevent the English from settling on the lands claimed by France.[48]

This fear of English expansion and imperialistic ambition was a constant factor in French colonial and international policies throughout this period. In one of the memoirs given the French delegates to the Congress of Soissons, for example, the plenipotentiaries were warned that, since the English were deliberately attempting both to encroach upon French territories in America and to infiltrate the commerce of the French colonies in the West Indies, the plenipotentiaries must be on their guard against English proposals relative to American territories and must join with the Spanish interests to block English ambitions, if necessary.[49] Again, about 1730, after the Treaty of Seville, the French policy-makers were still disturbed by the uncompromising expansiveness of the English in America:

Besides, it is not only today that we have negotiated with the English with regard to boundaries [between the two empires] in America; but they have never wished to carry to its conclusion any discussion which they felt could never be advantageous to them. So that it seems desirable to await other circumstances, while nevertheless taking all necessary measures to prevent the English from getting a foothold in our territories.[50]

By 1739, on the eve of the War of Jenkins' Ear, this line of thought was an important influence in the support the French ministry gave Spain to encourage that country to take a firm stand against England.[51] Amelot wrote to Ambassador la Marck on January 27, 1739, expressing his surprise that Spain had signed the agreement of the Pardo with England. It was not, he said, that France wished to see war break out between Spain and England, but, rather, that he thought the time had come to put an end to the excessive fraud and territorial aggrandizement which Englishmen practiced in Spanish America without punishment—"Which, with the other advantages that they already have, gives them a superiority in commerce

---

[47] "Limites pour les terres de l'Amérique appartenant aux français et aux Anglais" (n.p., n.d.), Paris, Bibliothèque National, Bureau des Estampes, Portefeuille Vd. 26.
[48] "Limites pour les terres de l'Amérique appartenant aux français et aux Anglais," *loc. cit.*
[49] "Mémoire concernant la propriété de la France sur l'Isle de Ste. Luci ou Ste. Alouzie en Amérique . . . ," A.N. Cols., C 10c/1.
[50] "Au Controlleur Général," Feb. 14, 1730, A.E., Corr. Pol., Ang., 369: fols. 150–151.
[51] "Réflexions sur les différences de l'Angleterre avec l'Espagne, 1739," A.E., Méms. et Docs., Ang., 9: fols. 104–110 vo.

which turns to the prejudice of all the other nations and especially France." [52]

The English were subject to almost exactly the same sort of fear of French expansion in America. The Board of Trade, at the moment of delivering to the Lords Justices the instructions for the English commissioners of 1719, expressed the conviction that the expansion of the French in America "frightens us" and seemed to threaten His Majesty's colonies there. For this reason, the commissioners were instructed, apart from their official negotiations, to keep a keen eye and ear open for news of what the French were doing, particularly in the matter of John Law's Mississippi enterprise;[53] and the Board concluded that it was to be hoped that England might extend its settlements to the Gulf of Mexico by the seizure of the Spanish establishment at St. Augustine. Such an enterprise would cost little and would be especially appropriate now that England was at war with Spain; this acquisition England "might possibly preserve by a future Treaty . . ." [54]

The imperialism of the English in America was a mixture of the urge for commercial expansion with a desire to acquire more land for settlement. English statesmen were convinced that the imperial rivalry of the French in America, which stood in the way of British expansion, was a product of a deliberate policy. Thus, in its famous report of 1721, the Board of Trade reviewed the activities of the French in North America as a great threat to the safety of the British colonies on the Atlantic seaboard and recommended the building of forts along the Alleghenies as a natural barrier against the French. However, the Board continued,

although these Mountains may serve at present for a very good frontier, we should not propose them for the boundary of your Majesty's Empire in America. On the contrary, it were to be wished, that the British Settlements might be extended beyond them, & some small forts erected on the great Lakes, in proper places, by permission of the Indian proprietors; & we would particularly recommend the building of a fort on the Lake Erie, as hath been proposed by Colonel Spotswood, your Majesty's Lieut Governor of Virginia, whereby the french communications from Quebec to the River Mississippi, might be interrupted, a new trade opened with some of the Indian nations, & more of the natives engaged in your Majesty's interest. . . .[55]

In other words, fortify the mountains but continue to penetrate the interior for the sake of tapping the Indian trade.

British distrust of France was fairly constant, after about 1733, and it became explicit in 1738, during the negotiations for a renewal of the Anglo-

[52] "Amelot to la Marck, Jan. 27, 1739, A.E., Corr. Pol., Esp., 452: fols. 54-57.
[53] Board of Trade to the Lords Justices, Aug. 26, 1719, *Labrador Boundary*, VIII, 4,073-4,074.
[54] *Labrador Boundary*, VIII, 4,073-4,074.
[55] N.Y.C.D., V, 623-625.

French alliance of 1716, when tension arose over the seizure of the English ship *Elizabeth* off Doña Maria Bay. The Duke of Newcastle instructed Ambassador Waldegrave on November 13, 1738, to reject limitations upon British ships using the Windward Passage proposed by the French, "which, it is apprehended, would be in effect destroying the Jamaica trade, and which there are not wanting people here [London] to say is the view of the French court in insisting upon this prohibition." [56]

At the time of the War of Jenkins' Ear, British expansiveness was, of course, focused upon the acquisition of Spanish territory. In 1739 the Earl of Carteret frankly expressed in Parliament the prevalent English rationalization of the impulse to acquire more territory in America:

We have met with such provocation from Spain, as must render this war just on our part, in the eyes of every impartial judge; and, in the prosecution of a just war, no power in Europe has a right, few of them can have an inclination to direct us, or to restrain us from making such conquests as may be sufficient for answering the charge of the war, as well as such as may be necessary for preventing our meeting with any injustice for the future.[57]

William Pulteney, Earl of Bath, echoed the same popular mood in 1740 when he said that although British fleets should ravage the coasts of Spain, England's true objective lay in "another place," that is, the West Indies. "What is the good of taking ships?" asked Carteret. "We shall take from Spain some countries in America, and we shall keep them in spite of the whole world." [58]

Underlying all the arguments on both sides for an "offensive defensive" sort of imperial expansion lay the nebulous concept of an international balance of colonial power. This idea, that the balance of power in Europe was in large measure dependent upon a balance of colonial power overseas, had already come to play a role of some importance in the deliberations of the Western powers during the seventeenth century. In the decades between the Peace of Utrecht and the War of Jenkins' Ear this doctrine was a factor of great weight in the deliberations of the diplomatic policy-makers of all the colonizing powers, but this was especially true of France and England.

Both of these powers gave lip service to the idea, for example, that the Spanish colonial establishment in America must be preserved intact in the hands of Spain, since domination by any other state would give that nation such a preponderance of power in the world as to threaten the

[56] Legg, ed., *Brit. Dip. Insts.*, 1689–1789, VI, *France*, 1727–44, 211.

[57] Cobbett, *Parliamentary History*, XI, 17, Nov. 15, 1739.

[58] Quoted in Pares, *War and Trade in the West Indies*, 66.

[59] For a discussion of the relation of colonial power to the balance of power in Europe in the eighteenth century, see Max Savelle, "The American Balance of Power and European Diplomacy, 1713–78," in R. B. Morris, ed., *The Era of the American Revolution*, 140–169. See also Chapter XII.

security of all the other states of Europe. But each of them did its utmost to build up its own colonial empire at the expense of the other, and of Spain, since the wealth derived from the colonies was a vital and indispensable element in the position of the mother country in the international power equilibrium.

This sort of thinking was essentially mercantilistic; finding the balance of international power to rest upon a balance in commercial wealth, and the balance of national wealth to rest upon the extent and profitableness of colonial commerce. Therefore, it would not do to allow any one nation to build up an overwhelming colonial empire and commerce. As one French memorialist pointed out with regard to England, all of Europe was concerned with the preponderant position acquired by England in Spain's colonial commerce by the Treaties of Utrecht and the abuses and frauds practiced by Englishmen under the terms of the *asiento*:

One must consider the inconveniences that result from according to one nation so many privileges, which, taken separately, might be fair, but which, being combined, amount to a matter of extreme prejudice to all of Europe.[60]

France was especially interested in establishing a commercial balance in America. Since its own profits from trade with the Spanish colonies were channeled through Cadiz and the voyages of the *flotas* and the *galeones,* France tried every means known to diplomacy to reduce England's privileged position, so largely illicit, and build up its own by acquiring a privileged position in the Cadiz trade.

Thus, as soon as the two nations signed the Treaty of Seville, France began its maneuvers at the Spanish court with this dual objective in mind. The Marquis de Brancas, French ambassador to Spain, was instructed, as soon as the treaty was ratified, to devote his chief efforts to winning France a preferential position in Spanish colonial commerce and to bring Spain to reduce the privileges of the English.[61]

This sentiment was written into the Bourbon Family Compact of 1733 [62] and was a powerful consideration in the thinking of Fleury and Amelot in the critical three-way negotiations of 1738:

It is universally agreed, that for the general good of Europe, it is necessary that the lands possessed by the Spaniards in America be and remain in their possession, and that no other nation, consequently, encroach upon their dominions. The French, the English, and the Dutch can never suffer any one of them to take any part [of the Spanish colonies] to the exclusion of the two others.[63]

[60] "Réflexions qui se presentent pour montrer l'intérêst que les Puissances Maritimes, et particulièrement la France, ont à faire annuller, ou du moins morifier le T^te d'Assiento qui est entre l'Esp.^e et l'Angl.^re," A.E., Corr. Pol., Esp., 343: fols. 511–514.

[61] The ministry to Brancas, Nov. 29, 1729, A.E., Corr. Pol., Espagne, 365: fols. 211–221 vo; "Mémoire du Commerce général," B.N., Ft., n.a., 23085, fols. 181–209.

[62] See Chapter XV.

[63] "Plan de Négotiation sur les Affaires Entre l'Espagne et l'Angleterre" (1739), A.E., Méms. et Docs., Angleterre, IX: fols. 111–120.

England was careless of the balance, if not deliberately determined to upset it in England's favor. The Duke of Newcastle was entirely frank about it:

This, my Lords, has always been looked upon as a necessary step towards preventing any one nation in Europe from becoming too rich and too powerful for the rest; and the preserving the sole right of navigation and commerce to and from the Spanish settlements in America, to the Spaniards themselves, was not the effect so much of the Spanish policy, as of the jealousy which the powers of Europe entertained among themselves, lest any other should acquire too great a property in that valuable branch of commerce. They knew that while the treasures of the Indies were the property of the Spaniards, or at least while they centred in Spain, that sooner or later their subjects must have a proportionable share; because that monarchy is destitute of many of the advantages, which the other nations of Europe enjoy, from their manufactures and the industry of their inhabitants; and that, consequently, it was not in the power of the Spaniards, let them have never such an aspiring and politic prince at their head, to monopolize these treasures. Whereas, should too large a share of them come into the hands of any other nation in Europe, whose situation, power or trade, render them perhaps already formidable to their neighbours, they might be employed to purposes inconsistent with the peace of Europe, and which might one day prove fatal to the balance of power, that ought to subsist amongst her several princes. In such a case there is no doubt but that a formidable alliance would be made against the power thus aspiring; and should the differences at last come to be made up by a treaty, it would be found that the most probable way to secure the general peace, is to suffer the Spaniards to remain in the same situation, as to their American settlements, they are now in.[64]

England's effort to upset the balance failed for the time being. The balance of power remained relatively stable, and none of the outstanding issues among the colonizing powers in America—least of all the issues between England and France—was to be finally settled until the arbitrament of war should settle them.

[64] Cobbett, *Parliamentary History*, X, 172, quoted in Pares, *War and Trade in the West Indies*, 139–140.

CHAPTER XVII

The War of Jenkins' Ear and the War
of the Austrian Succession, 1739-48

1. The War of Jenkins' Ear

FOR A NUMBER of months after the outbreak of the War of Jenkins' Ear in 1739, Cardinal Fleury, in his capacity as director of French foreign policy, maintained a belligerent attitude toward England in the interest of Spain. He repeatedly warned the Earl of Waldegrave, the British ambassador, that if England should seize any of Spain's American territories, France would be compelled to enter the war on Spain's side. He sent a fleet to the West Indies under the Marquis d'Antin, whose instructions were certainly of a highly belligerent and provocative nature,[1] while at the same time explaining to Waldegrave that, as Waldegrave reported, "It was incumbent upon him to protect his own commerce and prevent as much as in him lay . . . our making ourselves [the British] masters of all the West Indian trade," which he was convinced England was determined to do, and "to hinder as much as he could our becoming more powerfull than we were already." [2] It was all in the name of France's vital interest in defending Spanish ownership of its colonies in America and, thereby, of preserving the American balance of power.

Yet, France remained neutral. A part of the price of French assistance to Spain in its conflict with England had been a commercial treaty which would have given France a favored position in the trade with the Spanish colonies by way of Cadiz, and, since Spain had refused to make the necessary concessions, France had refused to make the alliance. Strangely

---

[1] Pares, War and Trade in the West Indies, 165–166.
[2] Waldegrave to Newcastle, Paris, Sept. 11, 1740, P.R.O., S.P., 78/223:385–387; quoted in Legg, ed., Brit. Dip. Insts., 1680–1789, VI, France, 1727–44, xxxix; see also, "Extracts of Letters from Lᵈ Waldegrave, relating to any Declaration, made to him by the Cardinal—and of the answers sent to Lᵈ Waldegrave" (n.d.), P.R.O., S.P., 78/221: fols. 276–279.

enough, when Spain, in August, 1740, finally broke down and agreed to make the commercial treaty, Fleury suddenly broke off the negotiations for both treaties, on the ground that such a drawing together of the two Bourbon countries might alarm the other European states and precipitate a general European war.[3]

However specious this pretext may have been, it did appear to be to France's interest to remain neutral and even to try to mediate between the two belligerents. As early as November, 1739, Fleury had exclaimed to Waldegrave that he would "give some of his life's blood," to bring about peace, if that were possible.[4] Waldegrave was of the opinion that a Spanish victory against England would not be to France's interest, because of the great accretion such a victory would give to Spanish power *vis-à-vis* France itself, and that Maurepas, the French minister of marine, hadn't the slightest interest in risking the French navy against the naval might of England.

Meanwhile, Holland, although technically an ally of England, had several good reasons for not getting drawn into the Anglo-Saxon war. Dutch ships had been seized by Spanish *guarda costas* in the Caribbean, to be sure, and the United Provinces were especially incensed by the Spanish seizure of Dutch goods in English ships, thus raising, in the minds of the Dutch ministers, the question of the right of neutrals to trade on the ships of belligerents, which, although the Dutch claimed the right, actually ran counter to the general practices of international law.[5] The Dutch attitude was conciliatory, nevertheless, because it was believed that the United Provinces had much more to gain from peaceful trade with both Spain and France than from war with either or both of them. The United Provinces were, in fact, in the midst of negotiations with France looking to the arrangement of a commercial treaty, and they were less than disposed to abandon those negotiations for the sake of England. In any case, it was argued, the alliance with England did not require Dutch aid to England unless France should enter the war; and it was firmly believed, in Dutch government circles, that France would not do so.[6]

Because of their desire to remain neutral, therefore, and to prevent the war from spreading, the United Provinces proposed to France that the two countries offer to mediate between Spain and England. Fleury welcomed the idea (he probably had already thought of it; he may even have suggested it, in the first place, through his ambassador at the Hague,

[3] Baudrillart, *Philippe V et la cour de France*, IV, 560.
[4] Waldegrave to Newcastle, Nov. 23, 1739, P.R.O., S.P., 78/221.
[5] Trevor to Harrington, Nov. 1, 1739, P.R.O., S.P., 84/328: fols. 76–79 vo; same to same, Nov. 10, 1739, *ibid.*, 84/382: fols. 84-85 vo.
[6] Trevor to Harrington, Dec. 4, 1739, P.R.O., S.P., 84/382: fols. 142–145 vo.

Gabriel-Jacques Fénelon), and tentative feelers were put out to test England's willingness to have its dispute with Spain mediated.

The proposed Franco-Dutch mediation never really materialized. Cardinal Fleury did intimate, in August, 1739, that England should agree to allow Spain to pay the 95,000 pounds it owed England under the terms of the Convention of the Pardo to a third party and withdraw Haddock's fleet from the Mediterranean and the reinforcements recently sent to Jamaica and Georgia.[7] But England was riding high and was hardly in a mood for mediation. Newcastle brusquely rejected Fleury's intimations as offering no prospect of a resolution of the real issues in dispute between England and Spain in America, and Robert Trevor, English minister at The Hague, was instructed to quash any proposal for mediation from the Dutch.[8]

Presently, news arrived in England of Admiral Vernon's capture and dismantling of Porto Bello, and all of England watched with enthusiasm as plans were made for a full-scale attack upon Cartagena. That expedition, staged in the spring of 1741, was a humiliating failure, and English enthusiasm for the war began to cool. In fact, events in Europe had already largely diverted the attention of all the European powers away from America and back to problems relative to the affairs of Europe itself. The War of Jenkins' Ear, fought almost entirely in America, ceased to be of prime importance to European diplomacy.

2. The War of the Austrian Succession

The year 1740 was marked by a concatenation of events that changed, for several years at least, the course of European diplomatic history, both for Europe and for America.

In the first place, the death of the Emperor Charles VI, King of Austria, on October 20, 1740, precipitated the question whether the other states of Europe would honor the famous Pragmatic Sanction providing for the succession of Charles's daughter, Maria Theresa, to the throne of Austria and its estates. That such an honoring of the Pragmatic Sanction was highly doubtful was indicated by the fact that the young King Frederick II of Prussia, who had succeeded to that throne in May, had designs upon Silesia, part of the Austrian inheritance. France, despite its acceptance of the Pragmatic Sanction, was almost certain to try to place its candidate, the Elector Charles Albert of Bavaria, upon the imperial throne, while England was concerned about what might happen to Hanover; and the Dutch desperately feared the effects of the ever-present threat of a French invasion of the Austrian Netherlands. Frederick II

[7] Pares, *War and Trade in the West Indies*, 145–146.
[8] Trevor to Harrington, Dec. 22, 1739, P.R.O., S.P., 84/382: fols. 182–187.

seized Silesia, and France sent an army into Bohemia; England allied itself with Austria, and the Dutch joined them informally, on the defensive against France. France, in order to secure the aid of Spain, turned once more to an effort to form a new alliance with that country.

Meanwhile, England's war with Spain had bogged down before Cartagena and Santiago de Cuba, while Walpole's reluctance to enter the continental war against France appeared to the English war party to be making for humiliation in Europe as well. The result was an attack upon Walpole that brought about his resignation in January of 1742 and the adoption, by England, now under the leadership of John Carteret, Earl of Granville, of a policy that led to the entry of England into the war on the side of Austria, unofficially in 1742, and officially in 1744.

The Dutch, egged on by England and always fearful for the preservation of the Austrian Netherlands (Belgium) as a barrier against France, and despite their reluctance to risk their profitable trade as neutrals, informally entered the war about 1743 by sending men and money to Maria Theresa; but the Dutch never declared war, preferring, under the fiction of neutrality, to reap the profits of a continued commerce with all the belligerents, both in Europe and in their colonies in the "new world".

3. The Second Bourbon Family Compact, 1743

After the death of Cardinal Fleury on January 29, 1743, Louis XV, more or less ably advised by his mistress, the Duchesse de Chateauroux, became "his own foreign minister." The war was going badly for France, and presently (September 13, 1743), Sardinia would defect from its alliance with France by the Treaty of Worms, which took that country out of the war. Desperately in need of allies, Louis XV, through his nominal minister, Jean-Jacques Amelot de Chaillou, revived Fleury's plan for a renewal of the Bourbon Family Compact.

The bases of the proposed new treaty of alliance were the Treaty of the Escorial of 1733 (the first Bourbon Family Compact) [9] and the project for an alliance proposed by Fleury in 1740, as modified by the circumstances of the present war. Aside from arrangements for mutual military assistance and plans, Spain now proposed that, in return for the alliance, all of the Emperor's possessions in Italy be assigned to the Spanish Infante, Don Felipe; France must formally join in Spain's war against England, and England must be forced to return Minorca and Gibraltar to Spain. With regard to America, Spain demanded that England be forced to evacuate Georgia and surrender the *asiento*. At the same time, Spain made it clear that it was not prepared at this time to make any favorable treaty of commerce such as France had demanded in the previous negotiations.

[9] See Chapter XV. See also, Baudrillart, *Philippe* V *et la cour de France*, V, 164 ff.

The price thus demanded by Spain for coming to the aid of France was high. But Louis XV was in no position to haggle. Within five weeks the treaty, the so-called Second Bourbon Family Compact, signed at Fontainebleau on October 25, 1743, was made.[10] By its provisions, the two signatories undertook mutually to guarantee each other's territories, and to secure each other's rights, "outside of Europe as well as within it." Since Don Felipe was the legitimate heir to the estates of the deceased Emperor Charles VI in Italy, those estates were to be seized and given to him. Because England had unreasonably and unjustly broken off the conferences begun under the provisions of the Convention of the Pardo in 1739 and had precipitated war, and since France, as well as Spain, had grave reasons, both in America and in Europe, to resort to force to bring England to a sense of its international obligations, the two signatories agreed to "determine the circumstances in which it might be convenient" for France to declare war on England; France promised not to make peace until England should have been forced to return Gibraltar and Minorca to Spain. As the security of Spanish Florida was threatened by the new English colony of Georgia, the establishment of which in Spanish territory could not be justified under any pretense of the English, England was to be compelled to destroy that colony, along with any other fort that the English might have constructed in the territory of His Catholic Majesty in America and to restore to him any of his territories there that they might have occupied, either before or during the war. Finally, with regard to America, England was to be forced to surrender the *asiento*, which Spain promised thereafter to award only to its own nationals, "having seen by experience how prejudicial to the interests of Spain has been the execution of this traffic by any other nation." [11]

France declared war on England April 27, 1744.

4. Diplomatic Juggling Relative to America, 1740-44

In the course of the kaleidoscopic changes in the shadings of European diplomacy in the first three years of the War of the Austrian Succession, there took place two sets of negotiations which bore upon the international history of America. One was the attempt of France to separate the Dutch from their ally, England; the other was the effort of England to separate Spain from its ally, France.

In the first case, Cardinal Fleury, wishing, as early as 1741, to take advantage of Dutch lukewarmness toward the war in order to secure Dutch neutrality, had offered the United Provinces a promise not to

---

[10] Cantillo, ed., *Tratados*, 367–373.
[11] Cantillo, ed., *Tratados*, 370.

invade the Austrian Netherlands, regarded by the Dutch as a barrier protecting their own territory, a treaty of commerce, and an assurance that
France would make no effort to change the dynasty in England.[12] Furthermore, France at that time offered to use its influence with Spain to
bring about the restoration of Dutch ships seized by Spanish *guarda costas*
in America and to achieve a clearer recognition by Spain of the principle
of the freedom of the seas in American waters.[13] The Dutch were definitely interested, and the negotiations for a commercial treaty progressed
until agreement seemed to be assured.[14]

Despite French efforts to hold the United Netherlands to neutrality,
however, fear of France and the need for assistance led the Dutch to send
informal aid to Austria, beginning in 1743, but without formally entering
the war.[15] In June, 1744, the Dutch made a last effort to win such concessions as might justify them in remaining neutral, among the terms for
which were demands that Spain recognize the right of the Dutch to go
freely to America and that Spain compromise its dispute with England.[16]

England was aware of the French-Dutch negotiations and, as the "informal" phase of the War of the Austrian Succession proceeded, brought
more and more pressure to bear upon the United Provinces to support
the Austrian cause, which they eventually did, albeit without enthusiasm.

Meanwhile, efforts were being made by England to separate Spain from
its alliance with France. Indeed, Spain itself, apparently, was by 1744
weary of the war in America, although still intensely interested in securing
estates for Don Felipe in Italy. Thus, in December, 1744, San Gil, a
Spanish diplomat in Germany, wrote secretly to the Marqués de Tabuerniga, then in London, that he had conferred on the subject of peace with
the Earl of Granville after the battle of Dettingen, in which King George
II of England personally participated, and, since Granville had not replied
to his suggestions, asked Tabuerniga to pursue the matter further. Tabuerniga sent San Gil's letter to Granville, now in London, who then replied
that England would deal with Spain only if that country would separate
itself from France. Tabuerniga persisted, however, and formulated a plan
for peace, according to which King Carlos of the Two Sicilies would be
guaranteed his crown, Parma and Placentia would be given to Don Felipe,
and relations between Spain and Maria Theresa could be settled amicably.
Spain would abandon the French alliance and would give England most-
favored-nation status in the commerce of Spain and its colonies. The King

---

[12] Wilson, *French Foreign Policy during the Administration of Cardinal Fleury*, 1726–
1743, 134, 323, 341.
[13] *Recueil des Insts., Espagne*, III, 222–233.
[14] Trevor to Harrington, Nov. 13, 1739, P.R.O., S.P., 84/382: fols. 90–93 vo; same
to same, Dec. 11, 1739, P.R.O., S.P., 84/382: fols. 156–159.
[15] Beer, "Holland und der österreichische Erbfölge-Krieg," *Archiv für Österreichische
Geschichte*, XLVI (1871), 297–418.
[16] Beer, "Holland und der österreichische Erbfölge-Krieg," *loc. cit.*, XLVI, 328.

of Spain went so far as to express a willingness to recognize the freedom of English ships to sail to America, provided they were not found too far from the most direct routes to the English colonies, and to reexamine Anglo-Spanish relations with regard to the colonies on the basis of the Treaty of Madrid of 1667. Matters pertaining to the *asiento*, the annual ship, and other disputes might be discussed amicably.[17] The Spanish King expressed himself as genuinely interested in peace, but he made it clear that Spain could not desert its alliance with France.[18]

Thus it fell out that both of these diplomatic gestures affecting international affairs in America, undertaken in the midst of the War of the Austrian Succession, came to nothing.

5. The Peace of Aix-la-Chapelle, 1748

After the defection of Sardinia from the Bourbon side by the treaty with the maritime and imperial allies signed at Worms on September 13, 1743, the War of the Austrian Succession degenerated into a sort of stalemate centering about the Austrian Netherlands. France, by reason of the military genius of Marshal Maurice de Saxe, was able to achieve a certain military advantage and to occupy the Austrian Netherlands and, eventually, some of the territory of the United Provinces. But French sea power was effectively destroyed by the British navy, which led to France being subjected to a strangling economic blockade, while its colonies in America were being economically paralyzed and almost totally cut off from the mother country. By the year 1746 all the participants were thoroughly sick of the war; the achievement of peace became a matter of dickering on the basis of a changing military situation in Europe usually favorable to France.

The first move toward peace was made by Marshal de Saxe, probably prompted by Louis XV, who, in 1747, intimated to Sir John Ligonier, an English prisoner of war, that he would be disposed to discuss peace with the English commander in chief, the Duke of Cumberland. He proposed that the basic principle in making the peace should be the restitution of all conquests, including Cape Breton, now held by the English, and an appeasement of Spain, which, since the accession of Ferdinand VI in 1746, was most intensely interested in acquiring an estate in Italy for Ferdinand's half-brother, Don Felipe.[19]

As early as the spring of 1746 the Marquis d'Argenson, French minister of foreign affairs, suggested, by way of the Dutch, who were technically still at peace, a program based upon his talks with the Comte de Was-

[17] Tabuerniga to Harrington, Dec. 28, 1744, P.R.O., S.P., 100/59.
[18] San Gil to Tabuerniga, Dec. 29, 1744, P.R.O., S.P., 100/59.
[19] Lodge, *Studies in Eighteenth-Century Diplomacy*, 267, 275, *et passim*.

sanaer,[20] that, he thought, might lead to peace. France would restore the conquests it had made in the Austrian Netherlands, and the neutrality of the Austrian Netherlands, as a barrier for the Low Countries, would be guaranteed. In return for this concession, Cape Breton would be returned to France. Spain and England would be expected to make peace on the basis of the abortive Convention of the Pardo of 1739.

This set of proposals was rejected by England as an effort by France to separate the United Provinces from their alliance with England. But England did not reject entirely the possibility of negotiation, and the Dutch made another effort. To satisfy England, the Marquis d'Argenson, the French foreign minister, agreed to repudiate the cause of the Stuart pretender to the English throne. He also agreed to demand from Spain a pledge not to interfere with the freedom of international navigation in the seas of America; but he said nothing about the *asiento* or the annual trading ship to the Spanish colonies. Neither the French nor the Dutch, of course, had any desire to see those monopolistic privileges of the English in Spanish America restored. With regard to Cape Breton, d'Argenson insisted that it must be restored to France.[21]

Such were the bases upon which negotiations for peace, insofar as they concerned America, began. But the American issues could not be separated from the European. France, for example, had promised Spain, in the family alliance of 1743, its support in the acquisition of an "establishment" in Italy for Don Felipe and in forcing England to restore Gibraltar and Minorca to Spain, as well as in compelling England to settle to Spain's satisfaction the American disputes left unsettled by the English declaration of war in 1739. For the moment, Spain's attention seemed to be focused more on the Italian problem than on America.

The Dutch, still technically neutral and enjoying a highly profitable neutral commerce with the belligerents on both sides, both in Europe and America, were vitally concerned with the status of the Austrian Netherlands as a sort of barrier against invasions of the United Provinces by the French. This "barrier" was, to them, a matter of survival; for its preservation they desperately needed the protection of England, while they feared to arouse the aggressive hostility of France. Thus, although they needed English support, they were not disposed to irritate France by insisting that England be allowed to keep Cape Breton. At the same time, the Dutch would have welcomed a dissolution of the favored English position in Spanish-American trade represented by the *asiento*, since they themselves would expect to benefit from such a dissolution.

In May of 1746 d'Argenson submitted a "project" of a general treaty to the Dutch envoys in Paris for communication to England. This "project" proposed, among other things, that France would promise not to attack the

---

[20] Wassanaer was the Dutch ambassador to Paris.
[21] Lodge, *Studies in Eighteenth-Century Diplomacy*, 150.

United Provinces through the Austrian Netherlands; England would restore Cape Breton to France. France would recognize the Hanoverian dynasty as the legitimate rulers in England. Peace between England and Spain would be made on the basis of the Peace of Utrecht and the Convention of the Pardo of 1739; the Dutch statement of the principle of the freedom of navigation in America was accepted. England and Spain would appoint commissioners to determine the boundaries of Georgia and Florida. Provision would be made for Don Felipe by a cession of Tuscany to him and his heirs so long as they did not occupy the throne of Spain.[22]

This "project" might have been the basis for a profitable negotiation had it not been for certain qualifications that d'Argenson added to it relative to the Stuart pretender to the English throne, thereby arousing a storm of protest in England. The negotiations were set back, therefore, but were renewed when d'Argenson sent the Marquis de Puysieulx to The Hague to continue them.

Puysieulx demanded that representatives of England and Spain be included in the negotiations and that conversations be held at some place other then The Hague. The result was a series of conferences at Breda, at which England was represented by the Earl of Sandwich, who succeeded Robert Trevor as English ambassador to the United Provinces; Spain was represented by Don Melchior de Macanaz.

News of the death of Philip V of Spain on July 9, 1746, with the succession of Ferdinand VI to the throne of Spain and the consequent removal of Elizabeth Farnese from the helm of the ship of state in Spain gave England reason to hope that a separate peace might be made with Spain. Ferdinand was thought of as more friendly to England and less than enthusiastic about the Bourbon Family Pact. Benjamin Keene was therefore appointed British ambassador to Lisbon, with instructions to make contact with the Spanish court, and the Marques de Tabuerniga, still living in London, was employed to assist Keene as a go-between.

Tabuerniga had, indeed, participated in a Spanish peace feeler as early as 1744 when, as already related, at the request of the Spanish diplomat San Gil he had approached Carteret on the subject of peace, only to be brushed off by Carteret with the remark that England could deal with Spain only if it separated itself from France. Now, in 1746, Newcastle sent Tabuerniga to Lisbon as "contact man" for Keene. He communicated with Villarias, the chief Spanish minister, and learned that Spain was willing to negotiate, provided only that England be prepared to guarantee some establishment for Don Felipe in Italy. This would mean that by giving such a guarantee England would recover its commercial privileges in Spanish America and, also, by forcing France to make peace by the elimination of Spain from the war, recover Cape Breton.

[22] Lodge, *Studies in Eighteenth-Century Diplomacy*, 153–155.

Keene's instructions would not permit him to go so far. He was not permitted to commit England to a guarantee in Italy, either for Don Carlos or for Don Felipe, and he was to insist on a reestablishment of the *asiento* and the annual ship; at least for the period during which those privileges were suspended, a period that the English reckoned at fifteen years. Even before Keene's negotiation got under way, however, military news from Italy caused Newcastle to tell Keene flatly that nothing could be done for Don Felipe; the best that could be hoped for was some sort of support for Don Carlos at Naples. Spain was committed to both Don Felipe and Don Carlos and had at least the paper backing of France in this enterprise. Therefore, Spain clung to France, and Keene's negotiation was a complete failure. England was not yet ready to trade guarantees in Italy for a recovery of the *asiento*.

Meanwhile, the Earl of Sandwich had been deliberately stalling at the conferences at Breda while Newcastle was awaiting the outcome of Keene's negotiations at Lisbon for a separate peace with Spain. Breda, too, was a failure for England, since the Dutch allies were willing to appease France by providing for Don Felipe in Italy and even to ask England to sacrifice Cape Breton in return for a French guarantee of the neutrality of the Austrian Netherlands. Thus, the conferences at Breda achieved nothing, chiefly because of the failure of the English and the Dutch to agree, and they were suspended when Puysieulx was recalled to France to replace d'Argenson as French foreign minister upon the latter's dismissal early in 1747.

The conferences at Breda did bring Sandwich and Macanaz, the Spanish representative, together, however, and there ensued yet another Anglo-Spanish negotiation with a view of concluding a separate Anglo-Spanish treaty of peace. Macanaz presented to Sandwich a list of Spain's terms, which were, if anything, even more impossible for England to accept than anything presented to Keene at Lisbon. He demanded that Gibraltar and Minorca be restored to Spain; Don Carlos was to remain King of the Two Sicilies, and Don Felipe was to be guaranteed an estate in Italy; the *asiento* must be cancelled; the slave-trade of the Spanish colonies would be thrown open to the traders of all countries.[23]

Such terms, of course, were unthinkable for England, although some members of the British ministry were willing to consider the possibility of trading Gibraltar for a restoration of the *asiento*. Macanaz presently reduced all his demands to one *sine qua non*, the restoration of Gibraltar. But this, also, was inadmissable to the cabinet as a whole, and the negotiation was broken off.[24]

Meanwhile, Sandwich had been endeavoring to hold the Dutch to the

[23] Lodge, *Studies in Eighteenth-Century Diplomacy*, 228.
[24] Conn, *Gibraltar in British Diplomacy*, 145–150.

British alliance and to prevent them from making a separate peace with France. In order to do so, Newcastle was beginning to consider the possibility of surrendering Cape Breton. Many people, he wrote Sandwich,

begin to think that Cape Breton alone without Quebeck and Canada will be such an immense expense and of so little use that the best we could do with it would be to purchase better conditions of peace. . . . The cession of Cape Breton, I should hope, might be avoided; the neutrality of the Low Countries can never, or ought never, to be consented to; the establishment for Don Philip may be settled as things turn out.[25]

The important thing, he said, was to hold the allies together.

During the year 1747, separate Anglo-Spanish negotiations were again revived. Don José de Carvajal, the Spanish minister, corresponded with Benjamin Keene, at Lisbon, and sent Major General Ricardo Wall secretly (but with the cognizance of France) to London to see what could be done. Wall had a series of secret meetings with Newcastle, in the course of which he presented Spain's claims to Gibraltar, demanded British support for an Italian estate for Don Felipe, and offered a conditional renewal of England's commercial concessions in America. Newcastle, although willing to make some arrangement in Italy for Don Felipe, would not budge on Gibraltar. Besides, since to make a separate peace with Spain would alienate his allies, especially Austria and Sardinia, he rejected Wall's proposals, and the general returned to Spain.[26]

In the course of 1747, several events took place to hasten the making of peace. A revolution in Holland brought an overthrow of the Republican party and the establishment of William of Orange as stadholder. France invaded Dutch territory. The conference at Breda came to an end, but the conversations were transferred to Aix-la-Chapelle, as being a more "neutral" place. Marshal de Saxe intervened with a letter, probably inspired by Puysieulx, proposing new negotiations based upon the return of all conquests, including Cape Breton in America and Madras, which had been seized by the French, in India. England was invited to submit proposals relative to American commercial issues and the provision of an Italian estate for Don Felipe.[27]

In the preliminary conversations that followed at Liège, France was adamant on the restoration of Cape Breton; if England insisted on keeping it, France would keep the Austrian Netherlands. In order to hold the Dutch, who were now in desperate straits, to the alliance, England was forced to concede the restitution of Cape Breton for the sake of French surrender of the Netherlands. Similarly, in order to win some sort of re-

[25] Quoted in Lodge, *Studies in Eighteenth-Century Diplomacy*, 239.
[26] Lodge, *Studies in Eighteenth-Century Diplomacy*, 295–296.
[27] Lodge, *Studies in Eighteenth-Century Diplomacy*, 278–279.

newal of England's commercial concessions in Spanish America, Newcastle was constrained to endorse a grant of Parma and Piacenza to Don Felipe.

The Spanish negotiator, the Duque de Sotomayor, went to the congress armed with documents and instructions empowering him to present a long list of Spanish claims against England, including the old right of the Guipuzcoans to fish on the Grand Bank of Newfoundland,[28] the expansion of British settlements in Honduras,[29] Georgia, illicit trade, and so on.[30] He had little or no occasion to argue these matters, however, as the other states at the congress were impatient for a quick general peace and were not disposed to debate such small issues. It was, however, apparently agreed by Sotomayor and Sandwich that the mutual claims of England and Spain against each other would be resolved by a joint commission after the treaty of peace should be signed.[31]

In the negotiations at Aix-la-Chapelle, early in 1748, preliminary articles were rather quickly agreed upon by France, England, and the United Provinces. The principle of the restitution of conquests was accepted all round, and in the Preliminary Articles of Peace, signed April 30,[32] it was agreed (Article 2) that "all conquests that have been made since the beginning of the present war, whether in Europe or in the East or West Indies, shall be restored, in the condition in which they are at present." The duchies of Parma, Piacenza, and Guestálla were to be ceded to Don Felipe. The treaty of the *asiento*, together with the permission to send an annual ship to trade in the Spanish colonies, was to be renewed. The Hanoverian dynasty in England was recognized, as was the Pragmatic Sanction.

Austria and Sardinia acceded to the Preliminaries on May 31, and Spain acceded on June 28. The Preliminaries were clarified by a series of joint declarations, the most important of which, for America, was the declaration of July 8, which provided that there should be named a joint commission to adjudicate claims relative to prizes taken after the agreed-upon term of six weeks after the signature of the Preliminaries.[33] The powers of this commission, which was to meet at St. Malo within two months of the date of the signature of the declaration, were afterward extended to include the territorial claims of France and England in America.[34]

As conditions went from bad to worse for England and its allies in the

[28] M.N.M., III, Doc. 116.
[29] M.N.M., Ms. 487, fol. 243.
[30] A.H.N., Estado, 3366/2, *passim*.
[31] Minuta de adicional articulo XIII sobre el Asiento de Negros y Navio de permiso . . ." (n.d.), A.H.N., Estado, 3368/2.
[32] Cantillo, ed., *Tratados*, 385–389.
[33] Paullin, ed., *European Treaties*, IV, 72. Prizes taken within six weeks after the signature of the Preliminaries were regarded as legitimate, since it was assumed that it would take at least that long for news of the signature to reach distant parts of the world.
[34] See Chapter XVIII.

summer of 1748, and as the English House of Commons began to clamor for peace at any price, the Duke of Newcastle instructed Sandwich to hasten the making of the definitive treaty. The chief difficulty arose with Spain over the article in the Preliminaries providing for the renewal of the *asiento*, and there ensued an argument as to the length of the term for which it should be renewed—whether for fifteen years, as claimed by the English, or for the four years between the outbreak of war in 1739 and the contractual expiration of the *asiento* in 1743, as claimed by Spain. France sided with Spain, and the Dutch felt no inclination to support the English mercantile monopoly in Spanish America, so the Duke of Newcastle was finally driven to accept the Spanish terms.

In the final treaty of peace, signed at Aix-la-Chapelle on October 18 by France, England, and the United Provinces,[35] there were only a few slight changes from the terms of the Preliminaries. All the signatories recognized and reaffirmed the Pragmatic Sanction, and it was agreed by all that (with certain specified exceptions) the territorial *status quo* that existed at the beginning of the war was to be restored. This meant the restitution of all conquests, and a number of international joint commissions were to be created to carry out the restorations of possession. Don Felipe was to be given the duchies of Parma, Piacenza, and Guastálla, in Italy.

It was agreed that, since France engaged (Article 18 of the Preliminaries) to give up its conquests in the Netherlands within six weeks, but since it must take much longer to effect the restitution of places in America, Great Britain would send to France, as hostages for the restitution of Cape Breton "two persons of rank and consideration" (afterward interpreted to mean two peers of the realm) to reside there until news of the restoration of that place should be received. The commissioners to be appointed by France and England to give and receive formal delivery of conquered territories "in the East or West Indies" were to be ready to set out immediately upon the exchange of ratifications of the treaty of peace.

The treaty of the *asiento* and the article providing for the annual ship were to be renewed, "for the four years during which the enjoyment thereof has been interrupted, since the commencement of the present war," that is, between 1739 and the contractual expiration of the *asiento* treaty in 1743.

[35] Chalmers, ed., *Collection of Treaties*, I, 424–467; Paullin, ed., *European Treaties*, IV, 73–75.

CHAPTER XVIII

The "Cold War" of 1748-55

THE PEACE OF Aix-la-Chapelle settled nothing with regard to America. The international *status quo* that had existed in the hemisphere prior to 1739 was supposed to be restored, nothing more. All the imponderables in the imperial rivalries of the "new world" came back into full play and all the local points of friction, whether arising from territorial expansion, relations with the Indian nations, licit and illicit commerce, or the freedom of the seas, reappeared wth intensified bitterness. The old issues between England and Spain over which the War of Jenkins' Ear had been fought flared up again and had to be resolved by a new negotiation which, *mirabile dictu*, did accomplish a certain measure of success in the Anglo-Spanish treaty of 1752. The expanding French and British empires faced each other at many critical points along the long North American frontier and in the islands of the Caribbean. Even the Dutch, silent partners of the English at the Peace of Aix-la-Chapelle, were drawn, as the Anglo-French conflict developed, by their activities as neutral carriers in America, into a series of bitter disputes with their long-time allies, the English.

The most pressing and significant of these sets of conflicts in America was, of course, that between the French and British empires (which was also going on in India and other parts of the world as well as in America). Most French and English statesmen probably realized, however vaguely, that the time was now come when there must be a showdown between them, either by peaceable means or by war. But most of them, apparently, were willing to try the peaceable method first, even though neither side had enough faith in the method to make it really effective.

1. The Anglo-French Commission on American Possessions, 1749-55

The treaty of peace had made no provision for the settlement of international disputes in America. The explanatory declaration of July 8, 1748, relative to the Preliminaries, had, indeed, provided that there should be set up a joint commission by the three signatories of the declaration (England, France, and Holland) to adjudicate claims relative to prizes made at sea after the agreed-upon term of six weeks after the signature of the Preliminaries.[1] The treaty itself had also included the vague provision (Article 18) that certain European problems "and the other articles, which could not be regulated so as to enter into the present treaty, shall be amicably adjusted immediately by the commissaries appointed for that purpose on both sides, or otherwise, as shall be agreed on by the Powers concerned."[2]

In the period between April 30, 1748, the date of the signature of the Preliminaries, and October 18, the date of the signature of the definitive treaty of peace, hostilities at sea had continued. It was to stop this activity that the declaration of July 8 had been issued and that the commission envisioned by it had eventually met, early in 1749. But this commission quarreled over the scope of its authority and broke up without accomplishing anything. England, in the meantime, had sent the Earl of Sussex and Lord Charles Cathcart to France as the hostages for the restitution of Cape Breton envisioned by the treaty of peace, and they had exchanged with the Marquis de Puysieulx, the French foreign minister, copies of the orders that had been sent to French and English governors and commanders for the restitution of conquered places in the East Indies and in America, particularly Cape Breton.

These orders called for the restoration of the *status quo* that had existed in America before the war. But, while the restitution of Cape Breton was achieved without any serious hitch, the restoration of the *status quo ante bellum* elsewhere was very difficult, since the colonial governors and commanders on both sides did not clearly know what that *status quo* had been or what it ought to be.

Differences of opinion arose almost immediately, in the first place, over the situation of the so-called "neutral islands," St. Lucia, St. Vincent, and Dominica, which France and England had agreed in 1730 to leave vacant until their ownership could be decided, and of Tobago, which had come informally to share a similar status. Since the neutral status of these islands had been a part of the *status quo ante bellum*, it was expected that they would remain unoccupied after the war, and orders were sent by the Kings of England and France to their governors of Barbados and Martinique, respectively, to make sure that the terms of the treaty of peace were effectuated. Because these islands had been infiltrated during the war, however, Joseph Yorke, secretary of the British embassy in Paris, was instructed (in the absence of any ambassador, as yet) to insist that strict orders be given Governor Caylus, of Martinique, who was also governor of all the French

[1] Paullin, ed., *European Treaties*, IV, 72.
[2] Chalmers, ed., *Treaties*, I, 440.

Caribbean colonies, to see to it that St. Lucia, St. Vincent, and Dominica were effectively evacuated. As for Tobago, however, since it was not included in the original agreement of 1730, and since England felt it had a strong claim to that island, Yorke was instructed to demand its complete evacuation by the French and to suggest the appointment of commissioners on both sides to decide the question of ownership.[3] These instructions, however, were only calculated to enable Yorke to open the question of the islands with Puysieulx and to prepare the way for the negotiation of a convention providing for the neutrality of all four islands.[4]

In the course of the conversations that ensued, the French ministers showed themselves disposed to enter into a full-scale discussion, not only of the ownership of the islands, but of all the other disputes between the two empires in America as well. They therefore proposed that a joint commission be set up to study and settle all questions at issue between France and England in America.

It was high time for such a comprehensive settlement. An intensive race for possession of the various areas of the North American continent, as well as for the occupation of unoccupied West Indian areas, had broken out almost immediately after the peace. On the side of the English there appeared the well-publicized project of Arthur Dobbs to expand the activities of the Hudson's Bay Company into the lands to the southwestward of the bay in territory claimed by France in virtue of the explorations of Pierre La Vérendrye and his sons. In Nova Scotia, Governor Mascarene, just after the preliminary articles of the Peace had been signed, and in view of the fact that Cape Breton was to be returned to the French, began to exact from the French *habitants* an oath of loyalty to the British crown, both on the peninsula and in the mainland west of the Bay of Fundy. Lieutenant Colonel John Gorham, sent to exact the oaths west of the bay, was fired upon by the French, and his visit elicited a violent protest from the Marquis de la Galissonière, French governor of Canada, who wrote to Mascarene that the lands west of the Bay of Fundy were not part of Nova Scotia, or Acadia, as ceded to England by the Anglo-French Treaty of Utrecht (1713),[5] but that they were, and always had been, a part of New France.[6] These actions and exchanges once more raised the old dispute about the boundaries of Acadia, or Nova Scotia, and de la Galissonière sent a detachment of men to the St. John River to build a fort to forestall any possible English occupation.

The English government, on its own side, founded the town of Halifax

[3] Bedford to Yorke, May 8, 1749, in Legg. ed., *Brit. Dip. Insts.*, 1689–1789, VII, *France*, 1745–89, 2–3. For the *de facto* situation in the islands, see Chapter XIII.
[4] Same to same, May 8, 1749, in Legg, ed., *Brit. Dip. Insts.*, 1689–1789, VII, *France*, 1745–89, 3–4.
[5] See Chapter XIII.
[6] N.Y.C.D., VI, 478–481.

in Nova Scotia as a British counterpart of Louisbourg, on Cape Breton, now returned to French possession. Edward Cornwallis, governor of the new military colony, was instructed to build a fort on the St. John River, since Acadia, in British eyes, included the mainland west of the Bay of Fundy as well as the peninsula; but he found himself anticipated and blocked by de la Galissonière's fort on the St. John.

Along the southern shores of the Great Lakes, also, the Anglo-French tension reappeared. The aggressive Marquis de la Galissonière, convinced that the proper boundary between the English colonies and the French in this area was the watershed south of the lakes, began to take steps to block English expansion, even before the peace, by strengthening the French fort at Crown Point on Lake Champlain and, after the peace, by sending French colonists there. He also considered Fort Oswego, on the south shore of Lake Ontario, as an intrusion upon French territory, similarly on the ground of the old French claim to ownership of all the land drained by the rivers that flowed into the St. Lawrence. He therefore took active steps to persuade the Indians, with French help, to destroy the fort. At the same time, he took steps to strengthen Fort Niagara, also on the south shore of the lake, and, to offset the influence of Oswego, founded a French port at Fort Rouillé (Toronto).

The English Governor Clinton of New York protested de la Galissonière's actions on the ground that the boundary of Canada was the St. Lawrence and the Lakes and that all the land involved in the Lake Champlain and Lake Ontario basins belonged to the Iroquois Indians, who had either ceded them to the English or had placed them under British protection, and that the Iroquois themselves had been recognized as allies of Britain in the Anglo-French Treaty of Utrecht.[7]

To the southwestward, in the Ohio Valley, de la Galissonière took additional steps to forestall English expansion. He had recommended, as early as 1748, that the Illinois country be settled with Frenchmen in order to block the English. The Miami Indian village of Pickawillany, on the Great Miami River, had become a center for the English fur trade in the Ohio Valley, and, presently, a small English village of traders was built at Logstown, on the Ohio River about twenty miles below the junction of the Allegheny and the Monongahela Rivers. Upon receiving news of the organization, in 1748, of the Ohio Company of Virginia, and of its project to settle the lands along the Ohio, de la Galissonière organized the famous expedition of Céloron de Blainville and sent it, in 1740, down the Ohio to reaffirm French possession of the entire Ohio drainage basin. This claim, of course, cut off the trans-Allegheny position of Pennsylvania and Virginia; de la Galissonière even wrote to Governor Hamilton of Pennsylvania to restrain the Pennsylvania fur traders from crossing the mountains into the

[7] N.Y.C.D., VI, 711–712.

Ohio Valley "with regard to which England has never had any pretensions." [8]

De la Galissonière was succeeded as governor of Canada by the Marquis de la Jonquière, who destroyed the Miami village at Pickawillany, and, in 1752, by the Marquis Duquesne, who carried the plans of de la Galissonière forward, most notably by building a line of forts down the Ohio Valley, beginning, in 1752, with Fort Presqu'isle (Erie, Pa.), on Lake Erie, and Fort le Boeuf, on the Rivière aux Boeufs, near the headwaters of the Allegheny River. These were followed by the erection, in 1754, of Fort Duquesne, at the junction of the Allegheny and the Monongahela Rivers in western Pennsylvania.

Still farther south, in the area around the southern end of the Appalachians and in the Gulf Coastal Plain, the French took other measures to block the English expansion. The Marquis de Vaudreuil, governor of Louisiana, reported in 1750 that British expansion in that area, signalized by William Livingston's plan for settling Protestant families on the western frontier of South Carolina, was moving westward into French territory and that the English had stirred up warfare between the pro-English and pro-French tribes.[9] The question of where the frontier might properly be, in the Gulf Coastal Plain, a question that must be studied by the joint commission in Paris, was very difficult to resolve; the French Fort Toulouse, on the upper waters of the Alabama, served as an easterly bastion of French holdings and as a point of "effective occupation" to try to force the English to accept a line farther east, perhaps along the Chattahoochee and Apalachicola Rivers.

In the West Indies, again, the rival expansion of the two empires was leading straight to conflict. Both sides, but especially the French, took steps to possess themselves of as many as posible of the "Neutral Islands." The French, influenced by the strategic position of Dominica between Martinique and Guadelupe, to say nothing of its potential richness as a producer of sugar, began actively to infiltrate that island in 1748. It was reported in 1753 that there were some four thousand French settlers there, who had organized a military government under the authority of Governor Bomipard, of Martinique.[10] The island of St. Vincent was similarly infiltrated by the French, beginning in 1748, although resistance by the Carib Indians slowed the penetration somewhat. Tobago, which was not one of the original "Neutral Islands," was also a focus of English-French tension. The French sent an expedition to settle the island in 1748, and a proclamation was issued by the Marquis de Caylus, governor of Martinique (that is, of all the French West Indies), which asserted Louis XV's ownership of it. In the exchange of diplomatic protests that followed, England and

[8] Margry, ed., *Méms. et Docs.*, VI, 667–726.
[9] N.Y.C.D., X, 219–220.
[10] Legg, ed., *Brit. Dip. Insts.*, 1745–80, VII, *France*, 1745–89, 39–40.

France agreed to make Tobago, also, one of the "Neutral Islands" until the joint commission, then hard at work in Paris, should decide which empire owned it.

It was St. Lucia that was the most important of the "Neutral Islands." Although it was supposed to have been evacuated under the Anglo-French agreement of 1730, the French settlers had never really evacuated it. When, therefore, the French began more actively to colonize the island, after the Peace of Aix-la-Chapelle, it became a sort of focal issue in the disputes of the commissioners in Paris. It is to be noted, however, that the English government was less sure of the validity of its title to this island than to the others, and that it was willing to have its commissioners surrender it to the French, provided England "shall have and enjoy the quiet and peaceable possession of the Island of Tobago . . ." [11], which was the one of the four islands to which England thought it had the most defensible title. The French hung on in St. Lucia, and by 1755 they were so firmly established that they could set up a formal military control there. Elsewhere in the West Indies, the English did evacuate the former French section of the island of St. Martin (jointly occupied by the French and the Dutch) from which the French had been driven during the war by the British from Anguilla. But in 1753 the French seized Turks Island and captured a number of American colonial ships loading salt.

Such was the long line of Anglo-French tension points in America when the joint Anglo-French commission began its work in Paris. On the continent of North America, France was clearly and consciously on the defensive against the universal and vigorous expansionism of the English colonies, the basic factors in which were the growth of their populations and a consequent movement toward the occupation of new lands west of the Appalachian watershed, an interest in the extension of the English fur and skin trade with the Indians, and the international military and strategic concerns of the mother country. In the Caribbean area, by contrast, the French were actively and aggressively moving into the hitherto unoccupied islands. In that area it was England that was on the defensive. It was to resolve these tensions and conflicts that the Anglo-French joint commission of 1750 was created.

The French suggestion for a joint commission to discuss all outstanding Anglo-French disputes in America was, at first, received coolly by the English ministers. The Duke of Bedford, now secretary of state for the Southern Department, was especially skeptical with regard to the possibility of achieving peace by this means. However, the ministry, in the interest of making a genuine effort to find peaceful solutions of the American disputes, acceded, and in July, 1749, it was agreed that the commission then meeting

[11] Quoted in Gipson, *The British Empire before the American Revolution*, V, 230.

in St. Malo should be liquidated and a new Anglo-French commission for American disputes set up in Paris. It was understood by the French that the commission was to be authorized to determine a boundary between the French and the English colonies in America and to decide the ownership of the "Neutral Islands" and other lands in dispute; the English vaguely expected it to discuss territorial questions, problems relative to the exchange of prisoners of war taken at sea, and the restitution of prizes taken at sea since the signature of the Preliminaries on April 30, 1748. But there was never any agreement as to the exact definition of the problem or problems to be discussed.

Early in 1750, while the situation in America was rapidly becoming more critical, the Anglo-French commission came into being.[12] England's representatives on the commission were William Mildmay, an English civil servant, and William Shirley, governor of Massachusetts Bay. The French members were the Marquis de la Galissoniére—the same who, as Governor-General of Canada, had taken so many steps to block British expansion in America—and Etiènne de Silhouette, a minor official in the French court. The British commissioners were instructed, apart from questions relative to prisoners of war and prizes, to demand a definition of the boundaries of Novia Scotia, or Acadia, according to what the English government understood those boundaries to be. They were to claim St. Lucia, St. Vincent, and Dominica for England, on the basis of the history of the occupation of those islands. Tobago, also, was to be claimed for England. The commissioners were authorized to discuss the question of a boundary between the French and the English possessions in North America, but they were to be extremely cautious not to surrender, by drawing a boundary, any part of Acadia, according to the English notion of what Acadia ought to be, or "any other lands or territorys which We or Our subjects may have a right to on the continent of America." This was interpreted as including all the land south of the St. Lawrence River; nothing was said of a boundary to the westward.[13]

The French commissioners were instructed to negotiate a boundary in North America and to discuss the ownership of the four "Neutral Islands." [14] Their instructions, in fact, were even more vague than those of the English commissioners; the specific details upon which the French claims on these and other matters were based appeared in extenso in the memorials presently offered on both sides.

[12] For a history of the work of this commission, see Savelle, *The Diplomatic History of the Canadian Boundary, 1749–63*, Chapter II.

[13] Legg, ed., *Brit. Dip. Insts., 1689–1789*, VII, France, 1745–89, 307–313.

[14] "Mémoire de la Cour de France pour les Instructions à donner aux commissionaires pour le règlement des limites en Amérique et des Prises faites en mer," "Réponse au Mémoire intitulé Projet des Instructions pour les Commissionaires qui doivent s'assembler à Paris," and "Mémoire d'Observations sur le Projet d'Instructions pour les Com.ʳˢ Anglais," C.L., Mildmay Papers, "Memorials."

The joint commission began its work on August 31, 1750. Several meetings were devoted to discussions of procedures and of the instructions on both sides, after which the commission settled down to the presentation of claims relative to two major areas, Nova Scotia (Acadia) and the Caribbean islands. The French commissioners began the conferences with a proposed statement of principles that might have led to compromise, that is, that both sides be prepared "to renounce anything that would give their respective colonists in America the temptation and the means to annoy, attack, or invade each other with ease and success, even in cases where a war might intervene and render such aggression legitimate." [15] Mildmay and Shirley understood this proposal to be intended to lay the groundwork for bargaining a large Acadia for England against the cession of St. Lucia to France, and stiffly replied that they would defend His Britannic Majesty's just rights, no matter where they lay, because justice and amity went hand in hand.[16] The commission, thus, began its work in a mood of mutual distrust and unwillingness to compromise; this mood became even more marked as the commissioners proceeded with their debates.

The first exchange of claims had to do with Acadia. Both sides submitted long memorials, based upon detailed histories, setting forth their claims relative to the boundaries of the Acadia ceded to Britain by the Anglo-French Treaty of Utrecht.[17] The English commissioners, starting from the provision in the Anglo-French Treaty of Utrecht that Acadia was to be ceded to England with its *"anciennes limites,"* [18] presented a claim that interpreted those "old limits" as being a line beginning at the mouth of the Penobscot River and following that river and a straight north-south line to the St. Lawrence, the south shore of that river to Cape Rosières, a line drawn from that cape across the Gulf of St. Lawrence south-eastwardly to the promontory of Cape Breton, and from thence by a line drawn in the Atlantic Ocean around Sable Island and the southern end of the peninsula to the mouth of the Penobscot, the place of beginning. This line, of course, included Cape Breton Island as a part of the original Acadia, but as that island had been specifically excepted and ceded to France by the Treaty of Utrecht, so now it was excepted and recognized as belong-

---

[15] C.A.O., A.E., Corr. Lol., Ang. 430: fols. 123–128.

[16] C.A.O., A.E., Corr. Pol., Ang. 430:123–128.

[17] The many memorials presented on both sides, during the life of this commission, were published in France contemporaneously, just after the commission ceased to function, as *Mémoires des Commissaires du Roi et ceux de Sa Majesté Britannique, Sur les possessions et les droits respectifs des deux couronnes en Amérique; avec les actes publics et pièces justificatives* (3 vols. Paris: Imprimerie Royal, 1755); a fourth volume, containing additional memorials relating to the French claims to ownership of Tobago, which had not been presented because of the rupture of diplomatic relations in 1756, was added in 1757. The English edition of the same Memorials was published as *The Memorials of the English and French Commissaries Concerning the Limits of Nova Scotia or Acadia*. London: [His Majesty's Printing Office?], 1755.

[18] See Chapter X.

ing to France. The commissioners were to demand that all other lands within the line indicated were to be recognized, once and for all, as belonging to England.[19]

To the English definition of the *"anciennes limites"* of Acadia the French proposed an opposite extreme, for, according to the French memorial of September 21, 1750, Annapolis (Port Royal) was not a part of Acadia. Rather, the *"anciennes limites"* of Acadia were defined as a line "beginning at the extremity of the Bay of Fundy at Cape St. Marie on Forked Cape, and extending around the coast to Cape Canseau [where it ends]."[20]

This French definition would have limited Acadia to a narrow strip of land along the Atlantic coast of the Acadian (Nova Scotian) peninsula. Since the Anglo-French Treaty of Utrecht specifically provided for the cession of Port Royal, the French commissioners were prepared to recognize that city as belonging to England, but neither the island of Canso, nor the isthmus, nor the land on the western shore of the Bay of Fundy were to be thought of as included in Acadia.

So far as Acadia was involved, the irreconcilable differences between the definitions of that province presented on the two sides characterized the protracted debates and the exchanges of many memorials and *"piéces justificatives"* through all the years of the commission's existence.

It was in this same uncompromising mood that the commissioners of the two nations attempted to arrive at a final settlement of the ownership of the "Neutral Islands" in the West Indies. The argument with regard to these islands centered chiefly upon St. Lucia.

The French commissioners presented their first memorial setting forth the French claim to St. Lucia on February 11, 1751.[21] Promising to present a memorial on Tobago later on, they disposed of discussion of the other two original "Neutral Islands" by saying that possession of those two islands "had been assured by the two Nations, and under the protection of France, to the Caribs, natives of the country."[22]

As for St. Lucia, the French memorial cited Grotius to justify the seizure of unoccupied lands as national property. It then went on to demonstrate the validity of the French claim to the island by a long and detailed recitation of the successive occupations of the island by the French, beginning with the Company for the American Isles, whose charter, issued by Cardinal Richelieu in 1626, covered an area of the West Indies that included St. Lucia. It was only for the sake of peace and good will that France had consented to leave the island in a neutral status.

It was not until November 15, 1751, that the English commissioners

---

[19] Legg. ed., *Brit. Dip. Insts.*, 1689–1789, VII, *France*, 1745–89, 310.
[20] *Mém. des Coms. du Roi* . . . , I, 10–11.
[21] *Méms. des Coms. du Roi* . . . , II, 3–42.
[22] *Méms. des Coms. du Roi* . . . , II, 4.

submited their reply to the French memorial on St. Lucia.[23] It began by re-
jecting the contention of the French memorial that the islands of St. Vin-
cent and Dominica had been left in possession of the Caribs "under the
Protection of France," and then went on to offer its own version of the his-
tory of the occupations of St. Lucia to show how incontrovertible was the
British title to the island, beginning with the charter issued by King Charles
I in 1627 to the Earl of Carlisle for "all the islands in the said Caribs or
Antilles," including St. Lucia, and settlements made on that island by the
Earl in 1635, 1638, and 1639.[24]

Memorial followed memorial and *pièces justificatives* followed *pièces
justificatives*, without softening in the slightest the inflexibility of either
side. Eventually, in 1755 or 1756, the French prepared a memorial on Tobago,[25] which repeated the procedures in the earlier memorial, but this
memorial was never presented to the English because of the breakdown of
all negotiations in 1755 and the official outbreak of the Seven Years War
in 1756.

The Anglo-French joint commission thus spent some five years wrangling over the boundaries of Acadia and the ownership of the "Neutral
Islands." Meanwhile, the British ministry, always skeptical of the possible
effectiveness of the commission, asked that the negotiations be placed in
the hands of the permanently accredited diplomats, and this was done in
1754, although the commission still remained technically in existence.

2. Direct Anglo-French Negotiations, 1754-56

During the years when the Anglo-French joint commission was gripped
in stalemate, incident after incident occurred along the frontiers of the
French and British empires in America to inflame colonial feelings and
arouse colonial fears. As tension heightened in America, the British ministry, increasingly impatient over the stalling of the Paris commission,
moved more and more definitely toward direct negotiations through the
usual channels of diplomacy. As early as 1750, before the commission had
been at work three months, the Duke of Bedford had suggested to the
Duc de Mirepoix, French ambassador in London, that the two countries
negotiate an arbitrary boundary line between their respective possessions
in America.[26] He had gotten no positive reply. He tried again in 1751,
when he suggested that both sides evacuate all disputed territories until a
satisfactory boundary could be drawn.[27] Again, the idea was received in
France without enthusiasm, even with suspicion, and the French minister

[23] *Méms. des Coms. du Roi* . . . , II, 44–153.
[24] *Méms. des Coms. du Roi* . . . , II, 50.
[25] *Méms. des Coms. du Roi* . . . , IV, iii–xxv.
[26] C.A.O., A.E., Corr. Pol., Ang. 429: fol. 335.
[27] C.A.O., A.E., Corr. Pol., Ang. 431: fols. 120–123.

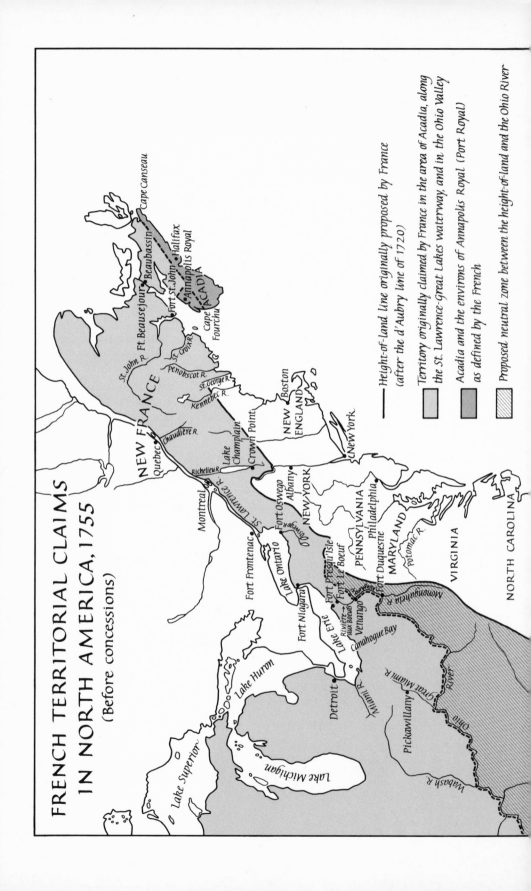

FRENCH TERRITORIAL CLAIMS IN NORTH AMERICA, 1755
(Before concessions)

Height-of-land line originally proposed by France
(after the d'Aubry line of 1720)

Territory originally claimed by France in the area of Acadia, along
the St. Lawrence-Great Lakes waterway, and in the Ohio Valley

Acadia and the environs of Annapolis Royal (Port Royal)
as defined by the French

Proposed neutral zone between the height-of-land and the Ohio River

Cape Canseau
Beaubassin
Fort St. John
Halifax
Annapolis Royal
ACADIA
Cape Fourchu
Ft. Beausejour
St. John R.
St. Croix R.
Penobscot R.
St. George R.
Kennebec R.
NEW FRANCE
Boston
NEW ENGLAND
Quebec
Chaudière R.
Lake Champlain
Crown Point
New York
Richelieu R.
NEW YORK
Montreal
St. Lawrence R.
Fort Oswego
Albany
Oswego R.
Fort Frontenac
Lake Ontario
PENNSYLVANIA
Philadelphia
MARYLAND
Fort Niagara
Lake Erie
Fort Presqu'Isle
Fort Le Boeuf
Rivière aux Boeufs
Venango
Fort Duquesne
Monongahela R.
Potomac R.
VIRGINIA
Canahogue Bay
Detroit
Miami R.
Great Miami R.
Pickawillany
Ohio River
Wabash R.
NORTH CAROLINA
Lake Huron
Lake Michigan
Lake Superior

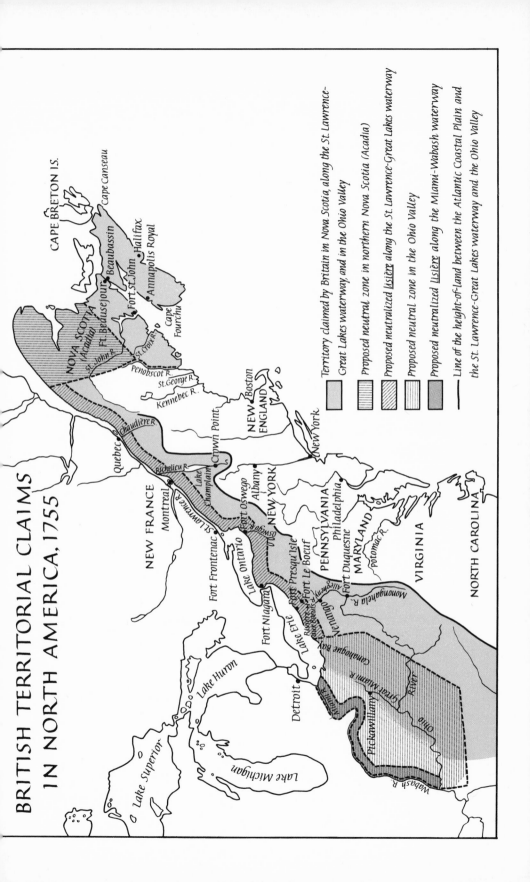

BRITISH TERRITORIAL CLAIMS IN NORTH AMERICA, 1755

Territory claimed by Britain in Nova Scotia, along the St. Lawrence–Great Lakes waterway and in the Ohio valley

Proposed neutralized zone in northern Nova Scotia (Acadia)

Proposed neutralized lisière along the St. Lawrence–Great Lakes waterway

Proposed neutral zone in the Ohio valley

Proposed neutralized lisière along the Miami–Wabash waterway

Line of the height-of-land between the Atlantic Coastal Plain and the St. Lawrence–Great Lakes waterway and the Ohio valley

CAPE BRETON IS.

Cape Canseau

Beaubassin

Halifax

Ft. Beauséjour

Fort St. John

Annapolis Royal

NOVA SCOTIA (Acadia)

Ft. St. John

Cape Fourchu

St. John R.

St. Croix R.

Penobscot R.

St. George R.

Kennebec R.

Boston

NEW ENGLAND

New York

Chaudière R.

Quebec

Richelieu R.

Crown Point

Lake Champlain

NEW FRANCE

Montreal

St. Lawrence R.

Fort Oswego

Albany

NEW YORK

Fort Frontenac

Lake Ontario

Oswego

Fort Niagara

Fort Presqu'Isle

Fort Le Boeuf

PENNSYLVANIA

Philadelphia

Lake Erie

Riv. aux Boeufs

Venango

Fort Duquesne

MARYLAND

Potomac R.

Allegheny R.

Canhogue Bay

Detroit

Lake Huron

Lake Michigan

Lake Superior

Monongahela R.

VIRGINIA

NORTH CAROLINA

Pickawillamy

Miami R.

Great Miami R.

Ohio River

Wabash R.

replied that the American negotiations should be left in the hands of the joint commission. In view of the French attitude, the British ministers suspected that a friendly French vote in an election of a new Holy Roman Emperor, then pending, might be made dependent upon a settlement of the American problem, at a considerable sacrifice of British interests in America. This made it all the more urgent, in the opinion of the British ministers, that the American problems be settled quickly and effectively; the way for doing this, they thought, was by direct negotiation *de cour à cour*.[28]

It was the personal opinion of French ambassador Mirepoix that the Paris commission could never succeed—that the problems involved were too complicated. "There is no court," he said, "where questions at issue between the King of France and the King of England can be brought to judgment." [29] But François Barberie de St. Contest, French minister of foreign affairs, refused to consider dissolving the commission, although he did express a willingness to carry on direct negotiations concurrently with the work of the commission.

In January, 1753, the Earl of Holdernesse instructed the Earl of Albemarle, English ambassador in Paris, again to broach the question of direct negotiations to St. Contest.[30] Holdernesse complained of French dilatoriness; the "Neutral Islands" were still not evacuated, and the French were on the aggressive in many parts of North America; it appeared to him that France was deliberately stalling for time, while carrying out a calculated policy of imperialistic expansion everywhere in America. Albemarle was instructed to make it clear that the King of England, despite his "strict adherence to the faith of treaties," would not be "deluded by ineffectual promises." [31]

Mirepoix was empowered to begin conversations with Albemarle in Paris, the two ambassadors to be the official channel for the direct negotiations between the two courts.[32] Albemarle was instructed by his government to approach the American problems with a certain degree of flexibility and to make such concessions as might guarantee "the mutual security of the undisputed possessions of each Crown." [33] As it was expected that French demands would focus upon St. Lucia, Britain was prepared to concede that island to France in return for a clear title to Nova Scotia, according to the British conception of what it was, together with the demolition of the

[28] Legg, ed., *Brit. Dip. Insts.*, 1689–1789, VII, *France*, 1745–89, 24–25.

[29] C.A.O., A.E., Corr. Pol., Ang. 434: fols. 187–192.

[30] Holdernesse to Albemarle, Jan. 4, 1753, in Legg, ed., *Brit. Dip. Insts.*, 1689–1789, VII, *France*, 1745–89, 34–36.

[31] *Ibid.*, VII, *France*, 1745–89, 35.

[32] St. Contest to Mirepoix, Feb. 15, 1753, C.A.O., A.E., Corr., Pol., Ang., 436: fols. 278–282.

[33] Newcastle to Albemarle, June 4, 1752, in Legg, ed., *Brit. Dip. Insts.*, 1689–1789, VII, *France*, 1745–89, 28.

French fortress at Crown Point, on Lake Champlain.[34] While the British claim to Nova Scotia included all the land up to the St. Lawrence, Britain was willing to entertain a proposal for a neutral zone between that river and the English colonies, provided France should promise not to make settlements in such a zone.

The instructions to Albemarle appear to have represented a genuine desire on the part of the British ministry to settle the Anglo-French disputes in America on the basis of compromise and exchange of concessions. But the French ministry was unwilling to go as far in the direction of concessions as was Mirepoix, He was given no instructions, apparently because the French ministers viewed with suspicion the vagueness of Albemarle's instructions. This ambassadorial negotiation, therefore, came to naught.

Direct negotiations were not seriously resumed again until the summer of 1754, after Mirepoix had returned to London in June of that year. The Paris commission had spent the year 1753 wrangling over procedures, while the irritation and counterirritations at the points of contact along the joint frontiers of the two empires in America were becoming more and more exacerbated. The events in America were beginning to lend a special feeling of urgency to the problem, especially when, in the summer of 1754, Canada and Virginia found themselves face to face in the upper Ohio Valley.

News of the defeat of George Washington and his Virginia militia at Fort Necessity by a party of French soldiers and Indians sent out from the new French Fort Duquesne and of the death of the French Lieutenant Jumonville in the skirmishing nearby was received in Paris and London in August of 1754.[35] This news infuriated the French, who regarded Washington's expedition as an intrusion upon French territory; on the other hand, the French resort to military action caused King George II to make a bristlingly belligerent speech from the throne in the fall,[36] and the British cabinet decided to send General Braddock to the Ohio to drive out the French.[37] The announcement of this decision in Paris, coupled with the developing events in America, only determined France to send *"aussi du monde,"* that is, reinforcements of its own, to America.[38]

Both sides were shocked into a realization of the danger of war, and in Albemarle's conversation with Antoine-Louis Rouillé, Comte de Jouy,

[34] L.C., B.M., Add. Mss., 32836: fols. 94–95, 97–99, 296–298, 300–301; see also, Legg, ed., *Brit. Dip. Insts.*, 1689–1789, VII, *France*, 1745–89, 28.
[35] Albemarle to Robinson, Aug. 21, 1754, C.L., Shelburne Mss., XXXVI, fol. 25.
[36] Cobbett, *Parliamentary History*, XV, 330 ff.
[37] Robinson to Albemarle, Oct. 3, 1754, in Legg, ed., *Brit. Dip. Insts.*, 1689–1789, VII, *France*, 1745–89, 48–49.
[38] Waddington, *Louis XV et le renversement des Alliances: préliminaires de la guerre de sept ans, 1754–1756*, 63.

the new French foreign minister, there was considerable mutual recrimination. Both thought themselves in the right and each saw the activities of the other as deliberately aggressive and imperialistic. Newcastle, for example, wrote, "All North America will be lost, if these Practices are tolerated, And no War can be worse to this Country, than the Suffering Such Insults, as These." [39] The French, in their own eyes, were only protecting what was theirs; and they were maintaining, by force, their old contention that the entire drainage basin of the Ohio belonged to them and that the true boundary of the English colonies was, and always had been, the Allegheny watershed.[40] Yet, both sides, however little they trusted each other, apparently sincerely desired to avoid war, and, despite the recriminations exchanged between the two ministries, both were prepared to make another try at a negotiated settlement of the American disputes.

It was apparently the French who made the first suggestion of a new negotiation. This time, however, it was the English who received the proposal coolly. Sir Thomas Robinson, now English secretary of state for the Southern Department, wrote to Albemarle that while the British ministry appreciated Rouillé's overtures as a personal expression of good will, the actions of France in America belied any possibility that they might represent a genuine desire on the part of France for peace. Indeed, French activities in America seemed to the British ministry to discover "a settled premeditated plan to distress the English trade in those parts, and to commit the most glaring encroachments and usurpations upon His Majesty's just rights and possessions." [41] If France really desired peace, Robinson wrote, let it show it,

1º. By executing the Treaty of Aix-la-Chapelle and fulfilling the subsequent promises which His Most Christian Majesty himself gave Your Excellency [Albemarle] as to the entire evacuation of the neutral islands;

2do. By relinquishing the forts which they have so unjustly built and the possession they have taken of so many posts in Acadie, or Nova Scotia, notwithstanding the positive agreement between the two Courts that no innovation should be made there during the negotiation of the commissaries; and

3tio. By withdrawing their forces from the Ohio and the countries adjacent thereto, so that everything may be previously put in these parts upon the footing it was at the signing of the said treaty of Aix la Chapelle.[42]

The French ministry paid little attention to this British "ultimatum," but it was really disturbed by the Braddock expedition. Vigorous steps were taken to augment French forces in the colonies, both in India and in America. The French ministry continued to negotiate, however, while the sud-

[39] L.C., B.M., Add. Mss., 32850: fol. 218.
[40] Albemarle to Robinson, Oct. 23, 1754, C.L., Shelburne Mss., XXXVI, fol. 69.
[41] Robinson to Albemarle, Sept. 12, 1754, in Legg, ed., Brit. Dip. Insts., 1689–1789, VII, France, 1745–89, 47–48.
[42] Legg, ed., Brit. Dip. Insts., 1689–1789, VIII, France, 1745–49, 47–48.

den death on December 22 of the Earl of Albemarle, who had carried on negotiations in Paris, threw the whole weight of the French side of the negotiation upon Mirepoix in London.

On January 16, 1755, Mirepoix presented to Robinson a memorial formally setting forth four proposals for steps to be taken preliminary to a negotiation of the issues. First, France proposed that both countries send strict orders to their governors in America to take no further actions that might affect the settlement of the points in dispute between the two countries; second, France proposed that the situation in the Ohio Valley be restored to the condition it was in before the recent war; third, it was proposed that the questions in dispute between the two empires in America be referred to the joint commission still sitting in Paris; finally, France asked the British King to explain the reason for the fervid build-up of armaments then going on in England and to indicate the destination of the troops that were being gathered for overseas duty.[43]

In the conversation that accompanied the delivery of Mirepoix's memorial, Robinson reminded the French ambassador that the French had never occupied the upper Ohio Valley prior to the War of the Austrian Succession, and that, in the communications with Louisiana, they had used the Lake Erie-Wabash-Ohio-Mississippi route. The upper Ohio region, he said, had been conquered by the Iroquois and must be regarded as belonging to the Iroquois and, therefore, to England. He thus rested the English title to the upper Ohio on Article 15 of the Anglo-French Treaty of Utrecht (1713), the conquest of the area by the Iroquois, and the actual purchase of these lands from the Indians by the English colonies.[44]

The English reply to Mirepoix's memorial, delivered on January 22, followed Robinson's argument. It proposed, thus, that the situation in the upper Ohio Valley be restored to the condtion it was in at the time of the Peace of Utrecht and not at the beginning of the recent war; similarly, all other situations in North America would be restored to the *status quo* of the year 1713. Logically, this would have meant the demolition of all the forts built by the French in North America since 1713: Niagara, Crown Point, the forts on the St. John River and on the isthmus of Nova Scotia, as well as those recently built on the upper Ohio. The English reply indicated that it would be easy to agree on the form of the orders to be sent to the French and English governors in America; as for the armaments then preparing in England, His Christian Majesty could rest assured that they were purely defensive in nature; the King of England had no aggressive designs against any of his neighbors![45]

To the English proposal Mirepoix could only reply that France stood

[43] Pease, ed., *Anglo-French Boundary Disputes*, 95–97.
[44] Mirepoix to Douillé, Jan. 16, 1755, Pease, ed., *Anglo-French Boundary Disputes*, 86–95.
[45] Robinson's Memoir, Jan. 22, 1755, Pease, ed., *Anglo-French Boundary Disputes*, 99–101.

unmoved from its first position. Thus, he proposed the same four steps: let the two Kings order their governors in America not to initiate any new moves; let the situation in North America be restored to the condition it was in before the last war; let the American disputes be referred to the Paris commission; and let the ministers of the two courts keep working on the problem of a peaceable solution of the American disputes. As for the warlike preparations going on in France, His Britannic Majesty could rest assured that they were purely defensive in purpose and not intended for aggression against any other nation! [46] Rouillé, in authorizing Mirepoix to negotiate, recognized that the focus of the American disputes was now upon the situation in the Ohio Valley. That valley had always belonged to France, he wrote, and the Treaty of Utrecht, in ignoring it, had tacitly recognized that it belonged to France. His Christian Majesty, therefore, could not recognize that the English had any rights there; to admit the English to the Ohio Valley would be to prepare the way for their seizure of Louisiana and Canada. It was up to London to demonstrate any possible validity to this new English pretension, which, of course, His Christian Majesty would not have the slightest difficulty in refuting! [47]

On February 6 Mirepoix presented to Robinson a project for a preliminary convention. In this project it was proposed: (1) that immediate orders be sent to the English and French governors in America to abstain from any aggressive action, (2) that the subjects of France and England in America evacuate all the territory between the Allegheny Mountains and the Ohio River: the French to the northwestward of the river and the English to the eastward of the mountains; the land between the river and the mountains would be left neutral during the life of the convention, and all the concessions made by either crown for the settlement of land in the area would be cancelled; [48] (3) the subjects of both countries would be prohibited from entering this territory; (4) all other areas in North America were to be restored to the condition they were in before the late war; (5) the convention was to be in effect for two years; (6) the diplomatic representatives of the two countries and the Paris commission were to be instructed to proceed with all possible speed to a settlement *"au fond"* of all the disputes between the two empires in America.[49]

In a series of meetings on February 7, 9, and 10, the British cabinet formulated its position relative to a preliminary convention. On February 7

[46] Project of Reply to Robinson's Memoir, Feb. 3, 1755, Pease, ed., *Anglo-French Boundary Disputes*, 102–106.

[47] Rouillé to Mirepoix, Feb. 3, 1755, Pease, ed., *Anglo-French Boundary Disputes*, 106–108.

[48] The reference is evidently to the cession made by Virginia to the Ohio Company.

[49] "Projet, d'une Convention préliminaire proposée par les ordres du Roi à la Cour de Londres," Feb. 6, 1755, *Mémoires des Commissaires du Roi, III: Mémoire contenant le Précis des Faits*, 171–173. See also, "Mémoire," C.A.O., A.E., Corr. Pol., Ang., 434: fols. 335–339 vo.

it authorized Robinson to continue his negotiations with Mirepoix, on the basis of an evacuation by both sides of the upper Ohio Valley and a demolition of the forts there, in such a manner that the territory between the Allegheny Mountains and the Great Lakes and westward to the Wabash River should be restored to the vacant condition it was in at the time of the Peace of Utrecht.[50] In a meeting on February 9 the cabinet further authorized an agreement with France that would provide specifically that orders should be sent immediately to the colonial governors of the two countries in America to carry out the evacuation of territories and the demolition of forts, and that there should be a suspension of arms for an unspecified number of months, during which time all the points at issue would be decided in a friendly manner; during the suspension of arms, neither side would send troops or armaments to America.[51] On February 10, the cabinet settled upon further details as to its preliminary conditions for a negotiated settlement: the upper Ohio Valley was to be evacuated by both sides, but it would be open to the traders of both the French and the English colonies. The navigation of the Great Lakes and the Niagara River, even "across that River, from and to the countries, lying within the Great Lakes," would be open to both French and English. All forts built on the westward [sic!] side of the Niagara River, as well as Crown Point, were to be demolished. France was to agree, as a preliminary condition, that the entire peninsula of Nova Scotia, together with a tract of land an unspecified number of leagues wide along the western shore of the Bay of Fundy, and extending from the Bay of Fundy to the eastern border of New and extending from the Bay of Fundy to the eastern border of New England, belonged to England as "Acadia," and to evacuate all that territory and demolish all the French forts built in it since the Peace of Utrecht. Beyond the coastal strip, the land between it and the St. Lawrence River was to be left neutral and uninhabited by either the French or the English. Once these conditions were accepted by France, orders were to be sent to the governors as proposed.[52]

This set of preliminary propositions was submitted to the Earl of Halifax, president of the Board of Trade, for comment, and Halifax pointed out a number of points at which the cabinet's position would be detrimental to the British case. If, for example, all the territory in the Ohio Valley between the Allegheny Mountains and the Wabash River were evacuated, that would mean the abandonment of about a third of the province of Pennsylvania, as already established, to the French; Halifax doubted whether the crown could constitutionally give up a part of the property

[50] Cabinet Minutes, Feb. 7, 1755, Pease, ed., Anglo-French Boundary Disputes, 109.
[51] Cabinet Minutes, Feb. 9, 1755, Pease, ed., Anglo-French Boundary Disputes, 109-110.
[52] Cabinet Minutes, Feb. 10, 1775, Pease, ed., Anglo-French Boundary Disputes, 110-111.

of a private proprietor. Moreover, a line drawn from the mountains to Lake Ontario would exclude Englishmen from the right of building forts or trading posts on the shores of Lakes Ontario and Erie west of the line, all of which lay within territory of the Iroquois, assumed, under the Treaty of Utrecht, to belong to England. Furthermore, even were the French to agree to the principle of free navigation of the lakes and of the Niagara River, it would be impossible to put it into practice if the French were to be allowed to retain the forts and trading houses they had already built on the north side of the lakes while the English were prohibited from building posts on the south side. As for Nova Scotia, Halifax advised insistence that Nova Scotia properly included all the land on the continent to the east-ward of the Penobscot and extending northward to the St. Lawrence River, and that any concession in that area be granted only in return for an equal concession by the French.[53] As a result of Halifax's critique of the cabinet position, the English communication to Mirepoix was stiffened, and the English reverted to a substitution of surveyable lines for delimiting the neutral zone, instead of the mountains.[54]

Meanwhile, Rouillé sent a statement of the French case to Mirepoix. To begin with, Rouillé interpreted Robinson's willingness to have both sides evacuate the upper Ohio Valley as an admission that the Allegheny Moun-tains constituted the true western boundary of the English colonies. There-fore, the willingness on the part of His Most Christian Majesty to evacuate the area, so obviously his own, must be regarded as a sure manifestation of his great desire for peace. He would not go so far, however, as to agree to the neutralization of the Wabash River. The English had never had any establishments in this area of the lower Ohio Valley, whereas the French had effectively occupied it for nearly a century. Rouillé rejected the English proposal to allow freedom of travel in the upper Ohio Valley to the nationals of both empires: the area was not necessary to any English colony; it was necessary, on the other hand, to the French as a route of communication between Canada and Louisiana. Commerce there could not be permitted to the English, since commerce must inevitably lead to the building of establishments of one sort or another. As for the forts the French had built in the upper Ohio Valley, their demolition, since they stood in territory so obviously French, would be a supreme sacrifice on His Most Christian Majesty's part; however, he was willing to demolish them if the English would demolish their own forts at Oswego and at Chignecto and Minas on the Acadian frontier.

Since the English had based their claim to the lands south of the St. Lawrence River and Lakes Ontario and Erie upon Article 15 of the Anglo-

---

[53] Halifax's Observations on Robinson's Proposals, Pease, ed., *Anglo-French Boundary Disputes*, 111–114.
[54] Hardwicke to Newcastle, Feb. 16, 1755, Pease, ed., *Anglo-French Boundary Dis-putes*, 115.

French Treaty of Utrecht, Rouillé took particular pains to point out that the Iroquois and other Indian nations of America were independent and sovereign and had never given their lands to any European king:

The American [Indian] nations have preserved their liberty and their independence; this is a universal principle, not only among the Iroquois nations; but also among all the other nations who are close enough to have intercourse with them. Everyone knows that England has neither governors nor magistrates among them; and it is certain that if any Englishman were to claim some authority over these peoples, the commission with which he was vested by his court would never insure his life against the danger with which it would be threatened on the part of the Indians.[55]

Furthermore, he said, the Indians have no idea of property; they move about constantly and their territory is only the territory they occupy at the moment; it is impossible, therefore, to fix any valid boundaries to the territory of the Iroquois, even if they had ceded it to England, which they had not.[56]

The English cabinet put into final form its counterproject for a preliminary convention on February 20, 1755. In the first place, the cabinet based its project upon its conviction that the boundaries in America should be fixed and surveyable lines. Thus, the English project proposed that the boundary between the English colonies and the French possessions be a line starting at Canagahogue Bay, on the south shore of Lake Erie, and running due south to 40° North Latitude; from the point of its intersection with that parallel it would run due southwest to 37° North Latitude. Any forts or other establishments erected to the eastward of this line by the French would be demolished. The eastern boundary of the French territory would be a line drawn from the mouth of the Miami River on Lake Erie to the source of the Wabash; it would follow that river to its confluence with the Ohio, and from that point it would run due south to 37° North Latitude. All the land between these two lines, 37° and the lakes, would be left completely free of settlement, although it would be open to the fur traders of both nations; all forts already built by either nation within this territory would be demolished. The French fort at Crown Point and the French settlements on Lake Champlain, as well as Fort Niagara, would also be destroyed; but the subjects of both crowns were to be free to use all the waterways and to traverse the territories surrounding the lakes and to trade with the Indians there.

With regard to Nova Scotia, or Acadia, its western boundary was to be recognized as the Penobscot River and a line drawn due north from its

[55] Rouillé to Mirepoix, Feb. 19, 1755, Pease, ed., *Anglo-French Boundary Disputes,* 116–125, especially 123, 124; see also, Rouillé to Mirepoix, Feb. 19, 1755, "No. 2," *ibid.,* 131-135.

[56] Rouillé to Mirepoix, Feb. 19, 1955, Pease, ed., *Anglo-French Boundary Disputes,* 124–125.

source to the St. Lawrence. A straight line was to be drawn from a point an unspecified number of leagues from its mouth northeastwardly to a point on the shore of the Gulf of St. Lawrence an unspecified number of leagues from Cape Tourmentin, and all the land between that line and the ocean was to be recognized as belonging to England; all the land between the line and the St. Lawrence River was to be left unsettled by the subjects of either crown, except for the purposes of trade with the Indians. All the lines described in the project were to be actually surveyed by joint commissions of surveyors.[57]

Despite the fact that both the French and the English projects represented genuine concessions, however slight, the two plans were well-nigh irreconcilable. The English found the French proposal to recognize the Alleghenies as the boundary between the English coastal colonies and the French colonies in the interior unacceptable for several reasons, chief among which were the fact that the true crest of the mountains was almost impossible to ascertain and the actual existence of long-standing British settlement on a number of the rivers flowing westward. Still more important, the English ministers warned Mirepoix that the very conceptual basis of the French claim to the Ohio basin ran so profoundly counter to what they understood to be the basic rights of the English in that area that there was little hope that the negotiation could be successful. Nevertheless, Mirepoix reported, Newcastle and Robinson seemed inclined to try once again and to offer France a choice of two alternate plans. One of these plans would envisage a provisional accommodation relative to the Ohio area only; the other would cover all the points at issue.[58]

When the English ministers delivered to Mirepoix their counterproject, which followed closely the cabinet minutes of February 20, the French ambassador thought all the points might be adjusted except the continental line proposed by the English for Acadia. But the French reply to the English counterproject only confirmed the English ministers in their fear that France had no intention of making a genuine settlement, but, rather, to play for time until France might be ready for war. The French claims with regard to Acadia, especially, would have left the English in possession of barely half of the peninsula of Nova Scotia.

The French reply to the English counterproject rejected the English concept of fixed surveyable boundary lines and returned to the old French insistence that mountain ranges and rivers were the best boundaries. It rejected the English claim to the land of the Iroquois, and the English demand for the demolition of Forts Frederick and Niagara, on the ground that the latter, at least, was built before the Treaty of Utrecht, in 1687.

[57] Cabinet Minutes, Feb. 20, 1755, Pease, ed., Anglo-French Boundary Disputes, 135–138.
[58] Mirepoix to Rouillé, Feb. 28, 1755, Pease, ed., Anglo-French Boundary Disputes, 138–143.

It also rejected the English proposal that trade with the natives be permitted to the traders of both nations. As for the right demanded by the English to trade on the Great Lakes and in the lands north of them, this proposal was particularly offensive to France, since that territory was thought of as being the heart of Canada, which was closed to the traders of foreign nations conformably with the current mercantilist custom in all the European colonies in the "new world." Such an infiltration into Canada by Englishmen would, in fact, threaten the safety of Canada itself, since it must lead to the establishment of English trading posts and strong points that would be independent of the King and the government of France! The English proposals with regard to Acadia were rejected as excessively imperialistic and out of all proportion to the true historical boundaries of Acadia, which would have defined it as only a part of the peninsula of Nova Scotia. Finally, the French reply insisted that France could not settle any of the American issues without settling all of them, including those relative to the West Indies, once and for all.[59] In the final passage of his commentary Rouillé eloquently deplored what he believed to be the implications of English imperialistic expansion:

It would be very sad and very unfortunate for humanity and for all of Europe if England were to rekindle a war of which no one can foresee either the extent or the outcome, for an interest which ought to be regarded as almost negligible from England's point of view, if considered apart from all designs to seize possession of our colonies.

A little more or a little less land in North America should not be permitted to cause a war in North America; each of the two nations already possesses more land there than it can develop within a very long time in the future.

It would seem that the object of each of the two powers ought to be, not to enlarge, but to insure the security of what it already possesses, and this is in the interest of all of Europe. The commerce or the trade of the River Ohio which has given rise to the present difficulties is not worth a thousand pistoles per year . . . but England has found ways to excite the spirits of its citizens as if France wished to invade and usurp all the commerce of the English colonies in North America.[60]

Both sides now realized that a reconciliation was next to impossible. Rouillé wrote to Mirepoix that "we see with regret, Sir, that only war can terminate our discussions," and he instructed the ambassador henceforth to assume a passive attitude toward the negotiation, "which we regard as absolutely broken," but to listen to anything the British ministers might have to say to him.[61] Robinson, on the English side, wrote to Benjamin

[59] Observations on the English Counter Project, Feb. 13, 1755 [incorrect; probably March], Pease, ed., Anglo-French Boundary Disputes, 164–177.

[60] "Observations on the English Counter Project, Feb. 13, 1755," Pease, ed., Anglo-French Boundary Disputes, 175–176.

[61] Rouillé to Mirepoix, Mar. 17, 1755, Pease, ed., Anglo-French Boundary Disputes, 159–164.

Keene, in Madrid, that it was evident "that France did intend to support, at all Hazards, a Claim to every Thing on the Back of the British Colonies as their own Right & Property . . ." [62] and that "Nothing is clearer . . . than that the only Meaning of his [Mirepoix's] Court, has been, to obtain a bare cessation of arms, and to keep Things in Suspence, during two Years, according as it shall please France to conciliate Matters definitely, or to have Recourse to Arms again." [63]

Yet, both sides made one more gesture toward conciliation. Robinson and Newcastle explained to Mirepoix that the British counterproject was in no sense an ultimatum and that the British must insist on only two points: the first was the English position that Acadia must include the entire Nova Scotia peninsula and a coastal corridor connecting it with the other colonies of New England; the other point was the unwillingness of the English to permit France to shut in the English colonies on the coast and to close the Ohio Valley to English fur traders and then build fortifications along the boundary which would be a constant menace to the security of the English colonies. Even these two points, they said, were subject to some modification.[64] Acadia was, in fact, more important to the English than the Ohio Valley, or, even, than the disputed islands in the West Indies; and the British ministers informed Mirepoix that, if France could satisfy England with regard to Acadia, England would reciprocate by making concessions with regard to the "Neutral Islands." [65] Mirepoix was convinced, by the tone of his conversations with Newcastle and Robinson, that they were sincere in their desire to settle the American disputes amicably.[66]

As a result of his conversations with Newcastle and Robinson, Mirepoix indicated a willingness on the part of France to grant the English demands with regard to Acadia, with slight modifications. He suggested the establishment of a *lisière*, twenty leagues in width, along the south shore of the St. Lawrence from the point where the Penobscot line touched that river, then along the river and the lakes as far as Presqu'isle, to provide a guarantee that the English would never intrude upon the river or the lakes, which were regarded as being, as it were, the heart of New France. Within the *lisière* neither the French nor the English would have any forts or other establishments, except only that the French might build upon the south bank of the St. Lawrence River proper. This represented a compro-

[62] Robinson to Keene, Mar. 11, 1755, Pease, ed., *Anglo-French Boundary Disputes*, 155–157.

[63] Robinson to Keene, Mar. 11, 1755, "Separate," Pease, ed., *Anglo-French Boundary Disputes*, 158–159.

[64] Mirepoix to Rouillé, Mar. 22, 1755, Pease, ed., *Anglo-French Boundary Disputes*, 178–189.

[65] Mirepoix to Rouillé, Mar. 22, 1755, Pease, ed., *Anglo-French Boundary Disputes*, 182–187.

[66] Mirepoix to Rouillé, Mar. 22, 1755, Pease, ed., *Anglo-French Boundary Disputes*, 188.

mise of the French "drainage-basin" theory of ownership, but it would involve the demolition of both the English post at Oswego and the French fort at Niagara.[67]

Similarly, Mirepoix suggested a twenty-league *lisière* along the east bank of the Wabash River, and he suggested a definition of the eastern boundary of the neutral zone proposed by the English as a line running from Venango to a point where it would strike the Allegheny Mountains and thence along the ridge of the mountains to their southern end. This suggestion appealed to Robinson, and he confided to Newcastle that

If the top of our line can be adjusted, I should humbly think the mountains stretching as they do so far to the West would be a very advantageous boundary for our Carolinas.[68]

Mirepoix reported to Rouillé his conversations with the English ministers as amounting to a sort of counterproject to the French objections to the original British project for a definitive treaty, to which Rouillé had so violently objected. According to his report, Robinson intimated that England might be willing to leave Lake Champlain in the possession of France, if France would demolish Fort Frederick at Crown Point. The English would insist, he said, upon free navigation of the lakes for their Indian allies; Robinson protested that it had never been the English intention to demand the right for their nationals to visit the lands north of the lakes; what they had intended was to make sure that the Iroquois traders might go anywhere around the lakes in search of furs and bring them to the English market. They envisaged leaving the lands north of the lakes, as those to the south of them, neutral; it was this consideration that had led them to suggest the demolition of the fort at Toronto.

The English would also insist upon the south shore of the lakes, beyond Lake Champlain, as the boundary. This land would remain in the possession of the Iroquois, but neither the French nor the English would be free to build any establishments on it. With regard to the Ohio, the English suggested a modification of Mirepoix's proposed boundary that would draw that line from Venango down the Rivière aux Boeufs toward Lake Erie but would limit the extent of the English possessions to a point twenty leagues from that lake. This line would be drawn from this point (Venango? The document is not clear.) to the Allegheny Mountains, of which the watershed would be the boundary of the English colonies to the southward. The boundary of the French colonies would be the Wabash River, including a *lisière* twenty leagues wide along its left bank, to the point where it joined the Ohio. The land between the two lines would be

[67] Robinson to Newcastle, Mar. 22, 1755, Pease, ed., *Anglo-French Boundary Disputes*, 189-191.
[68] Robinson to Newcastle, Mar. 22, 1755, Pease, ed., *Anglo-French Boundary Disputes*, 190.

left vacant, to be occupied only by the Indians, but the English still proposed that the Indian trade be left open to the traders on both sides.[69]

The impossibility of reconciliation of the two positions was manifest in Rouillé's comments upon this English memorandum. The English demand for a land communication between Nova Scotia and New England he found "absolutely impracticable"; what the English hoped to get, he believed, was a base for the invasion of Canada. Besides, the land along the western shore of the Bay of Fundy was absolutely essential for communication with Quebec in winter, since the St. Lawrence River was frozen at that season. As for the English idea that the boundary in the interior should be the St. Lawrence River and the lakes, "the king [Louis XV] will never consent that his sovereignty over the south shore of the St. Lawrence River and Lakes Ontario and Erie be brought into the question, and that these parts of Canada, which have always been considered its center, should become its boundaries." On the Ohio, France had already offered to recognize the territory between the Ohio and the Allegheny Mountains as a neutral zone. France could go no farther: the English proposal to set the zone between the Ohio and the Wabash would cut off French communication between Canada and Louisiana. It appears, he said, that it is "totally useless" to discuss these matters any further.[70] As a final word, two weeks later, in response to an informal conversation between the Earl of Granville and Mirepoix, Rouillé instructed Mirepoix to say to the English that if they would desist from their impossible demands relative to the lisière along the Bay of Fundy, the St. Lawrence-Great Lakes boundary, and the neutral zone between the Ohio and the Wabash, all other points could easily be adjusted.[71] But the English could not abandon their claims on these three points; they were willing, nevertheless, to discuss them.[72]

What was probably the ultimate extent of British concessions was reached in a conversation between Robinson and Mirepoix on April 30. The ambassador reported to Rouillé that, according to Robinson, if the French would concede to England the entire peninsula of Nova Scotia and agree not to build any establishments in the lands west of the Bay of Fundy, England would consent to a "prohibited zone" opposite the isthmus. As for the south bank of the St. Lawrence up to the beginning of the lakes, Robinson said England never had denied French sovereignty, and would not; what England really desired was a definition of the area involved. Robinson even intimated that England would not deny French

[69] Mirepoix to Rouillé, Mar. 24, 1755, Pease, ed., Anglo-French Boundary Disputes, 192–197.

[70] Rouillé to Mirepoix, April 13, 1755, Pease, ed., Anglo-French Boundary Disputes, 207–210.

[71] Rouillé to Mirepoix, April 24, 1755, Pease, ed., Anglo-French Boundary Disputes, 211–212.

[72] English Note, April 25, 1755, Pease, ed., Anglo-French Boundary Disputes, 214–216.

sovereignty over Lakes Ontario and Erie; what he must insist upon was the free navigation of the lakes for the Iroquois, in view of the fact that some of the English Indians (the Iroquois) were established there and were dependent upon their trade across the lakes; if the south bank were recognized as French, those savages and their trade would become entirely dependent upon the French. With regard to the upper Ohio, Robinson told Mirepoix that if the French would consent to a line drawn from Lake Erie to the sources of that river, the English would consent to French ownership of all the land beyond the Ohio, provided the river itself were neutralized; they would also be willing to declare the land between the Ohio River and the Allegheny Mountains a prohibited zone, closed to the subjects of both nations. Robinson cautioned Mirepoix that he could not say all these things "ministerially," but he assured the ambassador that an agreement might still be reached on the basis of these concessions if France were willing. Mirepoix recognized that what Robinson had told him did represent genuine concessions by the English in all three of the chief areas in dispute, and he was convinced of Robinson's sincerity. Perhaps, he said, the strength of the French armaments might have impressed them with the danger involved in precipitating a war.[73]

Five days later, Mirepoix advised Rouillé to disregard Robinson's apparently sincere overture for peace. The English, he said, were determined to make war. He had just learned that Admiral Boscawen had sailed for America with orders to intercept and attack the French fleet under Admiral MacNémara that had sailed from Brest with six battalions of soldiers for the reinforcement of Canada.[74]

Still, the exchange of ideas continued, although neither side had any real hope it might have any effect. On May 9 Mirepoix handed the English minister a memoir on the major issues in the negotiation, the boundaries of Canada, the Ohio Valley, and the disputed islands in the West Indies.

With regard to Acadia, according to this memoir, although that territory really was only that part of the peninsula which lay east of a line drawn from Cape Sable to Canso, His Christian Majesty, out of his deep love of peace, was now willing to cede to England the entire peninsula—provided, however, a) that the French *habitants* living in it should be given three years in which to remove, with all their movable effects; b) that the isthmus and Beaubassin should be reserved to France, since this area and its hinterland were absolutely essential to France, especially during the winter, as a route of communication between Quebec and Isle Royal (Prince Edward Island); c) that there be left a neutral zone along the shore of the peninsula upon the Gulf of St. Lawrence; d) that the English desist from their demands for a *lisière* along the western shore of the Bay of Fundy, since

---

[73] Mirepoix to Rouillé, May 1, 1755, C.A.O., A.E., Corr. Pol., Ang., 439: fols. 4–13.
[74] Mirepoix to Rouillé, May 5, 1755, C.A.O., A.E., Corr. Pol., Ang., 439: fols. 24–26.

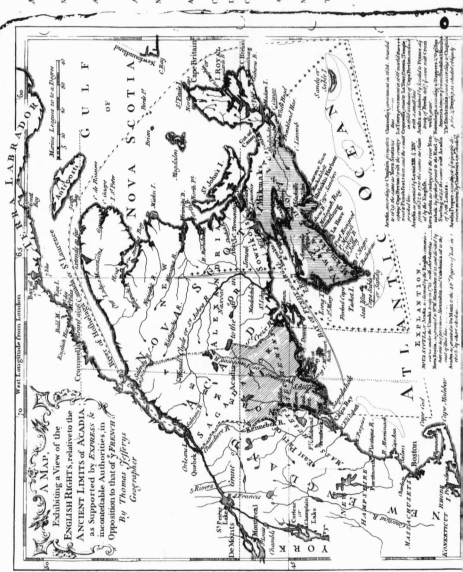

EXPLANATION

NOVA SCOTIA, or Acadia, as claimed by the English, (comprehensive under the Utrecht Treaty in 1713, with short strokes) ......

Nova Scotia, as granted to Sir Alexander, and divided by him into two provinces, Alexandria and Caledonia, all to the west of this line ——————

Acadia, according to Champlain, from 1603, to 1629, the same, as Nova Scotia (sawyers Cape-Breton) with the country west to Penobscot river, and the small pricked line ......

Acadia, as granted by Louis XIII. and XIV, from 1632, to 1702, the same as claimed by the English ———

Nova Scotia, as enlarged to the river Kennebek, by farther grant to the Earl of Sterling, 1635, the same with Acadia of Louis's ———

Acadia Proper, according to the tripart, its division, mentioned by Charlevoix, upright shades, ‖

Charnesay's government in 1638, bounded thus ......

La Tours government in 1638, marked thus ✛✛✛

Cromwells grant to La Tour, Crown, and Temple, in 1656, exclusive of Cape Breton; enclosed with a ∴, all line ......

Acadia, as claimed by, and ceded to France, at the treaty of Breda, 1667, the same with Cromwells, grant ———

Norembega, according to Dapper's, and Ogilby's America, between the rivers Penobskot and Kennibek ......

The Etechemins coast, according to Champlain, p. 60, and Denys, p. 51, shaded obliquely. ‖‖‖

A MAP, Exhibiting a View of the ANCIENT LIMITS of ACADIA, as Supported by EXPRESS & incontestable Authorities, in Opposition to that of ye FRENCH. By Thomas Jefferys Geographer

BRITISH CLAIMS WITH REGARD TO ACADIA, 1755. (In its original form this map was first published in *The Memorials of the English and French Commissaires concerning the Limits of Nova Scotia or Acadia* [*and St. Lucia*], [London, 1755]. The present map is a slightly revised copy from *A General Cartography of North America and the West Indies* [London, 1768], plate 17. Courtesy of the Library of Congress.)

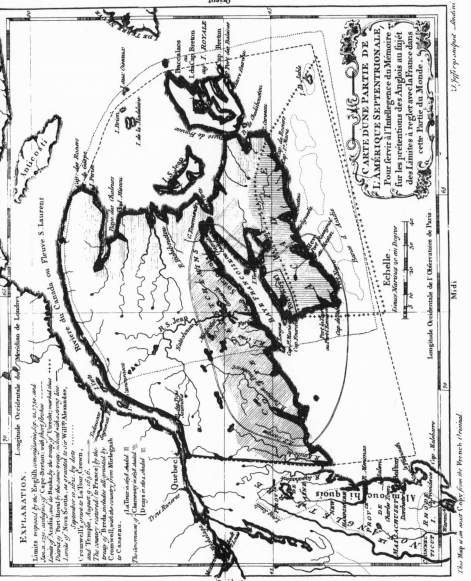

FRENCH CLAIMS WITH REGARD TO ACADIA, 1755. (From *Mémoires des Commissaires de Sa Majesté très-chrétienne et de ceux de Sa Majesté britannique...*
[Amsterdam and Leipzig, 1755], Vol. 1, facing page 1. Courtesy of the Library
of Congress.)

the English had neither title to that land nor use for it, whereas that land, with the St. John River, was absolutely indispensable to France for the purposes of communication with Quebec, especially in winter time. France would cede to England, nevertheless, the land between the Sagadahoc River and the Penobscot.[75]

With regard to the limits of Canada along the lakes, France again rejected the English claim that the boundary of Canada should be the south bank of the St. Lawrence River and of Lakes Ontario and Erie. One must begin by recognizing that the St. Lawrence River was "the center of Canada"; once this fact were accepted on both sides, it would be possible to negotiate a boundary that would be acceptable to both. The French memoir rejected again the British claims to the Iroquois lands based on the Anglo-French Treaty of Utrecht, since the Indians neither had any fixed territory nor anything even resembling the European idea of property. The savages were free and independent; they were the "subjects" neither of France nor of England; the Treaty of Utrecht was faulty and could not alter the nature of things: no Englishman would dare, "save at the risk of getting himself massacred," to assert to the Indians that they were the "subjects" of England. The real questions at issue in the Great Lakes region, then, were simply a) the question of mutual security and b), the question of commerce. France would always be prepared to negotiate a permanent arrangement, relative to both questions, which would be satisfactory to both nations.[76]

As for the Ohio Valley, the French memoir repeated again the old French arguments. The entire Ohio Valley belonged to France as a dependency of Canada and as a route of communication between Canada and Louisiana; furthermore, the French had effectively occupied it, while the English had never had any settlements in the valley; the only English penetration was that of a few English traders with the Indians, but they had been driven out or arrested by the French, and England had not protested. France, nevertheless, as "a lively proof of its love for peace," was willing to consent to the neutralization of all the territory between the Ohio River and the Allegheny Mountains, into which the nationals of both countries would be prohibited from going.[77]

Finally, with regard to the disputed islands in the West Indies, the French representatives on the joint commission still meeting in Paris had demonstrated that the island of St. Lucia belonged incontestably to France, and that St. Vincent and Dominica belong to the Carib Indians. The commissioners had not yet presented their case relative to Tobago, but they were prepared to show, just as conclusively, that France's title to that

[75] "Memoir on American issues," Joint à la lettre de M. de Mirepoix, May 9, 1755, A.E., Méms. et Docs., Amérique, 24: fols. 218–226.

[76] A.E., Méms. et Docs., Amérique, 24: fols. 221–222 vo.

[77] A.E., Méms. et Docs., Amérique, 24: fols. 223–224.

island was clear and uncontestable.[78] In view of the sacrifices France was prepared to make elsewhere, it was only just that France's title to St. Lucia and Tobago be recognized and that Dominica and St. Vincent be left to the Caribs, but under the protection of His Most Christian Majesty! [79]

France demanded that the convention which it hoped might be made upon the basis of these proposals be regarded as provisional and that its duration be limited to two years. Otherwise, the arrangements conceded by France would become permanent, and the English might, in the meantime, occupy the disputed areas and thereby despoil France of its rights.[80]

Mirepoix reported that the French memoir of May 9 was well received by the English, but that Robinson complained the French had "moved away" again. The Earl of Granville, who was assuming more and more importance in English public affairs, told Mirepoix that, although the British ministers could not, because of their "responsibility," express themselves in writing, they could offer the following comments:

With regard to St. Lucia, England was prepared to recognize the French title to that island; since Tobago was of no use to France anyway, Granville suggested that that island, also, be left in the possession of the Caribs. But England must insist upon title to the peninsula of Nova Scotia, the isthmus of Chignecto and the lisière along the western shore of the Bay of Fundy; on this last point Mirepoix thought they might consent to a neutralization of the lands west of that Bay. The British would not deny France's ownership of the south bank of the St. Lawrence and of Lakes Erie and Ontario, but they would ask for negotiation of a boundary somewhat to the south of these waters; they would also ask for the demolition of Fort Niagara. However, in view of the great outcry that would take place in England if the lakes were recognized as French, Robinson proposed that no explanations be given and that the proposed agreement state only that the situation along the lakes would remain as it had existed previously. The British appeared to Mirepoix to be uncertain in their own minds as to just what they would demand relative to the Ohio Valley, but he guessed that they might insist upon the Ohio River as the boundary and then consent to leave the area between the river and the Allegheny Mountains "prohibited" to the subjects of both nations.[81]

In a formal reply, dated June 7, 1755,[82] the English again reasserted the

---

[78] The French memoir on Tobago was never presented in the commission because of the outbreak of war. It was printed, however, in the Mémoires des Commissaires du Roi, in the edition of 1756.

[79] A.E., Méms. et Docs., Amérique, 24: fol. 225.

[80] A.E., Méms. et Docs., Amérique, 24: fol. 226.

[81] Mirepoix to Rouillé, May 15, 1755, C.A.O., A.E., Corr. Pol., Ang. 439: fols. 76–80.

[82] Mémoire, "Sur les 4 points à discuter relatifs à l'Amérique," June 6, 1755, A.E., Méms. et Doc., Amérique, 24: fols. 227–232; also B.M., Add. Mss., 6862: fols. 90–96 vo.

reasonableness of their proposal for Acadia. As for the French demand that the French Acadians in the peninsula be allowed three years in which to remain with their belongings, the English objected, because, they said, this "would deprive Great Britain of a very considerable number of useful subjects, if such a migration should include all the French who were established there at the time of the Peace of Utrecht and their descendants." [83] The memoir pointed out that the French inhabitants of Acadia did have, under Article 14 of the Treaty of Utrecht, the right to depart with their possessions within one year; but this term having expired fory years ago, there was not now the least reason why it should be supposed that the right still existed. It was to be supposed that all who wished to leave had done so; those who had chosen to remain, and their descendants born in the country, "would leave their establishments only with deep regret." [84] It was not possible, therefore, for the King to consent to such a disadvantageous proposal.[85] Similarly, the English memoir rejected the French demand for the isthmus of Chignecto, which was essential to the security of the peninsula, and for a neutral *lisière* along the north coast, where the thickness of the forest would be a sufficient deterrent to either of the two nations having designs on the other. The memoir also repeated the English insistence upon a *lisière* along the western shore of the Bay of Fundy, "without which the possession of the Peninsula and of the Bay of Fundy would be entirely precarious." [86] To leave the Bay of Fundy as a common possession would be to sow new seeds of discord.[87]

As for the boundaries of Canada, the English memoir flatly rejected the French contention that the St. Lawrence River was the "center" of Canada. Furthermore, England could not agree that the land between the south bank of the St. Lawrence and the north (west) coast of the Bay of Fundy, which England had already offered to leave neutral, should be regarded as part of Canada. Nor could England accept the French contention that Lakes Ontario and Erie, with the navigation of these lakes and the Niagara River, belonged to France exclusively, since the subjects of Great Britain and the Iroquois Indians had always enjoyed the navigation of these waters whenever they needed to do so. However, England was prepared to negotiate with France an agreement relative to the south bank of the St. Lawrence River itself—exclusive of the part it had proposed to leave neutral —that would fix a boundary, but without prejudice to the rights and

[83] Mémoire, "Sur les 4 points à discuter relatifs à l'Amérique," A.E., Méms. et Docs., Amérique, 24: fol. 228.

[84] Mémoire, "Sur les 4 points à discuter relatifs à l'Amérique," A.E., Méms. et Docs., Amérique, 24: fol. 228.

[85] A curious argument, indeed, in the light of the forced deportation of the Acadians that presently took place.

[86] Mémoire, "Sur les 4 points à discuter relatifs à l'Amérique," A.E., Méms. et Docs., Amérique, 24: fol. 228 vo.

[87] Mémoire, "Sur les 4 points à discuter relatifs à l'Amérique," A.E., Méms. et Docs., Amérique, 24: fols. 228 vo–229.

possessions of the Iroquois Indians. The English could not accept the French interpretation of Article 15 of the Treaty of Utrecht; the language of this article was clear and precise: the Five Nations of Indians were recognized as subject to the dominion of Great Britain; by the principles of all treaties this provision must apply to the land of these people as well as to their persons. Forts Frederick (Crown Point), Niagara, Presqu'isle (Erie) and le Boeuf were on the lands of the Iroquois; they were, therefore, on English land and must, if France desired peace, be demolished.[88]

With regard to the Ohio, Great Britain rejected the French claim to the river and its valley on the basis of effective occupation, since France had never had, prior to the Peace of Aix-la-Chapelle, any genuine establishments in the valley. France's best claim to the valley was that which was based upon the use of the Miami and the Wabash Rivers as a route of communications with Louisiana. But even this use had been only occasional or secret, so that it did not give the French claim the force of right or of title to the valley. On the other hand, since the Ohio Valley was part of the land ceded to England by the Iroquois, and since the English had had effective settlements in the upper valley, as far as Pickawillany, for the past twenty years, the territory rightfully belonged to England. Despite the validity of the English title, however, England, "for the love of peace," had already proposed, to prevent any dispute in the future, that this part of the valley be left neutral. England was now prepared to define the boundaries of the proposed neutral area amicably, if France so desired.[89]

As for the disputed islands in the West Indies, the English memoir took the position that, although Great Britain could not acquiesce in the arguments advanced in the last memoir of the French commissioners in Paris with regard to the island of St. Lucia, it would not be profitable at the present time to enter into a discussion of the details involved in the question of title to this island, or to St. Vincent, Dominica, and Tobago. England would be disposed to discuss all the questions involved in the proposed negotiations, confident that it would find the same friendly disposition in the French court.[90]

This exchange of memoirs, although couched in diplomatic language and although it introduced as a new issue the question of the loyalty of the Acadians, really represented a hardening of the attitudes of both France and England. It was evident that neither side had any confidence in the other and that both sides now fully expected that the American issues could only be settled by war. The French court did prepare another memoir, in answer to the English memoir of June 6, but this new statement

[88] Mémoire, "Sur les 4 points à discuter relatifs à l'Amérique," A.E., Méms. et Docs., Amérique, 24: fols. 229–230 vo.
[89] Mémoire, "Sur les 4 points à discuter relatifs à l'Amérique," A.E., Méms. et Docs., Amérique, 24: fols. 230 vo–231 vo.
[90] Mémoire, "Sur les 4 points à discuter relatifs à l'Amérique," A.E., Méms. et Docs., Amérique, 24: fols. 231 vo–232.

did little more than reiterate all the old arguments against the English claims relative to North America. It did, however, frankly face the probability of war: the court of France "still desires with the same intensity that a prompt conciliation may prevent the griefs that would be the inevitable consequences of a new war. It never ceases to hope that the Court of Great Britain may finally reciprocate its good will with a disposition for peace equally sincere and compatible with public peace and happiness with that of France." [91] Rouillé agreed with Mirepoix that the English were only trying to gain time and to deceive France with their assurances of good intentions. He therefore instructed the ambassador to "waste no more time in London" and to return to France. Mirepoix was to excuse himself on the ground that his absence should be considered a "leave," and because the Earl of Hertford, appointed English ambassador to France to succeed Albemarle, had never made any move to go to his post. Mirepoix was to assure the British ministers, however, that he would always be ready to return should it seem desirable.[92]

This was really the end of the negotiation. In the meantime, actual fighting was taking place in America. General Braddock had arrived in Virginia with instructions to drive the French from the upper Ohio Valley. The French Admiral MacNémara had sailed for Canada with six battalions of French troops and the English Admiral Boscawen had sailed from England to intercept him. On June 10 the two fleets met in the fog off Newfoundland, but the French fleet escaped, except for two ships, the *Alcide* and the *Lys*, which Boscawen seized, with two hundred thousand livres and eight companies of soldiers. On land, the French faced the English at the isthmus of Chignecto, where an English force under General Monckton easily captured the as yet unreinforced Forts Beauséjour and Beaubassin. In July, General Braddock was beaten back from the Ohio. Governor William Shirley marched against Fort Niagara, but he got only as far as Oswego. Sir William Johnson led an expedition against Crown Point, but he was met by a French force on the shore of Lake George. He defeated the French and built Fort William Henry, but he was unable to proceed and the French remained in possession of Lake Champlain. Upon receipt in Paris of news of Boscawen's seizure of the *Alcide* and the *Lys*, Rouillé ordered Mirepoix, who was still in London, to return to Paris immediately, without taking leave.[93]

War was, thus, actually going on in North America in the summer and fall of 1755. There was no declaration of war, however, until the two antagonists had found allies on the continent of Europe. England formed an

[91] "Projet de réponse au mémoire remis le 6 de juin 1755 par M. le Chev. Robinson à M. le Duc de Mirepoix," C.A.O., A.E., Corr. Pol., Ang., 439: fols. 242–245.
[92] Rouillé to Mirepoix, July 14, 1755, C.A.O., A.E., Corr. Pol., Ang., 439: fols. 239–241.
[93] Rouillé to Mirepoix, July 18, 1755, C.A.O., A.É., Corr. Pol., Ang., 439: fols. 255–256.

alliance with Prussia in January, 1756, and France allied itself with its ancient enemy, Austria. Russia, largely to thwart the ambitions of Frederick II of Prussia in Poland, joined the Franco-Austrian coalition against him. With this "diplomatic revolution" achieved, formal war was declared in May. The Seven Years War had begun.

3. The End of the Asiento—and After

The Treaty of Aix-la-Chapelle, to which Spain acceded on October 28, 1748, provided, with regard to Anglo-Spanish American affairs, only that the treaty of the *asiento* and the annual ship (1713) was to be renewed for a term of four years to cover the years 1739–43, during which it was suspended because of the War of Jenkins' Ear (the thirty-year life of the *asiento* envisaged by the original treaty would normally have expired in 1743).[94] Nothing was said about other disputes between the British and the Spanish colonial empires in the "new world."

Benjamin Keene, already in Lisbon as British minister to Portugal, was named minister to Madrid immediately after the peace. He was instructed to work for two ends: to separate Spain from the Bourbon Family alliance of 1743 and to form an Anglo-Spanish alliance, if possible; and he was to seek a renewal of the treaty of the *asiento*.[95] His prospects for success seemed reasonably good, because the new Spanish King, Ferdinand VI, resented French dominance over Spain and because his wife, Maria Magdalena Teresa Barbara Braganza, was a Portuguese princess from a dynasty traditionally friendly to, and allied with, Britain.

Keene was enthusiastically received in Madrid and reported that both the King and the Queen, of whom the King was "excessively fond" and who had a decisive influence over her husband, were very friendly toward him and toward England.[96] But he recognized the jealousies that existed between the two chief ministers Don José de Carvajal, Minister of State,

[94] See Chapter XVII. See also, Lodge, "Sir Benjamin Keene, K.B.: A Study in Anglo-Spanish Relations," *Transactions of the Royal Historical Society*, 4th Series, XV, 1–43.

[95] Bedford to Keene, n.d., *Bedford Correspondence*, II, 30–35; Bedford to Keene, July 13, 1769, *ibid.*, II, 36–37.

[96] Keene wrote of the Queen: "The reigning queen, though not increased to such a size as had been represented to me, has a good deal more than *embonpoint*. The least motion puts her into a difficulty of breathing, and anxieties, which deprive her of her two favorite diversions, singing and dancing; and though both by her looks and her humour she appears to be in good health, I am told her physicians imagine she has *tubercula* in her lungs, and may finish her days without giving any warning. She has parts, and is of a frank and easy conversation; is reckoned very covetous, and consequently not averse to presents; so fond of music that the famous Farinelli is supposed to have her sole confidence; and her ambition seems only to aim at passing her life with the King in tranquility, and to make provision in the mean time against such events as may happen if she should have the misfortune to lose him" (Keene to Bedford, Feb. 25, 1749, *Bedford Correspondence*, II, 5–6).

and the Marqués de Enseñada, Minister of Finance and of the Indies, and he realized that his task would not be easy.

The Spanish court was in fact divided in its thinking with regard to Spain's relations with Britain. The King himself resented the influence that France had had in Spain's affairs in the time of his father, Philip V, and, under the influence of his wife, his attitude toward England was a friendly one. The foreign minister, Carvajal, was also devoted to the maintenance of Spanish independence, from France in particular, and, in general, to a friendly policy toward England. On the other hand, Philip V's widow, Elizabeth Farnese, was now pro-French and still very powerful, and the pro-French party was led by the Marqués de Enseñada, who held the four ministries of marine, finance, war, and the Indies. This faction, inspired and encouraged by the Comte de Vaulgrenant, the French ambassador to Madrid, used its influence, whenever possible, to prevent a *rapprochement* between Spain and England.

In the year 1749, however, French policy in Spain was one of neutrality relative to most questions pertaining to England. Vaulgrenant was instructed to maintain a friendly relationship with Keene but to watch carefully Keene's negotiation with the Spanish ministers. France understood that Keene would be working for some sort of guarantee of the freedom of the seas for English vessels in the Caribbean area and for a renewal of the *asiento* with the privilege of the annual ship. With regard to the problem of the freedom of the seas, Vaulgrenant was informed that Engilsh traders had really abused both the freedom of the seas and their privileges under the *asiento* by carrying on a scandalous illicit trade with the Spanish colonies, while the Spanish *guarda costas* had carried the seizure of British vessels, on the ground of Spanish commercial laws, to an absurd and unreasonable extreme. It was well known that Spain had always chafed under the terms of the *asiento*, and it was expected that the Spanish ministers would not renew it. However, the French ministry believed that Spain might be willing to renew the *asiento* in return for a cession of Gibraltar to Spain; it was even thought that Spain might go so far as to cede the island of Puerto Rico to England as part of a setlement for Gibraltar. His Most Christian Majesty was indifferent to the possibility of a renewal of the *asiento*,

But it would be strongly to be wished [said Vaulgrenant's instructions] that the idea of exchanging Portorico for Gibraltar might never be realized. The English are only too powerful already, by reason of their naval forces, and if their possessions in America were to be augmented, especially by the cession of Portorico which is close to Santo-Domingo, they would be in a position to make themselves masters of the commerce and navigation of America; and however detrimental such a cession might be to the commerce of the King of France, it would be still more so for that of the Spaniards.[97]

[97] *Recueil des Insts., Espagne, III*, 1722–93, 293–295.

Upon the basis of this supposed threat to the American and, therefore, the European balance of colonial and commercial power, the French ambassador was instructed to watch the progress of the Anglo-Spanish negotiation, and, if possible, by devious means to prevent any such cession from taking place.[98]

Keene's basic problem, in any case, was an extremely difficult one, since all of the well-nigh irreconcilable conflicts between Spain and England relative to America remained as far from resolution as they had been in 1739, or, for that matter, ever since the Peace of Utrecht. Illicit English trade with the Spanish colonies continued to flourish, and the Spanish *guarda costas* continued to commit what the English called "depredations" upon English ships. The English continued, also, over Spanish protests, to cut logwood in Honduras and elsewhere in Central America, which Spain claimed as Spanish territory.

Even before he received his official instructions, Keene had begun to negotiate with Carvajal and Enseñada for a renewal of the *asiento* according to Article 16 of the Treaty of Aix-la-Chapelle and for a settlement of the old debt theoretically due the South Sea Company from the King of Spain. Unfortunately for Keene, while he dealt with Carjaval on general commercial matters, he had to deal with the pro-French Enseñada on matters relative to the colonies and to finance. When he broached to Enseñada the matter of renewing the *asiento* that minister presented him with an agreement signed at Aix-la-Chapelle on June 24, 1748, by the Earl of Sandwich and the Duque de Sotomayor, English and Spanish representatives respectively, but not included in the formal treaty. This agreement provided that, after the peace, English and Spanish commissioners should be appointed to consider the question whether Spain might end the *asiento* by payment of a sum of money that would equal the value to the South Sea Company of the remaining four years of the life of that agreement. Enseñada also pointed out that Spain had claims of its own against England.[99] Keene was compelled to ask for instructions on both these points.

When Keene's formal instructions finally arrived, he found that he was directed by the Duke of Bedford, new secretary of state, to demand the reestablishment of the *asiento*, an increase in the value of the goods that English merchants were permitted to import into Spain itself, a renewal of the so-called "Doddigton Treaty" of 1715 with Spain, which, somehow, had not been mentioned in the list of those renewed by the Treaty of Aix-la-Chapelle, and the other points at issue between Spain and England in America, "particularly freedom of navigation." [100]

With regard to British trade with continental Spain, Keene was to ask

[98] *Recueil des Insts., Espagne*, III, 1722–93, 293–295.
[99] Lodge, "Sir Benjamin Keene, K.B.," *loc cit.*, 4th Series, XV, 13–14.
[100] Bedford to Keene, n.d. [1749], *Bedford Correspondence*, II, 30–35.

that it be reestablished on the basis of the Treaty of Madrid of 1667 and the usages of the time of Carlos II. He was to suggest that, in return, England might be disposed to facilitate the admission of Spanish commodities into the British dominions, both in Europe and in America.[101] As for the other issues bearing upon America, Bedford expressed the opinion that

The settling of the points between the two nations, and the freedom of navigation,—will meet with little difficulty, as I know of no points depending except commercial ones; and I think the freedom of navigation is clearly on our side, by the treaties now indisputably existing. Besides, it is to be hoped, that in case the trade with Old Spain could be put on this footing [i.e., as of the time of Carlos II], the contraband trade with the Spanish West Indies, the great bone of contention between the two nations, and the cause of most of the wars that have happened betwixt them, might be kept under without the Spaniards taking such violent measures, by means of their *guarda costas*, in searching our ships and committing such depredations on our merchants as were the causes of the last war.[102]

As for the *asiento*, Bedford informed Keene that the South Sea Company was not unwilling to be guided by the Sandwich-Sotomayor Declaration and would prepare an estimate of what it considered to be the value of the four-years continuation of the *asiento* provided for in the Treaty of Aix-la-Chapelle. Bedford, therefore, instructed Keene to proceed with his negotiation on the basis of a cash settlement.[103] The company estimated the value of the *asiento* and the annual ship for four years, after deducting the amounts due the King of Spain as a partner in the company and the amounts due the company from the King, at £200,000 Sterling. In return for the surrender of the *asiento*, Great Britain asked for a privileged position in the trade of Spain and its colonies. However, Keene was authorized to accept £100,000 as a cash settlement for the *asiento*, if, thereby, the Spanish ministers could be brought to make concessions to British commerce in other areas.[104]

A treaty was finally concluded on October 5, 1750,[105] the most significant provision of which was that England surrendered the *asiento* treaty, in return for £100,000 Sterling in cash with a mutual cancellation of all debts owed by the South Sea Company to the King of Spain or by the King to the company. Commercial relations between the two countries were to be based upon the Anglo-Spanish Treaty of Madrid of 1667, and the subjects of each nation were to have all the privileges of the "most favored nation" in the territories of the other. His Catholic Majesty agreed to limit the duties upon English goods imported into continental Spain to those

[101] Bedford to Keene, n.d. [1749], *Bedford Correspondence*, II, 33.
[102] Bedford to Keene, n.d. [1749], *Bedford Correspondence*, II, 35.
[103] Bedford to Keene, May 11, 1749, *Bedford Correspondence*, II, 29–30.
[104] Bedford to Keene, August 30, 1750, *Bedford Correspondence*, II, 51–57.
[105] Cantillo, ed., *Tratados*, 409–410.

charged upon such goods in the time of Carlos II, and promised that English subjects in Spanish territories should not be required to pay higher taxes than Spanish subjects resident in those territories. English subjects were specifically permitted to gather salt on the island of Tortuga, also as in the time of Carlos II. All the differences and disputes between the two nations (in which other nations had no interest) were to be considered as extinguished by this treaty.

Keene's treaty with Spain was acclaimed in England, despite the fact that the South Sea Company felt it had been cheated by it, and Keene was raised to the rank of ambassador. But it was considered by France, and not without reason, to be a breach in the Franco-Spanish *entente* relative to England established by the Bourbon Family Compact of 1743. "Spain," wrote Keene, "has in some measure declared her divorce from France." [106]

These developments were of prime importance to France, coming, as they did, at a moment when the tensions between France and England in North America were becoming acute and when English diplomacy was consciously trying to separate Spain from its French alliance by promoting a *rapprochement* between Spain and Austria.[107] France, therefore, sent the Duc de Duras to Spain in the fall of 1752 with instructions to rebuild French influence in Madrid and to exploit the pro-French party, led by Enseñada, to bring this about.[108] Duras was briefed on the still outstanding disputes between England and Spain in America, particularly the insoluble conflict over the Spanish claim to the right of search of English vessels near the coasts of Spanish colonies and the continued practice of the English logwood cutters of cutting wood on the Mosquito Coast and the coast of Honduras. The French ministry expressed the opinion that despite the Anglo-Spanish treaty of 1750, the continuing disputes between the two nations in America would never be resolved. Duras was to take advantage of every opportunity to increase the irritations between them. Most important of all, he was to work, as subtly and as effectively as possible, toward a "union" of the two crowns of France and Spain in the form of a renewal of the Second Bourbon Family Compact of 1743.[109] At the same time, France was instructing its ambassadors and ministers in all the courts of Europe, including Spain, to point out to the rulers to whom they were accredited the imperialistic expansion of England overseas and the consequent threat to the commerce, navigation, and colonies of the other European powers. The cause of France in the West Indies was also the cause of Spain, it was argued, because, once England had

---

[106] Quoted in Lodge, "Sir Benjamin Keene, K.B.," *loc. cit.*, 4th Series, XV, 16 n.
[107] Lodge, "Sir Benjamin Keene, K.B.," *loc. cit.*, 4th Series, XV, 16–26.
[108] *Recueil des Insts., Espagne, III,* 1722–93, 314.
[109] *Recueil des Insts., Espagne, III,* 1722–93, 314.

driven the French out of that area, the Spanish colonies would be next, and Spain, alone, could not stand against the English fleets.[110]

But Keene had the support of a number of outstanding Spanish leaders, including the Duque de Huescar (later Duque de Alva), the Conde de Valparaiso, and the pro-English Spanish ambassador to London, Don Ricardo Wall, who were convinced that Spain's disputes with England could be settled, and should be, by negotiation. Keene's negotiations with the Spanish ministers, during 1752 and 1753, therefore, proceeded in a friendly fashion, despite the intrigues of the pro-French faction.

Thus it came about that, when Keene, in June, 1752, presented to Carvajal a protest against the continued seizures of British vessels in the Caribbean area by Spanish *guarda costas*, the minister read Keene's communication to the Spanish rulers and argued in favor of acceding in some way to Britain's demand for a greater freedom of the seas in that area. Keene reported that the Spanish court now found itself facing a dilemma,

whether by refusing to give us [the British] Satisfaction & preventing the Injustices complained of Spain would prefer a War with England, which must necessarily throw Her back under her old Yoke to France, to the Tranquillity, Security & Independency she enjoys at present by her Friendship with a Crown [England], whose Interest Obliges it to look upon the Happiness & Grandeur of this of Spain, as necessary to its own." [111]

The choice of the Spanish court, Keene was happy to report, "has fallen where Good Sense, Justice & Good Policy should direct it" [112]—that is, a policy of continued amicable relations with England. Negotiations looking toward an adjustment of Engand's claims for the ships seized since the Treaty of Aix-la-Chapelle began immediately, and Keene confidently expected that the Spanish would soon revise their policy with regard to the seizure of British ships in America.[113]

A permanent modification of Spanish policy with regard to the seizure of British ships was, in fact, more important to Britain than the immediate settlement of claims; and Keene was urged to endeavor to get Spain to liberalize its policy. At the same time, the British ministry acknowledged the explosive nature of the operations of British logwood cutters on the Mosquito Coast and the coast of Honduras, which Spain had threatened to close completely to the British, and Keene was instructed to endeavor tactfully to get from the Spanish court some positive statement that would recognize the right of the British to go into those areas. This question was especially pressing, since the Spanish *guarda costas*, as Newcastle put it,

[110] Newcastle to Keene, Mar. 5, 1752, L.C., Add. Mss., 32834, fols. 178–180. See also, "Instructions au Marquis d'Hautefort," 1750, *Recueil des Insts.*, *Autriche*, 309–328.
[111] Extract of a letter from Keene to Holdernesse, June 30 and July 2, 1752, L.C., B.M., Add. Mss., 32837: fols. 284–286 vo.
[112] Keene to Holdernesse, L.C., B.M., Add. Mss., 32837: fol. 284.
[113] Keene to Holdernesse, L.C., B.M., Add. Mss., 32837: fol. 285–286.

"took Every Ship, That had a Stick of Logwood on board, under Pretence, That That was a Proof of Their having sail'd in illicit Places." [114]

These two problems, which revolved about Spain's right to patrol the waters "adjacent" to its colonies (even many miles away from them) and His Catholic Majesty's sovereignty over the logwood coasts, were matters of great delicacy to the Spanish court, and they demanded all of Keene's skill as a negotiator. At the same time, the British ministry insisted that "Visiting Our Ships, upon the Open Seas, is a real Grievance, for which We must have Redress!" If the practice were to continue, Newcastle wrote to Keene, the British King would have no recourse but to issue letters of reprisal to the British merchants.[115]

The negotiations dragged on, and the fragile Anglo-Spanish friendship survived. On December 2, 1753, Carvajal wrote Keene a lengthy commentary on the issues then existing between the two countries. "Great Britain," he said,

in order to live in Friendship & Harmony, ought to put a Stop to the Contraband Trade that is carried on by her subjects in the Dominions of her Friends, & to punish them for such Proceedings; but if her Form of Government makes it difficult for her to take these just Measures, or to reduce her Subjects in This manner to their Duty, let her abandon them to their Fate, which is far from being a severe one,—for their Causes are tried by rational People, and are re-examined in a Catholick Kings Supreme Tribunal. If this was to be agreed to, I should be satisfied if they were to lose only one, out of ten Vessels laden with Contraband Goods; for at present I am persuaded, that We [the Spaniards] do not take one out of Thirty, & of those, that are taken the greatest Part are restored.[116]

That was a frank suggestion that the old rule of "no peace beyond the Line" be applied to the problem presented by the conflict between the Spanish claim to the right of visit and search in American waters and the British claim to a complete freedom of the seas. As for the logwood cutters, Carvajal argued that it was just as unlawful for the British to cut logwood in Honduras as it would be for them to cut timber for their ships in the forests on the Spanish coasts along the Bay of Biscay. Why not let Spanish cutters cut the wood and sell it to the English? Spain would surely be able to guarantee a plentiful supply.[117]

Although Keene knew that there was little probability that his country would accept either of Carvajal's proposals, his exchanges with the Spanish minister were conducted in a spirit of friendship and an apparently sincere

[114] Newcastle to Keene, Aug. 6, 1752, L.C., B.M., Add. Mss., 32839: fols. 24–28.
[115] Newcastle to Keene, Jan. 15, 1753, L.C., B.M., Add. Mss., 32842: fols. 152–154.
[116] Carvajal to Keene, December 2, 1753, L.C., B.M., Add. Mss., 32847: fols. 177–183.
[117] Carvajal to Keene, L.C., B.M., Add. Mss., 32847: fols. 177–183.

desire on both sides for an accommodation. Indeed, Keene and the British ministry were emboldened to pursue the possibility, apparently first hinted at by Carvajal himself of an alliance with Spain against France that might include Austria, with which England was attempting to negotiate an alliance at that very moment.

The greatest obstacle to this policy, of course, was Enseñada and his pro-French party. Newcastle lamented the division of the Spanish ministry and court in a long letter on the international situation in Europe and America that he wrote to Keene in January of 1754. The only way to block Enseñada and his anti-English intrigues, he wrote, was to push through the proposed Anglo-Spanish alliance; to do this, however, it would be necessary to get Enseñada out of the way. Even if the alliance could not be achieved, a neutrality of Spain relative to the Anglo-French disputes in America would be of the utmost value to Britain: "That may secure the Peace of Europe," he wrote; "But, If France was sure of having Spain against them [in an alliance with Britain], If they broke it, No Consideration, No King of Prussia, could engage them to do it." [118]

Newcastle reported to Keene that France was now instructing its ambassadors in the courts of Western Europe to explain the Anglo-French diplomatic duel relative to America from the French point of view and to try to win their sympathy and support. In Spain, in particular, the French ambassador, the Duc de Duras, was instructed to counteract, by every possible means, Keene's influence and to cultivate a pro-French policy by working through Enseñada and his pro-French party.[119] Newcastle expressed to Keene his conviction that France genuinely desired peace. But, he said, France, presuming upon the British desire for peace, was encroaching upon the British empire everywhere—in America, in Africa, and in the East Indies. In America, they were building forts, taking possession of unoccupied territory, and "Endeavouring, à la Sourdine, to confine our great, valuable, & extensive Dominions, in North America, to a bare *Lisière* of Country towards the Sea." [120] British policy, Newcastle continued, must be to have the fleet ready to go anywhere in the world where France was encroaching upon British interests and to draw to England's side all the powers that really desired peace, such as Holland, Austria, Spain, and Russia, to present a united front to France and to Prussia, which, at the moment, appeared to be menacing European peace, more or less in collaboration with France.[121]

British policy, in its relations with France and in Keene's negotiations with Spain, was thus thrown into a worldwide perspective; and Keene was instructed to negotiate the proposed alliance with Spain accordingly.

[118] Newcastle to Keene, Jan. 24, 1754, B.M., Add. Mss., 32848: fols. 142–149.
[119] Newcastle to Keene, Jan. 24, 1754, B.M., Add. Mss., 32848: fols. 142–149; *ibid.*; same to same, Jan. 25, 1754, B.M., Add. Mss., 32848: fols. 155–171.
[120] Newcastle to Keene, Jan. 24, 1754, B.M., Add. Mss., 32848: fol. 147.
[121] Newcastle to Keene, Jan. 24, 1754, B.M., Add. Mss., 32848: fol. 147.

Keene was proceeding with his negotiations with a highly qualified optimism, when, on March 8, 1754, Carvajal died. This event precipitated a crisis at the Spanish court, because the King was forced into the position of having to choose Carvajal's successor from either the pro-French or the pro-English party. Happily for Keene, Ferdinand VI's choice fell upon General Ricardo Wall, Keene's old friend and the pro-English ambassador of Spain in London, and Keene was emboldened to take the rash step of intervening in Spanish internal politics for the purpose of overthrowing Enseñada.

Keene felt sure of himself because he had come into possession of incontrovertible evidence that Enseñada, behind Carvajal's back, without the approval of the King, and apparently with the clear purpose of precipitating war with England, had sent orders to certain Spanish governors in America to take violent actions against the English, the most dramatic of which was an expedition to drive the English logwood cutters out of Campeche.[122] Such orders, if carried out, could hardly have failed to cause immediate war with England, into which France was to be expected to enter, both to support Spain against British imperialism and to gain France's own American ends.

Keene's exposure of Enseñada's orders, together with proof of his "combination with France," caused consternation both at the court of Madrid and that of Paris. Ferdinand VI exclaimed, when shown the documents, that he "would not be a vice-roy to the King of France." Enseñada was shown to be a creature of France and of the French ambassador, Duras. He was immediately divested of his ministries and banished from Madrid to Grenada. War with England was averted, but by the narrowest margin.[123]

The advent of the pro-British Ricardo Wall to the Spanish foreign ministry did not, however, end the American disputes between Spain and England. For, before new orders countermanding those sent out by Enseñada could be sent from Spain and received in America, Spanish soldiers had driven the English logwood cutters out of Honduras and had destroyed the settlement at the mouth of the Belize River. Keene was instructed to demand readmission for the logwood cutters and reparations for the damage done,[124] but he realized that for Spain to restore the territory to the English would be tantamount to recognizing English ownership, and this, he knew, Spain could not grant. To make matters worse, the English governor of Jamaica, Charles Knowles, sent the logwood cutters

[122] Keene to Robinson, June 17, 1754, B.M., Stowe Mss. 256: fols. 211–212; Keene to Newcastle, July 31, 1754, L.C., B.M., Add. Mss., 32849: fols. 441–452.

[123] Keene to Robinson, July 21, 1754, B.M., Stowe Mss., 256: fol. 218; Keene to Robinson, July 31, 1754, ibid., 256: fols. 221–231; see also, Lodge, "Sir Benjamin Keene, K.B.," loc. cit., 4th Series. XV, 28–30.

[124] Robinson to Keene, Dec. 12, 1754, B.M., Add. Mss., 32851: fols. 307–308.

back to the coast under the protection of a contingent of soldiers, who had instructions to build a fort, where there had been none before, to protect the logwood cutters. This, as Wall pointed out to Keene, was going a good deal further than a restoration of the *status quo ante*.[125]

This new tension, arising, as it did, just at the moment when Anglo-French disputes over American issues were reaching the breaking point, dispelled the good feeling that had existed between Spain and England since Wall had assumed power and set the stage for a resurgence of French influence at the Spanish court. In September of 1754, Keene reported that Duras had intimated that His Most Christian Majesty would be willing to submit his disputes with England to the mediation of the King of Spain.[126] This intimation was rejected by the Spanish King on the ground that it would be improper for him to undertake any such mediation, since he himself had a number of outstanding disputes pending with the English.[127] However, Duras continued to press for the renewal of the Family Compact, while promising that France would immediately come to Spain's aid against England to drive the English out of the logwood coasts, Jamaica, and the former Spanish possessions of the Mediterranean.[128]

Keene's conversations with Wall continued, but the mood of amity between the two countries had been dispelled by the actions in America, and it became increasingly evident that the old disputes between the two countries, despite the optimism of the British ministers, were not to be settled by a diplomatic formula. Spain was becoming nervous over the Anglo-French conflict in America, and this nervousness was accordingly cultivated by the French ambassador in Madrid. About the middle of July, 1755, when news of Boscawen's naval action off Newfoundland reached Europe, and Anglo-French negotiations were broken off, Duras was instructed again to point out to the Spanish monarchs the ruthless nature of British imperialism: the British would try to take the French colonies in America, but the real aim of England was the seizure of the Spanish colonies. Spain could not remain neutral in this struggle; the safety of its American empire could be protected only by a new Franco-Spanish alliance against England.[129] But Duras overplayed his hand: his vehement insistence that Spain now go to war with England and join forces with France aroused all of Ferdinand VI's old resentment of French domination, and Duras had to be recalled.[130]

Still, the Anglo-Spanish disputes with regard to American issues continued, and, with the outbreak of war between England and France in

---

[125] Lodge, "Sir Benjamin Keene, K.B.," *loc. cit.*, 4th Series, XV, 31.
[126] Keene to Robinson, Sept. 21, 1754, L.C., B.M., Add. Mss., 32850: fols. 362–364.
[127] Keene to Robinson, Oct. 25, 1754, L.C., B.M., Add. Mss., 32851: fols. 110–112.
[128] Keene to Robinson, Dec. 14, 1754, L.C., B.M., Add. Mss., 32851: fols. 319–321.
[129] Rouillé to Duras, July 27, 1755, A.É., Corr. Pol., Esp., 518: fols. 85–89.
[130] Rouillé to Duras, Aug. 13, 1755, A.É., Corr. Pol., Esp., 518: fols. 121–122.

1756, initial English defeats in America and in the Mediterranean weakened English influence in Madrid and strengthened the pro-French party. Furthermore, while the quarrels over the logwood cutters in Honduras and over the Spanish right of search in American waters continued unameliorated, Spanish ships, as neutral traders, began to carry French goods to and from the French colonies, despite the fact that foreign traffic with them was stringently prohibited in time of peace. This wartime commerce was justified by Spain under the right of neutrals to trade with belligerents in time of war and the principle that in such neutral trade "free ships make free goods." England, which, hitherto, had been invoking the principle of the freedom of the seas against the Spanish *guarda costas*, promulgated the famous "Rule of the War of 1756" against all neutrals, a group that included not only Spain, but Portugal, the Dutch, the Danes, and the Swedes as well. The new "Rule," needless to say, was a sharp redefinition of the freedom of the seas, insofar as that principle was affected by neutral trade. Its origins, however, are to be found in the problems presented by neutral trade in the War of Jenkins' Ear and the War of the Austrian Succession.

4. The Problem of Neutral Commerce: the Rule of the War of 1756

During the War of Jenkins' Ear and the War of the Austrian Succession, Portugal, Holland, Denmark, and Sweden had engaged, with considerable profit to themselves, in trade with all the belligerents. Portugal and Holland, in particular, while both ostensible allies of England, were particularly active in trafficking with France and Spain and their colonies in America, thus enabling these enemies of England to evade much of the damage that might have been done to their economic life by the British navy. These practices by England's allies were intensely displeasing to Britain and were the subject of many complaints.

Benjamin Keene, who had gone to Lisbon in 1746 as British minister to Portugal with the purpose of attempting to separate Spain from the allies of France, observed the activities of the Portuguese as neutrals and their effects upon the fortunes of England. He reported, for example, that Portuguese ships were carrying Spanish goods from Rio de la Plata to Lisbon, whence they were transshipped to Spain.[131] Keene commented that it was a criminal offense, under Spanish law, for a Spaniard in the colonies to export money to any country but Spain itself. But the Spanish colonists were now shipping money to Nova Colonia, a Portuguese colony, whence it was shipped in Portuguese ships to Lisbon, in order to escape capture

[131] Keene to Newcastle, Jan. 22, 1748, H.L., El., 10330; Keene to Bedford, Apr. 9, 1748, *ibid.*

by the British. The last fleet from Rio de Janeiro, he reported, carried three million Spanish dollars, which were to be sent on from Lisbon to Madrid.[132] Furthermore, Portuguese ships were carrying Spanish goods to the Spanish colonies under licenses from Spain. This practice continued, even after the signing of the Preliminaries in the spring of 1748, but Keene supposed that

the Court of Spain since the signing of the Preliminaries, and re-validating the Treaty of Utrecht, will have that Regard to its Obligations, its own Honour and Interest, and to the Complaints of its subjects, as not to permit for the future any Nation whatever to navigate to Spanish Ports in America, except those who are entitled to such Privileges in virtue of Public Contracts.[133]

Keene was instructed to protest, in the most vigorous terms, against the traffic with the Spanish colonies which, in peacetime, was stringently prohibited by the Spanish navigation system, a traffic which, said Bedford, was "so highly prejudicial to His [Britannic] Majesty and his allies, and so contradictory to that Sacred Neutrality, which His Portuguese Majesty is both in Honour and Interest, so strictly bound to observe." [134] If the Portuguese court failed to respond to Keene's protest, he was instructed to say that, if the Portuguese continued to abuse their "sacred neutrality," Britain would be compelled to take "disagreeable measures." [135]

Keene duly delivered his protest. Meanwhile, the Portuguese court protested, on its own account, the many violations of Portuguese neutrality by the English. Azevedo Continho, the Portuguese minister of foreign affairs, complained, for example, of the arbitrary use of Portuguese harbors by English warships and the enlistment of Portuguese sailors for the British navy. Efforts were made by the English to proselytize the Portuguese Catholics to English Protestantism. The English had refitted the Spanish prize ship *Glorioso* in Lisbon Harbor.[136]

Keene reported in July that he did not expect to have any significant success with his protest. He expected, on the contrary, that Portugal would defend its practices on the ground of the rights of neutrals and that Azevedo would cite the Anglo-Portuguese Treaty of 1654,

wherein they alledge not only that free Ships make free Goods, but that the English had likewise a Permission to carry even Arms to the Spaniards, during the long War between that Crown & Portugal, provided they were not exported out of the Portuguese Dominions.[137]

The Portuguese reply to Keene's protest followed the line that Keene

[132] Keene to Bedford, Apr. 9, 1748, H.L., El., 10330; Keene to Bedford, May 13, 1748, *ibid.*
[133] Keene to Bedford, Aug. 8, 1748, H.L., El., 10330.
[134] Bedford to Keene, Apr. 26, 1748, H.L., El., 10330.
[135] Bedford to Keene, May 10, 1748, H.L., El., 10330.
[136] Keene to Bedford, Apr. 29, 1748, H.L., El., 10330.
[137] Keene to Newcastle, July 7, 1748, H.L., El., 10330.

had anticipated. Azevedo rejected the protest on the ground that it infringed upon Portugal's rights as a neutral. The British protest, he said, reduced the matter to the question "whether as often as Great Britain shall think proper to declare War against Spain, all Commerce must cease between Spain and Portugall? And whether a Neutrality obliges a neutral Power to suspend its Trade with one of the Powers at War—at the same time that it carrys it on with the other?" [138] What would the British king think, Azevedo asked, if, because of the neutrality of Portugal, Madrid and Paris should demand that Portugal suspend its trade with England? [139]

Shortly after this exchange, Keene was transferred to Madrid, and, since peace became a reality in October, neither side pressed its claims against the other. The incident was of considerable significance, however, since it evoked a clear restatement of the right of neutrals to trade with belligerents and their colonies in time of war, while the English argument that the carrying-on by neutrals in time of war of commerce not permitted in time of peace was a violation of their neutrality and, therefore, not to be tolerated, clearly anticipated the famous "Rule of 1756" pronounced by Great Britain against the Dutch in the Seven Years War.

In its declaration of war against Spain at the beginning of the War of Jenkins' Ear (October 19, 1739), England had warned all neutrals

not to transport, or carry any soldiers, arms, powder, ammunition, or other contraband goods, to any of the territories, lands, plantations, or countries of the said king of Spain; declaring, that whatsoever ship or vessel shall be met withal, transporting, or carrying any soldiers, arms, powder, ammunition, or other contraband goods, to any of the territories, lands, plantations, or counties of the said king of Spain, shall be condemned as good and lawful prize.[140]

This pronouncement relative to neutral carriers and the freighting of contraband to the enemies of England was entirely in conformity with existing international practice, for it indirectly recognized the principle that free ships made free goods, except for such contraband articles as were listed.

After the war had gotten under way, merchants of the neutral nations, Portugal and the Low Countries (and even, to a certain degree, the Danes and Swedes), had engaged in an active and profitable trade with Spain and its colonies. Then, when France entered the war, the neutrals entered into a similar commerce with France and its colonies.

This commerce, carried on by two nations that were ostensibly allies of England, presented Britain with a dilemma. Not only did the Dutch, in particular, carry contraband that was bound to be used against England,

---

[138] Azevedo to Keene, Aug. 8, 1748, enclosed with Keene to Bedford, Aug. 27, 1748, H.L., El., 10330; Keene to Bedford, Apr. 29, 1748, *ibid.*
[139] Keene to Bedford, Apr. 29, 1748, H.L., El., 10330.
[140] The Declaration of War against Spain, Oct. 19, 1739, in Douglas, ed., *English Historical Documents*, X, 1714–83, 849–851.

but the foodstuffs and other materials carried to the Spanish and French colonies made it possible for the enemies of England to evade capture by English ships and to penetrate the blockades that England established on the enemy colonies in America. Under a system of licenses, for example, Dutch ships would carry merchandise from Spain to the Spanish colonies and return, and claim complete exemption, as neutrals, from capture by English warships. Two facts were obvious: the neutrals were now engaged, in time of war, in a trade with Spanish and French colonies from which they were absolutely prohibited in time of peace, and such participation in this commerce by England's allies was of substantial and significant assistance to the enemies of England in their prosecution of the war against that country. England's command of the seas was effectively nullified by the behavior of its own allies.[141]

The first English response to the Dutch trade with Spain and its colonies was a series of seizures of Dutch ships by British privateers in the West Indies. A number of Dutch ships were taken to the English continental colonies, where the prize courts sharply scrutinized the legal aspects and the practices of this neutral trade. Judge Lewis Morris, of New York, in particular, exposed the weakness of the legal position of the Dutch traders.[142] Morris condemned a number of Dutch ships engaged in the trade with the French colonies on the ground that a Dutch ship traveling in the protection of a French convoy was, in effect, a French ship and, therefore not Dutch and not neutral.[143] Popular opinion in England rose high against the neutrals, especially the Dutch, while the government and the prize courts sought to arrive at a valid distinction between neutral ships which traded *with* the enemy and those who traded *for* him.

When the English government protested to the government of the Low Countries the Dutch appealed on the principle that "free ships make free goods," and claimed immunity from interference under the Anglo-Dutch Marine Treaty of 1674 and the explanatory convention of 1675.[144] The Marine Treaty had provided that the subjects of either signatory should be free to trade with any other nation, even in time of war; and this freedom was to extend to "all commodities which shall be carried in time of peace," except those listed as contraband. It also provided that goods belonging to the subjects of either signatory, even if not contraband, found on enemy ships, should be subject to confiscation along with the enemy ship and its enemy goods. The explanatory convention interpreted these

---

[141] For excellent discussions of this situation and its effect upon English policy, see Pares, *Colonial Blockade and Neutral Rights, 1739–63*, Chapters III and IV, and *War and Trade in the West Indies, 1739–63*, Chapter VIII.

[142] Hough, ed., *Reports of Cases in the Vice-Admiralty of the Province of New York,* 185, 195, *et passim.*

[143] Pares, *Colonial Blockade and Neutral Rights,* 119.

[144] See Chapter V. The treaty is printed in Chalmers, ed., *Treaties,* I, 177–189; the explanatory convention of 1675 is printed *ibid.,* I, 189–191.

provisions to apply, not only to the foreign trade of a belligerent, but also to the coastwise trade, so that a Dutch or English vessel, for example, might engage in the coastwise trade or trade between a mother country and its colonies, of a nation at war with one of the two signatories.[145]

The British prize courts, faced with the apparent fact that seizures of Dutch ships during the War of the Austrian Succession appeared to be violations of these old treaties, generally released the ships.[146] However, the fact that the Dutch were now engaging, in time of war, in commerce, especially in the Spanish and French colonies, that was hermetically sealed to them in time of peace, and which, in fact, made it possible for the belligerents to evade the dangers of capture in the course of the war, threw a new light upon the whole matter. Such a trade amounted, in actual practice, to a sort of "benevolent neutrality" which was a definite aid to the enemy in the prosecution of the war.

In the light of these facts, the English claimed that the treaty of 1674 did not apply to America, thus reviving the old doctrine of two spheres. But it was easy for the Dutch to show that it had been the English who, in 1674, had insisted upon making the treaty apply to the whole world, and that this provision was clearly and incontestably written into Article 1 of the treaty.[147] Whereupon the English prize courts turned to the principle that neutral ships trading *for* belligerents were no longer neutral, but, in effect, must be regarded as ships of that belligerent nation, and, therefore, liable to seizure and confiscation. It is to be noted that this principle did not apply to smugglers who traded with French or Spanish colonies contrary to the exclusive national laws relative to foreign trade with the colonies, but only to cases in which those laws were suspended in favor of the neutral carrier, thus giving the neutral ship the national character and privileges of a Spanish or French ship.[148]

Curiously enough, neutrals trading with France had not been molested by the British during the War of the Austrian Succession, while those trading with Spain were. The explanation seems to be that the voyages made for France, in the cases that arose, either did not originate in France or did not constitute round trips within the French empire, whereas the voyages for Spain did.[149]

The new basic position taken by England relative to neutrals engaging, in time of war, in trades with the colonies of England's enemies was, thus, the position that if, in effect, neutral ships became ships having the character of vessels belonging to the nation they were serving, they were no longer neutral, and that they were, therefore, subject to seizure. With the

---

[145] Chalmers, ed., *Treaties*, I, 190.
[146] Pares, *Colonial Blockade and Neutral Rights*, 184–185.
[147] Chalmers, ed., *Treaties*, I, 172.
[148] Pares, *Colonial Blockade and Neutral Rights*, Chapter III, especially 196 ff.
[149] Pares, *Colonial Blockade and Neutral Rights*, 194–195.

advent of the Seven Years War, this doctrine was broadened into what became known in international law as the "Rule of the War of 1756." When it became obvious that the Dutch would again enter upon commerce with the French and Spanish colonies in America, both of which empires were closed to Dutch traders in time of peace, the British government announced that it would seize neutral ships engaged in commerce that was closed to them in time of peace, and it extended the rule to trade with the French colonies as well as to that with Spain. As the Earl of Hardwicke said, in September, 1756,

All the European nations exclude foreigners from their American colonies, and so things stood at the time of the treaty of 1674. It is the general rule still, and cannot possibly be varied, except as a new invention fraudulently to screen French effects from capture, and the question is whether England shall suffer them to trade thither in time of war, without seizure, when the French themselves will not suffer them to trade thither, in time of peace, on that very account.[150]

This implied, in effect, a drastic modification of the Marine Treaty of 1674 and the explanatory convention of 1675, or, rather, a complete abandonment of that treaty, since ships in the trade with French colonies were, in effect, French ships. England hesitated to apply the principle rigorously against the Dutch because it was hoping to keep them neutral in the war that was just beginning. But it was determined to stop this loophole for the enemy, now France, and in the case of the ship *America*, Hardwicke, as judge in the Court of Prize Appeals, pronounced the rule in its final form:

That the ship *America* in question in this cause having been freighted in French account and employed in a voyage to a port in St. Domingo, a French settlement in the West Indies, having delivered her outward-bound cargo by allowance of the French Governor there, and her homeward-bound cargo having been put on board after a survey made of the ship subject to the ordinances, and to the payment of duties ordinary and extraordinary and under penalties according to the laws of France, and the master having thrown overboard and destroyed the bills of lading and many other of the ship's papers, and a cargo laden and found on board being admitted to be the property of French subjects, [we, the court] declare that the said ship ought by law to be considered in this case as a French ship; and therefore affirm the sentence of the court of admiralty condemning both the ship and cargo.[151]

It is to be noted that this judgment made no reference to the Marine Treaty of 1674 and treated the case as arising in circumstances not considered by that treaty. The basic point was that the neutral ship was trading in the French colonies with the sanction of the French government,

---

[150] Quoted in Pares, *Colonial Blockade and Neutral Rights*, 197.
[151] Quoted in Pares, *Colonial Blockade and Neutral Rights*, 198.

whereas, in time of peace, any such official sanction had never been given and was never likely to be. It is also to be noted that this doctrine of condemnation on the basis of "authoritative trading" would incriminate any ship trading with the French colonies and the goods in it, no matter whose the ownership of them.[152]

It is also to be noted that, given this British legal principle, it was only a matter of time before either the Dutch would enter the war against England or the principle would have to be compromised. Such a compromise with the Dutch was effected about 1759.[153] Similarly, England's anxiety to preserve the neutrality of Spain, which it feared more than it feared the Low Countries, led to a special consideration for Spanish ships, with the result that by an order-in-council as early as the year 1756, Spanish ships were admitted to enjoy the principle that "free ships make free goods," even when trading with French colonies. The real explanation, however, in the Spanish cases which arose, seems to have been that it was more difficult, if not impossible, to show that they enjoyed "authoritative trading." [154]

[152] Pares, *Colonial Blockade and Neutral Rights*, 201–202.
[153] See Chapter XIX.
[154] Pares, *Colonial Blockade and Neutral Rights*, 203–204.

CHAPTER XIX

Angloamerica in the Diplomacy
of the Seven Years War, 1756-63

FOR GREAT BRITAIN and France, the war that began in 1756 was almost purely a colonial war; Anglo-French diplomacy, and now Anglo-French military conflict, had been set in motion by events in America, India, and Africa. It was a world war, in the sense that the conflict took place in and around four continents and that, for the chief protagonists, the main issues were extra-European, colonial, or imperial interests. The colonies were no longer pawns on a European diplomatic chessboard. European diplomats danced, and European armies marched, as colonial issues piped the tune.

In the actual fighting in America, an English expedition occupied the French island of Guadeloupe in 1759; Dominica, one of the "Neutral Islands" long since occupied by the French, was conquered in 1761; Martinique fell to the English in February of 1762. The English then proceeded to complete their conquest of the French West Indies and the "Neutral Islands" by occupying St. Lucia and Grenada. On the continent of North America, after several unsuccessful efforts in 1756 and 1757, the British (English and American) forces again took Louisbourg in 1758, then went on to take Quebec in 1759 and Montreal in 1760. This long series of British victories virtually swept French authority out of the hemisphere, and the successful British siege of Havana in 1762, after Spain entered the war on the side of France, rendered that country, too, practically helpless to offer effective resistance to British demands in America.

1. The Neutrals: Neutral Traders and "the Doctrine of Continuous Voyage"

With the outbreak of the Seven Years War in 1756, the merchants of the neutral states, particularly Denmark, Holland, and Spain, entered

[436]

eagerly upon the agreeable business, at high profits to themselves and under the protection, as they thought, of the international convention that "free ships make free goods," of carrying on the American and East Indian colonial trades for France, in this way assisting that country to evade the damaging effects of British mastery of the seas and British blockades of both continental France and its colonies. It was this neutral trade that evoked the famous pronouncement of the English prize courts in England and in North America of the so-called "Rule of the War of 1756," which prohibited to neutrals participation, in time of war, in national and colonial trades that were closed to them in time of peace.[1]

But this rule was not enough. England perceived, as the war progressed through the year 1757 and into the year 1758, that the neutrals were successfully evading even this stringent pronouncement. The outcome was a further extension of the "Rule" in the form of what came to be known as the "doctrine of continuous voyage."

The most brazen and successful evaders of the "Rule of the War of 1756" were the Dutch. To begin with, they protested, with considerable success, against the enforcement of the "Rule," itself. It was extremely difficult for the English officials and English courts to distinguish between a cargo of a Dutch ship that originated in, or was destined for, the Dutch colonies of St. Eustatius or Curaçao and a similar cargo that might have originated in France or a French colony. The Dutch ship carrying which cargo might, in reality, be carrying the cargo under license from France or on account for French merchants. This was made especially difficult by the practice of the Dutch, and the Danish and Spanish carriers as well, of allowing the French shippers to make the comparatively short run from a French colony to St. Eustatius or to Curaçao (or, in the case of the Danes, to St. Thomas or St. Croix, or, in the case of the Spaniards, to Monte Cristi, in Spanish Santo Domingo, or some other Spanish colony), and there transship the French cargo into Dutch (or Danish or Spanish) bottoms, for shipment to France, or, more deceptively, to Amsterdam, for reshipment to France, and *vice versa*.

Early in 1758 the British began to seize all Dutch ships going into or coming out of St. Eustatius and Curaçao, and later, even Surinam, on suspicion that they were engaged in this evasive trade. These seizures aroused the Dutch to a high pitch of anger. They also presented a new set of problems to the British prize courts; for even though a ship sailed directly from a Dutch colony, such as Curaçao, to Amsterdam, if the cargo was manifestly of French origin and could be presumed to be destined for France, the Dutch ship partook, thereby, of the nature of a French ship,

[1] See Chapter XVIII.

and was, therefore, subject to seizure and confiscation under the provisions of the "Rule of the War of 1756." [2]

In order to justify the seizure of neutral ships that evaded the strict interpretation of the "Rule," the English courts laid down the dogma, as expressed by the Earl of Holdernesse, the secretary of state, "That a voyage begun on a bottom that would render the cargo confiscable, is not to be continued by the ship of a friend, but would still be confiscable as the continuation of the same voyage." [3] This meant, in effect, that it was really the cargo that mattered, and that a cargo that made a continuous voyage from a French port to a French destination, even if carried part way by a neutral ship, was confiscable and, in the case of the neutral carrier, contaminated the ship with its enemy character and made the ship confiscable along with the cargo. It was this ruling that came to be called the "doctrine of continuous voyage."

The increased number of seizures of Dutch ships in 1758, whether under the "Rule of the War of 1756" or its corollary, the "doctrine of continuous voyage," brought on a diplomatic crisis between the Netherlands and England. The English ministers stoutly maintained that the Dutch, if they were to be respected as neutrals, must not carry on French commerce with the French West Indies for France, since such activity went so far toward enabling the French to escape the British fleet as to amount to *de facto* belligerency by the Dutch on the side of France.

The Dutch, on their side, argued that, under the provisions of the Anglo-Dutch Marine Treaty of 1674,[4] the right of neutrals to trade with belligerents under the principle that "free ships make free goods" was fully recognized, and that they, the Dutch, under that treaty must be left free to trade as neutrals with France in any way that they chose. On the basis of this argument, the Dutch demanded the release of the seized Dutch ships, even by extra-legal action of the British government, if necessary. If this were done, and if the English government would provide bona fide Dutch shipping to the Dutch colonies an absolute security from seizure in the future, the Dutch might be willing to give up their trade to the French West Indies. To which the English ministers could only reply that it was unthinkable for the English government to interfere in the regular processes of the English courts; but if the Dutch would voluntarily abandon their trade with the French colonies, England might extend the principle of "free ships, free goods" to the Dutch ships trading with continental Spain and Portugal.

The Dutch did not desire war; neither did the English. So the impasse continued. The tension was eased somewhat in 1759 by the passage of the

[2] See Pares, *Colonial Blockade and Neutral Rights*, Chapter III and 242–292, for a detailed discussion of England's disputes with the neutrals over this matter.

[3] Quoted in Pares, *Colonial Blockade and Neutral Rights*, 223.

[4] See Chapter V.

English Parliament of the "Privateers Bill," which strictly regulated the conduct of English privateers, while the Dutch set up a convoy system for the protection of their ships which significantly diminished the number of British seizures. The two countries got through the war without actual warfare over the colonial trade, the "Rule of the War of 1756," and the "doctrine of continuous voyage," but, as Richard Pares puts it, "the crises of the Seven Years War is a milestone on the road from the Anglo-Dutch alliance of King William III to the Anglo-Dutch war of 1781." [5]

The case of the Danish neutral traders was very similar to that of the Dutch. But Denmark was not strong enough to enforce their insistence upon the principle that "free ships make free goods," and Danish warships were instructed not to protect Danish ships that had French goods on board. Count J. H. E. Bernstorff, Danish minister of foreign affairs, vigorously protested British seizures of Danish ships, and with a somewhat better case than the Dutch, since St. Croix and St. Thomas actually produced sugar for export, and some, at least, of the Danish ships seized were bona fide cases of Danish ships carrying on legitimate Danish trade.

The Anglo-Danish tension reached a crisis toward the end of 1758, at which time Bernstorff proposed that the seized ships be freed to proceed to their destination with the understanding that if they were condemned by the prize courts on appeal, the Danish owners would pay the amounts of the judgments against them. The British government accepted the proposal, and Bernstorff dropped his insistence upon the principle that "free ships make free goods." The essential question of right was not solved by this *detente*, but, at least, actual war was avoided. [6]

England's disputes with Spain over neutral trade and the "doctrine of continuous voyage" were a very different matter, for in the case of Spain the problem was much more complicated. These new disputes, which arose out of the war, were coupled with Spain's other, older quarrels with England over such matters as English smuggling into Spanish colonies and the activities of the English logwood cutters on the Mosquito Coast, in Honduras and on the coasts of Yucatán. The disputes themselves became increasingly bitter as the war progressed, and the English ambassadors, Benjamin Keene and his successor, the Earl of Bristol, had to work against the constant pressure upon the Spanish court of the French ambassador, the Marquis d'Aubeterre, who, with the support of several of the Spanish ministers, sought to bring Spain into the war on the side of France.

As early as 1755, Don José Antonio d'Abreu y Bertodano, Spanish

---

[5] Pares, *Colonial Blockade and Neutral Rights*, 279.
[6] Pares, *Colonial Blockade and Neutral Rights*, 279–285.

minister to London, asked Sir Thomas Robinson, then secretary of state, to issue strict orders to English naval ships and privateers not to molest Spanish ships, on the ground that the Treaty of Madrid of 1667 [7] extended to Spanish ships the principle that "free ships make free goods." Robinson's answer was evasive, and he instructed Benjamin Keene, in Madrid, to say to General Ricardo Wall, the Spanish minister of foreign affairs, only that England would faithfully observe its treaties. The next year, 1756, after the English privateers had begun to seize Spanish ships on suspicion of violating the "Rule of the War of 1756," d'Abreu protested to Henry Fox, the new English secretary of state, against these seizures, on the ground that, since Spain effectively enforced its laws prohibiting the trade of foreigners in the Spanish colonies, a Spanish ship traveling from the Spanish colonies to Spain must be considered to be wholly Spanish, and, therefore, exempt from seizure. Fox accepted this point but refused to admit that the principle that "free ships make free goods" was embodied in the treaty of 1667. As he wrote to Keene, this was exactly what the Dutch were incorrectly claiming under the Anglo-Dutch Marine Treaty of 1674. If England were to admit that these treaties covered the present cases, it would have to grant the principle to all other neutrals. It "would end in the Maxim," he wrote, "which England does not allow, that *Free ships make Free Goods*, and that the Enemy's Trade can be carried on in Neutral Bottoms." [8] Fox appealed to his own interpretation of international law to justify the "Rule of the War of 1756" and "the doctrine of continuous voyage," an interpretation that held that the "unlawful," or enemy goods in a neutral ship, "may infect" the "lawful" part, as well as the ship. Now that war had been declared, he reasoned, England had a right, under this principle, to demand that neutrals not take over the business of carrying the enemy's commerce for him. [9] As evidence of England's desire for good relations, nevertheless, Keene was instructed to assure Wall that strict orders would be issued to stop "all illegal and vexatious visitings;" [10] the orders were issued in October. This action eased the tension a little, but the seizures of Spanish ships on suspicion of violating the "Rule of the War of 1756" and the "doctrine of continuous voyage" continued, despite the orders, and Spanish anger steadily mounted. [11]

Meanwhile, other issues had arisen to embitter Anglo-Spanish relations. Wall complained to Keene, in September, 1756, that the English logwood

---

[7] See Chapter VI.

[8] Fox to Keene, July 11, 1756, C.L., Shelburne Mss., XXII, 255–264.

[9] Fox to Keene, Aug. 18, 1756, C.L., Shelburne Mss., XXII, 311–324.

[10] Fox to Keene, Aug. 18, 1756, C.L., Shelburne Mss., XXII, 311–324.

[11] "Additional Instructions" for privateers against the King of France, Oct. 5, 1756, P.R.O., Chatham Mss., XCII. See also, Pares, *Colonial Blockade and Neutral Rights*, 286–287.

cutters in Honduras had recently built a fort in that Spanish territory and pointed out to him that Spanish anger against England was rising. Keene proposed a compromise, promising that the fort would be abandoned and suggesting that if Spain would sell the logwood to England that country might withdraw from the Spanish coasts—at least the parts occupied since the Peace of Aix-la-Chapelle—and pay for the logwood by payments in the form of Negro slaves from Jamaica.[12]

England, in fact, in 1756 and 1757, when the tides of war were running heavily against it, greatly feared that Spain might join France against England in a third Bourbon Family Compact. William Pitt, who became secretary of state in December, 1756, shared this fear and made a desperate effort to appease Spain. He had hardly assumed office when he instructed Keene to convey to General Wall an obsequious and flattering personal message, along with assurances that the differences between the two countries, especially in the matter of the seizure of Spanish ships in America, would be settled to the satisfaction of both courts.[13]

Pitt even hoped that Spain might be tempted to join England in the war against France. In the summer of 1757 he prevailed upon the British Council of Ministers to try to form, if possible, "a more Intimate Union with the Crown of Spain." The offer was high: nothing less than the restoration of Gibraltar, provided only that Minorca, already in French possession, be returned to England. Spain was also to be given complete "satisfaction" in the matter of English logwood-cutting establishments on the Mosquito Coast and the Bay of Honduras made "since the Treaty concluded at Aix-la-Chapelle in October, 1748, in order that all Establishments, so made, be evacuated." [14] This decision of the British ministers relative to the logwood problem was conveyed to d'Abreu by Pitt on September 9, 1757.[15]

Meanwhile, Benjamin Keene was instructed to sound out General Wall as to the possibility of an alliance on these terms. Pitt reviewed to Keene the deplorable situation in which Britain and its allies then found themselves, both in Europe and in America, and instructed the minister to point out to the Spanish court the upset of the balance of power caused by French victories. Surely Spain must realize, he wrote, that such an upset was of extreme danger to Spain itself, "who can no longer indulge the little, false, selfish interest of a lucrative but inglorious and dangerous

[12] Keene to Fox, Sept. 8, 1756, C.L., Shelburne Mss., XXII, 365–374; Fox to Keene Oct. 5, 1756, C.L., Shelburne Mss., XXII, 381–391.
[13] Pitt to Keene, Dec. 14, 1756, Chatham Corr., I, 209–211.
[14] Minutes of Council, Aug. 18, 1757, C.P.O., Chatham Mss., XCII; Pitt to Keene, Aug. 23, 1757, Chatham Corr. I, 247–256.
[15] Pitt to d'Abreu, Sept. 9, 1757, P.R.O., Chatham Mss., XCII.

neutrality at the expense of the subjection of Europe. . . ." [16] Keene was also to cultivate, through the Sicilian ambassador in Madrid, the good will of King Carlos of the Kingdom of the Two Sicilies, who was the presumptive heir of Ferdinand VI of Spain, expected soon to die, by promising Carlos that his second son might become King of the Two Sicilies when Carlos himself should become King of Spain. Furthermore, Keene was to fan Carlos's resentment against Austria, France's ally, and Austria's designs upon Italy.[17]

To Keene's chagrin—and Pitt's—this desperate effort to bribe Spain into an alliance with England was coolly received. General Wall's mood was already highly inflamed against England, and before Keene could present his proposal Wall bitterly complained of the continued unpunished "insults" of the English privateers and the "usurpations" of the English logwood cutters on the coasts of Central America. He also reminded Keene of Spain's expression of willingness to mediate between France and England, a gesture that England had ignored. He himself, he complained, had been severely criticized in the Spanish Council of Ministers for his willingness even to discuss with England matters that touched so closely upon Spain's sovereignty and the integrity of its American territories. Spain, said Wall, must do itself justice, if England would not.[18]

It was in the face of such a storm of anger and recrimination that Keene finally intimated the English plan for an alliance. Wall heard Keene's suggestions "with a cool politeness," but he bitterly reminded Keene that all his best and genuine efforts to build a solid Spanish friendship with England had been frustrated by England itself. It was now too late; and he had no hope of bringing Spain into the war against France. Keene concluded that the Spanish minister would not even mention the English proposal to the King or the Council of Ministers. Indeed, Keene wrote, even if he should bring the proposal before the King and his Council, there was not the least prospect, in view of the divided counsels that characterized the entire Spanish court, that it might be favorably considered.[19]

Thus ended Pitt's desperate and futile effort to draw England and Spain together. Indeed, it seemed to Keene to worsen relations between the two countries and to take them one step further on the road toward war. Keene quoted Wall as heatedly exclaiming,

Are these times and circumstances to talk on such points as the liberties of Europe and a closer union with Spain, when you have given *us* so much room to be dissatisfied with you? . . . What worse can happen to *us*, when the liberties of Europe are gone, than what you do to us? If we are to be despised,

[16] Pitt to Keene, Aug. 23, 1757, *Chatham Corr.*, I, 247–256.
[17] Pitt to Keene, Aug. 23, 1757, *Chatham Corr.*, I, 247–256.
[18] Keene to Pitt, Sept. 26, 1757, *Chatham Corr.*, I, 263–277.
[19] Keene to Pitt., Sept. 26, 1757, *Chatham Corr.*, I, 263–277.

let it be by the strong, and by our own blood and relations. . . . You may possibly make peace; and I hear there are already some overtures made to France [20] . . . but I shall leave it as a legacy, not to be friends with England after her peace with France, if we have not satisfaction for the [American] complaints I have mentioned.[21]

Which Keene interpreted to mean that though England might make peace with France, Spain would continue to insist upon its rights and sovereignty in America, even at the cost of war, if necessary.[22]

As for Pitt's suggestion that Keene cultivate the good will of the King of the Two Sicilies, Keene could be no more hopeful than he was as a result of his talks with Wall. The court of Madrid and that of the Kingdom of the Two Sicilies were not on the best of terms with each other. Matters pertaining to the succession were considered family matters, and neither the ruling family of Spain nor any of its branches would welcome intermeddling by an outside power. In fact, Keene reported that the Spanish nation in general expected the thrones of Spain and the Kingdom of the Two Sicilies again to be united upon the death of Ferdinand VI, which was thought to be imminent.[23]

Pitt's effort to align Spain with England was, thus, a complete failure, and when the Earl of Bristol went to Madrid in 1758 as Keene's successor [24] he was instructed to "consider that idea *entirely at an end.*" If Wall should bring it up, Bristol was to plead lack of instructions and refer the matter back to the British prime minister.[25]

The failure of Pitt's friendly gestures toward Spain left relations between the two countries in the perilous condition they had been in when Pitt came to power, or worse, and, as time went on, relations between Spain and England became increasingly strained.

To begin with, Keene had had repeatedly to protest, but without any satisfactory result, against the use made of Spanish ports by French privateers.[26] Worse still, French ships laden with East or West India goods made a practice of putting into Spanish ports, where they "sold" their cargoes to figurehead Spanish merchants, who then loaded the goods on Spanish or Dutch ships and sent them on up the Channel to France. Since this practice contravened the French navigation laws that products of French colonies could only be carried in French ships, the English seized

---

[20] See pp. 446–455.

[21] Keene to Pitt, Sept. 26, 1757, *Chatham Corr.*, I, 263–277.

[22] Keene to Pitt, Sept. 26, 1757, *Chatham Corr.*, I, 263–277.

[23] Keene to Pitt, Sept. 26, 1757, *Chatham Corr.*, I, 263–277. It is to be recalled that it was this same "Don Carlos" who had been placed on the ducal thrones of Tuscany and Placentia, nearly three decades earlier, with the assistance of England. See Chapter XIV.

[24] Keene died in Madrid on Dec. 15, 1757.

[25] Pitt to Bristol, Aug. 1, 1758, P.R.O., Chatham Mss., XCII.

[26] Keene to Pitt, Jan. 11, 1757, *Chatham Corr.*, I, 212–213.

such Spanish ships when they could, as violating the "Rule of the War of 1756" and "the doctrine of continuous voyage." [27]

Spain was infuriated by these seizures, as, also, by violations of Spain's territorial waters by English warships and privateers lying in wait for French ships going to and from the French colonies. The most famous of these cases, and the most disastrous in its effects upon Anglo-Spanish good will, was that of a French West Indiaman which, in the spring of 1759, was chased by two English frigates off the coast of Spain. In the course of the chase a Spanish warship, the *Guerrero*, intervened and—or so it appeared to the English captains—took the French ship under its protection. When night came the English ships seized the French ship from under the protection of the Spanish flag and took it to Gibraltar for adjudication in the prize court there. This flouting of the Spanish flag was a gross national insult in Spanish eyes, and it was particularly damaging since it occurred in the period when Ferdinand VI died and Carlos III was ascending the Spanish throne.[28]

Another contention growing out of English efforts to suppress the neutral carrying trade in the service of France arose out of the seizure of Spanish ships ostensibly fishing on the Grand Banks off Newfoundland. These ships were evidently intended for carrying provisions to the northern French colonies, since Spanish fishing boats had long since ceased going to the Newfoundland banks; but their seizure was interpreted by Spain as a violation of the right of its subjects to fish there—a right vaguely acknowledged by England in the Anglo-Spanish Treaty of Utrecht and in the treaty of 1721.[29]

When, therefore, d'Abreu protested the Newfoundland seizure in June, 1758, Pitt denied that Spanish subjects had any right to participate in the Newfoundland fisheries, alleging that the Anglo-Spanish Treaty of Utrecht did not recognize any such right.[30] The Earl of Bristol, the new British minister in Madrid, was instructed to deny Spain's right to a share of the Newfoundland fisheries on the ground that King William had prohibited "strangers" from fishing there in 1699 and that Spain was

[27] Pares, *Colonial Blockade and Neutral Rights*, 217–224.

[28] Bristol to Pitt, Dec. 19, 1759, *Chatham Corr.*, I, 473-474. See also, Pares, *Colonial Blockade and Neutral Rights*, 290–291.

[29] D'Abreu's Memoir to Pitt, June 16, 1758, P.R.O., *Chatham Mss.*, XCII; d'Abreu to Pitt, Aug. 1, 1758, *ibid.*; Pitt to Bristol, Aug. 15, 1758, *ibid.*

[30] Pitt to d'Abreu, Aug. 11, 1758, P.R.O., Chatham Mss., XCII. Pitt's statement was not precisely true. The preliminary treaty of peace, signed at Madrid on March 27, 1713, provided that "Her Britannic Majesty promises to maintain the Guipuzcoans and the rest of his Catholic Majesty's subjects in all their rights of whatever nature, and in the liberty hitherto enjoyed by them in the Newfoundland whale and cod fishery. . . ." The final treaty of peace, signed at Utrecht on July 13, was more equivocal: "her Britannic Majesty consents and agrees that all such privileges as the Guipuzcoans and other people of Spain are able to claim by right, shall be allowed and preserved to them." This equivocal language was repeated in the Anglo-Spanish treaty of 1721. See Chapters X and XIV.

excluded from the fisheries by Articles 7 and 8 of the Anglo-Spanish Treaty of Madrid of 1670.[31]

Yet, although Pitt was inflexible on the point of the fisheries, he did hope to keep Spain out of the war. He therefore instructed Bristol to adopt a conciliatory attitude on the question of logwood cutters in Honduras. As for the activities of English privateers, Pitt promised to do all he could to satisfy His Catholic Majesty, within the limits of the English constitution; he could not interfere with the due process of law in the prize courts.[32] It was this issue relative to the privateers that seemed to lie closest to the Spanish temper, and Wall continued to excoriate England on this point, both through Bristol and through the Conde de Fuentes, who succeeded d'Abreu as the Spanish minister to England late in 1758.

While Spanish feelings with regard to England continued to mount, through 1758 and into 1759, the fortunes of war in Europe began to turn against France and Austria and in favor of England and Prussia, and, in America, emphatically in favor of England. In 1758, the Abbé Bernis, the French foreign minister, frightened by the turn of the fortunes of war, proposed that Spain, Denmark, and Saxony offer a mediation between the two contending alliances. France would have preferred, of course, to have Spain enter the war on the Franco-Austrian side, and Bernis offered Minorca, seized by France at the beginning of the war, in return for Spain's accession to the Treaty of Versailles (the Franco-Austrian alliance of 1756). In June of 1758 Louis XV wrote a personal letter to Ferdinand VI, admitting the ebb in French fortunes and pointing out the danger to Spain of an English victory in the war. Ferdinand VI was not, as yet, prepared to enter the war, and the best he could offer was a new effort at mediation.[33] But Louisbourg fell to English forces on July 26, 1758, and Pitt was determined to go on to the conquest of Canada and the French islands in the Caribbean, with the result that Wall's suggestion of the possibility of mediation was politely evaded.[34]

Meanwhile, Bernis was succeeded by the more vigorous and resourceful Duc de Choiseul, who preferred accelerating the war to making peace with England, while the death of Ferdinand VI late in 1759 brought to the throne of Spain the Francophile and anti-English Carlos, King of the Two Sicilies, as Carlos III of Spain.

A much more vigorous, strong-minded, and imaginative man than Ferdinand, Carlos was determined to stand up to England on the disputes

[31] Pitt to Bristol, Aug. 1, 1758, P.R.O., Chatham Mss., XCII. These articles of the Treaty of 1670 did not mention the fisheries. They provided merely that the subjects of each nation would stay away from the American possessions of the other!

[32] Pitt to Bristol, Aug. 1, 1758, P.R.O., Chatham Mss., XCII.

[33] *Recueil des Insts.*, XII bis: Espagne, III, 323–324.

[34] D'Aubeterre to Choiseul, Dec. 18, 1758, A.É., Corr., Pol., Esp., 521: fols. 210–223.

between the two countries in America. He readily shared Wall's anger at England's flouting of Spanish sovereignty and rights, and it was easy for the Duc de Choiseul to fan his resentment to the point, eventually, of entering the war. He was not yet, at the time of his accession, ready to take that step, but that event may be taken as marking the real end of Spanish neutrality and the beginning of a mounting attitude of pro-French belligerency toward England.

2. Early Negotiations for Peace, 1757-60

The Seven Years War had hardly gotten under way before the participants began to put out feelers toward peace. Thus, in the autumn of 1757, Frederick II attempted to start a secret negotiation with Louis XV on his own account, but the only apparent result was to arouse Austrian suspicions of France.[35] Earlier in the same year, Rouillé, through Louis-Auguste-Augustin d'Affry, French minister to Holland, had sounded out Joseph Yorke, British minister to the Hague, on the prospects of a separate treaty. Great Britain quickly responded that a peace without the concurrence of Prussia was unthinkable, whereupon these negotiations came to an abrupt end.[36] In June, 1757, Rouillé was succeeded as French minister of foreign affairs by the Abbé Bernis, who constantly toyed with the idea of peace. Partly because of French losses at Kloster Seven and Rossbach, and partly because of a desire to separate England from Prussia, he revived the d'Affry-Yorke negotiations at the Hague in January, 1758. Great Britain again refused to be interested.[37] A similar overture was made in Copenhagen, with the same result.[38] As the fortunes of war turned increasingly against France, particularly in the colonies, Bernis became more and more disposed to bring the war to an end, but he did not have the confidence of Louis XV and Madame de Pompadour and was replaced in December, 1758, by the Duc de Choiseul.[39]

Choiseul had criticized Bernis for permitting the colonial war to be obscured by the European conflict, and his chief attention was now de-

---

[35] Waddington, La guerre de sept ans, I, 584–590.

[36] C. L., Shelburne Mss., XXII: 447–449, 459–464; B.M., Add. Mss., 6814: fols. 26–27. 59–62.

[37] Waddington, La guerre de sept ans, I, 732–735.

[38] Waddington, La guerre de sept ans, II, 475.

[39] Waddington, La guerre de sept ans, II, 433–465. Etienne-François de Choiseul, Comte de Stainville, Duc de Choiseul, was minister of foreign affairs from Dec. 8, 1758, until Oct. 15, 1761, when he surrendered his portfolio to his cousin, César-Gabriel de Choiseul, Comte de Choiseul, Duc de Praslin. The Duc de Choiseul continued to direct French relations with Spain, however, until his retirement in 1770.

voted to the campaign of 1759. While preparing fleets at Brest and Toulon, he sought to win the good will of Holland. But the Toulon and Brest fleets were beaten back when they emerged, the French were defeated at Minden, and Quebec was taken by the expedition of General Wolfe. These events made hopeless Choiseul's efforts with the Dutch, and he next turned for aid to Russia. Meanwhile, he had come to realize that France greatly needed peace, if it could be had without abandoning Austria, and he began to seek the latter's consent to an attempt to obtain it. Austria was at first utterly opposed to the idea, but the disasters of 1759 forced Empress Maria Theresa to consider it seriously. Austria had little to lose and much to gain by a continuation of the war, and the most that Choiseul could obtain was a reluctant consent to the opening of negotiations between France and England looking toward a separate Anglo-French peace.[40]

Choiseul's enemies were almost an anxious for peace as he was. As early as June 10, 1759, Frederick II, despairing of decisive ultimate victory, wrote a personal letter to George II, suggesting the advisability, at the first "favorable events" of the campaign, of calling a general congress of the belligerent powers for the purpose of making an "honorable and useful" peace.[41] But the campaign of the year 1759 was more than "favorable." For England this was "the wonderful year," the "annus mirabilis." For France, however, it was a year of many woes. From America came the news that the English had taken Guadelupe, Basse-Terre, and Marie-Galante; and then followed the victories at Ticonderoga and Niagara, and the fall of Quebec. In Africa the English seized Gorée and with it the valuable trade in slaves and rubber. From India came tidings that the English had successfully defended Madras and had taken Surat; while "the Marathon of Minden" saved Hanover for the English King. Frederick could say, in his enthusiasm, that "England has been long in labor, and has suffered much to produce Mr. Pitt; but at last she has delivered herself of a man!" [42]

The idea of a congress, meanwhile, had not been dropped. On the contrary, the successes of the year placed the Anglo-Prussian allies in a position to hope that such a proposition might be successful and to their advantage. They therefore prepared a declaration to this purpose and sent it to Duke Louis Ernest of Brunswick for transmission to the representatives of the belligerents at the Hague. At the same time, full information as to this step was transmitted to the new King of Spain, Carlos III, now on his way from Naples to Madrid.[43]

The determination to propose a peace congress, as a matter of fact, was

---

[40] Soltau, *The Duke de Choiseul*, 32–44.
[41] *Chatham Corr.*, I, 413–414.
[42] P.R.O., *Chatham Corr.*, I, 444–445.

hastened by Great Britain's desire to politely avoid offers of mediation between itself and France by the importunate Carlos. As King of Naples, even before his brother's death, this prince had indicated his sympathy for the French cause, and Choiseul took advantage of his benevolence to set on foot a move which he calculated would either force mediation or bring Spain into the war on the side of France. Early in the summer of 1759, the Prince of San Severino, Neapolitan ambassador to London, approached Pitt with the suggestion that his master would like to mediate the Anglo-French dispute. Pitt delayed making a definite reply, on the ground that the campaign then under way must be terminated, for better or for worse, before he could commit himself. The day after the arrival of news of Ferdinand's death, San Severino again tendered Carlos's good offices and received much the same answer as before.[44]

Choiseul, however, instructed the Marquis d'Ossun,[45] French minister at Naples, to accept Carlos's offer of mediation. The repeated defeats of France made peace almost imperative, he said, but he professed to be convinced that the balance of power in Europe now depended upon the balance of power in the colonies. France could not give up its possessions to Great Britain without greatly fearing that the resultant increase in British power would threaten the Spanish empire in America, and reduce both France and Spain to the position of second-rate states in Europe. He therefore reemphasized the desirability of a strong union between them, and, while accepting the mediation of His Catholic Majesty, he expressed the hope that it would be an armed mediation, with a clear warning to both belligerents that, for the preservation of the balance of power in America, Spain would take up arms against either nation that refused its good offices.[46]

Choiseul probably would have preferred Spanish interference in the war on the side of France to a successful Spanish mediation, but to give the color of sincerity to his acceptance of Carlos's offer, he outlined to the new Spanish monarch the bases of his own terms for peace. The conflict between England and France had begun, he wrote, as a quarrel over their colonial boundaries in the regions of Acadia and the Ohio River under the provisions of the Treaty of Utrecht. This conflict, with its potential effect upon the balance of power in the world, was the chief issue in the war. Now, to show its desire for fairness and justice, France proposed to leave the interpretation of the Treaty of Utrecht entirely to the impartial judgment of the King of Spain. France proposed, moreover, to restore Minorca to Great Britain in return for permission to fortify Dunkirk, and would consent to raze Louisbourg and to agree

[43] B.M., Add. Mss., 6818: fols. 113–114, 124; *Chatham Corr.*, I, 460–461, 461 n.

[44] B.M., Add. Mss., 6818: fols. 144–146.

[45] Pierre Paul d'Ossun, Marquis d'Ossun.

[46] *Recueil des Insts.*, XII *bis*, Espagne III, 349–350, 352–359.

never to rebuild it. Finally, France was willing to withdraw its troops from Germany on the condition that the army of Hanover be disbanded, but that both Great Britain and France might continue to support their respective allies with subsidies.[47]

The French line of argument apparently impressed Carlos, for in October San Severino again approached Pitt on the subject of mediation, using his master's interest in the balance of power in America to justify his insistence. Pitt, apparently now seeing this phase of the situation for the first time, immediately softened the tone of his refusal and urbanely explained to the Neapolitan envoy that England had no idea of retaining all her conquests in America. He compared the American situation with that in Italy and hinted that Great Britain would rejoice with Spain over any increase in the latter's power in America at the expense of France. Meanwhile, he promised that Bristol would be instructed to negotiate with Carlos's ministers at Madrid.[48]

It was at this juncture that news of the fall of Quebec arrived, and in the midst of the rejoicing Great Britain and Prussia launched their proposal for a peace congress. Pitt wrote Bristol of San Severino's overtures and instructed him to assure the new Spanish monarch, when he arrived in Madrid, that the British unwillingness to accept his mediation was not due to any want of confidence. On the contrary, Bristol was to express great appreciation of the Spanish effort and to say that His Catholic Majesty's offer of mediation was certainly not precluded by the Anglo-Prussian proposal for a peace congress, of which he was now "in great secrecy" to inform the Spanish King.[49]

Thus softly did the British minister turn aside the embarrassing attentions of Carlos III, even while Choiseul was desperately endeavoring to win that King's commitment to a policy of war. The internal condition of France was one of great disorder, and reverses everywhere were forcing it to contemplate great sacrifices for the cause of peace. Choiseul professed to see in the proposed Spanish mediation the only means to obtain a peace that would be just and honorable. He did not see how Spain could compel England to agree; but just in case the English should accept Spanish mediation, he sent d'Ossun a note on the colonial issues in the war which outlined the possible compromises that France was prepared to accept.[50] This document surveyed the regional colonial conflicts that had brought on the war, in North America, the West Indies,

[47]*Recueil des Insts.*, XII bis, *Espagne* III, 351–352; cf. Waddington, *La guerre de sept ans*, III, 433–434.

[48] L.C., B.M., Add. Mss., 32897: fols. 285–287; Waddington, *La guerre de sept ans*, III, 435.

[49] Thackeray, *William Pitt*, I, 458–461.

[50] A.É., Corr. Pol., *Espagne*, 525: fols. 325–329; L.C., A.É., Méms. et Docs., *Amérique*, 21: fols. 27–37.

Africa, and Asia. The conflict in North America, it said, resolved itself
into two questions, that of Acadia and that of the frontiers of Canada.
After a review of the dispute over Acadia, the French note proposed the
arbitration of that question; failing that, it would become a question of
choosing "the lesser evil." Whatever happened, France ought to preserve
its communications between Quebec and the sea by way of the St. John
River, perhaps by neutralizing it. But if England should now find itself
in a position successfully to insist upon the cession of an Acadia which
would include the south bank of the St. Lawrence, it would be better
for France to abandon Canada altogether and transport its inhabitants to
Louisiana. France must also insist, in the proposed negotiation, upon the
restitution of Cape Breton, for its loss would make it impossible to defend
Canada. As to the frontiers of Canada, nothing short of complete defeat
should be allowed to force the French to concede the Great Lakes to
England, for this, too, would make Canada useless and untenable, because
it would block communications between Canada and Louisiana and
place the British in a position to seize both. As for the frontier in the
Ohio region, it ought to follow the watershed, and no means should be
spared to avoid the hard necessity of surrendering more, especially because
a foothold in the Ohio Valley would make it easy for the English to attack
Louisiana. But the English would surely demand more; in which case the
French must try to confine the cession to the right bank of the river as far
as the Wabash. It was to be feared that the English might demand the
territory as far as the confluence of the Cherokee (Tennessee) River and
the Ohio, which would place them in dangerous proximity to the Mississippi.[51]

Thus Choiseul outlined the terms of a possible American peace. In his
desire to establish the Appalachian watershed as the boundary, he followed
the ideas of the Marquis de la Galissonnière. France was still in dread of
the irresistible expansion of the westward-moving English. The concessions
envisaged there were still inspired by a hope for the security of New
France; but by their very nature they were almost a confession of the futility of that hope and an acknowledgment that the war in America was
being fought in vain. Whether or not this was true, the French plea fell on
receptive Spanish ears, and until his arrival in Madrid, Carlos's tone,
under the pressure from d'Ossun, became increasingly belligerent. Soon
after he landed at Barcelona he confessed his desire to join the French
as soon as his forces might be made ready. Moreover, Carlos was not
happy over the way Pitt had put aside his proposed mediation, and he
ordered d'Aubreu to renew his offer.[52]

[51] L.C., A.E., Méms. et Docs., Amérique, 21: fols. 27–32.
[52] Recueil des Insts., XII bis, Espagne, 338; A.É., Corr. Pol., Espagne, 526: fols.
144–149, 181–188; Waddington, La guerre de sept ans, III, 436–437.

D'Abreu, Spanish minister in London, conformably with his orders, expressed to Pitt his master's extreme desire to bring about peace and his concern over the status of the balance of power in America established by the Peace of Utrecht, which His Catholic Majesty considered as already seriously disturbed by the extent of the British successes.[53] Pitt replied by again pointing to the Anglo-Prussian call for a peace congress as a step which precluded Spanish mediation. As for the American balance of power, said to have been established by the Peace of Utrecht, he declared there was no such thing.[54] D'Aubreu's orders had been written by the Marqués de Squillace, the finance minister, from Saragossa, before the King had talked to Wall, and apparently without Wall's knowledge. This fact gave Pitt an opportunity to complain about the irregularities involved in communicating with the Spanish government and to insinuate that Spain's concern over the pretended "balance of power" in America was due to the influence of the French ambassador.[55]

It was true that d'Ossun was attempting to force the Spanish King's hand. He expressed to Carlos his opinion that the Anglo-Prussian declaration was only an effort to avoid Spanish mediation and even advised the King to insist that Great Britain lay before him the British terms of peace. Carlos was completely convinced and agreed to demand that both belligerents submit their peace terms. "They [the British] will have to make peace," he cried. "If not, they will force me, against my will, to make war; but, in one way or another, I will not suffer them to remain the masters of Europe and America." [56]

The new ruler arrived in Madrid about the middle of December, 1759, and there he met Wall. That minister soon brought him to his diplomatic senses by pointing out that Great Britain would not negotiate a separate peace and that Spain could do nothing to force it to do so. Spain, in any case, was certainly in no condition to undertake a war. More than that, the British conquest of Canada affected Spain little, if at all. The only alternative to accepting Britain's refusal of Spanish mediation was war, and Spain had so little at stake in the conflict that war in support of France would be ridiculous.[57] At the same time, Wall met Bristol's complaints with soft words. Although obviously embarrassed by his sovereign's precipitate action, Wall insisted that Spain could not see the extensive

---

[53] B.M., Add. Mss., 6818: fols. 137–139; L.C., B.M., Add. Mss., 32899: fol. 303.

[54] B.M., Add. Mss., 6813: fols. 140–143.

[55] B.M., Add. Mss., 6818: fols. 140–143, 147–149; cf. Waddington, La guerre de sept ans, III, 489; Thackeray, op. cit., I, 461–468.

[56] D'Ossun to Choiseul, Dec. 7, 1759, A.É., Corr. Pol., Espagne, 526; fols. 175, 176–179, 181–188.

[57] A.É., Corr. Pol., Espagne, 526: fols. 203–214; Waddington, La guerre de sept ans, III, 439.

British conquests in America without concern; but he was careful to point out that "good offices" had been extended to both France and Great Britain in the same terms.[58]

Nothing came of the Spanish offer of mediation for the time being, because the British could now evade the Spanish proposals by referring to the congress at the Hague, while Anglo-Spanish relations took a momentary turn for the better. In February, 1760, d'Aubreu was replaced as ambassador in London by the Conde de Fuentes, probably at the suggestion of Great Britain,[59] who came instructed to seek to temper the attitude of the British government. He was to take a firm stand, nevertheless, on the desire of Spain to see its offer of mediation accepted and on the Anglo-Spanish disputes over the contraband trade and the British logwood cutters on the Mosquito Coast and in Honduras.[60] Fuentes was well received in England, and it began to appear as though the Anglo-Spanish quarrel might be patched up. It was even suggested that some sort of *entente cordiale* might be arranged between the two countries.[61] As a matter of fact, however, the quiet of apparently good relations was only the lull before the storm.

The Anglo-Prussian declaration of November 25, 1759, was now bearing fruit. Choiseul recognized in the declaration a move to obviate the proposed Spanish mediation for a separate peace between Great Britain and France. But he saw in it also an evidence of distrust between Great Britain and its ally, Prussia, and he accepted the plan for a congress with the twofold hope that it might result in a split between them and throw Great Britain back upon the choice between either accepting the Spanish mediation or forcing Spain into the war on the side of France.[62] Great Britain, on the other hand, took its peacemaking seriously, and the British ministers began to consider just what they should demand of France as the price of peace. The victories of the year had lifted British spirits high. The King was for keeping all conquests, as was also popular opinion,[63] but the ministers were more cautious. "The Nonsense of ye Populace, and ye printed Papers, about holding and keeping everything, and reducing France to Nothing, should be batter'd down, and discountenanced," wrote Hardwicke to Newcastle. "If you keep Quebec, you must keep all Canada, and Louisbourg as the Key to it, and is That possible

---

[58] B.M., Add. Mss., 6818: fols. 70–71, 80–81, 82–83.

[59] *Chatham Corr.*, II, 22–23. Joaquin Atanasio Pignatelli de Aragón y Moncayo, Conde de Fuentes.

[60] *Recueil des Insts.*, XII bis, Espagne, 338–339; A.É., Corr. Pol., Espagne, 527: fols. 140–151; *ibid.*, 528: fols. 38–48.

[61] A.É., Corr. Pol., Espagne, 528: fols. 65–67; L.C., B.M., Add. Mss., 82908: fols. 34–38; Corbett, *England in the Seven Years War*, II, 85; *Chatham Corr.*, II, 46–47.

[62] A.É., Corr. Pol., Espagne, 528: fols. 20–24; cf. Corbett, *op. cit.*, II, 75–76.

[63] L.C., B.M., Add. Mss., 82897: fols. 512–520.

without fighting on for ever?" [64] The basic principle of the peace, as of the prewar negotiations, and, indeed, the chief objective of the war, Hardwicke thought, was the security of the British possessions in America, and British demands must be based on that.[65] Pitt, however, was not ready to commit himself. He desired peace, but he ridiculed the King's exorbitant expectations and indicated to Newcastle a desire to keep Gorée and Senegal, in Africa, and the Bay of Fundy, Crown Point, Niagara, and the lakes in North America. With regard to Quebec, Louisbourg, and Montreal, he was disposed to negotiate and indicated a willingness to surrender them, for a consideration.[66] Negotiations never reached a point where he felt called upon to express himself definitely, but his cautious position in the autumn of 1759 was in distinct contrast with his exorbitant demands a little more than a year later.[67]

[64] L.C., B.M., Add. Mss., 82897: fols. 138–140. Many suggestions were made to the British ministry as to what the terms of peace ought to be. The Earl of Kinnoull, ambassador to Lisbon, an expert on American affairs, and one of Newcastle's confidants, suggested that Great Britain must demand Lake Ontario as a boundary, and Crown Point as a bulwark against possible French aggression from Canada. Louisbourg must now be taken in order to control both the navigation of the St. Lawrence and the fishery, and Nova Scotia must be carefully delimited for the security of all the colonies (L.C., B.M., Add. Mss., 328297: fols. 178–180). One anonymous adviser of the government proposed that the "Neutral Islands" be divided between France and Great Britain. The British islands should be peopled with emigrants from Georgia, which would be assigned to France—though for what reason is not stated (L.C., B.M., Add. Mss., 32897: fols. 890–891). Still another pointed out the desirability of leaving the French in Canada as a check upon the "Sturdiness . . . of our American Colonists towards his Majesty's Governours and Measures" (L.C., B.M., Add. Mss., 32900: fol. 874).

[65] L.C., B.M., Add. Mss., 32897: fols. 178–180.

[66] L.C., B.M., Add. Mss., 32897: fols. 512–520.

[67] The most thoroughgoing terms suggested for the anticipated treaty were submitted to Pitt by William Patterson, on Dec. 20, 1759. Patterson's memorandum, dated Oct. 30, has sometimes been attributed to Pitt himself, because signed "W.P." (Cf. Wad dington, La guerre de sept ans, III, 540, and Pease, Anglo-French Boundary Disputes, lxxviiin). A postscript, dated Dec. 4, indicates that it was not delivered until after that date, and the presence of a copy in the Newcastle Papers (L.C., B.M., Add. Mss., 32897: fols. 484–491) indicates that it may have been submitted to Newcastle first, and then, at his encouragement, sent to Pitt. The covering letter to Pitt, together with a copy of the memorandum, is in P.R.O., Chatham Mss., XCVI.

Patterson's memorandum proposed that Great Britain keep all conquests in America; thus Great Britain would have no more troublesome boundary questions with France, and would have a monopoly of the fur trade, the fisheries, the lumber and naval stores of North America. The retention of Senegal and Gorée would give it control of the slave and rubber trades. If other nations should take umbrage at Britain's increased empire, let them come on; Great Britain was never so well prepared to receive them. As for the rest of North America, Patterson proposed that the boundary of Acadia be the St. Lawrence, which would, indeed, become the boundary between Canada and the British colonies as far as Montreal; the navigation of the river he would leave open to both French and British. Beyond Montreal, he proposed that the boundary follow the Ottawa and the forty-seventh degree of latitude to the eighty-third degree of longitude and the north shore of Lake Huron, through the middle of Lake Michigan, the Illinois River and the Mississippi to the Gulf of Mexico. Thus, he says, "by settling

Negotiations at the Hague began in December, 1759. D'Affry, for France, informed Duke Louis Ernest of Brunswick that France and its allies would prepare a joint response to the Anglo-Prussian statement,[68] but he began secretly to propose that the Anglo-French dispute over American boundaries be separated from the European disputes.[69] Joseph Yorke, English minister at the Hague, parried the proposal, and he was promptly instructed to say to d'Affry that Great Britain would hear of no negotiations save as an ally of Prussia.[70] On the other hand, if France, separating itself from its allies—Austria, for example—was willing to negotiate with Prussia alone, he was to listen to what d'Affry had to propose.[71] D'Affry pointed out the difficulty of settling the Anglo-French disputes by a general congress and the corresponding impossibility of ending the European war before the Anglo-French quarrel was cleared away, and he intimated that the best way to avoid Spanish mediation would be by direct negotiations between Great Britain and France.[72] A few days later, in a dramatic secret meeting in a carriage on the road near the castle of Ryswick, d'Affry explained to Yorke that France, having accepted the Spanish offer of mediation, could not take matters out of Spain's hands without knowing how things stood between Spain and Great Britain, but that the Duc de Choiseul was ready to negotiate in any way Great Britain might suggest, provided he could transmit copies of the transactions to Spain, for that country's satisfaction. D'Affry intimated, further, that France was tired of the Austrian alliance, and that, could the American disputes only be settled, France would gladly get out of Germany and leave the balance of power there undisturbed.[73] Choiseul similarly proposed to Frederick, who had sounded him out, that the Franco-Prussian disputes be settled separately.[74]

Obviously, Choiseul desired to separate the Anglo-French colonial quarrel from the war in the Germanies, whether because he genuinely believed this to be the most effective means to peace or because he hoped thereby to weaken the Anglo-Prussian alliance. For whatever motive, he succeeded in injecting the principle of separation into the counterdeclaration of France and its allies that was made early in April, 1760. That

---

our Boundaries, the great Point in Dispute, in North America, [our possessions there would be] extensive enough, as above run out, for all the British who shall resort thither or be born there for a thousand years to come."

[68] B.M., Add. Mss., 6818: fols. 150, 152.
[69] B.M., Add. Mss., 6818: fols. 5, 9, 11–12.
[70] B.M., Add. Mss., 6818: fol. 13.
[71] B.M., Add. Mss., 6818: fols. 15, 17–18.
[72] B.M, Add. Mss., 6818: 28.
[73] B.M., Add. Mss., 6818: fols. 64–67; cf. Recueil des Insts., XII bis, Espagne, 338–339, and Corbett, op. cit., II, 72–73.
[74] Frederick II to Chevalier de Froulay [Feb. 14, 1760]; Froulay to Frederick, Mar. 19, 1760; "Choiseul's article toward peace" [Mar. 17, 1760]; all in P.R.O., Chatham Mss., LXXXV.

document proposed, for the purpose of peacemaking, the separation of the Anglo-French conflict from the continental war; for the former, it suggested the acceptance of the Spanish offer of mediation; for the latter, it proposed a congress to settle the issues in Germany and elsewhere in Europe.[75] At the time the counterdeclaration was made, however, d'Affry, under instructions from Choiseul, assured Yorke that these articles in no way precluded a direct settlement between England and France, if England preferred it that way.[76] Choiseul later agreed to include in the Anglo-French negotiations the questions of Hanover, Hesse, and Brunswick, as being essentially parts of the Anglo-French war. But the war between Austria, Russia, and Prussia, he said, must be settled separately, by a congress. If England could not agree to this, France would break off negotiations.[77]

Yorke's suspicions were aroused by the repeated insistence by France that Spain be informed and by the close association of d'Affry with the Marqués de Grimaldi,[78] Spanish minister at The Hague. Further, the French proposals for separate, secret, and direct negotiations convinced Holdernesse that the whole French maneuver was an attempt to exclude Prussia, and Yorke was told to say plainly that Prussia must be included in any settlement made between England and France. Upon the delivery of this message, d'Affry abruptly brought the negotiations to an end.[79]

3. The Third Bourbon Family Compact, 1761

The accession of Carlos III to the throne of Spain marked the opening of a new phase in Anglo-Spanish relations having to do with America. Carlos, son of Elizabeth Farnese, was, in contrast with his half-brother, Ferdinand VI, well-disposed and trustful toward France and antagonistic and distrustful toward England.[80] In any case, the fundamental issues be-

---

[75] B.M., Add. Mss., 6818: fols. 142–143.

[76] B.M., Add. Mss., 6818: 137–139, 148–149; note on dispatch from Choiseul to d'Affry, Mar. 31, 1760, P.R.O., Chatham Mss., LXXXV.

[77] B.M., Add. Mss., 6818: fols. 172–173.

[78] Jeronimo Grimaldi, Marqués de Grimaldi.

[79] B.M., Add. Mss., 6818: fols. 168–171, 178–180; A.É., Corr. Pol., Espagne, 528: fols. 232–235.

[80] It might be added that, although England had helped him to ascend the ducal thrones of Placentia and Parma in 1732, he had a personal animus against England that stemmed from an incident in the course of the War of the Austrian Succession, When Commodore William Martin, of the English navy, with his squadron lying within cannon range off Naples and his watch in his hand, had forced Carlos to declare himself neutral within thirty minutes on pain of an immediate and thorough bombardment of Carlos's capital city. It was said that this personal humiliation remained strongly embedded in his feelings throughout his life and that it accounted, in large measure, for his anti-English bias.

tween Spain and England remained exactly as they had been at the time of the death of Benjamin Keene in December of 1757. The Earl of Bristol had had to take up the problem of keeping Spain neutral where Keene had left off, but with this difference, that the Anglo-Spanish American quarrels had been exacerbated by the British seizures of Spanish ships, both in European waters and in American, and the continued British successes in America had aroused, in the Spanish monarch's mind—with the help of French pressure, if any help were needed—a real fear that a radical expansion of British colonial holdings in America would, in itself, constitute a threat to the integrity of Spain's American empire.

From the very beginning of the war, French ambassadors to Madrid had been instructed to use discreetly their best influence to lead Spain to join France in the war against England. Thus, when the Marquis d'Aubeterre had gone to Spain in 1757 to succeed the Duc de Duras, he had been instructed to avoid recriminations over the pro-English attitudes of General Wall and to point out to the Spanish monarchs and their ministers how indispensable for the welfare of both countries "a union of the two elder branches of the house of Bourbon" was, if they were to avoid being humiliated and ruined by Great Britain. In any case, d'Aubeterre was to suggest that Spain accede to the Treaty of Versailles of May 1, 1756 (the Franco-Austrian alliance), as a guarantee of Spanish interests in Italy.[81]

The perspicacity of Benjamin Keene and the cool-headedness of Ricardo Wall, coupled with Ferdinand VI's distrust of France, had prevented the insinuations of the French ambassador from bearing any significant fruit, and Keene had been able to report, early in 1757, that Wall had replied to the Austrian ambassador's invitation to accede to the Treaty of Versailles that Spain was but little concerned over the slight British successes in America.[82] D'Aubeterre had, however, succeeded in fanning Wall's resentment over British abuse of Spanish neutrality, especially the British habit of taking French prize ships into Spanish ports.[83]

During the year 1758, while the timid Abbé Bernis was French foreign minister, French policy was focused, in large part, upon the possibility of arranging a general peace. Yet the French ambassador continued to point out to the Spanish court the danger to Spain of an upset of the American balance of power by a great expansion of the British empire there, and he continually insinuated the desirability, for Spain, of a union with France.[84] At one time Wall asked d'Aubeterre, "But what profits can you offer

[81] Recueil des Insts, XII bis, Espagne, III, 321–322.
[82] Keene to Pitt, Jan. 11, 1757, B.M., Add. Mss., 6814: fols. 38–42.
[83] Recueil des Insts., XII bis, Espagne, III, 322–323.
[84] D'Aubeterre to Bernis, Mar. 27, 1758, A.É., Corr. Pol., Espagne, 523:152–157.

Spain from this war?" To which d'Aubeterre replied that France would give Spain Minorca, which France then held.[85] If Spain would join the war, France would gladly drop the project for Spanish mediation.[86] D'Aubeterre reported, however, that he did not expect Spain to come to any decision that year; the Spanish government would await the return of the treasure fleet from America and news of the fate of Louisbourg, at the moment under siege by the British.[87]

So low were French fortunes sunk in America and Europe, however, that Louis XV wrote a personal letter to Ferdinand VI desperately asking for Spanish aid, or, failing that, Spanish mediation for the securing of peace.[88] D'Aubeterre reported that the Spanish court reacted coolly to the offer of Minorca but that it might consider entry into the war if assured of recovering Gibraltar. At the same time, he said, Spain was waiting for news of the fate of Louisbourg; the fall of Louisbourg might, in fact, mean that Spanish help in America could do France no good.[89] Meanwhile, Ferdinand VI replied to Louis XV's personal letter, saying Spain could not join France in the war.[90]

News of the fall of Louisbourg reached Madrid about the beginning of September, 1758. D'Aubeterre again raised the question of Spanish aid and the difficulty of getting food into Canada. To which Wall replied "that the greater part of the necessary provisioning of that colony is done by the English themselves." [91] Of more importance to the French ambassador was that Wall had apparently become worried over the increase of British power in America and his remark that it was important to Spain that the British not be allowed to become masters of the French possessions in America.[92]

This may, indeed, have been the moment at which Spain began to think seriously of throwing its weight into the struggle in America on the side of France. D'Aubeterre took a genuine pleasure in reporting that Wall's attitude toward England was perceptibly stiffening. Wall had said to Bristol that it began to appear that Spain might have to resort to force to defend

---

[85] D'Aubeterre to Bernis, May 10, 1758, A.É., Corr., Pol., Espagne, 523: fols. 208–212; "Projet de Mémoire," enclosed with d'Aubeterre's letter to Bernis of May 17, 1758, *ibid.*, fols. 523:228.

[86] D'Aubeterre to Bernis, May 17, 1758, A.É., Corr. Pol., Espagne, 523: fols. 229–234.

[87] D'Aubeterre to Bernis, May 22, 1758, A.É., Corr. Pol., Espagne, 523: fols. 239–244.

[88] Louis XV to Ferdinand VI, June 10, 1758, A.É., Corr. Pol., Espagne, 523: fols. 275–277.

[89] D'Aubeterre to Bernis, June 12, 1758, A.É., Corr. Pol., Espagne, 523: fols. 278–287.

[90] Ferdinand VI to Louis XV, June 27, 1758, A.É., Corr., Pol., Espagne, 523: fols. 310–312.

[91] D'Aubeterre to Bernis, October 5, 1758, A.É., Corr. Pol., Espagne, 524: fols. 68–73.

[92] *Ibid.*

its flag and its possessions. When Bristol protested England's desire for peace, Wall told him that, now that the English had taken Louisbourg, they should be ready to talk peace with France. He repeated that Spain always stood ready to employ its good offices to that end.[93]

The Duc de Choiseul had succeeded Bernis at the French foreign ministry in December of 1758. An ambitious, energetic, imaginative, and resourceful man, he had abandoned at the beginning of his ministry, all direct efforts to make peace with England and had plunged into preparations for a continuation of the war. He had turned his back, as it were, on the European struggle, leaving that to France's ally, Austria, and had concentrated his efforts on the colonial conflict while increasing as much as possible his pressure on Spain to enter the war on France's side.[94] Ferdinand VI had become ill, and Choiseul, anticipating that King Carlos of the Two Sicilies would soon inherit the Spanish throne, had turned his attention to that monarch. He had instructed the Marquis d'Ossun, French minister in Naples, to explain the American situation to King Carlos and urge upon him the need of Spanish mediation in the war. Carlos had responded favorably, and his Neapolitan minister in London, Prince San Severino, had immediately proposed to England that the Anglo-French war be mediated, as already noted. While San Severino was negotiating with Pitt, news arrived of the fall of Quebec, and Carlos became all the more alarmed at this new and vast expansion of British colonial power. French ambassador d'Ossun reported, even before Carlos had arrived in Madrid to assume the Spanish throne, that Carlos strongly favored a union of Spain with France, although he was not yet ready to take a positive stand on a defensive alliance for the protection of the colonies of the two powers in the American hemisphere.[95]

Two weeks later, d'Ossun reported to Choiseul that Wall had expressed to him the opinion that England would not make a separate peace with France relative to America because of its responsibilities to Prussia; Wall also expressed a belief that England would not accept a Spanish mediation. D'Ossun also reported that Wall had offered Carlos III's mediation to England and had asked for a statement of the conditions on the basis of which England would make peace with France.[96]

The proposal for mediation had, in fact, been presented to Pitt on December 5. His Catholic Majesty, wrote d'Abreu, the Spanish minister in London, interested, as were France and England, in the affairs of America, "cannot witness with indifference the derangement that these conquests [of England] cause to the equilibrium established there by the

[93] D'Aubeterre to Bernis, Oct. 23, 1758, A.É., Corr. Pol., Espagne, 526: fols. 116–123.
[94] Renaut, Le Pacte de Famille, 13–23, et passim.
[95] D'Ossun to Choiseul, Dec. 3, 1759, A.É., Corr. Pol., Espagne, 526: fols. 144–149.
[96] D'Ossun to Choiseul, Dec. 15, 1759, A.É., Corr. Pol., Espagne, 526: fols. 203–214.

Treaty of Utrecht." He was instructed to say, however, that this remark sprang only from the vigilance of a sovereign "who must foresee future dangers, and whom the events in America touch . . . very closely, by reason of the close contiguity of the possessions of His Majesty with those in dispute [between England and France]." It was for this reason that His Catholic Majesty urgently wished that the Anglo-French disputes might be adjusted and that he offered his services with candor and the purest of intentions in the hope of bringing about this end.[97]

But Pitt was riding high and was in no mood to accept mediation. He assured d'Abreu that His Britannic Majesty was sincerely devoted to making peace, but he cited the Anglo-Prussian proposal for a congress of the belligerents for making peace as indicating the way in which England thought it ought to be done. As for the "equilibrium" supposedly established by the Peace of Utrecht, there was no such thing. It is evident, he said,

that it was never a question at that time [of the Treaty of Utrecht] of establishing in North America any balance between France and England. Besides, it was France's responsibility alone to see that the respective rights of the two nations in that part of the world should remain without change, in the condition in which they were established by the said Treaty, which so clearly defined them, and of which the shameful and perpetual infractions [by France] during a long period of years, were the unique cause of the present war between the two crowns.[98]

Pitt pointed out to d'Abreu the fact (as he saw it) that the King of England had scrupulously abstained from carrying his arms into any areas in which, by contiguity with Spanish territories, the presence of British arms might give the Spanish King reason to be in the least disturbed.[99] Finally, Pitt arrogantly gloated,

Since it has pleased Divine Providence to put into the hands [of his Britannic Majesty] certain gages for the security of his people, the King will gladly submit to the well-known candor and rectitude of His Catholic Majesty [the question] whether, after such a long sequence of wrongs [by France] and so many recent usurpations, this same *vigilance of the sovereign* that calls into action His Catholic Majesty's foresight relative to a distant future and with regard to dangers that are highly improbable, could permit His Majesty [of England] . . . to carry his moderation beyond what the protection of his subjects demands, at the risk of the return of the same evils that have so severely affected them.[100]

Thus did Pitt haughtily dismiss d'Abreu and his King on the question of mediation at the very moment when Carlos III was mounting the

---

[97] D'Abreu to Pitt, Dec. 5, 1759, B.M., Add. Mss., 6813: fols. 137–139.
[98] Pitt to d'Abreu, Dec. 13, 1759, B.M., Add. Mss., 6813: fols. 140–143.
[99] Pitt to d'Abreu, Dec. 13, 1759, B.M., Add. Mss., 6813: fols. 140–143.
[100] Pitt to d'Abreu, Dec. 13, 1759, B. M., Add. Mss., 6813: fols. 140–143.

Spanish throne. Pitt correctly guessed that the Spanish overture was prompted by "the French Ambassador's Infusions," and he expressed to Bristol his surprise that the gesture should have been made even before Carlos arrived at his capital. But he was made cautious by the apparent collusion of Carlos with the French, and he instructed Bristol to take pains to keep on good terms with Wall, if possible, and to watch the French ambassador while he and the British ministry adopted a conciliatory attitude toward d'Abreu in London.[101]

On the Spanish side, Carlos III's ardor for vigorous and aggressive action *vis-à-vis* England was distinctly dampened after his arrival in Madrid and his conferences with General Wall, who pointed out to him the realities of the bleak international situation. Not only that, he found Spain in a sad state of economic, political, and military demoralization, and he genuinely desired to build up his country before engaging in any risky international adventures.[102] The result was a distinct toning down of Spanish demands on England, and the Conde de Fuentes went to London to succeed d'Abreu, with instructions to continue Spanish demands for settlement of the old disputes between Spain and England over British smuggling and seizure of Spanish ships in America, the expansion of English logwood cutting in Central America, and the revived claim of Spain to a right to share the Newfoundland fisheries.[103]

It was at about this time that d'Ossun, having followed Carlos III to Madrid as the French ambassador at the King's request, renewed French diplomatic pressure upon Carlos to join the war on the side of France, while doing all he could to win the confidence of Wall. Carlos intended to hold the main authority in his realm and to rule with only the assistance of his ministers, d'Ossun reported, and was now so deeply concerned over the threat to Spanish possessions in America that seemed implicit in the British seizure of Quebec and the expansion of British power in the Caribbean that he was beginning to show again his inclination to take a firm stand against it. D'Ossun expressed the opinion that Spain might, at last, join France, but France must hold on to all that remained to it in America. "If we make our separate peace [with England], so much the better. If not, Spain will be in a condition to come to our assistance next year." [104] For the present, Carlos III had sent instructions to Fuentes to demand the British evacuation of the Mosquito Coast and Honduras; if the English refused, Carlos would send orders to eject them by force. It now appeared all too probable, to His Catholic Majesty, that if France and En-

---

[101] Pitt to Bristol, Dec. 14, 1759, B.M., Add. Mss. 6813: fols. 147–149.
[102] D'Ossun to Choiseul, Mar. 21, 1760, A.É., Corr., Pol., Espagne, 528: fols. 53–57.
[103] Newcastle, "An Account of My Conference with the Spanish Ambassador," July 3, 1760, L.C., B.M., Add. Mss., 32908: fols. 34–38.
[104] D'Ossun to Choiseul, Mar. 21, 1760, A.É., Corr. Pol., Espagne, 528: fols. 53–57; same to same, Apr. 21, 1760, A.É., Corr. Pol. Espagne, 528: fols. 172–180.

gland were to make a separate peace at the present juncture, Spain might have to face England in America alone.[105]

Still, Spain was not yet ready to move. Wall agreed with d'Ossun that England did not desire Spanish mediation but preferred to make peace with France directly; it had no intention of settling its disputes with Spain on terms acceptable to that country; once it had finished with France, it would be in a position to *"parler haute"* with Spain. For these reasons, Wall recommended that France make its peace with England quickly. That done, France could rebuild its navy and fortify its colonies; Spain could fortify its own colonies and supply them with troops, and strengthen its fleet. All these things done, the two nations could unite their forces to bring Great Britain to its senses. On the other hand, if Britain did not sincerely desire peace now, things would be different: Spain's proper course would be to come to France's aid. In any case, d'Ossun was convinced that Spain would not enter the war now, but was playing for time. This seemed to be borne out by Wall's approval of the negotiations of M. d'Affry at the Hague.[106]

The thing that most shocked d'Ossun was Wall's remark that Spain could not look with favor upon a division by France and England of the disputed islands in the Caribbean (St. Lucia, Dominica, St. Vincent, and Tobago). After all, these islands really belonged to Spain, said Wall, and always had, by right of prior discovery. Spain would cede two of these islands to France and two to England, as compensation for the evacuation of terrain "usurped" by the English. For these reasons, said Wall, France should not even discuss these islands with England without the knowledge of His Catholic Majesty! [107] D'Ossun was still further shocked by the Spanish King's remark, a little later, that Louisiana, too, really belonged to Spain, and that the French had established themselves there, not only without the knowledge of Spain, but despite the measures taken by Spain to prevent it. And the King had said, "after the peace I must arrange with France for Louisiana, perhaps by giving France something in exchange." D'Ossun suggested that Spain officially recognize French possession of the western part of Santo Domingo, but Carlos was not prepared to discuss the matter as yet.[108]

Meanwhile, the Spanish King, despite his indications of his conviction that Spain had claims against France as well as against England, was moving steadily toward the union that France so desperately desired. France and Spain are "natural allies" he said, with the same interests and the

[105] D'Ossun to Choiseul, Apr. 21, 1760, A.É., Corr. Pol., Espagne, 528: fols. 172–180.
[106] D'Ossun to Choiseul, Apr. 24, 1760, A.É., Corr. Pol., Espagne, 528: fols. 187–193.
[107] *Ibid.*
[108] D'Ossun to Choiseul, July 4, 1760, A.É., Corr. Pol., Espagne, 529: fols. 22–34.

same enemies, and were necessary to each other. And d'Ossun could report that the king and the court were *"très Bourbon."* [109]

This sort of talk made no deep impression upon Choiseul. He was surprised at His Catholic Majesty's intimation about Louisiana. He informed d'Ossun that France could not be interested in any such exchange and that it was absolutely necessary to drop the idea that Spain's interest in the "recovery" of Louisiana could even be discussed. [110]

Meanwhile, the negotiation of the Conde de Fuentes with Pitt was not prospering. On September 9, 1760, Fuentes presented to the English minister his memorials, setting forth the Spanish position relative to the points at issue, one relative to the logwood question, the other dealing with other matters. In the first, Fuentes demanded the complete evacuation of all the establishments made by the English in the logwood coasts of Central America. Honduras, Yucatán, and Campeche, he said, all belonged to Spain; the establishments of the English there were unjust and illegal. Spain had often driven out the English woodcutters, and the English had not protested. On the contrary, the Anglo-Spanish treaties of Utrecht (1713) and Madrid (1721) had stipulated that there should be no alienation of Spanish territories in America. The English settlements had been originally made, he said, without Spain's knowledge or consent; now, since the Peace of Aix-la-Chapelle, the English had actually expanded their establishments. In 1754, the English had been chased out of their new establishments in the Wallis River area, but, because of Spain's desire for peace, they had been allowed to return. [111] Thereupon, England had responded to Spain's generosity by building forts on Spanish soil to protect the woodcutters and had evaded an honest settlement of the problem. In view of the long history of arbitrary British occupation and refusal to negotiate a reasonable *modus operandi*, Fuentes now demanded complete evacuation by the English of all the areas occupied by the woodcutters in Honduras, the Mosquito Coast, Yucatán, and Campeche. Not only that, he demanded that England formally declare that it owned no establishment in those areas and that anyone attempting to create such an establishment would not be considered a British subject and would be left to the mercies of His Spanish Majesty and his agents! [112]

On other points, Fuentes was less peremptory but no less firm. [113] The right of Spain to participate in the Newfoundland fisheries, he told Newcastle, was a right, long established by treaties, that could not be infringed

[109] D'Ossun to Choiseul, July 4, 1760, A.É., Corr. Pol., Espagne, 529: fols. 22–34.
[110] Choiseul to d'Ossun, July 15, 1760, A.É., Corr. Pol., Espagne, 529: fols. 73–75.
[111] This was the incident that led to Enseñada's downfall. See above, Chapter XVIII.
[112] Fuentes to Pitt, memoir, Sept. 9, 1760, P.R.O., Chatham Mss., XCIII.
[113] Memorial [No. 2], Fuentes to Pitt, Sept. 9, 1760, P.R.O., Chatham Mss., XCIII.

upon by England, and he demanded that this right be recognized and that the Spanish ships seized there be promptly returned to Spain.[114] With regard to Spanish prizes seized by English privateers, Fuentes demanded a restoration of those prizes, as neutral ships, without the necessity of being tried in English admiralty courts; he cited the Treaty of Madrid of 1667 as providing that "free ships make free goods," a principle that would make Spanish ships immune from seizure.[115]

Pitt had no desire to drive Spain into the war. His reply to Fuentes, therefore, was deliberately mild but evasive. With regard to the logwood problem, Pitt said Britain was ready to satisfy Spain as to the expansion of the activities of the cutters and as to forts built, and to enter into an agreement with Spain with regard to the future cutting of wood. But he insisted upon England's "right" to cut wood under a series of treaties, and he refused to evacuate all the old British cutting stations on the logwood coasts. He demanded that the settlement of the problem be achieved by discussion and not merely by the arbitrary demands of Spain.[116]

On the point of Spain's right to a share of the fisheries, Pitt argued that the Newfoundland fishery was an English monopoly, except for certain specific rights granted the French by the Peace of Utrecht, and he took the position that any concession in this matter, so important for the British navy and economy and "a principle Basis of the Maritime Power of Great Britain," was an "utter impossibility." [117]

With regard to the Spanish prizes taken by English privateers, and Fuentes' appeal to the principle that "free ships make free goods" as set forth in the Treaty of Madrid of 1667, Pitt admitted that the principle was there and that the English Court of Prize Appeals was proceeding upon that basis. But he pointed out that in England the King's government could not constitutionally intervene in the processes of justice; Spanish ships really covered by the treaty of 1667 could count upon legal release. He took advantage of the opportunity to deliver a homily to Fuentes on the abuse of the principle by those who sold their neutral services to belligerents.[118]

Pitt worked himself into a high dudgeon over the part of Fuentes' memorial in which the Spanish ambassador said that a copy of his memorial had been communicated to France. Pitt protested "such an extraordinary communication to a court in open war with England, and which,

[114] Newcastle, "An Account of my Conference with the Spanish Ambassador," July 3, 1760, L.C., B.M., Add. Mss., 32908: fols. 36–38.
[115] Newcastle, "An Account of my Conference with the Spanish Ambassador, loc. cit. "Mr. Pitt's answer to the Spanish Memorial, delivered to the Conde de Fuentes, on the 1st September, 1760," printed in Thackeray, William Pitt, II, 487–491; D'Ossun to Choiseul, Aug. 4, 1760, A.É., Corr. Pol., Espagne, 529: fols. 123–131.
[116] Pitt to Bristol, Sept. 26, 1760, P.R.O., Chatham Mss., XCIII.
[117] Pitt to Bristol, Sept. 26, 1760, P.R.O., Chatham Mss., XCIII.
[118] "Mr. Pitt's answer to the Spanish Memorial, delivered to the Conde de Fuentes, on the 1st September, 1760," printed in Thackeray, William Pitt, II, 487–491.

besides, cannot, at any time, presume to meddle in Spain's claims upon us with regard to the fishery at Newfoundland . . ." [119] He then enlarged upon the incident in such a way as to accuse Spain of partiality toward France.[120]

Thus, Pitt gave a mixed reply to Spain's claims. With one hand he held out an olive branch; with the other he apparently sought to cut off Spain's obsequiousness to France with the ax of his anger over Spain's apparent appeal to France for sympathy and support.

Despite all Pitt's efforts to straddle the line between preserving Spanish neutrality and an arrogant assertion of the rightness of almost every one of England's actions, Anglo-Spanish relations with regard to America now reached a dramatic and paralyzing climax. In mid-September news was received in Europe that a Spanish expedition, ordered by Carlos III, had destroyed the English logwood settlements on the Campeche River. The Marquis d'Ossun reported to Choiseul that King Carlos had remarked to him, upon hearing the news, that he, the King, would also drive them out of the Rio Tinto and other areas, and that he would not allow them to return.[121] The King was hurt, said d'Ossun, by what he regarded as Pitt's cavalier treatment of Fuentes, and d'Ossun reported that, in general, Carlos knew Spain's interests were tied up with those of France; he hated Wall, who was too tolerant of English insults, and he was determined to oppose the English by force. Carlos wished only time to get ready. "I should not be surprized," wrote d'Ossun, "if there should be a rupture between Spain and England very soon. From that time on, His Catholic Majesty will seek, in his turn, the aid of France." [122] In October, news arrived in Europe of the fall of Montreal.[123]

It was at this moment that a crisis was reached in the relations between France and Spain relative to America and the war. D'Ossun told Carlos III that France, now, having failed to get the aid of Spain, must, perforce, make peace in any way possible. Yet Carlos knew, d'Ossun told him, how disastrous a British victory in America must be for Spain's colonies there, for it was to be expected that England might make a soft peace with France in order to be able to refuse Spain the satisfaction it had a right to demand from England in America, especially with regard to illicit commerce in Spanish dominions. England, he said, will try to separate

[119] "Réponse Verbale faite à Mons.ʳ Le Comte de Fuentes par Mons.ʳ Pitt, ce 16ᵉ Sept.ʳᵉ 1760," P.R.O., Chatham Mss., XCIII. See also, *Chatham Corr.*, II, 69 n.

[120] D'Ossun to Choiseul, July 4, 1760, A.É., Corr. Pol., Espagne, 529: fols. 22–34.

[121] D'Ossun to Choiseul, Sept. 15, 1760, A.É., Corr. Pol., Espagne, 529: fols. 243–249.

[122] D'Ossun to Choiseul, Oct. 13, 1760, A.É., Corr. Pol., Espagne, 530: fols. 49–63. See also, same to same, Sept. 28, 1760, *ibid.*, 529: fols. 293–299; same to same, Oct. 6, 1760, *ibid.*, 530: fols. 11–25.

[123] Choiseul to d'Ossun, Oct. 13, 1760, A.É., Corr. Pol., Espagne, 530: fol. 46.

Spain from France and prevent their union now in order to be able to fall upon Spain separately later on. Carlos replied that he realized that the salvation of both France and Spain depended upon their close union. Louis XIV had been right in believing that the family union of the Bourbons of France and Spain should guarantee the equilibrium of Europe. Yes, replied d'Ossun, especially with regard to the colonies in America and to mutual interests in Italy.[124]

The way now seemed clear for the formation of a Franco-Spanish alliance, and d'Ossun at once presented a "project," setting forth the amount and kinds of aid the two prospective allies would furnish in their common war against England.[125] It was to be expected that the English would seize Louisiana; in order to forestall an English invasion of Mexico, which d'Ossun anticipated, the French minister proposed a joint invasion of one or more of the British West Indian islands.[126]

Wall, always cautious, demanded time to reflect on this proposal, which led d'Ossun to suspect that Wall was representing France to Carlos III as already beaten and was cautioning the King not to risk his all in the interest of a cause that was already lost. But the Spanish King was ready; he was convinced, moreover, that if Spain did not help France out of its present desperate straits and stop England, that country would certainly fall upon Spain's empire immediately after France was disposed of. For Carlos, the survival of Spain's colonial empire depended upon going to France's rescue as soon as possible. Unfortunately, Spain itself was not yet ready and must have time to prepare. D'Ossun accepted Carlos's insistence upon delay and promised that France would manage to stall England off for long enough to give Spain the necessary time; but he blamed Wall and the finance minister, Julián de Arriaga, for His Catholic Majesty's slowness.[127]

Both Choiseul and d'Ossun were now convinced that the moment had arrived when Spain could be brought to sign an alliance with France. In January, 1761, Choiseul authorized d'Ossun formally to propose to the Spanish government two treaties, one a treaty of commerce, the other a treaty of alliance.[128] When the ambassador broached this proposal to Wall, the Spanish minister received it coolly; he reacted more vigorously to d'Ossun's remarks about the conduct of the English, which Wall described as "completely insupportable." [129] His Catholic Majesty was more enthu-

---

[124] D'Ossun to Choiseul, Oct. 17, 1760, A.É., Corr. Pol., Espagne, 530: fols. 64–82.
[125] D'Ossun to Choiseul, Oct. 17, 1760, A.É., Corr. Pol., Espagne, 530: fols. 64–82.
[126] D'Ossun to Choiseul, Oct. 23, 1760, A.É., Corr. Pol., Espagne, 530: fols. 109–119; same to same, Oct. 30, 1760, ibid., 530: fols. 136–147.
[127] D'Ossun to Choiseul, Nov. 28, 1760, A.É., Corr. Pol., Espagne, 530: fols. 242–254.
[128] Recueil des Insts., XII bis, Espagne III, 1722–93, 340–341.
[129] D'Ossun to Choiseul, Feb. 9, 1761, A.É., Corr. Pol., Espagne, 531: fols. 148–158.

siastic. He accepted the idea of two treaties, both to be made on the basis of perfect equality between the two nations. He asked d'Ossun for further explanations and an outline of the proposed provisions.[130]

Choiseul replied that d'Ossun should propose, with regard to the alliance, that it be both defensive and offensive, that the two countries agree mutually to guarantee each other's possessions everywhere, whether in Europe or in any other part of the world, both those presently held and those they might possess after the war. As for the treaty of commerce, it should embody the principles of equality and reciprocity.[131] Still, Carlos III was cautious. He suspected that France was on the point ot making peace with England, and he thought it wise to limit his engagement to a simple defensive treaty. He also drew back from allying himself with France's continental allies. In any case, the treaty of commerce would require a long time and much negotiation; therefore, he proposed that it be postponed, to which d'Ossun agreed.[132] Finally, in May, Choiseul drew up a double project: one part was for a Bourbon Family Compact, to cover the interests of all the rulers belonging to that family; the other part was to be a defensive military treaty between France and Spain, to take effect if Spain should go to war with England.[133] This double proposal was accepted by Spain; it remained only to work out the details.

Those details were worked out quickly, and the treaty called the Third Bourbon Family Compact was signed in Paris for Spain by the Marqués de Grimaldi, Spanish ambassador to France, and, for France, by the Duc de Choiseul, French foreign minister, on August 15, 1761. It was assumed that the Duke of Parma, brother of Carlos III, and the King of the Two Sicilies, Carlos's son, would also join in this family alliance.[134]

The basic principle expressed in the treaty, as signed, was that "whoever attacks one crown attacks the other." It provided that the two Kings mutually guaranteed their possessions, in whatever part of the world. Both signatories also extended the same guarantee to the King of the Two Sicilies and to the Infante Don Felipe, now Duke of Parma, provided those two members of the Bourbon family extended the same guarantee to France and Spain (France also agreed not to ask Spanish aid for its wars in northern Europe). Each signatory promised to make no separate peace without the consent of the other, and they agreed that, at the making of peace, the losses of one in the common cause would be compensated by

---

[130] D'Ossun to Choiseul, Feb. 9, 1761, A.É., Corr. Pol., Espagne, 531: fols. 148–158.

[131] Choiseul to d'Ossun, Mar. 3, 1761, A.É., Corr. Pol., Espagne, 531: fols. 280–281.

[132] D'Ossun to Choiseul, Mar. 15, 1761, A.É., Corr. Pol., Espagne, 531: fols. 345–352.

[133] *Recueil des Insts.*, XII bis, *Espagne*, III, 1722–93, 340–341. See also, Renaut, *Le Pacte de Famille et l'Amérique*, 29 ff.

[134] Cantillo, ed., *Tratados*, 468–473.

the gains of the other, "in such fashion that, in the operations of the war and in the making of the peace, the two monarchies of Spain and France, in all the extension of their dominions, are to be considered and are to proceed as though they formed one sole and single power." To cement further the "family" ties between France and Spain, the old law for foreigners (*droit d'aubaine*) was to be lifted for the citizens of each living in the territory fo the other; the citizens of one living in the territory of the other (in Europe) were to enjoy all the immunities and privileges of the citizens of the host country; their flags were to be treated with the same respect and honor; subjects of one living in the territory of the other were to pay the same taxes as native citizens; no third nation was to enjoy privileges in either country greater than those mutually guaranteed by this treaty; each signatory was to enjoy in the territory of the other full most-favored-nation treatment.[135]

While it was expected that Spain would now enter the war against England, the Duc de Choiseul still had hopes that his direct negotiations with England, begun in the spring of 1761, might bring peace and that Spanish participation might not be necessary. Thus it came about that it was only after those negotiations had obviously failed and England turned upon Spain that Spain actually entered the war, early in January, 1762.

4. The Pitt-Choiseul Negotiations of 1761

In the spring of 1761 the Duc de Choiseul was playing a three-cornered game. He desired peace with England, but his engagements to Vienna forestalled his impulse to make a separate peace that might involve the prerequisite evacuation of the lands of England's ally, Prussia. He saw in Spanish mediation a way to peace, or, failing that, the entrance of Spain into the war on the side of France; but his chief desire was peace, and he would use the Spanish menace only in case everything else failed. Meanwhile, he would keep the Spanish negotiations alive. Because he was absolutely convinced of the futility of the idea of a general congress for the settlement of the colonial and maritime conflict with England, he must negotiate for Austria's permission to settle the English quarrel separately; for peace, to be made at all, must first be made with England. Thus it was that, early in 1761, while continuing his negotiations with Spain, Choiseul entered upon negotiations with Austria and Russia looking toward a joint move for peace, a necessary part of which would be a preliminary arrangement between the two chief protagonists, France and England.

For France, peace was a dire necessity. The country was in desperate financial straits, and the year 1760 had added to the number of colonial

[135] Cantillo, ed., *Tratados*, 468–473.

disasters: a series of victories in India all but completed the English conquest there; the fall of Montreal in September gave England all of Canada;
while the tide of war in Germany had turned—at Warburg, Liegnitz,
and Torgau. Nevertheless, France would not negotiate as a completely
beaten country but as one which had a strong potential ally in Spain.
France's allies, too, were opposed to peace: Maria Theresa was determined
that Frederick must be completely and forever crushed. Choiseul's negotiations with Vienna and St. Petersburg were of the stormiest, therefore, and
it was only with the greatest difficulty and by the threat of abandoning
them altogether that he won their collaboration in a joint declaration
for peace—a sort of belated acceptance of the Anglo-Prussian declaration
of November 25, 1759.[136]

The joint declaration of the allies, dated March 26, 1761, was presented
to the British ministry by Prince Galitzin, Russian ambassador at London.
The declaration proposed that all the belligerents send plenipotentiaries
to a congress to be held at Augsburg, for the purpose of making peace.[137]
But with the tacit recognition of all the belligerents that the success of
the congress must depend upon a preliminary agreement between France
and Great Britain, Choiseul sent with the declaraton a note and a personal
letter to Pitt, proposing that the two countries proceed directly to a settlement of their private disputes before the opening of the congress. As a
basis for the negotiations, Choiseul proposed the principle of *uti possidetis*, that is, that each side keep whatever territories it then possessed by
right of conquest, to be applied as of May 1 in Europe, July 1 in America
and Africa, and September 1 in the East Indies.[138]

Great Britain accepted the proposal for a congress for itself and Prussia
on April 3 [139] and proceeded to name plenipotentiaries.[140] But Choiseul's
plan for an Anglo-French peace had to be debated by the cabinet before
direct negotiations could proceed. To begin with, the British ministry was
divided within itself, and its members were in a sensitive mood over a
recent shake-up that had placed the Earl of Bute in the office of the
secretary of state for the Northern Department as a teammate of the
fractious Pitt.[141] Most of the ministers, particularly Newcastle, favored
peace and were disposed to proceed; but Pitt was hesitant. While in a sense
desirous of peace, he had on foot plans for a series of campaigns which
he hoped to push to a successful conclusion, and, in March, he had inter-

---

[136] Waddington, *La guerre de sept ans*, IV, 481–496; cf. Williams, *The Life of
William Pitt, Earl of Chatham*, II, 80.

[137] B.M., Add. Mss., 32921: fols. 76–77.

[138] B.M., Add. Mss., 6819: fols. 37, 39–40.

[139] B.M., Add. Mss., 6819: fols. 83–84.

[140] Thackeray, *William Pitt*, I, 505, II, 516–517.

[141] *Com. Hist. Brit. Emp.*, I, 488–489. John Stuart, third Earl of Bute, the favorite
of George III, had succeeded Holdernesse as secretary of state for the Northern Department on March 25.

cepted several letters exchanged by the Spanish ambassadors in London and Paris that informed him of Choiseul's negotiations for an alliance with Spain.[142] To accept the dates suggested by Choiseul for the application of the *uti possidetis* principle would rob him of the fruits of his expected military successes, and his knowledge of Choiseul's parallel negotiations with Spain apparently made him suspicious of that minister's good faith, a suspicion that probably was chiefly responsible for the eventual failure of the negotiations.[143] But the sentiment for peace was too strong to be opposed, and Pitt himself believed Choiseul to be more disposed to make peace than to continue the war.[144] His reply to the French minister was, therefore, couched in friendly terms. He accepted the principle of *uti possidetis*; but because of the possibility of delays in the negotiations, and, probably, with one eye on his projected campaigns, he declined the dates suggested by Choiseul for the application of the principle and proposed that it be applied only with reference to the date of the anticipated treaty. He agreed to Choiseul's proposed exchange of agents for the further conduct of the negotiations and named Hans Stanley as British representative in Paris. He made it perfectly clear, however, that the interests of his Prussian ally would be considered at every stage of the discussions.[145]

The negotiations were now assured. Most of the British ministers were optimistic as to the outcome and set about clarifying their ideas as to what the peace should include. Pitt was apparently determined to retain Canada and to exclude France from the Newfoundland fisheries. Beyond this, his ideas seem to have been vague.[146] In true mercantilistic fashion he thought of North America as a source of raw materials for Great Britain and as a market for its products, and of the fishery as the foundation of British naval power. Thus his long-range view of the national interest impelled him to demand a settlement that would guarantee to Great Britain not only all Canada, both for its economic value and for the security of British North America, but also a monopoly of the fishery as a nursery for the British marine.[147] On both these points he was opposed by the peace advocates among the followers of Newcastle and the Duke of Bedford, who argued that it would be a mistake to ask so much of France. The removal of the French from Canada, they said, would tend to encourage the continental colonies in their growing mood of "independency"; and the claim of Britain to a monopoly of the fishery in the open sea was both untenable

[142] P.R.O., Chatham Mss. XCIII; *Chatham Corr.*, II, 92–93.
[143] Cf. Corbett, *op. cit.*, II, 142–143, 155; cf. also Ruville, *William Pitt, Earl of Chatham*, II, 365.
[144] L.C., B.M., Add. Mss., 32921: fol. 272.
[145] Pitt to Choiseul, Apr. 8, 1761, and accompanying note, P.R.O., Chatham Mss., LXXXV; *Chatham Corr.*, II, 116–119.
[146] L.C., B.M., Add. Mss., 32921: fol. 272.
[147] L.C., B.M., Add. Mss., 32921: fols. 340, 381; *ibid.*, 32922: fols. 15–21; cf. Williams, *op. cit.*, II, 82–83.

under international law and certain to arouse the combined opposition of the other maritime nations, particularly Spain.[148]

Choiseul's reply to Pitt, on April 19, accepted the British reservation regarding Prussia but reiterated the French desire for putting the "given periods" for the application of *uti possidetis* at the dates already suggested. Meanwhile, he notified Pitt of the appointment of François de Bussy as French agent for the negotiations and invited the British minister to reciprocate.[149] Pitt, in his turn, then notified Choiseul of the appointment of Hans Stanley and proposed that the question of the given periods be made a matter of negotiation, along with the question of the compensation, if any, for the conquered territories to be ceded by the respective belligerents.[150] There remained only the business of exchanging agents, which was accomplished about the middle of May.

Thus the negotiations got under way, but it was not without the attendance of evil omens. Austria and Russia were skeptical and critical,[151] and Spain was becoming increasingly interested. Choiseul, conscious of the difficulties surrounding him and rendered suspicious of British intentions by the vagueness of Pitt's replies,[152] which had begun earlier, pursued his Spanish negotiations with as much avidity as though they were his sole diplomatic objective.

Choiseul humored Spain, hoping to use that country as a makeweight in the rectification of France's balance with England. He suggested that if England refused the overtures which were to be made, Spain might bring about the making of an advantageous settlement by threatening to join forces against that country which refused to accept reasonable terms.[153] In fact, the Marquis d'Ossun, in Madrid, was already far advanced toward the completion of the proposed offensive and defensive alliance, as already related.[154] At the moment, with the announcement of the English negotiations, His Catholic Majesty thought it prudent to make the proposed alliance defensive only, as France would need several years of rest and recuperation before undertaking a new struggle with England.[155]

Thus far had Choiseul's game with Spain proceeded when Bussy went to London. Copies of the documents connected with the negotiations had been sent to the Spanish court promptly;[156] Bussy was instructed to keep the Spanish ambassador in London informed of every step in the negotia-

[148] L.C., B.M., Add. Mss., 32921: fols. 340, 381; *ibid.*, 32922: fols. 449–451.
[149] Thackeray, William Pitt, II, 514–516.
[150] Thackeray, *William Pitt*, II, 514–515, 517–518.
[151] A.É., Corr. Pol., Espagne, 532: fol. 221; C.A.O., A.É., Corr. Pol., Ang., 443: fol. 99; Waddington, *La guerre de sept ans*, IV, 55 ff.
[152] A.É., Corr. Pol., Espagne, 532: fol. 221.
[153] A.É., Corr. Pol., Espagne, 531: fols. 226–228.
[154] A.É., Corr. Pol., Espagne, 531: fol. 325.
[155] A.É., Corr. Pol., Espagne, 532: fols. 7–18.
[156] A.É., Corr. Pol., Espagne, 531: fols. 392–393; Waddington, *La guerre de sept ans*, IV, 514.

tions and to ask his counsel on all important questions. Choiseul doubted whether Pitt would really make peace, and, while he was willing to limit the proposed Family Compact to one of defensive purposes, he had no intention of throwing away his Spanish trump just on the chance that he might be wrong about the British minister. To Bussy he said that, if Great Britain were really disposed to make peace, France would make no offensive alliance against it; and he probably meant what he said.[157] But he directed d'Ossun to ask Wall directly whether, should England not make peace by May 1, 1762, Spain would declare war on the side of France.[158] Should the Spanish answer be in the affirmative, France would be prepared for eventualities, whether British action directed the course of events toward peace or toward war.

Meanwhile, Bussy and Stanley had gone to their posts late in May. As it was expected that the major part of the negotiations would take place in London, the British agent's instructions, dated May 18, 1761, were brief and noncommittal. He was told to listen to any proposals France might present for making effective the principle of *uti possidetis*; he might negotiate as to the dates to be set for the application of this principle. He was to say that Great Britain agreed to a separate peace, but he was to inform the French minister plainly that Great Britain would continue to support Prussia in the German war.[159]

Bussy, on the other hand, coming as he did from the nation which had proposed the negotiations, was more particularly instructed as to the definite proposals he should make. Recognizing that France had little with which to bargain, Choiseul offered to give up Minorca in return for Guadelupe, St. Lucia, Tobago, Marie-Galante, and the island of Gorée off the coast of Africa. The influence of the Spanish game could be seen in Choiseul's demand that Great Britain secure the acquiescence of Spain— who had, itself, always claimed these West Indian islands—in the recognition of France's title to them. Acadia, "in its entirety," was to be ceded to England; but Canada, entirely or in part, and Cape Breton were to be restored to France in consideration for the restoration of other territory won by French armies from Hanover and Prussia.[160] Bussy was instructed to keep in close touch with the Spanish ambassador and to urge upon the British minister, if necessary, the threat of a war with Spain; but if Pitt should prove to be reasonable Bussy was not to forget that the first object of his mission was peace, and that "it can only be when we lose hope [of success in the negotiations], that we shall be obliged to give ourselves up to the ideas of Spain." [161]

[157] Waddington, *La guerre de sept ans*, IV, 514–515.
[158] A.É., Corr. Pol., Espagne, 532: fols. 221, 334–338.
[159] Waddington, *La guerre de sept ans*, I, 506–508.
[160] C.A.O., A.É., Corr. Pol., Ang., 448: fol. 119.
[161] Quoted in Waddington, *La guerre de sept ans*, IV, 515–516.

The conversations in London and Paris began early in June. Stanley was well received, generously entertained, and convinced of Choiseul's determination to make peace. Bussy was not so devoted to peace as his master and adopted an almost preemptory tone, despite his mortal terror of Pitt. Early exchanges turned upon the "given periods" for the application of the principle of *uti possidetis* and the relations to be maintained between Great Britain and France and their respective allies.[162] On June 17, after news had arrived that Belle Ile, off the mouth of the Loire River, in France, had fallen to Commodore Keppel, Choiseul submitted to Stanley a memorandum expressing the minister's ideas as to the colonial settlement.[163] In it he now proposed that Guadelupe, Marie-Galante, and Gorée be returned to France in exchange for Minorca. The islands of St. Lucia and Tobago, which, according to Bussy's first instructions were to have been included in the cluster of islands to be given for Minorca, were not mentioned. Choiseul now proposed, also, to cede all Canada to Great Britain, with its southern limits to be fixed at the watershed between the lakes and the Ohio. He asked, however, that the island of Cape Breton be left to France. He would agree never to fortify it, but, although Stanley discouraged him, he persisted in demanding the island for French fishermen.[164] As a consideration for the cession of Canada, he demanded a continuation of the French right to the cod-fishery as established by the Treaty of Utrecht. France would evacuate the territories of Great Britain's allies in Germany. Nothing was said about Spain's title to the islands in the West Indies.[165]

This set of proposals, which Choiseul hoped would be "the foundation of a treaty," [166] split the British cabinet. All the ministers were agreed that the island of Cape Breton could not again be returned to France and that "all Canada" must be insisted upon. On the question of the fisheries, Pitt, representing the interests of the British mercantile world, differed widely from his colleagues, who were more moderate. He desired never again to surrender any part of this source of British wealth to France or any other nation and was ready to break off negotiations if France insisted upon it. He finally agreed to distinguish between the St. Lawrence fisheries and the Newfoundland or open-sea fisheries and to offer France the latter in return

[162] Thackeray, *William Pitt*, I, 514–537, II, 523, 525; *Chatham Corr.*, II, 124–128.
[163] Memorandum, June 17, 1761, P.R.O., Chatham Mss. LXXXV.
[164] Thackeray, *William Pitt*, I, 540–541.
[165] Memorandum, June 17, 1761, P.R.O., Chatham Mss. LXXXV. As a matter of fact, the reference to the Spanish title in Bussy's instructions was not intended really to be called to the attention of England. Choiseul confessed to Bussy in a private letter a little later: "I know very well that we are masters of St. Lucia and Tobago; and in your instructions you will see that I spoke of these islands, which have been considered neutral in other countries, only to establish the fact of our possession, and to bind our negotiation to Spain, in case, the peace failing, that liaison should become necessary to us" (C.A.O., A.É., Corr. Pol., Ang., 443: fol. 220).
[166] Thackeray, *William Pitt*, I, 540–541.

for some important compensation, such as, perhaps, the demolition of the fortifications at Dunkirk.[167]

This being agreed, Pitt drew up a set of instructions which, in part, amounted to an ultimatum. The document expressed the desires of the cabinet, but it was couched in terms which even Pitt's colleagues deprecated as being offensive and ill calculated to promote good feeling between the two courts.[168] In the first place, the territories of Great Britain's German allies, which belonged to neither France nor England, were ruled out of the discussion as subjects for exchanges between those two nations. With regard to the cession of Canada, Pitt rejected Choiseul's "new limits" in the Ohio country. To accept them, he said, would be "to shorten thereby the extent of Canada, and to lengthen the boundaries of Louisiana," as also to establish the principle "that all which is not Canada is Louisiana; whereby all the intermediate nations and countries, the true barrier to each province would be given up to France." [169] As he explained to Bussy, the course of the Ohio did not belong to France at all but was part of Virginia; nevertheless, he was willing to leave the territory between the Ohio and the mountains uninhabited, provided only that the Virginia title were recognized.[170]

Pitt likewise rejected the "mutilation" of Canada by the amputation of Cape Breton. Acadia, which belonged to England by prior right, the whole of Canada, and the Gulf of St. Lawrence fishery, one and all came within the *uti possidetis* arrangement, he maintained, and must be surrendered on the basis of that principle. As for the Newfoundland fishery, said Pitt, the Treaty of Utrecht was in force no longer; therefore, the French demand for a restoration of privileges under that treaty might be granted only in return for some important concession. Discussion of this proposal he postponed until the renewal of the other terms of that treaty, particularly those with regard to the fortifications at Dunkirk, should come to be discussed. For Minorca, instead of the constellation of islands demanded by Choiseul, Pitt offered Belle Ile. Guadeloupe and Marie-Galante he made the price of French evacuation of the territory of England's allies in Germany.[171]

Pitt specified the following points as essential: (1) the cession of Canada "without new limits," Cape Breton, and the other islands in the Gulf of St. Lawrence, together with the St. Lawrence fishery; (2) the cession of Senegal, which had not appeared in Choiseul's memorandum, and the island of Gorée; (3) the demolition of the fortifications at Dunkirk; (4) the evacuation of the "Neutral Islands," or their division between France

[167] L.C., B.M., Add. Mss., 32924: fols. 311–322; cf. Williams, *Life of William Pitt*, II, 92–93, and Ruville, *William Pitt*, II, 877.
[168] L.C., B.M., Add. Mss., 32924: fol. 320.
[169] Thackeray, *William Pitt*, I, 545.
[170] Pease, *Anglo-French Boundary Disputes*, 319.
[171] Thackeray, *William Pitt*, I, 543–547.

and England; (5) the restoration of Minorca and Benkulen (on the island of Sumatra); (6) the evacuation of the territories of England's allies in Germany, and, specifically, of Hesse, Brunswick, Wesel, and Hanover, as also those parts of Prussia occupied by French armies. These points expressed what Pitt called the unalterable intention of His Britannic Majesty; others were left for Stanley to negotiate with Choiseul.[172] The statement amounted, in effect, to a settlement dictated to the vanquished by their vanquisher and it could not fail to arouse the indignation of the French court.[173]

The extreme tone and vigor of Pitt's reply to Choiseul's offer can hardly be explained unless they had their source in his suspicions of a French liaison with Spain. For his distrust, aroused by the interception of the letters between Fuentes and Grimaldi, had not abated; on the contrary, it had apparently been increased by the differing tones of Bussy and his master and by Stanley's reports of the adverse pressure being exerted upon Choiseul by the ambassadors of Austria and Spain.[174] In any case, France was not as desperate as Pitt seemed to assume, and this communication seems to have convinced Choiseul that England was not yet ready to make peace. He decided to expose his Spanish cards, in the hope either that Pitt would grow milder in the face of the Spanish threat, or that France, with a new ally at sea, might be able to recoup some of its losses. In this he shared the revulsion of feeling that was now general in the French court,[175] and he wrote to Bussy that, henceforth, his policy would be to cultivate the Spanish alliance and delay peace negotiations long enough to prevent further military action that summer and to give Spain time to prepare. "It will be August," he said, "before they can answer my note: to their answer I shall have to reply in my turn, and I shall do so in such a way as to provoke another answer from England. This will bring us to September, when it will be too late for attempts on our coast." [176]

Choiseul's reply to Stanley was therefore of a temporizing nature. In conference he told Stanley that he could turn the German territories to good advantage elsewhere, should Pitt persist in refusing to consider them legitimate material for exchanges; and this statement was of such good effect that Stanley was convinced that Austria, and perhaps Spain, had made some effort to induce France to continue the war. Nevertheless, Choiseul apparently took Pitt's equivocal suggestion of a restitution of Guadelupe as an offer of that island as compensation for the French evacuation of the Germanies and indicated that he might agree on that

[172] Thackeray, William Pitt, I, 547–549.
[173] Cf. Ruville, William Pitt., II, 378–379.
[174] Thackeray, William Pitt, I, 500, 540, 560–562; II, 525, 526; cf. Corbett, England in the Seven Years War. II, 173.
[175] Von Ruville, William Pitt, II, 382.
[176] Quoted in Williams, Life of William Pitt, II, 93.

basis. Canada, Choiseul agreed, should be ceded "undismembered"; but because he believed strongly in the value of the cod-fishery to France, he fought hard for Cape Breton, almost to the point, as Stanley thought, of breaking off the negotiations; and he finally suggested that England might name some port which would take the place of Louisbourg as a shelter for French vessels engaged in the open-sea fishery.[177] Choiseul accepted the disposition of the "Neutral Islands" proposed by Pitt, giving preference to a division between France and England. With regard to India, Stanley thought Choiseul would make no trouble if the other questions were successfully adjusted and reported that the minister agreed to the restitution of Minorca and Senegal. Choiseul also insisted upon the return of Gorée and displayed anger at Pitt's demand for it. Both the French slave trade and the "sugar islands" dependent upon that trade, he said, would suffer if the French were left with only that one small slave-trading station which would then remain to them on the African coast. He hinted, however, that, if given a slave station elsewhere, France would not insist upon retaining Gorée.[178]

The conversations reported in these dispatches of July 1 and July 5 were of an informal nature and did not constitute an official reply to Pitt's instructions to Stanley. They did indicate, however, that Choiseul was far from accepting the *sine qua non* points in Pitt's demands. Without definitely rejecting those demands, Choiseul had parried them so skillfully as to make further discussion necessary. Meanwhile, he clearly intimated to Stanley that if England remained inflexible in its demands, France would continue the war and, in that case, would have the aid of Spain. Stanley rejected Choiseul's suggestion that Spain be asked to guarantee the peace and his hint of Spanish aid to France as an empty threat made to force England to soften its demands. He admitted the possibility that Spain might come to France's aid, but he scoffed at the idea of France fighting to settle Spain's quarrel. "She who acquiesces in the loss of Canada, will not soon enter into a war for the logwood of Honduras." [179]

Choiseul's warning was no idle threat. As he explained to Bussy, there

---

[177] Choiseul thought little of the old de la Galissonnière assumption that Canada and Louisiana would be lost if the English were allowed to go beyond the mountains. "Even though one were to admit," he wrote, "as I do not admit, that Canada is the highroad to Louisiana, which pays no profit to France; and even though one admits that a highroad might be eight hundred leagues long, and that a maritime power like England would attack Louisiana by land and by traversing these eight hundred leagues, I would still wager that the codfishery in the Gulf of St. Lawrence is worth infinitely more for the realm of France than Canada and Louisiana" (Pease, *Anglo-French Boundary Disputes*, 338). This explains why Choiseul gave up Canada and the interior so easily and struggled so persistently to preserve a foothold for French fishermen in the Gulf of St. Lawrence.

[178] B.M., Add. Mss., 36798: fols. 112–123.

[179] Quoted in Thackeray, *William Pitt*, II, 544; B.M., Add Mss., 36798: fols. 119, 122, 127.

were three points with regard to which France would rather continue the war than surrender. The first was the question of an island or port in the Gulf of St. Lawrence to serve as a haven, or *abri*, for French fishing ships. Even if Great Britain ceded Cape Breton, Ile St. Jean (Prince Edward Island), the Island of Canso, or the port of Canso on the Acadian peninsula, and even if it were willing to cede Newfoundland in exchange for French Guiana and its port of Cayenne, in no case would France make peace without some provision being made for such a haven. Choiseul's second point was his demand for Gorée or some other slave station on the coast of Africa, and the third was his refusal to agree to the demolition of the fortifications at Dunkirk. He was willing to negotiate as to terms on these last two points, but he was adamant upon the general principles involved.[180] The "neutral islands," Choiseul indicated to Bussy, constituted another point which made for trouble. Spain claimed these islands, and France could not make any agreement as to their final disposition unless Spain concurred in it.[181]

Bussy told Pitt of the three points on which his master would never consent to yield, only to find the British minister obstinately intransigent on every one of them. Pitt disavowed Stanley's expressed concession of the St. Lawrence and Newfoundland fisheries as due to Stanley's misunderstanding of his instructions, and frankly gave Bussy to understand that his own personal conviction was that France should be excluded from the fishery entirely. Bussy's hint that France would cede Guiana for Newfoundland he dismissed with the remark that the British were a northern people and would not desire establishments so far south. Pitt was equally immovable on the cession of Gorée and the demolition of Dunkirk. When Bussy spoke of the Spanish title and of his master's feeling that he must conduct the negotiations relative to the "Neutral Islands" with Spain as a fellow negotiator, Pitt exploded. "Oh, my God," he cried, "I certainly hope that will not happen. Spain has nothing to do with the negotiations between these two courts, and England will never permit her to be admitted to them!" [182] Bussy would have despaired of the negotiations, then and there,

[180] C.A.O., A.É., Corr. Pol., Ang., 443: fols. 324–327.
[181] C.A.O., A.É., Corr. Pol., Ang., 443: fol. 327. As a matter of fact, Choiseul, in his negotiation of the Family Compact, was at this moment proposing that an article ceding these islands to France be included in the proposed Franco-Spanish treaty (A.É., Corr. Pol., Espagne, 533: fols. 34–37). When this idea was presented to Wall by d'Ossun, the Spanish minister indicated a willingness to acknowledge France's title both to the islands and to Louisiana, but he suggested, in his turn, that the proposed treaty ought also to contain a provision that the boundary between Louisiana and Mexico should be definitely settled by a joint commission (A.É., Corr. Pol., Espagne, 533: fols. 122–128). Shortly afterward, Wall informed the English ambassador that His Catholic Majesty, at last despairing of obtaining justice at the hands of Great Britain, had placed his interests in the hands of France (L.C., B.M., Add. Mss., 32926: fol. 4; A.É., Corr. Pol., Espagne, 533: fols. 137–141).
[182] C.A.O., A.É., Corr. Pol., Ang., 443: fols. 334–347.

had he not believed Pitt would be overruled on all these points by his cabinet's peace party led by Bute. In this belief he was, as events were to show, largely justified.[183]

These conversations in Paris and London indicated the direction of French policy and the willingness of France to identify the Spanish cause with its own. Their net effect was to increase the stiffness of Spain toward Great Britain, to strengthen the conviction in Choiseul's mind that Pitt would not make a reasonable peace, and to increase Pitt's suspicions of Choiseul. That minister, indeed, was willing to present the Spanish case, if it became absolutely necessary, for he probably hoped England would accept it. If so, it would increase French prestige at Madrid; if not, it would inevitably draw Spain closer to a defensive union with France. He therefore instructed Bussy to present the Spanish case if it should seem desirable after consultation with the Spanish ambassador.[184]

Choiseul's formal reply to Pitt's demands was presented in a memorial dated July 13, which was delivered by Bussy on July 20. As both Stanley and Bussy had already anticipated, there were three points on which Choiseul refused to budge. He was willing to cede Canada with the boundaries it had had while owned by France, but with four reservations for the protection of the French inhabitants.[185] As a consideration for this cession, France would expect England to renew France's fishing privileges on the Banks of Newfoundland as provided for in the Treaty of Utrecht, with Cape Breton as a base and shelter for the French fishermen. Choiseul offered England its choice of either Senegal or Gorée but insisted that it be simply one or the other. Dunkirk was not mentioned. As for the "Neutral Islands," France was willing to let Dominica and St. Vincent continue to remain neutral and to divide the other two by giving Tobago to England and keeping St. Lucia. Bussy was instructed to say that this provision could have effect only upon the prior settlement of His Catholic Majesty's dis-

---

[183] C.A.O., A.É., Corr. Pol., Ang., 443: fol. 343.

[184] D'Ossun reported it to be his conviction that, in view of the ease with which the Anglo-Spanish disputes could be settled, England would not risk a new war with Spain over them, but that their successful conclusion under the auspices of France would tremendously increase French prestige at Madrid (A.É., Corr. Pol., Espagne, 533: fols. 203–209).

[185] First, the free exercise of the Roman Catholic religion; second, the freedom of the inhabitants to retire with their possessions to French territory; third, the delimitation of boundaries for Canada which would leave no room for future quibbling; fourth, the right to dry fish on the shores of Newfoundland (Thackeray, William Pitt, II, 547–548). With regard to the boundaries between Louisiana and the English territories, old and new, Choiseul sent Bussy a note on the boundaries of Louisiana, which vaguely defined that province as including Mobile and the valleys of the Alabama and the Coosa, the valley of the Tennessee up to the Appalachian Mountains, the lower part of the Ohio Valley, and the territory between the Great Lakes and the Mississippi from the lands of the Miamis to Lake Nipigon. The upper part of the Ohio Valley was spoken of as a part of Canada (C.A.O., A.É., Corr. Pol., Ang., 443: fols. 358–359. Cf. the translation of this text given in Pease, Anglo-French Boundary Disputes, 321–324).

putes with England. Because Spain's interests were thus so inextricably bound up with the Anglo-French dispute, Bussy was instructed to present a separate memorial on the Anglo-Spanish disputes and to demand that those disputes be settled.[186]

At several other points the French memorial showed a stiffening in Choiseul's attitude. With regard to the Germanies, he tried to escape the evacuation of Wesel, Gelderland, and Frankfort, which he had formerly agreed to evacuate, on the ground that they were conquered territory and were now occupied in the name of the Empress-Queen of Austria; he suggested that Belle Ile be restored as a counterbalance for the evacuation of Hesse, Hanau, and Hanover.

The thing that most infuriated Pitt and his colleagues was the presentation of two other memoranda calculated to promote the interests of Austria and Spain. The first of these, purporting to submit Austria's conditional approval of a separate peace, demanded that France retain possession of the territories belonging to Prussia and that both England and France refrain from aiding their allies with troops or otherwise.[187] The second memorandum, which Bussy presented only after considerable hesitation and upon the insistence of the Spanish ambassador,[188] definitely proposed that Spain be invited to guarantee the peace. Its author professed to fear a future disturbance of peace by the Anglo-Spanish disputes. Spain, Bussy said, had communicated to France the three chief points in dispute between Spain and His Britannic Majesty; these were so easy of adjustment that His Most Christian Majesty earnestly desired Great Britain to consent to settle them now and to invite Spain to participate in the general settlement.[189]

Choiseul must have known that Pitt would never accept such an extraneous proposal, yet he acquiesced in its submission with the thought that Great Britain, which he knew to be in considerable financial distress, would never undertake a war with Spain; that the threat of a Spanish alliance with France would force Britain to moderate its demands; and that, whether successful or not, it could not fail to put Spain squarely on the side of France and bring to the latter the full strength of Spain for the continuance of the war. He played his Spanish trump in the shape of what was really a desperate appeal over the head of William Pitt to the ministers in the cabinet who favored a reasonable peace. Choiseul realized what sort of reception these memoranda would probably have, and he was forced to agree to present them, against his better judgment, by the insistence of his allies, particularly Carlos III and his ambassador in London. If they suc-

---

[186] Thackeray, *William Pitt*, II, 546–552; Étienne-François Choiseul, *Mémoire historique sur la négociation de la France et de l'Angleterre, depuis le 26 Mars 1761, jusqu'au 20 Septembre de la même année*; 25–30.

[187] Thackeray, *William Pitt.*, II, 553.

[188] C.A.O., A.É., Corr. Pol., Ang., 444: fols. 59–72.

[189] Thackeray, *William Pitt*, II, 552–553.

ceeded, so much the better; if they failed, at least he would gain time while Spain was preparing for war.[190]

Whatever may have been in Choiseul's mind, the reaction of his opponent was immediate, peremptory, and final. Pitt was at his best in the dramatic hours of a crisis; and here was a crisis to satisfy even his histrionic nature. With the full approval of the cabinet, he returned to Bussy the note on the Prussian territories as "totally inadmissible" and as "implying an attempt upon the honor of Great Britain." [191] The memorandum on Spanish questions he likewise returned: Great Britain would not permit Spain to inject its quarrel into the negotiations with France, nor would it permit France to meddle in Britain's quarrels with Spain; any further mention of them by France would be considered "an affront to his Majesty's dignity." [192]

Having delivered himself of this blast, which he must have thoroughly enjoyed, Pitt turned to the points in Choiseul's formal reply to his own proposals and sent to Stanley a note based upon the instructions of June 26 which France was to consider as the British ultimatum and to which Great Britain demanded a categorical answer.[193] In this ultimatum, Pitt again listed his irreducible minima, practically without change. As for the boundaries between Louisiana and the British colonies, whether in the Canadian areas or in the south, he rejected in advance any idea that all that was not Canada was Louisiana and injected the principle that the Ohio Valley was a third area, owned by Great Britain, and distinct from both Canada and Louisiana.[194] On one point alone Stanley was authorized to compromise: should the success of the negotiations seem to turn upon it, he was to accept the mild and practically meaningless provisions of the Treaty of Aix-la-Chapelle with regard to Dunkirk in place of those of the Treaty of Utrecht.[195]

While he was pouring out the vials of his wrath upon France, Pitt also turned on Spain and instructed Bristol to protest against "the enormity" of mixing Great Britain's disputes with Spain, a neutral, with its negotiations with France, an enemy. Bristol was to demand a categorical statement of Spain's intentions, as well as an explanation of Spain's warlike preparations and the destination of her fleets. At the same time, he was to keep the door open for a friendly adjustment of the Anglo-Spanish quarrel.[196] All of which Bristol did, only to receive from Wall, who had now ratified the

[190] C.A.O., A.É., Corr. Pol., Ang., 44: fols. 59–72; A.É., Corr. Pol., Espagne, 533: fols. 122–128, 203–209, et passim; Renaut, Le pacte de famille et l'Amérique, 88. Cf. Williams, Life of William Pitt, II, 93–94.
[191] B.M., Add. Mss., 36798: fol. 144; Thackeray, William Pitt, II, 553–554, 555–556.
[192] Thackeray, William Pitt, II, 553–556.
[193] Thackeray, William Pitt, II, 556–557.
[194] L.C., B.M., Add. Mss., 3542: fols. 34–37.
[195] Thackeray, William Pitt, II, 556–557.
[196] B.M., Add. Mss., 36807: fols. 89–96.

Family Compact, an equivocal reply which successfully threw dust in Bristol's eyes and compelled his superior, albeit convinced of Spain's duplicity, to carry the discussions further.[197]

Pitt's conditions had been submitted to Choiseul by Stanley, and Choiseul was angry. He expostulated against Pitt's unbearable language and against his intransigence on the essential questions of the fishery and the obligations of France to its allies. All he asked, he told Stanley, was "a Rock that would afford shelter to the Barks of their Fishermen, which they were ready to receive on almost any Terms that England would prescribe." As for the evacuation of Wesel, "it would be impossible for France, without incurring the most indelible stain of Perfidy to consent to any Peace by which the Army under Prince Ferdinand of Brunswick should be let loose upon the Empress-Queen." This latter point, Stanley believed, would be easily resolved if some solution could be found to the question of a haven in the Gulf of St. Lawrence for French fishermen. The British agent realized that his attempt to negotiate had failed; and he was convinced that this question of the haven, or *abri*, was the one essential cause of that failure.[198]

In his report to his superior, Stanley made an effort to explain the apparent French inconsistencies and to soften the imperious minister's attitude. At the same time, Choiseul sent to Bussy a new memorial which was to constitute France's reply to the British ultimatum. France insisted upon the conditions previously attached to the cession of Canada [199] and to the fishery, both in the Gulf of St. Lawrence and off Newfoundland, together with some shelter for French fishermen. As for Louisiana, Choiseul accepted, with some asperity, Pitt's idea of regarding as neutral the "Nations intermediate between Canada and Louisiana, as well as between Virginia and Louisiana." [200] With regard to Africa, if Great Britain insisted on both Senegal and Gorée, France would be willing to make some other arrangement to provide for French needs in the slave trade. Pitt's proposal as to Dunkirk Choiseul was willing to accept on condition that France's demand

[197] B.M., Add. Mss. 36807: fols. 105–120, 124–129. Pitt had just intercepted another letter from Grimaldi to Fuentes, dated August 31, which spoke of the "Family agreement and the Convention," and said that "both instruments were signed on the 15th" (*Chatham Corr.*, II, 139–141).

[198] B.M., Add. Mss., 36798: fols. 150–173.

[199] The boundaries of Louisiana were now redefined, but hardly more clearly than before. The line now proposed would extend from the River Perdido between the Bay of Mobile and that of Pensacola, passing by Fort Toulouse in the lands of the Alabamas, to the western end of Lake Erie in such a way as to include the Miami River, and through the eastern end of Lake Huron to the height of land between Hudson Bay and the lakes, and thence northward to the Lake of the Abitibis. Such a line was intended to leave Lakes Michigan and Superior in the possession of France (C.A.O., A.É., Corr. Pol., Ang., 443: fols. 150–159, 182).

[200] Reported in Bussy's letter to Choiseul, July 3 (Pease, *Anglo-French Boundary Disputes*, 819).

for an *abri* in the Gulf of St. Lawrence be satisfied. The evacuation of Wesel, Gelderland, and Westphalia he refused as being extraneous to the Anglo-French war and part and parcel of the war between Austria and Prussia; this question, he said, must be left to the congress at Augsburg. Pitt's demands as to India he accepted. Spain was not mentioned.[201] In a covering letter to Bussy, Choiseul authorized his agent to delimit, with Pitt, the boundary line in the Mississippi Valley on duplicate maps. Bussy was also to insist on the question of the *abri* and on Choiseul's proposal to refer the question of Prussian territories to the proposed congress at Augsburg. If Pitt failed to give a favorable reply within eight days after the presentation of the French ultimatum, Bussy was to return to France.[202]

The negotiations had now to all intents and purposes been reduced to the question whether Great Britain would grant France an island in the Gulf of St. Lawrence. When Pitt saw Choiseul's memorial he expressed the belief that there could be no peace, but the more reasonable members of the British cabinet—Hardwicke, Bedford, Devonshire, Newcastle, and Bute—were all in favor of giving in, for the sake of a peace so nearly made, both in the matter of making the Gulf of St. Lawrence a *mare clausum*, and that of assigning a shelter for French fishermen in the gulf. At last, despite much thumping on the table and Pitt's refusal to have his draft of a reply "cobbled with," the irascible minister was constrained to concede to France the tiny island of St. Pierre, at the entrance to the gulf, and the "cobbled" reply was sent on August 30.[203]

More conciliatory than its predecessors, this note conceded to France the island of St. Pierre, together with a share in the fishery both in the Gulf of St. Lawrence and on the Banks of Newfoundland. Further, it substituted the provisions of the Treaty of Aix-la-Chapelle which dealt with the fortifications at Dunkirk for the more rigorous terms of the Treaty of Utrecht and went so far as to express a willingness on the part of Great Britain to aid its Prussian ally only with money subsidies; Prussian territory, however, must be evacuated by the French armies.[204] For the first time Pitt now expressed himself in detail on the subject of the northern boundaries between the British colonies and Louisiana. Rejecting the line proposed by Bussy, he claimed that the western boundary of Canada, as drawn by the Marquis de Vaudreuil at the capitulation of Montreal, was the Wabash River and the height of land from its source to the Mississippi,

[201] L.C., B.M., Add. Mss., 35421: fols. 40–44.

[202] C.A.O., A.É., Corr. Pol., Ang., 444: fols. 114–117.

[203] L.C., B.M., Add. Mss., 35421: fols. 50–51, 32926: fols. 308–310, 358–359; Bedford Corr., III, 35–36; Williams, *Life of William Pitt, op. cit.*, II, 97–98.

[204] Thackeray, *William Pitt*, II, 591–597. While the terms of the note were conciliatory, the language of Pitt's covering letter to Stanley was insulting and humiliating in the extreme, and doubtless greatly lessened its good effect (*ibid.*, II, 604–607).

thus including Lakes Huron, Michigan, and Superior in that province.[205]
With regard to the land to the southward, he was not specific upon its
boundaries, although he rejected the line of the Perdido River, stating
merely that "the King . . . might consent to leave intermediate countries
under the protection of Great Britain, and particularly the Cherokees, the
Creeks, the Chickasaws, the Choctaws, and other nations situated between
the British settlements and the Mississippi"—which modest proposal would
have given Great Britain a protectorate over all the lands between the
Alleghenies and the Father of Waters. Choiseul's reservations in favor of
the French inhabitants, Pitt accepted.[206]

Unfortunately, this genuinely conciliatory gesture came too late. "I most
ardently wish," wrote Stanley, "that the cession of the Island of St. Peter's
[St. Pierre], if now advisable, had been Earlier made. I have secretly seen
an Article drawn up between France and Spain in which the former engages to support the Interests of the latter." [207] Pitt's suspicions and arrogant intransigence had finally driven Choiseul into the arms of Spain. For
the British reply to the French note of July 13 had apparently convinced
that minister that France had more to gain by continuing the war with the
aid of Spain than by a peace so humiliating and disastrous as that which
Pitt now seemed to be seeking to impose. By August 1 he had made up his
mind. He was convinced that Pitt would make no reasonable peace and
advised the King to continue the war in close alliance with Spain.[208] He
therefore pushed the Spanish negotiations to a conclusion, and the Franco-
Spanish alliance was signed on August 15, as already noted. But Choiseul
did not wish to wait until the following spring for Spain to enter the war.
He saw great advantages in a surprise move upon Great Britain, and asked
His Catholic Majesty to declare war immediately. "At the moment of the
declaration," he said, "we will deliver to him, according to the Convention,
the island of Minorca, and we will propose to him some arrangement as to
Louisiana." [209] He proposed that Spain declare war on Great Britain in the

[205] Vaudreuil himself did not draw the line. Frederick Haldimand, acting for General
Amherst, asked Vaudreuil for a map of Canada, and, when told there was none, traced
on a map of North America the course of the line, as dictated to him orally by
Vaudreuil, while the marquis looked over his shoulder (B.M., Add. Mss., 21661: fol.
257; L.C., A.É., Méms. et Docs., Amérique, 21: fol. 96). The line drawn followed the
Ohio and Wabash Rivers from the confluence of the Ohio with the Mississippi to the
source of the Wabash, and thence followed the height of land to Lac Rouge, at the
headwaters of the Mississippi. Vaudreuil evidently thought of the Wabash as flowing
into the Mississippi, and of the Ohio as flowing into the Wabash. The map is reproduced in Pease, Anglo-French Boundary Disputes, opposite 568.

[206] Thackeray, William Pitt, II, fols. 591–597; cf. Pease, Anglo-French Boundary
Disputes, 383–389.

[207] L.C., Add. Mss., 32927: fol. 336.

[208] Pease, Anglo-French Boundary Disputes, 389.

[209] Quoted in Waddington, La guerre de sept ans, IV, 571. This arrangement was
nothing less than an immediate loan of 3,600,000 piastres, in return for which His
Most Christian Majesty was disposed to cede Louisiana to his Spanish cousin (A.É.,
Corr. Pol., Espagne, 533: fols. 210–212, 240–245, 320–325).

approaching autumn; but Spain demurred, on the ground of unprepared-
ness and a desire to wait till the treasure fleet from America was safely in
port.[210]

Pitt's conciliatory reply of August 30 to the French ultimatum of
August 5 therefore arrived at Paris after the Third Bourbon family alliance
between France and Spain had been sealed. The door to peace had not
been completely closed by that alliance, because there was nothing in it to
prevent an Anglo-French treaty, except, perhaps, France's agreement not
to make peace until the Anglo-Spanish disputes were settled. Even that, as
Choiseul informed Bussy, could be so arranged as to allow of a treaty between France and England first and, afterward, a friendly mediation of the
Anglo-Spanish matter by France, provided England was so disposed.[211]
Choiseul was playing his double game very skillfully and according to plan;
and Stanley, his own suspicions now aroused, doubted whether the volatile
Frenchman might not, on some pretext or other, repudiate the treaty now
so nearly made, should it suit his convenience to do so.[212]

Choiseul probably still desired, most of all, to make peace with England;
in any case, he continued the negotiations in apparent good faith and
framed a response to England's conciliatory gesture of August 30. There
was little that remained to be adjusted. On the question of the North
American boundary, Choiseul complained to Stanley of the extreme nature
of Pitt's claims. The governors of Canada and Louisiana had long disputed,
he said, as to what constituted the real boundary between the two provinces. Nevertheless, when Stanley showed him the Vaudreuil-Haldimand
map, he agreed that the boundary should be as it had there been drawn.
He then proposed that the map should be so divided that it would make
clear which Indian nations of the south were to be considered as being,
respectively, under the protection of each of the two signatory powers.
Pitt's offer of St. Pierre as an *abri* for French fishermen he tentatively accepted: he had asked for a rock, he said, and he had been given it. He
asked for St. Lucia in the proposed division of the "Neutral Islands" and
agreed to cede to England both Senegal and Gorée, which was now held by
England, on condition that England grant some other depot, and proposed,
for this purpose, Anamabu and Accra.[213]

This apparent progress was encouraging, but two days later Stanley wrote
that Choiseul, after having made inquiry as to the suitability of St. Pierre
and having discussed with the council the humiliating conditions under
which England proposed to cede it,[214] now protested and refused, though

[210] A.É., Corr. Pol., Espagne, 533: fols. 231–239.
[211] L.C., B.M., Add. Mss., 32927: fol. 336
[212] L.C., B.M., Add. Mss., 32927: fols. 367–376.
[213] L.C., B.M., Add. Mss., 32927: fols. 339, 367–376.
[214] No fortifications, residence of an English commissary, and periodic inspections by
the British naval commandant on the Newfoundland station.

not absolutely, to accept it. He insisted upon Anamabu and Accra in exchange for Senegal and Gorée. He refused to evacuate Wesel but said he
would welcome any expedient proposed by England that would protect
Maria Theresa from the armies of Prince Ferdinand of Brunswick and proposed a new method for regulating British aid to Prussia after peace should
have been made.[215] Stanley, however, was convinced that peace was now
impossible. He heard reports that Spain had given great sums of money to
France and would soon declare war. Choiseul, indeed, again informally
mentioned the right of France to sponsor Spain's claims against England.
The French minister was being severely criticized at home for the apparent
supineness with which he had surrendered Canada, a French possession,
and his anxiety to protect Maria Theresa, a foreigner whom the French
detested. Choiseul's desire for peace was frustrated by constant pressure
from Austria and Spain, along with the criticism at home, which were
making the chances of peace ever more remote. Still, Pitt's offer of St.
Pierre had not been definitely rejected, and his suggested line for the Carolina boundary would probably be accepted; Choiseul, moreover, had asked
England for a compromise proposal for the adjustment of the German
question. Under the circumstances, Stanley did not feel authorized to ask
for his passport and go home; on the contrary, he asked Pitt for further
instructions.[216]

The final French note, the *"ultimatissimum"* of France, was presented
by Bussy on September 13. As Choiseul had previously explained to Stanley, France accepted with slight modifications all but one of the British
conditions. The note asked for a definition of the word "dependencies" as
used by Pitt with regard to Canada and a clarification of the terms defining
the boundary in the south; it accepted St. Pierre as an *abri*, but, because
of the inadequacy of that tiny island, asked that Miquelon, which adjoined
it, be ceded also; France accepted the British plan for the division of the
"Neutral Islands," provided it were awarded St. Lucia. It merely refused to
evacuate the territories held for the Empress-Queen, while at the same
time it asked Great Britain to make new proposals of a kind that might
free it from its difficult position.[217]

Such was the narrow margin of difference by which the chance of making peace was lost. The French ministry did not expect their note to be
accepted; they may not even have wished that it might be. But Choiseul
could hardly have sent it had he been unprepared to have it accepted.[218]

[215] To the effect that soldiers actually in the pay of England would not be allowed
to serve Prussia; he inferred, however, that as soon as their home service had expired,
they might be free to enter that of Prussia.
[216] B.M., Add. Mss., 36798: fols. 236–249.
[217] Thackeray, *William Pitt*, II, 619–623.
[218] C.A.O., A.É., Corr. Pol., Ang., 444: fols. 264–265; cf. Pease, *Anglo-French
Boundary Disputes*, cxix, cxx.

Certainly it was the last chance England was to have to bring the negotiations to a successful conclusion.[219]

Pitt regarded this French note as an obstinate failure to meet the final English conditions and as a proof positive that Choiseul was only playing for time. As a matter of fact, it appears that that was exactly what Choiseul was doing, in the light of his "plan" for negotiations after his receipt of Pitt's conditions in June and his present statement that he would never have made such concessions had he expected Pitt to accept them.[220] Technically, France failed to comply with England's conditions. Because of this fact, coupled with Wall's unsatisfactory answer to Bristol's demand for an explanation of Spanish intentions, the cabinet authorized Pitt to recall Stanley from Paris,[221] and on September 20, Stanley demanded his passport.[222]

So ended Mr. Pitt's negotiations—but only to the great regret of many of his colleagues. "We lost l'Heure de Bergier [sic]" wrote Newcastle, sadly,[223] and it is impossible to escape the conclusion that responsibility for the failure of the negotiations rests squarely upon the shoulders of William Pitt. He was a great conqueror, but his ambition to extend the Empire, coupled with his hatred of France and his extreme suspiciousness, irascibility, and intractability made him a poor diplomat. On the other hand, Choiseul, under pressure from Austria and Spain and compelled as the loser to play as high as possible while still keeping open every avenue of escape in case of failure, was personally desirous of peace. Had he had a diplomat for an opponent, the peace would probably have been made.[224]

Pitt, upon the failure of his negotiations with Choiseul, had not been satisfied merely to renew the war with France; he also wished to strike immediately at Spain. But this was too much for the "precise old gentlemen" of his cabinet. In a series of cabinet meetings he had laid before them the unsatisfactory state of British relations with Spain and the evidences of a Bourbon alliance inimical to the safety and the interests of Britain. He desired to open hostilities at once, but the most he could get the cabinet to do was to send Bristol instructions to demand an explana-

[219] "For God's sake what are the material Points, France and England differ about?" exclaimed Bedford. "Those two trifling ones I have mentioned (the *abri* and the slaving station), which may be easily accommodated, the evacuation of Wesel, and the assistance to be given our respective Allies, the King of Prussia and the Empress Queen" (L.C., B.M., Add. Mss., 32928: fols. 158–159).
[220] C.A.O., A.É., Corr. Pol., Ang., 444: fol. 264.
[221] L.C., B.M., Add. Mss., 32928: fols. 182–184; B.M., Add. Mss., 32928: fols. 170–171.
[222] C.A.O., A.É., Corr. Pol., Ang., 444: fol. 332.
[223] L.C., B.M., Add. Mss., 32928: fol. 211. He meant *"l'heure du berger."*
[224] *Cf.* Stanley's opinion to Newcastle, in Newcastle to Hardwicke, Sept. 26, 1761, L.C., B.M., Add. Mss., 32898: fols. 362–363; and Waddington, *La guerre de sept ans,* IV, 600–601.

tion of Spain's intentions. As an assurance of British good will, Bristol was to say that Great Britain stood ready to evacuate her establishments on the coasts of Central America, if His Catholic Majesty would permit the British logwood cutters to continue their labors until some other way of supplying Great Britain with dyewood could be found.[225]

Pitt was not satisfied.[226] On October 5 he resigned and was succeeded by the Earl of Egremont. As directed by the cabinet Egremont wrote to Bristol, on October 28, instructing him "gently" to insinuate, "in the most polite, and Friendly Terms," England's desire for an explanation and its willingness to evacuate the dyewood-coast establishments if Spain would guarantee England the privilege of cutting there.[227] This was no concession from the prior English position, but it was couched in far friendlier terms than most of the dispatches of Egremont's predecessor.

In the meantime, however, Bristol had reported the arrival at Cadiz of the fleet from America and a notable stiffening of Wall's attitude toward the English question.[228] Wall confessed that Spain had renewed its "family compacts" and expressed his country's fear that England was determined, after annihilating France's colonial empire, to turn on Spain itself.[229] Wall personally desired peace, and it is to be assumed that his complaints of Pitt's insatiable vindictiveness were genuine. He realized that the French alliance did not preclude peace and, apparently in the hope that Pitt's resignation might admit some moderation into the British ministry and certainly with a desire to gain time for warlike preparations, he delayed his answer to the British demand for an explanation. He delayed until, late in November, Egremont instructed Bristol to demand a categorical answer as to Spain's intentions, and, if the answer proved to be unsatisfactory, to leave Madrid.[230] But neither the Spanish ambassadors in Paris and London nor the Spanish court looked with sympathy upon Wall's desire for peace, nor did Choiseul, his ally, see any hope for conciliation. It was true, he said, that most of the British ministers now desired peace; but France

[225] "Mem^{dums} of Spanish Partialities to France," P.R.O., Chatham Mss. XCII; L.C., B.M., Add. Mss., 32928: fols. 225, 233, 248–250, 259–262.
[226] *Bedford Correspondence*, III, 48–50. Upon Pitt's resignation, Bute offered him the governorship of Canada. Recognizing that the governor of a colony could not sit in Parliament, Bute offered to push through Parliament a bill which would make this possible. The assumption probably was that Pitt would not go to America, in any case; but it is an interesting approach to the principle of colonial representation (*Chatham Corr.*, II, 146–148).
[227] L.C., B.M., Add. Mss., 32930: fols. 78–84.
[228] Bristol to Pitt, Oct. 21, 1761, L.C., H.L. Mss.; L.C., B.M., Add. Mss., 32930: fols. 268–275.
[229] L.C., B.M., Add. Mss., 32930: fols. 268–275, 276–277.
[230] B.M., Add. Mss., 32981: fols. 134–139; A.É., Corr. Pol., Espagne, 534: fols. 15–24, 35–41, 305–308. Wall wrote to Fuentes describing his negotiations with Bristol. To the Spanish ambassador in London he said, "We wait to see, whether the changes of ministry will produce greater Moderation, than that court has hitherto shown. God grant it, for the Repose of Europe, which It is in such Need of!" (L.C., B.M., Add. Mss., 32930: fols. 276–277).

could not accede to their demands in full, and no British minister would dare to accept less.[231] Wall was compelled to subscribe to the policy of war; and, on December 10, writing to Bristol, he replied to the British demands tersely and to the effect that their haughty and peremptory tone was in itself a declaration of war.[232] Bristol immediately left Madrid and went to Portugal;[233] and England declared war on January 4 of the new year.

5. The Franco-Spanish Military Alliance of 1762

The Third Bourbon Family Compact, of August 15, 1761, was intended to be a permanent union among the princes of the Bourbon family for the mutual guarantee of their dominions in Europe, America, Africa, and Asia, in case of attack by any outside power. The military alliance between France and Spain pertaining to the war that was expected to result from an "attack" upon Spanish territories by England, was not signed until February 4, 1762, a month after England's declaration of war on Spain on January 4, 1762.

This military convention [234] was directed specifically at England. Its preamble justified the joint action of France and Spain against England in terms of the international balance of maritime, colonial, and commercial power:

All Europe should now know the danger to which the balance of maritime power is exposed by the ambitious projects of the British court and the despotism that it intends to arrogate unto itself in all the seas of the world. The English nation has shown, and clearly shows . . . that it wishes to make itself the absolute mistress of navigation, and to leave to other nations only a passive and dependent commerce. With this objective it began and sustains the present war against France . . . its ministry has obstinately refused to restore the territories that the English have usurped in the Spanish dominions in America, and has appropriated to England an exclusive monopoly of the cod-fisheries . . .[235]

Furthermore, according to this preamble, the English ministry had arrogantly insulted His Catholic Majesty by its demand to see the text of the Family Compact and had actually declared war on Spain on the fourth of January just preceding. In view of all this, His Catholic Majesty had decided to unite his forces with those of France in the present war against England. This treaty was, therefore, a private agreement between France

[231] A.É., Corr. Pol., Esp., 534: fols. 305–308.
[232] Wall to Bristol, Dec. 10, 1761, L.C., H.L. Mss.
[233] Bristol to Egremont, Dec. 11, 1761, L.C., H.L. Mss.
[234] Cantillo, ed., Tratados, 482–485.
[235] Cantillo, ed., Tratados, 482.

and Spain, as distinguished from the Family Compact, for the execution of the terms of which it was now made.[236]

It was accordingly provided that Spain would come to France's aid against England with all its forces, with the purpose of "obliging it [England] to turn of itself toward a reasonable peace." France promised to include Spanish interests in any future negotiation for peace and to compel England to restore the prizes seized from Spain during the time when Spain was a neutral, to admit Spain's right to share in the cod-fisheries off Newfoundland, and to evacuate all the territories the English had seized in Spain's colonies on the mainland of America (for cutting logwood), so that Spain's objectives in the war would be integrally joined with those of France in the final negotiation of peace. France would not accept an end of hostilities until the King of Spain should indicate his willingness to do so on the basis of the fulfillment of his objectives. The war was to be conducted in common; losses and gains were to be shared and were to be equalized, in the peace, "as though they had pertained to one single power." The two monarchs agreed that neither would make a separate peace but would negotiate the peace jointly, as one power. His Catholic Majesty confirmed "the generous cession" of its right to the islands of Dominica, St. Vincent, St. Lucia, and Tobago that France had offered England in its efforts to make peace with that country, and gave his approval to French use of this right, as though it belonged to France, in case it should be necessary to cede them to England as compensation for some other territory lost during the war. France promised to restore Minorca to Spain immediately, and Spain was to retain it forever, that is, "if God bless the combined arms of the two monarchs . . . and if it be not absolutely necessary for France to use it as a compensation for restitutions [France] may be compelled to ask of England." [237]

The two monarchs were to communicate their union to the King of Portugal and to invite him to join them against England for the same objective for which they were fighting, since the Portuguese suffered, they said, more than any other nation under the yoke that England imposed upon all the nations that had any seaborne commerce and possessed overseas dominions. It would not, indeed, in the language of the treaty, be just for Spain and France to sacrifice themselves in this war for such an objective, which was common to Portugal as well as to them, without Portuguese participation. Should Portugal, therefore, refuse to join them and continue to enrich the enemy and open to him the ports of Portugal, France and Spain were to inform His Most Faithful Majesty that they could not permit him to remain neutral in the war; it was clearly implied that, in such a case, they would attack Portugal as, in effect, an ally of England.

[236] Cantillo, ed., *Tratados*, 482–483.
[237] Cantillo, ed., *Tratados*, 484.

Other powers who had reason to "humble the pride of England" were to be invited to join the alliance. In this or any other war fought jointly by the allies against England, neither signatory would permit any foreign nation to introduce into its dominions certain enumerated textiles, particularly woolens, or hardware; France alone, during the war, should have the privilege of importing such commodities into Spain, and Spain alone the privilege of importing them into France, so that, in any case, none should be permitted to be imported into either country from the common enemy, England. Finally, the two monarchs agreed to work together to guarantee to Don Felipe, Duke of Parma (brother of Carlos III), some compensation for the part of Placentia awarded to the King of Sardinia by the Peace of Aix-la-Chapelle.

To the demands of Spain and France that Portugal join the Bourbon Family Alliance, José I gave a series of evasive answers. Confronted, finally, with an ultimatum, the King replied that he would adhere to his alliance with England, and declared war on France and Spain on May 18.[238]

6. The Bute-Choiseul Negotiations of 1762 and the Treaty of Paris, 1763

The renewal of the Anglo-French war had taken place over three or four questions which, as Bedford pointed out, were tragic in their insignificance; and a new war had been begun between England and Spain over a dispute that reduced itself to the question whether England should evacuate its illegal establishments on the dyewood coasts before or after Spain guaranteed the British a supply of dyewoods. But the real motive in the mind of the Spanish monarch was his desire to maintain the balance of power in America in the face of the threat to the Spanish dominions inherent in the anticipated elimination of France and the extension of the British North American boundary westward and also southward toward the Gulf of Mexico. The British, he said, were on the march and must be stopped. They had already taken all of Florida except St. Augustine and Pensacola.[239] They would soon take Louisiana, and it would not be long before they would seize Mexico. In view of this very accurate forecast of later Anglo-Saxon "manifest destiny," His Catholic Majesty urged France to take vigorous steps to defend Louisiana, the last barrier between his own American possessions and that expansive race, and to strengthen the barrier by moving the French population of Canada

---

[238] Cantillo, ed., *Tratados*, 483–485, 495–496.
[239] The reference is to Carolina and Georgia. *Cf.* Lanning, *The Diplomatic History of Georgia, passim.*

to the southern colony.[240] In his fear of British preponderance in North America, the Spanish monarch was now, if possible, more belligerent than his ally.

In any case, the campaign that followed was a parade of British victories. In the Caribbean England made a clean sweep of the French West Indies. It possessed itself of Martinique, Grenada, St. Lucia, and St. Vincent. Then the English forces turned against the possessions of Spain. They took Puerto Rico and Cuba, which gave England a stranglehold upon the routes of trade into and out of the Caribbean and the Gulf of Mexico. On the other hand, George III, who cared little about the ancestral domains of Hanover, and his minister, the Earl of Bute, who cared less, decided to discontinue the Prussian subsidies. Russia had withdrawn from the war, and it appeared that Frederick could safely be left to take care of himself; besides, if the subsidies were continued and if Frederick were given too much voice in the matter of peace, the war might go on indefinitely. This change of policy antagonized Newcastle and Hardwicke, both of whom retired from the cabinet in the spring of 1762. Its peace faction, meanwhile, had been strengthened by the addition of the Duke of Bedford, whose influence was in turn balanced by the belligerent Egremont and Grenville.

In view of these circumstances, it was easy for Bute to reopen negotiations for peace in the spring of 1762. As a matter of fact, the negotiations had never been entirely discontinued. It is indicative, probably, of Choiseul's desire for peace that he had made a last desperate appeal to Stanley, before that British minister left Paris, for a continuation of the negotiations,[241] and that he had apparently appealed to Stanley again after the latter's arrival in London, through the medium of Count Viry, the Sardinian minister to Great Britain.[242] Choiseul had to be shown that the British ministry dared to make a moderate peace.

The fall of Pitt had made the chance of success much more likely, and toward the end of November, 1761, there had appeared in London a Monsieur de Choiseul, a cousin of the Duc de Choiseul, who was assured that Great Britain would now make every effort to negotiate a satisfactory

---

[240] A.É., Corr. Pol., Espagne, 534: fols. 218–223, 305–308.

[241] L.C., B.M., Add. Mss., 32928: fols. 325–328.

[242] Count Viry to the Bailli de Solar de Breille, Sardinian minister in Paris, November 17 and 27, 1761, C.L., Shelburne Mss., IX. This is the beginning of the famous Viry-Solar correspondence, in the course of which the preliminary negotiations between France and England were arranged. The Duc de Choiseul turned over to his cousin, the Comte de Choiseul, the actual conduct of French foreign relations, with the exception of those dealing directly with Spain. Much of the Viry-Solar correspondence, therefore, passed through the hands of the count; but the duke was still the real director of French foreign policy, and he continued personally to conduct the relations of France with Spain. There are copies of the Viry-Solar correspondence in A.É., Corr. Pol., Espagne, 536: fols. 887 ff.

treaty.[243] The Duc de Choiseul intimated to the Bailli de Solar that he would make a separate peace, and Solar communicated the message to Viry. Viry sent back a reply suggesting that the British ultimatum of July 29, 1761, and the French ultimatum of August 5 be made the basis of the negotiations, and that confidential agents be exchanged between the two courts.[244] Such agents were not exchanged; but on January 5, 1762, Viry improved the occasion afforded by the declaration of war on Spain to assure his correspondent that the break between Great Britain and Spain should not interfere with an Anglo-French peace, because the questions relative to Campeche logwood and prizes made in violation of Spanish neutrality could easily be settled at the same time.[245] Thus encouraged, Solar again communicated with Count Viry and the Duc de Choiseul. The latter, on January 23, wrote Solar a cautious letter to the effect that the loss of Martinique would not affect his policies and that if Great Britain genuinely desired peace, the British ministry should make France a definite offer.[246] This stand was reiterated by the French ministers at a conference with Solar a few days later, in which they again suggested that England send a confidential agent to Paris. They intimated that they did not wish to use the memorials of the preceding summer as a basis for the negotiations, but proposed that, if Great Britain did not wish to send an agent, it might send Solar a memorandum containing definite proposals, to which they promised to reply.[247]

Meanwhile, Solar had communicated to the British government a request for the release of the young Comte d'Estaing, then a prisoner of war at Plymouth. D'Estaing was released, as requested, and a ship was provided for his return to France; Egremont seized upon the opportunity to open direct communications with the French ministers.[248] The result of this exchange was an interview between Viry and Bute, on March 8, and a memorandum from Egremont to the Sardinian minister, two weeks later, in which the British cabinet outlined its idea of the proper terms of peace.

In general, the British agreed to boundaries for Canada and Louisiana such as had been proposed by the French ultimatum of August 5. They

[243] L.C., B.M., Add. Mss., 32931: fols. 347, 388, 425. This was apparently a third member of the Choiseul family.

[244] Viry to Solar, Nov. 27, Solar to Viry, Dec. 13, Viry to Solar, Dec. 13, Dec. 15, 1761, C.L., Shelburne Mss., IX: fols. 1–18.

[245] Viry to Solar, Jan. 5, 1762, C.L., Shelburne Mss., IX: fols. 29–31.

[246] Solar to the Comte de Choiseul, Comte de Choiseul to Solar, Duc de Choiseul to Solar, Jan. 23, 1762, C.L., Shelburne Mss., IX: fols. 44–49.

[247] Solar to Viry, Feb. 1, 1762, C.L., Shelburne Mss., IX: fols. 50–58.

[248] Viry to Solar, Feb. 9, 22, 23, Solar to Viry, Feb. 25, Egremont to the Duc de Choiseul, Feb. 22, 1762, C.L., Shelburne Mss., IX: fols. 41–43, 67–68, 68–69, 71–74; A.É., Corr. Pol., Espagne, 536: fols. 62–69.

were willing to divide the "Neutral Islands" so as to give St. Lucia and St. Vincent to France, and Dominica and Tobago to Great Britain. They would allow a compromise arrangement in the case of Dunkirk and would return the island of Gorée to France. In the Gulf of St. Lawrence, they offered France both St. Pierre and Miquelon, with the right of maintaining fifty men in garrison there. Finally, on the question of Wesel and Gelderland, Bute proposed that in their case neutral garrisons be substituted for the French armies; but he would not make this a *sine qua non*. The British ministers also showed an inclination to negotiate in the case of the Spanish dispute with Great Britain, although they preferred to negotiate separately with Spain. On this subject they displayed a willingness to accept the demands of Spain with regard to the logwood coast; that is to say, Great Britain would immediately evacuate the objectionable establishments on the coast, if Spain would in return give a bona fide assurance that British logwood cutters might continue their work until some arrangement could be made that would be satisfactory to both parties. The Spanish demand for a share of the fisheries would not be granted; cases of prizes made in violation of Spanish neutrality must be submitted to British courts of admiralty. If Spain were willing, negotiations might begin on this basis immediately, and it was Egremont's sanguine belief that they could be settled in a single day.[249] This beginning having been made, the British cabinet on March 29 officially sanctioned negotiations by making France a definite offer based upon the informal suggestions already made,[250] and on April 8 Viry forwarded to the Duc de Choiseul a letter from Egremont and an official declaration by the King formally proposing a reopening of the negotiations of the preceding year by a new exchange of ministers.[251]

The Duc de Choiseul, for his part, immediately notified Spain of the British overture and expressed his determination to make peace. Sweden had proposed to make peace with Prussia, he said, and Russia had deserted the allies; the German situation would now take care of itself. News had just come of the capture of Martinique and the seizure of the "Neutral Islands" by Great Britain; France had absolutely nothing left in America for which to continue the war and must now accept peace on the basis of Bussy's ultimatum of the previous summer. As for Spain, the French

[249] Viry to Solar, Mar. 23, 1761, C.L., Shelburne Mss., IX: fols. 83–90: L.C., B.M., Add. Mss., 32935: fols. 249–251; *ibid.*, 32936: fols. 1–6. An attempt was made through the Dutch ambassador in Madrid to open negotiations on this basis, but the overture was rejected (L.C., B.M., Add. Mss., 32936: fol. 459).

[250] Great Britain, Royal Commission on Historical Manuscripts, *Tenth Report*, Appendix 1, "Underwood Manuscripts," 449. Hereafter cited as HMC X App. 1, Underwood MSS.

[251] Viry to Solar, Apr. 8, Egremont to Choiseul, Apr. 8, "Déclaration de Sa Majesté le Roy de la Grand Bretagne," April 8, 1762, C.L., Shelburne Mss., IX: fols. 100–107.

minister proposed that the Anglo-Spanish quarrel be settled in Paris by negotiations paralleling the British settlement with France.[252]

The terms which Choiseul now proposed to Great Britain in reply to its formal overture departed sharply from at least two of the points covered in the informal preliminary conversations. In the first place, he pleaded his inability to negotiate a peace separately from Spain and advised the British ministry of an invitation he had already extended to Spain to join in the making of the peace. For the rest, he divided the issues of the war into three groups: the differences between Spain and Britain; the colonial conflict of France and Britain in America, Africa, and Asia; and the war in Germany. In the first group, he admitted the justice of having the cases of Spanish prizes made in time of peace submitted to British admiralty courts. Spain was in the right, he said, with regard to the logwood coasts, but he believed an arrangement could be made that would satisfy both parties. As for Spain's right to a share in the Newfoundland fishery, there had not been two Spanish ships on the fishing banks in a century, and he assured his correspondent there would not be ten more in the hundred years to come; this point, he said, was purely a point of honor, and easily settled—though he did not say precisely how.

In the second group of questions for negotiation, he took as a basis of discussion the last ultimatums exchanged in the preceding summer. He acknowledged the cession of Canada, with boundaries in the direction of Louisiana, which it would be easy to arrange. The fishery in the Gulf of St. Lawrence and on the Banks of Newfoundland he demanded, with an *abri* that would be "convenient, not illusory, as that of St. Pierre." He asked the restitution of Martinique, Guadelupe, and Marie-Galante, and an equitable decision as to the "Neutral Islands." He demanded a "solid" establishment on the coast of Africa, presumably Gorée, and proposed that England outline a plan for the settlement of the question of India. Minorca he proposed to return to England. As for the third group of considerations, those relating to the Germanic allies of France and Great Britain, he felt sure that these allies genuinely desired peace; and, ambiguously, he expressed the conviction that, if France and Britain could agree, a peace in Germany would be easy.[253] He agreed to evacuate the German territory occupied by French troops, under any conditions that would protect France from any allegation of having failed in its duty to its allies.

It was over the question of the West Indies that the British cabinet was most disturbed. Choiseul's demands were staggering, for they envisaged

[252] A.É., Corr. Pol., Espagne, 536: fols. 60–61, 62–69; L.C., B.M., Add. Mss., 32986: fol. 306

[253] Duc de Choiseul to Egremont, Apr 14, Comte de Choiseul to Solar, Apr. 16, 1762, C.L., Shelburne Mss., IX: fols. 112–114, 115–118, 127–128, 135–142; L.C., B.M., Add. Mss., 32937: fols. 111–116.

nothing less than a restoration of all the French islands that had been seized in the war. Further, they revived the troublesome old debate over the question whether one potential "sugar island" in the West Indies was not worth more than the whole of Canada.[254] Egremont proposed to cede Martinique to France and keep Guadelupe; but if France wished to keep both, Great Britain would then cede both and accept Louisiana as compensation for them. Once this was settled, one might proceed to a consideration of the possible restitution of Marie-Galante and the fate of the "Neutral Islands." [255] At the suggestion of Bute, who feared these conditions would be refused by France and result in a continuation of the war, it was finally decided to offer a compromise plan, according to which Great Britain would offer France Martinique, Guadelupe, and Marie-Galante, keeping for itself the "Neutral Islands" and Grenada, and demand the Mississippi River as the western boundary of the British colonies in North America.[256]

Egremont's reply to Choiseul, therefore, conformed, with some slight modifications, to the French proposals at almost every point. The three points in the Spanish dispute were provided for as suggested: the cases of Spanish prizes would be submitted to British admiralty courts; Britain would give up its establishments on the dyewood coasts for a guarantee of continued cutting privileges; Egremont was sure that, as soon as this article was arranged, Spain would end its demand for a share in the Newfoundland fishery. As for the Anglo-French contest, Egremont accepted the cession of Canada with Choiseul's conditions; France was given the right to fish in the Gulf of St. Lawrence[257] and on the Banks of Newfoundland, and the island of Miquelon was added to St. Pierre as an *abri*; Gorée was to be ceded to France; the British ministers promised to accept any reason-

---

[254] The "Canada versus Guadelupe" controversy entered, both in 1761 and in 1762, into the deliberation of the cabinet. It was discussed and dismissed by Choiseul and Stanley, albeit informally. The controversy is treated by William L. Grant, in "Canada versus Guadelupe," *Amer. Hist. Rev.*, XVII, 735 ff. The idea of taking Guadelupe instead of Canada now cropped up again, in a new form: the Earl of Hardwicke suggested the possibility of keeping all the West Indies and returning Canada to France. The security of the colonies in North America, he suggested, could never be assured, in any case, so long as the French remained in Louisiana. Besides, Canada, he said, "is a cold northern climate, unfruitful; furnishes no Trade to Europe, that I know of, but the Fur Trade, the most inconsiderable of all Trades. . . . Its products are mostly or nearly of yᵉ same kind with those of Great Britain, and consequently will take off not much of our's. Besides, if you remove the French Inhabitants, this Kingdom and Ireland cannot furnish, or procure, People enough to settle and inhabit it in Centuries to come; And, if You don't remove the French Inhabitants, they will never become half Subjects, and this Country must maintain an Army there to keep them in Subjection" (L.C., B.M., Add. Mss., 32936: fol. 311). *Cf.* Grant, "Canada versus Guadelupe," *loc. cit.*

[255] L.C., B.M., Add. Mss., 3293: fols. 341–346.

[256] *Bedford Correspondence*, III, 75–77; *cf.* Pease, "The Mississippi Boundary of 1763," *American Hist. Rev.*, XL, 278–286.

[257] But not to dry fish on its English-owned shores.

able offer France might make for the Coromandel coast; Belle Ile would be returned to France in exchange for Minorca and the evacuation of German territory occupied by French troops; Great Britain would accept the provisions of the Treaty of Aix-la-Chapelle covering Dunkirk and would also accept the French assurance that Louis XV had no intention of retaining Ostend and Nieuport, cities in the Austrian Netherlands garrisoned by France during the war.[258]

It was only on the combined point of the West Indies and the Mississippi that Egremont proposed any serious modification of Choiseul's terms. With regard to the West Indies he explained that Great Britain now held not only the islands it had held in 1761 but had added Martinique and St. Lucia, and that, while he was writing, news had come of the British seizure of Grenada and the Grenadines and of the expected occupation of St. Vincent and Tobago. His proposal for the return of Guadelupe, Marie-Galante, and Martinique in consideration of a clear title to the "Neutral Islands" and the Mississippi boundary seemed modest enough. In his covering letter he urged that the French government make haste, for, he said, the anticipated success of the projected expedition against Havana would make a moderate peace more difficult and would jeopardize even the British concessions with regard to the French islands.[259]

Up to this time, the British minister had not been explicit as to the meaning of his demand for the Mississippi River as a boundary. Did it mean the Mississippi River throughout its course, or only south of its confluence with the Ohio? When Viry pressed him for a definition, Egremont avoided going further than the language of his memorandum. Whereupon Viry turned for light to another "person of credit," and received the following statement:

The line of the limits of Canada to the Westward traced by M. de Vaudreuil ended at the Confluence of the Ohio and the Mississippi. From this Confluence to the sea the course of the Mississippi shall serve as limits between the two nations; but as the Mississippi has several mouths, that one is meant that is the most easterly: that is to say, the one which flows through the little Iberville River, Lakes Maurepas and Pontchartrain, and from thence communicates with the sea.[260]

Choiseul accepted the Mississippi as a boundary, but he objected strenuously to the proposed cession of all the "Neutral Islands" to England.

---

[258] Egremont to Viry, May 1, 1762, C.L., Shelburne Mss., IX: fols. 164–175.

[259] Egremont to Viry, May 1, 1762; same to same, same date, C.L., Shelburne Mss., IX: fols. 164–165.

[260] "Note au sujet de la Limite du Cours du Mississippi entre les deux Nations," C.L., Shelburne Mss., IX. The boundary thus proposed would have given Mobile and Biloxi to England, but it would have left New Orleans in the hands of France. The "person of credit" was probably Bute, and the statement was apparently made without the knowledge of his colleagues. Cf. Pease, "The Mississippi Boundary," op. cit., XI, 281.

St. Lucia, he said, was particularly necessary to the French because of its strategic domination of the other French islands. He proposed, as a substitute for the British demand, that St. Lucia and Grenada be allocated to France, and that Great Britain keep Dominica (or, possibly, Grenada), St. Vincent, and Tobago. As for the Mississippi boundary, he would make that river the boundary between British and French territories above its confluence with the Ohio, thus abandoning the Vaudreuil line and including the Illinois country in British territory. Below the Ohio, however, as France had settlements on both shores, he demanded sovereignty of both banks of the river and proposed that the boundary be drawn parallel to, and one league from, the left bank, through Lakes Maurepas and Pontchartrain to the sea. This, he said, would give Great Britain the port of Mobile and would put Louisiana and Florida in an "absolute dependence" upon the British colonies.[261]

Choiseul also objected to St. Pierre and Miquelon as an *abri*. They were too small, he said; and he again proposed that Cape Breton be restored to France, with the condition that it should never be fortified. If Britain was still unwilling to cede Cape Breton, he expressed a willingness to accept some other sizable island in the gulf. Should the worst come to the worst, however, he would accept St. Pierre and Miquelon rather than wreck the negotiation, asking only that, in that case, the French should enjoy the same liberty to dry fish on the coasts of Cape Breton as they were to enjoy on the northern coasts of Newfoundland. As for India, he indicated that France needed nothing but certain trading stations, which would remain unfortified. Gorée he accepted; but he demanded, with it, the right to trade in the Senegal River. Finally, he proposed certain detailed arrangements for the Germanies, which might be modified should Great Britain so desire.[262]

To the British cabinet, in his covering letters, Choiseul appealed for a speedy peace. He predicted that the expedition against Cuba would fail, Spain would succeed against Portugal, and Spanish demands would soar. It would be a pity if the one small island of St. Lucia were to cause a continuation of the war, but he was determined to continue, if necessary. Against a cession of that small island he could cite his generosity with regard to the Mississippi. France, he said, would never have made such a concession in 1761. To cede the eastern half of the Mississippi Valley was to give away almost the whole of Louisiana, which, with the proposed boundaries, no longer had any communication with Florida. "Spain will perhaps make difficulties over this article," he wrote, "on account of her

[261] Solar to Viry, May 12, 1762, C.L., Shelburne Mss., IX: fols. 208–212; Memoir of the Duc de Choiseul, May 25, 1762, C.L., Shelburne Mss., IX: fols. 261–279.
[262] Memoir of the Duc de Choiseul, May 25, 1762, C.L., Shelburne Mss., IX: fols. 261–279.

colony of Florida; but we will make her listen to reason. If she takes it badly, we will propose to her the exchange of Florida, though I know not what we should do with it, for whatever remains to us of Louisiana." [263]

Choiseul's chief objective, now more than ever, was a speedy and generous peace, to promote it, he used all his wiles on the inexperienced Bute. But he was too able a statesman to abandon his plans for the war simply because of the apparently favorable attitude of the British cabinet toward peace. He therefore made his arrangements for war at the same time that he was seeking peace; and, while inviting Spain to join him in his negotiations with Great Britain, he was also urging his ally to strike quickly and effectively at Portugal. His plan for war was based upon a projected invasion of England calculated to force that country to accept reasonable terms. Such an invasion would depend upon at least a temporary control of the English Channel, which, in turn, would be possible only if British ships and men were diverted to the defense of Portugal. Thus, while urging Spain to strike, he was playing upon the disturbance in the British cabinet caused by Newcastle's resignation to hasten the making of an early and reasonable peace, and was at the same time suggesting to Viry, with a treacherous apparent candor, that, because a victory for Spain in Portugal would go to the heads of the Spanish and make it difficult to bring Spain into the peace, Great Britain should rush all possible troops to Portugal, as the chief action of the year's campaign would take place there.[264]

Spain had been kept informed of the negotiations by Choiseul, and at his suggestion Great Britain had extended to His Catholic Majesty the same invitation to make peace that had been sent to Louis XV.[265] As a preliminary basis for negotiations, the British ministers had expressed a willingness to evacuate the military posts at Rio Tinto, Wallis River, and

[263] Choiseul to Solar, May 28, 1762, C.L., Shelburne Mss., IX: fols. 284–297. Choiseul indulged in a lengthy exposition of his colonial views in justification of his demand for St. Lucia. With a mercantilism somewhat watered down by physiocratic doctrine, he declared himself an enemy of large colonial empires. The "American system," in particular, had been pernicious in its effects upon France; "I consider it more essential to cultivate the grain, the vines of the realm, and to sustain its manufactures, than to supply foreigners with sugar, coffee and indigo." Since these products were become necessities in France, however, he added, "I think a great power should not export any money from its own territory for these commodities . . . and, consequently, it pertains to the perfection of its constitution to have enough American possessions to supply its needs of this sort . . . [but] at the same time that the said possessions should be secure and that the commerce of the metropolis may be carried on without fear of unforeseen events, such as the effects of the ill-humor of a governor, or of a sea-captain from a neighboring isle." St. Lucia was so important with regard to all these considerations, he said, that he would continue the war rather than give it up.
[264] Corbett, *England in the Seven Years War*, II, 298–311; Solar to Viry, June 17, 18, 1762, C.L., Shelburne Mss., X: fols. 18–25.
[265] A.É., Corr. Pol., Espagne, 536: fols. 60–61, 62–69; Solar to Viry, May 12, 1762, C.L., Shelburne Mss., IX: fols. 203–208; Declaration by the British King, May 19, 1762, C.L., Shelburne Mss., IX: fols. 217–218.

Laguna Azul, in exchange for a guarantee by Spain of the right to continue cutting dyewood on the above coastal areas. The claims of Spain to a share in the Newfoundland cod fishery were to be left as they had been by the Anglo-Spanish Treaty of Utrecht.[266]

Great Britain's invitation to make peace was forwarded to Spain by Choiseul,[267] who was already urging His Catholic Majesty both to join promptly in such negotiations,[268] and at the same time to push forward his plans for war in order to force Great Britain to make a reasonable settlement.[269] He trusted neither the Spanish ambassador nor the ambassador's master,[270] and his distrust was intensified by the reports he was receiving from his ambassador at the Spanish court. For His Catholic Majesty, who had but recently entered the war, was still in the first flush of his enthusiasm and reluctant to make peace before there had been some signal feat of arms, such as he hoped might soon take place in Portugal.[271]

In addition to this reluctance to make peace, Choiseul had also anticipated trouble from Spain over the Mississippi boundary. True to his predictions, it came when the Spanish accepted the British declaration for peace, which Grimaldi handed Choiseul on June 24.[272] In this reply to the suggested terms, the Spanish ambassador merely stated that Spain would adhere, on the three vital points at issue, to the demands made upon Great Britain before the war began.[273] But when Choiseul had prepared to draft the articles which he was to forward to England, Grimaldi strenuously objected to the Mississippi boundary, as accepted by Choiseul in May, on the ground that it would bring the British into the Gulf of Mexico. Choiseul made light of the objection: the boundary he had proposed, he said, would not give Great Britain a single port large enough to receive a frigate. But Grimaldi insisted. Spain, he declared, would never admit the British to the gulf; as for Mobile, he demanded that the important port be not even mentioned in the negotiation. Choiseul, who

---

[266] Viry to Solar, May 22, 1762, C.L., Shelburne Mss., IX: fols. 237–239.

[267] Duc de Choiseul to Solar, May 27, 1762, C.L., Shelburne Mss., IX: fols. 281–282.

[268] A.É., Corr. Pol., Espagne, 536: fols. 221–222, 308–313.

[269] A.É., Corr. Pol., Espagne, 536: fols. 221–222; Solar to Viry, June 17, 18, 1762, C.L., Shelburne Mss., IX: fols. 18–25.

[270] Of Grimaldi, he said, "Il n'y a pas de Sottise dont je ne crois le Bavard capable; mais Je vous prie de dissimuler jusqu'à la Fin; Nous avons besoin de Lui et nous le conduirons par son Foible Jusqu'au bout; après quoi nous nous moquerons de Lui" (Duc de Choiseul to Solar, May 25, 1762, C.L., Shelbourne Mss., IX: fols. 258–261).

[271] A.É., Corr. Pol., Espagne, 536: fols. 281–283; Duc de Choiseul to Solar, May 28, 1762, C.L., Shelburne Mss., IX: fols. 283–297.

[272] Grimaldi to the duke de Choiseul, June 24, 1762, C.L., Shelburne Mss., X: fols. 103–107.

[273] Reply of Spain to the British declaration, June 12, 1762, C.L., Shelburne Mss., X: fols. 103–107; A.É., C.P., Espagne, 526: fols. 389–390.

was already committed to the line of the Iberville, felt constrained at least to appear to cede to the intransigent Spaniard, and, therefore, inserted in his note a vague article which apparently shut the British off from the sea.[274]

Choiseul's proposals of June 28 were little more, therefore, than a formal statement of his more informal suggestions of May 25.[275] The outstanding part of his note, of course, was that relating to the Mississippi boundary. This article, as formulated to meet the objections of Grimaldi, provided that "France will agree to the fixation of the boundaries of Canada with the greatest extent, it being understood that they will not extend beyond the Mississippi River, nor encroach upon the dependencies of Louisiana along the seacoast." This Choiseul recognized as a radical departure from the line as drawn by the British; but he explained to Solar that he had no intention of varying his preceding offer, and Great Britain had only to insist, to break down Spain's resistance.[276]

Shortly after this Franco-Spanish communication was sent off, Egremont's reply to the French proposals of May 25 at last arrived. This reply was anything but encouraging and should have cleared Choiseul's mind of the delusion that he could play upon the divisions within the British cabinet to win British acquiescence to a generous peace. The French insistence upon St. Lucia, and Choiseul's half refusal of the *abri* offered, had stirred the resentment of the British ministers. Bedford, to be sure, was disposed to accede to Choiseul's demands; Bute, too, was for conceding St. Lucia. But the majority of the ministers were for taking a firm stand. Egremont's answer therefore rejected all the proposed French compromises. He stood firm on St. Pierre and Miquelon, and scoffed at the *quid pro quo* offered in return for the rich "sugar islands" which Great Britain was willing to restore to France. The islands offered Britain, he said, were worth absolutely nothing; the additional lands along the upper Mississippi were "desert and useless plains," which, "if they belonged to France, make part of the cession of Canada"; and Mobile was only a "little establishment stuck in between those of France and Spain." But his strongest argument was against the proposed French *lisière* on the left

[274] A.É., Corr. Pol., Espagne, 536: fols. 380–382, 385–386; Solar to Viry, June 30, 1762, C.L., Shelburne Mss., X: fols. 139–147.
[275] He again asked for Cape Breton instead of St. Pierre and Miquelon; if England insisted on retaining Cape Breton, France would acquiesce, provided only that she were granted the privilege of drying fish on the shores of Cape Breton as well as on those of Newfoundland. He insisted upon having St. Lucia for France, and asked for the privilege of trading on the Senegal River. With regard to the Germanies, he proposed that Wesel and Gelderland be garrisoned by French troops, and that England agree not to let her Hanoverian troops go to the aid of Prussia.
[276] "Projet des Articles de Paix dressés par la France," June 28, 1762, C.L., Shelburne Mss., X: fols. 108–121; Choiseul to Solar, June 29, 1762, *ibid.*, X: fols. 132–138; Colar to Viry; June 30, 1762, *ibid.*, X: fols. 139–147.

bank of the Mississippi. The British intention in proposing the river as a boundary, he said, was to provide a line that would avoid forever any possible disputes in that region. Not only did the French proposal contain the germs of endless broils, but it also "totally prohibits us from the navigation of the Mississippi, which we have understood should be in common for the commerce of the two nations." [277]

Bute attempted to soften the effect of this reply by informally suggesting that the Duke of Bedford, the most ardent English advocate for peace, might be the plenipotentiary who would bring the negotiations to a conclusion.[278] Bute and Egremont were both becoming genuinely apprehensive as to their success; finally, on June 28, Egremont, with the knowledge only of Bute, assured Viry that if France accepted the other British conditions, Great Britain would give up St. Lucia, despite the recent decision of the cabinet.[279] This concession eased the strain considerably and probably saved the negotiations from complete failure. The question of the Mississippi was still far from settled, however, and the French ministers expressed amazement that the British insisted upon the Mississippi River as the boundary, from its source to its mouth, apparently without realizing that this would give New Orleans, the capital and the key to the whole of Louisiana, to Great Britain. To clarify the British ministerial mind, therefore, Choiseul sent a map to Viry, whereon was a tracing of the boundary as proposed by France, a boundary which was now extended to include everything the British demanded, except the island and city of New Orleans.[280]

The arrival of Choiseul's proposals of June 28 did not help matters in the British mind. Egremont had to express the disappointment which he and his colleagues felt that the French had made no real concessions on the vital points. He reiterated the British determination to cede nothing beyond St. Pierre and Miquelon as an *abri*, made no observable concession on St. Lucia, and demanded that the Mississippi River, from its source to the sea, be the boundary in North America.[281] In the three Spanish points he saw little difficulty, except that he insisted upon a Spanish guarantee of the British privilege of cutting dyewood before England evacuated the forts on the dyewood coasts.[282] Bute worked hard with

[277] Egremont's memoir of June 26, 1762, C.L., Shelburne Mss., X: fols. 44–61; Egremont to Viry, June 26, *ibid.*, X: fols. 37–44.

[278] Bute to Viry, June 26, 1762, C.L., Shelburne Mss., X: fols. 184–189; Viry to Solar, June 27, 1762, *ibid.*, X: fols. 61–92.

[279] Viry to Solar, June 27, 1762, C.L., Shelburne Mss., X: fols. 61–92; Viry to Solar, June 28, 1762, *ibid.*, X: fols. 192–194.

[280] Solar to Viry, July 4, 5, 1762, C.L., Shelburne Mss., X: fols. 204–210, 216–224.

[281] Egremont's memoir to Viry, July 10, 1762, C.L., Shelburne Mss., X: fols. 257–271.

[282] Egremont to the Comte de Choiseul, July 10, 1762, C.L., Shelburne Mss., X: 243–246.

Viry over the article on the Mississippi and finally produced a secret provision which would give New Orleans to France. Viry warned his correspondent in Paris that he must reply to the English note with great caution as Bute and Egremont would probably be destroyed were their secret concessions on Louisiana, St. Lucia, and the Germanies to become known. Choiseul was requested to word his next communication as if the secret concessions of Bute and Egremont had never been made. He was to insist upon St. Lucia as a *sine qua non*, but he must admit the Mississippi River as a boundary, following the Iberville River outlet to the sea in order to leave Now Orleans in the hands of the French, while guaranteeing the navigation of the river to both nations.[283]

Choiseul now acceded to all the British demands. And well he might, for he saw all his well-calculated schemes failing before his eyes. Carlos III, unfortunately, was a gentleman and had hesitated to strike his neighbor, Portugal, without warning. He had waited so long that he had given Great Britain time to send to Portugal's aid sufficient reinforcements to make Spanish success in that quarter extremely unlikely. When a Spanish army finally invaded Portugal it bogged down, after a series of minor successes, in the muds of the autumnal rains, and the war there became a miserable stalemate. In England, George Anson, First Lord of the Admiralty, had penetrated Choiseul's scheme for an invasion and had long since prevailed upon the cabinet to strengthen its home defenses.[284] Finally, Viry was now persistently warning the French ministers that they must make peace quickly. A continuation of the war would inevitably make the British terms harder; France might lose St. Lucia; and the seizure of Cuba, which was generally expected in London, would make it impossible for Bute to make peace without some considerable compensation.[285]

Choiseul himself was now convinced that the limit of British concession had been reached, and he made up his mind to sign the preliminaries as Great Britain wished to have them. [286] The only obstacle in the way was Spain; but Choiseul had now determined to make peace, regardless of the Spanish ambassador's "verbiage." Grimaldi wrestled with the French ministers for three successive days over the article on the Mississippi. Choiseul had tried to reassure him by saying that the British, under the article as he proposed to draw it, would have no access to the Gulf of Mexico, but Grimaldi would not be satisfied. He submitted his "preliminary articles" for the Anglo-Spanish treaty, in which apparently he did not budge from his previous demands in the matter of the British evacuation of the posts on the dyewood coast and the question of Spanish participation in the

---

[283] Viry to Solar, July 12, 1762, C.L., Shelburne Mss., X: 302–320.
[284] Corbett, *England in the Seven Years War*, II, fols. 315–322.
[285] Viry to Solar, July 12, 1762, C.L., Shelburne Mss., X: fols. 302–320.
[286] Duc de Choiseul to Solar, July 15, 1762, C.L., Shelburne Mss., X: fols. 322–325.

Newfoundland fishery. Worst of all, Spain refused absolutely to sign any peace that would give England a footing on the continental shore of the Gulf of Mexico, and Grimaldi demanded from Choiseul a written assurance that France would not make any such concession.[287]

Choiseul's note of July 21, therefore, was written under difficulties, to say the least. But he did not flinch before the logical implications of his determination to make peace. As he put it, there were now only three points separating France and England: St. Lucia, New Orleans, and the Prussian territories occupied by French troops; and Bute and Egremont had secretly accepted the French conditions on these three. In his draft he traced the boundary "between Canada and Louisiana" down the Mississippi and the Iberville Rivers; he insisted upon St. Lucia as a *sine qua non*, giving Grenada to England; and he submitted three different articles to cover Wesel and Gelderland, drawn up by Starhemberg, the Austrian ambassador in Paris, from which England might choose the one that seemed most acceptable. On the latter point, he recommended the article providing for joint occupation of these places by French and English troops.[288] Because of the strenuous objection of Grimaldi, the article on the Mississippi boundary was so worded in the draft treaty as to indicate that the line would run only to Lake Pontchartrain and that the English possessions would not extend to the shore of the gulf. A separate article, making it perfectly clear that the line ran to the sea and that the English territory included the shoreline from the Perdido River, the boundary of Spanish Florida, to Lake Pontchartrain, was to be kept secret until the signing of the definitive treaty. If the Spanish still balked at the terms, France was prepared, said Choiseul, to sign without them.[289]

To all intents and purposes, the Anglo-French peace now seemed to be made, but it still had to be passed upon by a divided and ill-disciplined British cabinet. George Grenville and the Earl of Granville led the opposition, which was determined not to give way either on St. Lucia or on New Orleans. It took all Bute's influence and the personal intervention of the King to overcome the objections of this opposition; and, even so, Bute could not bring his colleagues to accept the French proposals in the case

[287] Duc de Choiseul to Solar, July 19, 1762, C.L., Shelburne Mss., X: fols. 325–326; Solar to Viry, July 21, 1762, *ibid.*, X: fols. 420–422; Spanish Project of Preliminaries, July 20, 1762, *ibid.*, X: fols. 345–353; A.É., Corr. Pol., Espagne, 536: fols. 512, 513–514, 521, 522.
[288] "Projet d'articles Préliminaires arrêtés entre la France et L'Angleterre," C.L., Shelburne Mss., X: fols. 376–388; Comte de Choiseul to Egremont, July 21, 1762, *ibid.*, X: fols. 369–373, 402–413; Duc de Choiseul to Solar, July 21, 1762, *ibid.*, X: fols. 361–365; Solar to Viry, July 21, 1762, *ibid.*, X: fols. 336–344.
[289] Duc de Choiseul to Solar, July 21, 1762, C.L., Shelburne Mss., X: fols. 361–365; Comte de Choiseul to Solar, July 21, 1762, *ibid.*, X: fols. 369–373; Solar to Viry, July 21, 1762, *ibid.*, X: fols. 428–433; "Projet d'articles Préliminaires," *ibid.*, X: fols. 376–388; "Note, Art. 6," *ibid.*, X: fols. 373–374.

of Wesel and Gelderland. Reserving these questions, therefore, for further discussion by the negotiators of the treaty in its final form, Egremont was at last instructed to inform Choiseul that England conceded St. Lucia and New Orleans to France and was ready to name an ambassador whenever France wished. He made certain new reservations as to the Mississippi boundary, however. Since it was very doubtful whether the Iberville River were deep enough to make English navigation of the Mississippi a reality, he asked that England be permitted, when navigating the Mississippi, to use the same channel the French used from the Iberville to the sea; and to forestall any possible French fortifications below the city of New Orleans that would block English entry to the river, he asked that any land east of the river below the island of New Orleans be included in the cession to be made to England—thus granting France the island of New Orleans alone. As for Spain, the British ministry was opposed to making a separate peace without that country and requested Choiseul to attempt to bring His Catholic Majesty to a settlement.[290]

Choiseul was desperate. Spain was adamant on the question of the Mississippi and showed no signs of growing less so. Early in August Wall proposed to d'Ossun that the southern boundary of "Canada" be drawn so as to leave no doubt as to the exclusion of the British from access to the Gulf of Mexico. Spain had never recognized either France's title to Louisiana or England's title to Georgia. It would do so now, he said, if England would consent to mark the southern limits of "Canada" by a line to be drawn directly from the western boundary of Georgia to the Mississippi, leaving the territory between this line, the Mississippi, Florida, and the sea to the natives. He apparently thought nothing, in proposing this prototype of the later line of 31°-31', of asking France and England to consent to the abandonment of such considerable places as Mobile and Biloxi.[291]

This was too much for Choiseul, and he crisply replied that France would do as it chose with its own. Unfortunately, the latest English reply had omitted any discussion of possible Spanish preliminary articles, and the French minister was under the necessity of mollifying the offended Spanish ambassador. In view of the English omission, Choiseul took it upon himself to compose a message for Spain, which he based upon Egremont's letter of July 31; in it he tactfully suppressed all of the British terms that he thought Grimaldi should not see. Then, in an effort to cajole Spain into speedy acceptance of the British terms and into naming a plenipotentiary, he sent his friend Jacob O'Dunne to Madrid to assist

[290] Egremont to the Comte de Choiseul, July 31, 1762, C.L., Shelburne Mss., XI: fols. 8–16; Egremont to Viry, July 31, 1762, ibid., XI: fols. 32–52; Viry to Solar, Aug. 1, 1762, ibid., XI: fols. 52–68.
[291] A.É., Corr. Pol., Espagne, 537: fols. 4–12.

d'Ossun in his negotiations at the Spanish court. He felt sure of success and named September 5 as the day on which the English and French ambassadors should be ready to depart for their respective posts.[292]

August passed while these preparations were being made. On August 21, Egremont corrected his omission with regard to Spain by saying he proposed to leave the Spanish questions in the hands of the ambassadors. But to make the British position clear, he said that the British plenipotentiary would be instructed to insist that the question of prizes be left with British courts of admiralty; that Spanish participation in the Newfoundland fishery be left as provided in treaties in existence prior to the war; and that questions of the restitution of conquered territory be left to the plenipotentiaries for discussion. On the vital question of dyewoods Spain and Great Britain would exchange agreements: Great Britain to evacuate its military posts, and Spain to guarantee to Great Britain the privilege of cutting.[293]

Two days later the news of a successful British action before Havana arrived in London, and a wave of national enthusiasm swept the country.[294] On August 26, Solar advised Viry that Spain's reply to the French mission was satisfactory and that Grimaldi had been named Spanish plenipotentiary for the negotiation of the treaty in Paris.[295] On the same day Solar communicated to Grimaldi the news from Havana, and Choiseul began to talk to him in a manner to *"rabattre son caquet"* ("to quiet his cackling"). It was assumed that, if occupied, Cuba would be restored; but everybody knew that if Havana itself should fall Great Britain would not make peace without some compensation for this important conquest. As Solar put it, Spain's war had been *"plus bruyante que brillante!"* ("more burning than brilliant!").[296]

It was thus in an atmosphere of excitement and of rising British temper that the Duc de Nivernais [297] and the Duke of Bedford received their instructions as ambassadors and plenipotentiaries. They were empowered to sign preliminary articles on the basis of the British and French notes of the preceding July 10 and 21. Only one point seemed to promise much

[292] Comte de Choiseul to Solar, Aug. 10, 1762, C.L., Shelburne Mss., XI: fols. 94–98; Comte de Choiseul to Egremont, Aug. 10, 1762, *ibid.*, XI: fols. 146–168; Duc de Choiseul to Solar, Ang. 12, 1762, *ibid.*, XI: fols. 103–113; Solar to Viry, Aug. 12, 1762, *ibid.*, XI: fols. 114–133.

[293] Egremont to Comte de Choiseul, Aug. 21, 1762, C.L., Shelburne Mss., XI: fols. 183–188.

[294] Viry to Solar, Aug. 23, 1762, C.L., Shelburne Mss., XI: fols. 214–217.

[295] Solar to Viry, Aug. 26, 1762, C.L., Shelburne Mss., XI: fols, 257–267; Comte de Choiseul to Egremont, Aug. 26, 1762, *ibid.*, XI: fols. 277–289.

[296] Viry to Solar Aug. 23, 1762, C.L., Shelburne Mss., XI: fols. 214–217; Solar to Viry, Aug. 26, 1762, *ibid.*, XI: fols. 289–294; Viry to Solar, Sept. 4, 1762, *ibid.*, XI: fols. 334–387.

[297] Louise Jules Bourbon Mancini-Mazarini, Duc de Nivernais.

difficulty, and that was the delicate position which France occupied with regard to Spain, whose approval of a British means of access to the Gulf of Mexico, hitherto rigorously denied, must be obtained before the peace could be made. It was to be hoped that future news from Havana might bring Spain to give in on this point. On the other hand, as the mutual returning of ships and territory captured by Spain and Great Britain was to be left to the British and Spanish ambassadors for settlement, Bedford was instructed merely to make as good a bargain as he could. But he was to sign no separate peace; Spain and France must sign together, and Portugal must be included.[298]

Bedford reached Paris on September 12, and negotiations began. He had little or no trouble with the French ministers, but Grimaldi presented almost insuperable difficulties on every point and injected a demand for new and revised commercial agreements between Great Britain and Spain. This being a point on which Bedford had no instructions, he was compelled to refer it to London. The French ministers had not yet dared to break to Grimaldi the true import of their secret article on the Mississippi, and they begged Bedford not to jeopardize the peace by betraying the secret before the signing of the preliminaries. They assured him that if Great Britain so desired France stood ready to sign a separate and secret article guaranteeing to Britain everything it wished on that head.[299]

The Spanish ambassador's obstructiveness was well-nigh fatal to the negotiations. Bedford's report to his government was received in an atmosphere already highly charged with hostility to Bute's peace. Popular clamor in England was mounting, cultivated and encouraged both by the opposition ministers and by the diplomatic representatives of the King of Prussia, who hated Bute. Furthermore, by his tact and address Nivernais had won certain slight concessions from Egremont that were significant only inasmuch as they increased British distrust of French sincerity. Bute himself trembled before the growing opposition, in genuine fear for both his office and his life.[300] The cabinet began to doubt the wisdom of having given Bedford plenary powers, and he was now instructed not to sign anything without first referring it to the ministry at home—a curtailment of his responsibility which he bitterly resented.[301]

It was at this juncture that the news came of the capture of Havana, and it cleared the atmosphere. Both France and Spain now showed a willingness to close with Great Britain's terms, but, as anticipated, the British cabinet raised its demands. On October 26, a new draft treaty was

[298] C.A.O., A.É., Corr. Pol., Ang., 447: fols. 28–36; Legg, ed., *Brit. Dip. Instr.*, VII, *France, 1745–1789*, 56–64, 64–66.

[299] *Bedford Correspondence*, III, 103–113.

[300] *Bedford Correspondence*, III, 114–116; C.A.O., A.É., Corr. Pol., Ang. 448: fols. 83–88; Corbett, *op. cit.*, II, 358–359.

[301] *Bedford Correspondence*, III, 116–117.

sent to Bedford, one that rejected all compromises in the articles as stated and instructed the ambassador to demand as compensation for Cuba either Florida or Puerto Rico. At the same time Bedford himself was mollified by a renewal of his full powers.[302]

Choiseul was more than ready to sign. He had asked Spain directly whether it chose to continue the war to keep England from gaining a foothold on the gulf and pointed out that, in that case, England would easily take both Florida and Louisiana.[303] Spain had decided in favor of the inevitable, with reservations; [304] but the news of the fall of Havana, reinforced by a personal appeal from Louis XV to Carlos III, obliterated the reservations. Louis, moved by Spain's sacrifices in a war undertaken in his behalf, foresaw a British demand for a *quid pro quo* for Havana. He therefore offered his Spanish cousin what remained of Louisiana, with New Orleans, to compensate him, in some measure, for his anticipated loss.[305] There was nothing else France could do. France was beaten, wrote Choiseul, and must submit to the English yoke, while preparing for a new war.[306] Carlos, although his first impulse was to decline the offer of Louisiana, accepted the expected English conditions and authorized Choiseul to proceed with the negotiations on that basis.[307]

The negotiators were thus prepared for the new draft treaty from London when it arrived in Paris. It came with a warning that France and Spain must sign, in view of the impossibility of getting further concessions through the Parliament that was shortly to meet, or else continue the war.[308] The French ministers complained of certain clarifying phrases pertinent to the St. Lawrence fishery,[309] but there was nothing for them to do but sign, which both France and Spain did, on November 3.[310]

At the same time, Choiseul and Grimaldi signed an agreement by which France ceded to Spain the western half of Louisiana, together with New Orleans.[311] At the last minute Choiseul had offered it to Great Britain, in order to relieve Spain of the necessity of ceding Florida, but the offer had been refused.[312] Spain had been treated harshly, wrote Choiseul; but

---

[302] A.É., Corr. Pol., Espagne, 537: fols. 227–230; *Bedford Correspondence*, III, 118–119.

[303] A.É., Corr. Pol., Espagne, 537: fols. 189–190.

[304] A.É., Corr. Pol., Espagne, 537: fol. 201.

[305] A.É., Corr. Pol., Espagne, 537: fols. 208, 210, 215–219, 221–222.

[306] A.É., Corr. Pol., Espagne, 537: fol. 223.

[307] A.É., Corr. Pol., Espagne, 537: fols. 266–273; C.A.O., A.E., Corr., Pol., Ang. 448: fols. 288–291.

[308] *Bedford Correspondence*, III, 139, 140–142, Legg, ed., *Brit. Dip. Instrs.*, VII, *France, 1745–1789*, pp. 69–71.

[309] C.O.A., A.É., Corr. Pol., Ang. 447: fols. 388–391.

[310] C.A.O., A.É., Corr. Pol., Ang., 448: fols. 10–11.

[311] Cantillo, ed., *Tratados*, 485.

[312] A.É., Corr. Pol., Espagne, 537: fols. 290–291, 292–293.

"as for us, the conditions are better than those of last year, and those which we might expect next year." [313]

There remained only the task of arranging the final and definitive treaty. The preliminaries had first to be ratified, and this promised to be most difficult in the British Parliament. There, the great debate took place on December 9. William Pitt spoke for three hours and forty minutes against the treaty, which, he said, cast a shadow upon Britain's glory and was both a surrender of British interests and a violation of her national

---

[313] A.É., Corr. Pol., Espagne, 537: fol. 307. As finally signed, the preliminary articles provided that (1) France was to cede to Great Britain Canada, including Acadia, Cape Breton, and all the islands in the Gulf of St. Lawrence. The French inhabitants were guaranteed the right to retain and practice the Catholic religion, "as far as the laws of Great Britain permit," and were to have the privilege of selling their property and withdrawing from Canada within eighteen months. (2) France was to be free to fish and dry fish in Newfoundland as provided by Article 13 of the Treaty of Utrecht, and to fish in the Gulf of St. Lawrence, except within three leagues of the shores of the continent and the islands in the gulf, and, outside the gulf, except within fifteen leagues of the shores of Cape Breton. (3) Great Britain was to cede to France the islands of St. Pierre and Miquelon, which France undertook to leave unfortified, and with a guard of only fifty men. (4) The fortifications of the town of Dunkirk were to be left as provided in the Treaty of Aix-la-Chapelle. (5) The boundary between French and British possessions was fixed as the course of the Mississippi and the Iberville Rivers to the sea. The river and port of Mobile, and all the land east of the Mississippi, except the island of New Orleans, were specifically ceded to Great Britain together with the right of navigation on the Mississippi from its source to its mouth, and especially that part of it between the island of New Orleans and the west bank below the Iberville. (6) Great Britain was to restore the former French West Indies and Belle Isle to France; and (7) France gave Grenada and the Grenadines to Great Britain. (8) The four "Neutral Islands" were to be divided: St. Vincent, Tobago, and Dominica were to go to England, and St. Lucia to France. (9) England was to restore Gorée to France and to retain Senegal. (10) In the East Indies, England was to restore the coast of Coromandel, Malabar, and Bengal to the *status quo* of 1749, and France was to renounce conquests on the Coromandel coast made since 1749. (11) Minorca was to be restored to England. (12) The territories of Hanover, Hesse, Brunswick, and Lippe were to be restored to their rulers by France. (13) France and England were to evacuate places and areas held by their arms in the Rhineland, Prussia, Westphalia, and "the Empire," and agreed to give no further help to their respective German allies. Finally, (14) France was to evacuate Ostend and Nieuport.

With regard to Spain, the articles provided that: (1) Cases of Spanish prizes made by British ships in time of peace were to be submitted to British courts of admiralty. (2) Great Britain was to demolish its forts on the coasts of Honduras and other Spanish territories in that part of the world, but was to continue to have the privilege of cutting logwood there. (3) Spain would no longer claim any share of the Newfoundland fishery. (4) Great Britain was to restore Havana and Cuba to Spain, and (5) Spain gave up to Great Britain all it possessed on the continent of North America, east of the Mississippi River. The inhabitants of this territory (Florida) were to have the same right to practice the Catholic religion and to move elsewhere as the French inhabitants of Canada.

"His Most Faithful Majesty" of Portugal was to be included in the treaty, and France and Spain agreed to restore to him all that had been won from him during the war. Unspecified conquests or countries were to be restored to the *status quo ante bellum*. Ships taken at sea after the expiration of certain given periods were to be restored (Almon, ed., *All the Treaties*, II, 261–271).

EUROPEAN POSSESSIONS IN NORTH AMERICA AND THE CARIBBEAN AREA
AFTER THE PEACE OF PARIS, 1763.

good faith so far as her German allies were concerned. But a cabinet shuffle and a shameless use of bribery in Parliament by Henry Fox overcame all opposition, and the preliminaries were ratified.[314] France and Spain, not being hampered by the obstructive tendencies of representative institutions, had no such difficulties.

Meanwhile, in Paris, Bedford was working over the final draft of the treaty with Choiseul. Certain questions of language and detail had arisen in the case of the British draft treaty sent to Choiseul on December 6,[315] and one, in particular, called forth strenuous objections. With a view to sharing in the control of the mouth of the Mississippi below New Orleans, the British ministers had taken advantage of the phrase giving Great Britain the ownership of everything east of the river "except the town of New Orleans and the island on which it is situated," to omit provision for the demarcation of a boundary line to be drawn through the Iberville River and Lakes Maurepas and Pontchartrain. But the French saw through this sophistry; the only island east of the Mississippi and south of the Iberville, they insisted, was the island of New Orleans. Besides, the British had constantly protested that their chief desire was for a clear and unequivocal line. It was precisely to provide a line leaving no possibility of future dispute that France had accepted the line of the Iberville and had now to insist upon it. Bedford was surprised to find Grimaldi joining strenuously in the debate over this line, and he began to suspect "that the report I have heard that France intended to cede New Orleans, to Spain has some foundation." [316] Choiseul privately expressed to Nivernais his willingness to accede to the British quibble, were it not for his commitments to Spain. But his feelings of national honor, he said, compelled him to insist. A few more conferences on the subject took place, and Egremont finally gave in.[317] With this point and the arrangements as to India finally out of the way, the work was completed by the end of January, and the definitive treaty was signed on February 10, 1763.[318]

The Treaty of Paris, as finally signed, provided that Canada was to be ceded to Great Britain, and that the boundary of the British territory on the continent should henceforth be the Mississippi and the Iberville Rivers. In the West Indies, Great Britain was to retain Grenada and the Grenadines, and the four "Neutral Islands" were to be divided, St. Lucia going to France, and St. Vincent, Tobago, and Dominica going to Great Britain. From Spain, Great Britain received Florida. The British now possessed all the land on the continent of North America east of the

---

[314] *Bedford Correspondence*, III, 166–167, 168–169.
[315] Legg. ed., *Brit. Dip. Instrs.*, VII, France, 1745–1789, 73–74.
[316] *Bedford Correspondence*, III, 173–183; C.A.O., A.É., Corr. Pol., Ang., 448: fols. 368–384; 449: fols. 30–31.
[317] C.A.O., A.É., Corr. Pol., Ang., 449: fols. 34, 72; Egremont to Bedford, Jan. 22, 1763, C.L., Shelburne Mss., XXXVIII: 5.
[318] *Bedford Correspondence*, III, 188; A.É., Corr. Pol., Espagne, 538: fol. 72.

Mississippi River, with the exception of the island and town of New Orleans.[319] This exception was of vast importance, however, because New Orleans, controlling all ingress to, and egress from the Mississippi Valley, was a gateway to the interior of North America that Spain could close at will.

[319] The text of the treaty is in Paullin, ed., *European Treaties*, IV, 92–98.

CHAPTER XX

The Growth of American Opinion Relative to International Affairs

IN THE COURSE of a century and a half of international experience, whether in the realm of intercolonial commerce, in the course of westward expansion, or in the constant reading of news of international activities among the states of western Europe,[1] the Angloamericans, by the middle of the eighteenth century, had become fully conscious of their position in the complex skein of relationships among the members of the Atlantic community of states and colonial empires. They knew what was going on, and in their own parts of the "great frontier" they participated in international activity. More than that, in the course of this activity, their spokesmen, their governors, or their agents in England, in many cases, especially in matters pertaining to territorial claims of expansion, prompted the mother country in its conduct of more formal diplomatic exchanges. In other cases, such as matters pertaining to trade with foreign colonies, where the powerful self-interests of the colonies conflicted with those of the mother country, the Americans formed ideas as to international policy that ran counter to the mercantilistic colonialism of the mother country.

But the Angloamericans were not involved merely in the actual conduct of international contacts. Many informed and enlightened Americans wrote letters, essays, sermons, and other commentaries upon the international scene in general and upon their own place in it—a corpus of writing that embodied an imposing expression of American thought and opinion relative to international affairs.

These commentaries touched upon many aspects of international relations that were of interest to the American colonies, such as Anglo-French

[1] Johnson, "The Content of American Colonial Newspapers Relative to International Affairs, 1704–1763," Unpublished Ph.D. dissertation in the University of Washington Library.

imperial rivalry in the hemisphere, their own interpretations of Anglo-French differences, the role of the Indians as factors in the international power struggle, the international repercussions of colonial disunity and the need for colonial union for the purposes of the common defense, freedom of international colonial commerce, cultural conflicts, and so on. Much, indeed, of the external policy-making of the English government was based upon reports and recommendations emanating from the colonies themselves, while English colonial and commercial imperialism in the eighteenth century coincided, for the most part, with the expansive "enlightened self-interest" of the colonies themselves. The feeling of cooperation with the mother country both formed the imperialistic impulses of the Angloamericans and encouraged them to call upon the metropolis for more and more help. In other words, English international relations, both with regard to the colonies and in them, coupled with the encouragement of colonial interest, greatly stimulated the awakening and the articulation of a body of conscious American deliberation on international affairs.[2]

Of supreme importance in the gestation of American opinions relative to international affairs was the fact that such thinking was the inevitable and natural rationalization of the experience of the Americans themselves in the day-by-day progress of their history. If they were vitally conscious of their contacts with the French, Dutch, Spanish, and Portuguese empires that surrounded them, it was because the people of many of the colonies were in almost daily contact or conflict with them or with the Indians who, in many instances, held the balance of power among them. If, on the other hand, they were vitally interested in commerce with their non-English neighbors, both in peace and during war, and if their thinking about it brought them into a position both of theoretical and of *de facto* conflict with the policies of the mother country in such matters, it was because their economic prosperity within the empire—even, it seemed at times, their very economic existence—was inseparably involved in that trade. So vital to them was it, indeed, that they would one day rebel for, among other things, the right to that trade's freedom.

Angloamerican colonial opinion relative to international affairs, then, although influenced by English opinion, was derived primarily from the actual day-by-day experiences and realistic self-interests of the Angloamericans themselves, and not, primarily, from the policies or the self-interests of the mother country.

1. *Fear of Encirclement*

The chief concern of all the colonists on continental North America, English and French, was the bitter imperial struggle between France and

[2] See Chapters XI and XIII.

England which reached its peak during the eighteenth century and made of America its chief arena of conflict. To each side the presence of a hostile power on its frontiers, threatening expansion into disputed territories during times of peace and total destruction of its neighbor in time of war, seemed to promise certain doom to all its establishments. The fact that the British and French thus confronted each other along a long and ill-defined frontier extending the length of the continent from the St. Lawrence to the Gulf of Mexico and in neighboring islands in the West Indies only intensified mutual fears.

Colonial spokesmen on each side with a good deal of justification attributed to the other deliberate intentions and plans to drive their imperial rivals from the continent, and expressed the fear that the enemy had the power to do so. At the same time, each side looked jealously at the holdings of the other and dreamed of the day when it, alone, would possess the wealth of the continent. The Angloamericans, indeed, were some of the loudest voices of British imperialism.

Such imperialistic ideas were expressed even before the end of the War of the Spanish Succession. Samuel Vetch, for example, was a Scottish-born colonial entrepreneur and prosperous trader of Albany and Boston, who hoped to become governor of Canada if it should be taken by the British and did become military governor of Nova Scotia after it was conquered. In 1708 Vetch presented to the British government a plan for the conquest of Canada. In the tract in which he presented his plan, "Canada Survey'd," Vetch expressed his wonder that a nation as strong as Britain would allow so troublesome a neighbor as France to live beside its colonies in America, with so few people to possess so much land and to hem the British colonies between the French colonies and the sea. He believed that with little expense the English could easily overpower the French, having "twenty times" the number of troops on the continent. Canada, in which Vetch included the Mississippi Valley, offered many advantages to the British, including fertile soil and an agreeable climate. Arguments of self-interest and self-preservation against French ruination of English trade and murder of English populations "must prevail upon every true Brittain, who hath any regard to the honour, interest or safety of his Country, to endeavour the reduction of that Country." [3]

Vetch believed that the acquisition of Canada would

infinitely advance the commerce of the Brittish over all America, and particularly make them sole masters of the furr, fish and navall stores trade over all the Continent, and H.M. sole Soveraign of the North Continent of America, and of hundreds of nations of new subjects, who will become intirely obedient to

[3] "Canada Survey'd, or the French Dominions upon the Continent of America briefly considered in their situation, strength, trade and number, more particularly how vastly prejudiciall they are to the British interest, and a method proposed of easily removing them," *C.S.P., Col., A.& W.I.,* 1708–09, No. 60, pp. 41–51.

her laws, when they have no preists to poyson them, nor no rivall Monarch to debauch them from her interest and make Canada a noble Colony, exactly calculate for the Constitutions and genius of the most Northern of the North Brittains.[4]

Vetch's plan won much colonial support, both from other imperialists and from those who saw that the continued presence of the French could lead only to continued conflict. After a survey of the colonies, Robert Quary, the agent of the British government in the colonies, reported from Philadelphia that there was little likelihood of the colonists driving out the French by themselves and added that "if some effectual means be not used [in] this war to remove the French, it will be too late afterwards."[5]

The French were not, however, driven from the continent during Queen Anne's War, and the Anglo-French struggle for dominion continued. In 1715, Colonel Caleb Heathcote, an articulate New York farmer, wrote to Governor Hunter of New York on the occasion of a series of Indian revolts in Carolina and New England, expressing his fears that they were instigated by the French, who planned "to angle us away, province by province, till at last all will be gon."[6] He urged that strong defensive measures be taken by the British colonies, because "it is impossible that we & the French can both inhabit this Continent in peace but that one nation must at last give way to the other, so 'tis very necessary that without sleeping away our time, all precautions imaginable should be taken to prevent its falling to our lotts to remove."[7] Heathcote was thus one of the earliest Angloamericans to anticipate the idea that one or the other of the two empires must inevitably drive the other from the continent.

The people of the southern colonies found themselves, in the eighteenth century, potentially confined to the narrow seaboard by French penetration of the country beyond the Appalachian Mountains. To them, therefore, it was vital that England establish its dominion in that area. Because the western boundaries of these colonies, as defined by their charters, ran on indefinitely to the "South Sea," the movement of the French into the lower Mississippi Valley was construed as trespassing, pleas to the British government to occupy those lands were many and urgent, and various schemes to promote English colonization in the west were developed to prevent the French from gaining control there.

One of the earliest of these plans for settlement was that of Price Hughes, a Welshman who arrived in South Carolina between 1712 and 1713 to promote the creation of a Welsh colony in the area around Natchez, on the Mississippi. Hughes attempted to make very clear the

[4] "Canada Survey'd," loc. cit., 51.
[5] Quoted in Waller, Samuel Vetch, Colonial Enterpriser, 106.
[6] Heathcote to Hunter, July 8, 1715, N.Y.C.D., V, 430.
[7] N.Y.C.D., V, 431.

justice of his plan; the Welsh had no intention of encroaching upon the acquisitions of the French at Mobile "but in an industrious way seek an honest Settlement in those Parts we've allready fixt upon to that purpose". The English had already possessed a great part of the Mississippi and Alabama Rivers long before the French settled at their mouths, "So that they are but encroachers at best"; he "flatly" denied that the French were the first discoverers of those regions, as they claimed to be. Hughes was particularly concerned that the French might learn of his scheme before he was able to put it into effect and that they would send settlers from Mobile to prevent British settlement in Natchez. He concluded that "probably they'll be little the better for it when we have a precedent title both by claim and possession. If the English think proper to follow their garbe [style in dress] at home: the Britains I believe will not be Subject to their Prescriptions in America, Having as yet some little of our old courage as well as discretion left." [8] Already an American sense of moral superiority over Britain!

The position of the southern colonies was particularly precarious because they were exposed to attack not only by the French and Spanish and their various Indian allies but by independent tribes as well who were dissatisfied by their treatment at the hands of the British. Alexander Spotswood, Lieutenant Governor of Virginia, feared that the combination would be too much: while the English forces were on the frontiers fighting Indians the cities were left open to attack by the French or Spanish and could easily be taken.[9] Spotswood therefore made frequent pleas for reinforcements for the colonial militia, with little success. He also encouraged British settlement of the southwest to offset the effects that French settlement there would have on the trade and security of the British colonies. He feared that the French there would begin to cultivate the chief exports of the British colonies, tobacco and rice, and thus compete with Britain for its markets and also that they would gain all of the Indian trade of the British. The French, he said, in reply to the Board of Trade's inquiry in 1720, in effect now surround the English from the Great Lakes to the Gulf of Mexico. They bid fair to dominate the Indian trade in all that area; by fortifying the passes over the Alleghenies they would be in a position to overrun all the British colonies.

And seeing [he said], by their late seizure of Pensacola, their design seems to be to extend their Dominions Eastward from Mississippi towards South Carolina, It is certainly the British Interest to put a stop to their Advancing any further that way, w'ch, in My Opinion, w'll be best Effected by possessing our selves with some places on the Coast of Florida, and forming a Settlement as

[8] Hughes to the Duchess of Ormande, Oct., 1713. Quoted in Crane, *The Southern Frontier*, 101–102.
[9] Spotswood to Secretary Stanhope, July 15, 1715. *The Official Letters of Alexander Spotswood*, Brock, ed., II, 120–125.

near as can be to cramp their's, w'ch leads me to consider the other part Yo'r Lord'ps desire to be informed in, vizt: the Importance of taking St. Augustine from the Spaniards.[10]

The possession of St. Augustine would allow the British to control the Bahama Channel, through which the French and Spanish ships passed on their way to Europe from the Caribbean and the Gulf of Mexico. In the case of a rupture with France, the trade of the French settlements on the Mississippi could be destroyed by the British in that channel. Spotswood also proposed that the British capture the Spanish fort of St. Mark, on the west side of Florida, as a base of operations against the French Mississippi settlements.[11]

Other American expressions of the fear of French encirclement and of the imperialistic urge to push the French out of the continent were formulated and communicated to England about this same time by the governor of Pennsylvania, Sir William Keith, and the Pennsylvania colonial secretary, James Logan. Keith, asked by the Board of Trade for a report on Pennsylvania's situation *vis-à-vis* the French, called upon Logan, who was deeply engaged in the Indian trade, for advice. He got it, in the form of a report from Logan, then added some reflections of his own and sent the whole to the Board of Trade.[12] The best way, Keith wrote, to forestall the French was by engrossing the trade with the Indians, "as far westwaid upon the Lakes and Rivers behind the great mountains" as might be possible. But this could be done most effectively by establishing a unified imperial control of Indian trade for all the colonies, "without any distinction made or regard had to their particular Societies as separate Governments." [13] He thus anticipated a step taken after the Albany Congress of 1754.

As for defense, Keith proposed that a fort be built on Lake Erie, another on Lake Ontario, one at the headwaters of the Potomac River, and a fourth at the headwaters of the Susquehanna. The first would be supported and commanded by Virginia, the one on Lake Ontario by New York, the one on the Potomac by Maryland, and that on the Susquehanna by Pennsylvania.[14]

At the moment when Spotswood and Keith made their comments on the Anglo-French situation in America, England and France were at war

[10] Spotswood to the Board of Trade, Feb. 1, 1720, *Official Letters of Alexander Spotswood*, Brock, ed., II, 328–335.

[11] *Official Letters of Alexander Spotswood*, Brock, ed., II, 328–335.

[12] C.S.P., Col., A.& W.I., 1719–20, No. 61 (1), pp. 32–41. See also, Wendel, "Sir William Keith, Lieutenant Governor of Pennsylvania and the Three Lower Counties, 1717–1726," unpublished Ph.D. dissertation in the University of Washington Library.

[13] C.S.P., Col., A.& W.I., 1719–20, No. 61 (I), pp. 36, 37.

[14] C.S.P., Col., A.& W.I., 1719–20, No. 61 (I), pp. 36, 37.

with Spain.[15] These governors' reports were among a number of similar reports sent in by British governors in America, made in answer to inquiries by the Board of Trade, which provided basic information and recommendations for the Board's famous "State of the British Plantations in America, 1721," made to the crown on the condition of the colonies and recommending measures to be taken to provide for colonial defense, including a unified military command.[16]

In 1727, Daniel Coxe of New Jersey, whose father, a speculator in American lands, had acquired in 1698 the area called "Carolana," in the Mississippi Valley, under a charter issued in 1629 by King Charles I to Sir Robert Heath, published a small booklet called A *Description of the English Province of Carolana*. In his booklet he warned against French aggression, which he blamed on the "levity and restlessness" of the Gallic temper, the enterprising genius of the French, and their ambition to extend their dominions and raise the glory and grandeur of their monarchs.[17] In contrast to the English, whom Coxe complained had too little regard for the welfare of their colonies,

the *French*, who all the world acknowledge to be an enterprizing, great and politick *Nation*, are so sensible of the *Advantages* of *Foreign Colonies*, both in reference to *Empire* and *Trade*, that they use all manner of *Artifices* to lull their *Neighbours* A Sleep, with fine *Speeches* and plausible *Pretences*, whilst they cunningly endeavour to compass their *Designs* by degrees, tho' at the hazard of encroaching on their *Friends* and Allies, and depriving them of their *Territories* and *Dominions* in time of *Profound Peace*, and contrary to the most *Solemn Treaties*.[18]

Coxe was far from being satisfied to recommend a defensive posture for the English colonies, whether along the seaboard or even in the Mississippi Valley. In his pamphlet, published in the hope of stimulating English interest in the Mississippi Valley, he emphasized the danger to the British colonies should the French gain control of Carolana, which they called Louisiana, and surround the British colonies. The ministry at the time of the Peace of Utrecht was to be criticized for not having insisted upon the surrender of Canada for the security of the northern colonies, but now, at least, Coxe hoped that the British would cease being inattentive to French usurpations and let them know that they had enough in Canada and Cape Breton and that they were expected to abandon their new acquisitions on the Mississippi and Gulf of Mexico because those places belonged to Britain.[19]

[15] See Chapter XIV.
[16] N.Y.C.D., V, 630 ff.
[17] Coxe, A *Description of the English Province of Carolana*, 10.
[18] Coxe, A *Description of . . . Carolana*, 9.
[19] Coxe, A *Description of . . . Carolana*, 10.

In the event that the British failed to assert their right to this "so useful and necessary" colony, Coxe believed it preferable that the Spanish be masters of it rather than the French, since the British had less reason to be apprehensive of a Spanish threat to their colonies, trade, or navigation. It was prudent, he said, to strive to maintain a balance of power in America as well as in Europe, and since the British had striven to check the growing power of France in Europe they should not allow them to encroach on their American possessions. The Spanish were uneasy about the presence of the French on the Mississippi, and with proper encouragement Coxe believed they could be induced to join the British to drive the French from the area and then divide the country with Britain, surrendering all their claims east of the Mississippi except St. Augustine. Nothing could be more reasonable than that the Mississippi River should be the boundary between the territories of Spain and Britain. "*Nature* seeming to have form'd it almost purposely for that end." [20]

The value of Carolana was enhanced by the possibility that there might be a river communication from the Mississippi to the Pacific, providing a passage to Asia. Moreover, the presence of so many useful minerals, plants, and animals in Carolana would allow the British to match the progress of Spain since the conquest of Mexico and Peru.[21]

A few years later James Logan offered his own interpretation of the French menace and his suggestion as to what England should do about it. Logan was convinced that Britain's commercial and naval power depended in large measure upon the prosperity and safety of the colonies. Similarly, the power of France and Spain derived from their colonies; therefore,

its plain that nothing but a Conjunction [of France] with Spain could more effectually Contribute to that than the Accession of the Trade & Navigation of America and its very certain that ever since the Peace of Utrecht they [the French] have constantly Studied and been Silently making Advances to this while the British Interest there appears to have been as much neglected.[22]

Logan was deeply impressed by the rapid expansion of the French in the West Indies and on the continent of North America; he was genuinely disturbed by the prospect of the upset of the balance of power in America and in Europe that might be caused by a union of the French and Spanish empires. He warned the British government that "the American Plantations are of such Importance to Britain, that the Loss of them to any other Power especially to France might be its own ruin," and he

[20] Coxe, A *Description of* . . . *Carolina*, 11–12.
[21] Coxe, A *Description of* . . . *Carolina*, 14–16.
[22] Logan, "Of the State of the British Plantations in America," printed in Joseph C. Johnson, ed., "A Quaker Imperialist's View of the British Colonies in America, 1732," *Pennsylvania Magazine of History and Biography*, LX, No. 2 (April, 1936), 97–130. The quotation is from *ibid.*, 128.

urged it to treat the colonies well and to take vigorous steps to protect them.[23]

William Douglass, similarly, writing in 1747, saw the French as troublesome neighbors, "the common Nusance and Disturbers of *Europe*, and will in a short Time become the same in *America*, if not mutilated at Home, and in *America* fenced off from us by Ditches and Walls, that is, by great Rivers and impracticable Mountains. They are a numerous, powerful, rich and polite Nation . . ." [24]

2. Enticement to Imperialism: Strategic Considerations, The Land and Its Boundaries, and the Indian Trade

The *desiderata* of greatest and most compelling attractiveness to the imperialists on both sides were land and the control of the Indian fur and skin trade, to which, as a part of their reasoning, must be added strategic considerations. Along every part of the frontier, from Acadia to Florida and including the West Indies, lay territories the title to which the British disputed with their French and Spanish neighbors. Some areas were desired for their strategic value, others for their economic promise; but all of these areas aroused deep desires in the hearts of the Angloamericans. The expressions of this interest were extremely numerous; both public and private persons seem to have inundated the British ministry with appeals to secure various territorial areas to British possession. But the range of colonial concern was generally limited. The most significant area to be acquired, in the mind of almost every writer, was that nearest his own province: New Englanders desired to see Acadia secured; New Yorkers demanded the Iroquois lands up to the lakes; and Virginians wanted the Ohio Valley; Carolinians and Georgians were interested in the southwest. British West Indians coveted the yet-unoccupied islands of the Antilles. Few people were fully aware of, let alone concerned about, the frontier claims of other provinces. There was not yet sufficient intercolonial loyalty or interest for most colonists to be able to consider the situation of Britain's American holdings in its entirety.

As a matter of strategic interest, the presence of the French on the island of Cape Breton was looked upon by New Englanders as a constant threat to New England. The great fortress Louisbourg, built by the French after the Peace of Utrecht, provided a harbor from which French ships could prey upon New England's ports and shipping. Consequently, when war broke out between Britain and France in 1744, there was much agitation in New England to organize an expedition against Louisbourg. The Mas-

[23] Logan, "Of the State of the British Plantations . . . ," *loc. cit.*, 113.
[24] Douglass, A *Summary, Historical and Political . . . of the British Settlements in North America*, I, 2.

sachusetts Assembly recommended that Governor Shirley report to the King the danger to New England from Louisbourg and promised that Massachusetts would join other provinces to reduce that "Great Fortress." The strategic value of Louisbourg was great: it provided a haven for French warships and privateers; it was the center of the thriving French fishery; it protected the entrance to Canada.[25] Thomas Hutchinson, in his *History of Massachusetts-Bay*, recalled that in New England minds Louisbourg in French hands was potentially "the Dunkirk of New England" and that the New Englanders hoped that

if we succeeded [in taking it] not only the coasts of New-England would be free from molestation, but so glorious an acquisition would be of the greatest importance to Great Britain and might give peace to Europe, and we might depend upon a reimbursement of the whole charge we had been at.[26]

Benning Wentworth, of New Hampshire, saw Louisbourg as the key to French power in America: "I am convinced," he said, "the Reduction of Louisbourg would so dispirit the Enemy that we might make an intire conquest of the French in North America & then the French war would be the happiest war New England ever engaged in." [27]

Louisbourg was finally captured in 1745 by an expedition of English colonists cooperating with the British fleet. But Britain's war with France ended as a stalemate, and when peace was concluded by the Treaty of Aix-la-Chapelle of 1748, one of the provisions of the treaty was that all colonial conquests, including Cape Breton Island, would be returned to their original owners. The restoration of Louisbourg to France produced loud protests from New Englanders, who once again felt themselves threatened by this French fortress. New Englanders blamed the British ministry for giving up too much too easily. Many evil consequences of the cession of Cape Breton were envisaged: the French could increase the numbers of their ships and mariners; they could exploit the colliery and fishery of the island and through such competition cause unemployment among the fishermen of New England; they would settle on the frontiers of New England.[28]

This reaction from New England provides an interesting illustration of the eighteenth-century Angloamerican mind. Americans at this time were strongly interested in European affairs and made frequent expressions of their concept of themselves as parts of the British empire and of their

[25] Shirley to the Duke of Newcastle, Jan. 14, 1744, *Correspondence of William Shirley*, I, 161–165.
[26] Hutchinson, *The History of the Colony and Province of Massachusetts-Bay*, ed. Lawrence Shaw Mayo, II, 311–312.
[27] Benning Wentworth to William Shirley, Apr. 12, 1745, *Correspondence of William Shirley*, I, 207.
[28] *Independent Advertiser*, Boston, No. 7, 1748. See also, Menig, "Public Opinion in Massachusetts Relative to Anglo-French Relations, 1748–1756," unpublished Ph.D. dissertation in the University of Washington Library.

concern for imperial welfare, although they never thought of themselves as participating in the empire's wars in Europe. Yet in the matter of the restoration of Cape Breton to France they were unable to understand or accept the point of view of the British ministry, which was prompted by the exigencies of European conditions, thus sacrificing American colonial interest to the expediencies of European diplomacy.

If Cape Breton was a strategic objective of supreme importance to the New Englanders, their interest in the area between the Isthmus of Nova Scotia and the eastern boundary of New Hampshire was focused upon that area's potential as a territory furnishing lumber, masts, furs, and land for the settlement of an expanding population. To the New Englanders, the territory lying along the western shore of the Bay of Fundy had always been a part of Acadia, despite the fact that it was attached to Massachusetts by the Charter of 1691. When Acadia, therefore, with its *"anciennes limites,"* was ceded to England by the Anglo-French Treaty of Utrecht, the New Englanders understood that that territory was part of the cession, and they steadily extended their settlements and their lumbering into it. The French, on the other hand, consistently argued that the territory, which they called "Norumbega," was not a part of Acadia and, therefore, was not a part of the cession.[29]

The significance of Acadia, of course, was not lost on the French, either. The Marquis de la Galissonière, in his famous memoir of 1750, reported that the claims of the British commissioners in Paris regarding the extent of Acadia and the measures which the British were using to reestablish themselves there demanded serious attention.[30] He feared that if they were not opposed, the British would place themselves in a position to invade the French colonies in the event of a new war.[31] De la Galissonière felt that the loss of Acadia had been one of the most serious consequences of the Treaty of Utrecht, for Louisbourg was only a "feeble recompense." Acadia in British hands could easily take Louisbourg. The most important part of this area, although not, strictly speaking, part of "Acadia," was the St. John River, which for six months of the year provided the only ice-free communication between Louisbourg and Quebec. De la Galissonière therefore recommended that the French members of the proposed Anglo-French commission to settle, among other disputes, the boundaries of Acadia take great care that this river be acknowledged as French. English territory, he believed, must end at Port Royal; the British must possess nothing on the Gulf of St. Lawrence or on the isthmus separating the peninsula of Acadia from the mainland. No part of the

---

[29] See Chapter XIII.
[30] See Chapter XIX.
[31] De la Galissonière, "Memoir on the French Colonies in North America," *N.Y.C.D.*, X, 220ff.

peninsula should be ceded except in return for advantages for the French.[32]

When de la Galissonière, believing in the rightness of France's claim to "Norumbega" and in the strategic value of the area for the preservation of Canada, moved settlers and soldiers into the valleys of the St. John and Kennebec Rivers, the New Englanders, believing equally sincerely in the rightness of their own claim, accused the French of trespassing on English soil. Numerous protests came from New England regarding this supposed "encroachment" on their province. William Shirley recommended that the English secure for themselves possession of this area so as to end French infiltration.[33] When war broke out again it was greeted by New Englanders as an opportunity to rid themselves of the French menace in the northeast.

The people of the province of New York had especial reason to be uneasy about the presence of the French on their frontiers. The French fortress at Crown Point, on the southern end of Lake Champlain, lay dangerously near to Albany, and the French establishments on Lake Ontario threatened the western part of the province and British control over the bitterly contested territories of the Iroquois. There was a certain amount of criticism of the "unwise frugality" of the British ministry for failing to prevent the French intrusions at Crown Point and Niagara.[34] There was also fear that the French might attack the port of New York by sea, sending ships from Louisbourg or their port on the St. John River.[35] The British were well aware of the attraction New York held for the French: possession of its harbor would open a year-around communication between the sea and the cities of Canada. The colonists also knew that the security of the other northern colonies depended upon the preservation of New York. For this reason, there were many pleas to the ministry and the colonial assembly for increased defenses for that province, pleas which either went unanswered or became inextricably ensnarled in the conflicts of provincial politics.

In New York, as elsewhere, strategic considerations were linked with others, particularly the control of the Iroquois lands and the Indian trade. Here, the conflict with the French centered around the part of the Great Lakes basin that lay to the southward of the lakes. To the French, possession of this area was vital for communication between Canada and Louisiana, and they did their best to establish their hegemony on both sides of the Great Lakes.

[32] De la Galissonière, "Memoir," N.Y.C.D., X, 225–26.
[33] Shirley to the General Court of Massachusetts; Mar. 28, 1754, Correspondence of William Shirley, II, 33.
[34] Kennedy, Serious Considerations on the Present State of the Affairs of the Northern Colonies, 4.
[35] "A Summary View of the PRESENT STATE of this Continent . . . ," New York Mercury, Sept. 23, 1754. William Livingston is believed to be the author of this article.

The pleas from the colonies of both sides that the mother countries undertake the settlement of boundaries in this area were therefore very strong. The Marquis de la Galissonière, concerned with the defense of Canada, enunciated the long-used French policy of claming the watershed or height of land as the boundary, a policy which, had the English accepted it, would have limited them to the narrow coastal plain east of the Appalachians.[36]

The British were by no means willing to accept this fate, nor, without qualification, the whole principle of boundary by height of land. Cadwallader Colden, corresponding with Governor William Shirley, who was then in France as a member of the Anglo-French joint commission set up in 1750, was suspicious of the very idea of setting boundaries: the "proposal from France to set bounds to the English Colonies westward," he said, "seems to have something insnaring in it as with design to restrain the English trade with & any influence on the numerous nations of Indians in the inland parts of this Continent."[37]

Colden also found objections to the use of the watershed as the boundary between French and English holdings in the New York area. It was possible, he thought, to use the heads of the large and undisputed rivers, the Hudson and St. Lawrence, for this purpose, but "if the smaller rivers were intended to be included in this agreement it would occasion such a kind of indenting of Territory as must occasion the greatest Confusion but indeed every thing consider'd most to the prejudice of the English."[38] He suggested a boundary between the French and English colonies which would run from the northernmost head of the Connecticut River in a straight line to the northern head of the Hudson River, and thence in a straight line to the place where the St. Lawrence issued from Cadaracqui Lake [Lake Ontario], then along the Niagara River and through Lake Erie, navigation of which would be open to both sides. This boundary would require that the English give up a large part of the territory of the Five Nations, but Colden believed the English had little advantage from it anyway, since the French on the Niagara obstructed all British commerce with the Iroquois beyond the lakes.[39]

Colden concluded that "it may be dangerous to settle the claims farther to the Southward or Westward & I think neither side have sufficient pretences to setle boundaries farther."[40] Like many colonial imperialists, Colden was reluctant to accept boundaries which, although convenient, would permanently restrict English expansion westward. As long as the

[36] De la Galissonière, "Memoir on the French Colonies in North America," N.Y.C.D., X, 225–226.

[37] Colden to Shirley, Nov. 1749, Cadwallader Colden Papers, New York Historical Society Collections, IX, 52–57.

[38] Colden to Shirley, Nov., 1749, Colden Papers, IX, 52–57.

[39] Colden to Shirley, Nov., 1749, Colden Papers, IX, 52–57.

[40] Colden to Shirley, Nov., 1749, Colden Papers, IX, 52–57.

boundaries remained unsettled the English (and the French) were free to exploit their various claims in their efforts to expand into one another's territories.

The area which, after the Peace of Aix-la-Chapelle, most attracted the eyes of the Angloamerican imperialists was the valley of the Ohio River. But this area was also one that was of great strategic importance to the French, for unbroken possession of all the lands west of the Appalachians, from Canada in the north to Louisiana in the south, was considered necessary not only to unite the two French colonies but also to provide a barrier against English penetration into Spanish territory and particularly the silver mines.[41] De la Galissonière believed the Ohio Valley to be of especial significance to the preservation of an unbroken line of communication between Canada and Louisiana and regarded English settlements there as particularly dangerous. The Ohio in British hands, he believed, would provide a route by which they could attack and destroy the French posts in Illinois, on the Mississippi and at Detroit. Moreover, it gave them greater opportunities to seduce the Indians from their French alliances and to interrupt communication between Canada and Louisiana. If the British ever attempted a conquest of Mexico he expected them to descend by this river.[42]

The British fully appreciated the importance to the French of maintaining a line of communication between Canada and Louisiana. Lieutenant-Governor Clarke of New York, writing to the Lords of Trade in 1741, had said that in the event of war with France it would be "absolutely necessary" for the British to capture the two French forts at either end of Lake Ontario and to destroy the French brigantines on the lake, thereby cutting off all communication with the Mississippi and giving the British opportunity to form alliances with the Indians to the north and west of the lakes. "If we do not drive the french from that Lake," he warned, "and thereby stop all intercourse between Canada and Mesasipi, the French will in time, by means of the Indians, drive all the planters in the English colonies from their settlements, and make them of little use to England, or put it to a vast charge to protect them." [43]

The lands beyond the Alleghenies were desirable for their fertility as well as for their strategic position. Benjamin Franklin believed that possession of that area would determine the future history of the continent. If the French were to establish themselves in the west the English would be confined to the seaboard and their numbers consequently limited; the French, on the other hand, would multiply in this felicitous area, provid-

[41] De la Galissonière, "Memoir on the French Colonies in North America," N.Y.C.D., X, 220.
[42] De la Galissonière, "Memoir," N.Y.C.D., X, 229.
[43] Clarke to the Board of Trade, Apr. 22, 1741, N.Y.C.D., VI, 186.

ing a haven for runaway English debtors and slaves and cutting the English off from all commerce and friendship with the western Indians. To prevent such an eventuality Franklin suggested that two strong English colonies be established between the Ohio River and Lake Erie, providing security to the frontiers of the other colonies and severing communication between Canada and Louisiana. From these colonies the English could easily attack French settlements and secure the friendship of the western Indians.[44]

Franklin's idea was appropriated by a Philadelphia merchant, Samuel Hazard, who published a plan for the creation of a colony west of Pennsylvania, of which he hoped to be made proprietor. Franklin was angered to see his plan stolen, as it were, but he admitted that "I wish to see it [the creation of the colony] done, and am almost indifferent how or by whom it is done." [45]

To Lewis Evans, the American geographer, the Ohio Valley was the choicest part of North America and more deserving of British attention than the conquest of Canada. He believed that if the French succeeded in establishing themselves on the Ohio, not only would that river fall to them but all the country southward to the Gulf of Mexico. And to him possession of the west was of fateful significance:

The Country between the British Settlements and Mississippi . . . must one Day determine, whether the Southern Colonies shall remain the Property of the British Crown; or the Inhabitants, to prevent the entire Defection of their Slaves, which the French will encourage . . . be obliged to fall under the Dominion of France. Let not the Public think this a remote Contingence: If the French settle back of us, the English must either submit to them, or have their Throats cut, and lose all their Slaves.[46]

In order to prevent the west from falling to the French, Evans recommended that the British establish forts along the Ohio River and in the lands between the Ohio and the French settlement at Mobile, on the Gulf of Mexico, in order to break communication between Canada and Louisiana. Evans had observed that the French rarely used the Mississippi to travel north because of its rapid currents and that they resorted, instead, to more easterly rivers, thereby making Mobile of greater strategic value than New Orleans.[47]

But it was for its great fertility that the Ohio Valley was most to be valued:

[44] Franklin, "A Plan for Settling Two Western Colonies," *Franklin Papers*, Labaree, ed., V, 456–463.
[45] Franklin to Peter Collison, June 26, 1755, *Franklin Papers*, Labaree, ed., VI, 83–90.
[46] Evans, *Analysis of a General Map of the Middle British Colonies*, 1755, in Gipson, *Lewis Evans*, 159.
[47] Evans, *Analysis of a General Map*, loc. cit., 160.

Were there nothing at Stake between the Crowns of Britain and France, but the Lands on that Part of Ohio included in this Map,[48] we may reckon it as great a Prize, as has ever yet been contended for, between Two Nations; but if we further observe, that this is scarce a Quarter of the valuable Land that is contained in one continued Extent, and the Influence that a State, vested with all the Wealth and Power that will naturally arise from the Culture of so great an Extent of good Land, in a happy Climate, it will make so great an Addition to that Nation which wins it, where there is no third State to hold the Ballance of Power, that the Loser must inevitably sink under his Rival. It is not as two Nations at War, contending the one for the other's Habitations; where the Conquered, on Submission, would be admitted to partake of the Privileges of the Conquerors; but for a vast Country, exceeding in Extent and good Land all the European Dominions of Britain, France and Spain, almost destitute of Inhabitants, and will as fast as the Europeans settle become more so of its former Inhabitants . . .[49]

To Evans the contest with the French over title to Fort Frontenac was unnecessary. He saw no need to drive the French out of Canada; rather, he would have seen them driven into it and out of the Ohio, where they were so eager to settle.[50] He believed that all efforts to gain this territory were worthwhile and vigorously defended Braddock's campaign there against the attacks of conservative opponents:

Had he [Braddock] been successful, the War had been probably over, and we in Possession of the finest Country on Earth. Not one who loves the Name of a Briton, Liberty or of GEORGE, but would rejoice in an Opportunity of another Attempt. A Country incontestibly ours, capable of maintaining, with moderate Cultivation, Fifty Millions of People at a Time, and those renewed every Generation, to be thrown away for the Sake of taking Frontenac! Madness. To let so many People be the Descendants of Frenchmen and not of Britons, the Sons of Slavery and not of Liberty, would be making a Waste of the most excellent Country that ever God created.[51]

The Angloamericans also looked with covetous eyes upon the lands of the Southeast and the lower Mississippi Valley. Daniel Coxe, early in the century, proposed settling a colony along the lower Mississippi River, as already noted.

William Douglass, on the other hand, in his proposal for boundaries in this area, was willing to accept the Appalachians as the western boundary, but was also interested in pushing south into Florida. Douglass believed the "natural and most effectual Boundaries" of countries and ter-

---

[48] Evans', Map of the Middle British Colonies.

[49] Evans, Analysis of a General Map, loc. cit., 175.

[50] Evans, Essays. Number II. Containing a Letter . . . containing Objections to those Parts of Evans' General Map and Analysis . . . with an Answer. . . . (1756), in Gipson, Lewis Evans, 203.

[51] Evans, Essays. Number II, loc. cit., 38.

ritories were large rivers and impassable mountains. He therefore suggested that an Anglo-French American boundary should employ the St. Lawrence, Lakes Ontario and Erie, and the Appalachian Mountains, "without any Advantage or Acquisition, Disadvantage or Loss on either Side; but merely for Peace and good Neighbourhood." [52]

He was content to accept the existing limits of British settlement as the limit of British claims on inland territories. His proposed boundary in the northwest closely followed the extent of British settlements.[53] The use of the Appalachians Douglass justified by their having been mentioned as a western boundary in numerous land deeds from the Indians to the proprietors of the Carolinas.[54] The boundary which he suggested between Georgia and Florida was a line running east-west at 29° North Latitude, which would have included the Spanish settlement at St. Augustine within British territory. This boundary was that of the original royal grant of Carolina and, according to Douglass's interpretation, was confirmed by the Anglo-Spanish treaties of 1667 and 1670.[55] He felt that St. Augustine had no advantage for the Spanish except as a base from which to annoy the British in time of war. The peninsula to the south Douglass believed "not worth contending for," being of barren soil.[56]

3. The Indians as Factors in the International Situation

The various tribes of Indians played roles of enormous significance in the conflict between Britain and France for control of North America. In many ways they were intermediaries in this conflict because as allies of the two powers the Indians carried on much of the frontier warfare by which the conflict was waged. The economic role of the Indians was also very great and the struggle to secure the Indian market and fur trade was one of the chief causes of Anglo-French bitterness. There was, consequently, much written by colonials on the subject of Indians and their role in international affairs.

Shortly after the Peace of Utrecht Caleb Heathcote had called attention to the importance of good relations with the Indians to the international interests of the British in America. Heathcote blamed the revolt of the Indians in the south on their mistreatment at the hands of the whites: the Indians' lands had been taken without payment and their children taken from them to be educated by Christians and instead sold as slaves.

[52] Douglass, *Summary*, I, 9.
[53] Douglass, *Summary*, I, 10–11.
[54] Douglass, *Summary*, I, 12.
[55] According to the terms of these two treaties, the Spanish recognized British possession of all American territories which were then occupied by British subjects. See Chapter VI.
[56] Douglass, *Summary*, I, 13.

Heathcote suggested that the British question the Indians about their grievances and give promise of redress in order to pacify them and keep them loyal. This should be done, he said, "that we may if possible keep the Indians quiet and in temper, till we have our country better settled & secured and the French rooted out, & then we may expect to have the heathen on better terms, altho' justice ought forever to be don 'em." [57] Apparently, Heathcote believed judicious treatment of the Indians was only an expedient rather than a permanent basis for policy; this was, indeed, the principle usually practiced by the Angloamericans.

A little later, in 1727, Daniel Coxe had pointed out the importance of the Indians in the international struggle for power in North America. Coxe suspected that the uprisings of the Carolina Indians had been clandestinely fomented by the French, who were also to be blamed for the defection of the Iroquois. The French, Coxe said, knew that the best way to destroy the Iroquois was to deprive them of their fishing and hunting grounds, which bordered on the Great Lakes. Forts were being built by the French to intercept the passage of the Iroquois to and from their hunting grounds. Coxe feared that if the French were to succeed in their efforts to establish communication between Canada and the Gulf of Mexico they would be able to subject the Iroquois to them,

the consequence of which will not only be very *Shocking*, but of the utmost *Concern* to the *Safety* of our *Northern Plantations*: for if we now, in so great measure, stand in need of, and depend on them as our *Friends*, for the *Security* of our *Frontiers*, what must we expect, when that *Barrier* is remov'd, and they become our *Enemies*; and not only they, but all the rest of our friendly *Indians* to the *Southwards*, which we may of *Course* depend on.[58]

Coxe blamed the inroads of the French among the English Indian allies on the poor defenses of the frontiers of the English colonies, which not only failed to provide defense against the French but provided no security for the Indians either.

The eighteenth century was not, in fact, a particularly bright period in the history of Anglo-Indian relations. Although the Five Nations of the Iroquois, and, presumably, their lands, had been recognized as "subject" to Britain by the Treaty of Utrecht, during the eighteenth century they began to drift away, many of them to the side of the French. There were several reasons for this defection. In the first place, the Indians frequently found themselves unjustly dealt with by British traders. Moreover, their traditional role had been that of economic intermediaries between the British and the pelt-gathering tribes of the west: the Iroquois purchased trade-goods which they then exchanged with the western Indians for furs,

[57] Heathcote to Lord Townshend, July 16, 1715, *N.Y.C.D.*, V, 432.
[58] Coxe, *A Description of . . . Carolana*, 5.

selling these for more trade-goods and commodities such as firearms and rum for their own use. During the eighteenth century many of these western tribes fell under French domination so that, in order to trade with them, the Iroquois had to be friendly with the French. Also, the French, whose trade-goods had formerly been more expensive and of lower quality than the English, found a new and superior source of trade-goods: they purchased them from New York merchants. Now the French were able to compete with the English for the Iroquois trade on equal or better terms. At the same time, French missionaries, who for many years had been laboring among the tribes, began to reap a small but significant harvest of converts and French sympathizers. A few tribes, formerly British allies, even moved into Canada so as to be closer to their new allies and religious companions.

This defection of their old allies greatly troubled the British and forced a reexamination of customary Indian policies. An examination of French practices in Indian relations was made by many Angloamericans in an effort to learn the secrets of French successes.

One of the advantages attributed to the French was a religious one. To be sure, the French government gave considerable encouragement to the conversion of the Indians, and to such colonial leaders as the Marquis de la Galissonière the conversion of the heathens was a "salutary" work of great importance.[59] But to the Protestant Angloamericans the Catholic religion of their French adversaries seemed ungodlike and conducive to primitive evils, "better framed to make Proselytes amongst uncivilized and ignorant Nations, than any of our Protestant Persuasions."[60] The Jesuit priests who were so active among the Indians were blamed for the success of their nation among the aborigines. By their "dishonest Arts and unrighteous Compliances" the Jesuits extended their influence "upon the Continent, over the Indians, so much more than we do."[61] The presence of French missionaries among the Five Nations was a constant concern to the English: the missionaries not only converted the Indians to the French religion but subverted them to the French interest as well. As the Indians gave their faith, so they gave their fur trade.[62] Other writers, too, blamed the French missionaries for French control over the Indians. William Keith, Governor of Pennsylvania, had reported to the Lords Commissioners in 1718 that the "artifices" of the Jesuit missionaries "daily debauched" the Iroquois from the British interest.[63] James Logan, in 1732, had said that the priests among the Indians conformed to Indian

[59] La Galissonière, "Memoir," N.Y.C.D., X, 222.
[60] "A Summary View of the PRESENT STATE of this Continent . . . ," New York Mercury, Sept. 23, 1754.
[61] "A Summary View . . . ," loc. cit., Sept. 23, 1754.
[62] Vetch, "Canada Survey'd . . . ," C.S.P., Col., A.& W.I., 1708–09, No. 60, p. 47.
[63] "The Report of the Honourable William Keith . . . , Feb. 16, 1718–19," Keith, A Collection of Papers and Other Tracts, 189.

ways and thus endeared themselves and the French nation to the Indians.[64] In 1754 William Shirley, Governor of Massachusetts, said that French missionaries had "chiefly conducted and managed this [Recent] War," having had charge of supplying the Indians and encouraging them against the British.[65]

To counteract these French successes the British were forced to examine their own Indian policies. The chief bond between the English and their Indian allies was trade, and within this trade were the seeds of much discord. The English-Indian trade was largely conducted by private traders who were more concerned with securing personal profits than with cementing friendly relations with the Indians, and consequently the Indians frequently suffered injustices at the hands of profiteering traders.

Archibald Kennedy, royal receiver-general for the province of New York in the middle of the eighteenth century, was very critical of the current economic relations with the Indians. In a tract entitled *The Importance of Gaining and Preserving the Friendship of the Indians to the British Interest Considered*, which he published in 1752, Kennedy examined various aspects of Anglo-Indian relations. The defection of the Iroquois he blamed on the faulty execution of their treaty of commerce; the treaty, he said, had been committed to the execution of commissioners who were mostly Anglo-Dutch traders in Indian goods who so greatly abused the Indians in their efforts to make profits that there were now few Indians left upon whom the British could depend. This situation he contrasted to that of the French: "What to me is most surprizing [is] that, tho' there is hardly a colony upon the continent but what is a match for all *Canada*; yet, by a proper management of their [the French] *Indians*, they keep us all, both in time of peace and war, in a constant dread and terror." [66] Elsewhere Kennedy wrote that however the French treated the Indians in other matters they were, unlike the British, always honest in trade.[67] The British, he wrote, were guilty of a "total Neglect" of Indian affairs; while the French had "for many Years been indefatigable in their Endeavours to seduce our Indians; we on the other Side, have been as indolent as they could wish." [68]

To regain the friendship of the Indians Kennedy said that laws must be enacted to regulate the Indian trade. He suggested that a single officer be appointed by the crown to superintend the Indian trade for all the continental colonies, an officer who must have no connection with either

---

[64] Logan, "Of the State of the British Plantations in America," *loc. cit.*, LX (1936), 120.

[65] Shirley to General Court of Massachusetts, Mar. 28, 1754. *Correspondence of William Shirley*, Lincoln, ed., II, 33.

[66] Kennedy, *The Importance of Gaining . . . the Indians*, 3.

[67] Kennedy, *Serious Considerations on the Present State of the Affairs of the Northern Colonies*, 5.

[68] Kennedy, *Serious Considerations . . .*, 5.

the trade or people of the colonies. This officer, as "Superintendent of Indian Affairs," would take his orders from and be responsible to the provincial governor and council and would make at least once a year a tour among the Six Nations to receive complaints and redress grievances. Interpreters should also be appointed, preferably one for each of the Six Nations, and smiths and apprentices should be sent to live among each nation, who could handle the sale of Indian goods at prices fixed in New York. Every person in this service would be strictly forbidden to participate in trade, and every effort possible should be made to undersell the French. Kennedy also recommended that an annual fair be held for the Indians where they could trade and which would serve as an attraction for distant Indians and would act as a check upon unfair practices by the traders of Oswego. Special means would have to be taken to improve the quality of guns sold by the English to the Indians and to undersell the French, who sold better arms at cheaper rates than the English did. Kennedy here suggested that the colonists be allowed to import powder from Holland and arms from France, or else to manufacture their own powder in the Mohawk country where saltpeter was abundant.

In order to pay the expenses of this plan, Kennedy suggested that, first, a duty be collected on all Indian goods sold and all furs and skins bought, under direction of customs officers. Second, he believed that every colony should be required to pay a portion of the expenses, since the plan would contribute to the security of all the colonies. If any colony should suggest that New York should pay all the expenses because it enjoyed all the trade, Kennedy recommended that each contributing colony establish its own township on the frontier with a trading house and a garrison and participate in the trade.[69]

Elsewhere Kennedy recommended that fortifications be erected in or near every Indian "castle" or village to prevent sudden attacks both by and upon the Indians. These forts could also be used as trading posts. A strong fort should be built at Wood Creek, to counterbalance that of the French at Crown Point. This, Kennedy said, should be staffed with Scottish Highlanders, because "there seems to be so much Affinity both in their Disposition and Dress . . . with that of our *Indians,* that I am confident they would be highly pleased with them, and I doubt not, have a very good Effect." [70] Since the Indians had been so hospitable to priests, Kennedy recommended that Protestant pastors be sent to each of the forts, where they could act as commissaries as well as missionaries. Trade between the British and the Indian allies of the French ought to be forbidden, for these Indians not only carried off English goods but specie as well. Moreover, the government should halt the selling of British trade-goods to the French, who then traded these goods with the Indians and in

[69] Kennedy, *The Importance of Gaining . . . the Indians,* 4–23.
[70] Kennedy, *Serious Considerations . . . ,* 14.

return gave the British only their coarsest furs.[71] Kennedy also suggested that all British fortifications in the Indian country between Montreal and Schenectady be demolished, in order to keep trade open and to convince the Indians that the English had their interest at heart, in contrast to the French, who, he said, desired the destruction of the Indians by preventing their trade and dominating their hunting grounds.[72]

The geographer Lewis Evans also recognized the bond of trade between the British and the Indians. "We charge the Indians with Fickleness," he wrote, "but with greater Propriety we should charge ourselves with great Want of Sense or Experience, in supposing any Nation is to be tied to another, by any Thing than Interest." [73] One tribe, the Welinis, had cultivated friendship with the English for the sake of trade and held to their alliance despite overtures from the French. But during the war the English abandoned them without arms or ammunition to the mercies of the French. The great fault in England's Indian policy was a lack of attention and loyalty to its Indian allies:

'Tis a Custom, established with the English, to purchase the Friendship of wavering Nations at a great Expense, and to abandon their Friends. Hence those who know this Mixture of Weakness and Baseness that possesses us, keep Members of Council in the French Interest as well as ours, as the Confederates do, to keep us under a perpetual Contribution; while those Nations who are truly in our Interest are entirely slighted.[74]

The giving of presents was another significant part of the program by which England won and maintained alliances with the Indians. This custom was practiced with particular care and generosity in relations with the Iroquois, who also accepted gifts from the French. Such competitive gift-giving placed a great strain upon the resources of the provincial government of New York, which was responsible for maintaining relations with the Iroquois, and it was consequently forced to seek help. In 1741 Lieutenant Governor Clarke suggested to the Board of Trade that the other colonies be obliged to make contributions for the annual gifts given the Iroquois in time of war. Although the province could afford the gifts given every two years in time of peace, the annual gifts were too great a burden, but, as Clarke said, "in my humble opinion we must do it or loose them." [75]

Another program for the management of Indian affairs was conceived by Governor William Shirley of Massachusetts. In 1756 he recommended to the Board of Trade that the Indians of North America be divided into

[71] Kennedy, *Serious Considerations* . . . , 18. This Anglo-French trade flourished during much of the eighteenth century. See Chapter XIII.
[72] Kennedy, *Serious Considerations* . . . , 19.
[73] Evans, *Analysis of a General Map*, loc. cit., 159.
[74] Evans, *Analysis of a General Map*, loc. cit., 160.
[75] Clarke to The Board of Trade, Dec. 15, 1741, N.Y.C.D., IV, 208.

four districts for more efficient administration. To bring the Indians into English dependence, means should be taken to protect their women, children, and old people from the French and France's Indian allies while their warriors were away. To prevent injustices, trade with the Indians should be regulated, as also regulations should govern the purchase of Indian lands and prevent encroachments on their hunting grounds. French missionaries should be expelled from among the English Indians and English Protestant missionaries introduced in their place. Relations with the Indians could further be cemented by gathering them into general councils and by establishing general interviews between the Indians and royal governors and commissioners.[76]

Elsewhere Shirley recommended that the colonies unite to create one general league of friendship with the Indians, with stipulations to build such forts as the Indians judged necessary for their protection against the French. Such a coalition, Shirley said, would convincingly prove to the Indians that they could safely depend upon the British for protection.[77]

To the Angloamerican of North America in the mid-eighteenth century, then, the Indians were not only fearsome enemies and profitable partners in the continent-wide fur and skin trades: they were factors of enormous, even decisive importance in the intercolonial relations and balance of power among the European nations on the continent. Whoever controlled the friendship of the Indians would control the continent. It was this international aspect of the Indian problem that outweighed in importance both Indian enmity, *per se*, and Indian trade, *per se*, in the policy calculations both of the colonial governors and of the ministry of England.

4. Maps as International Propaganda

Of considerable importance as expressions of opinion relative to international relations between the colonial empires were the maps printed on both sides, ostensibly to give true representations of the European possessions in America, but really to set forth cartographically the territorial claims of the rival empires. Thus, a series of maps by the French cartographer Guillaume Delisle illustrated that country's territorial claims in America. Maps published by Delisle in Paris in 1700, 1703, and 1718 all showed the same interpretations of boundaries between the French and British lands: New France or Canada covered most of the eastern half of the continent, limiting "Nouvelle Angleterre" to a narrow strip along the coast, extending from the Bay of Fundy to Virginia and bounded on the

[76] Shirley, "Sketch for a System for the Management of Indian Affairs in North America under one General Direction," Jan. 5, 1756, *Correspondence of William Shirley*, II, 373–377.
[77] Shirley to The General Court of Massachusetts, Apr. 2, 1754, *Correspondence of William Shirley*, II, 42–43.

west by the ridge of the Appalachians. France claimed the country of the Iroquois (Western New York and Pennsylvania), and British Carolina was considered part of Spanish Florida.[78]

Such maps as these were met by protests and other maps from the British. Archibald Kennedy accused the French of employing their maps as part of their "political system of encroachments upon the territories of other Nations." [79] James Logan, the Pennsylvania imperialist, feared that the French, on the basis of Delisle's maps, would easily extend their territorial claims so far as to drive the British from the continent.[80]

By the middle of the eighteenth century the population of the colonies had grown to the extent that it had begun to push west of the Alleghenies, and the British government began to take an official interest in establishing its possession of the western lands. The Board of Trade therefore commissioned Dr. John Mitchell of Virginia to make a map of the colonies which would show the British territorial claims in North America in their fullest extent. Based on official British documents, charts, surveys, French maps, and the reports of traders, Mitchell's *Map of the British and French Dominions in North America* was published in 1755 as part of official British propaganda in the struggle with France for control of North America. The map made the broadest possible interpretation of the extent of Britain's American territories: Nova Scotia comprised both the peninsula and the mainland north to the St. Lawrence; New England also was bounded in the north by the St. Lawrence; the western boundary of the British territories was the Great Lakes and the Mississippi River; the southern boundary of Georgia ran directly across the northernmost part of the Florida peninsula. According to Mitchell's map, the French were confined to an area north of the British settlements and had no territory south of the Great Lakes.[81] The map was eagerly accepted by colonial imperialists such as William Livingston and Archibald Kennedy, who were ambitious to see France driven completely from North America.

Lewis Evans, another colonial map maker, was less imperialistically inclined, and his maps were more directed toward a reasonable settlement of intercolonial boundary disputes and the description of actual western settlement. Evans's most famous work was his *General Map of the Middle British Colonies in America*, which he published in 1755.[82] With the map Evans also published an *Analysis* in which he described the lands of the west and discussed the conflicting territorial claims. He, like many of his

[78] Paullin, *Atlas of the Historical Geography of the United States*, Plate 24.

[79] Kennedy, *Serious Considerations* . . . , 4.

[80] Logan, "Of the State of the British Plantations in America," *loc. cit.*, LX (1936), 97–130.

[81] Mitchell's map is reproduced in Miller, ed., *Treaties and other International Acts of the United States of America*, III, end-pocket.

[82] Evans, *A General Map of the Middle British Colonies in America*, in Gipson, *Lewis Evans*.

contemporaries, was concerned with the progress of French settlement in the west and feared that the French might eventually drive the British from the continent. French penetration into the Ohio country particularly concerned Evans, for he saw the potential prosperity of this territory and wished to awaken the British ministry to its value.

While he was concerned to establish British possession in the Ohio, Evans by no means intended to exaggerate the extent of British claims. He acknowledged French rights to Fort Frontenac and, indeed, the whole of Canada on the basis of their possession of that land at the time of the Peace of Ryswick. Imperialistic critics, including William Livingston, attacked Evans for his "generosity," but Evans defended his position, claiming that it would be little to the British interest to contest those French claims; for such a contest would only give the French proof of the British encroachments upon which they blamed the conflicts in North America. Evans believed it wiser to expend men and money to enforce actual claims; false claims, he said, could only lead to fruitless expeditions and would be harmful to the honor of the British king. He acknowledged French rights to share the navigation of Lake Ontario with the British by virtue of the Treaty of Whitehall (Treaty of American Neutrality) of 1686, which provided that both nations should retain all dominions which they held at that time, the French having had at that time ships on the lake. Lake Erie, however, Evans believed was closed to the French, being entirely surrounded by the country of the Five Nations, which was recognized as British by the Treaty of Utrecht. The parts of Lakes Huron and Michigan bordered by the Iroquois country were also open to British navigation, but the other parts of these lakes were undetermined as to ownership and rights of navigation.[83]

Evans was scrupulously honest in his description of the extent of British settlement. After listing the areas and extent of British settlements he concluded that

There have been British Subjects scattered over many Places, besides those above-mentioned, especially on Ohio, Wawyaghtas, and the Branches of Cherokee River to the West; and the Lake Ontario Northward; but they cannot with any Propriety be said to be *Settlers*, because they have not acquired *Titles to the Soil under their King*, nor *cultivated the Land by Husbandry*; two Things absolutely necessary to denominate a Settlement.[84]

The corpus of maps portraying European empires in America published in the eighteenth century was thus of great importance as a form of publication giving visible definition to the territorial claims of the European empires in America. Evidently, not all the maps produced either by French or British cartographers agreed with each other as to the boundaries of

[83] Evans, *Essays, Number II, loc. cit.*, 203–210.
[84] Evans, *Analysis of a General Map, loc. cit.*, 146.

the European possessions in North America. The French maps agreed with English maps even less, naturally. But the maps themselves were important vehicles of opinion, and some, such as Delisle's maps and Mitchell's map, were actually used as guides for the diplomats attempting to rationalize the claims of one empire or the other to territory in America.

5. International Conflict and the Problem of Colonial Disunity

Whatever policies the Angloamericans might suggest or encourage to improve their position in the general international situation, it became increasingly evident to colonial thinkers of the eighteenth century that they could hope for little success unless some means were found to bring about the participation and support of all the colonies. There had been in the past several efforts to unite the colonies for common action, but they were mostly intended to meet particular emergencies and most of them proved to be abortive. Efforts by the British government to create any permanent colonial union were stubbornly resisted by the colonies, each of which feared colonial union as a threat to its own autonomy and was suspicious of the financial and military demands of its neighbors. But as the French menace grew, thoughtful men were ever more conscious that the colonies, individually, could not hope easily to survive, and that, therefore, some sort of military union, at least, was fast becoming a necessity.

One of the dangers of disunity was that the French knew how to exploit it for their own advantage. During King William's War, as Caleb Heathcote recalled in 1715, the other colonies evaded their duty to send men and money to the assistance of embattled New York, and the French would not allow their Indians to make war on more than one colony at a time, "& the others were so besotted, as all ways to sitt still." When the French attacked New York, Connecticut, which was unmolested, refused to give any assistance, and when at the end of the war Connecticut, instead, was attacked, New York refused to assist that colony. "After this unaccountable management on our side, the crafty French, who are but a handful in comparison of the English, on this Continent, have generally out done us." [85]

The disunited state of the colonies served also to encourage French incursions. While the French enjoyed the advantage of being under a single direction and a single purse, the British colonies were handicapped by the "extreme Difficulty of Bringing so many different Governments and Assemblies to agree in any speedy and effectual Measures for our common Defense and Security." [86] Robert Dinwiddie, Governor of Vir-

[85] Heathcote to Lord Townshend, July 12, 1715, N.Y.C.D., V, 431–432.
[86] *Pennsylvania Gazette* (May 9, 1754), *Franklin Papers*, Labaree, ed., V, 272–275.

ginia, complained that the "French too justly observe the want of connection in the Colonies, and from thence conclude (as they declare without reserve) that altho' we are vastly superiour to them in Numbers, yet they can take and secure the Co't'y before we can agree to hinder them." [87] Archibald Kennedy, criticizing the failure of the British to continue to cultivate the friendship of the Indians, said that "the very *French* themselves openly upbraid us with our Indolence and Divisions, which they acknowledge to be their greatest Security." [88]

Disunity even within the individual colonies created other problems of defense. The source of this problem lay in the struggles between the royal governors and the provincial assemblies for primacy over provincial affairs. The assemblies could best assert their independence by refusing to vote the funds requested by the governors, and thus they frequently thwarted the efforts of the governors to reinforce the defenses of their provinces. Governor Dinwiddie of Virginia complained to the Board of Trade in 1754 that the House of Burgesses "have been extremely Obstinate and Self Opiniated, at [the] same Time infatuated and unactive, w'n the enemy is so near Us as to have robbed many of our frontier Settlers of their Cattle and Corn." Dinwiddie continued that "I think it impossible to conduct any Expedit'n in these Parts with a dependence of Supplies from the Assemblies, with't a B. Act of Parliam't to lay a Poll Tax on the whole Subjects of these Provinces, to bring them to a sense of their duty to the King, to awaken them from their Indolence, to take care of their Lives and Fortunes." [89] The idea of an imperially imposed poll tax to support colonial defenses was one which Dinwiddie long advocated as a means of bypassing the colonial assemblies. Elsewhere, referring again to his problems with the Virginia assembly, Dinwiddie exclaimed, "A Gov'r is really to be pitied in the discharge of his Duty to his King and Co't'y, in having to do with such obstinate, self-conceited People." [90]

Governor Clinton also had difficulties with the legislature of New York and complained that he had no use of the money in the provincial treasury, although, he thought, the leaders of the faction which opposed him were using it to support their own interests. The French, he said, "are too well informed of the publick dissentions in this and the neighbouring Colonies, and lay hold of this opportunity to weaken our interest among the Indian nations." The only way Clinton could secure the friendship of the Indians was by advancing large sums from his own pocket.[91]

Internal dissensions also created great difficulties with the defense of

[87] Dinwiddie to Sir Thomas Robinson, June 18, 1754, *The Official Records of Robert Dinwiddie* (*Collections of the Virginia Historical Society,* New Series, Vol. III–IV), I, 201–205.

[88] Kennedy, *Serious Considerations* . . . , 5.

[89] *Dinwiddie Papers,* I, 327–330.

[90] Dinwiddie to Governor Hamilton, Sept. 6, 1754, *Dinwiddie Papers,* I, 307–308.

[91] Clinton to the Duke of Bedford, Mar. 19, 1749/50, N.Y.C.D., VI, 550–552.

Pennsylvania, as William Smith revealed in his tract. A *Brief State of the Province of Pennsylvania*. Smith claimed that the provincial assembly, after having received sole control of the public money in 1723, had become intoxicated with its power and quite careless of the defense of the colony. He said that the assembly must be assured of the friendship of the French, for only this could explain its refusal to defend the colony. The Quakers of the assembly were motivated by interests other than religious, he said, in refusing to provide for a provincial militia; Smith believed that if a militia were created its officers would influence the soldiers to vote the Quakers out of power. "Hence it is that this Province is reduced to the most miserable Condition.—The People at variance, and distrustful of each other! A French Enemy and their Savage Allies advanced far into our Territory! The People on our Frontiers liable to be murdered or driven from their Habitations! Our Lives and all our sacred Rights exposed on easy Prey!— And all this owing to the Infatuation and detestable Policy of a Set of Men who mind no Consequences, provided they can secure their own Power and their Seats in the Assembly." [92]

The idea of a union of all the colonies to provide for their mutual defense had been discussed many times in the eighteenth century. In 1715 Caleb Heathcote had suggested to Governor Hunter of New York that he arrange a congress of as many governors as possible to take measures to extinguish the Indian revolts, "for as every part of North America is struck at, so all our interests are the same, & what number soever is wounded or hurt, the whole ought to reckon themselves agrieved, and not carelessly suffer the French to angle us away, province by province, till at last all will be gon." [93] Governor William Keith of Pennsylvania had envisaged a colonial union to regulate the Indian trade and to make treaties and alliances with as many Indian nations as possible.[94] Cadwallader Colden of New York reported a proposal from Governor Shirley of Massachusetts to Governor Clinton of New York that commissioners be appointed by the colonies to meet to make some plan for their joining together to carry on the war and the mutual defense of the colonies; the congress was a failure for the few commissioners who did appear "treated together more like the Ministers of independent States than the Subjects of the same Prince." [95] Daniel Coxe, also, discussing the problems of colonial defense in 1727, had noted the reluctance of the individual colonies to send aid to the defense of distressed neighbors and concluded that "The only *Expedient* I can at present think of, or shall presume to mention . . . to help and

[92] Smith, A *Brief State of the Province of Pennsylvania*, 10–25.
[93] Heathcote to Governor Hunter, July 8, 1715, *N.Y.C.D.*, V, 430–431.
[94] "The Report of the Honourable *William Keith* . . . , Feb. 16, 1718/19," in Keith, *A Collection of Papers and Other Tracts*, 193.
[95] Colden to Dr. John Mitchell, July 6, 1749, *Colden Papers*, IX, 27.

obviate these *Absurdities* and *Inconveniences,* and apply a *Remedy* to them, is, that all the *Colonies* appertaining—to the Crown of Great Britain on the *Northern Continent* of *America,* be united under a *Legal, Regular* and firm *Establishment;* over which, it's propos'd, a *Lieutenant,* or *Supreme Governour,* may be constituted, and appointed to preside on the *spot,* to whom the *Governours* of each *Colony* shall be *subordinate."* [96]

Clearly, then, when Benjamin Franklin in 1751 proposed the organization of a union of the continental colonies, his proposal represented a realization of the need for colonial union that was both widespread and deeply rooted in American experience. To be sure, the congress that met at Albany in 1754 and formulated the so-called "Albany Plan of Union" was inspired by the Earl of Halifax, President of the Board of Trade, and was held in accord with instructions to the colonial governors from the crown. The interest of the crown seems to have been chiefly in a union for defense and in restoring and maintaining good relations with the Indians, and the idea of a genuine colonial political union seems to have been originated by leaders in the colonies themselves. Thus, Governor Shirley of Massachusetts as spokesman for the crown, urged the General Court of his colony to send commissioners to the Albany congress because he believed a coalition of the colonies for defense and the creation of "one general League of Friendship" with the Indians the best means to combat the French.[97]

The failure of the colonial assemblies to ratify a union of the colonies disturbed many men, and the general consensus of the thought of the advocates of union was that it would have to be imposed on the colonies by the British Parliament. William Clarke of Boston wrote in despair to his friend and fellow union-advocate Benjamin Franklin that

. . . this Union is hardly to be expected to be brought about by any confederacy, or voluntary Agreement, among our selves. The Jealousies the Colonies have of each other, with regard to their real or imaginary different interests, &c. will effectually hinder any thing of this kind from taking place. But were everything else to be got over, we should never agree about the Form of the Union, or who should have the execution of the Articles of it. So that however necessary a Step this may be, for the mutual Safety and preservation of these Colonies; it is pretty certain, it will never be taken, unless we are forced to it, by the Supreme Authority of the Nation.[98]

William Shirley, giving up hope for a union formed by the colonies themselves, advised Robert Morris, who had just assumed the government of Pennsylvania that

[96] Coxe, *A Description of . . . Carolana,* 6.
[97] Shirley to the Massachusetts General Court, Apr. 2, 1754, *Correspondence of William Shirley,* II, 40–46.
[98] *Franklin Papers,* Labaree, ed., V, 270.

The Best Advice I can give you, is to lose no time for promoting the Plan of a Union of the Colonies for their mutual Defence to be concerted at home [England], and establish'd by Act of Parliamt, as soon as is possible. The proceedings of the Commrs at Albany, from the general Governmts, will shew you the necessity of it. I am labouring this point, totis viribus. It would ease you of a great part of the burthen, your Government may probably bring upon you otherwise, in the management of Military and Indian Affairs . . .[99]

Shirley recognized that any common measures would have to be imposed by Parliament: "the common fund . . . will never be agreed upon by the Assemblies among themselves, tho' acknowledg'd to be necessary to all; that, and a plan of Union must be establish'd by an authority from home or neither of them will be effected. . . ." [100]

6. American Opinion Relative to Intercolonial Commerce

While much of the opinion of the Angloamericans relative to international affairs dovetailed with that of the mother country and even prompted some of it, especially in the area of imperialistic expansion, and while the Americans took pride in standing shoulder-to-shoulder with Britain in the face of their common enemies, in one very significant area the colonies not only resisted or evaded the policies of the imperial government but developed a way of thinking that ran directly counter to the mercantilist foreign and colonial policies of the Empire as a whole. This was the area of international intercolonial trade.

The close mercantilistic regulation of colonial trade by the European metropoli was practically universal in the eighteenth century; that of Spain, France, and England was particularly vigorous. Nevertheless, a thriving international trade, sometimes "licit," sometimes "illicit," between the British colonies and those of Spain, France, Portugal, Holland, and Denmark flourished, within, as well as despite, the British navigation system.

While there are no figures available to show how many Angloamericans were involved, directly or indirectly, in this vast and active intercolonial trade, it is certain that it was of direct and vital concern to a substantial percentage of the individual colonists in British America. Those who were directly concerned in commerce and government were acutely conscious of its importance; many of them wrote rationalizations and justifications of it and even urged a more liberal policy, a policy at times amounting to freedom of commerce, upon the mother country.[101]

[99] Shirley to Morris, Oct. 21, 1754. *Correspondence of William Shirley*, II, 95–97.
[100] Shirley to Sir Thomas Robinson, June 20, 1755. *Correspondence of William Shirley*, II, 204.
[101] For a narrative of the direct international relations between the British colonies and foreign colonies relative to this trade see Chapter XIII.

One of the branches of the trade of the northern colonies that was of international significance was that of New York and New England with the French in Canada and Cape Breton.

Trade with the French in Canada had begun in the seventeenth century and by the beginning of the eighteenth century it was flourishing. In 1705 Governor Dudley of Massachusetts was severely criticized by certain Bostonians for countenancing trade with the French and their Indian allies. He was accused of having sent his son and Samuel Vetch to Canada in 1705, ostensibly to redeem captives of Queen Anne's War but actually to trade. There is no proof that Dudley engaged in trade with the French, but Vetch certainly did, an enterprise which whetted his appetite for the conquest of Canada.[102]

The trade between New York and Montreal was particularly active. New York merchants sold to the French goods which were used in the French fur trade with the Indians, where the French previously could not compete because their goods were more expensive and of poor quality. By means of the New York trade the Canadians were able to undersell the Iroquois in trading with the Indians of the west. The Iroquois complained to the English and asked them to stop this trade, for without it the French could not supply the western Indians who would then be obliged to trade with Albany through the Iroquois. In 1720 Governor Burnet had passed by the legislature a law forbidding the sale of goods to the French under penalty of confiscation and fine, but the Manhattan merchants greatly opposed this law and means were found to evade it.[103]

This trade was severely criticized, with no success, by the royal governors of New York. Reporting to the Board of Trade in 1747, Governor Clinton complained that a powerful faction had been established against him in the colony, composed of merchants and their supporters who wished to maintain a state of neutrality with the French so they could carry on their trade unimpeded.[104] This conflict between Clinton and the neutralist party went on for many years, during which the merchants and their adherents in the assembly resisted all Clinton's efforts to carry on war with the French or to provide for the defense of the frontiers or the mobilization of the Iroquois.

The problem of regulating trade continued into the administration of William Shirley. In his "Sketch for a System for the Management of Indian Affairs" Shirley wrote that a free trade with French Indians was carried on at Albany, enabling the French to trade with the Indians of the north and west at prices cheaper than the English charged for their goods at Oswego. The Albany trade, Shirley said, was the cause of the defection of the Cagnawaga Indians, who were now supplied by the French with

[102] Waller, *Samuel Vetch*, Chapter V.
[103] Flick, ed., *History of the State of New York*, II, 140–141.
[104] Clinton to Lords of Trade, Nov. 30, 1747, *N.Y.C.D.*, VI, 412–413.

goods from Albany. Shirley proposed that the Albany trade with the French be prohibited and that a free trade with the Indians of the west be opened at Oswego.[105]

A large segment of public opinion, both at Boston and at New York, favored continuing the Canadian trade because it was so profitable. Indeed, in New York, the "assembly party" espoused the trade as a political issue. The fact that this profitable trade, so detrimental to British imperial policy generally, lay so close to the self-interest of the colonials engaged in it, led them not only to practice it in defiance of all law and regulation, but, also, to develop a set of ideas and a political program to rationalize and justify it.

Another branch of foreign intercolonial trade which was enthusiastically supported by the British continental colonies was carried on with the French West Indian islands.[106] It was an advantageous trade for both sides: the French islands could buy foodstuffs and other necessities more cheaply from the British continental colonies than from France, and the British colonies could purchase sugar from the French islands more cheaply than from the British islands, where prices were protected by their legal monopoly. The continental colonies tried very hard, therefore, to persuade the British government to lift its restrictions on such international trade. Most blame was placed on the greed of the British "sugar islands," which were "not content with the great gains they yearly make from their rich Plantations" and thus endeavored, "by Misrepresentations," to obtain an act of Parliament barring the continental colonies from all commerce in America with any others than themselves. The certain consequence of this policy, according to the provincial assembly of Pennsylvania, would be "a vast Diminution to the Navigation of Great Britain, an Increase of the Shipping of Our foreign Neighbours, a large Reduction to the Exportation of the British Manufactures, and by the Decay of their Trade would extremely impoverish these your Majesty's colonies, and by that means not only render us useless to Our Mother Country but expose Us to great Dangers from our powerfull Neighbours, the French, by whom we are now surrounded . . ." [107]

James Logan also defended the continental colonies' foreign West Indian trade. He claimed that the British islands were languishing in luxury and careless administration and, to relieve their disorders, they sought to prohibit all trade between the continental British colonies and foreign plantations. Logan believed such a prohibition would prove injurious to all

[105] Shirley to the Board of Trade, Jan. 5, 1756, *Correspondence of William Shirley*, II, 373–377.
[106] See Chapter XIII.
[107] Petition of the Lieutenant Governor, council, and assembly to the King, Dec. 4, 1731, *Minutes of the Provincial Council of Pennsylvania* (*Colonial Records of Pennsylvania*, III), III (1717–36/7), 423.

the British dominions: Britain would be injured by having to pay more for all West Indian commodities because the British islands, by their monopoly, could control prices; the continental colonies would suffer by being forbidden to participate in this trade, which was a service to Britain and a disservice to the French islands, which "can furnish themselves with more Advantage to the General Interest of France with the same necessarys from their own Colonies"; the British islands would suffer by being made richer and therefore indolent and more vulnerable to enemy attacks.[108]

The historian Thomas Hutchinson eloquently rationalized New England's international trade. Some colonies, he said, such as the grain-growing colonies between Pennsylvania and Virginia, raised only one crop. They needed, therefore, to sell or barter this grain for produce and manufactured goods which they lacked. But the trade with the British West Indies, where the continental colonies customarily disposed of their produce, had declined since 1713 because those colonies had learned to produce their own food and had much less need for northern produce. At the same time, the prices of their products had increased so that it was difficult for the northern colonies to supply all their needs in West Indian goods. It was only through trade with the French and Dutch islands that the northern colonies were able to buy British West Indian produce. Nevertheless, the British West Indians were trying to restrain this trade with foreign islands and colonies, although if this trade were restrained both the continental colonies and Great Britain would be greatly burdened by a still greater increase in the price of West Indian goods. Moreover, if New England's trade with foreign colonies were suppressed and their supplies of West Indian goods confined to those purchased at British islands, then the northern colonies would have to pay the balance of what was owed above the amount of what the West Indians purchased in gold or silver and exchange upon England, both of which would lessen the returns to England and reduce the amount of British manufactures consumed by New England and the other continental colonies.

Hutchinson concluded that the continuation of this intercolonial trade was beneficial to the entire British empire:

If the question be, which is most for the Interest of the British dominions in general, to restrain the French American trade or to give it all possible encouragement, it must be given in favor of encouragement. The speedy settlement of this vast continent is generally supposed to be advantageous to Great-Britain. Every new house, new farm, and new subject adds to the consumption of British manufactures. Nothing more contributes to this speedy settlement than a vent for the lumber, a great help in clearing the lands near the sea and upon navigable rivers, and for provisions the produce of settlement when made. But, on the other hand, admit that raising the price of West India produce

[108] Logan, "Of the State of the British Plantations," loc. cit., 129.

tends to increase the number of plantations in the islands, yet those plantations, although more valuable, will never bear any proportion in number to the plantations and settlements upon the continent, and the increase in white subjects will be still less in proportion. Blacks eat and drink nothing and wear next to nothing of British manufacture.[109]

The problems presented to the empire by the international intercolonial trade of the British colonies became most acute during the Seven Years War, when the Angloamericans engaged in trade with all the non-English colonies in America but, most flagrantly, with the colonies of England's enemies France and Spain—in a war, be it noted, actually in large part undertaken by Britain in defense of the colonies.[110] Opinion in the British West Indies opposed this trade; but much North American opinion, even in this time of war, excused it, rationalized it, and urged the British government to tolerate it, despite the fact that it both violated the navigation laws and encouraged and assisted Britain's enemies.

Thus, Lieutenant Governor Cadwallader Colden, of New York, while assuring Prime Minister William Pitt that Pitt's instructions for the suppression of illicit trade would be carried out, made bold, nevertheless, to inform the Prime Minister, with evident approval "what has been said in excuse":

It is aver'd that this trade has been highly advantageous to Great Britain, by the great quantities of British Manufactures, in value far exceeding the value of the Provisions, & by the large returns in Sugars; & some pretend they can demonstrate this against the force of all contradiction.[111]

A little later he clarified the question thus:

I observed that the Gentlemen of the Council distinguished between trade with the Enemies Colonies and trade with Neutral Ports. All trade with the Enemy was allow'd to be prohibited; but that the trade with the Neutral ports in the West Indies is only illegal under certain circumstances, & in certain commodities, & that this trade came not under the view of his Majesties orders of the 23rd August last. . . . As the plain view of the Act [of 1757] is only to prevent the Enemies being supplied with provisions, it cannot be intended to prevent sending of provisions to the Portiguies & Spanish Islands,[112] from whence all the Wines consumed in America are imported; because all the provisions imported to these Islands are consumed in them, & never reexported; and if no provisions be allowed to be sent thither for the purchase of Wines, they must be paid in Cash, or by Bills of Exchange with evident prejudice to the trade of Great Britain.[113]

Again, Colden reported the New York council as arguing that, although

[109] Hutchinson, History of . . . Massachusetts-Bay, II, 338–340.
[110] See Chapters XIII, XVII, and XIX.
[111] Colden to Pitt, Oct. 27, 1760, Colden Letter Books, I (Collections of the New York Historical Society, 1876, IX), 26–28.
[112] Both Portugal and Spain were still neutral. See Chapters XVIII and XIX.
[113] Colden to Pitt, Dec. 27, 1760, Colden Letter Books, I, 49–53.

the colonies were not permitted to ship provisions to neutral ports, the merchants of Great Britain and Ireland were. This, he said,

is evidently of prejudice to the trade of the Colonies, & in its consequence of prejudice to Great Britain, for without freedom in trade the Collonies are not able to pay for the British manufactures consum'd in them.[114]

As a positive suggestion, Colden wrote that "It seems evident to me that could a mutual intercourse in trade be obtain'd, between the British & Spanish colonies it must be highly advantageous to Great Brittain." [115] He suggested that Spanish colonists be allowed to purchase provisions from the northern colonies and that British colonists be permitted to sell provisions in the Spanish colonies; even if such a trade were to be limited to provisions only, "it would greatly advance the trade & riches of Great Brittain & cannot in any case be detrimental to it." [116]

The northern colonies, said Colden, cannot pay for the British manufactures they consume by their sales to the British colonies alone. Further, the consumption of British manufactures in the northern colonies increased in proportion to their ability to purchase them; those colonies consume far more British manufactures than the British West Indies. Finally, he said, it is difficult to prosecute people under the laws restraining colonial foreign trade "while they are under the prejudice to think that the Sugar Islands have gain'd a preference inconsistent with the true interest of the Mother Country." [117]

The international intercolonial trade of the British colonies was of vital importance to a vast number of individual Angloamericans, private merchants especially, whose property, even their very solvency, might depend on that trade's prosperity. While figures are not available, it is highly probable that more Americans were thinking about international commercial problems than about any other subject relative to international matters, with the exception of the Anglo-French imperial rivalry. And the trend of their thinking about that commerce showed a tendency toward a philosophy of free trade that ran directly counter to the intent and the policies of the English navigation system. While Angloamericans generally stood shoulder-to-shoulder with the mother country in the drives of imperial expansionism, their position with regard to international commerce rested upon a fundamentally different basis of self-interest. It seems, therefore, hardly too much to say, to suggest that this one international issue and the conflicts of opinion between colonies and mother country that arose from it may have been one of the most profound causes of the American Revolution.

[114] Colden to Pitt, Dec. 27, 1760, *loc. cit.*, I, 50.
[115] Colden to Pitt, Dec. 27, 1760, *loc. cit.*, I, 52.
[116] Colden to Pitt, Dec. 27, 1760, *loc. cit.*, I, 52.
[117] Colden to Pitt, Dec. 27, 1760, *loc. cit.*, I, 52.

7. Cultural Differences, Cultural Conflict, Cultural Nationalism

The thinking of the Angloamericans relative to their own international relations was not confined to matters of defense or of territorial imperialism, to questions relative to the role of the Indians in international affairs and the need for intercolonial union, or to the enlightened colonial self-interest in international intercolonial commerce that was leading them into frank, open, and official criticism of English policy calculated to suppress or restrain that commerce. The Angloamericans were also intensely conscious of the cultural differences between them and their foreign neighbors, particularly the Spanish and the French; this consciousness of difference, and the fear of the destruction of their own culture that sprang from it, became an integral part of the American thinking and feeling that lay behind the aggressive Angloamerican imperialism of the 1750s. This cultural and nationalistic fear was expressed by many voices.

A corresponding sense of cultural difference, indeed, and the nationalism that was associated with it, also characterized the international thinking of French leaders. Practically all of them expressed the same mood. One of the most eloquent was the Marquis de la Galissonière, who had such a powerful influence in French policy with regard to the colonies at the mid-century:

Motives of honor, glory and religion forbid the abandonment of an established Colony; the surrender . . . to a nation inimical by taste, education and religious principle . . . the giving up of so salutary a work as that of the conversion of the heathen who inhabit that vast continent.[118]

De la Galissonière, as has been noted, made numerous recommendations for the preservation of Canada and the establishment and advancement of its boundaries, and concluded that

it is of the utmost importance and of absolute necessity not to omit any means, nor to spare any expense to secure Canada, inasmuch as that is the only way to wrest America from the ambition of the English, and as the progress of their empire in that quarter of the globe is what is most capable of contributing to their superiority in Europe [that is, their preponderance in the balance of power].[119]

No matter how much it might cost, the French colonies on the continent must be preserved; to be preserved, they must be extended, peopled, and

[118] De la Galissonière, "Memoir on the French Colonies in North America," N.Y.C.D., X, 222.
[119] De la Galissonière, "Memoir on the French Colonies in North America," N.Y.C.D., X, 224.

fortified; with settlement there must go the French language, French religion, French governmental institutions, French culture.

On the English side, this cultural element in the international thinking of the Americans was expressed by many publicists, governors and officials, ministers, doctors, lawyers, and essayists. Archibald Kennedy saw the French as "the Disturbers of the Peace of Mankind, and worse than a Pest." Britain alone had prevented them from "enslaving the World and Mankind"; encroachments on Britain's American territories was only part of their strategy, "their national Polity being one continued Train of Chicane and Deceit." [120] The Canadians were the lowest of the Gallic troublemakers: they "are esteemed, even in France, a Race of Men lost to all those Principles of Honour upon which that Nation pique themselves." However, the English had much more at stake and better reason to fight than the French, who had "little to fight for but the Glory of their Monarch; we have the Glory of *Britain*, our Religion, our Liberties and our Properties, and upwards of a hundred Years Labour in these wild Deserts for the Sake of our Posterity." [121]

William Livingston saw the origins of the French nature and their political advantage in their popish religion, "an *impious*, an *absurd*, a *persecuting*, Blood *shedding* Religion:—a Religion as disgraceful to human Understandings, as it is injurious to the sacred Ties of social Benevolence . . . *It* is a Religion chiefly calculated to support the tyrannical Power, and the insatiable Avarice of their Clergy." [122] The Reformation was not yet dead! Because Catholicism trained people to absolute submission it formed them to obey the will of an absolute monarch. The subjects of the French king were thus blindly obedient to him, which gave the French an advantage over the free subjects of Britain in raising men and money and in disciplining their soldiers.

Other writers also found French religion sufficiently distasteful to be reason for resistance. Lewis Evans, the geographer, warned his countrymen against the possibility of the French settling in the Ohio Valley: "As bad as French Government and Religion is to those who have any Remains of British Spirit, it is easy to guess what Alternative the most zealous of us would chuse." [123]

To William Livingston, the loss of Britain's possessions in America would be a blow "of the most tremendous consequence . . . to the Protes-

---

[120] Kennedy, *Serious Considerations* . . . , 3.

[121] Kennedy, *Serious Considerations* . . . , 15. For a study of Angloamerican nationalism and other loyalties see Wilson, "Angloamerican Loyalties, 1739–1756," Unpublished M.A. thesis in the University of Washington Library.

[122] "A Summary View of the PRESENT STATE of this Continent in general, and of this Province in particular, with Regards to our neighbouring Enemies the French," *New York Mercury*, Sept. 23, 1754.

[123] Evans, *Analysis of a General Map of the Middle British Colonies, loc. cit.*, 159.

tant religion—to the peace of Europe—yes—and to the peace and happiness of all mankind." [124]

So bitter were feelings against the French that, in the mind of one writer at least, the French became synonymous with, and exemplified by all the vices he observed around him. This writer, the "Antigallican," as he called himself, published a series of moral essays in the *American Magazine* during 1757 and 1758. In the initial essay he set forth his purpose:

As an *Antigallican*, and an irreconcilable foe to *French* power, *French* customs, *French* policy and every species of *Slavery*, it is my purpose, as far as I am able to expose and check the enormous growth and influence of those evils, especially in these remoter parts of the globe. In a word, I am to devote a series of papers in order, if possible, to reluminate the dying virtue of our country, and bear my testimony against every sentiment, notion, measure or thing, either in *Religion, Manners* or *Government*, whereby the unrighteous designs of our enemies may be promoted against us.[125]

The "Antigallican" makes no further mention of the French: he was only a moralist who, like moralists of other times, had seized upon the most popular external enemy as the source of domestic decay.

The Angloamerican mood of imperialistic and cultural antigallicanism reached a shrill fortissimo in the sermons of such preachers as Samuel Davies, in Virginia, Aaron Burr, president of Princeton, and Jonathan Mayhew, of Boston.

To Davies, for example, the presence of French enemies in the back country along the Virginia frontier excited him to call upon his "countrymen," the Virginians, to rise in the name of religion and liberty and patriotism, to the defense of their "country," Virginia, against the French and their Indian allies:

Shall Virginia incur the Guilt and everlasting shame, of tamely exchanging her Liberty, her Religion, and her all, for arbitrary Gallic Power, and for Popish Slavery, Tyranny and Massacre? . . . And must I give thee up for lost, O my Country, and all that is included in that important Word? [126]

For the Reverend Aaron Burr,

God has in his sovereign Goodness, chosen the *British Nation* to be the *Bulwark* of the Reformation; to hold up a Standard against those *Superstitions* and *Impostures* [of Rome]. . . . On the one Hand, ther is *Poverty, Slavery*, Persecution and Death; on the other, a fruitful Country, pleasant Habitations, *British* Liberty, and what is dearer than all, undefiled Christianity.[127]

[124] Livingston, *Review of the Military Operations in North America*, in Mass. Hist. Soc. Colls., 1st Series, VII, p. 189.
[125] "The Antigallican, No. I," *American Magazine*, Vol. I, No. 2 (Nov., 1757), 78–82.
[126] Davies, *Religion and Patriotism the Constituents of a Good Soldier*, 5.
[127] Burr, *A Discourse Delivered at New-Ark, in New Jersey, January 1, 1755*, 29, 40.

President Burr urged his fellow Americans on to war:

'Tis high Time, to awake, to call up all the *Briton* in us, every spark of *English* Valor, cheerfully to offer our Purses, our Arms, and our Lives, to the Defence of our Country, our holy Religion, our excellent Constitution, and invaluable Liberties. . . . A *free-born Briton*, should disdain the Life of a Slave;—better, —far better, bravely to *sacrifice* it to the Defence of our Religion and Country, than to *survive* the dismal Day, when these Regions of Light and Liberty, shall be overspread with Ignorance, Superstition, and Tyranny. And had we but the *Spirit* of our brave *Ancestors.* . . . I doubt not, by the Smiles of Heaven, we should soon make our Enemies flee before us, and again sit quietly under our Vines and Fig-Trees, and eat the Good of the Land.[128]

Jonathan Mayhew was the most eloquent cultural-nationalist-imperialist of them all. Before the governor and the General Court of Massachusetts he preached a veritable anti-French crusade:

And what horrid scene is this, which restless, roving fancy, or something of a higher nature, presents to me; and so chills my blood? Do I behold these territories of freedom, become the prey of arbitrary power? . . . Do I see Christianity banished for popery! the bible, for the mass-book! the oracles of truth, for fabulous legends! Do I see the sacred Edifices erected here to the honour of the true God, and his Son, on the ruins of pagan superstition and idolatry; erected here, where Satan's seat was; do I see these sacred Edifices laid in ruins themselves! and others rising in their places consecrated to the honour of saints and angels! Instead of a train of Christ's faithful, laborious ministers, do I behold an heard of lazy Monks, and Jesuits, and Exorcists, and Inquisitors, and cowled, and un-cowled Imposters; Do I see a Protestant, there, stealing a look at his bible, and being taken in the fact, punished like a felon! What indignity is yonder offered to the matrons, and here, to the Virgins! . . . Do I see all liberty, property, religion, happiness, changed, or rather transubstantiated, into slavery, poverty, superstition, wretchedness! . . . O dishonest! profane! execrable sight! O piercing sound! that *entereth into the ears of the Lord of Sabbath!* Where! in what region! in what world am I! Is this imagination? . . . Or is it something more divine? I will not, I cannot believe 'tis prophetic vision; or, that God has so far abandoned us! [129]

Mayhew also urged his people to war:

Shall the sword rust? . . . Shall our military garments be moth-eaten for want of use, when such things are doing! It is impossible, Gentlemen, you should be any ways backward, or parsimonius, in such a cause as this; a cause wherein the glory of God, the honour of your King, and the good of your country, are so deeply concerned; I might perhaps add, a cause, whereon the liberties of Europe depend. For of so great consequence is the empire of North America, . . . that it must turn the scale of power greatly in favour of the only Monarch, from whom those liberties are in danger; and against the Prince, who is the

---

[128] Burr, A *Discourse Delivered at New-Ark, in New Jersey*, 29, 40.
[129] Mayhew, A *Sermon Preach'd in the Audience of His Excellency William Shirley, Esq; . . . , May 29th, 1754*, 32–47.

grand support and bulwark of them. . . . It is even uncertain, Gentlemen, how long you will have an House to sit in, unless a speedy and vigorous opposition is made to the present encroachments, and to the further designs, of our enemies! [130]

These were Angloamerican voices which, among many, expressed the cultural and nationalistic self-consciousness which provided a deeper and broader emotional and ideological rationalization of the imperial conflict between the British and the French in North America. That conflict, now, was not merely territorial, or commercial, or directed at the control of Indians, or political: it was religious and cultural, the very basis of civilization itself now seeming to be at stake.

8. The Inevitable Conflict

Through much of the writing of the colonial publicists on both sides of the Anglo-French conflict in America there ran a note of inevitability. The Marquis de la Galissonière, most eloquent of French colonial spokesmen, clearly expressed, in his famous "Memoir on the French Colonies in America," his fears of English success and his deep conviction that France must, at all costs, preserve New France as a wall against English expansion.

Canada, he wrote, constituted "the strongest barrier that can be opposed to the ambition of the English," for Canada alone was in a position to wage war against them in all their continental possessions, "possessions which are as dear to them as they are precious in fact, whose power is daily increasing, and which, if means be not found to prevent it, will soon absorb not only all the Colonies located in the neighboring islands of the Tropic, but even all those of the Continent of America." [131] De la Galissonière was especially fearful for the French Windward Islands and the Spanish islands of Cuba and Santo Domingo, which he believed could easily fall to forces sent from the British continental colonies. If the English were not stopped, the outcome was inevitable: the French would be driven from the continent.

This sense of inevitability also characterized the writings of many English commentators. William Shirley, Governor of Massachusetts, reporting his correspondence with de la Galissonière, expressed somewhat the same idea: "I can't but look upon the point now coming on in Dispute, as what must finally determine the Mastery of this Continent between His Majesty and the French King." [132] So did the *Boston Evening Post*:

[130] Mayhew, *A Sermon Preach'd in the Audience of . . . William Shirley.*
[131] De la Galissonière, "Memoir on the French Colonies in North America," *N.Y.C.D.*, X, 223.
[132] Shirley to the Duke of Bedford, May 10, 1749, *Correspondence of William Shirley*, Lincoln, ed., I, 487.

It is very easy to penetrate the Designs of the *French*, and without the Spirit of Prophecy to foretel, that if there is not a vigorous and united Opposition effectually to prevent it, they will, in a few Years, lay a solid and lasting Foundation, for making themselves in Time Masters of all *North America*.[133]

The Albany congress met in 1754 in response to what its supporters believed was a desperate need for united action by the colonies against the French. In July of that year the congress issued its "Representation of the Present State of the Colonies" in which it outlined French aggressions against British territories and concluded, "That it is the Evident Design of the French to Surround the British Colonies . . . To be in a Capacity of making a General Attack on the Several Governments . . . there is the utmost danger that the Whole Continent will be subjected to that Crown." [134]

But the congress came to nothing, and the war became formal early in 1756. William Livingston, a New Yorker who had supported the congress and its aborted plan for union, wrote, after the adjournment of the congress, an essay attacking those who had opposed colonial union, emphasizing the French danger and the need for colonial action:

There is too much reason for general concern: and I venture to predict, what every judicious person foresees, that unless some successful blow is struck, at the power of France, Britain must inevitably lose her possession in America. . . . Canada, my Lord, Canada must be demolished—Delende est Carthago—or we are undone.[135]

The outbreak of the undeclared French and Indian War in 1754 had already produced a flood of comment from the Angloamericans. Fearful of engulfment by the French, the colonists bombarded their press and the British ministry with warnings, dire predictions, and agitation for the permanent and complete conquest of French America. The "present state of the colonies," usually regarded as desperate, was a popular theme developed by numerous writers.

Archibald Kennedy, for example, wrote in his *Serious Considerations on the Present State of the Affairs of the Northern Colonies* that the Anglo-French conflict was not merely territorial but one in which the British were the sole force preventing France from "enslaving the World and Mankind." One part of the policy of the French King, "an ambitious, all-grasping Monarch," was the possession of the whole continent, "in which he has made not a little progress." [136]

Governor William Shirley of Massachusetts made the same interpretation of French ambitions:

[133] *Boston Evening Post*, Apr. 1, 1754.
[134] *Franklin Papers*, Labaree, ed., V, 366–374.
[135] Livingston, *A Review of the Military Operations in North America* in Mass. Hist. Soc. Colls., 1st Series, VII, p. 189.
[136] Kennedy, *Serious Considerations* . . . , 3, 5.

The French seem to have advanced further towards making themselves Masters of this Continent within these last five or six Years, than they have done ever since the first Beginning of their Settlements upon it; and how determined they are to accomplish their Scheme as soon as possible, Appears from their breaking thro' the most recent solemn Treaties and Agreements made between the two Crowns in order to effect it.[137]

When the inevitable conflict eventually came, all the motives of territorial and commercial imperialism, of fear of French and Indian encirclement, and of cultural and religious self-consciousness combined in the expression of American opinion relative to the war. The colonies were probably more united with each other and with the mother country in the prosecution of the common cause than they had ever been before. In 1760, after the fall of Quebec to the English, Benjamin Franklin expressed what was probably the prevailing opinion among Angloamericans when he wrote to Henry Home, Lord Kames, "No one can rejoice more sincerely than I do on the Reduction of Canada; and this, not merely as I am a Colonist, but as I am a Briton." And in his famous pamphlet on the question whether Britain should retain Canada at the peace, *The Interest of Great Britain Considered, With Regard to her Colonies, and the Acquisition of Canada and Guadaloupe . . .*, he wrote, "I hope it will appear before I end these sheets, what if ever there was a *national war*, this is truly such a one; a war in which the interest of the *whole* nation is directly and fundamentally concerned." For him, as for most Angloamericans, this was a war by and for the entire British nation. He demolished the argument that the war in progress was a war for the colonies: "The inhabitants of them [the colonies] are, in common with the other subjects of Great Britain, anxious for the glory of her crown, the extent of her power and commerce, the welfare and future repose of the whole British people." To call this a war for the colonies, he said, was no more correct than to call a war for British commerce a war for the weavers of Yorkshire, Norwich, or western England, or for the button-makers of Birmingham.[138]

Here was an expression of British imperial nationalism, a feeling shared by most Angloamericans along with Englishmen. Franklin's was unquestionably the most distinguished American voice; it certainly expressed a British nationalistic attitude toward the international situation that was shared by most, if not all, articulate Angloamericans.

9. Conclusion

While the Angloamericans of the eighteenth century were most concerned with finding their place within their respective French or British

---

[137] Shirley to the General Court of Massachusetts, April 2, 1754, *Correspondence of William Shirley*, Lincoln, ed., II, 46.
[138] *The Papers of Benjamin Franklin*, Labaree ed., IX, 6–7, 72, 75.

empires, they were, the British colonists at least, learning at the same time to find their separate identity and individual worth. One of the means the colonists used to try to persuade the home government to pursue various advantageous policies was to emphasize the particular value of the colonies and the magnitude of their potential loss.

One of the values of the American colonies in the international scheme of things, according to the Angloamericans, lay in the common belief that they controlled the balance of power among the various colonizing nations. The British colonists insisted that whichever nation controlled North America would hold the hegemony of power over the rest of Europe. Such opinions were expressed in the many warnings sent to the home government to try to win more attention for America.

The colonies also saw themselves as of immeasurable economic importance to their mother countries, and this was another point which the Americans used to try to win support and defense from England. There were many warnings that Britain would be able to maintain its power only so long as it held its American colonies. Such, for example, as the opinion of William Clarke that

These Colonies are of such Consequence to the Trade, Wealth and Naval Power of *Great-Britain*, and will in future Time make so much larger Additions to it, that whilst she keeps them entire, she will be able to maintain not only her Independency, but her Superiority as a Maritime Power. And on the other Hand, should she once lose them, and the *French* gain them, *Great-Britain* herself must necessarily be reduced to an absolute Subjection to the *French Crown*, to be nothing more than a *Province of France*.[139]

Or, again, that of Elias Huske that

The Mother Country must needs rejoice in the Security and Prosperity of every one of her Colonies, because it is her own Security and Prosperity; and the Colonies are to her as the Feet are to the Natural Body, the Support of the whole Political Frame. And they have enabled us to make the Figure we do at present, and have done for upwards of a Century past, in the Commercial World, from whence we have derived Wealth, Power and Glory, and the greatest Blessings given Man to know.[140]

This sort of self-consciousness must also have produced feelings that, as valuable and useful as the colonies and their resources and men were, they might possibly have been able to exist independently of their European masters. Such ideas were not openly expressed until the latter part of the eighteenth century, but they must have existed earlier, for one finds, in the earlier part of the century, numerous denials from colonials that independence was possible or even thinkable. Apparently, there existed a fear in some circles in Britain that if the colonies were given too much aid in

[139] Clarke, *Observations on the Late and Present Conduct of the French*, 47.
[140] Huske, *The Present State of North America*, 58.

defense against the French they would use it to achieve their own independence. Such assertions were vigorously denied by Americans pleading for more help against the French.

Lewis Evans insisted that the colonies would never be able to achieve independence, being tied as they were to Britain by blood, friendship, and mutual dependence and being at the same time too divided among themselves ever to unite. But he warned that

repeated and continued ill Usage, Infringements of their dear-bought Privileges, sacrificing them to the Ambition and Intrigues of domestic and foreign Enemies, may not provoke them to do their utmost for their own Preservation, I would not pretend to say; as weak as they are. But while they are treated as Members of one Body, and allowed their natural Rights, it would be the Height of Madness for them to propose an Independency, were they ever so strong. If they had any ambitious Views, a strong Colony, of a natural Enemy to England, on their Borders, would be the only Article that would render any Attempt of Independency truly dangerous; and for that Reason it becomes those who would regard the future Interest of Britain and its Colonies, to suppress the Growth of the French Power, and not the English, in America.[141]

The Americans had discovered themselves and their importance, not only as members of the British empire but, also, as important members—if only junior members, as yet—of the community of Western states.

[141] Evans, *Analysis of a General Map, loc. cit.*, 176.

Bibliography

I. Unpublished Archival Material

Archives du Ministère des Affaires Étrangères, Paris.
    Correspondance Politique: Angleterre
                                Autriche
                                Danemark
                                Hollande
                                Portugal
                                Naples
Archives du Ministère des Affaires Étrangères, Paris. Divers.
Archives du Ministère des Affaires Étrangères, Paris.
    Mémoires et Documents.   Amérique
                                France
Archivo General de Indias, Seville.
    Papeles procedentes de Cuba.
    Papeles procedentes de Santo Domingo.
Archives of the State of Massachusetts.
    Documents collected in France.
Archivo Historico Nacional, Madrid. Papeles del Estado.
Archives Nationales, Paris.
    Documents des Colonies: Series A
                                Series $C_{11}E$
                                Series C_{13}
                                Series K
Biblioteca Nacional, Madrid. Manuscritos diversos.
Bibliothèque Nationale, Paris. Bureau des Estampes.
Bibliothèque Nationale, Paris. Manuscrits: Fonds Français, nouvelles acquisitions.
British Museum, London. Additional Manuscripts.
British Museum. London. Harleian Manuscripts.
British Museum. London. Lansdowne Manuscripts.
British Museum, London. Stowe Manuscripts.

W. L. Clements Library, Ann Arbor, Michigan. Shelburne, The Earl of. The Papers of the Earl of Shelburne.

W. L. Clements Library, Ann Arbor, Michigan. Mildmay, William. The Personal Papers of William Mildmay.

Huntington Library. Blathwayt Papers.
          Elesmere Manuscripts.

Huntington Library. Rare Book Room, 137888.
          "Convention for explaining the articles of the Asiento. Madrid 26/15 May, 1716."

Library of Congress, Washington. Additional Manuscripts. Transcripts of Documents in the British Museum, London, deposited in the Library of Congress, Washington, D.C.

Library of Congress, Washington. Colonial Office Papers. Transcripts of documents in the British Public Record Office, London, deposited in the Library of Congress, Washington.

Library of Congress, Washington. House of Lords Manuscripts. Transcripts and photostats of documents in the Library of the House of Lords, London, deposited in the Library of Congress, Washington, D.C.

Library of Congress, Washington. Mémoires et Documents: Amérique. Transcripts and Photostats of Documents in the Archives du Ministère des Affaires Étrangères, Paris, deposited in the Library of Congress, Washington, D.C.

Library of Congress, Washington. Papeles procedentes de Santo Domingo. Transcripts of Documents in the Archivo General de Indias, Seville, deposited in the Library of Congress, Washington.

New York Historical Society. Rufus King Papers.

New York Public Library. New York. Chalmers Manuscripts: "Canada."

New York Public Library, New York. Copies of documents in the Archivo General de Simancas (Spain) made for Alexander Brown.

New York Public Library. New York. Hardwick Papers.

Public Archives of Canada, Ottawa. Foreign Office Papers [British]. Transcripts of documents in the Public Record Office, London, series "Foreign Office," deposited in the Archives of the Dominion of Canada, Ottawa.

Public Archives of Canada, Ottawa. Correspondence Politique: Angleterre. Transcripts of documents in the Archives du Ministère des Affaires Étrangères, Paris, series Correspondance Politique, Angleterre, deposited in the Archives of the Dominion of Canada, Ottawa.

Public Record Office, London. Chatham Manuscripts.
          Foreign Office Papers.
          State Papers. France
                          Spain

II. Printed Materials

A. Collections of Treaties

Abreu y Bertodano, José Antonio de, ed. Colección des los Tratados de Paz, Alianza, Neutralidad, Garantia . . . [y] Comercio . . . de España . . . desde antes del establecimiento de la Monarchia Gotica hasta el . . . reynado del Rey . . . Felipe V. 12 vols. Madrid, 1740–52.

Actes et Mémoires des Négociations de la Paix de Nimèque. 2nd ed. 4 vols. Amsterdam and the Hague, 1680.

Actes et Mémoires des Négociations de la Paix de Ryswick, compiled by J. Bernard. 2nd ed. 5 vols. The Hague, 1707.

Actes et Mémoires touchant la Paix d'Utrecht. 6 vols. Utrecht, 1714.

Actes, Mémoires et autres pièces authentiques concernant la Paix d'Utrecht, depuis l'année 1706 jusqu'à présent. 6 vols. Utrecht, 1712–15.

The Acts and Negotiations, Together with the Particular Articles at Large, of the General Peace, concluded at Ryswick, by the French King. To which is premised, the Negotiations and Articles of the Peace, concluded at Turin, between the same Prince and the Duke of Savoy. Translated from the Original Publish'd at the Hague. London, 1698.

Almon, J., ed. *A Collection of the Treaties of Peace, Alliance and Commerce, between Great-Britain and other Powers, from the Revolution in 1688, to the Present Time.* 2 vols. London, 1772.

Calvo, Carlos. *Recueil complet des traités, conventions, capitulations, armistices et autres actes diplomatiques de tous les états de l'Amérique latine compris entre le golfe du Méxique et le cap de Horn, depuis l'année 1493 jusqu'à nos jours . . .* 11 vols. Paris, 1862–68.

Cantillo, Alejandro del, ed. *Tratados, Convenios y Declaraciones de Paz y de Comercio que han hecho con las Potencias Estranjeros los Monarcas Espanoles de la Casa de Borbon. Desde el Año de 1700 hasta el Dia.* Madrid, 1843.

Chalmers, George, ed. *A Collection of Treaties between Great Britain and Other Powers.* 2 vols. London, 1790.

Davenport, Frances Gardiner, and Charles O. Paullin, eds. *European Treaties bearing on the History of the United States and its Dependencies.* 4 vols. Washington, 1917–37.

Dumont, Jean, ed., *Corps universel diplomatique du droit des gens; contenant un recueil des traitez d'alliance, de paix, de trève, de neutralité, de commerce, d'échange . . . & autres contrats, qui ont été faits en Europe, depuis le règne de l'Empereur Charlemagne jusques à présent . . .* 8 vols. Amsterdam, 1726–31.

Ferreira Borges de Castro, José, ed. *Collecção dos Tratados, Convencões, Contratos e Actos Publicos celebrados entre a Corôa de Portugal e as mais Potencias desde 1640 ate ao presente.* 30 vols. Lisbon, 1856–79.

Hertslet, Lewis, ed. *Hertslet's commercial Treaties. A Collection of Treaties and Conventions, between Great Britain and Foreign Powers, and of the Laws, Decrees, Orders in Council, Ec., concerning the same, so far as they relate to Commerce and Navigation, Slavery, Extradition, Nationality, Copyright, Postal Matters, Ec. . . .* 31 vols. London, 1827–1925.

Jenkinson, Charles, Earl of Liverpool, ed. *A Collection of all the Treaties of Peace, Alliance, and Commerce between Great-Britain and other Powers; from the treaty signed at Münster in 1648 to the treaties signed at Paris in 1783 . . .* 3 vols. London, 1785.

Koch, Christophe Guillaume and F. Scholl. *Histoire abrégée des traités de paix, entre les puissances de l'Europe, depuis la Paix de Westphalie . . . Ouvrage entièrement refondu, augm. et continué jusqu'au Congrès de Vienne et Traités de Paris de 1815.* 15 vols. Paris, 1817–18.

Leonard, F., ed. *Recueil des traitez de paix, de trève, de neutralité, de conféderation, d'alliance, et de commerce, faits par les rois de France, avec tous les princes et potentats de l'Europe.* 6 vols. Paris, 1693.

Martens, Georg Friedrich von. *Nouveau Recueil général des traités, conventions et autres transactions remarquables . . .* Continued and revised by C. Murchard *et al.* 20 vols. Göttingen, 1843–75.

Miller, David Hunter, ed. *Treaties and other International Acts of the United States of America.* 8 vols. Washington, 1931–48.

Vast, Henri, ed. *Les grands traités du règne de Louis XIV.* 3 vols. Paris, 1893–99.

B. Contemporary Imprints

The American Magazine and Monthly Chronical for the British Colonies. Philadelphia, 1757–58.

The Annual Register, and Virginian Repository. London, 1759–80.

"The Antigallican, No. I," *American Magazine,* Vol. I, No. 2 (Nov., 1757), 78–82. Philadelphia, 1757.

Arredondo, Antonio de. *Arredondo's Historical Proof of Spain's Title to Georgia, a Contribution to the History of One of the Spanish Borderlands.* Edited by Herber E. Bolton. Berkeley, Calif., 1925.

Auchmuty, Robert. *The Importance of Cape Breton to the British Nation.* London, 1745.

Barreto, João Franco. *Relacão da embaixada a França em 1641,* ed. Carlos Roma du Bocage and Edgar Prestage. Coimbra, 1918.

Bolingbroke, Henry Saint-John, First Viscount. *Letters on the Spirit of Patriotism: on the Idea of a Patriot King: and on the State of Parties at the Accession of King George the First.* London, 1749.

Boston Evening Post. Boston, 1739–75.

Bradford, William. *Of Plymouth Plantation,* ed. S. E. Morison. New York, 1962.

Burnet, Gilbert. *Bishop Burnet's History of His Own Time.* 6 vols. Oxford, 1823.

Burr, Aaron. *A Discourse Delivered at New-Ark, in New Jersey. January 1, 1755.* New York, 1755.

Butel-Dumont, Georges Marie. *Histoire et Commerce des Antilles Angloises. Où l'on trouve l'état actuel de leur population & des détails curieux sur la constitution de leur gouvernement.* Paris, 1757.

Camden, William. *Annales. The True and Royall History of the Famous Empresse Elizabeth, Queene of England, France and Ireland, &c., True Faith's Defendresse of Divine Renowne and Happy Memory. Wherein all such memorable things as happened during hir Blessed Raigne, with such Acts and Treaties as past betwixt Hir Matie and Scotland, France, Spaine, Italy, Germany, Poland, Sweden, Denmark, Russia, and the Netherlands, are exactly described.* London, 1625.

Castro, Fratris Alfonsi a. *De Potestate legis poenalis libri duo.* Salamanca, 1551.

Charlevoix, Pierre François Xavier de. *Histoire de l'Isle Espagnole ou de S. Domingue.* 2 vols. Paris, 1730–31.

Charlevoix, Pierre François Xavier de. *History and General Description of New France.* Translated and edited by J. G. Shea. 6 vols. New York, 1900.

Charlevoix, Pierre François Xavier de. *Journal d'un voyage fait par ordre du Roi dans l'Amérique Septentrionale.* Paris, 1744.

Choiseul-Stainville, Étienne François, Duc de. *Mémoire historique sur la négociation de la France et de l'Angleterre depuis le 26 Mars 1761, jusqu'au 20 Septembre de la même année, avec les pièces justificatives.* London, 1761.

Choiseul-Stainville, Étienne François, Duc de. *Mémoires du Duc de Choiseul, 1719–1785,* ed. Fernand Calmettes. Paris, 1904.

Clarendon, Edward, Earl of. *The Life of Edward, Earl of Clarendon: a Continuation of his History of the Grand Rebellion.* 3 vols. Dublin, 1759–60.

Clarke, William. *Observations on the Late and Present Conduct of the French with regard to their Encroachments upon the British Colonies in North America.* Boston, 1755.

Colden, Cadwallader. *The History of the Five Indian Nations of Canada.* London, 1747.

Considérations sur les consequences que l'on doit craindre de l'établissement des français sur le Mississippi par rapport au commerce et à la sûreté des colonies anglaises en Amérique et dans les Indes Occidentales. London, 1720.

Coxe, Daniel. *A Description of the English Province of Carolina.* London, 1722.

Davies, Samuel. *Religion and Patriotism the Constituents of a Good Soldier.* Philadelphia, 1755.

Denys, Nicolas. *The Description and Natural History of the Coasts of North America (Acadia).* Tr. and ed. by William F. Ganong. Toronto, 1908.

A Description of Georgia by a Gentleman who has resided there upwards of Seven Years and was one of the First Settlers. London, 1741.

Douglass, William. *A Summary, Historical and Political, of the First Planting, progressive Improvements, and present state of the British settlements in North America.* 2 vols. Boston, 1747–52.

Dummer, Jeremiah. *A Defense of the New-England Charters.* London, 1721.

Dutertre, Jean Baptiste. *Histoire générale des Antilles habitées par les Français.* 4 vols. Paris, 1667–71.

Edwards, Bryan. *The History Civil and Commercial of the British West Indies.* 5th ed. 5 vols. London, 1819.

Egmont, John Perceval, Second Earl of. *Faction detected by the Evidence of Facts.* London, 1743.

d'Eon de Beaumont, Charles. *Lettres, mémoires et négociations particulières du chevalier d'Eon, ministre plénipotentiare de France auprès de Roi de la Grande Bretagne . . .* The Hague, 1764.

Evans, Lewis. *Geographical, Historical, Political, Philosophical and Mechanical Essays.* Philadelphia, 1756; New York, 1756. In Lawrence Henry Gipson, *Lewis Evans.* Philadelphia, 1939.

A Fair Representation of His Majesty's Right to Nova Scotia or Acadia. Briefly Stated from the Memorials of the English Commissaries; with an answer to the objections contained in the French memorials, and in a treatise entitled, Discussion summaire sur les anciennes limites de l'Acadie. London, 1756.

Forbes, Patrick, ed. *A Full View of the Public Transactions in the Reign of Q. Elizabeth.* 2 vols. London, 1740–41.

Forman, Charles. *Mr. Forman's Letter to the Right Honourable William Pulteney, Esq.; Shewing how Pernicious, the Imperial Company of Commerce and Navigation, lately established in the Austrian Netherlands, is likely to prove to Great Britain, as well as to Holland . . .* London, 1725.

Franklin, Benjamin. *The Interest of Great Britain considered with regard to her colonies, and the acquisitions of Canada and Guadaloupe. To which are added, Observations concerning the Increase of Mankind, Peopling of Countries, etc.* London, 1760.

Freschot, Casimir. *The Compleate History of the Treaty of Utrecht, as also that of Gertruydenberg; containing all the Acts, Memorials, Representations, Complaints, Demands, Letters, Speeches, Treaties and other authentick Pieces Relating to the Negotiations there.* 2 vols. London, 1715.

Gaceta de Madrid, 1732, 1733, 1734. Museo Nacional, Madrid.

Gage, Thomas. *The English-American, his Travail by Sea and Land: or, A New Survey of the West-India's . . .* London, 1648.

Gentilis, Albericus. *De Iure Belli Libri Tres (The Classics of International Law,* ed. James Brown Scott, No. 16). 2 vols. Oxford and London, 1933.

Gentilis, Albericus. *Hispanicae advocationis libri duo.* Amsterdam, 1661.

The Gentleman's Magazine and Historical Chronicle. 303 vols. London, 1731–1907.

Grotius, Hugo. *De Jure Praedae Commentarius (The Classics of International Law,* ed. James Brown Scott, No. 22). 2 vols. Oxford, 1950.

Hakluyt, Richard. *A Discourse concerning Western Planting, written in the Year 1584,* ed. Charles Deane (*Collections of the Maine Historical Society.* 2nd Series. Vol. II). Cambridge, Mass., 1877.

Hakluyt, Richard. "A particular discourse concerning the greate necessitie and manifolde comodyties that are like to growe to this Realme of Englande by the Western discoveries lately attempted. . . ." *Collections of the Maine Historical Society,* 2nd Series, II, 1–167.

Hakluyt, Richard. *The Principal Navigations. Voyages, Traffiques & Discoveries of the English Nation, made by Sea or Overland to the Remote and farthest Distant Quarters of the Earth at any Time within the Compass of these 1600 years.* 10 vols. London and Toronto, 1927–28.

[Hoadly, Benjamin]. *A Defense of the Enquiry into the Reasons of the Conduct of Great Britain.* London, 1729.

[Hoadly, Benjamin]. *An Enquiry into the Reasons of the Conduct of Great Britain, with Relation to the Present State of Affairs in Europe.* London, 1727.

Hubner, Martin. *De la Saisie des Batimens Neutres, ou, Du droit qu'ont les nations belligérantes d'arrêter les navires des peuples amis.* 2 vols. The Hague, 1759.

Huske, Elias. *The Present State of North America.* 2nd ed. London, 1755.

Hutchinson, Thomas. *The History of the Colony and Province of Massachusetts-Bay.* ed. Lawrence Shaw Mayo. 3 vols. Cambridge, Mass., 1936.

The Importance of the British Plantations in America to this Kingdom. London, 1731.

The Importance of the Ostend Company Considered. London, 1726.

The Important Question Discussed, or, a Serious and Impartial Enquiry into the Interest of England with Respect to the Continent. London, 1746.

Independent Advertiser. Boston, 1748–49.

An Inquiry concerning the Trade, Commerce, and Policy of Jamaica. London, 1759.

The Instructor. New York, 1755.

[Jeffreys, Thomas]. *The Conduct of the French, with Regard to Nova Scotia; from its First Settlement to the Present Time. In which are exposed the*

Falsehood and Absurdity of their Arguments made use of to elude the Force of the Treaty of Utrecht, and support their unjust Proceedings. London, 1754.

Jeffreys, Thomas. *Remarks on the French Memorials concerning the limits of Acadia, printed at the Royal Printing House at Paris, and distributed by the French Ministers at all the foreign courts of Europe, with two maps exhibiting the limits: one according to the system of the French, the other conformable to English rights. To which is added an answer to the Summary Discussion, etc.* London, 1756.

Jenkinson, Charles, First Earl of Liverpool. *A Discourse on the Conduct of Great Britain in respect to Neutral Nations during the Present War.* London, 1758.

Keith, Sir William. *A Collection of Papers and other Tracts, written occasionally on Various Subjects.* London, 1740.

Kennedy, Archibald. *The Importance of Gaining and Preserving the Friendship of the Indians to the British Interest, Considered.* London, 1751.

Kennedy, Archibald. *Serious Considerations on the Present State of the Affairs of the Northern Colonies.* New York, 1754.

Lahontan, Louis Armand de Lom d'Arce, Baron de. *Nouveaux voyages de m le baron de Lahontan, dans l'Amérique Septentrionale, qui contiennent une relation des différens peuples qui y habitent; la nature de leur governement; leur coutumes, leur réligion, & leur manière de faire la guerre. L'intérêt des François & des Anglais dans le commerce qu'il font avec ces nations; l'avantage que l'Angleterre peut retirer dans ce pais, étant en guerre avec la France.* 2 vols. The Hague, 1703.

Lettres-patentes du Roy, du mois de Mars mil sept cens treize; par lesquelles Sa Majesté a admis la Renonciation faite à la Couronne de France par le Roy d'Espagne son Petit-fils. Besançon, 1713.

Livingston, William, et al. *The Independent Reflector; or, Weekly Essays on Sundry Important Subjects,* ed. Milton M. Klein. Cambridge, Mass., 1963.

[Livingston, William]. "A Summary View of the PRESENT STATE of this Continent . . ." *New York Mercury,* New York, Sept. 23, 1754.

Livingston, William. *A Review of the Military Observations in North America from 1753–1756.* Dublin, 1757 (Reprinted in *Massachusetts Historical Society Collections,* 1st Series, Vol. VII, 67–113).

Logan, James. "Materials for Governor Keith's Memorial to the Board of Trade, relating to the Indians." Printed as "Logan's Account of the French Settlements in the West in 1718," *Historical Magazine,* VI (1862), 19–22.

Logan, James. "Of the State of the British Plantations in America." In Joseph C. Johnson, ed. "A Quaker Imperialist's View of the British Colonies in America, 1732," *Pennsylvania Magazine of History and Biography,* LX, No. 2 (Apr., 1936), 97–130.

London Gazette. London, 1665–1827.

London Magazine: or, Gentleman's Monthly Intelligencer. London, 1732–83

[Marchmont, Hugh H., Earl of Marchmont]. *A State of the Rise and Progress of Our Disputes with Spain, and of the Conduct of Our Ministers relating thereto.* London, 1739.

Martin, Benjamin. *An Account showing the Progress of the Colony of Georgia in America from its First Establishment.* London, 1741. Reprinted in *Georgia Colonial Records,* III, 368–403.

Mauduit, Israel. *Considerations on the Present German War.* London, 1760.

Mayhew, Jonathan. *A Sermon Preach'd in the Audience of His Excellency William Shirley, Esq. . . . May 29, 1754.* Boston, 1754.

Mémoires des Commissaires du Roi et de ceux de sa Majesté Britannique, sur les possessions et les droits respectifs des deux Couronnes en Amérique; avec les Actes publics & Pièces justificatives. 3 vols. Paris, 1755.

The Memorials of the English and French Commissaires concerning the Limits of Nova Scotia or Acadia [and St. Lucia]. 2 vols. London, 1755.

Miscellaneous Thoughts on the Present Posture of our Foreign and Domestic Affairs. London, 1742.

[Mitchell, John]. *The Contest in America between Great Britain and France.* London, 1757.

Moreau, Jacob Nicolas, compiler. *Mémoire contenant le précis des faits, avec leurs pièces justificatives. Pour servir de Réponse aux Observations envoyées par les ministres d'Angleterre, dans les cours de l'Europe.* Paris, 1756.

New York Mercury, New York, 1754.

Observations on the Conduct of Great-Britain, with Regard to Negotiations and other Transactions Abroad. London, 1729.

Observations on the Present Conventions with Spain. London, 1739.

[Oglethorpe, James]. *A New and Accurate Account of the Provinces of South-Carolina and Georgia; with Many Curious and Useful Observations on the Trade, Navigation and Plantations of Great Britain, Compared with her Most Powerful Maritime Neighbors in Ancient and Modern Times.* London, 1733. (Georgia Historical Society, *Collections,* I, 42–78).

Papers relative to the Rupture with Spain. London, 1762.

Pichardo, José Antonio. *Pichardo's Treatise on the Limits of Louisiana and Texas.* Edited and translated by Charles Wilson Hackett. 3 vols. Austin, Tex., 1931–41.

Pidanzet de Mairobert, Mathieu François. *Discussion sommaire sur les anciennes limites de l'Acadie et sur les stipulationes du Traité d'Utrecht.* Basel, 1755.

Political State of Great Britain. London, 1739.

Postlethwayt, Malachy. *Britain's Commercial Interest Explained and Improved . . .* 2 vols. London, 1757.

Postlethwayt, Malachy. *A. Dissertation on the Plan, Use and Importance, of the Universal Dictionary of Trade and Commerce.* London, 1749.

[Pulteney, William, Earl of Bath]. *Review of all that hath pass'd between the Courts of Great Britain and Spain, Relating to Our Trade and Navigation from the Year 1721, to the Present Convention . . .* London, 1739.

[Pulteney, William]. *A Series of Wisdom and Policy, Manifested in a Review of our Foreign Negotiations and Transactions for several years past.* London, 1735.

Raynal, Guillaume Thomas François. *A Philosophical and Political History of the Settlements and Trade of the Europeans in the East and West Indies.* 8 vols. London, 1783.

The Report of the Committee of both Houses of Assembly of . . . South Carolina [on] . . . the Late Expedition against St. Augustine. London, 1743.

Rousset de Missy, Jean. *Recueil de pièces authentiques pour servir à l'histoire de la Paix d'Aix-la-Chapelle conclue en 1748.* London, 1653.

Scott, Thomas. *The Second Part of Vox Populi. Or Gondomar appearing in the likeness of Matchiavell in a Spanish Parliament, wherein are discovered his treacherous & subtile Practices To the ruine as well of England, as the Netherlandes. Faithfully Translated out of the Spanish Coppie by a well-willer to England and Holland.* Utrecht, 1624.

[Scott, Thomas]. *Sir Walter Ravvleighs Ghost, or Englands Forewarner. Discovering a secret Consultation, newly holden in the Court of Spaine. Together, with his tormenting of Count de Gondomar; and his strange affrightment, Confession and publique recantation: laying open many treacheries intended for the subversion of England.* Utrecht, 1626.

Scott, Thomas. *Vox Populi, or Newes from Spayne, translated according to the Spanish coppie. Which may serve to forewarn both England and the United Provinces how farre to trust to Spanish pretences.* London, 1620.

Selden, John. *Mare clausum, seu De dominio maris libri duo.* London, 1635.

Smith, William. *A Brief State of the Province of Pennsylvania.* London, 1755.

Smith, William. *The History of the Late Province of New-York, from its Discovery, to the Appointment of Governor Colden, in 1762. (Collections of the New York Historical Society, IV–V).* 2 vols. New York, 1829.

Some Considerations on the National Debts. London, 1729.

Some Farther Remarks on a Late Pamphlet, intitled, Observations on the Conduct of Great Britain. London, 1729.

Southwell, Robert. *The History of the Revolutions in Portugal . . . to . . . 1667, . . . with Letters of Sir Robert Southwell during His Embassy There.* London, 1740.

Suarez, Francisco. *Selections from Three Works of Francisco Suarez, S.J.: De legibus, ac Deo legislatore, 1612. Defensio fidei catholicae, et apostolicae adversus anglicanae sectae errores, 1613. De triplici virtute theologica, fide, spe, et charitate, 1621 (The Classics of International Law,* ed. James Brown Scott, No. 20). 2 vols. Oxford and London, 1944.

Temple, Sir William. *Nouveaux mémoires du Chevalier Guillaume Temple . . . Contenant un détail intéressant & curieux des intrigues de la cour d'Angleterre, des briques de différens partis, des négociations des ministres & de lui même dans les cours étrangères, depuis la paix de Nimèque jusqu'à la retraite de l'auteur . . . The Hague, 1729.*

The Treaty of Seville and the Measures that have been taken for the four last years, impartially considered. London, 1730.

Trumbull, Benjamin. *A Complete History of Connecticut, Civil and Ecclesiastical, from the Emigration of its First Planters from England, in the Year 1630, to the Year 1764; and to the Close of the Indian Wars.* 2 vols. New Haven, 1818.

Ulloa, Bernado de. *Rétablissement des Manufactures et du Commerce d'Espagne. Traduit de l'Espagnol. . . . Dedié à Philippe V. & publié à Madrid en 1740.* Amsterdam, 1753.

Ulloa, Jorge Juan. *Disertación historica y geografica sobre el meridiano de demarción entre los dominios de España y Portugal, y los parages por donde passa en la America meridional, confirme a los tratados y derechos de cada estado, y las mas seguros y modernos observaciones.* Madrid, 1749.

Uztariz, Geronimo de. *Theorica, y practica de comercio, y de marina, en diferentes discursos, y calificados exemplares, que, con especificas providencias, se procuran adaptar a la monarchia española, para su prompta restauración . . . Madrid, 1742.*

Vattel, Emmerich de. *Le Droit de Gens; ou, Principes de la loi naturelle appliqués à la conduite et aux affaires des nations et des souverains (The Classics of International Law,* ed. James Brown Scott No. 4). 3 vols. Washington, D.C., 1916.

Vittoria, Francisco de. *De Indis et de Iure Belli Relectiones*, ed. Ernest Nys, trans. John P. Bate (*The Classics of International Law*, ed. James Brown Scott, No. 7). Washington, D.C., 1917.

"The Watch-Tower." *New-York Mercury*. New York, Nov. 25, 1754; Nov. 17, 1755.

Whitelocke, Sir Bulstrode. *A Journal of the Swedish Ambassy, in the Years MDCLIII and MDCLIV. From the Commonwealth of England, Scotland, and Ireland*. 2 vols. London, 1772.

C. Collected Letters and Documents

Adams, Charles F., *et al.*, eds. *Commerce of Rhode Island, 1726–1800* (*Collections of the Massachusetts Historical Society*, 7th Series, Vol. IX). Boston, 1914.

Akins, Thomas B., ed. *Selections from the Public Documents of the Province of Nova Scotia*. Halifax, 1869.

American State Papers: Documents, Legislative and Executive. 38 vols. Washington, D.C., 1832–1861.

Angelis, Pedro de, ed. *Colección de Obras y Documentos relativos a la historia antigua y moderna de las provincias del Rio de la Plata*. 2nd ed. 5 vols. Buenos Aires, 1910.

Arneth, Alfred von, ed. *Die Relationen der Botschaften Venedigs über Österreich im achtzehnten Jahrhundert*. Vienna, 1863.

d'Avaux, Jean Antoine de Mesmes, Comte. *Négociations de Monsieur le Comte d'Avaux ambassadeur extraordinaire à la cour de Suède, pendant les années 1693, 1697, 1698* . . . Edited by J. A. Wijnne (*Werken van het Historisch Genootschap, Gevestigd te Utrecht. Nieuwe Reeks*. No. 33–36). 4 vols. Utrecht, 1882–83.

Bartlett, J. R., ed. *Records of the Colony of Rhode Island and Providence Plantations in New England (1636–1792)*. 10 vols. Providence, 1856–65.

Baxter, James Phinney. *A Memoir of Jacques Cartier, Sieur de Limoilou, his Voyages to the St. Lawrence*. New York, 1906.

Baxter, James Phinney, ed. *The Baxter Manuscripts* (*The Documentary History of the State of Maine*, 2nd Series, Vols. IX–XXIV). 16 vols. Portland, 1907–16.

Beazley, C. R., and Edgar Prestage, eds. *The Chronicle of the Discovery and Conquest of Guinea by Gomes Eames de Azuraro*. London, 1896.

Bedford, John Russell, Fourth Duke of. *Correspondence of John, Fourth Duke of Bedford*, ed. Lord John Russell. 3 vols. London, 1842–46.

Blanchet, Jean, ed. *Collection de Manuscrits contenant lettres, mémoires, et autres documents historiques relatifs à la Nouvelle-France, recueillis aux archives de la Province de Québec, ou copiés à l'étranger mis en ordre et édités sous les auspices de la Législature de Québec*. 4 vols. Quebec, 1883–85.

Bolingbroke, Henry Saint-John, 1st Viscount. *Letters and Correspondence, Public and Private, of the Right Honourable Henry St. John, Lord Visc. Bolingbroke*. 4 vols. London, 1798.

Bolingbroke, Henry Saint-John, Viscount. *Lettres historiques, politiques, philosophiques et particulières de Henri Saint-John, lord vicomte Bolingbroke, depuis 1710 jusqu'au 1736*. 3 vols. Paris, 1808.

Bolingbroke, Henry Saint-John, 1st Viscount. *The Works of Lord Bolingbroke. With a Life . . . containing additional Information relative to his Personal and Public Character, selected from the Best Authorities.* 4 vols. Philadelphia, 1841.

Bouton, Nathaniel, *et al.*, eds. *Documents and Records Relating to the Province [Towns and State] of New Hampshire (1623–1800).* 40 vols. Concord, 1867–1943.

Boyd, Julian P., and Carl Van Doren, eds. *Indian Treaties printed by Benjamin Franklin, 1736–1762.* Philadelphia, 1938.

Brants, V., ed. *Recueil des Ordonnances des Pays-Bas, Règne d'Albert et Isabelle, 1597–1621.* Brussels, 1909.

Bridges, George Wilson. *The Annals of Jamaica.* 2 vols. London, 1828.

British Guiana Boundary, Arbitration with the United States of Venezuela, Appendix to the [British] Counter-Case. London, 1898. Part II: "Special appendix to illustrate Chapter V of the Counter-Case: the Treaty of Münster."

Brown, Alexander, ed. *The Genesis of the United States. A Narrative of the Movement in England, 1605–1616, which resulted in the Plantation of North America by Englishmen, disclosing the Contest between England and Spain for the Possession of the Soil now occupied by the United States of America.* 2 vols. Boston, 1890.

Browne, W. H. *et al.*, eds. *Archives of Maryland.* 65 vols. Baltimore, 1883–1952.

Brymner, Douglas. "Transactions between England and France relating to Hudson's Bay, 1687," *Report on Canadian Archives for 1883.* Ottawa, 1884, 173–200.

Buckingham-Smith, Thomas. *Colección de varios documentos para la historia de la Florida y terras adyacentes.* London, 1857.

Burden, J. A., ed. *Archives of British Honduras.* London, 1931.

Canada. Public Archives. *Report Concerning Canadian Archives for the Year 1905.* 3 vols. Ottawa, 1906–7.

Carroll, Bartholomew Rivers, ed. *Historical Collections of South Carolina . . . relating to the History of that State from its first Discovery to its Independence, in the Year 1776.* 2 vols. New York, 1836.

Cartier, Jacques. *The Voyages of Jacques Cartier,* ed. and trans. by H. P. Biggar. Ottawa, 1924.

A. Chervel, ed. *Lettres du Cardinal Mazarin pendant son ministère (1642–1661) (Collection de Documents inédits sur l'histoire de France, Sér. 1).* 9 vols. Paris, 1872–1906.

Chesterfield, Philip Dormer Stanhope, Earl of. *The Letters of Philip Dormer Stanhope, Fourth Earl of Chesterfield.* 6 vols. London, 1932.

Chesterfield, Philip D. S. *Private Correspondence of Chesterfield and Newcastle, 1744–46,* ed. Sir Richard Lodge (*Royal Historical Society, Publications.* Camden (3rd Series, Vol. 44). London, 1930.

Clark, George N., and Jonkheer W. J. M. Van Eysinga, eds. *The Colonial Conferences between England and the Netherlands in 1613 and 1615* (Bibliotheca Visseriana. *Dissertationem Jus Internationale Illustrantinem.* Vol. XXXII). Leyden, 1940.

Clement, Pierre, ed. *Lettres, Instructions, et Mémoires de Colbert.* 10 vols. Paris, 1861–82.

Cobbett, William. *Parliamentary History of England from the Norman Conquest in 1066 to the Year 1803.* 36 vols. London, 1806–20.

Colden, Cadwallader. *Colden Letter Books* (*Collections of the New York Historical Society*. Publication Fund Series, IX–X). 2 vols. New York, 1877–78.

Colden, Cadwallader. *The Letters and Papers of Cadwallader Colden . . . 1711–1775* (*Collections of the New York Historical Society*, L–LVI, LXVII–LXVIII). 9 vols. New York, 1918–1937.

Colonial Records of Pennsylvania. 16 vols. Harrisburg, Pa., 1851–53.

Connecticut Historical Society. *Collections*. 23 vols. Hartford, 1870–1948.

"Correspondence between the Colonies of New Netherland and New Plymouth, 1627," *Collections of the New York Historical Society*, 2nd Series, I (1841), 355–368.

Coxe, William, ed. *Memoirs of the Administration of the Right Honourable Henry Pelham*. 2 vols. London, 1829.

Coxe, William, ed. *Memoirs of Horatio, Lord Walpole, selected from his correspondence and papers and connected with the history of the times, from 1678 to 1757*. 2 vols. 3rd ed. London, 1820.

Coxe, William, ed. *Memoirs of the Life and Administration of Sir Robert Walpole, Earl of Orford*. 3 vols. London, 1798.

Coxe, William, ed. *Memoirs of the Kings of Spain of the House of Bourbon, from the Accession of Philip V to the Death of Charles III, 1700 to 1788. Drawn from original and unpublished documents*. 5 vols. 2nd ed. London, 1815.

Dalrymple, Sir John. *Memoirs of Great Britain and Ireland; from the Dissolution of the Last Parliament of Charles II till the Capture of the French and Spanish Fleet at Vigo . . .* 3 vols. London, 1790.

Dinwiddie, Robert. *The Official Records of Robert Dinwiddie, Lieutenant-Governor of the Colony of Virginia, 1751–1758* (*Collections of the Virginia Historical Society*, New Series, III). 2 vols. Richmond, Va., 1883.

Donnan, Elizabeth, ed. *Documents illustrative of the History of the Slave Trade to America*. 4 vols. Washington, D.C., 1930–35.

Doughty, A. G., ed. *Report of the Work of the Archives Branch for the Year 1912*. Ottawa, 1912.

Douglas, David C., gen. ed. *English Historical Documents*. 12 vols. New York, 1953–59.

Druillettes, Gabriel. "Rapport du R. P. Druillettes, envoyé en deputation à la Nouvelle-Angleterre pour y conclure un traité de neutralité entre les colonies anglaises et françaises, 1651," *Canada Française*, XX (1933), 941–949.

Edits, ordonnances royaux, déclarations et arrêts du Conseil d'état du Roy concernant le Canada. 3 vols. Quebec, 1854–56.

Essex Institute. *Abstracts of English Shipping Records relating to Massachusetts Ports. From original records in the Public Record Office, London*. 5 vols. Salem, Mass., 1931–33.

d'Estrades, Godefroi Louis, Comte. *Correspondance authentique de Godefroi comte d'Estrades, de 1637 à 1660, publiée pour la Société de l'Histoire de France par A. de Saint-Léger et le docteur L. Lemaire*. Paris, 1924.

d'Estrades, Godefroi Louis, Comte. *Lettres, Mémoires et Négociations de Monsieur le Comte d'Estrades, tant en qualité d'ambassadeur de S.M.T.C. en Italie, en Angleterre, & en Hollande, que comme Ambassadeur Plénipotentiare à la Paix de Nimèque, conjointement avec Messieurs Colbert & Comte d'Avaux*. New ed. 9 vols. London, 1743.

d'Estrades, Godefroi Louis, Comte. *Lettres, Mémoires, et Négociations de Monsieur le Comte d'Estrades, servant à l'éclaircissement de l'histoire de la République des Provinces-Unies, pour les Années 1674 & 1675.* London, 1763.

Fabie y Escudero, Antonio Maria, ed. *Documentos legislativos de Indias.* (*Colección de Documentos Ineditos Relativos al Descubrimiento, Conquista y Organización de las Antiguas Posesiones Españoles de Ultramar.* 2nd Series, Vols. V, IX–X). 3 vols. Madrid, 1890–97.

Fanshawe, Richard. *Original Letters of His Excellency Sir Richard Fanshawe, during his Embassies in Spain and Portugal: which, together with divers Letters and Answers from the Chief Ministers of State of England, Spain and Portugal, contain the whole Negotiations of the Treaty of Peace between those three Crowns.* London, 1701.

Fénelon, François de Salignac de La Mothe. *Oeuvres choisies: De l'éducation des filles—Fables—Mémoires politiques—Lettres.* London, 1913.

Fénelon, François de Salignac de La Mothe. *Oeuvres de Fénelon, archévêque de Cambrai.* 23 vols. Versailles, 1820–30.

Fernow, Berthold, ed. *Calendar of Council Minutes, 1668–1783.* Albany, 1902.

Fernow, Berthold, ed. *Records of New Amsterdam, 1653–1674.* 7 vols. New York, 1897.

Firth, Sir Charles Harding, comp. *Notes on the Diplomatic Relations of England, 1603–1762.* 4 vols. Oxford, 1906–13.

Firth, C. H., ed. "Secretary Thurloe on the Relations of England and Holland," *English Historical Review,* XXI (1906), 319–327.

Firth, C. H., and R. S. Rait, eds. *Acts and Ordinances of the Interregnum, 1642–1660.* 3 vols. London, 1911.

Force, Peter, ed. *American Archives . . . a Documentary History of . . . the North American Colonies . . .* 9 vols. Washington, D.C., 1837–53.

Force, Peter, ed. *Tracts and other Papers relating Principally to the Origin, Settlement, and Progress of the Colonies in North America, from the Discovery of the Country to the Year 1776.* 4 vols. Washington, D.C., 1836–46.

Fotheringham, J. G., ed. *The Diplomatic Correspondence of Jean de Montereul and the Brothers De Bellièvre, French Ambassadors in England and Scotland, 1645–48.* Edinburgh, 1898–99.

France. Ministère des Affairs Étrangères. *Recueil des instructions données aux ambassadeurs et ministres de France depuis les Traités de Westphalie jusqu'à la Révolution Française.* 26 vols. Paris, 1884–1929.

Franklin, Benjamin. *The Papers of Benjamin Franklin,* ed. Leonard W. Labaree *et al.* 9 vols. to date. New Haven, 1959–

French, Benjamin F., ed. *Historical Collections of Louisiana.* 5 vols. New York, 1846–53.

Gachard, Louis Prosper, ed. *Actes des États-Généraux de 1660 (Collection de Documents sur les Anciennes Assemblées Nationales de Belgigue).* Brussels, 1849.

Gardiner, Samuel Rawson, and C. T. Atkinson, eds. *Letters and Papers relating to the First Dutch War, 1652–1654.* 6 vols. London, 1899–1930.

George III. *The Correspondence of King George the Third from 1760 to December 1783,* ed. by Sir John Fortescue. 6 vols. London, 1927–28.

Georgia Historical Society. *Collections.* 7 vols. Savannah, 1873–1916.

Gist, Christopher. *Christopher Gist's Journals,* ed. William M. Darlington, Pittsburgh, 1893.

Great Britain. Parliament. House of Commons. *Journals of the House of Commons*. 155 vols. London, 1803–1954.

Great Britain. Parliament. House of Commons. *Reports from Committees of the House of Commons*. 16 vols. London, 1803–6.

Great Britain. Parliament. House of Lords. *Journals of the House of Lords*. 72 vols. London, n.d.

Great Britain. Privy Council. *Acts of the Privy Council of England. Colonial Series. 1630–1783*. 6 vols. London, 1908–12.

Great Britain. Privy Council. Judicial Committee. *In the Matter of the Boundary between the Dominion of Canada and the Colony of Newfoundland in the Labrador Peninsula, between the Dominion of Canada of the One Part and the Colony of Newfoundland of the Other*. 12 vols. London, 1927.

Great Britain. Public Records Office. *Calendar of Letters, Despatches and State Papers, Relating to the Negotiations between England and Spain, Preserved in the Archives at Vienna, Simancas, Besançon and Brussels . . . 1485–1558*. 13 vols. London, 1862–1954.

Great Britain. Public Records Office. *Calendar of Letters and State Papers relating to English Affairs, preserved principally in the Archives of Simancas. Elizabeth 1558–1603*, ed. Martin A. S. Hume. 4 vols. London, 1892–99.

Great Britain. Public Records Office. *Calendar of State Papers and Manuscripts relating to English Affairs, existing in the Archives and Collections of Venice and in other Libraries of Northern Italy, 1202–1675*. 38 vols. London, 1864–1940.

Great Britain. Public Record Office. *Calendar of State Papers, Colonial Series*. 40 vols. to date. London, 1860.

Great Britain. Public Records Office. *Calendar of State Papers, Domestic Series*. 88 vols. London, 1856–1960.

Great Britain. Public Record Office. *Journal of the Commissioners for Trade and Plantations, from April, 1704, to May, 1782*. 14 vols. London, 1920–38. Also known as *Board of Trade Journals*.

Great Britain. The Royal Commission on Historical Manuscripts. *Reports of the Royal Historical Manuscripts Commission on*

"The Manuscripts of Charles Fleetwood Underwood, Esq., of Somerby Hall, Lincolnshire." Tenth Report, Appendix 1, 199–520. London, 1885.

The Manuscripts of His Grace the Duke of Portland preserved at Welbeck Abbey. Thirteenth Report. Appendix 1–2; Fourteenth Report, Appendix 2; Fifteenth Report, Appendix 4, 33–36; Twenty-Ninth Report, Appendix 9–10. 10 vols. London, 1892–1931.

The Manuscripts of the Earl of Lonsdale. Thirteenth Report, Appendix 7. London, 1893.

"Trevor MSS." Fourteenth Report, Appendix 9, 1–154. London, 1895.

"Hare MSS." Fourteenth Report, Appendix 9, 200–266. London, 1895.

The Manuscripts of the Earl of Carlisle preserved at Castle Howard. Fifteenth Report, Appendix 6. London, 1897.

Report on the Manuscripts of Lady Du Cane. Sixteenth Report, Appendix 2. London, 1905.

Report on the Manuscripts of Lord Polwarth, formerly preserved in Mertoun House, Berwickshire. Seventeenth Report, Appendix 1–2; Vol. 67, pts. 1–2, 5. 5 vols. London, 1911–61.

Calendar of the Manuscripts of the Marquis of Bath. Fifteenth Report, Appendix 64–66. 3 vols. London, 1904–8.

Manuscripts of the Earl of Egmont. Vol. 63. 3 vols. London, 1923.

Manuscripts of the House of Lords. Ninth Report, Appendix 2 (1670–8); Eleventh Report, Appendix 2 (1678–88); Eleventh Report, Appendix 6, Thirteenth Report, Appendix 5, Fourteenth Report, Appendix 6 (1689–93). London, 1884–94.

Grimblot, Paul, ed. *Letters of William III and Louis XIV and their Ministers; illustrative of the Domestic and Foreign Politics of England, from the Peace of Ryswick to the Accession of Philip V of Spain, 1697 to 1700.* 2 vols. London, 1848.

Hardwicke, Philip Yorke, Earl of. *The Life and Correspondence of Philip Yorke, Earl of Hardwicke,* ed. Philip C. Yorke. 3 vols. Cambridge, 1913.

Hardwicke, Philip Yorke, Second Earl of. *Miscellaneous State Papers . . . 1501 to 1726.* 2 vols. London, 1778.

Hazard, Ebenezer, comp. *Historical Collections; consisting of State Papers, and Other Authentic Documents; intended as Materials for a History of the United States of America.* 2 vols. Philadelphia, 1792–94.

Heinsius, Anthonij. *Het Archief van den Road pensionaris Antonie Heinsius,* ed. H. J. Van der Heim. 3 vols. The Hague, 1867–80.

Hening, W. W., ed. *Statutes at Large; being a Collection of all the Laws of Virginia.* 2 vols. Roanoke, Virginia, 1934–36.

Hervey, Baron John. *Some Materials towards Memoirs of the Reign of King George II,* ed. Romney Sedgwick. London, 1931.

Hoadly, Charles H., ed. *Records of the Colony and Plantation of New Haven, from 1638 to 1649.* Hartford, 1857.

Hoadly, Charles H., ed. *Records of the Colony or Jurisdiction of New Haven, from May, 1653, to the Union.* Hartford, 1858.

Hough, Charles Merrill, ed. *Reports of Cases in the Vice-Admiralty of the Province of New York and in the Court of Admiralty of the State of New York, 1715–1788.* New Haven, 1925.

Hutchinson, Thomas, comp. *A Collection of Original Papers Relative to the History of the Colony of Massachusetts-Bay.* Boston, 1769.

Hutchinson, Thomas. *The Diary and Letters of His Excellency Thomas Hutchinson,* ed. P. O. Hutchinson. 2 vols. Boston, 1884–86.

Hutchinson, Thomas. *The Hutchinson Papers,* ed. W. H. Whitmore and W. S. Appleton (Prince Society. *Publications,* II–III). 2 vols. Albany, 1865.

Insh, G. P., ed. "Papers relating to the Ships and Voyages of the Company of Scotland trading to Africa and the Indies," *Publications of the Scottish History Society,* 3rd series, VI (1924).

Jameson, John Franklin, ed. *Narratives of New Netherland, 1609–1664.* New York, 1909.

Jameson, J. F., Gen. ed. *Original Narratives of Early American History.* 19 vols. New York, 1906–19.

Jensen, Merrill, ed. *American Colonial Documents to 1776 (English Historical Documents,* gen. ed. David C. Douglas, Vol. IX). London, 1955.

Johnson, Amandus, ed. and tr. *The Instruction for Johan Printz, Governor of New Sweden.* Philadelphia, 1930.

Johnson, Samuel. *The Works of Samuel Johnson.* 11 vols. Oxford, 1825.

de Jonge, Johan Karel Jakob. *De opkoniat van het Nederlandsch gezog in*

Oost-Indie (1595–1610). *Versameling van onnitgegenen stukken uit het Oud-kolonial Archief.* 13 vols. Amsterdam and the Hague, 1862–88.

Jouon des Longrais, Frédéric, ed. *Jacques Cartier; Documents nouveaux.* Paris, 1888.

Keene, Benjamin. *The Private Correspondence of Sir Benjamin Keene, K.B.,* ed. Sir Richard Lodge. Cambridge, 1933.

Kellogg, Louise P., ed. *The French Regime in Wisconsin and the Northwest.* Madison, Wisconsin, 1925.

Kimball, Gertrude Selwyn, ed. *The Correspondence of the Colonial Governors of Rhode Island, 1723–1775.* 2 vols. Boston and New York, 1902.

Kingsbury, Susan M., ed. *The Records of the Virginia Company of London.* 4 vols. Washington, 1906–35.

Labaree, Leonard Woods, ed. *Royal Instructions to the British Colonial Governors, 1670–1776.* New York, 1935.

Lasene, Ricardo. *Comercio de Indias. Documentos para la Historia Argentina.* Buenos Aires, 1915.

Le Clerc, J., ed. Négociations sécrètes touchant la Paix de Münster et d'Osnaburg . . . 1642 . . . 1648. 4 vols. The Hague, 1725–26.

Legg, Leopold George Wickham, ed., *British Diplomatic Instructions, 1689–1789* (Royal Historical Society. *Publications.* Camden 3rd Series, Vols. XXXII, XXXV–XXXVI, XXXVIII, XXXIX, XLIII, XLIX). 7 vols. London, 1922–34. Volume I was edited by James Frederick Chance.

Legg, Leopold George Wickham, ed. "Torcy's Account of Matthew Prior's Negotiations," *English Historical Review,* XXIX (1914), 525–532.

Legislature of Quebec. *Nouvelle France: Documents Historiques; Correspondance échangée entre les autorities français et les gouverneurs et intendants.* 2 vols. Quebec, 1893.

Lexington, Robert Sutton. *The Lexington Papers; or, Some Account of the Courts of London and Vienna; at the Conclusion of the Seventeenth Century. Extracted from the Official and Private Correspondence of Robert Sutton, Lord Lexington,* ed. E. Manners Sutton. London, 1851.

Lodge, Richard, ed. *Private Correspondence of Chesterfield and Newcastle, 1744–46* (Royal Historical Society. *Publications.* Camden 3rd Series. Vol. XLIV). London, 1930.

Lomas, S. C., ed. *Letters and Speeches of Oliver Cromwell.* 3 vols. New York, 1904.

Lopez de Gomara, Francisco. *Annals of the Emperor Charles V,* ed. Roger Bigelow Merriman. Oxford, 1912.

Louis XV. *Correspondence sécrète inédite de Louis XV sur la politique étrangère avec le comte de Broglie, Tercier, etc. . . . ,* ed. M. E. Boutaric. 2 vols. Paris, 1866.

Louis XV. *The King's Secret: being the secret correspondence of Louis XV with his diplomatic agents, from 1752–1774,* ed. the Duke de Broglie. 2 vols. London, 1879.

McDowell, William L., Jr., ed. *Documents relating to Indian Affairs* [in South Carolina], *May 21, 1750–Aug. 7, 1754.* Columbia, S.C., 1958.

McIlwaine, H. R., ed. *Journals of the House of Burgesses of Virginia, 1619–1658/9.* Richmond, Va., 1915.

Macpherson, David. *Annals of Commerce, Manufactures, Fisheries and Navigation.* 4 vols. London, 1805.

Maine Historical Society. *Collections.* 21 vols. Portland, 1831–1906.

Maine Historical Society. *Documentary History of the State of Maine* (Col-

lections of the Maine Historical Society, 2nd Series). 24 vols. Portland, 1869–1916.

de Malonet, P. V. *Collection de mémoires et correspondances officielles sur l'administration des colonies, et notamment sur la Guiane française et hollandaise.* 5 vols. Paris, 1802.

Marchmont, Hugh Hume, Third Earl of. *A State of the Rise and Progress of our Disputes with Spain, and of the Conduct of our Ministers relating thereto.* London, 1739.

Margry, Pierre, ed. *Découvertes et établissements des Français dans l'ouest et dans le sud de l'Amérique Septentrionale, 1614–1698: Mémoires et documents inédits.* 6 vols. Paris, 1879–88.

Marlborough, John Churchill, 1st Duke of. *The Letters and Dispatches of John Churchill, First Duke of Marlborough, from 1702–1712,* ed. Sir George Murray. 5 vols. London, 1845.

Marsden, R. G., ed. *Documents relating to the Law and Custom of the Sea.* London, 1915.

Massachusetts Bay Province. *A Collection of the Proceedings of the Great and General Court or Assembly of his Majesty's Province of the Massachusetts Bay, in New England* . . . Boston, 1729.

Massachusetts (Colony). *The Acts and Resolves, public and private, of the province of the Massachusetts Bay: to which are prefixed the charters of the province.* 21 vols. Boston, 1869–1922.

Massachusetts Historical Society. *Collections.* 78 vols. Boston, 1792–1941.

Masson, Frédéric, ed. *Mémoires et lettres de François-Joachim de Pierre, Cardinal de Bernis (1715–1758).* 2 vols. Paris, 1878.

The Memorials of the English and French Commissaries Concerning St. Lucia. 2 vols. London, 1755.

Memorials of the English and French Commissaries concerning the Limits of Nova Scotia or Acadia. London, 1755.

Mignet, F. A. A., ed. *Négociations relatives à la Succession d'Espagne sous Louis XIV (Collection de Documents inédits sur l'histoire de France,* 1st Series). 4 vols. Paris, 1835–42.

Minutes of the Provincial Council of Pennsylvania from the Organization to the Termination of the Proprietary Government . . . (*Mar.* 10, 1683–*Sept.* 27, 1775) (*Colonial Records of Pennsylvania,* Vol. I–X). 10 vols. Philadelphia, 1851–52.

Moreau de Saint-Méry, Médéric L. E., ed. *Loix et constitutions des colonies françoises de l'Amérique sous le vent* . . . 6 vols. Paris, 1784–90.

Myers, A. C., ed. *Narratives of Early Pennsylvania, West New Jersey and Delaware, 1630–1707.* New York, 1912.

Navarrete, Martín Fernández de. *Colección de los viages y descubrimientos que hicieron por mar los españoles desde fines del siglo XV, con varios documentos inéditos concernientos a la historia de la marina castellana y de los establecimientos españoles en Indias.* 5 vols. Madrid, 1825–37.

Neill, Edward Duffield. *Virginia Company of London. Extracts from their Manuscript Transactions.* Washington, D.C., 1868.

New Hampshire Historical Society. *Collections.* 11 vols. Concord, 1824–1939.

Newton, Arthur P., ed. *Travel and Travellers of the Middle Ages.* London, 1926.

New York. *Report of the Regents of the University on the Boundaries of the State of New York.* 2 vols. Albany, 1874–84.

New York Historical Society. *Collections.* 80 vols. New York, 1811–1943.

Nova Scotia. Public Records Commission. *Nova Scotia Archives.* 3 vols. 1869–1908.

O'Callaghan, Edmund B., ed. *Laws and Ordinances of New Netherland, 1638–1674.* Albany, 1868.

O'Callaghan, Edmund B. *The Documentary History of the State of New York.* 4 vols. Albany, 1849–51.

O'Callaghan, Edmund B., and Berthold Fernow, eds. *Documents Relative to the Colonial History of the State of New York.* 15 vols. Albany, 1853–87.

Pacheco, Joaquin Francisco, *et al.*, eds. *Colección de documentos inéditos relativos al descubrimiento, conquista y colonización de las posesiones españolas en America y Oceania, sacados, en su mayor parte, del Real Archivo de Indias.* 42 vols. Madrid, 1864–84. 2nd Series, 25 vols. Madrid, 1885–1932.

"Papers relative to the Rival Chiefs D'Aulney and La Tour, Governors of Nova Scotia," *Collections of the Massachusetts Historical Society,* 3rd Series, VII (1938), 90–121.

Pease, Theodore Calvin, ed. *Anglo-French Boundary Disputes in the West, 1749–1763 (Collections of the Illinois State Historical Library,* Vol. XXVII). Springfield, Ill., 1936.

Pennsylvania. *Archives.* 101 vols. Philadelphia, 1852–56; Harrisburg, 1874–1914.

Pickering, D., ed. *The Statutes at Large, from Magna Carta to . . . 1761.* 46 vols. Cambridge, 1762–1807.

Pitt, William. *Correspondence of William Pitt,* ed. William Stanhope Taylor and Captain John Henry Pringle. 4 vols. London, 1838–40.

Pitt, William. *Correspondence of William Pitt, when Secretary of State, with Colonial Governors and Military and Naval Commissioners in America,* ed. Gertrude S. Kimball. 2 vols. New York, 1906.

Prestage, Edgar. *Portugal and the War of the Spanish Succession: A Bibliography, with Some Diplomatic Documents.* Cambridge, 1938.

Proceedings of the Council of Maryland, 1636–1770 (Archives of Maryland, Vols. 3, 5, 8, 15, 17, 20, 23, 25, 28, 31, pt. 1; 32, pt. 1). 11 vols. Baltimore, 1885–1912.

Rebello da Silva, Luiz Augusto, ed. *Corpo Diplomatico Portuguez.* Lisbon, 1862.

Richelieu, Armand Jean du Plessis, Cardinal, Duc de. *Lettres, Instructions diplomatiques, et Papiers d'État du Cardinal de Richelieu,* ed. Vicomte G. d'Avenel. 8 vols. Paris, 1853–77.

Richelieu, Armand Jean du Plessis, Cardinal, Duc de. *Maximes d'État, ou Testament Politique d'Armand du Plessis, Cardinal Duc de Richelieu,* ed. E. Lauréault de Foncemagre. 2 vols. Paris, 1764.

Richelieu, Armand Jean du Plessis, Cardinal, Duc de. *Mémoires authentiques du Maréchal de Richelieu* (1725–1727), ed. A. de Boislisle (La Société de l'Histoire de France, *Publications,* No. 120). Paris, 1918.

Rousset de Missy, Jean. *Recueil historique d'actes, négotiations, mémoires et traitez, depuis la Paix d'Utrecht jusqu'à . . . celle d'Aix-la-Chapelle.* 21 vols. The Hague, 1728–55.

Rowland, Dunbar and A. G. Sanders, eds. *Mississippi Provincial Archives: French Dominion, 1729–1740.* 3 vols. Jackson, 1927–32.

Roy, P.-G., ed. *Ordonnances, Commissions . . . des Gouverneurs et Intendants de la Nouvelle France, 1639–1760.* 2 vols. Beauceville, 1924.

Salley, A. S., ed., *Journal of the Commons House of Assembly of South Carolina* (1692–1726/7). 19 vols. Columbia, S.C., 1907–46.

Sée, Henri, ed. "Documents sur le Commerce de Cadix (1691–1752), *Revue de l'Histoire des Colonies Françaises,* XIX (1926), 465–520; XX (1927), 33–80, 259–276.

Sée, Henri, and Léon Vignols, eds. *Les Documents sur le Commerce de Cadix.* Paris, 1927.

Sée, Henri, and Léon Vignols, eds. "Mémoires sur le commerce rédigés en vue du Congrès de Soissons (1728), etc." *Notices, Inventoires et Documents; Études et Documents divers,* XII (1926), 1–33.

Serrano, Luciano, ed. *Correspondencia diplomática entre España y la Santa Sede durante el Pontificada de S. Pio V.* 4 vols. Madrid, 1914.

Serrano y Sanz, Manuel L., ed. *Documentos Historicos de la Florida y la Luisiana, Siglos XVI al XVIII.* Madrid, 1913.

Shirley, William. *Correspondence of William Shirley, Governor of Massachusetts and Military Commander in America, 1731–1760,* ed. Charles Henry Lincoln. 2 vols. New York, 1912.

Shurtleff, Nathaniel B., and David Pulsifer, eds. *Records of the Colony of New Plymouth, in New England.* 12 vols. Boston, 1855–61.

Shurtleff, Nathaniel B., and David Pulsifer, eds. *Acts of the Commissioners of the United Colonies of New England, 1643–1679* (*Records of the Colony of New Plymouth, in New England,* Vols. IX–X). 2 vols. Boston, 1859.

Shurtleff, N. B., ed. *Records of the Governor and Company of the Massachusetts Bay in New England,* 6 vols. Boston, 1853–54.

South Carolina Historical Society. *Collections.* Charleston, 1857–97.

Spotswood, Alexander. *The Official Letters of Alexander Spotswood, Lieutenant-Governor of the Colony of Virginia, 1710–1722,* ed. R. A. Brock. 2 vols. Richmond, Va., 1882–85 (*Collections of the Virginia Historical Society,* New Series, Vol. I–II).

Stock, Leo Francis, ed. *Proceedings and Debates of the British Parliaments Respecting North America.* 5 vols. Washington, 1924–41.

Talbot, Charles, Duke of Shrewsbury. *Private and Original Correspondence of Charles Talbot, Duke of Shrewsbury, with King William, the Leaders of the Whig Party and other distinguished Statesmen,* ed. William Coxe. London, 1821.

Temple, Sir William. *Memoirs of the Life and Negotiations of Sir William Temple,* ed. A Boyer. London, 1714.

Temple, Sir William. *The Works of Sir William Temple.* 2 vols. London, 1750.

Thurloe, John. *Collection of the State Papers of John Thurloe . . . Containing Authentic Memorials of the English Affairs from the Year 1638 to the Restoration of King Charles II,* ed. Thomas Birch. 7 vols. London, 1742.

Tommaseo, Niccolò, ed. *Relations des ambassadeurs vénitiens sur les affaires de France au XVIᵉ siècle* (France. Comité des Travaux Historiques et Scientifiques. *Collection de Documents Inédits sur l'Histoire de France.* 1st Series. Histoire Politique). 2 vols. Paris, 1838.

Torcy, Jean Baptiste Colbert, Marquis de. *Memoirs of the Marquis of Torcy, Secretary of State to Lewis XIV containing the History of the Negotiations from the Treaty of Ryswic to the Peace of Utrecht.* 2 vols. London, 1757.

Towle, Dorothy S., ed. *Records of the Vice-Admiralty Court of Rhode Island, 1716–1752.* Washington, D.C., 1936.

Trumbull, J. H., and C. J. Hoadly, eds. *Public Records of the Colony of Connecticut* (1636–1776). 15 vols. Hartford, 1850–90.

Vazquez Menchaca, Fernando. *Illvstrivm controversiarum, aliarumque vsu freqventivm libri sex in duas partes divisi.* Frankfort, 1668.

Virginia Magazine of History and Biography, published by the Virginia Historical Society. Richmond, 1893–date.

Walpole, Horace, Earl of Orford. *The Letters of Horace Walpole, Fourth Earl of Orford*, ed. by Mrs. Paget Toynbee. 16 vols. Oxford, 1903–5.

Walpole, Horace, Earl of Orford. *Memoirs of the Reign of King George the Second*, ed. Lord Holland. 2nd ed. 3 vols. London, 1847.

Washington, George. *The Writings of George Washington from the Original Manuscript Sources, 1745–1799*, ed. John C. Fitzpatrick. 39 vols. Washington, D.C., 1931–44.

Weaver, F. J., ed. "Anglo-French Diplomatic Relations, 1558–1603," *Bulletin of the Institute of Historical Research*, IV (1926), 73–86; V (1927), 13–22; VI (1928), 1–9; VII (1929), 13–26.

Westlake, John. *The Collected Papers of John Westlake on Public International Law*, ed. L. Oppenheim. Cambridge, 1914.

Winthrop, John. *Winthrop's Journal, "History of New England," 1630–49*, ed. James Kendall Hosmer. 2 vols. New York, 1908.

Winthrop, John. *Winthrop Papers . . . 1498–1649 (Collections of the Massachusetts Historical Society*, 4th Series, Vol. VI–VII; 5th Series, Vol. I; 6th Series, Vol. III, V). 5 vols. Boston, 1929–47.

Winwood, Sir Ralph. *Memorials of Affairs of State in the Reigns of Q. Elizabeth and K. James I.* 3 vols. London, 1725.

Wraxall, Peter. *An Abridgment of the Indian Affairs contained in Four Folio Volumes, transacted in the Colony of New York, from the Year 1678 to the Year 1751*, ed. C. H. McIlwain. Cambridge, Mass., 1915.

Wright, Irene A., ed. "John Clark of the Mayflower," *Proceedings of the Massachusetts Historical Society*, LIV (1920–21), 61–76.

III. A Selected List of Secondary Works

General

Andrews, Charles McLean. *The Colonial Period of American History.* 4 vols. New Haven, 1934–38.

Ballestros y Beretta, Antonio, gen. ed. *Historia de America y de los pueblos americanos.* 14 vols. Barcelona, 1936–56.

Beer, George L. *The Old Colonial System, 1660–1754.* 2 vols. New York, 1912.

Beer, George L. *Origins of the British Colonial System, 1578–1660.* New York, 1908.

Bonnassieux, Louis Jean Pierre Marie. *Les Grandes Compagnies de Commerce; Étude pour servir à i'historie de la Colonisation.* Paris, 1892.

Bourgeois, Emile. *Manuel historique de politique étrangère.* 4 vols. Paris, 1900–26.

Brymner, Douglas. "Canadian Archives." *Papers of the American Historical Association*, III, 395–407. New York, 1889.

Burns, Alan C. *History of the British West Indies*. London, 1954.

The Cambridge History of the British Empire, ed. J. H. Rose *et al.* 8 vols. New York, 1929–59. Vol. I: *The Old Empire from the Beginnings to 1783* (1929). Vol. VI: *Canada and Newfoundland* (1930).

Cambridge History of British Foreign Policy, 1789–1919, ed. A. W. Ward and G. P. Gooch. 3 vols. New York, 1922–23. Vol. I.

Cambridge Modern History, ed. A. W. Ward *et al.* 13 vols. New York, 1907–25. Vol. V: *The Age of Louis XIV*. New York, 1908.

Chapman, Charles E. *A History of Spain*. New York, 1918.

Clark, George Norman. *The Later Stuarts, 1660–1714*. Oxford, 1934.

Conn, Stetson. *Gibraltar in British Diplomacy in the Eighteenth Century*. New Haven, 1942.

Davenport, Frances Gardiner. *American and European Diplomacy to 1648*. Washington, 1917.

Dessalles, Adrien. *Histoire générale des Antilles*. 5 vols. Paris, 1847–48.

Dorn, Walter L. *Competition for Empire, 1740–1763* (*The Rise of Modern Europe* Series). New York, 1940.

Egerton, Hugh E. *British Foreign Policy in Europe to the End of the 19th Century*. London, 1918.

Flassan, Gaetan de Raxis de. *Histoire générale et Raisonnée de la diplomatie française, ou de la politique de la France, depuis la fondation de la monarchie, jusqu'à la fin du règne de Louis XVI*. 2nd ed. 7 vols. Paris, 1811.

Friederici, Georg. *Der Charakter der Entdeckung und Eröberung Amerikas durch die Europäer; Einleitung zur Geschichte der Besiedlung Amerikas durch die Völker der alten Welt*. 3 vols. Stuttgart-Gotha, 1925–26.

Ganshof, François-Louis. *Histoire des Relations Internationales: Le Moyen Age*. Paris, 1953.

Garden, Guillaume de, Comte. *Histoire générale des traités de paix et autres transactions principales entre toutes les puissances de l'Europe depuis la paix de Westphalie*. 15 vols. Paris, 1848–87.

Gaxotte, Pierre. *Le Siècle de Louis XV*. 2 vols. Paris, 1935.

Gerbi, Antonello. *La Disputa del Nuovo Mundo: Storia de una Polemica, 1750–1900*. Milan and Naples, 1955.

Graham, Gerald Sandford. *Empire of the North Atlantic: The Maritime Struggle for North America*. Toronto, 1950.

Hassall, Arthur. *The History of British Foreign Policy from the Earliest Times to 1912*. Edinburgh and London, 1912.

Hauser, Henri. *La prépondérance espagnole* (1559–1660). (*Peoples et civilizations, Histoire Générale*, ed. L. Halphen. Vol. IX). Paris, 1933.

Hauser, Henri, and Augustin Renaudet. *Les débuts de l'âge moderne, la renaissance et la réforme*. Paris, 1929.

Hertz, G. B. *British Imperialism in the Eighteenth Century*. London, 1908.

Hill, David Jayne. *A History of Diplomacy in the International Development of Europe*. 3 vols. New York, 1905–14.

Horn, *David Bayne*, ed. *British Diplomatic Representatives, 1689–1789* (Royal Historical Society. *Publications*. Camden 3rd Series, Vol. XLVI). London, 1932.

Horn, D. B. *The British Diplomatic Service, 1689–1789*. Oxford, 1961.

Hubbard, William. *A General History of New England, from the Discovery to MDCLXXX*. Cambridge, Mass., 1815.

Immich, Max. *Geschichte des europäischen Staatensystems von 1660 bis 1789.* Munich, 1905.

Innis, Harold Adams. *The Cod Fisheries: The History of an International Economy.* New Haven, 1940.

Innis, Harold A. *The Fur Trade of Canada.* Toronto, 1927.

Ireland, Gordon. *Boundaries, Possessions, and Conflicts in Central and North America and the Caribbean.* Cambridge, Mass., 1941.

Ireland, Gordon. *Boundaries, Possessions and Conflicts in South America.* Cambridge, Mass., 1938.

Jobex, Alphonse. *La France sous Louis XV* (1715–1774). 6 vols. Paris, 1864–73.

Judah, Charles B. *The North American Fisheries and British Policy to 1713.* Urbana, Illinois, 1933.

Knorr, Klaus. *British Colonial Theories, 1570–1850.* Toronto, 1944.

de Lannoy, Charles, and Herman Van der Linden. *Histoire de l'expansion coloniale des peuples éuropeens.* 3 vols. Brussels, 1907–21.

Lavisse, Ernest, ed. *Histoire de France depuis les origines jusqu'à la Révolution.* 9 vols. Paris, 1900–11.

Lecky, W. E. H. *History of England in the Eighteenth Century.* 8 vols. New York, 1878–87.

Lounsbury, Ralph G. *The British Fishery at Newfoundland, 1634–1763.* New Haven, 1934.

Malcolm-Smith, E. *British Diplomacy in the Eighteenth Century.* London, 1937.

Mowat, Robert Balmain. *A History of European Diplomacy, 1451–1789.* New York, 1928.

Muret, Pierre. *La prépondérance Anglaise* (1715–1763). 2nd ed. Paris, 1942.

New Cambridge Modern History, ed. G. R. Potter *et al.* 14 vols. Cambridge, 1957–61.

Newton, Arthur Percival. *The European Nations in the West Indies, 1493–1688.* London, 1933.

Ogg, David. *Europe in the Seventeenth Century.* London, 1931.

Osgood, Herbert L. *The American Colonies in the Eighteenth Century.* 4 vols. New York, 1924–25.

Parry, J. H. *England and a Wider World.* London, 1949.

Paullin, Charles Oscar. *Atlas of the Historical Geography of the United States,* ed. John K. Wright. Washington, D.C., 1932.

Penson, L. M. *Colonial Background of British Foreign Policy.* London, 1930.

Petrie, Sir Charles Alexander. *Diplomatic History, 1713–1933.* New York, 1949.

Petrie, Sir Charles Alexander. *Earlier Diplomatic History, 1492–1713.* New York, 1949.

Rain, Pierre. *La diplomatie française de Mirabeau à Bonaparte.* Paris, 1950.

Ranke, Leopold von. *A History of England Principally in the Seventeenth Century.* 6 vols. Oxford, 1875.

Rein, Adolf. *Das Problem der europäischen Expansion in der Geschichteschreibung.* Hamburg, 1929.

Roberts, Penfield. *The Quest for Security, 1715–1740.* New York, 1947.

Sagnac, Philippe. *La prépondérance française: Louis XIV* (1661–1715) (*Peuples et Civilizations, Historie Générale,* ed. L. Halphen. Vol. X). Paris, 1935.

Santarem, Manuel Francisco de Barros, ed. *Quadro elementar das relacões politicas e diplomaticas de Portugal com as diversas potencias do mundo, desde o principio da monarchia portugueza ate aos nosses dias.* 18 vols. Paris, 1842–76.

Sorel, Albert. *L'Europe et la Révolution Française.* 8 vols. Paris, 1885–1904.

Stanhope, Philip Henry Stanhope, 5th Earl (Lord Mahon). *History of England from the Peace of Utrecht to the Peace of Versailles. 1713–1783.* 7 vols. London, 1836–54.

Thomson, Mark A. *The Secretaries of State, 1681–1782.* Oxford, 1932.

Vidal de La Blache, Paul Marie Joseph. *Principes de Géographie humaine,* ed. Emmanuel de Martonne. Paris, 1922.

Viner, Jacob. "Power versus Plenty as Objectives of Foreign Policy in the Seventeenth and Eighteenth Centuries," *World Politics,* I (1948), 1–29.

Walsh, Edmund A., ed. *The History and Nature of International Relations.* New York, 1922.

Williams, Basil. *The Whig Supremacy, 1714–1760 (The Oxford History of England).* 2nd ed. Oxford, 1962.

Wrong, George M. *The Canadians: The Story of a People.* New York, 1938.

Zavala, Silvio. *The Colonial Period in the History of the New World,* abridgement in English by Max Savelle. Mexico, 1962.

Zeller, Gaston. *Les temps modernes (Histoire des rélations internationales,* ed. Pierre Renouvin. Vol. II–III). 2 vols. Paris, 1953–55.

Chapter I. The Pre-Columbian Precedents

Beazley, Charles R. *Prince Henry the Navigator.* New York, 1908.

Beazley, C. R. "Prince Henry of Portugal and the African Crusade of the Fifteenth Century," *American Historical Review,* XVI (Oct., 1910), 11–23.

Boxer, C. R. *Four Centuries of Portuguese Expansion, 1415–1825: A Succinct Survey.* Johannesburg, 1961.

Cheyney, Edward P. *The Dawn of a New Era, 1250–1453 (The Rise of Modern Europe* Series). New York, 1936.

Heawood, Edward. "The World Map before and after Magellan's Voyage," *Geographical Journal,* LVII (1921), 431–446.

Mattingly, Garrett. *Renaissance Diplomacy.* London, 1955.

Morison, Samuel E. *Portuguese Voyages to America in the Fifteenth Century.* Cambridge, Mass., 1940.

Newton, Arthur P., ed. *The Great Age of Discovery.* London, 1932.

Oliveira Martins, Joaquim Pedro. *The Golden Age of Prince Henry the Navigator,* trans. by J. Johnston Abraham and W. Edward Reynolds. London, 1914.

Parry, John Horace. *The Spanish Theory of Empire in the Sixteenth Century.* Cambridge, 1940.

Perez Embid, Florentino. *Los Descubrimentos en el Atlantico y la rivalidad castellano-portuguesa hasta el Tratado de Tordesillas.* Sevilla, 1948.

Prestage, Edgar. *The Portuguese Pioneers.* London, 1933.

Renault-Roulier, Gilbert. *The Caravels of Christ,* trans. by Richmond Hill. New York, 1959.

Schäfer, Heinrich. *Geschichte von Portugal.* 5 vols. Hamburg, 1836–54.

Verlinden, Charles. *Précédents médiévaux de la colonie en Amérique.* Mexico, 1954.

Chapter II. Columbus and the Hispano-Portuguese Lines of Demarcation

Bourne, Edward Gaylord. "The Demarcation Line of Pope Alexander VI," *Essays in Historical Criticism.* New York, 1901.

Brebner, John Bartlet. *The Explorers of North America, 1492–1806.* London, 1933.

Dawson, S. E. "The Lines of Demarcation of Pope Alexander VI, 1493, and the Treaty of Tordesillas, 1494," *Transactions of the Royal Society of Canada,* 2nd Series, V (1899), 467 ff.

Hamilton, E. J. "The Role of Monopoly in the Overseas Expansion and Colonial Trade of Europe before 1800," *American Economic Review,* XXXVIII (May, 1948), 33–53.

Harrisse, Henry. *The Diplomatic History of America: Its First Chapter, 1452–1492–1494.* London, 1897.

Harrisse, Henry. *The Discovery of North America: A Critical, Documentary, and Historic Investigation.* London, 1892.

Morga, Antonio de. *History of the Philippine Islands, from their Discovery by Magellan in 1521 to the Beginning of the XVII Century,* trans. and ed. by E. H. Blair and J. A. Robertson. 2 vols. Cleveland, 1907.

Nowell, C. E. "The Discovery of Brazil—Accidental or Intentional?" *Hispanic American Historical Review,* XVI (1936), 311–338.

Peres, Damião. *O descobrimento do Brasil por Pedro Álvares Cabral; antecedentes e intencionalidade.* Porto, 1949.

Peschel, O. F. *Die Theilung der Erde unter Papst Alexander VI und Julius II.* Leipzig, 1871.

Rein, Adolph. *Der Kampf der Westeuropäer im Nordamerika in XV und XVI Jahrhunderten.* Stuttgart and Gotha, 1925.

Van der Linden, H. "Alexander VI and the Demarcation of the Maritime and Colonial Domains of Spain and Portugal," *American Historical Review,* XXII (1916), 1–20.

Chapter III. The French, English, and Dutch Challenges to the Hispano-Portuguese Monopoly

Beer, George L. *Origins of the British Colonial System, 1578–1660.* New York, 1908.

Blok, Petrus Johannes. *History of the People of the Netherlands,* trans. Oscar A. Bierstadt and Ruth Putnam, 5 vols. New York, 1898–1912.

Connell-Smith, Gordon. "English Merchants trading to the New World in the Early Sixteenth Century," *Bulletin of the Institute of Historical Research,* XXIII, No. 67 (May, 1950).

Connell-Smith, Gordon. *Forerunners of Drake; A Study of Trade with Spain in the Early Tudor Period.* London, 1954.

Corbett, Julian Stafford. *Drake and the Tudor Navy, with a History of the Rise of England as a Maritime Power.* 2 vols. London, 1898.

Corbett, Julian S. *Sir Francis Drake.* London, 1901.

Crouse, Nellis M. *French Pioneers in the West Indies, 1624–1664.* New York, 1940.

Froude, J. A. *English Seamen in the Sixteenth Century.* London, 1922.

Fruin, Robert Jacobus. *Tien jaren uit den tachtigjarigen oorlog, 1588–1598.* 5th ed. The Hague, 1899.

Guénin, E. *Ango et ses pilotes.* Paris, 1901.

Haring, Clarence Henry. *Trade and Navigation between Spain and the Indies in the Time of the Habsburgs.* Cambridge, Mass., 1918.

Jameson, J. F. "William Usselinx, Founder of the Dutch and Swedish West India Companies," *Papers of the American Historical Association,* II (1887), 149–382.

Martin, Gaston. *Jacques Cartier et la découverte de l'Amérique du Nord.* Paris, 1939.

Mattingly, Garrett. *The Defeat of the Spanish Armada.* London, 1959.

Means, Philip A. *The Spanish Main; Focus of Envy, 1492–1700.* New York, 1935.

Motley, John Lothrop. *History of the United Netherlands from the Death of William the Silent to the Twelve Years' Truce—1609.* 4 vols. New York, 1868–71.

Newton, Arthur Percival. "The West Indies in International Politics, 1550–1850," *History,* New Series, XIX (1935), 302–310.

Pirenne, Henri. *Histoire de Belgique.* 7 vols. Brussels, 1900–32.

Roncière, Charles de la, Joannes Tramond and Emile Lauvrière. *L'Amérique* (*Histoire des colonies française,* Vol. I). Paris, 1929.

Roncière, Charles de la. *Histoire de la marine française.* 6 vols. Paris, 1909–32.

Williamson, James A. *The Age of Drake.* London, 1938.

Williamson, James A. *Hawkins of Plymouth: A New History of Sir John Hawkins and of the Other Members of His Family Prominent in Tudor England.* London, 1949.

Williamson, James A. *Sir John Hawkins. the Time and the Man.* Oxford, 1927.

Williamson, James A. *The Foreign Commerce of England under the Tudors.* Oxford, 1883.

Williamson, James A. *Maritime Enterprise, 1485–1558.* Oxford, 1913.

Wood, William C. H. *Elizabethan Sea-Dogs.* New Haven, 1918.

Chapter IV. Virginia, the Thirty Years War, and the End of the Hispano-Portuguese Monopoly

Barbour, Violet. "Dutch and English Merchant Shipping in the Seventeenth Century," *Economic History Review,* II (1930), 261–290.

Bougeant, G. H. *Histoire du traité de Westphalie.* 3 vols. Paris, 1751.

Burr, G. L. "Report as to the Meaning of Articles V and VI of the Treaty of Münster." United State Commission to Investigate and Report upon the True Divisional Line between Venezuela and British Guiana. *Report and Papers.* 9 vols. Washington, 1896–97. I, 71–96.

Colby, Charles William. *The Founder of New France: A Chronicle of Champlain* (*Chronicles of Canada* Series, Vol. 3). Toronto, 1915.

Davies, Godfrey. *The Early Stuarts.* Oxford, 1945.

Edmundson, George. *Anglo-Dutch Rivalry during the First Half of the Seventeenth Century.* Oxford, 1911.

Edmundson, George. "The Dutch on the Amazon and Negro in the Seventeenth Century," *English Historical Review,* XVIII (1903), 642–663; XIX (1904), 1–25.

Edmundson, George. "The Dutch Power in Brazil," *English Historical Review*, XI (1896), 231–259; XIV (1899), 676–699.

Foxcroft, Helen Charlotte. *The Life and Letters of Sir George Savile, Bart., First Marquis of Halifax.* 2 vols. London, 1898.

Hauser, Henri. "Les Rélations Commerciales entre la France et l'Espagne et la politique de Richelieu," *Revue d'Histoire Économique et Sociale*, XXIV (1938), 5–13.

Julien, Charles André, ed. *Les Français en Amérique pendant la première moitié du XVIe siècle.* Paris, 1946.

Kramer, F. J. L. *De Nederlandsch-Spaansche Diplomatie voor den Vrede van Nijmegen.* Utrecht, 1892.

Lefroy, Sir John Henry. *Memorials of the Discovery and Early Settlement of the Bermudas or Sommers Islands, 1515–1685.* 2 vols. London, 1877–79.

Lodge, Sir Richard. *The Life of Cardinal Richelieu.* New York, 1903.

Morton, Richard Lee. *Colonial Virginia.* 2 vols. Chapel Hill, N.C., 1960.

Newton, Arthur P. *Colonizing Activities of the English Puritans.* New Haven, 1914.

Parkman, Francis. *A Half-Century of Conflict.* 2 vols. Boston, 1894.

Waddington, A. *La République des Provinces-Unis, la France, et les Pays-Bas Espagnols de 1630 à 1650.* 2 vols. Paris, 1895–97.

Weslager, Clinton Alfred. *Dutch Explorers, Traders, and Settlers in the Delaware Valley, 1609–1664.* Philadelphia, 1961.

Wright, Irene A., ed. "Spanish Policy toward Virginia, 1606–1612; Jamestown, Ecija, and John Clark of the *Mayflower*," *American Historical Review*, XXV (Apr., 1920), 448–479.

Wright, James Letch, Jr. "English-Spanish Rivalry in North America, 1432–1763." Unpublished Ph.D. Dissertation, University of Virginia, 1958.

Chapter V. Anglo-Dutch Relations Bearing upon America, 1648-89

Beer, George L. *Cromwell's Policy in its Economic Aspects.* Boston, 1902.

Bischoffshausen, Sigismund von. *Die Politik des Protectors Oliver Cromwell in der Auffassung und Thätigkeit seines Ministers des Staatssecretärs John Thurloe.* Innsbruck, 1899.

Catterall, R. C. H. "Anglo-Dutch Relations, 1654–1660," *Annual Report of the American Historical Association for 1910* (1912), 103–121.

Clarke, G. N. *The Dutch Alliance and the War against French Trade.* Manchester, 1923.

Colenbrander, Herman Theodoor. *Koloniale Geschiedenis.* 3 vols. The Hague, 1925–26.

Lannoy, Charles de, and Herman Vander Linden. *L'Histoire de l'expansion coloniale des peuples européens: Néerlande et Danemark.* Brussels, 1911.

Dexter, F. B. "Early Relations between New Netherland and New England," *Papers of the New Haven Colony Historical Society*, III, 443–469.

Edmundson, George. "The Dutch in Western Guiana," *English Historical Review*, XVI (1901), 640–675.

Elias, Johan E. *Het Voorspel van den eersten Engelschen Oorlog.* 2 vols. The Hague, 1920.

Firth, Charles Harding. *Oliver Cromwell and the Rule of the Puritans in England.* New York, 1900.

Gardiner, Samuel Rawson. *History of the Commonwealth and Protectorate, 1649–1660.* 4 vols. London, 1894–1903.
Japikse, N. "Louis XIV et la guerre anglo-hollandaise de 1665–1667," *Revue Historique,* XCVIII (1908), 22–60.
Sluiter, Engel. "Dutch-Spanish Rivalry in the Caribbean Area, 1594–1609," *Hispanic American Historical Review,* XXVIII (1948), 165–196.

Chapter VI. Anglo-Spanish Diplomacy Relative to America, 1648-89

Barbour, Violet. "Privateers and Pirates of the West Indies," *American Historical Review,* XVI (1910), 529–566.
Craik, Sir Henry. *The Life of Edward, Earl of Clarendon.* 2 vols. London, 1911.
Dunn, William E. *Spanish and French Rivalry in the Gulf Region of the United States, 1678–1702.* Austin, Tex., 1917.
Girard, Albert. *Le Commerce français à Seville et à Cadiz au temps des Hapsbourgs.* Paris, 1932.
Haring, Charles H. *The Buccaneers in the West Indies in the XVII Century.* London, 1910.
Haring, Charles H. *Trade and Navigation between Spain and the Indies in the Time of the Hapsbourgs* (Harvard Economic Studies, XIX). Cambridge, Mass., 1918.
Harlow, V. T. *History of Barbados, 1625–1685.* Oxford, 1926.
Hussey, Roland D. "Spanish Reaction to Foreign Aggression in the Caribbean to about 1680," *Hispanic American Historical Review,* IX (August, 1929), 286–302.
Strong, Frank. "Causes of Cromwell's West Indian Expedition," *American Historical Review,* IV (1899), 228–245.
Watts, Arthur Pryor. *Une histoire des colonies anglaises aux Antilles (de 1649 à 1660).* Paris, 1924.
Wright, Irene A., ed. "The English Conquest of Jamaica (1655–1656)," *Publications of the Royal Historical Society,* Camden 3rd Series, Vol. XXXIV; *Camden Miscellany,* XIII (1924), 1–29.

Chapter VII. Anglo-Portuguese Colonial Diplomacy, 1648-89

Brazão, Eduardo. *The Anglo-Portuguese Alliance.* London, 1957.
Chapman, A. B. Wallis. "The Commercial Relations of England and Portugal, 1487–1807," *Royal Historical Society Transactions,* 3rd Series, I (1907), 157–179.
Grose, Clyde L. "The Anglo-Portuguese Marriage of 1662," *Hispanic American Historical Review,* X (1930), 313–352.
Harris, Frank Reginald. *The Life of Edward Mountagu, K.G., First Earl of Sandwich (1625–1672).* 2 vols. London, 1912.
Jones, Guernsey. "Beginnings of the Oldest European Alliance: England and Portugal, 1640–1661," *Annual Report of the American Historical Association for 1916,* Vol. I, 405–418.
Mendosa, Renato de. *Historia da Politica Exterior do Brasil, 1500–1825.* Mexico, 1945.

Prestage, Edgar. "The Anglo-Portuguese Alliance," *Transactions of the Royal Historical Society*, 4th Series, Vol. XVII (1934), 69–100.

Prestage, Edgar. *The Diplomatic Relations of Portugal with France, England, and Holland from 1640 to 1668*. Watford, England, 1925.

Shillington, Violet Mary, and A. B. Wallis Chapman. *The Commercial Relations of England and Portugal*. London, 1907.

Stone, Thora G. *England and the Restoration, 1660–1688*. London, 1923.

Chapter VIII. The Swedes, the Danes, and the Brandenburgers, 1648-89

Brodhead, John R. *History of the State of New York*. 2 vols. New York, 1853–71.

Higham, C. S. S. *The Development of the Leeward Islands under the Restoration, 1660–1688*. Cambridge, 1921.

Pribram, A. F. *Franz Paul Freiherr von Lisola und die Politik seiner Zeit.* Leipzig, 1894.

Schuck, Richard. *Brandenburg-Preussens Kolonial-Politik unter dem grossen Kurfürsten und seinen Nachfolgern* (1647–1721). 2 vols. Leipzig, 1889.

Sprinchorn, C. K. S. "History of the Colony of New Sweden," trans. G. B. Keen. *Pennsylvania Magazine of History and Biography*, VII (1883), 395–419; VIII (1884), 17–44, 129–159, 241–254.

Waddington, A. *Le Grand Electeur Frédéric Guillaume de Brandebourg: sa politique extérieure, 1640–1688*. 2 vols. Paris, 1905–8.

Westergaard, Waldemar. *The Danish West Indies under Company Rule, 1671–1754*. New York, 1917.

Chapter IX. Anglo-French Diplomacy with Regard to America, 1648-1702

Bolton, H. E. "The Location of La Salle's Colony on the Gulf of Mexico," *Mississippi Valley Historical Review*, II (Sept., 1915), 165–182.

Clément, Pierre. *Histoire de la Vie et de l'administration de Colbert*. Paris, 1846.

Cole, Charles Woolsey. *Colbert and A Century of French Mercantilism*. 2 vols. New York, 1939.

Durant, R. "Louis XIV et Jacques II à la veille de la révolution de 1688. Les trois missions de Bonrepaus en Angleterre," *Revue d'histoire moderne et contemporaine*, X (1908), 28–44, 111–126, 192–204.

Eccles, W. J. *Frontenac, the Courtier Governor*. Toronto, 1959.

Feiling, Keith Grahame. *British Foreign Policy, 1660–1672*. London, 1930.

Fox. Charles James. *A History of the Early Part of the Reign of James the Second*. London, 1808.

Guttridge, George Herbert. *The Colonial Policy of William III in America and the West Indies*. Cambridge, 1922.

Hannay, James. *The History of Acadia from its First Discovery to its Surrender to England, by the Treaty of Paris*. St. John, N.B., 1879.

Jacobsen, Gertrude Ann. *William Blathwayt: A Late Seventeenth Century English Administrator*. New Haven, 1932.

Jaray, Gabriel Louis. *Les principes de la politique américaine de la France sous Henri IV, Richelieu, et Colbert," *Revue Synthèse*, XIII (1937), 97–113.

Jusserand, J. J. *A French Ambassador at the Court of Charles the Second: le

Comte de Cominges, from his unpublished Correspondence. London, 1892.

Klopp, Onno. *Der Fall des Hauses Stuart und die Succession des Hauses Hanover in Gross-Britannien und Irland, im Zusammenhange der europäischen Angelegenheiten von 1660–1714.* 14 vols. Vienna, 1875–88.

Koch, Gallus. *Die Friedensbestrebungen Wilhelms III. von England in den Jahren 1694–1697. Ein Beitrag zur Geschichte des Rijswijker Friedens.* Tübingen and Leipzig, 1903.

Legg, Leopold George Wickham. *Matthew Prior: A Study of His Public Career and Correspondence.* Cambridge, 1921.

Levae, Adolphe. *Essai historique sur les Négociations de la Trève de Vingt Ans, conclue à Ratisbonne en 1684.* Brussels, 1844.

Lodge, Sir Richard. *The History of England from the Restoration to the Death of William III (1660–1702).* London, 1910.

Macaulay, Thomas Babington Macaulay, 1st Baron. *The History of England, from the Accession of James the Second,* ed. Charles Harding Firth. 6 vols. London, 1913–15.

Mims, Stewart L. *Colbert's West India Policy.* New Haven, 1912.

Morgan, William T. "English Fear of 'Encirclement' in the Seventeenth Century," *Canadian Historical Review,* X (1929), 4–22.

Parkman, Francis. *Count Frontenac and New France under Louis XIV.* Boston, 1877.

Parsons, C. W. "Thomas Willett, the First Mayor of New York City," *Magazine of American History,* XVII (1889), 233–242.

Prowse, D. W. *History of Newfoundland from the English, Colonial and Foreign Records.* London, 1895.

Wolf, John B. *The Emergence of the Great Powers, 1685–1715.* 2nd ed. New York, 1951.

Chapter X. Angloamerica in the Diplomacy of the War of the Spanish Succession and the Peace of Utrecht, 1702-1713

Alison, Sir Archibald. *The Life of John, Duke of Marlborough, with Some Account of His Contemporaries and of the War of the Succession.* 2nd ed. 2 vols. Edinburgh, 1852.

Bourne, Ruth. *Queen Anne's Navy in the West Indies.* New Haven, 1939.

Clark, G. N. "War Trade and Trade War, 1701–1713," *Economic History Review,* I (Jan., 1928), 262–280.

Coombs, Douglas. *The Conduct of the Dutch: British Opinion and the Dutch Alliance during the War of the Spanish Succession.* The Hague, 1958.

Corbett, Sir Julian Stafford. *England in the Mediterranean. A Study of the Rise and Influence of British Power with the Straits, 1603–1713.* 2 vols. London, 1904.

Dahlgren, Erik Wilhelm. *Les rélations commerciales et maritimes entre la France et les côtes de l'Océan Pacifique (commencement du XVIIIᵉ siècle).* Paris, 1909.

Dahlgren, Erik Wilhelm. *Voyages français à destination de la mer du Sud avant Bougainville (1695–1749).* Paris, 1907.

Du Casse, Robert Emmanuel Léon. *L'Amiral Du Casse, Chevalier de la Toison d'Or (1646–1715). Étude sur la France maritime et coloniale (règne de Louis XIV).* Paris, 1876.

Fisher, Margaret Anne. "America in European Diplomacy relative to the Spanish Succession 1668–1713." Unpublished Ph.D. dissertation. University of Washington Library, 1967.

Girard, James W. *The Peace of Utrecht*. New York, 1885.

Giraud, Charles Joseph Barthélemy. *Le Traité d'Utrecht*. Paris, 1847.

Harkness, D. A. E. "The Opposition to the 8th and 9th Articles of the Commercial Treaty of Utrecht," *Scottish Historical Review*, XXI (1924), 219–226.

Langdon-Davies, John. *Carlos II: The King Who Would Not Die*. Englewood Cliffs, N.J., 1962.

Legrelle, Arsène. *La Diplomatie française et la Succession d'Espagne*. 4 vols. Ghent, 1888–92.

McLachlan, Jean O. *Trade and Peace with Old Spain, 1667–1757; A Study of the Influence of Commerce on Anglo-Spanish Diplomacy in the First Half of the Eighteenth Century*. Cambridge, 1940.

Morgan, William T. "The Origins of the South Sea Company," *Political Science Quarterly*, XLIV (1929), 16–38.

Nettels, Curtis. "England and the Spanish-American Trade, 1680–1715," *Journal of Modern History*, III (1931), 1–33.

Prestage, Edgar. *Portugal, Brasil e Grã-Bretanha*. Coimbra, 1925.

Preuss, G. T. *Wilhelm von England und das Haus Wittelsbach im Zeitalter der spanischen Erbfolgefrage*. Breslau, 1904.

Rheaume, Cordelia E. "The Treaty of Utrecht (1713)," *Transactions of the Women's Canadian Historical Society of Ottawa*, VI (1915), 40–46.

Rich, E. E. "The Hudson's Bay Company and the Treaty of Utrecht," *Cambridge Historical Journal*, XI (1954), 183–197.

Scelle, Georges. *Histoire politique de la traite négrière aux Indes de Castille*. 2 vols. Paris, 1906.

Sichel, Walter Sydney. *Bolingbroke and His Times*. New York, 1901.

Somerville, Dorothy H. "Shrewsbury and the Peace of Utrecht," *English Historical Review*, XLVII (1932), 646–647.

Stanhope, Earl (Lord Mahon). *History of England . . . comprising the Reign of Queen Anne until the Peace of Utrecht, 1701–1713*. 2 vols. London, 1872.

Stanhope, Philip Henry Stanhope, 5th Earl. *History of the War of the Succession in Spain*. 2nd ed. London, 1836.

Trevelyan, George Macauley. *England under Queen Anne*. 3 vols. London and New York, 1930–34.

Weber, Ottokar, *Der Friede von Utrecht. Verhandlungen Zwischen England, Frankreich, dem Kaiser und den Generalstaaten 1710–1713*. Gotha, 1891.

Wright, James Letch, Jr. "English-Spanish Rivalry in North America, 1432–1763." Unpublished Ph.D. dissertation. University of Virginia Library, 1958.

Chapter XI. Direct Intercolonial Relations in America during the Seventeenth Century

Adams, James T. *The Founding of New England*. Boston, 1927.

Barbour, V. "Privateers and Pirates of the West Indies," *American Historical Review*, XVI (1911), 529–566.

Bruce, P. A. *Economic History of Virginia in the Seventeenth Century.* 2 vols. New York, 1907.

Bryce, George. *The Remarkable History of the Hudson's Bay Company, including that of the French Traders of North-Western Canada and of the North-West, XY, and Astor Fur Companies.* London, 1900.

Buffinton, A. H. "The Isolationist Policy of Colonial Massachusetts," *New England Quarterly,* I (1928), 158–179.

Burrage, Henry Sweetser. *The Beginnings of Colonial Maine, 1602–1658.* Portland, Me., 1914.

Clark, George Norman. *The Later Stuarts, 1660–1714 (The Oxford History of England).* Oxford, 1944.

Crane, Verner W. "The Southern Frontier in Queen Anne's War," *American Historical Review,* XXIV (1919), 379–395.

Crouse, Nellis M. *French Pioneers in the West Indies, 1624–1664.* New York, 1940.

Dexter, F. B. "Early Relations between New Netherland and New England," *Papers of the New Haven Colony Historical Society,* III (1882), 443–469.

Drake, Samuel Adams. *The Border Wars of New England, Commonly Called King William's and Queen Anne's Wars.* New York, 1897.

Flick, Alexander C., ed. *History of the State of New York.* 10 vols. New York, 1933–37.

Ganong, W. F. "A Monograph of the Evolution of the Boundaries of the Province of New Brunswick," *Transactions of the Royal Society of Canada,* 2nd Series, VII (1901), Sect. 2, 139–449.

Halsey, Francis Whiting. *The Old New York Frontier . . . 1614–1800.* New York, 1901.

Higham, Charles Strachan Sanders. *The Development of the Leeward Islands under the Restoration, 1660–1688. A Study of the Foundations of the Old Colonial System.* Cambridge, 1921.

Hunt, George T. *The Wars of the Iroquois.* Madison, Wisc., 1940.

Johnson, Amandus. *The Swedish Settlements on the Delaware: Their History and Relation to the Indians, Dutch and English, 1638–1664.* 2 vols. Philadelphia and New York, 1911.

Lounsbury, Ralph Greenlee. *The British Fishery at Newfoundland, 1634–1763.* New Haven, 1934.

Moreau, Célestin. *Histoire de l'Acadie françoise (Amérique Septentrionale) de 1598 à 1755.* Paris, 1873.

Murdoch, Beamish. *A History of Nova Scotia, or Acadie.* 3 vols. Halifax, 1856–67.

O'Callaghan, Edmund Bailey. *History of New Netherlands; or, New York under the Dutch.* 2 vols. New York, 1846–48.

Palfrey, John Gorham. *A Compendious History of New England from the Discovery by Europeans to the First General Congress of the Anglo-American Colonies.* 4 vols. Boston, 1873.

Parkman, Francis. *La Salle and the Discovery of the Great West.* Boston, 1896.

Parkman, Francis. *The Old Regime in Canada.* Boston, 1894.

Philips, Paul Chrisler. *The Fur Trade.* 2 vols. Norman, Okla., 1961.

Ward, Christopher. *The Dutch and Swedes on the Delaware, 1609–1664.* Philadelphia, 1930.

Watts, A. P. *Une histoire des colonies anglaises aux Antilles de 1649 à 1660.* Paris, 1924.

Williamson, W. D. *History of the State of Maine . . . 1602 . . . to 1820.* 2 vols. Hallowell, Maine, 1832.

Wilson, Beckles. *The Great Company (1667–1871), being a History of the honourable Company of Merchants-Adventurers trading into Hudson's Bay . . .* 2 vols. London, 1900.

Winsor, Justin, ed. *The Memorial History of Boston, including Suffolk County, Massachusetts, 1630–1880.* 4 vols. Boston, 1880–81.

Winsor, Justin. *Narrative and Critical History of America.* 8 vols. Boston, 1884–89.

Wrong, George M. *The Conquest of New France; A Chronicle of the Colonial Wars.* New Haven, 1918.

Wrong, George M. *The Rise and Fall of New France.* 2 vols. New York, 1928.

Chapter XII. The Impact of the New World of the Colonies upon the Evolution of the Theory and the Practice of International Law

Barcia-Trelles, Camilo. "La Doctrine de Monroë dans son Développement historique . . . ," Hague Academy of International Law, *Recueil des Cours*, XXXII (1930), 2, 391–405.

Brown, Louise Fargo. *The Freedom of the Seas.* New York, 1919.

Brunhes, Jean, and Camille Vallaux. *La Géographie de l'histoire: géographie de la paix et de la guerre sur terre et sur mer.* Paris, 1921.

Deak, Francis. *Neutrality. Its History, Economics and Law.* 4 vols. New York, 1935–36.

Dupuis, Charles. *Le Principe d'équilibre et le concert européen de la Paix de Westphalie à l'acte d'Algéciras.* Paris, 1909.

Fulton, Thomas W. *The Sovereignty of the Sea.* Edinburgh and London, 1911.

Garneau, François Xavier. *Histoire du Canada depuis sa découverte jusqu'à nos jours.* 2nd ed. 9 vols. Quebec, 1852.

Gidel, Gilbert Charles. *Le Droit International Public de la Mer.* Chateauroux, 1932.

Hall, William Edward. *International Law.* Oxford, 1880.

Hall, William Edward. *Treatise on International Law.* 3rd ed. Oxford, 1890.

Hamilton, Bernice. *Political Thought in Sixteenth-Century Spain: A Study of the Political Ideas of Vitoria, De Soto, Suarez, and Molina.* Oxford, 1963.

Knight, William Stanley Macbean. *The Life and Works of Hugo Grotius.* London, 1925.

Kulsrud, C. J. *Maritime Neutrality to 1780.* Boston, 1936.

Lapradelle, Paul de. *La Frontière: Étude de droit internationale.* Paris, 1928.

Margry, Pierre. *Les navigations françaises et la révolution maritime du XIVe au XVIe siècle, d'après les documents inédits tirés de France, d'Angleterre, d'Espagne et d'Italie.* Paris, 1867.

Martens, Karl, Freiherr von. *Causes célèbres du droit des gens.* 2nd ed. 5 vols. Leipzig, 1858–61.

Maulde-La-Clavière, Marie Alphonse René de. *La Diplomatie au temps de Machiavel.* 3 vols. Paris, 1892–93.

Mendosa, Renato de. *Alexandre de Guzman, El Precursor de Monroe.* Mexico, 1941.

Moore, John Bassett. *A Digest of International Law as embodied in Diplomatic Discussions, Treaties and other International Agreements, International Awards, the Decisions of Municipal Courts, and the Writings of Jurists.* 8 vols. Washington, D.C., 1906.

Moore, John Bassett. *Principles of American Diplomacy.* New York, 1918.

Nys, Ernest. *Le droit des gens et les anciens jurisconsultes espagnols.* Brussells, 1914.

Nys, Ernest. *Le droit international; les principes, les théories, les faits.* New ed. 3 vols. Brussels, 1912.

Nys, Ernest. "La théorie d'équilibre européen," *Revue de Droit Internationale et de Législation Comparée,* XXV (1893), 34–57.

Oppenheim, Lassa Francis Lawrence. *International Law, A Treatise.* 2 vols. London, 1905–6.

Pillet, A., *et al. Les fondateurs du droit international.* Paris, 1904.

Potter, Pitman B. *Freedom of the Seas in History, Law and Politics.* New York, 1924.

Reeves, J. S. "Two Conceptions of the Freedom of the Seas," *American Historical Review,* XXII (1917), 535–543.

Savelle, Max. "Colonial Origins of American Diplomatic Principles," *Pacific Historical Review,* III, No. 3 (Sept., 1934), 334–350.

Scaife, W. B. "The Development of International Law as to Newly Discovered Territory." American Historical Association, *Annual Report,* IV, No. 3 (1890), 69–93.

Scott, James Brown. *The Spanish Conception of International Law and of Sanctions.* Washington, 1934.

Scott, James Brown. *The Spanish Origin of International Law: Lectures on Francisco de Vitoria (1480–1546) and Francisco Suárez (1548–1617).* Washington, 1928.

Ségur-Dupeyron, P. de. *Histoire des négociations commercials et maritimes du règne de Louis XIV considerées dans leurs rapports avec la politique générale.* Paris, 1863.

Snow, Alpheus Henry. *The Question of Aborigines in the Law and Practice of Nations.* New York, 1921.

Supan, Alexander Georg. *Die territoriale Entwicklung der europäischen Kolonien.* Gotha, 1906.

Vattel, Emmerich de. *Le Droit des Gens, ou, principes de la loi naturelle, appliqués à la conduite & aux affaires des nations & des souverains.* 3 vols. London, 1758.

Walker, Thomas Alfred. *History of the Law of Nations.* 2 vols. Cambridge, 1899.

Walsh, Edmund A., ed. *The History and Nature of International Relations.* New York, 1922.

Wheaton, H. *Histoire des progrès du droit des gens en Europe depuis la Paix de Westphalie jusqu'au congrès de Vienne.* Leipzig, 1841.

Wheaton, H. *History of the Law of Nations in Europe and America.* New York, 1845.

Williamson, James Alexander. *Maritime Enterprise, 1485–1558*. Oxford, 1913.
Zeller, Gaston. "La Monarchie d'ancien Régime et les frontières naturelles," *Revue d'Histoire Moderne*, VIII (1933), 305–333.

Chapter XIII. International Relations on the "Great Frontier" in America, 1713-54

Alvord, Clarence W. *The Illinois Country, 1673–1818*. Springfield, Ill., 1920.
Audet, F. J. *Jean-Daniel Dumas, le Héros de la Monongahela*. Montreal, 1920.
Bell, Herbert C. "The West India Trade before the Revolution," *American Historical Review*, XXII (1917), 272–287.
Bolton, Herbert Eugene, and Mary Ross. *The Debatable Land: A Sketch of the Anglo-Spanish Contest for the Georgia Country*. Berkeley, Calif., 1925.
Bradley, Arthur Granville. *The Fight with France for North America*. New York, 1900.
Brebner, John B. *New England's Outpost: Acadia before the Conquest of Canada*. New York, 1927.
Breen, Henry Hegart. *St. Lucia: Historical, Statistical, and Descriptive*. London, 1844.
Carny, John Pitts. *Indian Affairs in Georgia, 1732–1756*. Philadelphia, 1936.
Cleland, Hugh. *George Washington in the Ohio Valley*. Pittsburgh, 1955.
Coulter, E. Merton. *Georgia: A Short History*. Revised ed. Chapel Hill, N.C., 1960.
Crane, Verner Winslow. *The Southern Frontier, 1670–1732*. Philadelphia, 1929.
Dodson, Leonidas. *Alexander Spotswood, Governor of Colonial Virginia, 1710–1722*. Philadelphia and London, 1932.
Douglas, Edward M. *Boundaries, Areas, Geographic Centers and Altitudes of the United States and the Several States, with a Brief Record of Important Changes in their Territory and Government* (United States Department of the Interior, Bulletin 817). 2nd ed. Washington, D.C., 1932.
Dunn, William B. *Spanish and French Rivalry in the Gulf Region of the United States, 1678–1702; The Beginnings of Texas and Pensacola* (University of Texas, *Studies in History*, No. 1). Austin, Tex., 1917.
Franz, Alexander. *Die Kolonisation des Mississippitales bis zum Ausgange der französischen Herrschaft*. Leipzig, 1906
Freeman, Douglas Southall. *George Washington, A Biography*. 7 vols. New York, 1948–57.
Gardner, William J. *A History of Jamaica*. London, 1909.
Gipson, Lawrence Henry. *The British Empire before the American Revolution*. 12 vols. New York, 1936–61.
Gould, Clarence P. "Trade between the Windward Islands and the Continental Colonies of the French Empire, 1683–1763," *Mississippi Valley Historical Review*, XXV (Mar., 1939), 473–490.
Hamelberg, J. H. J. *De Nederlanders op de West Indische Eilanden*. 4 vols. Amsterdam, 1901–9.
Hamer, P. M. "Anglo-French Rivalry in the Cherokee Country, 1754–1757," *North Carolina Historical Review*, II, 303–322.

Heinrich, Pierre. *La Louisiane sous la Compagnie des Indes, 1717–1731*. Paris, 1908.

Higgins, Ruth L. *Expansion in New York, with especial Reference to the Eighteenth Century*. Columbus, Ohio, 1931.

Johnson, James G. *The Colonial Southeast, 1732–1763: An International Contest for Territorial and Economic Control* (*University of Colorado Studies*, XIX). Boulder, Colo., 1932.

Lanctot, Gustave. *Les Canadiens français et leurs voisins du sud*. Montreal, 1941.

Lanning, John Tate. "American Participation in the War of Jenkins' Ear," *Georgia Historical Quarterly*, XI (1927), 191–215.

Lanning, John Tate. *The Diplomatic History of Georgia: A Study of the Epoch of Jenkins' Ear*. Chapel Hill, N.C., 1936.

Lanning, John Tate. *The Spanish Missions of Georgia*. Chapel Hill, N.C., 1935.

Lucas, Charles Prestwood. *A Historical Geography of the British Colonies*. Oxford, 1888.

McLennon, J. S. *Louisbourg from its Foundation to its Fall*. London, 1958.

Meriwether, Robert Lee. *The Expansion of South Carolina, 1729–1765*. Kingsport, Tenn., 1940.

Pares, Richard. *Yankees and Creoles: The Trade between North America and the West Indies before the American Revolution*. Cambridge, Mass., 1956.

Penson, Lillian N. *The Colonial Agents of the British West Indies: A Study in Colonial Administration, mainly in the 18th Century*. London, 1924.

Pitman, Frank Wesley. *The Development of the British West Indies, 1700–1763*. New Haven, 1917.

Raymond, W. D. "Nova Scotia under English Rule, from the Capture of Port Royal to the Conquest of Canada, A.D. 1710–1760," *Proceedings and Transactions of the Royal Society of Canada*, 3rd Series, Vol. IV, Section II, 55–84.

Reese, Trevor R. *Colonial Georgia: A Study in British Imperial Policy in the Eighteenth Century*. Athens, Ga., 1963.

Stevens, W. B. *A History of Georgia*. 2 vols. Philadelphia, 1859.

Surrey, Nancy M. M. *The Commerce of Louisiana during the French Regime, 1699–1763*. New York, 1916.

Taylor, Ira W. "Massachusetts Trade with the French West Indies, 1686–1733." Unpublished M.A. Thesis, University of Washington, 1959.

TePaske, John Jay. *The Governorship of Spanish Florida, 1700–1763*. Durham, N.C., 1964.

Turner, Frederick Jackson. "The Diplomatic Contest for the Mississippi Valley," *Atlantic Monthly*, XCIII (1904), 676–691, 807–817.

Whitson, Agnes Mary. *The Constitutional Development of Jamaica, 1660 to 1729*. Manchester, 1929.

Williams, Basil. "The Foreign Policy of England under Walpole," *English Historical Review*, XV (1900), 251–276, 479–494, 665–698; XVI (1901), 67–83, 308–327, 439–451.

Williams, S. C. *Early Trade in the Tennessee Country, 1540–1800*. Johnson City, Tennessee, 1928.

Winsor, Justin. *The Mississippi Basin: The Struggle in America between England and France, 1697–1763*. Boston, 1898.

Wood, William C. H. *The Great Fortress*. Toronto, 1915.

Woodcock, Henry Iles. *A History of Tobago*. Ayr, 1867.

Chapter XIV. The "Concert of Europe" and the Colonial Problem, 1715-29

Aiton, Arthur S. "The Asiento Treaty as reflected in the Papers of Lord Shelburne," *Hispanic American Historical Review*, VIII (1928), 167–177.

Aragon, Marcel. "La Compagnie d'Ostende et le grand commerce en Belgique au début du XVIIIᵉ siècle," *Annals des Sciences Politiques*, XVI (1901), 219–233.

Bateson, Thomas. "The Relations of Defoe and Harley," *English Historical Review*, XV (1900), 238–250.

Baudrillart, Alfred. *Philippe V et la cour de France d'après des documents inédits tirés des archives espagnoles de Simancas et d'Alcala de Henares et des Archives du Ministère des Affaires Etrangères à Paris.* 5 vols. Paris, 1890–1901.

Chance, James Frederick. *The Alliance of Hanover: A Study of British Foreign Policy in the Last Years of George I.* London, 1923.

Dept, Gaston. "La Compagnie d'Ostende. Voyages et projects de colonisation," *Bulletin de la Société d'histoire et d'archéologie de Gand*, XXXIII (1926), 34–55.

Donnan, Elizabeth. "The Early Days of the South Sea Company," *Journal of Economic and Business History*, II (1930), 419–450.

Geike, Roderick and Isabel A. Montgomery. *The Dutch Barrier, 1705–1719.* Cambridge, 1930.

Goslinga, Ariaan. *Slingelandt's Efforts towards European Peace.* The Hague, 1915.

Hassal, Arthur. *The Balance of Power, 1715–1789.* London, 1929.

Hertz, Gerald B. "England and the Ostend Company," *English Historical Review*, XXII (1907), 255–279.

Höfler, C. von. *Der Congress von Soissons.* 2 vols. Vienna, 1876.

Horsfal, Lucy F. "British Relations with the Spanish Colonies in the Caribbean, 1713–1739." Unpublished M.A. Thesis in the University of London Library, 1935.

Huisman, Michel. *La Belgique commerciale sous l'empereur Charles IV: La Compagnie d'Ostende.* Brussels, 1902.

Levac, A. *Recherches historiques sur le commerce des Belges aux Indes pendant le XVIIᵉ et le XVIIIᵉ siècle.* Brussels, 1842.

Lewis, Warren Hamilton. *The Scandalous Regent: A Life of Philippe, Duc d'Orleans, 1674–1723, and of His Family.* London, 1961.

Lodge, Sir Richard. "The Treaty of Seville," *Transactions of the Royal Historical Society*, 4th Series, XVI (1933), 1–43.

Pantaleão, O. *A Penetração comercial da Inglaterra na América espanhola de 1713 a 1783.* São Paulo, 1946.

Pergameni, H. "La Compagnie d'Ostende," *Revue de Belgique* (Oct., 1902), 155–177.

Scelle, Georges. "The Slave Trade in the Spanish Colonies of America: The Asiento," *American Journal of International Law*, IV, 618 ff.

Sée, Henri, and Léon Vignols. *La Fin du commerce interlope dans l'Amérique Espagnole.* Paris, 1925.

Sée, Henri, and Léon Vignols. "L'envers de la diplomatie officièlle de 1715 à 1730: La Rivalité commerciale des puissances maritimes et les doléances des négotiants français," *Revue Belge de Philologie et d'Histoire,* V (1926), 471–491.

Vignols, Léon. "L'Asiento français (1701–1713) et anglais (1713–1750) et le commerce franco-espagnol vers 1700 à 1730. Avec deux mémoires français de 1728 sur ces sujets," *Revue d'Histoire Économique et Sociale,* XVII (1929), 403–436.

Wiesener, Louis, Abbé. *Le Régent, l'Abbé Dubois et les Anglais.* 3 vols. Paris, 1891–99.

Williams, Basil. *Stanhope, a Study in Eighteenth-Century War and Diplomacy.* Oxford, 1932.

Wilson, Arthur McCandless. *French Foreign Policy during the Administration of Cardinal Fleury, 1726–1743.* Cambridge, Mass., 1936.

Wilson, Charles. *Anglo-Dutch Commerce and Finance in the Eighteenth Century.* New York, 1941.

Chapter XV. Anglo-Spanish Colonial Diplomacy from the Treaty of Seville (1729) to the Convention of the Pardo (1739)

Armstrong, Edward. *Elizabeth Farnese: "The Termagant of Spain."* London, 1892.

Berindougue, H. *Le Mercantilisme en Espagne.* Paris, 1929.

Bolton, H. E. *Texas in the Middle Eighteenth Century: Studies in Spanish Colonial History and Administration.* Berkeley, Calif., 1915.

Brown, Vera Lee. "Contraband Trade: a Factor in the Decline of Spain's Empire in America," *Hispanic American Historical Review,* VIII (1928), 178–189.

Brown, Vera Lee. "The South Sea Company and Contraband Trade," *American Historical Review,* XXXI (1926), 662–678.

Chatelain, Verne Elmo. *The Defenses of Spanish Florida, 1565 to 1763.* Washington, 1941.

Dunn, W. E. *Spanish and French Rivalry in the Gulf Region of the United States, 1678–1702.* Austin, Tex. 1917.

Hanotaux, Gabriel. "L'influence française en Amérique du Nord," *France-Amérique,* XXIV (1933), 105–107.

Hertz, Gerald B. *British Imperialism in the Eighteenth Century.* London, 1908.

Hildner, Ernest C. "The Role of the South Sea Company in the Diplomacy leading to the War of Jenkins' Ear, 1729–1739," *Hispanic American Historical Review,* XVIII (1938), 322–341.

Hussey, Roland Denis. *The Caracas Company: A Study in the History of Spanish Monopolistic Trade (Harvard Historical Studies, XXXVII).* Cambridge, Mass., 1924.

Lanning, John Tate. "The American Colonies in the Preliminaries of the War of Jenkins' Ear," *Georgia Historical Quarterly,* XI (1927), 129–155.

Laughton, John Knox. "Jenkins' Ear," *English Historical Review,* IV (1899), 742–43.

Lodge, Richard. "English Neutrality in the War of the Polish Succession. A Commentary upon Diplomatic Instructions, Vol. VI, France, 1727–1744," *Transactions of the Royal Historical Society,* 4th Series, XIV (1931), 141–173.

McLachlan, Jean O. *Trade and Peace with Old Spain, 1667–1750*. Cambridge, 1940.

Nelson, George H. "Contraband Trade under the Asiento, 1730–1739," *American Historical Review*, LI (Oct., 1945), 55–67.

Reese, Trevor R. *Colonial Georgia: A Study in British Imperial Policy in the Eighteenth Century*. Athens, 1963.

St. John, James H. "Anglo-Spanish Commercial Relations, 1700–1750." Unpublished M.A. Thesis, University of Iowa, 1927.

Sée, Henri. "Esquisse de l'histoire du commerce français à Cadix et dans l'Amérique espagnole au XVIIIᵉ siècle," *Revue d'Histoire Moderne*, III (1928), 13–31.

Seeley, J. R. "The House of Bourbon," *English Historical Review*, I (1886), 86–104.

Temperley, Harold W. V. "The Causes of the War of Jenkins' Ear, 1739," *Transactions of the Royal Historical Society, 3rd Series*, III (1909), 198–236.

Temperley, H. W. V. "Relations of England with Spanish America, 1720–1744," *Annual Report of the American Historical Association for the Year 1911*. Washington, 1913. 2 vols. I, 229–237.

Wilson, Arthur M. "The Logwood Trade in the Seventeenth and Eighteenth Centuries." In Donald C. McKay, ed., *Essays in the History of Modern Europe*. New York and London, 1936.

Zaragoza, Justo. *Piraterías y Agresiones de los Ingleses en la America Española*. Madrid, 1883.

Chapter XVI. Anglo-French Diplomacy with Regard to America, 1716-39

Andrews, Charles M. "Anglo-French Commercial Rivalry, 1700–1750: The Western Phase," *American Historical Review*, XX (Apr., 1915), 539–556; XX (July, 1915), 761–780.

Biggar, H. P. *Early Trading Companies of New France*. Toronto, 1901.

Bourgeois, Emile. *La Diplomatic secrète au 18ième siècle*. Paris, 1892.

Bourgeois, Emile. *Le Secret du régent et la politique de l'Abbé Dubois (triple et quadruple alliances, 1716–1718)*. Paris, 1909.

Coquelle, P. *L'Alliance Franco-Hollandaise contre l'Angleterre, 1735–1788*. Paris, 1902.

Darcy, Jean. *Cent ans de rivalité coloniale [entre] France et Angleterre*. Paris, 1904.

Girard, Albert. *Le Commerce français à Seville et Cadix du temps des Hapsbourgs*. Paris, 1932.

Hanotaux, G., and A. Martineau, eds. *Histoire des colonies françaises et de l'expansion de la France dans le monde*. 6 vols. Paris, 1920–33. Vol. I.

Klassen, Peter. "Die englische-französische Rivalität und die Wandlung der europäischen Friedensidee im 18. Jahrhundert," *Die Welt als Geschichte*, III (1937), 368–377.

Lodge, Sir Richard. "The Anglo-French Alliance, 1716–1731," in *Studies in Anglo-French History*, ed. G. A. Coville and H. W. Temperley. Cambridge, 1935.

Miller-Surrey, Nancy M. *The Commerce of Louisiana during the French Regime, 1699–1763*. New York, 1916.

Nulle, Stebelton Henry. *Thomas Pelham-Holles, Duke of Newcastle; His Early Political Career, 1693–1724.* Philadelphia, 1931.

Parkman, Francis. *A Half-Century of Conflict.* 2 vols. Boston, 1892.

Plumb, J. H. *Sir Robert Walpole: The King's Minister.* Boston, 1961.

Prud'homme, L. A. "La baie d'Hudson," *Proceedings of the Royal Society of Canada,* 3rd series, III, Sec. 1, 3–36.

Reese, Trevor R. "Georgia in Anglo-Spanish Diplomacy, 1736–1739," *William and Mary Quarterly,* 3rd Series, XV, No. 2 (Apr., 1958), 168–190.

Savelle, Max. "The Forty-Ninth Degree of North Latitude as an International Boundary, 1719: The Origin of an Idea," *Canadian Historical Review,* XXXVIII, No. 3, (Sept., 1957), 183–201.

Taylor, George Robert Stirling. *Robert Walpole and His Age.* London, 1931.

Vaucher, Paul. *Robert Walpole et la Politique de Fleury (1731–1742).* Paris, 1924.

Vaucher, Paul. "Une convention franco-anglaise pour régler le commerce et la navigation dans les Indes Occidentales, 1737–1740." In *Mélanges d'histoire offerts à M. Charles Bémont.* Paris, 1913.

Chapter XVII. The War of Jenkins' Ear and the War of the Austrian Succession, 1739-48

Ballayntyne, A. *Lord Carteret, a Political Biography, 1690–1763.* London, 1887.

Beer, Adolf. "Holland und der österreichische Erbfölge-Krieg," *Archiv für österreichische Geschichte,* XLVI (1871), 297–418.

Bernstein, Harry. *Origins of Inter-American Interest, 1700–1812.* Philadelphia, 1945.

Broglie, Duc de. *La Paix d'Aix-la-Chapelle.* Paris, 1895.

Caldwell, Norman Ward. *The French in the Mississippi Valley, 1740–1750.* Urbana, Ill., 1941.

Coquelle, P. *L'Alliance franco-hollandaise contre l'Angleterre, 1735–1788.* Paris, 1902.

Fernandez, Olbes L. *La Paz de Aquisgran.* Pontevedra, 1926.

Hartmann, Cyril Hughes. *The Angry Admiral: The Later Career of Edward Vernon, Admiral of the White.* London, 1953.

Laughton, J. K. "Jenkins' Ear," *English Historical Review,* IV (1889), 742–743.

Lodge, Sir Richard. "The Continental Policy of Great Britain, 1740–60," *History,* XVI (1931–32), 298–305.

Lodge, Sir Richard. *Studies in Eighteenth-Century Diplomacy, 1740–1748.* London, 1930.

Ogelsby, John C. M. "The Maritime Struggle in the West Indies, 1739–1748." Unpublished Ph.D. Dissertation, University of Washington, 1963.

Owen, John Beresford. *The Rise of the Pelhams.* London, 1957.

Pares, Richard. *Colonial Blockade and Neutral Rights, 1739–1763.* Oxford, 1938.

Pares, Richard. *War and Trade in the West Indies, 1739–1763.* Oxford, 1936.

Richmond, Herbert W. *The Navy in the War of 1739–1748.* 3 vols. Cambridge, 1920.

Santai, M. *Les Préliminaires de la guerre de la Succession d'Autriche.* Paris, 1907.

Temperley, H. W. V. "The Causes of the War of Jenkins' Ear (1739), *Transactions of the Royal Historical Society,* 3rd Series, III (1909), 197–236.

Williams, Basil. *Carteret and Newcastle: A Contrast in Contemporaries.* Cambridge, 1943.

Zabola y Lera, Pío. *El Marques de Argenson y el Pacto de 1743.* Madrid, 1928.

Chapter XVIII. The "Cold War" of 1748-55

Aranda, M. J. de. *El Marques de la Enseñada.* Madrid, 1898.

Bailey, Kenneth P. *The Ohio Company of Virginia and the Westward Movement, 1748–1792.* Glendale, Calif., 1939.

Beer, Adolf. *Zur Geschichte des Friedens von Aachen, im Jahre 1748.* Vienna, 1871.

de Bonnault, Claude. "M. de la Galissonière, gouverneur-général du Canada," *Franco-American Review,* II (1937), 27–36.

Brown, Vera Lee. "Anglo-Spanish Relations in America in the Closing Years of the Colonial Era," *Hispanic American Historical Review,* V (1922), 329–483.

Brown, Vera Lee. *Studies in the History of Spain in the Second Half of the Eighteenth Century (Smith College Studies in History,* XV, Nos. 1 and 2). Northampton, Mass., 1929.

Christelow, Allan. "Contraband Trade between Jamaica and the Spanish Main, and the Free Port Act of 1766," *Hispanic American Historical Review,* XXII (1942), 309–343.

Edmundson, George. "Spain and Portugal (1746–94)," *Cambridge Modern History,* VI, 361–392.

Gipson, Lawrence H. "British Diplomacy in the Light of Anglo-Spanish New World Issues," *American Historical Review,* LI (1946), 627–648.

Harris, George. *The Life of Lord Chancellor Hardwicke; with selections from his correspondence, diaries, speeches and judgments.* 3 vols. London, 1847.

Horn, D. B. *Sir Charles Hanbury Williams and European Diplomacy (1747–1758).* London, 1930.

Koontz, Louis K. *Robert Dinwiddie.* Glendale, Calif., 1941.

Lodge, Richard. "Sir Benjamin Keene, K.B.: A Study in Anglo-Spanish Relations," *Transactions of the Royal Historical Society,* 4th Series, XV (1932), 1–43.

Manning, W. R. "The Nootka Sound Controversy," *Annual Report of the American Historical Association for the Year 1904.* Washington, 1905. 279–478.

Newbold, Robert C. *The Albany Congress and Plan of Union of 1754.* New York, 1955.

Pares, Richard. *Colonial Blockade and Neutral Rights, 1739–63.* New York and Oxford, 1938.

Pease, Theodore C., and Ernestine Jenison, eds. *Illinois on the Eve of the Seven Years' War, 1747–1755 (Collection of the Illinois State Historical Library,* Vol. XXIX; French Series, Vol. III). Springfield, Ill., 1940.

Richmond, Herbert. *The Navy in the War of 1739–1748.* 3 vols. Cambridge, 1920.

Russell, Nelson Vance. "The Reaction of England and America to the Capture of Havana, 1762," *Hispanic American Historical Review,* IX (1929), 303–316.

Savelle, Max. *The Diplomatic History of the Canadian Boundary, 1749–63.* New Haven, 1940.

Savelle, Max. "Diplomatic Preliminaries of the Seven Years War in America," *Canadian Historical Review,* XX (1939), 17–36.

Schutz, John A. *Thomas Pownall, British Defender of American Liberty: A Study of Anglo-American Relations in the Eighteenth Century.* Glendale, Calif., 1951.

Schutz, John A. *William Shirley, King's Governor of Massachusetts.* Chapel Hill, N.C., 1961.

Villa, Antonio Rodriguez. *Don Cenon de Somodevilla, Marqués de la Ensenada.* Madrid, 1878.

Waddington, Richard. *Louis XIV et le renversement des alliances: préliminaires de la guerre de sept ans, 1754–1756.* Paris, 1896.

Wainwright, Nicholas B. *George Croghan, Wilderness Diplomat.* Chapel Hill, N.C., 1959.

Chapter XIX. Angloamerica in the Diplomacy of the Seven Years War, 1756-63

Aiton, Arthur S. "A Neglected Intrigue of the Family Compact," *Hispanic American Historical Review,* XI (1931), 387–393.

Aiton, Arthur S. "Diplomacy of the Louisiana Cession by France to Spain, 1763," *American Historical Review,* XXXVI (July, 1931), 701–720.

Atard, Vicente Palacio. *El Tercer Pacto de Familia.* Madrid, 1945 (Publicaciones de la Escuela de Estudios Hispano-Americanos de la Universidad de Sevilla, 17, Series 2, Monografias No. 4).

Baker-Crothers, Hayes. *Virginia and the French and Indian War.* Chicago, 1928.

Beer, George Louis. *British Colonial Policy, 1754–1765.* 2nd ed. Gloucester, Mass., 1958.

Blart, Louis. *Les rapports de la France et de l'Espagne après le Pacte de Famille, jusqu'à la fin du ministère du Duc de Choiseul.* Paris, 1915.

Bourquet, Alfred. *Études sur la politique étrangère du duc de Choiseul.* Paris, 1907.

Bourquet, Alfred. "Le Duc de Choiseul et l'alliance espagnole, après le Pacte de Famille," *Revue Historique,* XCIV (1907), 1–27.

Boyer de Peyreleau, E. E. *Les Antilles françaises, particulièrement la Guadeloupe.* 3 vols. Paris, 1823.

Broglie, Jacques Victor Albert, Duc de. *L'Alliance Autrichiènne.* Paris, 1897.

Christelow, Allan. "Economic Background of the Anglo-Spanish War of 1762," *Journal Modern History,* XVIII (1946), 22–36.

Christelow, Allan. "French Interest in the Spanish Empire during the Ministry of the Duc de Choiseul, 1759–1771," *Hispanic American Historical Review,* XXI (1941), 517–537.

Coquelle, P. L'Alliance franco-hollandaise contre l'Angleterre, 1735–1788. Paris, 1902.

Corbett, Julian S. England in the Seven Years War. 2 vols. London, 1907.

Danvila y Collado, Manuel. El Reinado de Carlos III. 6 vols. Madrid, 1893–96.

Daubigny, Eugène. Choiseul et la France d'outre-mer après le Traité de Paris. Paris, 1892.

Dorfman, Joseph. The Economic Mind in American Civilization, 1606–1918. 3 vols. New York, 1959.

Gipson, Lawrence H. "A French Project for Victory Short of a Declaration of War, 1755," Canadian Historical Review, XXVI (Dec., 1945), 361–371.

Gipson, Lawrence H. The Great War for the Empire (The British Empire before the American Revolution, Vols. 6–8). 3 vols. New York, 1946–54.

Grant, William L. "Canada versus Guadeloupe, an Episode of the Seven Years' War," American Historical Review, XVII (1911), 735–743.

Grant, William Lawson. La Mission de M. de Bussy à Londres en 1761. Paris, 1906.

Grant, William Lawson. The Colonial Policy of Chatham (Bulletin of the Departments of History and of Political and Economic Science in Queen's University, No. 1). Kingston, Canada, 1911.

Hall, Hubert. "Chatham's Colonial Policy," American Historical Review, V (1900), 659–675.

Hotblack, Kate. Chatham's Colonial Policy. London, 1917.

Hotblack, Kate. "The Peace of Paris, 1763," Transactions of the Royal Historical Society, 3rd series, II (1908), 235–267.

Lyon, E. W. Louisiana in French Diplomacy, 1759–1804. Norman, Okla., 1934.

Pease, Theodore. "The Mississippi Boundary of 1763," American Historical Review, XL (1935), 278–86.

Peñaranda y de Angulo, Agustin de. Consideraciones generales sobre el segundo Pacto de Familia . . . 1761, entre Francia y España y las dos Sicilias. Madrid, 1906.

Ramsey, John F. Anglo-French Relations, 1763–1770; A Study of Choiseul's Foreign Policy. Berkeley, Calif., 1939.

Rashed, Zenab Esmet. The Peace of Paris, 1763. Liverpool, 1957.

Renaut, O. P. Le pacte de famille et l'Amérique: la politique coloniale franco-espagnole de 1760 à 1792. Paris, 1922.

Ropes, Arthur R. "The Causes of the Seven Years' War," Transactions of the Royal Historical Society, New Series, IV (1889), 143–170.

Rousseau, François. Règne de Charles III d'Espagne (1759–1788). 2 vols. Paris, 1907.

Ruville, Albert von. William Pitt, Earl of Chatham. Translated by H. J. Chaytor. 3 vols. London and New York, 1907.

Savelle, Max. "The American Balance of Power and European Diplomacy, 1713–78," in The Era of the American Revolution: Studies inscribed to Evarts Boutell Greene, ed. Richard B. Morris. New York, 1939. 140–169.

Shepherd, W. R. "The Cession of Louisiana to Spain," Political Science Quarterly, XIX (1904), 439–458.

Sirtema van Grovestins, Carel Frederik, Baron. Histoire des luttes et rivalités politiques entre les puissances maritimes et la France durant la seconde moitié du XVIIIe siècle. 8 vols. Paris, 1851–54.

Soltau, Roger Henry. *The Duke de Choiseul: the Lothian Essay*, 1908. Oxford, 1909.

Soulange-Bodin, André. *La Diplomatie de Louis XV et le Pacte de Famille.* Paris, 1894.

Stourzh, Gerald. *Benjamin Franklin and American Foreign Policy*. Chicago, 1954.

Strangeways, Giles S. H. Fox. *Henry Fox. First Lord Holland.* 2 vols. London, 1920.

Tanner, E. P. "Colonial Agencies in England during the Eighteenth Century," *Political Science Quarterly*, XVI (Mar., 1901), 24–49.

Temperley, H. W. V. "Pitt's Retirement from Office, 1761," *English Historical Review*, XXI (1906), 327–332.

Thackeray, Francis. *A History of the Right Honourable William Pitt, Earl of Chatham: containing his Speeches in Parliament; a considerable Portion of his Correspondence, when Secretary of State, upon French, Spanish, and American Affairs, never before Published* . . . 2 vols. London, 1827.

Van Alstyne, Richard W. "The Significance of the Mississippi Valley in American Diplomatic History, 1686–1890," *Mississippi Valley Historical Review*, XXXVI (Sept., 1949), 215–238.

Vignols, Léon. "L'ancien concept monopole et la contrabande universelle," *Revue de l'Histoire Économique et Sociale*, XII, 239–299.

Waddington, Richard. *La guerre de sept ans: histoire diplomatique et militaire.* 5 vols. Paris, 1899–1919.

Waddington, Richard. *Louis XIV et le renversement des Alliances: préliminaires de la guerre de sept ans, 1754–1756.* Paris, 1896.

Williams, Basil. *The Life of William Pitt, Earl of Chatham.* 2 vols. London, 1913.

Chapter XX. The Growth of American Opinion Relative to International Affairs

Gedosch, Waldo Robert. "Samuel Davies, New Side Presbyterian Minister and Advocate of Religious Toleration in Colonial Virginia." Unpublished M.A. Thesis, University of Washington, 1962.

Gilbert, Felix. *Through the Farewell Address: Ideas of Early American Foreign Policy*. Princeton, 1961.

Johnson, Warren B. "The Content of American Colonial Newspapers Relative to International Affairs, 1704–1763." Unpublished Ph.D. Dissertation, University of Washington, 1962.

Menig, Paul Henri. "Public Opinion in Massachusetts Relative to Anglo-French Relations, 1748–1756." Unpublished Ph.D. Dissertation, University of Washington, 1962.

Rippy, J. Fred, and Angie Debo. *The Historical Background of the American Policy of Isolationism (Smith College Studies in History*, Vol. IX, Nos. 3 and 4). Northampton, Mass., 1924.

Savelle, Max. "The Appearance of an American Attitude toward External Affairs, 1750–1775," *American Historical Review*, LII (July, 1947), 655–660.

Waller, G. M. *Samuel Vetch, Colonial Enterpriser.* Chapel Hill, N.C., 1960.

Wendel, Thomas Harold. "The Life and Writings of Sir William Keith, Lieutenant Governor of Pennsylvania and the Three Lower Counties, 1717–1726." Unpublished Ph.D. Dissertation, University of Washington, 1964.
Wilson, Judith. "Angloamerican Loyalties, 1739–1756." Unpublished M.A. Thesis, University of Washington, 1966.

INDEX